BERNARD SHAW'S BOOK REVIEWS
VOLUME 2: 1884–1950

BERNARD SHAW'S BOOK REVIEWS

Volume 2
1884–1950

Edited and with an Introduction
by
Brian Tyson

The Pennsylvania State University Press
University Park, Pennsylvania

Library of Congress Cataloging-in-Publication Data

Shaw, Bernard, 1856–1950.
   Bernard Shaw's book reviews: 1884–1950 / edited and with an introduction
by Brian Tyson.

        p.   cm.
Includes bibliographical references and index.
   ISBN 0-271-01548-9
   1. Books—Reviews.   1. Tyson, Brian, 1933–   .   II.   Title.
PR5364.B47   1991
028.1—dc20   90-39579
                                                                    CIP

For Jill, who made it possible

CONTENTS

ACKNOWLEDGMENTS

My thanks are first of all due to the Society of Authors for permission to edit these reviews and to quote from Shaw's other printed works. Second, I must express my gratitude to those frontiersmen of Shavian scholarship, Dan Laurence and Stanley Weintraub, whose reputations for generosity of scholarly spirit are well founded. I also offer my heartfelt thanks and acknowledgment for their help to Marina Chiste and Rosemary Howard of the University of Lethbridge Library, and to John St. Clair Chafen, Bernard Dukore, Gudrun Hesse, Isidor Saslaf, and the Reverend Fergus Tyson.

INTRODUCTION

In *Major Barbara,* when Stephen Undershaft has exhausted his father's patience and the audience's laughter at his complete absence of aptitude for any form of employment, Undershaft remarks, "Stephen: Ive found your profession for you. Youre a born journalist. I'll start you with a high-toned weekly review . . ."

Shaw, too, when he first arrived in London in 1876, lacked aptitude for gainful employment. As he admitted, "Impecuniosity was necessarily chronic in the household." Allegedly refusing invitations to dine in case they led to the commercial employment he feared, Shaw calls himself at that time an "incorrigible Unemployable," plying his trade as an unsuccessful novelist, which he remained until 1885 when he was rescued by the discovery that he was a "born journalist" and began his first regular London job, reviewing books for the *Pall Mall Gazette.* Later he was to graduate to the "high-toned" *Saturday Review.*

Half a century later, he reflected on his profession. "Among the drudgeries by which the aesthetic professions have to save themselves from starvation, reviewing is not the worst." So wrote Bernard Shaw in 1943. "When one thinks of Mozart and Beethoven having to 'give lessons,' and Sterndale Bennett, our English Mendelssohn, being extinguished as a composer by having to teach five-finger exercises to fashionable young ladies and charge them four shillings for 'pieces' of sheet music which the music shops let him have for two shillings ('professional terms'), we reviewers can at least congratulate ourselves on the mercy that though we have to read each other's books we are not forced to teach children to read them."

"Even so," Shaw ruminates, "reviewing is, like gathering samphire, a dreadful trade. I earned my first income in literature by practising it."[1] And, one may add, his last. Reviewing was a constant in Shaw's literary life. During the two world wars his playwriting slowed almost to a halt. Toward the end of his life, he abandoned the political platform and the debate. But he never stopped reviewing books. One reason, no doubt, was the one that had impelled him toward a journalistic career in the first place. For though Shaw's income steadily increased until (in 1898) he could afford to marry; and though his playwriting subsequently made him a wealthy man, he lived through a century in which inflation and taxation doubled or trebled the price of goods, while income tax took 50 percent of his income and, once over a certain amount, super tax robbed every pound sterling of 97 percent of its value, making him, as he said, "one of the poor rich, not the rich rich." To make ten guineas, he had to earn four hundred and twenty pounds! Lump sums of money (such as those paid for film rights) were particularly vulnerable to the tax man; and in 1920 Shaw finds himself "lapsing into ephemeral journalism because it means ready money from America." The journalism in question was, for the most part, book reviewing. But a simpler reason for the steadiness of this occupation is the one given by Blanche Patch, his secretary for thirty years, who speaks of the compulsive element in Shaw's writing: "He wrote because he had got to write about something or other. . . . When he arrived in London as a youth he had already drilled himself to filling his five quarto pages a day." And she ends by saying, with the heartfelt sigh of a person whose task was to transcribe the results of such terrific industry, "I have always thought that he wrote too much."[2]

It is my hope that the reader of the following pages will not agree with her. In this second volume of the book reviews of Bernard Shaw, I have excluded those that pertain to the special areas of art, music, theater, and photography, which might be expected to find a place in more specialized collections, while including a scattering of early book reviews that were reprinted (unannotated) in the Collected Edition of Shaw's work in the 1930s. I have also included some of those reviews that have been reprinted since Shaw's death, but that are not now

1. Bernard Shaw, "Reviewing Reviewed," *The Author* 3 (summer 1943), 71.
2. Blanche Patch, *30 Years with G.B.S.* (London: Victor Gollancz, 1951), 243.

readily available. In all, this amounts to seventy-three articles by Shaw, fifty of which have never been reprinted, articles that incidentally trace Shaw's life and the exciting century through which he lived from the age of twenty-eight to the age of ninety-four. The uncollected reviews are no longer discoverable by anyone who does not have the leisure to pore through newspaper libraries, where they are scattered throughout the pages of a score of mostly obsolete journals. It may be that some of these articles have been rescued just in time: "Playing the resurrection man in the old newspaper rooms of our public libraries," can be a pretty depressing experience. Too many of these articles now exist only in faded and brittle newsprint, or on imperfectly reproducible microfilm. The twenty-first century may have something to say about the twentieth-century film technology that has preserved so poorly the journals of the nineteenth.

The date at the head of each review is that of first publication. The titles are (with the exception of the "Books of the Day" articles, which have been amplified by the addition of the book titles) Shaw's own. The code references that follow are those of the 1983 Laurence Bibliography. The rarity not mentioned in that volume is marked NIL. And I have endeavored to preserve the (sometimes eccentric) format of the articles as printed in their respective journals, without standardizing spelling or punctuation, in order to retain as far as possible the intellectual and aesthetic impact of each review as it first appeared.

Although I believe this collection constitutes a good companion volume to *Bernard Shaw's Book Reviews*[3] and it follows a similar format, it differs from that book in one important way. The reviews in the first book belong to only four years of Shaw's writing life; they all appeared in the same journal (the *Pall Mall Gazette*); and Shaw had to review them whether he liked them or not. As he remarks in one of the reviews in this volume: "Every season brings its budget of scamped, faked, and worthless books, feverishly pushed, to prove that those eminent and typical publishers Alnaschar & Co., have again had their belly filled with the east wind by some duffer whose pretensions would not take in an ordinarily sharp bookstall boy." The only possible escape from the torrent of sentimental novels, second-rate biographies, and third-rate poetry with which he was inundated in his early years was first derision, and finally resignation (in both senses of the term). Accordingly

---

3. Brian Tyson, ed., *Bernard Shaw's Book Reviews: Originally published in the "Pall Mall Gazette" from 1885 to 1888* (University Park: Pennsylvania State University Press, 1991). Hereafter referred to as *Bernard Shaw's Book Reviews*.

Shaw left the staff of the *Gazette* with something of a sigh of relief, and turned his attention initially to musical and then to theatrical criticism. Whenever he returned to book reviewing after 1888, he did so on his own terms. The reviews after that date, therefore, reveal Shaw fully engaged in the task at hand, usually expressing a personal enthusiasm or antipathy for the book in question. He tended, moreover, to choose significant works; in consequence the present volume contains few authors who are obscure, although there are still one or two early ones who remain stubbornly undiscoverable: information about Thomas Common, for instance, is anything but, while G. Chaplin Piesse seems to be the one that passeth all understanding.

The reviews are presented in chronological order, and therefore we can observe Shaw's developing style. But Oscar Wilde says somewhere, "Talent develops: genius goes round in circles"; and in a sense the genius of Shaw shapes this collection. Themes recur, like musical *leitmotifs*. Shaw reviews William Dawson's factual treatment of Ferdinand Lassalle ("The Messiah of Social Democracy") and Meredith's fictional treatment of the same figure in *The Tragic Comedians;* he reviews Tolstoy's view of Art and Aylmer Maude's view of Tolstoy; he gives his estimate of the military capabilities of Viscount Montgomery of Alamein, and his views on the love life of the Duke of Wellington; and he returns more than once to discuss Samuel Butler, G. K. Chesterton, H. G. Wells and Sidney Webb. He even manages a final fling at the doctors in his review of Douglas Guthrie's *History of Medicine* in 1945. Thus these book reviews find familiar Shavian paths across the wide territory scarred by two world wars and the enormous social upheaval in Europe that surrounded them. But there is still wide variety in them, the collection sparkles with wit and wisdom, and takes us briskly through Shaw's own writing life, beginning when he was relatively unknown and concluding when he was a legend.

The fact that Shaw felt strongly about the books he chose for discussion led to his increasing tendency to present views rather than reviews; to use the book he is supposed to be reviewing merely as a jumping-off point, almost omitting consideration of the work itself. Shaw himself draws attention to the fact. Concluding a review of Vernon Lee's *Satan the Waster* (which has not to this point mentioned the book) he says:

> The book, of first-rate workmanship from beginning to end, is far too thorough to leave the reviewer anything to say about it that is not better said in the book itself.

And of Chesterton's *Short History of England,*

> There is nothing worth saying left to be said of his book, be-
> cause he has said it all himself.

While in his review of *Diary of a Dean* in the last year of his life, Shaw
writes,

> All a reviewer has any right to say of another man's book is
> "Read it" unless his verdict is "Dont read it," in which case he
> should give his reasons.

In fact, increasingly Shaw tends to choose only those books he wishes
us to read; and, finally, that is all he wishes to say about them. As he
explained to Lena Ashwell who, angered by the preface to *Heartbreak
House,* had written a caustic review of it:

> As a journalist you must never write about anything that an-
> noys you. You mustnt use your articles as safety valves: you
> must always think "Can I get an article out of this? Have I any
> experiences or ideas that I can hang on to this book I am
> reviewing or this subject that I am treating?"[4]

In short, the great advantage of saying little about the book is that one
has more space to speak about its subject; and it is fascinating, in the
course of these articles, to watch Shaw's experiences chiming or clash-
ing with those of the authors he reviews, and his pragmatism straining
itself to accommodate the political changes in the world around him.
His 1921 attack on the previously praised H. M. Hyndman for having
"mellowed," for the internationalist turning patriot, for the revolutionist
becoming a pacifist, is ironic in view of Shaw's own changing view of
democracy. There are comments in the same article on the impossibility of educating the majority into the ways of Socialism, and change
always coming (with, apparently, attendant force and necessary atrocities) from an "energetic minority." Strange words from the Fabian
whose original quarrel with Hyndman's Social Democratic Federation
had been its revolutionary, rather than evolutionary, tendencies! As is

---

4. Bernard Shaw, letter to Lena Ashwell, 31 October 1919, in *Bernard Shaw. Collected
Letters 1911–1925,* ed. Dan H. Laurence. (London: Max Reinhardt, 1985), 644. Hereafter
referred to as *Collected Letters 1911–1925.*

implied above, politics feature largely in the nonfiction works that he reviewed. Shaw reviews books of Socialist theory by H. M. Hyndman, J. L. Joynes, Frederick Engels, and Beatrice and Sidney Webb, and monitors its practical appearance in the newly emergent Soviet Union (for which he remains stubbornly apologist, rebuking the suspicions of such authors as Chesterton, Wells, and Dean Inge); but he balances these by sensitively examining the Individualism of J. H. Levy, the anti-Socialism of Thomas Mackay, and the economics of E. C. K. Gonner and Philip Wicksteed. However, these reviews also reveal Shaw's growing frustration with the political process, and chronicle the collapse of his belief in democracy which, although usually dated from World War I, can be seen in 1913, when he uses Sir Almroth Wright's attack on female suffrage as an excuse for liberating his own growing disbelief in male suffrage! Throughout the First World War Shaw's distrust of democracy deepened:

> When one recalls the wars of the French Revolution, when Members of Parliament went single-handed into camp to arrest generals in the presence of their troops, and send them to the guillotine for insubordinations and failures which would secure them baronies in England today, one realizes how hopelessly our governors have failed to educate the rank and file to a pitch of democracy at which an army of six millions is a guarantee of liberty instead of a bodyguard of military tyranny.

Despairing of effecting educational change on the large scale necessary for Democratic Socialism to work, Shaw fell back on the views of Ibsen's Dr. Stockmann that the majority are never right and, for a dangerous time, admired the fascist dictatorships of Hitler and Mussolini. But Shaw soon distinguished between Democratic and National Socialism, and saw how the line had been crossed:

> . . . we could not publish [Fabian Socialism] for the workers without publishing it for the capitalists as well. And the capitalists, cleverer than the workers, seized it and turned it to their own account by combining the enormous productiveness, power and scope of State financed enterprise with their private property on its sources, and thus producing the new form of Capitalism called Fascism or Nationalism—Nazi for short in Germany.

So National Socialism was not Socialism at all: it was simply a new form of Capitalism. But the problem with Democratic Socialism was still the level of general education required for it to function effectively. Indeed, the world war had widened the scope of the education necessary:

> Our common democrats must, if they are to vote with any intelligence and exercise any real power, know not only the history of their own country but that of all other countries as well.

Shaw knew that the Fabian Society, whose chief aim had been to educate, had failed to change the mindset of the masses. To the end, Shaw wanted the Fabians to make Socialists of the proletarianized businessmen and professional intelligentsia in order to defeat the Fascist financiers. But for a time the only pragmatic alternative seemed to be to educate their leaders, and then apply Cromwell's rule: not what they want but what's good for them. Consequently, when Shaw saw the dictatorship emerging in the Soviet Union, he defended its repressive policies, saying:

> It is precisely those freedoms which the Soviet Government has had to abolish that the Fabians must disclaim also, because they are the most potent weapons of Capitalism, being in fact the right to be idle and do what you like . . .

As the decades passed, Shaw continued to express his exasperation with the Western form of democracy (which he characterized as the "election of anybody by everybody"):

> The real use of votes for everybody is to prevent us from being governed better than we can bear, as in the case of Prohibition of intoxicating drink in the U.S.A., which had to be repealed in spite of its proved betterment. The Welfare State is not possible with an Illfare constitution.

And toward the end of his life one hears a familiar note of resignation:

> . . . instead of democratic authority there are constitutional guarantees to the man in the street that he shall not be governed at all, which is just what the poor mug desires. And so Britons always will be slaves . . .

What he and the Fabian Society had failed to accomplish, Shaw looked to the Life Force to do. Yet the political despair of *Heartbreak House* is followed by the spiritual despondency of *Saint Joan,* where the inspired leader chosen by the Life Force to enlighten her contemporaries is ruthlessly put to death, and her canonization deferred until she is no longer a social danger.

The works Shaw reviews are frequently by authors whom he knew personally, like H. G. Wells and G. K. Chesterton; and there is often an immediacy about their subjects: discussions of books on women's suffrage, censorship, the Irish question, and the two world wars take place alongside the events themselves, or while the issues are being hotly debated; and because many of the political events of the day have now become, in Shaw's words, "the idlest of library curiosities," I have endeavored in the notes to elucidate obscure contemporary references. I have also tried to make occasional (but significant) connections between the reviews and Shaw's own plays (trying to minimize what Shaw calls "those exultant little discoveries of plagiarism which are the sure sign of a bad critic in all departments of the critic's art").

Finally, however, it is not the ephemeral but the enduring qualities of these articles that makes it necessary to bring them out of obscurity; and quarrying in the old newspapers often throws up Shavings of gold. Who else but Shaw would write:

That is the worst of knowing a poet: he is always longing for you to die, in order that he may have an opportunity of mourning you in verse.

Does not patriotism consist mainly in covering your own country with fictitious whitewash, and the enemy with fictitious soot?

Whilst Arab children were taught to respect Jesus in the name of Mahomet, English children were taught to despise and slander Mahomet in the name of Jesus.

[The] intellect is still so new a toy in evolution that those who possess it are often more interested in their intellectual processes than in their conclusions.

Nor is it only Shaw's gnomic utterances which demand that these occasional pieces be given to the world. One is increasingly struck with the inventive aptness of his analogies, extended metaphors that illuminate the personalities of the authors whose books he is reviewing, or their subjects. "The method of nature ... is a dramatic method," says Shaw. And so is the Shavian method: the eye of the playwright transforms his contemporaries into the dramatis personae of Shaw's personal *Traumwelt*. Thus, H. M. Hyndman is cast as a publican who might have "drawn it mild," but instead has drawn it "with a startling head to it." Sir Edward Carson becomes a policeman who misdirects the nurserymaid [Lloyd George] because he has "rashly undertaken fixed point duty in a strange district much too big for his powers of comprehension." Asquith features as a second-rate cricketer who, if he had read the works of Sidney Webb, might have "often caught out Lloyd George instead of being bowled helplessly by him"; whereas Tolstoy becomes a first-rate fighting man in defense of his definition of Art; and "our generation has not seen a heartier bout of fisticuffs, or one in which the challenger has been more brilliantly victorious." Shaw's favorite sport is a frequent figure: Natural Selection, we are told, "knocked Paley and the Book of Genesis clean out." Chesterton, too, is characterized as a first-rate boxer "with a knock-out punch which is much more deadly than Carpentier's," and his book as "another round in the exhibition spar with Sidney Webb."

Occasionally Shaw rebukes authors whose books he is reviewing for poor characterization—almost, poor casting! He objects to Frank Harris's dramatization of the man Shakespeare as "a snivelling, broken-hearted swain, dying because he was jilted"; on another occasion he complains about Gilbert Murray's portrait of Sir Edward Grey as though Murray were a fellow playwright [Euripides] *inventing* Sir Edward. Given the choice of inflating Sir Edward Grey until he was large enough to fit the world-shaking circumstances surrounding the outbreak of World War I, or diminishing the circumstances until they fitted Grey, Murray allegedly chose the latter. And Shaw grandly excuses him on the grounds that "to falsify Sir Edward Grey by making him up as Bismark would have coarsely violated the veracity of his dramatic instinct. The modern Euripides could not have done it: his hand would have refused the task in spite of him." By contrast, Meredith in *The Tragic Comedians* has "belittled his hero (based on Lassalle) in order to magnify the dramatic situation." Chesterton, too, says Shaw, "could no more hate the Kaiser than Shakespear could hate Iago or Richard." And yet, perversely, on another occasion, Shaw does not scruple to complain that Chesterton "invents [opponents] and imposes monstrous opinions on them for the sake of leading a crusade against them"! The fact is that this is Shaw's own method. His dramatic instinct causes fact and fiction to become strangely merged. The flesh-and-blood Chesterton is imagined kicking the fictional Mr. Honeythunder "into the horsepond"; while Shaw cheerfully accepts the portrait of himself as "the son of Donizetti's Lucrezia Borgia."

Shaw's extended metaphors are not simply dramatic: they also have poetic resonance. When we are told that the First World War "is a fire burning itself out as best it may, because the poker is too big for party politicians to wield," the metaphor is a vivid one of destructive force encouraged by tactical clumsiness; it also brings with it, however, the faint ghost of the funny man with the red-hot poker, suggesting that the clowns are running the circus.

Moreover, if the people Shaw speaks of become figures in his mental landscape, then his deeper analysis of them discovers further landscapes in the minds of his figures. In another review, for example, he captures exactly the difference between the drawing-room politics of Ruskin and Carlyle and the popular Socialism of Robert Blatchford in the image of the latter "transposing the tune from their eternal D flat major (good for the trombone) into the plain G and B flat of their favorite songs and cornet marches." Blatchford is immediately seen as a man leading a street parade rather than an orchestra; and the unspoken limitations of both are an important part of Shaw's political analogy: a street parade moves; it has direction and vigor; whereas an orchestra, though producing nobler, deeper, and more thoughtful sounds, is both cumbersome and static. But again, the street parade, however cheerful and energetic, carries with it the suggestion of a directionless monster, the mob, carrying more emotion than intellect on its journey. Thus we have a choice of Socialisms: the intellectually appealing, which remains, however, at the ideal stage; or the practical variety, which might lose its energy in noisy demonstration. A more complex example of such "landscaping" is found in Shaw's analysis of the mind of Chesterton, depicted as a man walking down a blind alley, but with imagination enough to spot diamonds instead of pebbles— perhaps even imagination enough to transform pebbles *into* diamonds. Shaw continues:

> By stopping to pick the diamonds up, like Atalanta, he may not get far enough to discover that the alley is blind. Even if he does, he may find a way out by pretending that he has found one, as the mathematician overcomes an intellectually insuperable difficulty by pretending that there is such a quantity as minus x. Searchlights in blind alleys have illuminated the whole heavens at times; and men have found courage and

insight within their limits after finding nothing but terror and bewilderment in the open desert.

This transformation of Chesterton's intellectual limitations into a landscape of the mind is modified by a figure drawn from Greek mythology and an anonymous mathematician: the Atalanta reference associates speed with both hunting and a hint of vanity, as the daughter of Iasus and Clymene was tempted to stop in her race by the golden apples dropped by Milanion, which allowed him to beat (and thus marry) her; while the mathematical reference reminds one (and is perhaps intended to remind Chesterton himself) that immediately prior to this passage Shaw had just invoked the name of Einstein, a member of a race for which Chesterton has an irrational dislike. The entire analogy exactly captures the powerful, precise but essentially narrow viewpoint Chesterton has of the world (the searchlight in the blind alley); while for the brilliance of his expression of it the diamond is a perfect metaphor. Finally, although Shaw manages to make it sound as though Chesterton himself would prefer to be dazzled by his own diamonds rather than face the bleakness of the blind alley, he does leave a loophole in the mathematical comparison that allows Chesterton's inward way to infinity to be as valid as Shaw's outward way.

To read these book reviews is to realize the truth of O'Casey's contention that Shaw is more the poet than has generally been acknowledged. Certainly Shaw, who once had ambitions to be an artist, and some of whose earliest published criticism originated in Burlington House and the Grosvenor Gallery, thinks in pictures. And they are pictures chosen to appeal to his immediate readership. In the late 1880s we are told that Lassalle's willpower went into people "like steam into a vaccuum." By 1916, in an age yet more mechanical and violent, Mr Chesterton's spirit is "so explosive that it bursts every strong modern prison"; and we are warned that "an error of a millimetre at the cannon's mouth may mean an error of a mile when the shell explodes." In 1917, reading Dixon Scott's criticisms for Shaw is "like watching revolver practice by a crack shot." The following year Belloc's *The Free Press* is "launched as a torpedo at poor Northcliffe"; and Hilaire Belloc has "conducted truth raids, and seen all England rush to the cellars every time." Between the wars Shaw's imagery keeps closer to its subject matter: Dean Inge is "like a refiner's fire" in the church; Bolshevism has a difficult birth "needing a strong hand and forceps." In the year of the General Strike, as at other times of great crisis, Shaw employs the nautical navigational imagery so pervasive in *Heartbreak House*. "Capitalist parties," we are told, "are as ignorant [of the fact that the Living Wage is a Capitalist principle] as an average forecastle hand is of astronomy and mathematics without which his captain dare not lose sight of land." In the same way the rulers of Europe are "like mutineers who throw the captain overboard, because they think that the art of navigation is only his tyranny." During World War II, however, Shaw reverts to military images: H. G. Wells dispersed his foes with a "one-man artillery barrage of vituperation" and "scattered invective in all directions as an R.A.F. pilot scatters bombs"; "Marx's torpedo hit [the Victorian golden age] between wind and water in its middle, and blew the golden lid off hell." While of Samuel Butler's attack on his father, we are informed that a "hydrogen bomb could not have blasted his reputation more devastatingly after his death than his undutiful son did with his novel called The Way of All Flesh."

The reviews, arranged chronologically, do toward the end reveal their author's diminishing energy and progressive isolation. First his friends, then his wife, eventually his generation, died; and by the time Shaw himself followed on 2 November 1950, he lay alone in a room with two nurses.[5] But all the world paid homage. Sir Sydney Cockerell speculated that his ashes might well be buried in Westminster Abbey; in New York, Broadway was ordered to black out for one minute its three-quarters of a million bulbs and quarter of a million feet of neon strip; and special tribute was paid in two Broadway theaters where *Mrs. Warren's Profession* and *Arms and the Man* were being staged. When news of his death reached India, schools and colleges throughout the country were closed. In Australia theater audiences stood for two minutes in silence. Tributes poured in, from the British prime minister Clement Attlee, from President Truman in the United States, from the French writer André Maurois, from the novelist Arnold Zweig in East Germany, from Pandit Nehru in India.

The obituary notices produced a sudden consciousness of how much better Shaw himself would have written them. J. B. Priestley, writing in the *News Chronicle*, said,

> with his passing, a great light goes out. We seem at once a smaller and grubbier lot of people. The world becomes a duller and stupider place.

5. Sisters Howell and Horan.

Though the sharp tongue was still forever, echoes of controversy lingered: the Conservative press wondered about Shaw's wealth, calling him "the richest of the rich Socialists"; the Labour press countered by stressing his financial generosity. All acknowledged his greatness. Perhaps the simple words of the *News Chronicle*'s editorial best summed up the general feeling:

> There will be no throng of writers to cast their quills beside his ashes. He first outstripped and then outlived those who vied with him for fame. He had no peer and he leaves no successors.

BERNARD SHAW'S BOOK REVIEWS

1 April 1884

Mr. H. M. HYNDMAN'S SOCIALISM*
[C81]

WHEN a nation, contemplating its own greatness in the record of its vast and constantly increasing wealth, congratulating itself on internal peace and public order unbroken for thirty-five years, [is] satisfied by the calculations of the head of the statistical department of its Board of Trade that the humblest of its units shares its prosperity, it may be excused for regarding its position with complacency, and awaiting its future with confidence. And if it happen to be the traditional guardian of liberty, the pioneer of political reform, the possessor of a constitution so perfect that foreign peoples are more blest when brought under its yoke by conquest than when abandoned to their own freedom, surely such a nation, if any, is justified in electing itself the best and happiest of all nations of the earth. Now when, in this reassuring state of affairs, an intelligent gentleman, in easy circumstances, publicly assumes that he is living in the midst of enforced anarchy, slavery, corruption, misery, slow-poisoning of children, prostitution of women, grinding to death of men before half their natural time is fulfilled, and systematic use as instruments of torture of machines intended to relieve human toil, there is a general disposition to believe that the intelligent gentleman, in easy circumstances, has either parted with his intelligence or lost his property. But when these hypotheses are successively discredited by the coherence of his utterances, and his undiminished expenditure, and when it becomes apparent that he is obtaining a growing constituency among persons of unquestioned sanity, and even among men of distinguished ability, then his more reasonable neighbours, asking themselves whether they are to be calmly told that their national greatness is a dream, naturally beg that intelligent and easily circumstanced gentleman either to explain himself or, familiarly, to draw it mild.

This is the relation in which England and Mr. H. M. Hyndman stand at present; and, in the book under notice, Mr. Hyndman has

---

* "The Historical Basis of Socialism in England." By H. M. Hyndman. (Kegan Paul, Trench, 1883.)

explained himself, and has not drawn it at all mild—has, indeed, drawn it with a startling head to it. "A more horrible state of things," he declares, "than the capitalists of England, as a class, created for the workers in the days when, having cleared away all the restrictions of the middle ages on reduction of wages or over-work, they had full power to take advantage of the freedom of contract they throve by, and could grind women and children into an early grave for their profit, never disgraced a civilised commu-nity." Comfortable members of the middle class will be struck at once by the extravagance of this statement as it stands isolated above. Readers of Mr. Hyndman's work will be compelled to admit that it is entirely justified, and that, outside the operation of the Factory Acts, it is as true of our half of the nineteenth century as of that in which Robert Owen worked. The process by which the condition of society which it describes arose upon the ruins of the general prosperity enjoyed by the producing classes in England during the fifteenth century, is the subject of Mr. Hyndman's book, as it is, in fact, the historic basis of modern scientific socialism. Such a book was urgently needed in England. Mr. Henry George's writings have suddenly opened the eyes of the reading public to the fact that there is something exceedingly rotten in our state; but his account of the expropriation of the rural population, though an important part of the shameful story of "Progress and Poverty," is not the whole of it. The extraordinary history of modern industrial civilisation, published by the late Karl Marx under the characteristi-cally curt and significant title "Capital," has not yet been translated into the language of the country in which it was written, and from which its illustrations were mainly drawn. Mr. Hyndman is, there-fore, practically in the field in England before the deceased founder of his school, whose views he has thoroughly assimilated and ap-plied independently to his own experience, instead of merely pick-ing them up and repeating them in different and inferior order and phraseology, or uselessly elaborating trifles which he passed lightly over, as so many followers of Adam Smith have gained a reputation by doing. Like Marx, Mr. Hyndman is free from academic pedantry, and from the literary vanity of merely verbal originality. Thus, when he has to say something which has been well said before, he simply quotes the writer, whether socialist or individualist, who has best expressed it. Again, he estimates economic facts according to their influence on the well-being of society, without reference to their convenience to the students of finance who regard treatises on political economy as technical instruction books for men who aspire to become budget cooks or bankers. Nor does he give the slightest encouragement to optimists who hope that the process of righting existing wrongs may be an entirely brotherly one. "Force, or the fear of force," he says, "is, unfortunately, the only reasoning which can appeal to a dominant estate, or will ever induce them to surrender any portion of their property or privileges." Here the word reasoning, which no sentimental socialist would use in such a context, expresses much of Mr. Hyndman's view of human motive. Again he says, "It was force, and the fear of force, which really enabled the workers to get any measures whatever passed for their benefit." These truths are wholesome for the class to which the book is addressed, and to whose ranks its price must for the present restrict its circulation. He does not hesitate to give dynamite its due as a factor in the evolution of society, but with Anarchism he has no sympathy; and, in an interesting chapter on International Labour Movements, he describes the tenets of Bakunin as "individualism gone mad." His last words on this subject are worth quoting. "Force," he says, "masters the world, but organised force should be used not to weaken and destroy the very basis of human happiness—physical well-being—but to strengthen and develop it for the common good."

The nature and source of surplus value, the immense moral scope of which was first adequately appreciated by Marx, is fully explained by Mr. Hyndman. As it is the basis of all the current socialistic accusations of theft, extortion, "socialisation of production, and anarchy of exchange," and so forth, which are so startling, and appear so unreasonable to those who have no material ground for dissatisfaction with the existing state of society, it deserves the most attentive consideration from readers of all classes. But neither the historic nor the economic parts of the book are pleasant reading, even when they are most interesting. That Mr. Hyndman could record so many events which could never have happened had men been humane, and analyse industrial conditions which could never have arisen had they been honest, without rising from his task an absolute pessimist, proves him, in spite of his severity towards the middle class, to be an incorrigibly indulgent man. He concludes his work by condensing material enough for an ordinary volume into a hopeful and suggestive sketch of the present and its outlook, similar to those which he has occasionally contributed to periodical literature, and in the execution of which he is unrivalled.

Editor's Notes

▪ This was published in *The Christian Socialist, a Journal for those who Work and Think* 1 (April 1884): 166–67. This journal had started the previous year as the organ of the Land Reform Union (see below, 180).

▪ There is no mention of Shaw's reviewing for this year, in his brief note on 1884; see *Bernard Shaw: The Diaries 1885–1897. With early autobiographical notebooks and diaries, and an abortive 1917 diary,* 2 vols., ed. and annotated by Stanley Weintraub (University Park: Pennsylvania State University Press, 1986), 33. Hereafter, this will be labeled simply *Diary.*

▪ H[enry] M[ayers] Hyndman (1842–1921). Converted to Socialism by reading a French translation of Marx's *Das Kapital* (1867–94), he later struck up an acquaintance with Marx himself, but when he wrote a book (*England for All*) in which he borrowed, without acknowledgment, many of Marx's views, a breach developed between the two men. On 8 June 1881, Hyndman started the Democratic Federation, which became the Social Democratic Federation (SDF for short), whose manifesto, *Socialism Made Plain,* advocated the overthrow of the Capitalist system. From the SDF a splinter group gave rise to the Fabian Society in January 1884. Five months after writing the above review, on 5 September, Shaw formally joined the Fabians. The two societies were not initially rivals, and Shaw was for a time a "candidate member" of the SDF, but he soon became irritated by Hyndman's rancorous and revolutionary speeches. In later years, however, Hyndman was to mellow somewhat politically (see below, "The Old Revolutionist and the New Revolution," 427 et seq.).

▪ In the original the phrase "is satisfied" reads "and satisfied," thus robbing the time clause of its finite verb, and rendering it ungrammatical.

▪ "To draw it mild" means to "tone it down a little," and clearly derives from the public house: "A pint of double X, and please to draw it mild." Shaw extends his metaphor later by saying that Mr. Hyndman has drawn it "with a startling head to it."

▪ The Factory Acts is the name given generally to a long series of parliamentary acts, beginning in the early nineteenth century that, among other things, restricted hours of work for women and young persons and improved working conditions.

▪ Robert Owen (1771–1858), Welsh social reformer who in his Scottish mills established schools, improvements in housing and sanitation, and a store at which goods could be purchased for little more than cost. When the Factory Act of 1819 contained only a few of his proposals, he sought instead to change the social structure of society by establishing cooperative communities in which members would share the products of their labor. However, union-owned industries provoked such government opposition that Owen was forced to dissolve the movement in 1834, and he withdrew from active participation in labor affairs, promoting his socialist and educational theories in books such as *A New View of Society* (1813), *Revolution in Mind and Practice* (1849), and his autobiography in 1857–58.

- Henry George (1839–97), American economist, whose pamphlet *Our Land and Land Policy* (1871) argued that the boom in the West, resulting from railroad development, was actually impoverishing most people and making only a few rich, because land ownership was concentrated in the hands of the few. The answer, according to George, was the imposition of a single tax on land values. He proposed to retain private ownership, requiring only that society appropriate the socially created value of land, which increases in value largely as a result of community growth. These ideas were set out in his book *Progress and Poverty* (1879), which made him famous as an opponent of injustice in modern Capitalism. In the 1880s George, lecturing on his ideas throughout the United States, Ireland, and Great Britain, was the author of Shaw's conversion to Socialism when, on 5 September 1882, he spoke at the Memorial Hall, Farringdon Street, London, on "Land Nationalization and the Single Tax." Shaw remained loyal to George for the rest of the latter's life, in 1886 supporting his candidacy for the mayoralty of New York City, and in a review in the *Pall Mall Gazette* briskly dismissing Laurence Gronlund's attempted demonstration of the insufficiency of Henry George's theory. In 1897, running as an Independent Democrat, George again made a bid for the mayoralty of New York, but died during the campaign. His other writings include *Social Problems* (1884), *Protection or Free Trade* (1886), and *The Science of Political Economy* (1897).

- The first two volumes of *Das Kapital* (1867 and 1885), carried to completion by Friedrich Engels, friend and collaborator of Karl Marx (1818–83), the German social, political, and economic theorist, had to wait three more years before they were translated into English by Samuel Moore and Edward Aveling, at which point Shaw would review them at length for the *National Reformer*. To this point he had read Marx only in G. Deville's 1883 French translation. Engels completed the final volume in 1895.

- "He does not hesitate to give dynamite its due" and so forth. A year later, Shaw himself said "startling things about dynamite" in a speech to the Bedford Debating Society; later these developed into an attitude shared by Shaw's character Andrew Undershaft, whose religion "must have a place for cannons and torpedoes in it."

- Mikhail Aleksandrovich Bakunin (1814–76), Russian anarchist and writer, whose property was confiscated, and he himself expelled from Paris, for advocating the overthrow of the Polish and Russian monarchies. Thereafter he was a revolutionary, sentenced to death in Austria, but extradited to Russia, where he was sent to Siberia. Escaping in 1861, he returned via Japan and the United States to Europe where for fifteen years he was the leading anarchist, and worked with Marx and Engels until he was expelled from the First International in 1872 for the violence of his views. The development of Bakunism followed *God and the State* (1882), whose primary tenets were atheism, destruction of the state, and ultra-individualistic rights.

1 August 1884
RECENT POETRY* [C85]

I have often wondered why Milton wrote *Paradise Lost*. Perhaps he could not help it. In that case there is nothing more to be said on the subject. Perhaps he thought that it would gratify his fellow-creatures. If so, I think he was wrong; for the humiliation of the literate but lazy persons who are ashamed of not having read his work, and the fatigue of the more resolute who have read it from a sense of duty, and disliked it, probably outweigh the pleasures of those who have relished it. Perhaps he thought he had something to tell which a few people would be the better for hearing. I am not in a position to deny that he had; although it remains to be considered whether the something might not have been put more briefly. But on the whole I do not think that Milton ever raised that question betwixt himself and his genius, because nothing had really occurred, from the time of Eschylus to that of Spenser, to discredit great poems as things admirable and desirable for their own sakes. Nor do the authors of the four books cited above, although their Muses are frequently low-spirited, seem to have been troubled with doubts any more than Milton was. They must have known, as Milton knew, that the faculty of writing a good poem cannot be acquired, and that the chances are a million to one against its existence in any particular individual. For venturing at these heavy odds they deserve some gratitude, which might perhaps be more practically expressed by leaving Milton out of the question in dealing with their works.

The chief piece in Miss Levy's volume is *Medea;* but that title having been anticipated by Euripides, she has put *A Minor Poet* in the place of honour. A Minor Poet is, presumably, one whose verse falls short, not only of Shakspere's and Shelley's, but of average excellence, just as a short man is not one who fails to attain gigantic stature, but one who is beneath the medium height. In the absence of any means of determining average excellence in an art which eludes analysis, I shall not now commit myself to any distinction between major and minor poets. I have an impression, nevertheless,

---

* "A Minor Poet, and other Verse." By Amy Levy. (London: T. Fisher Unwin, 1884.)
"Marcia. A Tragedy." By Pakenham Beatty. (London: Hamilton, Adams, 1884.)
"Measured Steps." By Ernest Radford. (London: T. Fisher Unwin, 1884.)
"Callirhöe: Fair Rosamund." By Michael Field. (London: Bell & Sons, 1884.)

that the great poets deal honestly with us by giving us their experiences rather than their fancies, and affect us by the irony—tragical or farcical, as may happen—of the contrast between the two. Minor poets, on the contrary, finding their experiences uninteresting because they have not much capacity for experience, give us their fancies exclusively. As the combinations and permutations of experience are inexhaustible, great poets, reproducing their experience, are original and interesting. And as the fancies of any two or two hundred imaginative people are as like as eggs, minor poets, reproducing their fancies, are common-place and dull. Miss Levy's minor poet, for example, has failed to persuade anyone to believe in him. Feeling out of sorts because he is not quite all that he ignorantly wishes to be, he demands whether mortal or divine brain ever devised a Hell more fraught with torment than the world for such as he. Tom Leigh, his friend, described as a philosopher, but evidently a twaddling imposter, replies with "neatest, newest phrases, freshly culled from works of newest culture." These fail to relieve the overcharged heart of the minor poet. He bids farewell to his books, to "lofty Shakspeare with the tattered leaves and fathomless great heart," to Goethe, with "triumphant smile, tragic eyes, and pitiless world-wisdom," and to "one wild singer of to-day, whose song is all aflame with passionate bard's blood lash'd into foam by pain and the world's wrong." As this wild singer is unnamed, Mr. Pakenham Beatty, Mr. Ernest Radford, and the author of *Callirhöe* are all in a position to draw the most flattering conclusions from the passage. Finally, the poet comes to the usual intolerable intimation that "there was a woman once," after which he wisely poisons himself. All this is told in Browningesque blank verse with an intelligence and taste which are in direct contrast to the common-place worthlessness of the subject. Curiously enough, on page 4 of the poem occurs a passage in which the writer comes within an ace of the truth, apparently not yet familiar to her, that we are so strongly affected by our mere fancies that the rudest criticism can hardly convince us that they are stale and uninteresting to others. The mock-tragic note of *A Minor Poet* runs through all the other poems, though it is occasionally made acceptable by description and versification which are throughout superior to the conceptions to which they are applied. Some of the smaller poems in the book deserve nothing but praise; and even when the immaturity of the writer is most evident, she is, for the moment at least, quite sincere. In *Xantippe*, which is good enough to suggest comparisons which it can hardly sustain, occur the following lines:—

> Then, as all youthful spirits are, was I.
> Wholly incredulous that Nature meant
> So little, who had promised me so much.

I hope to find, in some future poem of Miss Levy's, a heroine incredulous that Nature means so much though she seems—in our Minor Poet stage—to promise so little.

Mr. Pakenham Beatty is an old offender in the jurisdiction of critics of poetry. Fortunate are the poets or patriots whom he admires; for they are certain of a sonnet, or at least a dedication, describing them in terms by comparison to which the Psalmist's praises of Jehovah are tame and qualified. Mazzini, Garibaldi, and "Orion" Horne, have passed out of reach of his hyperbole; but Victor Hugo, Mr. Swinburne, and several less known gentlemen who apparently enjoy Mr. Beatty's private acquaintanceship, must find considerable difficulty in fulfilling the expectations which his references to them are calculated to raise. He has enthusiasm enough for four poets, and discrimination enough for rather less than one. He does not take up his subjects by halves. His erotic poems, published in 1879, though free from coarseness and from the ineptitudes of most first essays in poetry, breathed infatuation rather than love. Two years later, in a transport of revolutionary fury, he issued a collection of poems in which his indignation at the tyranny of Napoleon III, revived after a lapse of ten years by the persecution of the Nihilists in Russia under the administration of Loris Melikoff, found vent in language of such astonishing rancour, that the unlucky editor of the *Freiheit*, then in prison for suggesting measures for which Mr. Beatty positively clamoured, must have felt the truth of the proverb that one man may steal a horse where another may not look over a hedge. Since then, Mr. Beatty's feelings on the state of affairs in Russia, far from having cooled, have led him to write a drama entitled *Marcia,* which issued from the press in June of the present year. Marcia is a Pole, and mistress of the Czar of Russia, whom the poet, possibly from a desire to spare the feelings of his original as far as possible, denominates "The Tyrant" without further particularization. She has gained the privilege of releasing at her discretion one of a batch of her countrymen who are on their way to Siberia. The forethought with which she exercises this dispensing power is apparent from her remark to an old man that the remainder of his life is not worth saving, and that his daughter does not look as if she should live much longer than he. Eventually she releases Michael Stolskoi, a poet, who repays her by an impressive lecture upon the infamy of her behaviour. She falls in love with him; and he, though coy at first, soon returns her affection. The Czar discovers this, and Stolskoi is arrested and tried with three confederates, one of whom an Englishman, has the impudence to boast, with reference to India, that

> The indignant spirit of an Englishman
> Chafes at the fetters on another's limbs,
> And freedom finds a champion of her cause
> Where'er her swords strike or her banners wave.

They are condemned to death. Marcia, however, obtains access to Stolskoi's cell with a pistol and some poison. The lovers drink the poison, and, on the Czar entering to superintend the execution personally, Stolskoi shoots him and expires. The story is not in any way founded on facts. The materialist conspirators of real Russia, plotting against a bigoted despot who is but the figure-head of a corrupt bureaucracy, are misrepresented in Mr. Beatty's imagination by pious victims appealing to heaven against a godless autocrat whose malicious disposition has made his people miserable, who gloats over instruments of torture, and who has state criminals hanged with a frayed rope, which breaks, and so prolongs their agony. The scenes between Michael and Marcia are the best in the play, and compel a measure of respect for the author's powers in spite of the commonplace fiction with which he has replaced the tragic truth of Russian history in 1880. Soberer than his *Three Women of the People,* and more mature than his early love poems, "Marcia" is an advance on both.

> I would be with the workers in the van
> For somehow, somewhere, rises godlike Man

says Mr. Beatty on the title page of *Three Women of the People,* quoting the late Arthur O'Shaughnessy. It may be worth while to suggest to him, and to all enthusiasts for liberty and progress, that the claims of collective Socialism to be the somehow and of the ranks of the Democratic Federation to be the somewhere, are worthy of consideration in view of the general paucity of results from the publication of fervid verse.

Mr. Ernest Radford is too shrewd, and has too keen a sense of the ridiculous, to disregard common sense and polite taste so outra-

geously as Mr. Beatty, in his wilder moments, has done. He is a
critic, and knows how to refine his verse. He is also a humourist, and
can, on occasion, help himself across the shallows of inspiration by
sportive essays in the vein of the late Mr. Calverley. Sometimes,
indeed, the humourist gets the better (or the worse) of both critic
and poet. Mr. Radford is not very industrious, apparently. His *Measured Steps* are short and do not carry him very far: *Fits and Starts,*
as he calls his humorous pieces, are more fitful than startling. Out of
twenty-seven of the former, ten were published at Cambridge in
1882; and five out of the twenty jocular trifles are also reprints,
whilst eight of the new ones are astonishing attempts to impart a
sane aspect to the repetitions of the triolet by taking familiar street
cries for the recurring lines, and intercalating them with bitter
asides. The remainder of the volume consists of translations from
Heine. The *Measured Steps* are so good as far as they go that it is
difficult to account for the feeling of dissatisfaction which some of
them leave. In two trivial verselets, *Christmas at Plymouth,* Mr.
Radford complains that he is "sad and seedy." And his pathos does
not at any place suggest deeper tragedy than this. Even at his sad-
dest and seediest, he tacitly refuses to be serious, having apparently
no settled convictions, and too much sincerity to excite himself without conviction. The comparative infertility of his Muse may be due to
his labour as an art-critic, or to his fastidiousness in selecting poems
for publication; but her egotistical disregard of any wider feelings
than the vague regrets and undefined aspirations of the sad and
seedy Individual is less excusable.

"Michael Field," the author of *Callirhöe* and *Fair Rosamund* is a
woman who, following the example of Charlotte Bronté and George
Eliot, pays the other sex the compliment of attempting to pass as a
member of it. Why this senseless mystification should be dealt with
more tenderly than any other species of fraud probably does not now
appear plainly to the generous critic who, in the *Spectator,* announced as a great poet the author who was unprovokedly duping
him by a misleading title page. In *Callirhöe,* however, the relations
between the heroine and the priest Coresus are such as women
invent for themselves with delight, whereas nothing analogous to
them is to be found in the work of any virile poet. It has been stated
on several hands—and certain expressions in the drama and preface
seem to countenance the opinion—that the moral of Callirhöe is that
people should be enthusiastic. With all my kindly feeling towards the
Californian parson who, whether swearing, praying, or gambling,

"done it with a zest," a cultus of pure enthusiasm seems to me so preposterous that I cannot believe that Michael Field really means it; nor is it made attractive by the Mænads of the drama, drunken furies whose tie to the altar of Bacchus is their jealous love of his priest. The scene is Calydon. The classical and the romantic—the respectable and the Bohemian—patience and impulse, are at war there as usual. Coresus, the priest of Bacchus, attempts to convert Callirhöe. His motives being obviously personal, she repels him; and he, irritated by the rebuff, calls upon his god to smite Calydon with a plague. This extraordinarily unreasonable demand being complied with (a circumstance which surely does not place the god of enthusiasm in a favourable light), the oracle is consulted by the citizens. The reply is that Callirhöe has offended the gods, and must either die or find a substitute willing to die for her. Coresus leads her to the sacrificial altar, but stabs himself. The plague is stayed; and Callirhöe, struck by the conduct of Coresus, embraces his faith, and enthusiastically commits suicide. The most remarkable character is her brother Emathion, a champion athlete, but a hopeless cur. He it is who is sent, because of his fleetness of foot, to consult the oracle. At the sacred grove he inspires passion in an old pythoness; and the scene in which the wind rises in the grove until the oracle is delivered, he almost beside himself with terror at the supernatural tempest and with loathing at the proffered caresses of the decrepit priestess, is so brutally grotesque, and at the same time so terrible and pitiful, that it is hard to decide whether it is above criticism or beneath it. Whichever it be, the drama is worth reading for its sake. Squeamish readers will be shocked by the tragi-comic old woman, in whose mouth a single tooth appears like a stalagmite in a vast cavern, and from whose peaky nose hangs "a drop." But squeamish readers will not take kindly to so vigorous and frank a writer as Michael Field, who, if she has not yet the originality of a mature poet, has a large share in the freshness of a young one. *Callirhöe,* however, is admirable only for the sake of such episodes as that cited above, and for a charming scene in which a Faun, like Taglioni in *La Sylphide,* or Cabel in *Dinorah,* dances to his own shadow. As an organic whole it comes to nothing. Machaon, a physician who takes a common-sense and somewhat sceptical view of the proceedings, and who sees, one would think, enough of the cultus of enthusiasm to prejudice him against it for the rest of his life, becomes its high priest in the last act on grounds which he fails to make clear. A cultus of pure enthusiasm is perhaps not unlikely to lead to a practice of pure inconsistency, or, as the modern American calls it, pure cussedness; but unfortunately for the dramatic effect, Machaon seems the last man in the antique world to give way to cussedness in the presence of an impressive national calamity, and a touching domestic tragedy.

In *Fair Rosamund,* Michael Field reminds us, not for the first time, of Charlotte Brontë, by the force of her execution, and by her entire want of sympathy with the evil personages she portrays. The old knight, Sir Topaz, seems to be the result of an attempt to create an interesting character out of a passing fancy without any substantial materials. The atmosphere of *Fair Rosamund* is Gothic, as that of *Callirhöe* is Greek, each play being as fresh after the other as if they were from different hands, although the individuality of the author asserts itself with equal force in both.

L. O. STREETER

Editor's Notes

▪ The above review was originally published in *To-Day,* n.s. 2 (August 1884): 156–64; but no dates for Shaw's reviewing occur in his 1884 notes. (see *Diary* 33)

▪ The pseudonym "L. O. Streeter" was one of several employed by Shaw in his early journalistic days. According to Dan H. Laurence it meant "Lives on Osnaburgh Street."

▪ Amy Levy (1861–89), English poet and fiction writer. She was educated at Brighton School and became the first Jewish woman to enter Newnham College, Cambridge. From an early age she showed literary talent, publishing short stories in *Victoria* magazine in 1880 and her first book of poetry (*Xantippe and Other Verse*) in 1881 while still a student. After leaving Cambridge, Amy Levy traveled through Europe, pursuing her interest in the Jewish experience. Her novel *Reuben Sachs* (1888) concerns the disparity between the affluent Jewish society with which she was familiar, and the more austere lifestyle of Jewish tradition. The book received adverse criticism from some Jewish quarters and this, plus her melancholic temperament, according to some, led her to take her own life on 10 September 1889 at the age of twenty-seven. In addition to the books mentioned above, Amy Levy published *The Romance of a Shop: a Novel* (1888), *Miss Meredith* (1889), and some short fiction. Her last book, *A London Plane Tree, and Other Verse* (1889), she corrected a week before her death, in preparation (as her best friends believed) for the end she had marked out for herself.

▪ [Robert] Browning (1812–89), according to Shaw, "saved English verse from utter emasculation." Shaw was elected "by mistake" in 1883 to the Browning Society, a wild group that discussed almost any topic. On 29 June 1887 Shaw and Edward Gonner tried to dissolve the society on the grounds that "it had ceased to exist," but the motion failed.

■ Pakenham Thomas Beatty (1855–1930), Anglo-Irish poet who settled in London in the 1870s, where he lived on a dwindling inheritance. Shaw's friendship with Beatty began at this time (in 1878 Beatty sent Shaw a copy of his first book of poetry, *To My Lady, and Other Poems.*) Himself an amateur boxer, Beatty interested Shaw in boxing, introducing him to Ned Donnelly (professor of boxing to the London Athletic Club), who became the model for Ned Skene in Shaw's novel *Cashel Byron's Profession* (1882–83). Beatty himself was satirized in Shaw's last novel, *An Unsocial Socialist* (1883), and later his nickname "Paquito" supplied the nickname of Captain Brassbound. Shaw's friendship with Beatty survived the latter's pursuit of Shaw's sister, and Beatty's alcoholism. During this period Shaw acted as advisor to his wife Edith "Ida" Beatty, in addition to which he paid toward her son Mazzini's education and lent money to Beatty in memory of the latter's subsidizing *him* in his impecunious youth.

■ Pakenham Beatty's dedications were occasionally fulsome. *Marcia,* for example, begins with the following:

> I dedicate this book,
> As an inadequate tribute of admiration and
> affection,
> To the greatest of living English dramatists,
> To the one epic poet since Milton,
> To my master and dear friend
> Richard Hengist Horne.

This is followed by twelve lines of verse that offer "what gifts are ours"

> Till our sun miss thee, and thou be
> Where Marlowe's spirit waits for thee.

■ In the late 1870s the Social-Revolutionary Party in Russia, though it had, by its own admission "no political reforms in view," sought to destroy despotism in the person of the Czar Alexander II (1818–81). After several bombs had exploded—some under the Czar's own roof—Loris-Melikov (1825–88), an Armenian soldier, was appointed to head a special executive commission to crush the terrorists in the empire. Loris-Melikov showed no mercy, and there were countless arrests and executions. Nevertheless on 1 March 1881 two bomb attacks took place on the Czar in his carriage en route to the Winter Palace in Saint Petersburg, the second of which injured him so severely that he died. Ironically, under Loris-Melikov there had been a liberalization of the regime; while the assassination of Alexander II, abruptly ending the age of reform associated with his name, brought about yet another reactionary period of repression in the Russian Empire.

- Shaw's reference to the imprisonment of the editor of the *Freiheit* is a reminder that, largely as a result of two assassination attempts on the life of Kaiser Wilhelm in May and June 1878, Bismarck, the German chancellor, proposed legislation against the Socialists and their peers. When the Reichstag reconvened in September of that year, there was an overwhelming vote in favor of the anti-Socialist law (passed on 21 October), which outlawed "social-democratic, socialistic, and communistic" organizations that aimed to overthrow the existing political order. Publications could be forbidden and organization members imprisoned.
- Ernest William Radford (1853–1919), English barrister, poet, and art critic, who married Caroline "Dollie" Maitland (?–1920) in 1884, in which year Shaw set some of her verse to music. She later became a prolific writer of verse for children. From 1885 to the early 1890s Shaw was a close friend of the Radfords. Ernest Radford was a fellow Fabian, member of the Browning Society, and frequenter of the British Museum. In addition to writing art criticism, Radford was a member, and for a time secretary, of the Rhymers' Club, a society of poets who met at the "Cheshire Cheese" in Fleet Street, and read their poems to one another; together with that of Ernest Dowson, Ernest Rhys, Arthur Symonds, Richard Le Gallienne, W. B. Yeats, and others his work was anthologized in *The Book of the Rhymers' Club* in 1892, and in the *Second Book of the Rhymers' Club* in 1893.
- Charles Stuart Calverley (1831–84), English parodist who had died that very February. He published *Verses and Translations* (1862) and *Fly Leaves* (1866), and became famous for the scholarly wit of his verse and for parodies of Browning, Macaulay, Tupper, and others.
- "Michael Field," joint pseudonym of two English women poets, Katherine Harris Bradley (1848–1914), and her niece Edith Emma Cooper (1862–1913). In 1881 they began their collaborations in verse, producing twenty-seven tragedies, a masque, and eight volumes of lyric poetry. From 1884 to 1914 they also kept a journal, which was bequeathed to T. Sturge Moore (their literary executor) with instructions for him to open it at the end of 1929 and "publish so much and whatever parts of it" he might think fit. Accordingly, a selection from this was published, together with some of their letters, in 1933 under the title of *Works and Days*. Shaw's view of their work is now the general one; nor was he impressed by it when it was staged: on 25 October 1893, at the Opéra Comique, he found the dress rehearsal of "Michael Field's" *A Question of Memory* "very tedious."
- Arthur William Edgar O'Shaughnessy (1844–81), English poet. The quotation

> I would be with the workers in the van
> For somehow, somewhere, rises godlike Man

is from "Europe" published in *Music and Moonlight* (1874), in which, anticipating history, the poet rejects "Polluted France" and "Spoiled" Italy, in anticipation of

a more splendid vision, as of grand
Unanimous Europe.

- Maria Taglioni (1804–84) Italian *danseuse,* born in Stockholm of Italian and Swedish parentage. She was acknowledged to be the finest dancer in the world when she created the title role in Jean Schneitzhoeffer's *La Sylphide* in 1832, with what Théophile Gautier described as "aerial and virginal grace."
- Marie Josèphe Cabel (1827–85), Belgian soprano who created the title role in Meyerbeer's opera *Dinorah, ou le Pardon de Ploërmel* when it was first performed at the Opéra Comique in Paris on 4 April 1859. In the opening scene of the second act she sang and danced the "Shadow Song."

1 December 1884
THE SOCIALIST CATECHISM* [C87]

THIS is a reprint, or rather a new edition, of a catechism recently published in *Justice.* Its value has been considerably enhanced by the addition of new matter; the rearrangement of many of the questions; their division into chapters under various heads; and a thoughtful revision of the original text, which now stands purged of a few inaccuracies of expression which left the portions which appeared in *Justice* open here and there to exception. The result is in every way worthy of the conscientious labour which Mr. Joynes has bestowed on his work. It reappears as a penny pamphlet, a price which can only prove remunerative in the event of the work attaining a very large circulation. This it certainly deserves; for we can recall no instance of a book containing so much carefully considered and stated economic information and costing so little to the purchaser. The question-and-answer form in which this information is conveyed has the advantages of exceptional conciseness; of stating objections in the shape in which they are most frequently raised; and of giving to many important points an emphasis which would be lost in the smoother web of a conventional treatise. Not that Mr. Joynes's conclusions always need artificial prominence of this sort. Such a statement as that "nothing

---

* "The Socialist Catechism." By J. L. Joynes. (London: Modern Press, 1884.)

short of a display of organised force" (on the part of the workers) "will enable the idlers as a body to perceive the advantage of taking their due share in the necessary work of society under a just system of Socialism" hardly requires to be specially recommended to the attention of ordinary readers. And again, "For what have the labourers really to thank the capitalists? For defrauding them of three-quarters of the fruits of their toil, and rendering leisure, education, and natural enjoyment almost impossible for them to attain"—is not likely to be overlooked. This somewhat bitter strain of sarcasm does not appear, however, until it has been justified by a plenteous array of evidence, presented in their logical order, and conducting the reader inevitably to the author's conclusions. A certain piquancy is imparted to the questions by the fluctuations of opinion and even of mental capacity exhibited by Mr. Joynes's suppositious catechist, who sometimes lays traps for his interlocutor and snubs him ruthlessly for falling into them, and sometimes asks the most feeble questions and is in turn made to feel his inferiority by a crushing reply. On the whole, Mr. Joynes's work, like others in a similar form, is not without occasional humour; but in no case have we detected unsound points in the views enunciated. Of all the shorter publications of the Modern Press on the subject of Socialism, we have seen none cheaper and none more likely to prove helpful to the student or interesting to the casual enquirer.

Editor's Notes

▪ The above review was published in *The Christian Socialist: a Journal for those who Work and Think* 2, no. 19 (December 1884), the year in which no accounts of Shaw's reviewing occur (see *Diary* 33).

▪ J[ames] L[eigh] Joynes (1853–93), English Socialist, teacher, and poet. Educated at Eton and Cambridge, he returned to Eton as an undermaster. Like Shaw, Joynes was a vegetarian, a Shelleyan, and, briefly, a Fabian; the two men were close friends in the 1880s. In August 1882, having agreed to write some descriptions of the Irish troubles for the *Times*, Joynes was arrested in Loughrea, Co. Galway, Ireland, while traveling with Henry George, both men being taken for Fenian organizers. Joynes's report of this incident in the *Times* (4 September 1882) springboarded George and his ideas of land nationalization into notoriety, and was no doubt responsible for the enormous crowd (which included Bernard Shaw) which went to hear his lecture on 5 September at the Memorial Hall, Farringdon Street, London. Joynes had already written *The Adventures of a Tourist in Ireland* (1882), and with

Belfort Bax (see below, 229), was coediting *To-Day,* which was currently serializing Shaw's novel *An Unsocial Socialist,* and was later to serialize *Cashel Byron's Profession.* In November 1889 Shaw tried to return the compliment by interceding for Joynes with the Bodley Head publishing house on behalf of Joynes's poems. The publishers wished certain poems omitted. Shaw rejected this notion; and they promptly rejected the poems, which were privately published as *On Lonely Shores and Other Rhymes* in 1892. By this time, Joynes was suffering from ill health, and he died in 1893.

▪ *Justice,* a Socialist weekly journal, edited by H. M. Hyndman, had been started in January 1884 with a gift of three hundred pounds from the poet Edward Carpenter. The penny newspaper was sold door to door in Fleet Street and the Strand by its staff, including William Morris, Henry Champion, R. P. B. Frost, and Joynes himself.

1 February 1885
LEAVES FROM A PRISON DIARY* [C89]

THESE leaves from a prison diary are presented in the form of lectures to a prison blackbird, to whom Mr. Davitt played the part of Mr. Barlow, interesting the bird at first by descriptions of crime and criminals, illustrated by many amusing anecdotes, and then, having entrapped its attention and raised its hopes of further entertainment to the highest pitch, extinguishing all its vivacity by a discourse in which political economy, ethics, and sentiment, Mill, Jevons, and Mr. Henry George, land monopoly, Collectivism, and the functions of the State in relation to the state ownership of railways, are brought to bear heavily on the blackbird, with a view to making plain before it "the path illumined by the Star of Hope." After this, Mr. Davitt "indulged the fond hope that he" (Joey, the blackbird) "would have remained" for further enlightenment. "I opened his door," says Mr. Davitt, "with a trembling hand, when, quick as a flash of lightning, he rushed from the cage with a wild scream of delight, and in a moment was beyond the walls of the prison." This was the fault of the second volume. The first almost gives a charm to penal servitude. The exclusiveness of the "magsman nobility"; the

---

* "Leaves from a Prison Diary." By Michael Davitt, Founder of the Land League. (London: Chapman and Hall, 1885.)

scorn of the "hook" for the snatcher; the jealousy with which the honourable title of thief is denied to pretentious cadgers and shoplifters; the vainglory of the "bruiser"; the wide toleration of all religions which permits a convict to change his faith, at a moment's notice, for the sake of sitting next an old friend or under a more gullible chaplain; the cynical philosophy of the swindler who, having improved his mind by the study of Pascal and Lafontaine, proves logically that there is no such thing as honesty; and the vaunted rectitude of the unfortunate person, condemned to penal servitude by jurors who fancied that the presence of a dead woman at the foot of a staircase is necessarily due to a swearing and heavily-booted man at the top;—all these might tempt a student of humanity to obtain admission to Dartmoor in the most usual way, if they were not so terribly like the castes, hypocrisies, and false pretences of the world at large.

Should the student, missing the similarity, wish to study life in a "push," and taste "toke" and "skilly," he will find the fullest instructions for picking a pocket or performing the three card trick in Mr. Davitt's pages, though he will be duly warned there that a sentence of seven years penal servitude is a sufficient expiation of any crime short of murder. This being so, it is impossible not to admire the spirit in which Mr. Davitt, in spite of the ardent temperament which makes his style so pronouncedly Irish at times, betrays no bitterness with regard to his severe sentence, and does not condescend even to mention the cancelling of his ticket-of-leave, subsequently admitted to be an act of mistaken meanness. Solitary confinement has not made him egotistical. His book is chiefly concerned with the criminals with whom he suffered. Regarding them as inevitable products of our civilization, he is fairly free from the old vindictive conception of the object of imprisonment as punishment, though it crops up once or twice in the use of such words as "expiation." He goes at some length into the question of education, and traces the evils of our present condition to private property in land, in the abolition of which he sees the remedy for poverty and for the crime which springs from poverty. Here he is following Mr. Henry George, to whose teaching in "Progress and Poverty" he adds nothing except some criticism of the schemes of Mr. Alfred Russell [sic] Wallace, and the Financial Reform Association for "nationalizing" the land. "I would abolish land monopoly," he says, "by simply taxing all land, exclusive of improvements, up to its full value. . . . The labourer would then have to purchase only the tenant right" (i.e., the improvements). Mr. Davitt, in fact, like Mr. George, goes too far for ordinary opinions in attacking the property of the landlord, and not far enough for the Socialist who will point out that the labourer could not compete successfully with the wealthy capitalist for the land so thrown open, and would thus remain a labourer to the end of his days, having changed nothing but his master. Mr. Davitt, indeed, finally announces that "complete co-operative production" is the only final solution of the Labour Question, and so declares himself a thorough Collectivist Socialist. This, however, is not new; and the portion of the book which is most interesting and most valuable is that which has grown out of his experience of penal servitude. The testimony of an observant and able man, guiltless of dishonesty, and conscious of no reason to be ashamed of his condemnation, is free from the suspicion which always attaches to the "confessions" of genuine rogues, even when they have the rare gift of being able to describe what has passed under their observation.

It is pleasant to be able to lay down this book with the knowledge that Mr. Davitt's prison hardships are over, and that, among the converts of Mr. George, he is one of the most popular men in England. From being bullied by a warder for chatting with a fellow-convict in a "push" at Portland, to being enthusiastically cheered by a packed audience in St. James's Hall, is an agreeable transition which Mr. Davitt has shared with only one man in England—the Tichborne claimant. About him there is a chapter in the prison diary which will attract many readers. A somewhat amateurish sketch of the writer in his cell, with the blackbird perched on the bedpost, has the merit of being a capital likeness.

Editor's Notes

• There is no indication in Shaw's *Diary* for 1885 of when he wrote this review, which was first published in *Time*, n.s. (February 1885). It was reprinted in the *New Edinburgh Review*, no. 29 (April 1975).

• E. M. Abdy-Williams [Mrs. Bernard Whishaw] (1857–1914), the editor of *Time*, had casually asked Shaw at a Fabian Society meeting to review Michael Davitt's book for her journal. Later a payment dispute arose over the review, which, Ms. Abdy-Williams understood, was to be paid for only by a copy of the book in question. Shaw accepted this ruling with a bad grace; and on 10 March his *Diary* reports "Rec'd: Sonnenschein & Co. for Davitt review in Feb. No. of *Time* 1/1/0" (a cheque for £1.1s.0d.)

• Michael Davitt (1846–1906), Irish nationalist, whose family was evicted and emigrated to Haslingden, Lancashire, in 1851, where Davitt lost his right arm in a factory accident in 1857. In 1866 he joined the Fenian movement. Imprisoned in Dartmoor in 1870, Davitt served seven of a fifteen-year prison sentence before being released on "ticket-of-leave," (which was an order of licence giving a convict his liberty under certain restrictions before his sentence had expired.) His leadership of the Mayo tenant farmers and subsequent alliance with Charles Stewart Parnell (1846–91) earned him the title "Father of the Land League" (the Irish National Land League), which was founded on 21 October 1879. But in February 1881 the Liberal government, unable to win a guilty verdict against Davitt on charges related to the land agitation, revoked his pass, and he spent fifteen months in Portland Prison. Shaw finally met him on 10 May 1888, at the Bedford Debating Society. (*Diary* 374). In 1895 Davitt was returned as member for South Mayo, but resigned in 1899. In addition to the above book, whose full title is *Leaves from a Prison Diary; or, Lectures to a "Solitary" Audience,* Davitt wrote numerous political works, including *Life and Progress in Australasia* (1898), *The Boer Fight for Freedom* (1902), and *Within the Pale. The true story of anti-Semitic persecutions in Russia* (1903).

▪ In convicts' slang, "magsmen" were cardsharpers, confidence-trick workers, begging-letter writers, bogus ministers of religion, professional noblemen, "helpless victims of the cruel world," and medical quacks; a "hook" was a Manchester term for a pickpocket; a "snatcher" was a young inexperienced thief or apprentice pickpocket; a "bruiser," a cowardly bully, "usually the hanger-on of some unfortunate creature who supports him out of the rewards of her shame"; a "push," a prison labor gang; "toke," a general name for food; and "skilly," a kind of gruel, served to prisoners.

▪ Henry George (see above, 23–24).

▪ Alfred Russel Wallace (1823–1913), Welsh naturalist. Primarily known for his foundation work on scientific zoogeography and his influence upon Darwin's *Origin of Species,* both before and after its publication (he published his own *Contributions to the Theory of Natural Selection* in 1870), Wallace yet found time to advocate land nationalization in a book of that name published in 1882. He proposed, however, that, following a complete valuation of the landed property of the kingdom, a distinction be made between the inherent value of the land and that which arose from improvements to it, the latter remaining the property of the landlord. Davitt objected to Wallace's proposal saying "it is . . . difficult to imagine a scheme more utterly neglectful of the interests of the community at large." Shaw adds an "l" to Wallace's second name.

▪ The Financial Reform Association, had proposed that a tax of four shillings on the pound be levied upon all landed property. Conceding that this would be a step in the right direction, Davitt nevertheless felt that once the revenue from such a tax had been collected, there would be pressure for the tax to cease until the next crisis; in the meantime the landlords would recoup their loss by increasing rents.

▪ The Tichborne claimant was Arthur Orton, who in 1872 claimed to be the heir presumptive to the Tichborne estates, Roger Charles Tichborne (1829–54), who had in fact been lost at sea. He was tried for perjury, imprisoned, and was a fellow prisoner of Michael Davitt for two years in Dartmoor.

1 April 1885

PROFESSOR KARL PEARSON ON THE THEORY AND PRACTICE OF SOCIALISM* [C97]

IN the matter of lectures on Socialism, the working classes of to-day may esteem themselves specially favoured. They know, by their daily experience, more of the subject than the middle class knows; and they are consequently less in need of instruction. Yet lecturers that are patient, conciliatory, forbearing, and minutely explanatory when addressing workmen attack the middle-class with fierce denunciation, biting sarcasm, bewildering paradox, or perhaps a combination of all three. Professor Pearson, in his preface to this admirable pamphlet, expressly states that had it been intended for a middle-class audience, its tone would have been harsher. "The selfishness of the upper classes," he says, "arises to a great extent from ignorance; but these are times in which such ignorance is itself criminal." He might have added that the upper classes have never admitted ignorance as an extenuation of the selfishness of such members of the working class as have occasionally attempted to appropriate the portable property of the rich, although it is certain, that stealing appears as rational to many cruelly punished thieves as rent does to a landlord. Professor Pearson, however, with a working-class audience in view, proceeds in a gentle but very earnest strain. After declaring, by way of preface, that the higher socialism of our time strives, not for mere political reorganization, but for a renascence of morality, he points out that the government of this country is not in the hands of the people. "It is mere self-deception," he says, "for us to suppose that all

---

* "Socialism in Theory and Practice; being a Lecture Delivered to a Working-Class Audience in Plain and Simple Language." By Karl Pearson, M.A. (William Reeves, 185, Fleet Street, London, E.C.) Price 2d.

classes have a voice in the management of affairs. The educative class (the class which labours with its head) and the productive class (the class which labours with its hands) have little or no real influence in the House of Commons. The governing class is the class of wealth, in both of its branches—owners of land and owners of capital. This class naturally governs in its own interests; and the interests of wealth are what we must seek for, would we understand the motive of any particular form of foreign or domestic policy on the part of either great state party." Mr. Pearson then shews that the state of things which the upper classes profess to have discovered for the first time from "The bitter cry of Outcast London," was fully made known forty years before that sensational pennyworth appeared; and he deals with the pretence that extreme poverty is proved by history to be inevitable and irremediable by stating that he has made special investigation of the condition of the working class in Germany some three to four hundred years ago, and that "anything like the condition of the courts and dwellings of poorer London was then totally unknown."

As Mr. Pearson's pamphlet costs only twopence, and is exceedingly well worth that sum, it is not necessary to condense his matter, which is lucidly and agreeably set forth, into a review. He does not shrink from the extreme Socialist position of objecting to the rent of exceptional ability as he does to rent of land or interest on capital; but he has no patience with claims to natural "rights," or appeals to "justice;" and he is careful to shew that mere rebellion is no remedy for existing evils, and that the hand workers, by attempting to help themselves by violence, would only alienate the head workers, who alone can organize a better system. He attaches great importance to the possible effect of extension of the franchise, provided the enfranchised be educated to understand that Society must be organized on the basis of labour; that all labour is equally honourable; and that the general law of a society based on wealth is that the misery of the labouring classes is directly proportional to the luxury of the wealthy. He advocates land nationalization, but objects to Mr. George's scheme of expropriation without compensation as too sudden, and to expropriation with full compensation as being really not nationalization at all. Instead of either, he offers the following suggestion: "Let a bill be passed to convert all freehold in land into a leasehold, say, of 100 years. Here there would be no question of compensation, and little real injury to the *present* landowner, because the difference between freehold and a hundred years' leasehold (at least in towns) is comparatively small. At the end of a hundred years the nation would be in possession of all land without having paid a penny for it, and without violently breaking up the present social arrangements. . . . Precisely as I propose to treat the land I would treat most forms of capital. With the land, of course, mines and factories would necessarily pass into the hands of the nation. Railways would have to be dealt with in the same fashion. The present companies would have a hundred years' lease instead of a perpetuity of their property."

This suggestion will probably meet with some criticism. One objection has been anticipated by Professor Pearson: that of the uselessness of striving for a measure that, if carried, would postpone the realization of Socialism until after our deaths. His reply is, that "the little streak of improvement which each man may leave behind him—the only immortality of which mankind can be sure—is a far nobler result of labour, whether of hand or head, than three-score years of unlimited personal happiness." It may be added that those who doubt this may also have reason to doubt whether, if Socialism were realized to morrow, they would be fit for it or happy under it. Men without sufficient virtue to induce them to work for posterity are probably happier as individualists than any truly socialist state could make them.

Editor's Notes

- The above review was published in *The Christian Socialist: a Journal for those who Work and Think* 2 (April 1885), the same edition which published Shaw's lecture on "Socialism" given to the Liberal and Social Union on 26 February 1885.
- Shaw's Diary for 23 March 1885 has the reminder "Send in review of K. Pearson's pamphlet to Reeves for *The Christian Socialist*." It was the following day, however, when Shaw "left review of Pearson with Reeves" (*Diary* 72).
- Karl Pearson (1857–1936), English mathematician, and founder of the science of statistics. After graduating from Cambridge in 1879 he went to Germany where he studied both physics and metaphysics and, under the influence of the two leaders of German Socialism, Karl Marx and Ferdinand Lassalle, became a committed Socialist. Returning to London, he was called to the Bar in 1881, in which year he also obtained his LL.B. from Cambridge. He was appointed Goldsmid Professor of Applied Mathematics at University College, London, in 1884, and was lecturer in geometry at Gresham College, London, from 1891 to 1894. In 1911 he relinquished the Goldsmid Chair to

become the first Galton Professor of Eugenics (at Galton's expressed wish.) Among Pearson's works are *The Moral Basis of Socialism* (1887), in which year a second edition of the above-reviewed pamphlet appeared, retitled *Socialism, its Theory and Practice; The Chances of Death* (1897), *The Grammar of Science* (1899), and *The Life and Letters of Francis Galton* (1915). Shaw was a friend of Pearson in the 1890s, sharing with him an interest in Socialism and Ibsen.

▪ *The Bitter Cry of Outcast London. An Inquiry into the Condition of the Abject Poor,* a penny pamphlet prepared by Nonconformist ministers, exposing the frightful conditions of the housing of the working classes, had appeared in the summer of 1883. Shaw had helped himself freely to the information it contained when he began his first play the following year.

27 March 1888

THE BOOKMAKER AS HE IS* [C417]

"SUPPOSE any one owed you £1,000, and your only security was the word of honor of a clergyman or of a bookmaker, which of the two would you prefer for your debtor? I believe that 99 out of 100 would feel surer of getting their money were it owed by a bookmaker rather than by the parson. What is the reason of this? Simply the fact that bookmakers, as a class, have a far higher sense of honor about money matters than the clergy." Thus Mr. Chaplin Piesse, holding a brief for the bookmakers against their detractors. He goes on to point out that great criminals never graduate as bookmakers: they have all been either lawyers, divines, doctors, or unprofessional men. These pleadings are very ingenious, and at times almost eloquent. In many particulars they are perfectly true. A clergyman can without any particular discredit or damage to himself be six months late in settling his bills, when a delay of six hours would ruin a bookmaker. But this is due, not to a more exquisite sense of honor in the bookmaker, but partly to the fact that prompt settlements are in the nature of his business, and partly to the extreme improbability—absent in the case of the clergy—that he will pay at all if he does not pay at once. Short

* "The Bookmaker as He is." By G. Chaplin Piesse. (London: *Sporting Life* Office, 1888.)

accounts make long friends; but it would be a grave mistake to infer that those who act most on this maxim are persons of exceptionally friendly disposition. It may be conceded to Mr. Piesse that the bookmakers are necessarily strict in their money dealings, and that to confound them with the roughs, the thieves, the welshers, and the advertising tipsters is to show crude ignorance of the turf. Further, no objection can be alleged to their occupation that does not apply equally to that of the stockbroker who does "speculative business." It is also true that whilst the turf flourishes the bookmakers minimise its evils instead of aggravating them; and it is at least possible to defend the assumption that the natural propensity to gamble necessitates for its orderly satisfaction either the turf or its foreign equivalent the State lottery. But, admitting all this, the fact remains that the bookmaker is the organizer of gambling, and that gambling is the meanest and most anti-social of the vices, because it is at bottom a desire to get money without earning it. The first qualification of the betting man is cupidity, the second laziness, the third willingness to gain by others' loss. It is, in short, a thoroughly aristocratic vice. When the working man condescends to it, he forfeits his right to denounce and resist those who live idly upon his labor, since they are only doing by law what he is trying to do by luck. Mr. Piesse's whole contention rests on the position that there is no harm in moderate gambling. Therefore the organizer of gambling is a useful and respectable member of society. One cannot help thinking how excellent a case the late Mrs. Jeffries could have made for her calling by simply assuming that, human nature being what it is, there is no harm in a moderate recourse to prostitution.

Editor's Notes

- This review was first published in the *Star*, 27 March 1888, 2:1. The *Star* had been founded in 1856 as the *Morning Star & Evening Star*, but in 1869 both papers were absorbed into the *Daily News*. In 1887 the *Star* made its reappearance, owned by Daily News Ltd. This was Shaw's sixteenth article in that periodical, but his first book review.
- Shaw's *Diary* for 20 March 1888 records that he "wrote and sent off review of a book in defense of bookmakers (*On the Turf*)" (*Diary* 359).
- G. Chaplin Piesse (n.d.), writer of books on gambling. He also wrote with W. F. Goldberg *Monte Carlo, and how to do it* (1890), which ran to three editions.
- The strong terms in which Shaw disapproves of gambling are repeated in

his Preface to *Mrs. Warren's Profession,* where the bookmaker is used as the male equivalent to Mrs. Warren, and gambling is condemned even more vigorously than prostitution.

- Shaw refers to the state lottery as the "foreign equivalent" of the turf because although such things still featured largely in the budgets of Germany, Holland, Spain, and Italy, they had been suppressed in Great Britain since 1826 (following the corruption of the British state lotteries from 1709 to 1824).

- "The late Mrs. Jeffries" was Mary Frances Jefferies (1819?–87), described as a "lodging house keeper," who had been convicted on 27 April 1885 at the Middlesex Quarter Sessions, and fined £200 for "keeping disorderly houses" in Church Street, Chelsea; and who had been arrested again on 27 September 1887, accused of keeping a brothel at 15 Brompton Square, of which she was the landlady, though she still resided in Chelsea. Shaw's spelling of her name (without the second "e") suggests he read of her case in the *Pall Mall Gazette. The Times* spelled her name "Jefferies."

3 April 1888

BOOKS OF THE DAY: "SONGS OF A REVOLUTIONARY EPOCH"* [C420]

MR. J. L JOYNES is known to the people as a gentleman who once sang a song of revolution to a tune that cost him a valuable mastership at Eton, which he had the honesty to sacrifice when the authorities forced upon him the alternative of resignation or perpetual silence as to his opinion that the land belongs of right to the people and not to the landlords. If that recommendation is not sufficient, it is only necessary to add that when Mr. Joynes visited Ireland he was put in prison. That clinches a good character for a man nowadays.

The songs translated in this shilling volume begin with certain fiery utterances of Freiligrath's inspired by the European revolutionary movement of 1848. Some of them breathe that fierce contempt for the law which is the most dangerous product of aristocratic governments, and which is worthy the serious consideration of democratic govern-

* "Songs of a Revolutionary Epoch." By J. L. Joynes. (London: Foulger and Co., 1888.)

ments who take advantage of septennial acts to violate their election pledges. "Black, Red, and Gold," with its terrible refrain, is a sinister echo of it.

> "Nay, Freedom reigns not there aright
>   Where men with all submission,
> Instead of arming them for fight
>   Present a fool Petition.
> God help the cowards who present,
> Petitions to a Parliament!
>   Powder is Black;
>   Blood is Red;
>   Golden flares the Flame!"

Less splendid and impetuous than Freiligrath, but also less artificial, and with a certain bitter homeliness and pathos that make a haunting impression on the imagination, are the songs of Georg Herwegh. Nothing could add to the burden of "The Birth of Lisa's Child."

> "Haste, Lisa, to the hospital:
> 'Tis there the common folk are born."

There is a pang in every repetition of it. "Poor old Jacob," dead after a lifetime of toil, is not the easier to read because so many die among us daily of whom it might have been written. Here is the first verse and the last:—

> "Yes, poor old Jacob died last night;
>   At early dawn they took his measure;
> Made him a coffin 'ere 'twas light,
>   And laid therein the treasure.
> "They coffined him with ne'er a shroud;
>   Yet sleeps he sound his boards between.
> No prince shall rise, however proud,
>   Whose linen shall be clean."

But Herwegh could vary these heartbreaking hymns to the poor by a strain not unlike that in which Mr. Joynes himself sometimes vents his humor. The most amusing example of this vein is "The Heathen," of whom we are told that—

> "To tyrants they were hardly fair,
>   Preferring mostly to be free.
> How sensible those heathen were!
>   The heathen: yes—but we?"

A less playful sarcasm is felt in some of the songs of labor by various writers at the end of the volume. The humor of "The Weavers—from an Employer's Point of View" is mordant; and the moral of "Content" may be gathered from the last verse:—

> "Content shall be my one delight:
>   Content shall all my glory be.
> In tatters and in rags bedight
>   No nobler virtue can I see.
> "And if in rags and tatters old
> I die of hunger and of cold,
>   Write o'er my grave, 'This good man went
>   And died at last of sheer content.'"

There is hardly one of the 176 pages from which a worker who has thought over his condition will not find a verse coming straight home to him. With the exception of a few of Freiligrath's more reckless calls to arms, the songs of '48 retain most of their point still. As to Mr. Joynes's share in the work, his success as a translator is unusually complete. The English dresses of the poems are homespun; there is in them no English as she is spoke in Germany. Force, freedom, felicity of phrase, apparent spontaneity—all the characteristics of original verse are preserved; and yet the translations are for the most part very close indeed. He has even grappled with the impossibilities of Heine, who is represented by six out of the 80 poems. It is unnecessary to add that he brought to the work a full measure of the spirit of democracy which filled the first authors of his remarkable revolutionary anthology.

Editor's Notes

- Shaw began his review of Joynes's translations "in the afternoon at the [British] Museum," on 13 March 1888, and the following day "added a few words to the Joynes review." However, since a differently worded and longer review by Shaw appeared in the *Pall Mall Gazette* almost two weeks later (on 13 April), it may be that the *Star* review occupied Shaw only one day; for on

15 March the Diary notes, "Went back to the Museum and wrote review of Joynes's book for *The Star*" (*Diary* 356).
- J[ohn] L[eigh] Joynes (see above, 32–33).
- [Ferdinand] Freiligrath (1810–76), who abandoned a commercial career for literature, and Georg Herwegh (1817–75), were German poets of the popular uprising and expression of German nationalism in 1848. Freiligrath, who had already spent some years in exile before the revolution, was expelled from Germany a second time for his poem *Die Toten an die Lebenden* (1848); Herwegh, also exiled earlier when he fled to Switzerland to avoid a court-martial during his military service, was severely criticized for leading an invasion of Baden in the same year (1848), and returned to Switzerland, where he died.
- [Heinrich] Heine (1797–1856), German poet and essayist. In the 1820s and 1830s his revolutionary opinions prevented his obtaining employment in Germany. He lived in England and Italy from 1827 to 1831, in which year, aroused by the revolution in Paris (which overthrew the Bourbon dynasty) he went there, and later married and settled; but contracted a spinal disease in 1848 that confined him to his "mattress-grave" as he called it until he died. Among poems published in 1851 occur the following stanzas:

> Now, where to? My foolish feet
> Want to go to Germany;
> But my reason shakes its head
> Wisely, and it says to me:
>
> "True, the war is ended now,
> But the wartime laws are not,
> And it's said that you once wrote
> Stuff enough to get you shot."

("Jetzt wohin?" trans. Hal Draper, in *The Complete Poems of Heinrich Heine* [Boston: Suhrkamp/Insel, 1982], 633)

8 June 1888

HOW TO EARN £400 A NIGHT!* [NIL]

IT is probable that Madame Adelina Patti is the most monstrously overpaid working woman in the world. Hence many of our daugh-

---

* "Maurice Strakosch's Ten Commandments of Music." Edited and compiled by M. le Roy. (London: Cramer, 1888.)

ters are ambitious to set up for themselves in her business, if only they could find out how it is done. What, then, could be more opportune than a full explanation of the whole mystery, as taught by the late Maurice Strakosch, Madame Patti's brother-in-law, impressario and teacher, he who taught Minnie Hauk, Belocca, Sessi, Kellogg, Nilsson, Emma Thursby, Sigrid Arnoldson, and Nikita? The whole art, in short, of earning £400 a night for five shillings. It is, indeed, excellent value—none better in the market if it can really do all it promises. Unfortunately, there is very little chance of its doing anything of the sort. Maurice Strakosch's "Ten Commandments of Music," pretentiously as they are put forth, are simply what all singers and teachers call "the scales," gravely set down in black and white, just as they have grown up out of the daily practice of the Italian school during the last two centuries. Their merit is that they are a growth and not a doctrinaire invention, like so many of the elaborate *solfeggi* and infallible "methods" of the music shops. If you sing them the right way every day for four years, you will be able to produce your voice as well as Patti—even to sing like her, if Nature has given you Patti's voice and Patti's brains. If you sing them the wrong way every day for four months, they will destroy your voice and your health as effectually as a daily gargle of vitriol. Experience proves that ninety-nine students out of a hundred, by trying to make their untrained voices produce at the first attempt something like the effect of the trained voices they admire, choose the wrong way. Worse still, nine teachers out of ten are no better than blind leaders of the blind. Consequently there is no present danger of the "Ten Commandments" perceptibly increasing the number of Pattis. And if it did, let us not forget that their competition would soon bring the £400 a night down to £40—or even, if they were numerous enough, to £4.

The letterpress in the book, tall talk about Patti apart, is fairly sensible as far as it goes, except in a few particulars. The sound "Ha" may be a very good one to practise on when you know what the actual sound is, and when you know how to breathe properly. But if, as is likely enough, the syllable conveys nothing to you but either the bleated "Haah" of the rustic or the "Haw" of the Cockney; and if, besides, you are apt to steady your notes by sheer force of aspiration (which is fatal to even the mildest mastery in singing), you may rue the day in which you invested your 5s. with Patti's preceptor. Furthermore, a singer whose skill was limited to vocalising on "Ha," and who could not sound the other vowels clearly and purely, would hardly succeed as a ballad singer. At the opera the words are not supposed to matter, and you simply scream on the most convenient syllable. Again, the urgent recommendation to keep the pianoforte "always in perfect tune" shows a curious ignorance of the very unsatisfactory limits to the art of tuning keyed instruments.When a pianoforte is tuned so as to make it possible to accompany all Strakosch's exercises, all intervals upon it except the octave are necessarily made false; and in some of them—the major thirds, for example, which are sharp— the unavoidable error is by no means imperceptible to a well-trained ear. Touching the remarks on diet, it passes our comprehension why a singer with good teeth and a sound digestion should be forbidden to eat nuts. Our remote ancestors knew better. The few old and simple calisthenic exercises will be found useful by students into whose ordinary education such wholesome physical training has not entered. The book is well printed on good paper; but we should recognize the old enterprising spirit of the proprietors of the *Magazine of Music* better if the price were a shilling, or half a crown at most. The "Ten Commandments" are too stale to be worth sixpence a piece at this time of day.

Editor's Notes

- The above review was published in the *Star,* 8 June 1888, 4:3.
- Shaw's *Diary* reports on 5 June 1888: "Went through Strakosch's singing exercise in the morning." The next day Shaw "wrote and sent off review of Strakosch to *The Star*" (*Diary* 382).
- Maurice Strakosch (1825–87), Bohemian impresario, who traveled as a pianist in Europe, came to America in 1848 and settled in New York as a teacher. After 1856, however, he was mainly known as an impresario. His first season of Italian opera was in 1857 in New York, where his own opera, *Giovanni di Napoli,* was first produced. He also wrote *Souvenirs d'un Impresario* (Paris, 2d ed., 1887); and his *Ten Commandments of Music for the Perfection of the Voice,* reviewed above, was published posthumously. He died in Paris.
- Adelina [Adela Juana Maria] Patti (1843–1919), Spanish-born coloratura soprano. She was of Italian parents who moved to the United States before she was ten. Her first formal debut in New York was in 1859 as Lucia; and her first appearance in London was two years later at Covent Garden. In 1877 she appeared nine times at La Scala, Milan, and four times in Venice; even then her fee was 8,000 fr. (£320) for each performance; see *The Theatre* (30 October 1877), 217. Shaw gave her limited praise: though he acknowledged

that she was a "consummate artist," he disparaged her dramatic quality; see the *World*, 26 November 1890. She retired from the stage in 1895, but continued to appear from time to time, finally giving an official "farewell concert" at the Albert Hall in London in 1906.

- Maurice Strakosch's "stable" of operatic talent seems to have been prodigious: Minnie Hauk [Amalia Mignon Hauck] (1851–1929) was a celebrated American soprano, whose German father emigrated to the United States as a political refugee in 1848. Minnie Hauk came to stardom at the age of fourteen, singing in *La Sonnambula;* after lessons in New York, sang in opera in Paris in the summer of 1868, and made her London debut at Covent Garden in the same year. She sang in Vienna two years later, and first appeared at the Metropolitan Opera, New York, in 1891. Anna di Belocca (n.d.) was the daughter of M. de Bellokh, a scholar from Saint Petersburg. She spoke five languages and was much in demand because of her fine contralto voice and her "unusually attractive" appearance—brown hair, large black eyes, and pale complexion. She made her début in 1874, and her first appearance in the United States under the auspices of Strakosch two years later. "Sessi" is undoubtedly Marianna Sessi (or Sessa) the Italian singer and composer (1776–1847) who began singing at the Italian opera in Vienna, where she became a celebrity. She made numerous concert tours in the early years of the nineteenth century. Again the dates make her acquaintance with Strakosch problematic. [Clara Louise] Kellogg (1842–1916) was another famous American soprano, who made her professional début at the Academy of Music in New York, sang Marguerite in the New York production of *Faust* in 1863, and made her London début in the same role in 1867. In 1887 she married Karl Strakosch, nephew of Maurice, and retired from the stage. [Christine] Nilsson (1843–1921), the celebrated Swedish soprano, studied in Paris, made her début as Violetta in *La Traviata* in 1864, and had successful tours in London, on the Continent, and in America. Emma Thursby (1845–1931), an American soprano, studied in New York, went to Italy in 1873 for further study, and in 1875 returned to the United States where she was engaged by the bandleader Gilmore for his summer concerts, touring with him both nationally and internationally. Sigrid Arnoldson (1861–1943), another Swedish soprano, studied in Paris with Maurice Strakosch, made her stage début in 1885 at the Prague Opera, and in 1886 had a sensational success at the Moscow Imperial Opera as Rosina in *Il Barbiere di Siviglia*. In 1887 she sang at the Drury Lane Theatre, London, and was hailed as "the new Swedish nightingale," successor to the famous Jenny Lind. Finally, Luise Nikita [Louisa M. Nicholson] (n.d.), was an American soprano whom Shaw would praise the following year at Covent Garden on 10 August 1889, for having been taught well, for not screaming her high notes, and for imitating feeling sympathetically.
- Shaw had made a similar point about books on voice-training that promise more than they can deliver in his review of Morell Mackenzie's *Hygiene of the Vocal Organs* on 26 July 1888, again using the wealthy Patti as his example.
- Shaw was familiar with "methods" of voice production. His mother's singing

teacher and friend George John Vandeleur Lee had imparted to her a "method," which she used as a singing teacher herself and lost no time in passing on to her son, one of whose earliest aspirations was to be an operatic baritone. Shaw was still enthusiastic about Lee's "method" in his ninety-fourth year.

1 August 1888

BOOKS OF TO-DAY: "THE UNIVERSITY ECONOMICS"* [C473]

PROFESSOR Gonner's handbook is a cautious and intelligent introduction to what takes the name and place of Economic Science in our University class rooms. That is to say, it is a handbook, not of Economics, but of the current adaptation of Economics to the needs of young gentlemen of the proprietary classes, who must not be told that they have no right in equity to a farthing of their incomes. The plan adopted is the usual one. The rent of land is dealt with in a chapter which is completely isolated from the rest of the book. It is explained that rent does not enter into price. That admitted, it follows that rent has nothing to do with the theory of exchange, which is accordingly treated without any reference to the varying productiveness or limited supply of accessible land. On these conditions it is easy to prove that if contracts were free, commodities would exchange normally in proportion to their cost of production, and everything would be for the best in the best of all possible worlds. Except for passing examinations, such a handbook is about as useful as a treatise on physics with gravitation relegated to a separate chapter, and the rest conducted on the assumption that atmospheric pressure might be treated as non-existent. It is really time to ask writers on political economy whether it is strictly honest to state without qualification that rent does not enter into price, when both the facts and the theory shew that part of the price of all commodities, except those produced at "the margin of cultivation," is rent. Also whether it is reasonable to declare that commodities tend to exchange in the

* "The University Economics." By E. C. K. Gonner. (London. R. Sutton, 1888.)

ratio of their expenses of production, when, as a matter again of both fact and theory, they neither exchange nor tend to exchange in any such ratio. As to treating wages as the result of an exchange of services for subsistence matter between equally free contractors, it is not necessary to ask whether that is ingenuous or not. The only question that arises is whether it is any longer expedient. Considering that the division of the "catallactic atoms" of the labour market into proprietors and proletarians has been not only admitted but stringently legislated upon for fifty years past, it is daily growing harder for even a university professor with any sort of countenance to affect ignorance of it and write futile chapters about wages as if it did not exist. Professor Gonner, however, admits by his title page the distinction between "University Economics" and real economics; and for this humorous stroke he is much to be applauded. He is also quite honest in his explicit refusal to defend private property in land. For the rest, he attempts to disclaim all concern with the moral aspect of his applications of economic law, an irresponsibility which may be conceded to writers who, like Jevons in dealing with value, do not *apply* economic laws at all; but which must emphatically be denied to writers like Professor Gonner, who commits himself to a distinct advocacy of Free Trade, and a qualified disparagement of Socialism, besides laying down the canon that taxation should be so contrived as to leave those on whom it falls in the same relative positions as if there were no taxation. That canon would be an excellent one in a perfectly socialized community. As a practical suggestion to Chancellors of the Exchequer under our present system—and it is apparently so intended—it is a mere pre-economic superstition. This point apart, Professor Gonner has done what he professes to do very capably. From the point of view of Socialism or even pure economics, his way is only a way of "holding a candle to the devil"; but it is due to him to point out that he holds it steadily and is acquainted with all the latest improvements—except, perhaps, the extinguisher.

Editor's Notes

- This review appeared in *To-Day: the Monthly Magazine of Scientific Socialism* 10, n.s. (August 1888): 61–63. Shaw reviewed Gonner's book again for the *Pall Mall Gazette* on 26 December 1888.
- Shaw's *Diary* reports that he was "reading Gonner's economics" in the British Museum on 13 June 1888, and he continued on and off for the next five days. On 19 June he began a review that he finished and corrected the

following day (*Diary* 385, 386, 387). This, however, must have been the longer review of the book for the *Pall Mall Gazette;* on 11 July he writes "wrote review of Gonner's *Political Economy* for *To-Day* and sent it off to Bland." The shorter and more succinct review was no doubt written for a more partisan and economically aware audience.

- [Professor][Sir] E[dward] C[arter] K[ersey] Gonner (1862–1922), English professor of economics was a graduate of Lincoln College, Oxford. Subsequently he became a lecturer for the London Extension Society in 1885, in which year he also became a lecturer at University College, Bristol. In 1888 he became a lecturer at University College, Liverpool, where he obtained a professorship in 1891. Gonner wrote other books, including *Commercial Geography* (1894), *The Socialist State* (1895),*The Social Philosophy of Rodbertus* (1899), and *The Economic History of Germany in the Nineteenth Century* (1912). Shaw knew Gonner well in the middle 1880s and, on 11 June 1888, Gonner persuaded Shaw to "write a textbook on Socialism for Sutton's University series. Terms—a royalty of fourpence a copy. I agreed, so far." The book was not started until 1891; but two days after talking to Gonner about it, Shaw was "at Museum all day reading Gonner's economics," no doubt as much to familiarize himself with the format of a university textbook, as to consider it for review.
- [Johann Karl] Rodbertus (1805–75), German economist, politician, and founder of scientific Socialism.
- "Everything would be for the best in the best of all possible worlds." The line is from Voltaire's satire on the optimistic theology of Leibniz, *Candide* (1759): "Tout est pour le mieux dans le meilleur des mondes possibles."

31 October 1888

THE MESSIAH OF SOCIAL DEMOCRACY* [NIL]

THE chapters in this book which will be read most eagerly are those which deal with Ferdinand Lassalle, a man who, without going once outside the ordinary surroundings of nineteenth century city life, ran a career so romantic in its outlines that novelists, rhapsodists, poets,

---

* "German Socialism and Ferdinand Lassalle." By William Harbutt Dawson. (London: Swan Sonnenschein, 1888.)

biographers, orators, statesmen, and essayists have been busy with
him ever since his strange end a quarter of a century ago, and are not
done with him yet, or likely to be. Among the novelists is Mr. George
Meredith, whose Count Alvan, "the tragic comedian," is an attempt to
portray Lassalle; and the statesmen include Prince Bismarck, who, in
an interview with this fabulously accomplished social democrat, was
out-talked as completely as the late Lord Beaconsfield is said to have
been on a similar occasion by Mr. H. M. Hyndman.

Lassalle was born in 1825 of parents named Lassal, rich Jewish
tradespeople in Breslau. He is supposed to have been virtually the
master of the house, even as a boy, just as he is said afterwards to have
made himself virtually governor of the gaol in which he was incarcer-
ated. He certainly generally had his own way, not as a dictatorial bully,
but as a man who thought more quickly than other people, and whose
will consequently went into them like steam into a vacuum. He was
intended for business, but it soon became evident that his mother was
right in thinking that her wonderful boy was made for higher concerns.
Off he went, accordingly, to Berlin, where he studied philosophy, and
cut such a figure at 20 that he was able to impress Heine, during a visit
to Paris, as an altogether extraordinary person. On his return to Berlin
he was introduced to the Countess Hatzfeldt, a lady of 40, handsome, a
bold horsewoman, able to share the cigars and conversation of clever
men, and quite emancipated from the drawing-room discipline of the
ordinary woman of fashion. She was, however, married to a Silesian
noble who would neither support her apart from him, nor behave tolerably when she was with him. Lassalle heard her story; was fired with
indignation; and challenged Hatzfeldt, who contemptuously declined
to meet "a silly young Jew." The silly young Jew promptly turned lawyer, followed his man up through 36 courts, and beat him handsomely
after eight years' hard fighting. In the meantime he had "done six
months" for attempting to bring about a rising in Düsseldorf in 1848,
the year of revolutions; and he had been tried and acquitted for obtaining a document from Hatzfeldt's mistress by the strong hand on the
highway. He had told two of his friends to obtain the document at all
hazards; and they had carried out his instructions to the letter, probably
much to his annoyance, though people insisted on accepting the romantic and lawless character of the transaction as exactly characteristic of
the young adventurer. When the Countess's property was won for her
at last, between seven and eight hundred a year was charged upon it for
his use; and he, thus provided for, returned to his old studies, wrote a
work on the philosophy of Heraclitus, and a poetic drama. He was

forbidden to enter Berlin on account of his 1848 exploit, but he entered it, nevertheless, in disguise, and stayed until the prohibition was cancelled by the King. In Berlin he soon became famous. He refused, on principle, to fight a duel, and his challenger, instead of safely posting him as a coward, rashly concluded that he actually was one, and lay in wait for him in the street with a stick, bringing another man along to help. Lassalle, however, had a stick also, and he used it with such zest that his assailants vanished precipitately. Förster, the historian, thereupon presented him with a stick which had been carried by Robespierre. In 1862, at a period of great political ferment, Lassalle cut himself adrift from all the political parties by recommending the workers to go straight for "universal suffrage," as it was then called. They were to use the democratic power, when it was won, to provide State capital for co-operative industries, and so solve the industrial problem. From that time Lassalle gave himself away completely to the cause of the workers. He showed them their historic destiny; he exposed to them the sordid class basis of mere Whiggery; he proved the futility of the petty joint-stockery preached by the ordinary co-operators; he stripped the mask of "culture" from the idle classes, and shewed, with all the authority of his own remarkable attainments, that history, philosophy, and economics were on the side of the laborer and against the gentleman. He succeeded in founding the German Social Democratic party; but the work that fell on his shoulders—not to mention social persecution and Government prosecutions—could not have been done by 10 men, much less one. He was deeply discouraged, too, by the dulness and narrowness of the workers. In spite of great meetings and ovations, he only enlisted 1,000 men where he had bargained for 100,000. His health gave way, and he went to Switzerland for a holiday. There he found a young lady with whom he had already fallen in love in Berlin. She immediately ran away from her parents to his hotel and proposed an elopement. He had the good sense to refuse to compromise her reputation, his own, and that of his cause by an unnecessary scandal. Unfortunately this was the last sensible step he took. When he pushed his suit with the girl's parents in the usual manner, they refused to have anything to do with a man who had been tried for a robbery. He persevered with his usual energy and confidence for a while in spite of repeated and insulting rebuffs; but when he at last received a cold letter from the girl herself announcing her approaching marriage with her cousin, he lost his temper and recklessly challenged both the father and the cousin. The father fled: the cousin accepted the challenge and practised hard with the pistol in order to meet his redoubtable antagonist, whose skill with weapons was supposed—out of sheer superstition, apparently—to be consummate. Lassalle, who had made no such preparation, fell, shot through the bowels, to die perhaps the most agonising death that a bullet can inflict. His death took place three days after the duel, on 28 August, 1864. The inscription on his tomb in Breslau, his native town, is "Hier ruht was sterblich war von Ferdinand Lassalle, dem Denker und dem Kämpfer"—(Here lies what was mortal in Ferdinand Lassalle, thinker and fighter).

Such a death, closing such a life, was certain to overwhelm his memory for a time with the tawdry romance which makes "good copy" for circulating libraries and magazines, leaving us little wiser than we were before as to why he threw away his life in so deplorable a fashion. There is no such contradiction in his political work. Among the founders of modern Social Democracy Karl Marx was the only man whose pretensions rival his. Both were pupils of Ricardo and Hegel. As a writer Marx was, on his own subject, unique and unapproached by any rival; but Lassalle had the advantage over Marx of working in his own country—an advantage which enabled him to play the orator, and saved him from the exile's dream that it is possible to skip over national socialism and begin by international organisation. He saw too that the complete Democratic State, founded on "universal suffrage," could alone provide the indispensable political machinery for State organisation of industry. He understood the importance of the next step: Marx was always full of the next step but one. In economics, too, he stuck to the one simple and unanswerable difficulty of the Ricardian "iron law of wages," whereas Marx insisted on deducing the law of exchange value anew in a way of his own, and only succeeded in making a very old blunder in a very novel fashion. It was the far-reaching and acute Marx who first saw what was going to happen, but it was Lassalle who first saw much more clearly and readily how it was going to happen.

Mr. William Harbutt Dawson's volume, with its remarkable portrait of the great German agitator, deserves nothing but thanks and praise. The judgment with which he has selected exactly what was wanted from an appalling mass of German literature—or rather letterpress—and the industry and conscientious fulness and accuracy of detail with which he has presented it, place him above all minor criticisms. His own standpoint is that of an admirer of Prince Bismarck, one whose intellectual conviction of the validity of the Socialist theory has not yet detached him in sympathy from the classes threatened by Socialism. His account of Lassalle gives a truer impression than Mr.

George Meredith's novel or Mr. Ludlow's able but bitter article in the *Fortnightly Review* for 1869. At that date the time had not come for a Christian Socialist and co-operator to do justice to the freethinking assailant of Schulze-Delitzsch. But now that Lassalle's name, nearly 25 years after his death, is better known than during his life, Mr. Dawson will find no difficulty in persuading English readers that his hero was much more than a profligate demagogue and duellist. They will not, like some of his wilder disciples, proclaim him a Messiah; but if they study his utterances in the light of subsequent events, they will find that his place is already secured among the prophets of the nineteenth century.

GEORGE BERNARD SHAW.

Editor's Notes

- This review was first published in the *Star*, 31 October 1888, 4:2
- It was on 24 September 1888 that Shaw "began review of *German Socialism and Lassalle* for *The Star*." On the twenty-fifth he "got to the Museum about 16 and worked at review of Lassalle. . . . Finished review and sent it off" (*Diary* 415).
- William Harbutt Dawson (1860–1948), English biographer and writer on social and educational subjects was educated at the University of Berlin, and his first publications were written to interpret German life and institutions to the English, but also had a political motivation. The one reviewed above, and its sequel, *Bismarck and State Socialism; an exposition of the social and economic legislation of Germany since 1870* (1890), were followed by *The Unearned Increment; or, Reaping without Sowing* (1890). *Germany and the Germans* (1894), and *German Life in Town and Country* (1901), which ran to several editions. More books on Germany followed, both before and during the First World War; but it was after the war that he produced perhaps his major work, the two-volume *The German Empire, 1867–1914, and the unity movement*. Between the wars, he constantly evaluated the relationship between England and Germany, in such books as *The Future of the Empire and the World Price of Peace* (1930), and *Germany under the treaty* (1933). He also managed to write books on South Africa, the thought of Matthew Arnold, Richard Cobden, and John Lambert. In 1936 he received an honorary doctorate from the University of Königsberg.
- Ferdinand Lassalle (1825–64). Shaw's outline of Lassalle's life in the above notice is substantially accurate.
- Shaw's own review of Meredith's novel appeared in the *Daily Chronicle*, 19 January 1892 (see below, 88 et seq.).

- Prince [Otto Eduard Leopold von] Bismarck (1815–98), Prussian states-
man and first chancellor (1871–90) of the German Empire, whose lifework
was to bring about the unification of Germany under Prussian leadership.
To accomplish this he provoked a series of conflicts including the defeat of
Denmark over Schleswig-Holstein, followed by the Seven Weeks' War
(which defeated Prussia's former ally over the same matter), and the
Franco-German War of 1870, after which all Germany was united as the
German Empire under its first emperor William I of Prussia, with Bismarck
as its "Iron Chancellor."
- The "late Lord Beaconsfield" was, of course, Benjamin Disraeli (1804–
81), first Earl of Beaconsfield, a title granted him by Queen Victoria in 1876
in recognition of his "services to the empire" (which included his proclaiming
Her Majesty Empress of India that very year.) He established a political
reputation as a reforming Tory, concerned with the plight of the very poor. His
novels *Coningsby; or, the New Generation* (1844), *Sybil; or, the Two Nations*
(1845), and *Tancred; or, The New Crusade* (1847), dealt with social problems
and a search for true morality. As a Conservative he was the polar opposite of
Hyndman (see above, 20); as a novelist, however, Disraeli plied the same
trade as Shaw, who may have been influenced by him: one remembers R. L.
Stevenson's declaration that Shaw's novel *Cashel Byron's Profession* was "$\frac{1}{2}$
part Disraeli."
- In Heinrich Heine's (1797–1856) third great collection of poems published in 1851, the poem "To the Young" was allegedly written with Ferdinand
Lassalle in mind (Lassalle was twenty-two in 1847). Its original final verse
(as translated by Hal Draper), replaced in the published version, reads

We are the heir. We smash in mid-air
The cup from which we've drunk all down!
We'll die for fair, but at last we share
A sweet death in triumph in Babylon town.
(in *The Complete Poems of Heinrich Heine: A Modern English Version*,
trans. Hal Draper [Boston:Suhrkamp/Insel, 1982], 953)

- Shaw refers to Lassalle's *Die Philosophie Herakleitos des Dunklen von
Ephesos* (1858), and his historical verse tragedy (in five acts) *Franz von
Sickingen* (1859).
- David Ricardo (1772–1823), English writer on economics and politician.
His major work *Principles of Political Economy and Taxation* (1817) con-
cerns itself chiefly with the causes determining the distribution of wealth.
In this, his famous theory of rent (which influenced Marx) played a part.
Simply put, Ricardo believed that wages are determined by the price of food,
which is determined by the cost of production, itself determined by the
amount of labor required to produce the food. In other words, labor determines value.
- [Georg Wilhelm Friedrich] Hegel (1770–1831), German philosopher. In
1807 he published his first great work *Phänomenologie des Geistes* [Phenome-

nology of mind], in which he traces the human mind from simple consciousness through self-consciousness, reason, spirit, and religion to absolute
knowledge. It was in his second great work *Wissenschaft der Logik* [Science
of logic], whose two volumes appeared in 1812 and 1816, that he set out his
famous dialectic: a triadic process in which thesis generates antithesis and
both are superseded by a higher synthesis that incorporates what is rational
in them, and rejects what is not.

▪ Ludlow's article in the *Fortnightly Review* for 1869 (also printed in the
Eclectic Magazine, New York) was entitled "Ferdinand J. G. Lassalle, the
German Socialist."

18 December 1888

MARGINALIA: A HOTCH-POTCH OF POETRY, ART, ECONOMICS, AND FICTION* [C518]

A batch of books like this provokes the remark that reviewing is not
what it used to be. Formerly the "serious" books issued for the general
reader were upon evolution, art or literature. Nowadays they are upon
political economy and the social question, and the minor anarchist has
taken the place of the minor poet as the established butt of critical
sarcasm. Here, for instance, is a volume—a typical volume—of 460
pages just issued by Messrs. Swan, Sonnenschein, and Co. Guess the
title or subject. The proximity of the next glacial epoch, perhaps; or,
"From Holbein to Herkomer," or "Wordsworth and other Essays"? Not
a bit of it. It is called "English Associations of Working Men," by J. M.
Baernreither, Doctor of Law and Member of the House of Deputies in
Austria. Dr. Baernreither knows much more about us than we know
about ourselves, and we are flattered to find that he has a prodigious
opinion of our aptitude for self-help and steady business-like solution

---

* "English Associations of Working Men." By J. M. Baernreither. Trans. Alice Taylor.
(London: Swan, Sonnenschein, 1888.)
    "The Alphabet of Economic Science." By Philip H. Wicksteed. (London: Macmillan.)
    "Great Minds in Art." By William Tirebuck. (London: Fisher Unwin, 1888.)
    "The Paradox Club." By Edward Garnett. (London: Fisher Unwin, 1888.)
    "Leaves of Life." By E. Nesbit, author of *Lays and Legends*. (London: Longmans.)

of the social difficulties which solve themselves by periodic explosions among less gifted peoples. "The power of union, the capacity for submitting to the lead of others, the pertinacity and energy which they display in the pursuit of fixed aims, is amazing. . . . The deep-rooted mistrust between capital and labor has been, even if not

ENTIRELY ERADICATED,

still essentially mitigated." Thus Dr. Baernreither, innocent and optimistic doctor of laws. If he only knew! However, let us accept his compliments with a modest air; though he really does us too much honor. The value of the book is in the mass of information it contains as to friendly societies. It is prefaced by a weighty recommendation from Mr. J. M. Ludlow, who takes care to say that "our country has to ask itself, in fear and trembling, whether it deserves, or will continue to deserve, so friendly a judgment as that of Dr. Baernreither." The translation is by Miss Alice Taylor.

Messrs. Macmillan, the publishers of most of the professional economists, have just issued a fascinating little half-crown volume uniform with Professor Marshall's "Economics of Industry." It is a book that no economist, no socialist, no housekeeper, no gambler should be without. It is even not too much to say that if

EVERY BURGLAR WERE PROVIDED WITH A COPY

we should hear no more of intelligent cracksmen, the flower of their profession, staking 20 years' liberty against a couple of Britannia metal forks and a case of stuffed birds, from want of scientific guidance in the balancing of "final utilities." This remarkable little text book is entitled "The Alphabet of Economic Science," by Mr. Philip H. Wicksteed, who is already known as a preacher, a linguist of Mezzofantian powers, a social reformer, and an exceptionally gifted interpreter of the highest poetry, who now comes into the field as an economist. Probably no writer ever ventured more unluckily than Mill did when he stated that "there is nothing in the laws of value which remains for the present or any future writer to clear up; the theory of the subject is complete." If Mill could have anticipated Mr. Wicksteed, he would have classed that statement among the things one would rather not have said. For we have here a demonstration, helped out by the most captivating curve diagrams, of a theory of value which has already left the Ricardian dogma as dead as the Doges—a theory worked out in England by Stanley Jevons, and first appreciated at anything like its full importance by Mr. Wicksteed. Students of Socialism who have slaved through the terrible first section of Karl Marx's "Kapital" will find with a certain vengeful satisfaction that the "abstract human labor" theory of value which is the very philosopher's stone of the fanatical Marxites shares the ruin of the Ricardian theory. Mr. Wicksteed, as may be gathered from the shockingly misprinted bibliography at the end of Messrs. Macmillan's new edition of Jevons's now famous "Theory of Political Economy," was the first to point out to the enthusiasts of the Democratic Federation that Marx's theory of value was out of date, and the term

"SURPLUS VALUE" A MISNOMER.

He has now provided them with an exposition of the sounder modern analysis of value, which is quite the best and cheapest in the language.

Mr. Fisher Unwin rescues us from the eternal social problem by Mr. William Tirebuck's "Great Minds in Art," a most readably printed collection of eight essays on Doré, Dürer, Raphael, Rembrandt, Wilson, Landseer, and Wilkie. The fashionable literature of Art has come to such a pass now that it is quite startling to find Raphael among the great painters. He had an old-fashioned reputation of that sort, as most of us learned from our boyish studies of Vasari and Quatremère de Quincy. How astonished we were on growing up to discover that Tintoretto was the true prince of painters, according to Mr. Ruskin, whilst the rest of the persons who are supposed to understand such matters were divided

BETWEEN VELASQUEZ AND MR. WHISTLER!

Yet now that we have learned to do justice to Tintoretto and Velasquez, and even to Mr. Whistler, it appears that, after all, Raphael is still "the divine." So much so, indeed, that the remark is as ridiculous a platitude as ever. Still, since Mr. Tirebuck, notwithstanding his appreciation of the prince of painters, has not ventured to place him before Gustave Doré, perhaps it may be permissible to suggest with due deference, and without the slightest disposition to share the excesses of the vulgar reaction against the French artist's great and deserved popularity, that on the whole Raphael was a greater "mind in Art" than Gustave Doré. But no doubt Mr. Tirebuck would not dispute that, and has put Doré first unawares.

Another book from Mr. Fisher Unwin is "The Paradox Club," by Mr. Edward Garnett, whose pages have much of the charm of immaturity without its ineptitudes and provincialities. The Paradox Club is one of those little circles which young people of a literary and artistic turn, well found in brains, conceit, and the illusions of youth, manage to form outside the vulgar visiting lists of money and class. There they talk a sort of transcendental politics of life made beautiful and women made free. When they get married to one another, nature's object in forming the club is achieved; she snatches away the now useless veil of illusions; and the circle dissolves, leaving not a rack behind. Mr. Garnett writes of all this, not with the coarse touch of one who has been through and come out on the other side, but rather as one who is still there, too shrewd to be a blind dupe, but too young to be an unwilling one. It is all very visionary and very inconclusive at bottom; but it "touches a chord," as Mr. Guppy hath it. The sketch of "Nina Lindon," which serves as frontispiece, is an unmistakeable portrait of a young lady of tried intellectual distinction, and may therefore presumably be accepted as an historical document.

"LEAVES OF LIFE."

Miss Nesbit (Mrs. Bland) has already established her right to be called a poetess. She is not without her debt to sisters and brothers of her art, possibly to Mrs. Browning for spirit, and less markedly to Mr. Swinburne for form. But she has a line of her own, and no one who has followed her contributions to fugitive literature will have failed to note in her a real touch of original inspiration. Miss Nesbit chooses to take as her motto the sad line from Fitzgerald's "Omar Khayyam,"

"The leaves of life are falling one by one,"

and perhaps she would be willing to confess that she had voluntarily stripped her tree of many leaves which were wont to deck its branches. The note of this very charming little book is to some extent a note of scepticism, of the half-regretful relinquishment of the scholar in one of Miss Nesbit's poems, who, sitting in his study, turns over the leaves of the Prayer Book where his own and his old sweetheart's names are written, and is reminded of the time when

"I believed in God, in love, in you,
In everything."

But it would be very far from true to say that Miss Nesbit has ceased to believe in anything. The strongest of all her beliefs is, no doubt, in man and in man's future in a new social epoch.

THE REVOLUTIONARY TOUCH

is, indeed, as conspicuous as the sceptical tendency, and we find in her work what we miss in Matthew Arnold's delightful musings and reflections—a real phoenix-like hope of a constructed society. As for style, Miss Nesbit's graces are a pure and restrained diction, which, without great variety of metre or depth of artifice, gives a sufficient quality of style to her work. There is also much strong stuff in the volume, and we suppose many readers will prefer such strenuous compositions as "The Ballad of Splendid Silence." Among the slighter pieces nothing is prettier than the "Morning Baby-song," which is as good as anything Mr. Swinburne has done in the same line, and is less ambitious:—

> Baby, darling, wake and see,
>   Morning's here, my little rose;
> Open eyes and smile at me
>   Ere I clasp and kiss you close.
>   Baby, darling, smile! for then
>   Mother sees the sun again.
>
> Baby, darling, sleep no more!
>   All the other flowers have done
> With their sleeping. You, my flower,
>   Are the only sleepy one;
>   All the pink-frilled daisies shout
>   "Bring our little sister out!"
>
> Baby, darling, in the sun
>   Birds are singing, sweet and shrill;
> And my bird's the only one
>   That is nested softly still.
>   Baby—if you only knew,
>   All the birds are calling you!
>
> Baby, darling, all is bright,
>   God has brought the sunshine here;
> And the sleepy, silent night
>   Comes back soon enough, my dear!
>   Wake, my darling, night is done—
>   Sunbeams call my little one!

Editor's Notes

- This review appeared in the *Star*, 18 December 1888, 2:5–6.
- On 12 December 1888, Shaw reports in his *Diary*, "Began reading Baernreither's *English Association of Working Men*," and that evening "wrote

a couple of notes for *The Star.*" When he wrote the other reviews must be a matter of conjecture. As early as 16 October, Shaw's *Diary* reveals that he went to hear "*Wicksteed on Curves*" (*Diary* 422); and on 11 December, Shaw was at the museum "where I stuck to the review books" (though which ones are not specified), and later that evening went again to Beeton's to hear Wicksteed on "Suggestions relating to the Curve of the Supply of Capital." Neither the work nor the persons of Tirebuck and Edward Garnett is mentioned in Shaw's *Diary;* and similarly Shaw's review of Edith Nesbit's poems is not noted by name; but it is possible that the review of this book of poetry was written on the same day (12 December) as his review of Baernreither's book, since he met and dined with the Blands on that day, and his *Diary* reports that he wrote "a *couple* of notes for *The Star*" (*Diary* 444).

- J[osef] M[aria] Baernreither (1845–1925), German nationalist. A doctor of law, he was twice (briefly) appointed to government service by Emperor Francis Joseph in 1898, resigning after a few months; and again was part of the government of Heinrich von Clam-Martinic in 1916, resigning a second time. He wrote a number of other books, perhaps the most notable being his *Fragments of a Political Diary.*
- Alice Taylor (n.d.), unidentified translator.
- J[ohn] M[alcolm Forbes] Ludlow (1821–1911), English social reformer who promoted social advances in India, spoke against slavery, and became a member of the anti–Corn Law League. In May 1848 "Politics for the People" was issued, which marked the beginning of the Christian Socialist movement. In 1851 Ludlow founded and edited a journal called the *Christian Socialist,* and was instrumental in founding the Working Men's College in Great Ormond Street, London, in 1854. In 1870, Ludlow was appointed secretary to the Royal Commission to inquire into all questions connected with Friendly Societies, and in 1875 he became chief registrar of Friendly Societies, an office he held until 1891.
- [Alfred] Marshall (1842–1924), English economist, who became interested in economics while lecturing in moral science at St. John's College, Cambridge, where he became a fellow in 1865. His marriage to a former pupil of his lost him his fellowship, however, and for four years he was principal of University College, Bristol; he resigned this principalship in 1881 and, after a year in Italy, returned to Bristol as a professor, before taking a position in 1883 at Balliol College, Oxford. From 1885 to 1908 he was professor of political economy at Cambridge. Shaw, visiting Cambridge on 18 February 1887 to deliver the lecture "Socialism: Its Growth and Necessity," had met Marshall and his wife. Marshall's *Principles of Economics* (1890) is still a standard textbook, and the adaptation of its first volume into *The Economics of Industry* is the book mentioned by Shaw in this review.
- [Philip Henry] Wicksteed (1844–1927), English classical scholar, clergyman, and economist. Shaw was friendly with Wicksteed at the time of the above article. From November 1885 he had met Wicksteed regularly at the house of Henry R. Beeton, a stockbroker, to discuss economics in a group that later became the British Economic Society. In fact in 1904 Shaw, inscribing

Wicksteed's copy of *The Common Sense of Municipal Trading,* called him "my master in economics." Wicksteed took Jevons's notion of "final degree of utility" and renamed it "marginal utility." He then developed the theory applying it to the pricing of labor and capital, and this, his integration of the theories of the value of goods and of resources, he set out in *An Essay on the Co-ordination of the Laws of Distribution* (1894). Wicksteed's background as a Unitarian minister was perhaps responsible for the humanitarian feelings he brought to the science of economics, and he was much involved with the Fabians, who utilized his economic expertise.

▪ [William Stanley] Jevons (1835–82), English economist and logician. Jevons introduced mathematical methods to economics, and was one of the first to use the concept of final or marginal utility (as opposed to the classical cost-of-production theories.) His work was enormously important to Shaw, who used it to refute parts of Marx's theory.

▪ William [Edwards] Tirebuck (1854–1900), English novelist and critic. Born in Liverpool, he became subeditor of the *Liverpool Mail,* and subsequently for six years subeditor of the *Yorkshire Post,* after which he devoted himself exclusively to writing books. In addition to the one reviewed above, he also authored *William Daniels, Artist* (1879), *Dante G. Rossetti: His Work and Influence* (1882), *The Discontented Maidens: A Dramatic Cantata* (1887), and a number of novels.

▪ According to Tirebuck: "The eight painters whose biographies appear in this volume may be regarded as the eight parts of speech in the one great language of pictorial art. Raphael's (1483–1520) part was grace in form and colour; Doré's (see below), imagination; Wilkie's (see below), pathos; Landseer's (see below), sentiment; Dürer's (1471–1528) was moral inference; Rembrandt's (1606–1669), contrast, or light and shade; Velásquez (1599–1660), realism or fidelity to what he saw; and Richard Wilson's (see below) was idealization, or the power of adding to what he saw something finer which he imagined" (William Tirebuck, *Great Minds in Art, with an Introduction on "Art and Artists"* [London: T. Fisher Unwin, 1888], 13).

▪ Gustave Doré (1832–83), German painter, who began by supplying caricatures (or cartoons) for such journals as *Le Journal pour Rire* and the *Journal Amusant* before turning his attention toward more serious book illustration, decorating impressively the works of Dante, Rabelais, Cervantes, and Coleridge, as well as the Bible. He was a prolific artist: in 1854 and 1855 he exhibited paintings in the Salon and the Universal Exhibition in Paris, although his paintings did not become as popular as his illustrations. Nevertheless, in 1868 an exhibition of his paintings was held in London, where public enthusiasm was immense.The following year Doré's paintings were removed to 35 New Bond Street, where they were still on exhibition at the time of Tirebuck's book's publication. His canvases (particularly those with religious themes) fetched large sums of money.

▪ [Richard] Wilson (1713–82), Welsh painter. He served a long apprenticeship in the studio of Thomas Wright, his first authenticated painting occurring when he was thirty-six. He next went to Italy to study the old masters, turned to landscape painting, and set his life to the task of interpreting nature. In this he preceded Reynolds, Gainsborough, and Constable. After six years in Italy he returned to England and a cool reception for the Continental "warmth" of his work. He was not merely neglected: he was ridiculed, and found it difficult to sell his work. However, in 1760 his painting *Niobe* was exhibited and did something to repair his artistic reputation, though he remained a financial failure. On the formation of the Royal Academy in 1768, he was included in the first list of members; even this, however, did not establish him in the public eye, and in 1770 poverty forced him to apply for the post of librarian to the Royal Academy. Finally, in 1780 he was relieved of his destitution by the bequest of a small property in Wales, where he lived out his last two years, becoming progressively senile.

▪ [Sir Edwin Henry] Landseer (1802–73). Landseer's early artistic training came from his father, a well-known engraver, and he was already competent at drawing from nature by the age of eight, and at thirteen exhibited in the Royal Academy. He was particularly gifted in drawing animals, perceiving the "personality" of each dog or sheep. Landseer's London studio was in a street just off Fitzroy Square (where Shaw was to reside fifty years later); however, in 1824 Landseer visited Scotland, and later when Sir Walter Scott visited London, the artist returned to Abbotsford with him; and these Scottish visits made a strong impression upon the artist, whose Scottish paintings such as *The Hunting of Chevy Chase, The Widowed Duck,* and particularly *The Monarch of the Glen* (1851) firmly established his reputation. At twenty-four he became an associate of the Royal Academy (that being the earliest age for that honor to be bestowed), and in 1830 a royal academician. He also modeled the famous bronze "lions" at the foot of Nelson's Column in Trafalgar Square, London.

▪ [Sir David] Wilkie (1785–1841), Scottish painter. He applied to the Edinburgh Academy, where his sketches were initially rejected, and his entry (in 1800) only assured by the good offices of Lord Leven, who admired the youth's talent. In 1805 he journeyed to London, and entered the Royal Academy as a probationer. Poverty was his lot until he obtained a commission from Lord Mansfield (for *The Village Politicians*), who had seen an early work of his (*The Country Fair*), and his work gradually became recognized. Canvases such as *Rent Day*—which took him months to finish— brought him money, reputation, and the friendship of Leigh Hunt, Coleridge, and Constable. In 1811 Wilkie (rather to his surprise) was elected a member of the Royal Academy, and the following year he sold his *Village Festival* for 800 guineas. At the Duke of Wellington's request he painted *The Chelsea Pensioners* (1822), a painting whose exhibition was a national event. For many years plagued by poor health, Wilkie was constantly traveling to different places in search of rest and refreshment of spirit. After one such trip to Smyrna and the Holy Land in 1841, he died aboard the steamer *Oriental,* outward bound from Alexandria, and his body was committed to the deep.

▪ [Giorgio] Vasari (1511–74), Italian artist, architect and art historian, whose most important paintings include those on the walls and ceiling of the Palazzo Vecchio in Florence, but who is principally remembered for his monumental *Vite de' Più Eccellenti Pittori, Scultori, ed Architetti Italiani* (1550), translated into English as the ten-volume *Lives of the Artists* (1912–14), which provides us with our chief knowledge of the artists of the Italian Renaissance.

- [Antoine Chrysostôme] Quatremère de Quincy (1755–1849), French archaeologist and politician. He was editor of a dictionary of architecture; he also contributed to *The Lives of the Italian Painters* (1846) the chapter on Raphael, and wrote *An Essay on the nature, the end and the means of Imitation in the Fine Arts* (1823, trans. 1837).

- [John] Ruskin (1819–1900), English writer, art critic, and reformer. The first Slade Professor of Fine Art at Oxford University, Ruskin was the greatest art critic of his age. Tintoretto was one of "five supreme painters" praised by Ruskin; and Shaw largely agreed with this estimate.

- [James Abbott McNeill] Whistler (1834–1903), American artist who left America in 1852 and went to Paris, where he studied under the Swiss classicist painter Charles Gabriel Gleyre (1808–74), was influenced by the work of other leading contemporary artists, and by the Japanese art then coming into fashion in Paris. Whistler's reputation as a painter began after his removal to London, when in 1860 *At the Piano* was shown by the Royal Academy. In 1863 *The White Girl* was highly acclaimed in Paris, and thereafter, his famous "butterfly" trademark became known, and his international reputation assured. In 1878 he brought an action for libel against Ruskin (see above) over the latter's review of his painting *The Falling Rocket*. He won his case, but was awarded only a farthing in damages, and the expenses of the trial forced him into bankruptcy. Thereafter he concentrated increasingly upon etching. Shaw frequently reviewed his work in the picture galleries of the 1880s, and cautiously admired it.

- [Jacopo Robusti, "Il" Tintoretto] (1518–94), Italian painter. Born in Venice, the son of a dyer (in Italian *tintore*, whence his name) he studied with the painter Titian and, conceiving the idea of uniting Michelangelo's sculptural design with the colors of Titian, made frequent studies from the two men. Among his own greatest works are *The Last Supper*, in San Giorgio Maggiore, and the decoration of the Scuola di San Rocco, also in Venice, which included paintings more than sixteen feet high, in his cycle the *Life of Christ*.

- Edward Garnett (1868–1937), English critic and playwright. As a publisher's reader and critic, he introduced many notable writers to the public, including D. H. Lawrence, and Joseph Conrad. For a time he was a permanent guest of the Rhymers' Club (see above, 30). He was also an active Fabian, and lived with his wife Constance [Clara] Black, translator (like Garnett himself) of Russian novels and plays, at Limpsfield in Surrey. Garnett's play *The Breaking Point* was refused a license by the Lord Chamberlain's reader of plays in 1907, and Garnett contacted Shaw at that time suggesting a combination of authors against censorship. The play was produced privately the following year by the Stage Society, but the furor over its being banned was one of the factors that led to the parliamentary hearings on censorship in 1909. Garnett also wrote two other plays, a book of criticism (*Turgenev*, 1917), and edited the letters of Conrad and Galsworthy.

■ The review of Garnett's book is appropriately brief, as the novel itself is little more than two hundred pages in length, but the kindly tone of Shaw's remarks may be a clue to his interest in the book's premise. Five years later, when he came to write *The Philanderer,* with its "Ibsen Club," whose candidates for admission must be, if female, not womanly, and if male, not manly, Shaw may well have remembered "The Paradox Club": "A social Club that has rooms in one end of the town instead of the other, that meets at ten instead of the fashionable eight, that includes women as well as men," and that is "so absolutely incomprehensible to the average mind that all its members are outside Society," (Edward Garnett, *The Paradox Club* [London: T. Fisher Unwin, 1888], 7–8). The leading figure in the book, Patrick, pursuing Nina Lindon, is introduced by her to the club and gives a paper "Men and Women," in which he proves the superiority of the latter over the former; Martell the Socialist (who may be his rival in love) gives a paper on Socialism, and Lofthouse the Poet discusses "Being Anticipated" (that is, every time he develops an original idea, he discovers that it has been developed by someone else.) The book, though no doubt originating in the male/female tensions within the Fabians, is too slight to have given more than a hint to Shaw; but it does contain occasional lines like "You see even you women, who go in for being independent," said Patrick to Nina, "are only independent within the recognized conventionalities" (*The Paradox Club* 107). This reminds one of Charteris's remark to Julia: "Advanced views, Julia, involve advanced duties: you cannot be an advanced woman when you want to bring a man to your feet and a conventional woman when you want to hold him there against his will."

■ Mr. [William] Guppy is the lawyer's clerk in Dickens's *Bleak House* who conceives a passion for its heroine, Esther Summerson, and makes her a ridiculous proposal of marriage. She refuses him, and, thereafter, when he is reminded of her he becomes upset, repeating "there are chords in the human mind . . ."

■ Miss [Edith] Nesbit [Mrs. Bland] (1858–1924), English novelist, poet, and writer of books for children. She began to write seriously in 1876, her first published piece (the poem "Dawn") appearing in the *Sunday Magazine* that year. She married Hubert Bland (1856–1914) in 1880. Like her husband, she was an active Socialist and one of the founders (in 1883) of the "Fellowship of New Life" out of which grew the Fabian Society in 1884. She had two daughters and two sons; but the Bland household was strange: Edith befriended her husband's mistresses (including Alice Hoatson, whose daughter Mrs. Bland brought up as her own child). Shaw was one of the frequent visitors to the Blands at Blackheath. For her part Mrs. Bland haunted the British Museum (where Shaw habitually worked) throughout the 1880s. On 26 June 1886, Shaw discovered that she had become "passionately attached" to him

(*Diary* 34), and spent some time dodging her amorous advances. On 10 November that year, Edith showed Shaw her new book of poems *Lays and Legends* (1886), for which he wrote a review, probably for the *Star* ("Found at last—a new poet") which was, however, never published at the time: it has recently been published in *SHAW: The Annual of Bernard Shaw Studies*, vol. 16. It was not until 1899 that "E. Nesbit" (as she habitually called herself as author) published *The Story of the Treasure Seekers*, and established herself as a children's author of great merit. In this and subsequent children's books, notably *The Railway Children* (1906), she presented children as realistic beings behaving naturally, and her steadiness of character drawing and excellence of style place her in the top rank of writers of children's fiction. She still wrote poetry and several novels, of which the best known was perhaps *The Red House* (1903). Shaw remained friendly with her all her life, and paid for her son John to go to Cambridge.

12 December 1889

POOR MISS J. THE SOFT SIDE OF THE IRON DUKE* [C662]

THIS is quite the most curious book of the season. Miss J. emerges from oblivion as an invincible egotist, a predestined, unredeemable fool. Wellington appears as a dreamer of heroic patience and simplicity. Those who laugh at the pair will run a risk of having their merriment likened to the crackling of thorns under a pot. The mere monstrosity of Miss J. may provoke a mirthless guffaw here and there; but the correspondence is not funny, not humorous, not to be made light of by any truly sympathetic reader.

In 1834, the Duke of Wellington had been a widower for three years, and was 65 years old. In the middle of January
A LETTER FROM AN UNKNOWN LADY
in Devonshire affected him strongly. It was a fervid appeal to him to be born again unto righteousness, in order that he might fulfil his momentous public duties in the true spirit of Christ. He acknowledged the letter; and the lady pursued her exhortation in further communica-

---

* "The Letters of the Duke of Wellington to Miss J." Ed. Christine Terhune Herrick. (London: T. Fisher Unwin, 1889.)

tions, and left a Bible for him at his town house. He then suggested a meeting. She invited him to call, and was informed that "although the Duke is not in the habit of visiting young unmarried ladies with whom he is not acquainted, he will not decline to attend Miss J." On calling, he found his correspondent a beautiful young lady of 20, highly connected, and in practically independent circumstances, her parents being dead, and her guardian content to leave her in the hands of her companion, Mrs. L. She describes the interview in the following terms:—

> "Since God must have influenced the Duke of Wellington to love me above every other lady on earth from the first moment he beheld me, I am not afraid, as in His sight, to imply such feelings were permitted to exist towards one, through the workings of His power, for the accomplishment of His own ends, be they *whatever* they may—*which* ends, *however* varying from those I had naturally anticipated, will, I trust, redound far more to *His Glory* than my anticipations, if realised, could possibly have done. I say *naturally anticipated!* And who can presume to think such were not *justifiable* when the individual *thus* brought into my presence
>
> BY THE LORD OF LORDS
>
> for the purpose of receiving instruction from His holy Word, never spoke, all power of speech seeming to be withdrawn, until he was compelled to exclaim: 'Oh, *how* I *love* you! *how* I *love* you!' repeating the same over and over again with increasing energy."

It is necessary to explain here that the Duke was not the first subject whom Miss J. had tried to regenerate. Rather more than a year before she had gone to a gaol to visit a condemned murderer named Cook, who had rejected the advances of chaplains of all persuasions as very evident attempts to fill his belly with the east wind. But he succumbed to the beauty and enthusiasm of Miss J.; and she, after receiving his confession, accompanied by edifying expressions of repentance, was able to celebrate his execution with the tranquil entry in her diary, "To-day poor Cook suffered; and I can now fancy him a glorious spirit, hovering near, ministering to those that are to be heirs of salvation." It was her brilliant success with Cook that stimulated her to try her 'prentice hand on the Iron Duke. Not that he was the Iron Duke to her. Such was fame and female education in those days, that Miss J. did not know that he had conquered Bonaparte, and had as vague an idea of the battle of Waterloo as a modern young lady has of the Schleswig-Holstein difficulty.

Miss J's letters had set the old Duke dreaming; and now her bodily presence

KINDLED HIS AFFECTIONS,

for their first two interviews contained the following passages:—

FIRST INTERVIEW. *12th Nov., 1834.*
Miss J's parlor. The Duke standing before the fire.
Enter Miss J. in a dark green merino gown.

MISS J. (*aside*) What a beautiful silver head! Not at all what I had expected. (*Aloud, offering her hand.*) This is very kind of your Grace. Be seated. (*They sit at the fire.*) I will show you my Treasure. (*Duke at a loss. She rises. So does he. She fetches a large Bible, he standing punctiliously until she sits down again. She reads the third chapter of St. John's Gospel down to—* "Ye must be born again.")

THE DUKE (*seizing her hand*): Oh, how I love you! how I love you!

MISS J. (*in the tone of a Church Catechist*): Who causes you to feel thus towards me?

THE DUKE: God Almighty. (*Curtain.*)

SECOND INTERVIEW. *23rd Dec., 1834. Same place.*

THE DUKE: This feeling of mine must be for life. Yes, for life. Do you feel sufficiently for me to be with me a whole lifetime?

MISS J.: If it be the will of God.

THE DUKE (*hurriedly*): I am going on a visit to the King.

MISS J.: I wish you were going on a visit to the King of kings.

THE DUKE: I shall return shortly. (*Exit. Miss J. locks the door and prays. She is interrupted by the return of the Duke, who knocks for admission. She lets him in.*) Why did you lock the door?

MISS J.: It is written, "When thou hast shut thy door, pray to thy Father which is in secret; and thy Father which seeth in secret shall reward thee openly." Therefore I locked the door when you were gone, your Grace, to kneel down and ask God to take care of me. (*His eyes drop and he says nothing.*)

THE DUKE (*presently*): Why did you not write to me during my absence from town?

MISS J.: Because God would not let me. (*Curtain.*)

Perhaps that was Wellington's last dream of
A BEATRICE OR A CLOTILDE.
If poor silly Miss J. could have lived up to it, their acquaintance would beyond a doubt have become a close union for a whole lifetime. But it only made her more foolish than before. The luckless Cook had turned her head in the direction of apostleship; and now the Duke, too great a man to despise instruction from the mouth of a babe and suckling, innocently turned her head again, this time in the baser direction of the position of Duchess of Wellington. She betrayed that in her very next letter by the clumsy coquetry of affecting to forbid him to come again.

> "*Saturday, 10 Jan., 1835.*
>
> *My Lord Duke,—Finding my peace, that perfect peace which for so many years I have uninterruptedly enjoyed, interfered with by your visits—visits which under present circumstances I cannot feel justified in receiving, as they are of so different a nature from those I anticipated when I gave you permission to call upon me—I think it my DUTY to entreat that they should cease, &c., &c., &c., &c., &c.*"

That settled her. The Duke awoke from his dream instantly, and never for a moment fell under its illusion again, though the recollection of it induced him to bear with her long after she had made herself an unmitigated nuisance. Here is his reply:—

> "My dear Miss J.,—I have received your letter and enclosures. I beg to remind you of what I said the second day that I saw you; and if you recollect it you will not be surprised at my telling you that I entirely concur in the intention which you have communicated to me.
>
> I am obliged for what you have sent me; and I am ever, yours most sincerely,
> WELLINGTON."

Of course, Miss J. did not see that
HER CHANCE WAS LOST.
She became more and more confirmed in her belief that the will of God was that she should become the wife of the Duke—that, as she wrote in her diary, "the end God had in view was my exaltation for his glory." Sometimes the Duke condescended to give her a practical

example of how much more experienced and skilful a hand he was at coquetry than she. Sometimes, again, he put the absurdity of her hopes bluntly to her. "What would be said," he wrote, "if I, a man of 70 years of age, were to take in marriage a lady young enough to be my granddaughter?" Yet he amused himself with occasional visits to her, during which she expounded Scripture to him, lectured him, tried to enlighten him on the subject of "true nobility," and expressed her yearning "to be hated of all men for Christ's sake," an aspiration which she appears subsequently to have in a considerable measure realised. Occasionally, when she got into trouble by rebuking casual profanities in stage coaches and the like, he would give her a little solid advice as to the good sense of practising a little Christian patience.

In 1835 there came a fearful quarrel. He sent her a letter sealed with a plain seal, and signed simply "W." The

REVELATION OF HER LITTLENESS

which followed would be condemned as mere burlesque in a work of fiction. In her diary she wrote:—

> "My feelings, were I not afraid of offending God, would incline me to seal up all the Duke's letters and return them, conscious that I merit an increase rather than a diminution of respect. Except such is bestowed, the Duke need not be surprised at any step the Lord may incline me to take."

The pages which follow this entry contain the most extraordinary boasts of the divine strength with which she felt inspired to bear the absence of the coronet from the seal. A genuine Christian martyr on the rack would have blushed to make so much of actual torture. The Duke was quite equal to the occasion:—

> "You will find this letter signed and sealed in what you deem the most respectful manner. And if I should write to you any more I will take care that they shall be properly signed and sealed to your satisfaction. I am very glad to learn that you intend to send back all the letters I ever wrote to you. I told you, heretofore, that I thought you had better burn them all. But if you think proper to send them in a parcel to my house, I will save you the trouble of committing them to the flames."

Of course, the letters were not returned because "dear Mrs. L. arrived, and on my telling her all, strongly advised my *not* returning the Duke his letters—which struck me forcibly, as I had asked the Lord to put it into her heart to advise me agreeably to His Will." Nevertheless, Miss J. sent just one complaint too many. It crossed the Duke's letter; and the result was that for a year he wrote to her in the third person only. Here are a couple of extracts from her heavily-underlined lamentations under this stern discipline.

> "Having written the accompanying Hymn for your acceptance, I take this opportunity of
> BIDDING YOU FAREWELL,
> being enabled, through God's Grace, which is all sufficient, to exclaim in *Scripture* language, 'The Lord GAVE and the Lord hath taken away *and* BLESSED BE THE NAME OF THE LORD!' "
> "The information that you have destroyed my letters is *anything* but gratifying, one and all being more or less marked with *Divine* Truth, calculated properly and *seriously* considered, to benefit your *immortal Soul*."

At last she pleaded for a renewal of the first person; and her plea found favor. But by this time the Duke's moral attitude towards her was unmistakably *de haut en bas*. The following is the conclusion of the last third person letter of this period (1836):—

> "Prudence and Discretion would appear to require that Miss J. should not rebuke a Gentleman for words spoken not to Her, not even in Her Presence, but to Her Landlady in the relation of a Lodger in the House.
> "The Duke may be wrong. But he considers the exercise of Prudence and Discretion virtues (*sic*) not unbecoming to any character, however exalted."

In 1836 the Duke began suggesting that she should not trouble herself to write any more, a policy which he pursued vainly to the end of his life. In October they had an interview, the first for two years. She complained in her diary that "he exclaimed, 'You shall do this and you shall do that' without any reference to God's Holy will," and also that "he appeared delighted,
BRUSHING UP HIS CHAIR
nearer to me, which of course met with the withdrawal on my part *due* to Christianity." She was injudicious enough to complain of this "presumption" presently in a letter, and was, as she might have anticipated

had she been a woman of the smallest real delicacy, promptly punished by a relapse into the third person and a crushing apology. She revenged herself by sending him a hymn "unsuited to the taste of any but the Regenerated Soul, which *blessed* state Miss J. has no good reason for believing his Grace the Duke of Wellington has yet experienced."

Her next move was an attempt to get into hortatory correspondence with the Throne. She wrote a letter to Queen Adelaide, warning her against trusting the Duke, and beseeching her "to lean to no Adviser or advice in comparison with Christ and His Gospel, which, if sedulously studied, will in itself enable you rather to instruct the Duke of Wellington than be instructed by him." This she gave to Wellington to hand to the Queen, which he of course declined to do. She then

HAD A SHOT AT SIR ROBERT PEEL,

who politely assured her that her communications were "received in the spirit in which they were dictated." Wellington was very indulgent to her. "There is nothing under heaven worth quarrelling about," he said. And again, "I am really much concerned that you should suppose that my last note to you was what you call cross. But I am not so foolish as ever to be cross, much less in writing." His humble confessions of his inability to understand the high subjects she wrote of would have pierced arrogance of any ordinary density; but hers was impenetrable. Sometimes, in spite of his wonderful forbearance, she brought down the lightning on her wretched head.

> "The Duke is very sensible of Miss J.'s offer of service in case the Duke should be sick or afflicted. The Duke is much obliged to her. He is quite well. He has no reason to believe that he will have occasion to trouble her upon any object whatever."

The only effect of this was to make her endorse the letter in these terms:— "Let not Him that girdeth on his harness *boast himself* as he that putteth it off. 1. Kings xx. 11."

At last, what with her bad handwriting and the impossibility of keeping up any interest in her incessant letters, he

MISTOOK A REFERENCE TO A LOAN

which she was raising, for a request that he himself would assist her with money. Without a moment's hesitation or circumlocution, he told her to name the sum she wanted, and her banker's address. She at once rushed to her diary and wrote: "Friday, 6 Sept., 1846. O my God, wherefore hast Thou thought proper to let Satan try and distress me in this unanticipated manner?" The unfortunate Duke apologised as humbly as a man could; but all he gained by his sincere anxiety to make amends was a letter in which, whilst she vouchsafed him her own forgiveness as a great favor, she expressed the gravest doubts as to whether he could ever hope for that of God. The Duke was deeply disgusted and took no more notice of her for some months.

In 1849, a fresh attempt on her part to induce him to give one of her letters to Sir Robert Peel, earned her another snubbing:—

"I have received your letter of the 17th inst., in which you have enclosed certain letters which you have written to Sir Robert Peel, which I return. I am not the postman, nor the secretary of Sir Robert Peel, nor your secretary."

She was greatly taken aback by this "unmerited angry letter"; but he only replied, "I thank God that I am never angry with anybody on any subject."

Finally she got into pecuniary difficulties, and actually did ask him to help her. He was as prompt as before in his response; but, instead of telling him how much she needed and to whom he should remit it, she only complained of his indelicacy and want of generosity. He,

WITH UNRUFFLED PATIENCE

told her that he should send her some money in a registered letter. She warned him that if he dared to send a postman to her with a receipt to be signed, she should refuse the letter. Then she sent him some family correspondence which he told her, not unkindly, showed that she was not so poor as she had led him to believe. The end of the storm which this raised was the following:—

"Strathfieldsaye, 21 Dec., 1850

Field-Marshal the Duke of Wellington presents his compliments to Miss J. He understood from her former letter that it was Miss J.'s desire never to hear from the Duke again.

Therefore he did not write, nor should he now excepting a mere matter of courtesy. He thus finally takes his leave. WELLINGTON."

But she was at him in no time about her health and his soul, and he acknowledged her letters, though long before this she had noted in her diary— "It is very evident that from this period Satan was permitted to work on the Duke's mind, weakening consequently the power I had been permitted to exercise, by making my communications tedious."

In 1851 [*sic*] death released the Duke from 17 years of Miss J., who went out to New York and died there, some 27 years ago, in the full odor of the worthless piety which had imposed on the great Duke to the last.

Editor's Notes

- The above review was first published in the *Star,* 14 December 1889, 6:6–7. The book's full title is *The Letters of the Duke of Wellington to Miss J. 1834–1851,* edited, with extracts from the diary of the latter.
- Shaw's *Diary* for 9 December 1889 reports: "Up very late. Reading *The Duke of Wellington's Letters to Miss J.* for review. Began to write review in the evening and finished the pen work at 24." (*Diary* 567)
- Christine Terhune Herrick (?–1944), American author. Born in Newark, New Jersey, she was educated by a governess, private schools, and teachers in Rome, and Geneva. In 1884 she married James Frederick Herrick (who died in 1893). She wrote mainly on domestic topics, some of her books being *Housekeeping Made Easy* (1888), the cookbook *Liberal Living Upon Narrow Means* (1890), *The National Cook-Book* (with her mother "Marion Harland") (1897), *The Expert Maid Servant* (1904), and *The ABC of Housekeeping* (1915).
- Arthur Wellesley, first Duke of Wellington (1769–1852), British soldier and statesman, who received his first independent command as a colonel in India in 1796. He took part in several successful military campaigns, subduing the Marathas—then the dominant people of India—and returned to England in 1805, where he was knighted and elected to the British Parliament. Wellesley distinguished himself in the struggle against the French emperor Napoleon I, particularly in the Peninsular War (1808–14) which expelled Napoleon's armies from Portugal and Spain. On Napoleon's escape from Elba the following year, Wellington (now a duke) again resumed command of the main allied armies, and, with the help of Prussian Field Marshall Gebhard Leberecht von Blücher, defeated Napoleon decisively at the Battle of Waterloo on 18 June 1815. In 1828, at the insistence of King George IV, Wellington was named prime minister. Predictably, his draconian tactics angered his Tory colleagues, and he was forced to resign in 1830; however, he remained in Parliament and, when the Tories returned to power, became foreign minister in the government of Sir Robert Peel (see below). In 1842 Wellington again became commander-in-chief of the army, a post he held until his death at his home, Walmer Castle, Kent, in 1852. The funeral took place "amidst an Empire's lamentation" on 18 November, through streets dense with mourners, many of whom had waited all night in the rain. Regiment upon regiment marched past, and Queen Victo-

ria's eyes were so full of tears that she was almost unable to see the great bronze funeral car that carried the mortal remains, as the "Iron Duke" was carried to his burial in Saint Paul's Cathedral.

- "Miss J." was a beautiful young evangelist named Anna Maria Jenkins (1814?–62), born into the minor gentry, and educated at a good English school. She was, by nature, an extremist, and her introspection and pondering over the Bible seems to have transformed her into a religious zealot, obsessed with a desire to convert all about her. The "conversion" to Christianity (with her friend "Mary") of the condemned prisoner "Cook" took place in the summer of 1833, and its success strengthened her devotion to evangelism. She now felt that she had been called by God to this great work, and the Duke of Wellington seemed a likely candidate. His great friend Mrs. Arbuthnot had just died, and Anna Jenkins pursued the duke until nearly the end of his own life, receiving her last letters from him in 1851. On the duke's death she sailed for New York to join her sister, but did not destroy the letters. As one of Wellington's biographers remarks, "She who was afraid to kiss was not afraid to tell" (Richard Aldington, *The Duke; being an account of the life and achievements of Arthur Wellesley, 1st Duke of Wellington* [New York: Viking Press, 1943], 350). More bigoted than ever in later years, she was unable to live in the same house as her sister, and finished her days alone in New York.
- The "Schleswig-Holstein difficulty" refers to the Seven Weeks' War, in which the rival powers of Austria and Prussia fought over the ownership of the state of Schleswig-Holstein, apportioned to their joint administration by the Treaty of Vienna. Shaw establishes a neat parallel by likening a "modern young lady's" ignorance of a battle won twenty years previously by an "Iron Chancellor (see above, 56), to one won by an "Iron Duke," twenty years before Miss Jenkins's time.
- Shaw's casting the dialogue in dramatic form makes this the first *published* Shavian drama! Though he never seriously considered this as a theme for a stage play, six years after writing this review, Shaw would write one (*The Man of Destiny*) in which a great man (Wellington's most famous adversary, Napoleon) is tricked by a mysterious lady over a packet of letters!
- Shaw likens Miss Jenkins to Dante Alighieri's (1265–1321) "Beatrice," perhaps Bice Portinari (1266?–90), but certainly the "glorious lady of his mind" whom the Italian poet first glimpsed when he was ten, and who inspired him thereafter; and to Saint Clotilda (474–545) daughter of the Burgundian king, Childeric, who married the Frankish King Clovis in 493 and converted him to Christianity.
- Shaw's statement that the Duke of Wellington was too great a man to despise instruction from the mouth of a babe and suckling he developed into Undershaft's paradox in *Major Barbara* (1905):

STEPHEN. Any further discussion of my intentions had better take place with my father, as between one man and another.
LADY BRITOMART. Stephen! [*She sits down again, her eyes filling with tears.*]

UNDERSHAFT [*with grave compassion*] You see, my dear, it is only the big men who can be treated as children.

- Queen Adelaide (1792–1849) was the consort of King William IV of Great Britain, predecessor of Queen Victoria.
- Sir Robert Peel (1788–1850), English statesman who entered Parliament as a Tory in 1809. He was undersecretary for the colonies in 1811, and from 1812 to 1818, as secretary for Ireland, "Orange Peel," as he was called, revealed a strong anti-Catholic bias, and was so severely attacked by O'Connell that he challenged the latter to a duel. In 1822 Peel became home secretary, in which capacity he organized the London Police Force, known therefore as "Peelers" or "Bobbies." In November 1834 he was briefly prime minister; but stepped aside for Lord Melbourne the following April. In the election of 1841, however, Peel's Conservatives won. His ministry was notable for introducing an income tax, and for revising the British banking laws. Peel also reversed his earlier views on free trade and urged repeal of the Corn Laws. Although repeal was approved in 1846, the controversy it caused was so great that Peel was forced to resign, though he continued to serve in Parliament until 1850, when he was thrown by his horse and injured so badly that he died.

14 December 1889
MR. DONISTHORPE'S INDIVIDUALISM*
[C665]

"AN INDIVIDUALIST" —Mr. Donisthorpe Writes a Book—What will the Liberty and Property Defence League say to it?

This big book of 400 pages will be read by many Londoners whose interest in its subject has already been roused by the author in person. Mr. Wordsworth Donisthorpe is not one of those champions of Individualism who fight Socialism from the safe cover of the study, the British Association platform, or the magazine which accepts no copy from Socialist contributors. He never joined the conspiracy of silence whilst it lasted; never pretended to hold Socialism as a thing of slight account; never, like Mr. Mallock, stooped to soothe and flatter the rich in his attacks on the aspirations of the poor; never, like Mr. Bradlaugh,

---

* "Individualism, a system of politics." By Wordsworth Donisthorpe.

went from the lecture hall where he had denounced State interference to concert extensions of it in the House of Commons. Whatever audience, rough or cultured, the Socialists addressed, he has faced with a courage and independence which seemed cynical to those who forgot that the one thing a cynic never does is to devote himself to the upholding of a principle, even though it were the principle of cynicism.

Nobody who knows anything of English public life will need to be told, after this, that Mr. Donisthorpe soon made the party which he formed much more uncomfortable than the party he opposed. The Liberty and Property Defence League, consisting originally of Mr. Donisthorpe alone, was not prepared, when it joined him, to forego those common hypocrisies and self-deceptions which are called the decencies of English society. Now, Mr. Donisthorpe's distinction lies precisely in the fact that he is neither a hypocrite nor a self-deceiver. He is what used to be called a materialist; and he disdained to conceal the fact. When Bastiat tried to justify *laisser-faire* to the people, he took them according to their customary professions, and blended the respectable man with the economist. To doubt the ultimate beneficence of the natural and unfettered action of competition was, he said, to doubt the goodness of God.

AMEN, SAID EVERYBODY

with £1,000 a year. Now, here Mr. Donisthorpe:—

> "When you ask, 'By what title do men exercise power over each other?' I answer simply enough, By the title of superior strength—*force majeure*—not necessarily muscular force, but force for all that; and what is more, physical force, by which expression I wish to exclude that which is metaphysical or supernatural. And every title, every right, can be resolved by analysis into physical force. There is no other. I regret that Mr. Auberon Herbert has complicated matters by dragging in altogether superfluous causation. If evolution will not explain morals and rights, then I think we had better take a deep draught of Fichte's 'Destiny of Man,' and tie ourselves to the apronstrings of Blind Faith."

In this uncompromising statement of the doctrine that might is right, Mr. Donisthorpe is not only turning his back on the Bible, but giving his countenance to the great Social-Democrat Ferdinand Lassalle, who, in 1862, opened a new political phase of the modern class war by an address ("Uber Verfassungswesen") based on this very doctrine.

But Mr. Donisthorpe did worse things than this in the eyes of the defenders of "Liberty" and Property. He faced the facts. Instead of bolstering up the pretence that the

HONEST, THRIFTY, SOBER

workman is a happy and contented scorner of the arts by which vile demagogues stir up sedition among the idle, drunken, and worthless, he started with the assumption that wagedom is but the latest form of slavery. He said such things, for example, as the following:—

> "Instead of serfdom, we have wagedom. The present system is one of labor hiring. At the bottom of the scale we find agricultural laborers standing out for a real wage, fair and square, without patronage or privilege. At the top we find the men in the large mills, the factories, the ironworks, and the mines, demanding something more than this. They are already in the happy position to which the agricultural laborers are aspiring; and yet they are discontented. No wonder! They have discovered by experience that they receive no more than is necessary to keep them in repair for the employers."

Here we have an individualist receiving Mr. Giffen and his "Improvement in the Condition of the Working Classes," not with open arms, but with a well-directed punch in the wind. Such language is that of a revolutionary individualist, not of a Conservative one. And like all revolutionists, instead of blinking the class war, he forces it on public attention.

> "The battle is now between employer and employed. Year by year the strife waxes hotter. We are now in the midst of it. Louder and louder roar the discontented hosts of wage earners. Inch by inch the baffled capitalists retire before the onward pressure of numbers. Masters quail; they offer terms; they
>
> BUY OFF THE ENEMY FOR A WHILE;
>
> and then again the billows swell and roll forward as before. Whither does all this tend? See, the millions are organizing: no longer a mob, they are an army. The battle cannot rage for ever with equal fortune. And which side shall win?"

When the property owners came to the conclusion that a Defence League on Donisthorpist lines was, on the whole, much more dan-

gerous than the Fabian Society, they showed that their instincts of
self-preservation were, as usual, in full working order. The League
is no longer Mr. Donisthorpe. His disciples founded Individualist
Clubs, which, by a curious freak of evolution, turned into chess
clubs; and he himself, like most original men, fights apparently
single-handed.

Mr. Donisthorpe's own system of individualism will be rejected by
Socialists as unsound, philosophically and economically. Philosophically, it is actually the negation of individualism, because it ignores
the first lesson that modern German philosophy taught us: namely,
that we should look on the individual as an end in himself, and not
as a means. Mr. Donisthorpe regards the individual purely as a
means to the evolution of a more successful type of man. Speaking of
a hypothetic case cited by him of an unjust transaction between a
draper and tailor, he says: "Under this arrangement, who would
pocket the 50 per cent. profit? The draper would; and quite right too.
Fools are made to be bled." It is hardly necessary to go beyond this
fundamental denial of individualism. The cleverest man nowadays
can be an expert in but a very few of the bargains he is called upon
to make during his life. In nine-tenths of them he is "a fool," in the
sense of being

AT THE MERCY OF THE HONESTY

of the other party. As we are all more or less "fools" in this sense, it
follows that if fools were made to be bled, the individual was made to
serve an end destructive to himself. If this is rightly called individualism, then individualism is its own *reductio ad absurdum.* The fact is
that this curious variety of evolutionary philosophy, though complete
within its own circular orbit as a specification of human mechanism,
is not a philosophy of human life, because it ignores not merely individualism but the fact of consciousness.

The economic basis upon which Mr. Donisthorpe builds is not
worked out; but it must be flagrantly heterodox, the conclusions he
has arrived at having no warrant in any known economic system.
"Unearned increment," he says, as if the fact were self-evident, "simply means the reward of successful risk." This extraordinary view
seems to be derived in some way from the fact that the power to
appropriate unearned increment—that enjoyed by the Duke of Westminster and Lord Cadogan, for instance—is as pure a

PIECE OF LUCK FOR THOSE GENTLEMEN

as the turning of sixes in a cast of the dice would be. Mr Donisthorpe
seems to have been misled by some analogy of this sort to the assump-

tion that their luck is attended, as in gambling, by a proportionate risk. Obviously neither gentlemen has risked a single farthing to bring about the unearned increment which has made him so wealthy. They could not have prevented it had they tried; and if Mr. Donisthorpe were to attempt to buy their prospects to-morrow, he would find that the sole risk affecting the price would be the risk of socialistic legislation, which, if it has any effect at all, equally depreciates consols. He pursues the subject in terms which leave no doubt that he means what he says. The following passage is calculated to make any economist or man of business rub his eyes:—

"If you invest in agricultural land you may think yourself lucky if you get $2\frac{1}{2}$ per cent. In town property the risk is greater, and the profits expected are consequently higher."

The notion that a good harvest is much more certain than that the usual $4\frac{1}{2}$ millions worth of unearned increment will be added to the property of the owners of the site of London next year is certainly a novel one. Mr. Donisthorpe does not go on to declare that the more out-of-the-way and uncertain of its traffic a railway is, the higher interest its shares will produce; nor does he mention that the relatively high dividend on North Metropolitan Tramway shares is due to the great risk their cars run of not picking up passengers in the primeval solitudes of Finsbury; but such statements would hardly add anything to the surprise of the reader. It does not even appear that the words are used in an unusual sense; for Mr. Donisthorpe evidently does not see that his "labor capitalisation" is rendered impracticable by the poverty in which the abstraction of the "unearned increment" leaves the laborer. It is useless to recommend a man to enter into productive business as a capitalist on the ground that his labor is capital. How is he to live until his capital begins to fructify—until the mine shaft is sunk, the railway constructed, the factory built and fitted? Only the man who has savings to live upon can do this. How can the laborer save, when, as Mr. Donisthorpe admits, he has barely enough to live on? How can the enjoyer of unearned income help saving when he is able to satisfy all the appetites that money can minister to, and yet have as much again lying idle at his banker's? The absurdity of the position leads Mr. Donisthorpe to the verge of cant—the very vice from which he is so conspicuously free. He actually speaks of interest as "the reward of abstinence." Surely if there is one proposition which is by this time too obvious to require more than a bare statement, it is that interest, in our society, is the reward of satiety.

The fact is, that Mr. Donsithorpe, who was fairly abreast of the rough-and-ready propaganda with which English Social-Democrats were breaking the ground as lately as 1885–6,

HAS NOT KEPT PACE

with the remarkable intellectual organisation and subsequent formulation of a practical political programme which has given such an impulse to the movement since that period. He criticises a Land Nationalisation Society which is extinct, for proposals which it abandoned before it became so. He selects Mr. J. L. Joynes's "Catechism" as a textbook of academic socialism, and flogs a dead horse vigorously by attacking the implied acceptance of the unfortunate value theory of Marx. If Mr. Joynes were to prepare a new edition of his little work, he would probably no more think of insisting on that value theory, or of using the terms "capitalist" and "employer" indifferently, than of introducing the economic harmonies of Bastiat.

To the ordinary reader whose interest in the personal criticisms in the volume is that of a looker-on only, its combative tone will be by no means disagreeable, and its entire freedom from dulness, the result partly of the author's intellectual alertness and partly of his very considerable literary skill, will be all in its favor. Economic students will find some interesting trains of thought started by his suggestions. Probably the people who will relish the book least will be the members of the Liberty and Property Defence League, if that organisation still persists.

Editor's Notes

- The above review was originally published in the *Star*, 14 December 1889, 4:1–2.
- Shaw's *Diary* records that on 8 December 1889 he "wrote review of Donisthorpe's *Individualism*. Had to break off at 16 to go to Beeton, who had telegraphed me last night. . . . I had to sit up until after 4 to finish the review."
- Wordsworth Donisthorpe (1847–1912?), English political writer. In the 1880s, Donisthorpe lived in Reigate, Surrey, was active in the Liberty and Property Defence League, and wrote and lectured on social matters. In addition to the above book, he wrote numerous others, including *Principles*

of Plutology (1876) ["Plutology" being his preferred word to Political Economy], *The Claims of Labour; or, Serfdom, Wagedom and Freedom* (1880), *Liberty or Law?* (1884), *Democracy. A Lecture on State Structure* (1886), *Socialism Analyzed, being a critical examination of Mr. Joynes's 'Socialist Catechism'* (1888), *Down the Stream of Civilisation* (1898), and *Uropa. A new simple philosophically-constructed language based on Latin roots* (1913). Shaw had written to Donisthorpe "about the new Liberty Club" on 22 February 1886 (*Diary* 148), and in the next few years attended debates in which Donisthorpe took part, heard him address the Fabians and met him at the Dialectical Society.

▪ [William Hurrell] Mallock (1849–1923), English author, whose *The New Republic* (1877), a symposium of extremist views, had considerable success. But Shaw is undoubtedly referring to his books *Social Equality* (1882), in which Mallock develops the view that various efforts to produce wealth are essentially unequal, and can only be stimulated by unequal circumstances, and *Property and Progress; or a brief enquiry into contemporary social agitation in England* (1884), which was an attack on the theories of Henry George. Mallock's attack on Socialism, "Fabian Economics," published in the *Fortnightly Review* in February 1894 led to Shaw's reply "On Mr. Mallock's Proposed Trumpet Performance," in the *Fortnightly Review,* April 1894, later augmented into *Fabian Tract No.146: Socialism and Superior Brains* (1909). As Shaw said in *The Intelligent Woman's Guide to Socialism and Capitalism* (1928): "It was a reply to the late William Hurrell Mallock, who took it as a matter of course, apparently, that the proper use of cleverness in this world is to take advantage of stupid people to obtain a larger share than they of the nation's income."

▪ Charles Bradlaugh (1833–91), English author and politician. In 1850 he published a pamphlet denouncing Christianity, in addition to which he was also concerned with social and political issues, lecturing in support of Garibaldi, visiting Italy and Spain to help their struggles for independence, and taking the part of the French in the Franco-Prussian War. In 1861 he founded the *National Reformer,* a weekly journal that championed the issues mentioned above, and two years later became its proprietor. Notwithstanding his radical views, however, he was never in favor of Socialism (largely because he associated it with violent revolution). In 1868 and 1874 he ran unsuccessfully for parliament, as the member for Northampton, but was finally successful in 1880. Ironically this moment of victory also saw his greatest controversy; for as an atheist he was unable to take the oath, and this led to a six year struggle over his right to take his parliamentary seat, which he finally did in 1886.

▪ [Frédéric] Bastiat (1801–50), French political economist and staunch advocate of free trade, believing that human interests, when left to themselves, tend to the general good. His great constructive work designed to prove this point entitled *Les Harmonies Economiques* was published early in 1850, at the end of which year Bastiat himself died in Rome.

▪ Auberon [William Edward Molyneux] Herbert (1838–1906), English politician and social philosopher. Strongly influenced by the writings of John Stuart Mill and Herbert Spencer, he became obsessed with individual freedom and unequivocally opposed to anything which smacked of uniformity. In 1885 he published *The Right and Wrong of Compulsion by the State*, a statement of the moral principles of the Party of Individual Liberty and the political measures founded upon them. For some years he edited *Free Life*, the journal of the Liberty Party, which, however, exerted only moral pressure, and never contested a parliamentary seat. Not surprisingly, in the 1890s Herbert was associated with the Anarchists, though he repudiated the connection in print.

▪ Johann Gottlieb Fichte (1762–1814), German philosopher who modified the Kantian system, believing that the only basic reality was the human mind (in opposition to the thesis that there could exist an unknowable object such as God or the soul, which reason might conceive but sense could not experience.) His *Destiny of Man* (sometimes translated *The Vocation of Man*) was published in 1800.

▪ Ferdinand Lassalle (see above, 51 et seq.).

12 September 1891

THE BOOK BILLS OF NARCISSUS* [C813]

OF all the consequences of that deluge of schooling which has taught everybody to read, and made cheap books remunerative to capitalists, none is more appalling than the ease with which a clever and imaginative young man may, for a few shillings, provide himself with an exhaustive second-hand experience of life. To read this book of Mr. Le Gallienne's one would suppose that he had been through three times as much as Ulysses, and was old enough and wise enough to be the father of Koheleth, the author of Ecclesiastes. Every page is pervaded by an assumption of elderly moderation, of gentle tolerance of the follies of passion, of resigned disillusion, of mellow paternal kindliness, which will move those who do not know the truth concerning the author's age to lay down the volume with a murmured blessing on his kindly voice and on his silver hair. This is the note of youth nowadays. From our riper men—our Morrises, Ruskins, Bradlaughs, Gladstones,

---

* "The Book-Bills of Narcissus, an Account rendered." By Richard Le Gallienne. The Moray Library. (Derby: Frank Murray, 1891.)

Tyndalls, and their contemporaries—we have strenuous words, urgency, combativeness, readiness to think every halfpennyworth of their convictions worth fighting for tooth and nail. How superior are our young men. How calm, how dispassionate, how full of conviction that nothing is worth quarrelling over, and yet how beautifully indulgent, how infinitely pitiful they are over the impetuosities and wilfulness of their elders. Later on, of course, when their knowledge of books is displaced by a knowledge of life, they become as little children again, and lose this fine philosophic *tout-comprendre-c'est-tout-pardonner* impartiality. But it is wonderfully perfect while it lasts, and keeps

OUR HOTHEADED OLD MEN

duly reproved and checked. As for me, though I am not yet quite old enough to be Mr. Le Gallienne's father, I feel a better and soberer man for having read this little book of his.

If an unusually fine literary instinct could make a solid book, Mr. Le Gallienne would be at no loss for an enduring reputation. One can see by his style how he appreciates Charles Lamb, Sterne, and the most delicate-handed of our modern bookmen. But though the manner is dainty, the matter is too superfine to be real; the author's wisdom is the outcome, not of his mother wit, but of his clergy. Nothing can be prettier than his pleas and persuasions on behalf of Narcissus and George Muncaster; but if I had the heart to ask what these highly praised gentlemen had ever said or thought or done to entitle them to five minutes' attention from any seriously busy man, I fear Mr. Le Gallienne, for want of a satisfactory answer, would have to abuse me for being a Philistine. These observations will not injure Mr. Le Gallienne (else they had not been made); for his publisher tells me that the whole edition of "Narcissus" was subscribed for before publication. So much can be done by

A GOOD WORKMAN

with his pen, even when he has but little first-hand material to put into his books.

One thing Mr. Le Gallienne has taught me. It is that Omar Khayyam must have been a very young man—probably not more than 17 when he wrote his "Fitzgeraldiana." I have even begun to suspect Browning's "Rabbi Ben Ezra" of being a schoolboy effusion touched up by the poet later in life. Let no one be saddened by the thought that in a year or so more Mr. Le Gallienne will gain knowledge otherwise than through his books, and with it temper, bias, one-sidedness, bigotry, and everything that is fatal to the polite negativeness of perfect taste. The change may impair his philosophy; but I think on the whole it will improve his books. No doubt that is only an opinion of mine; but I do not think the readers of *The Star* will undervalue any opinion which appears over the once-familiar signature of

C. DI B.

Editor's Notes

▪ The above was first published in the *Star,* Saturday, 12 September 1891, 4:4. An extract of it was reprinted in Grant Richards's *Author Hunting by an Old Literary Sportsman* (London: Hamish Hamilton; New York: Coward-McCann), 1934.

▪ Shaw's *Diary* on 10 September 1891 reports, "Wrote review of Le-Gallienne's *Narcissus* for *The Star*" (*Diary* 753).

▪ Richard Le Gallienne (1866–1947), English poet and novelist. Born in Liverpool and educated at Liverpool College, where he became a close friend of the actor James Welch (1867–1917), who was to play "Lickcheese" in the original production of Shaw's first play *Widowers' Houses* in 1892. Through the offices of Welch, who was then acting with Wilson Barrett's company in London, Le Gallienne obtained a post as literary secretary to Barrett (assisting in the writing of the latter's biography). He had published a volume of verse (*My Ladies' Sonnets*) in 1887 (dedicated to Welch), and in June 1891 he became a book reviewer to the *Star* under the pseudonym "Logroller." In the same year he married and published the book reviewed above. Oscar Wilde—whom Le Gallienne had met and knew slightly—after *The Book Bills of Narcissus* was published, is alleged to have declared that he could not believe that Le Gallienne would be "so unkind to so true a friend." Le Gallienne, who idolized Wilde, blushed and replied, "Why Oscar, I don't know what you mean. Unkind to you in *The Book-Bills of Narcissus* . . . why, I can't remember that I even mentioned your name in it." "Ah, Richard, that was just it"; see Richard Whittington-Egan and Geoffrey Smerdon,*The Quest of the Golden Boy: The Life and Letters of Richard Le Gallienne* (London: Unicorn Press, 1960), 182. The following year his *English Poems* were published, and reviewed by Shaw for the same newspaper (see below, 151 et seq.). In April 1894 *The Yellow Book* was published, containing work by Le Gallienne. In 1903, after the collapse of a second marriage, Le Gallienne left England permanently, initially for New York (where he had previously lectured) and, although fighting frequent bouts of sickness, continued to publish books of poetry and fiction. By 1930, now married a third time, Le Gallienne decided not to live in America, preferring to spend summers in Paris, and winters in Menton, which became the couple's permanent home in 1935. There Le

Gallienne died on 17 September 1947. He had been a prolific author and editor: he wrote volumes of poetry, fairy tales, fables, and romances; he translated the work of Wagner, edited the work of writers such as Hazlitt, Burns, Walton, and De Quincey, and wrote critical monographs on authors like Meredith, Stevenson, and Kipling.

- "Blessing on his kindly voice and on his silver hair." Shaw will repeat this form of words in his derisive picture of the absent clergyman in Conan Doyle's *A Story of Waterloo* (*Saturday Review*, 11 May 1895), the point in each case being the same, the audience's (false) vision, created by carefully chosen words.
- Shaw chooses men of principle. Morris (see below, 165), Ruskin (see above, 65), and Bradlaugh (see above, 83), were all prepared to fight for their convictions, as were the two that follow.
- [William Ewart] Gladstone (1809–98), English Liberal statesman. He became prime minister four times, in 1868 (when he effected the first National Education policy in England, and measures to compensate Irish tenants), in 1880, in 1886 (for a very short period, the rock upon which this administration split being the famous Home Rule for Ireland Bill, which caused division in his own ranks and defeated his government in the July of that year, and in 1892. On the same page as the above review appeared a line drawing of Gladstone's favorite dog and his youngest grandchild Dorothy Drew, with a note to the effect that "an excellent photograph" of the same could be obtained from Mr. Rowland Hawarden. Gladstone finally retired from public life because of his advanced age in 1894.
- [John] Tyndall (1820–93), Irish physicist and natural philosopher, whose views on the relationship between science and religion were made known in his presidential address to the British Association at Belfast in 1874—an event that caused him to be denounced as a materialist. Shaw claimed to have "read Tyndall and Helmholtz" in his youth.
- In choosing the poet and essayist Charles Lamb (1775–1834) and the novelist [Laurence] Sterne (1713–68), Shaw cites two very different but unique and highly personal literary stylists whose writing influenced numerous writers.
- The original author of the *Rubáyát of Omar Khayyám of Naishápúr,* which was freely translated from the Persian and published anonymously in 1859 by Edward FitzGerald (1809–83), was a twelfth-century astronomer and poet; Browning's "Rabbi Ben Ezra" (first published in *Dramatis Personae,* 1864) also concerns the historical character Abenezra, or Ibn Ezra [Abraham Ben Meir Ben Ezra] (c. 1090–c. 1168), one of the most eminent Jewish literati of the Middle Ages. Both poems are philosophical, but offer widely different approaches to life: the *Rubáyát,* marked by a world-weary romantic melancholy, offers an escape from the fashionable scientific determinism of Shaw's day, speculates on the mysteries of existence, but advises the reader to drink and make merry while life lasts; whereas, according to Rabbi Ben Ezra, man's life is to be viewed as a whole: God's plan in our creation has arranged for youth and age, and no view of life is consistent with it that

ignores the work of either. God is the Potter; we are the clay, receiving our shape and form and ornament by every turn of the wheel and faintest touch of the Master's hand.

19 January 1892
THE TRUTH ABOUT "THE TRAGIC COMEDIANS"* [C836]

WHEN "The Tragic Comedians" first appeared twelve years ago its importance as a historical study was little understood. The novel-reading public did not then suspect that the loves of Dr. Alvan and Clotilde von Rüdiger, otherwise Ferdinand Lassalle and Helena von Dönniges, were destined to become as famous in history as those of Antony and Cleopatra. Almost the only Lassallean document then in the hands of the British public was an article in the *Fortnightly Review* by Mr. Ludlow, our registrar of friendly societies, formerly known to insiders as the possessor of more than his equal quota of the capacity shown by the Christian Socialists of 1848–52, of whom Kingsley became the best known in the literary world. This article, one of the ablest yet written upon Lassalle, was a criticism by a Christian Socialist of a boastfully godless one, and by an ardent co-operator of the man who turned the German working classes from co-operation to Social Democracy, and whose fiercest polemic was directed against the "self-help" doctrine of Schulze-Delitzsch, the apostle of modern co-operation in Germany. It is therefore not surprising that the very ability with which the article was written only helped to infect the reader with the intense mistrust and dislike with which Mr. Ludlow regarded Lassalle.

When Mr. Meredith's novel appeared in the same review after-wards, it is doubtful whether any of its readers connected Dr. Alvan with the Luciferous hero of the article. Mr. Meredith himself vouch-safed no clue whatever, and yet did not hesitate to make the full effect of his book depend on the power of the reader to interpret it in

---

* "The Tragic Comedians." By George Meredith. 3d ed., revised and corrected by the Author. (London: Ward, Lock.)

the light of an easy familiarity with the whole Lassallean tradition, personal and political. The inevitable result was that the "The Tragic Comedians," instead of ranking as a Meredithian masterpiece, which it undoubtedly is, came to be classed by the author's disciples as a sort of by-blow or bastard offspring of his genius; and it is questionable whether we should have had this revised edition, with its portraits of Lassalle and Helen, and its introductory historical sketch by Mr. Clement Shorter, were it not that the success of Mr. William Harbutt Dawson's book on Lassalle, itself the result of the remarkable spread of Socialism in this country during the past decade, and the consequent priming of the public with the necessary historical information, has completely changed the conditions under which the novel reaches its readers. Now that we have access to the story of the Hatzfeldt case and the robbery of the casket, the allusions which used to fog us light up our path through the story, and the mysterious Baroness Lucie von Crefeldt becomes a real and interesting personality; whilst the apparently insane and impossible political position of Alvan, and his conversations with a certain "old Ironsides," who was plainly meant for Bismarck, become quite actual and credible in view of the history of the foundation of the *Allgemeiner Deutscher Arbeiterverein* in 1863.

The severest test to which a writer of fiction can be put is that of making a book out of a true story. From the hands of the ordinary novelist, an undisguised historic fact appears as a ridiculously obvious patch on the stuff his dreams are made of. The first-rate hand finds it otherwise: the more Shakespeareanly any passage strikes you in Shakespeare's historical plays the surer you are to find that it is pure Plutarch. Scott, too, was never embarrassed by history: when he is patchy it is the romance that is the patch and the history the fabric. As with Scott, so with Meredith. In "The Tragic Comedians" the touches which fail to convince are those which are against the historical evidence. For instance, in order to sharpen the irony of fate as exhibited in Lassalle's fall in a duel at the hand of a consumptive stripling, who died a few months later, Alvan is represented as being a consummate swordsman and marksman, and a man of gigantic health and strength, with "great breast and head," "massive column of throat," and so on. Prince Marko (Racowitza) is said never to have handled pistols, and to have killed Alvan with a shot "accidentally well-directed." This leads to a jarring passage, in which Alvan brags to Clotilde as follows:— "I will challenge any man that needs a lesson to touch buttons on a waistcoat with the button on a foil, or drill fives and eights in cards at twenty paces, &c." Now Lassalle, in his play hours, as everybody knows by this time, was fond of exuberating into comparisons of himself with Caesar, Hannibal, or any other hero who might be in question, not to mention lions, mountains, eagles, thunderbolts, and so forth; but there is all the difference in the world between these humorous bombastics and the passage quoted above, in which we have a man of nearly forty boasting seriously of his fencing and shooting to a girl of nineteen, and threatening to give an exhibition of his skill as "a lesson" to any challenger. It was the speciality of Lassalle's intelligence that he was able to sweep away all such academic tests of true fighting capacity—witness his celebrated definition of the Constitution in the crisis of 1862. He had an instinct for reality, which Mr. Meredith has on other pages done deep-sighted justice to, not only in the description of Alvan's keen sympathy with the same instinct in Bismarck, but in such speeches as, "Politically, also, we know that strength is the one reality, the rest is shadow: behind the veil of our human conventions power is constant as ever; and to perceive the fact is to have the divining-rod—to walk clear of shams." Besides, there is no reason whatever to suppose that Lassalle was an expert with either sword or pistol. He refused to practise before meeting Racowitza, who, on his part, very sensibly practised as hard as he could, with the natural result that his bullet hit Lassalle anything but "accidentally" before the latter had succeeded in pulling his trigger. Again, so far from there being any likelihood that but for the duel Lassalle would be at this moment a magnificently vigorous man on the verge of seventy, the medical testimony as to the state of his lungs goes to show that an insurance company would not have thought his life a much better one than Racowitza's. A glance at the woodcut which accompanies Mr. Shorter's memoir, and which is an unsuccessful attempt to reproduce the well-known 1864 photograph, disposes of the great breast and massive throat as utterly as it fails to convey the dazzling effect of the bold eyes and splendid brow which led to all the eagle comparisons, and which made Lassalle so imposing as an orator.

In truth, on these points Mr. Meredith is almost as arrantly romantic as Helen herself. He even, in hinting (page 68) that Lassalle had not been "the quietest of livers," gives the final touch to the Don Juan tradition which attaches itself so persistently to personally fascinating heroes. And he alludes to the lawless robbery of the casket in the Hatzfeldt case as having been planned by Lassalle. In sober truth, Lassalle—who was probably as little of a libertine and certainly as great a stickler for legality as the late Mr. Bradlaugh—succeeded in convincing a tolerably hostile tribunal that nothing more contrary to his wish and mischievous to his case could possibly have occurred than Oppenheim's impulsive blunder in running away with the Baroness von Meyendorff's jewel-case. If Mr. Meredith had stuck to these facts, he would have got rid of all his patches. He should have worked throughout in the spirit of that fine descriptive stroke of calling Alvan "a great prose giant" in contrast to Prince Marko, the "sprig of poetry." The real Alvan was no more a Claude Duval than a Don Juan or a D'Artagnan. As a man of action he was, on the whole, more like Daniel O'Connell than any other man of the century; and one notes in him a prodigious power of prosaic drudgery, down even to the careful rehearsal of his oratorical effects. As a political thinker, of course, no man of action—O'Connell less than most—can be compared to him for a moment. All the same, patches or no patches, it cannot be said that Mr. Meredith has failed to realise at least the feminine side of the character of his chief tragic comedian. There are superb strokes of portraiture in the book—the sixth and seventh chapters are magnificent; but there is a certain failure to realise the historical situation which vitiates the analysis of Alvan's state of mind at a critical point. The moment in which he says to Clotilde, "Why have I ever [always] unfailingly succeeded?" is the moment at which Lassalle knew himself to have failed, beaten by the "damned wantlessness" of the German working classes. His health was wrecked: a protracted period of inhuman over-exertion had ended in disappointment; he had a sentence of imprisonment hanging over him which, though it was only for six months, threatened death to him just then; and he had probably determined not to return from Switzerland to Germany.

This was the broken Lassalle who, after one more immense display of perseverance, energy, and self-restraint under the most galling treatment, lost his temper, and frantically coupled a savage vilification of a girl of nineteen with the challenge to her father, which was subsequently taken up by her affianced husband. Lassalle himself saw clearly, even in the agonies of his painful death, that he had his fit of rage to thank for his fate: there is no other possible explanation of his statement that he himself, and nobody else, had brought about his own death. The bearing of all this on the novel is that Mr. Meredith, by representing Alvan as being in 1864 what Lassalle was from 1848 to 1863, when he refused challenges instead of sending them, and was marching from success to success, has belittled his hero in order to magnify the dramatic situation. And though he plainly enough paints the disaffection of the friends who were going between Lassalle and the Dönniges family in the matter, he very considerably flatters them, and conveys no idea of the extent to which Lassalle seems to have been duped and under-estimated by his entourage at this crisis. If, as Mr. Meredith rightly says, "Among his gifts the understanding of women did not rank high," he erred equally in his dealings with men, and in the same way, by overrating them. In the mass he knew them well enough. And, by-the-by, Dr. Alvan's claims for the Jew in modern society—claims which might have been written by the author of "Daniel Deronda"—are far from harmonising with the recorded observations of Lassalle on the subject. Mr. Meredith has not quite caught the Social Democratic view of the successes cited by Alvan. It will be noted, too, that Lassalle's final interview with old Dönniges has been dropped in the novel.

Turning from the study of Lassalle in Alvan to that of Helen in Clotilde, all patchwork disappears, and it becomes impossible to doubt that here we have the real woman; and that if Madame von Racowitza-Shevitch were to come over from Riga expressly to assure us that Clotilde is not in the least bit in the world like her we should yet have to believe that Mr. Meredith knows her better than she knows herself. Though there are three or four pages of the book upon which you can lay your finger and say, "Lassalle never said that," there is not a line which is not veritable Helen. All the heroine-mongering of our standard novelists is the merest journeyman's work beside the analysis of Clotilde's relations with Alvan on the one hand and Marko on the other. It would be useless to indicate points; the work is as nearly perfect as can be, and must be read to be appreciated.

Mr. Shorter's little historical sketch is peculiar chiefly in its tenderness to Helen. The peculiarity is altogether creditable to the writer, as it is the custom for Lassalleans, in their mortification at the idea of so feather-headed a young lady causing the death of "the Messiah of Social Democracy," to abuse her as if she had been an experienced adventuress instead of a girl of nineteen, all but spoiled by the worst sort of petty aristocratic training. None of the exceptions commonly taken to her subsequent career will bear examination. Vulgarly romantic people find her marriage with Racowitza heartless; whilst conventional people are shocked at her breaking with her parents and going on the stage, not to mention her finally marrying a Socialist. But as Racowitza, to whom she was engaged before she met Lassalle, behaved bravely and honourably according to his somewhat dim lights, the charge of heartlessness would have been better founded had she refused to marry him. As to her family, their unscrupulous sacrifice of her chance of marrying the most brilliant and lovable man in Europe to their own mean and shortsighted social ambitions would place her repudiation of them beyond all need of apology, even if the results of their action had not included the slaughter of her lover. The people who regard actresses and Socialist's wives as disgraceful persons can hardly, at this time of day, aspire to the dignity of being argued with.

On the whole, Mr. Shorter's note of sympathy with Helen is sensible and timely. His sketch practically leaves Lassalle's political career out of account, and deals only with the episode which forms the subject of the novel. Mr. Meredith has done much the same thing; for in his normal mood he echoes the growing disillusion of the middle class rather than the rising hope of the working class, feeling himself to be a part of the funeral cortège of the old order rather than one of the family at the christening festival of the new. He is still full of the illusion, rampant in our literature from Shakespeare to Thackeray, that life is a farce and mankind but a company of paltry comedians, merely because he perceives that our narrow class ideals of life and character will not stand the test of experience. But it is Mr. Meredith's distinction from Shakespeare that his moments of exaltation, instead of making him more tragic, make him rejoice. Take, for example— and to conclude—this passage, in which the new spirit can be clearly recognised, especially by those who can penetrate to the significance of the word "needs" as it is used here:— "With the golden light came numbers, workmen still. Their tread on the stones roused some of Alvan's working thoughts, like an old tune in his head; and he watched the scattered files passing on, disciplined by their daily necessities, easily manageable if their necessities are but justly considered. These numbers are the brute force of the earth, which must have the earth in time, as they had it in the dawn of our world, and then they entered into bondage for not knowing how to use it. They will have it again: they have it partially, at times, in the despot, who is only the reflex of their brute force, and can give them only a shadow of their claim. They will have it all, when they have illumination to see and trust to the leadership of a greater force than they—in force of brain; in the spiritual force of ideas—ideas founded on justice, and not the justice of these days, of the governing few whose wits are bent to steady our column of civilised humanity by a combination of props and jugglers' arts, but a justice coming of the recognised needs of majorities, which will base the column on a broad plinth for safety and will be the guarantee for the solid uplifting of our civilisation at last."

Editor's Notes

- The above review was first published in the *Daily Chronicle*, 19 January 1892, 3:3–4. This national daily newspaper began in 1855 as the *Business and Agency Gazette,* and in 1870 was called the *Daily Chronicle and Clerkenwell News.* In 1876 it was purchased by Edward Lloyd; in 1892 Frank Lloyd became the proprietor, and Alfred Ewan Fletcher its editor. This was Shaw's first *Chronicle* review, and half a century later his reviewing for this journal prompted the following reminiscence: "Later on, when a local paper owned by Lloyds suddenly blossomed into the *Daily Chronicle,* and became a leading London daily, I reviewed for it, and, to my great indignation, was offered remuneration at the rate of so much (I think it was $3\frac{1}{2}$ d.) per compositor's 'stick.' I flung this back in the face of the reigning Lloyd, denouncing him as a sweater, and demanding £3 per thousand with a minimum of £5. This was considered so monstrous Lloyd, a most benevolent man, I believe, was seriously upset by it; and even my friends H. J. Massingham and Henry Norman, then on the editorial staff, sympathized with him, and agreed that I should never again contribute to the paper. However, I did contribute, and on my own terms. It was a successful stroke of literary trade unionism" (Bernard Shaw, "Reviewing Reviewed," *The Author* 52 [summer 1943], 72). The *Daily Chronicle* ceased in 1930.
- Shaw's *Diary* for 12 January 1892 records that he "spent most of the morning reading Shorter's edition of Meredith's *Tragic Comedians* for review." On the thirteenth, fourteenth, and fifteenth Shaw was "Working at review," which he finished and sent off on 16 January (*Diary* 785–86).
- George Meredith (1828–1909), English novelist and poet. Articled to a solicitor in London, he began submitting poems to journals. In 1860 Meredith became a journalist and a reader for Chapman and Hall the publishers (a post he retained until 1894), in which capacity he encouraged the young Thomas Hardy and George Gissing, and discouraged Bernard Shaw. Meredith was one of the publisher's readers of Shaw's early novels, who, according to Shaw "vetoed me without apology" (Bernard Shaw, "Reviewing Reviewed," *The Author* 52 [summer 1943], 71). Meredith's first published work had been poetry, and, indeed, his *Modern Love* (1862), a sonnet sequence written under the influence of the Pre-Raphaelite painters, has ensured him a permanent place among poets; but in 1859 began the series of novels for which he is famous: *The Ordeal of Richard Feverel, Evan Harrington* (1861), *Sandra Belloni* (1864), *Rhoda Fleming* (1865), *Vittoria* (1867), *The Adventures of Harry Richmond* (1871), *Beauchamp's Career* (1876), *The Egoist* (1879), and *The Tragic Comedians* (1880). He returned to poetry with *Poems and Lyrics of the Joy of Earth* (1883), and wrote more novels, of which *Diana of*

the Crossways (1885) was perhaps the first of his novels to become generally popular.

- Clement [King] Shorter (1857–1926), English journalist and author. From 1877 to 1890 he was a clerk in the Exchequer and Audit Department of Somerset House, still advancing his formal education by taking classes at the Birkbeck Institution. In 1888 Shorter was reviewing books for the *Star* and a little later for the *Queen*. In 1890 he left Somerset House (at the invitation of Sir William Ingram) to edit both the *Illustrated London News* and the *English Illustrated Magazine*. By 1897 he was editing five newspapers at once (in addition to the two mentioned, the *Sketch,* the *Album,* and *Pick-me-up*). He became very interested in German literature, and in 1890 annotated a reprint of Goethe's *Wilhelm Meister*. He also wrote books on the Brontës, Napoleon, and George Borrow.

- Meredith's novel first appeared serially in the *Fortnightly Review* from October 1880 to February 1881, and in book form on 15 December 1880.

- William Harbutt Dawson's book on Lassalle was reviewed by Shaw on 31 October 1888 (see above 51).

- The *Allgemeiner Deutscher Arbeiterverein* was the General German Workers' Union.

- One may wonder whether Shaw himself stood the "severest test" of making a book out of a true story when he wrote such plays as *Caesar and Cleopatra* and *Saint Joan.*

- Shaw refers here to Shakespeare's sourcebook for *Julius Caesar, Antony and Cleopatra, Coriolanus,* and some of *Timon of Athens,* namely Thomas North's translation of Jacques Amyot's *The Lives of the noble Grecians and Romans, compared together by that grave and learned Philosopher and Historiographer, PLUTARCH of Chaeronea* (1579).

- Shaw had read the novels of Sir Walter Scott (1771–1832) from childhood, encouraged in this, according to the preface to his own novel *Immaturity,* by his father, and was thoroughly familiar with the more than thirty historical romances known as the Waverley Novels (written between the years 1814 and 1832) as is clear from his frequent references to them.

- Charles Bradlaugh (see above, 83).

- Shaw's reinforcement of Lassalle's "bold eyes and splendid brow" is a further reminder of his interest in physiognomy as seen in the stage directions of his plays. In the next three years we shall have the "proudly set brows" of Grace Tranfield in *The Philanderer* (1893), the "clear quick eyes and good brows" of Bluntschli in *Arms and the Man* (1894), and the "serene brow" and "courageous eyes" of Candida (1895)

- Claude Duval (1643–70) was a highwayman notorious for his daring and gallantry.

- Don Juan (according to the Spanish account of Gabriel Tellez in *El Burlador de Sevilla y Convidado de Piedra* (1630) was Don Juan Tenorio of Seville, who seduced the daughter of the military commander of Seville. After killing the commander in a duel, Don Juan ironically invites his statue to a feast, whereupon the statue comes to life, seizes the hero, and drags him down to hell. There are famous dramatic representations of the character by Molière, Shadwell, Mozart, and, of course, Shaw himself in *Man and Superman* (1903). D'Artagnan is one of the characters of Alexandre Dumas *père*'s *Les Trois Mousquetaires* (1844), a great swordsman, based on a real Gascon gentleman (born c. 1611) and killed at the siege of Maastricht.

▪ Daniel O'Connell (1775–1847), Irish political leader, who was a leader in the fight for Catholic emancipation, ironically, since when he was elected M.P. for Clare in 1828, he was prevented, as a Catholic, from taking his seat. He was elected again in 1830, by which time the Catholic Emancipation Act had passed, and thereafter devoted his political energy to repealing the Union.

▪ The high-souled eponymous hero in *Daniel Deronda* by George Eliot [real name Marian Evans](1819–80) turns out to be Jewish, and is a highly sympathetic portrait.

▪ Shaw's quotation from Meredith differs slightly from the final version of the novel in respect of its punctuation, and the spelling of "civilized" and "civilization" with an "s."

1 February 1892

MR. BERNARD SHAW'S WORKS OF FICTION* [C839]

REVIEWED BY HIMSELF

The need for getting me to review my own works of fiction has arisen through the extreme difficulty of finding anyone else who has read them. This is not to be wondered at, as one of my novels has never been published at all; two others are buried in the pages of an extinct magazine; and of the two which enjoy a separate public existence only one has as yet shown any serious symptoms of immortality. I need hardly add that this one, "Cashel Byron's Profession," is, at bot-

---

* "Immaturity "(unpublished at this time); "Love Among the Artists" (serialized in *Our Corner*, November 1887–December 1888); "The Irrational Knot" (serialized in *Our Corner*, April 1885–February 1887); "Cashel Byron's Profession" (serialized in *To-Day*, April 1885–March 1886; published London: Modern Press; New York: George Munro; Harper and Bros., 1886; London: Walter Scott, 1889); "An Unsocial Socialist" (serialized in *To-Day*, March 1884–December 1884; published London: Swan Sonnenschein, 1887)

tom, a mere boy's romance. It has a sort of cleverness which has always been a cheap quality in me; and it is interesting, amusing, and at one point—unique in my works—actually exciting. The excitement is produced by the brutal expedient of describing a fight. It is not, as usual in novels, a case in which the hero fights a villain in defence of the heroine, or in the satisfaction of a righteous indignation. The two men are paid to fight for the amusement of the spectators. They set to for the sake of the money, and strive to beat each other out of pure ferocity. The success of this incident is a conclusive proof of the superfluity of the conventional hypocrisies of fiction. I guarantee to every purchaser of "Cashel Byron's Profession" a first class fight for his money. At the same time he will not be depraved by any attempt to persuade him that his relish for blood and violence is the sympathy of a generous soul for virtue in its eternal struggle with vice. I claim that from the first upper cut with which Cashel Byron stops his opponent's lead-off and draws his cork (I here use the accredited terminology of pugilism) to the cross-buttock with which he finally disables him, there is not a single incident which can be enjoyed on any other ground than that upon which the admittedly brutalized frequenter of prize-fights enjoys his favourite sport. Out of the savagery of my imagination I wrote the scene; and out of the savagery of your tastes you delight in it. My other novels contain nothing of the kind. And none of them have succeeded as well as "Cashel Byron's Profession."

The late James Runciman himself, I understand, an amateur boxer of some distinction, wanted to dramatise "Cashel Byron's Profession," an enterprise from which I strongly dissuaded him on the ground that the means by which I had individualised the characters in the novel would prove quite ineffective on the stage; so that all that could be done was, not to dramatise the novel, but to take the persons out of it, and use them over again on the stage in an otherwise original play. Lest there should be any heir to Runciman's design, I may as well point out that the two incidents in the story which have dramatic potency in them have already been used prominently on the stage. All the essentials of the glove fight in which the hero vanquishes an antagonist personally much less attractive than himself in the presence of a fashionable audience which includes the heroine, are to be found in a play of Shakespeare's called "As You Like It." Rosalind, Orlando, Charles the Wrestler, and Le Beau are sufficiently close copies of Lydia, Cashel, Paradise and Lord Worthington. The second instance is the episode of Bashville, the footman who loves his mistress. His place on the stage is already occupied by Victor Hugo's Ruy Blas, the valet who loves the

Queen of Spain. And Bulwer Lytton disputed the novelty of "Ruy Blas" on the ground that the central idea was to be found in Claude Melnotte's passion for the Lady of Lyons. But as the only unusual feature in Victor Hugo's play springs from his perception that a domestic servant is a human being, Fielding's Joseph Andrews is more nearly related to Ruy Blas and Bashville than Claude, who was a gardener. If I had not seen quite clearly that the fact of my not being a footman myself was the merest accident (a proposition which most of our novelists would undoubtedly repudiate with the greatest indignation) I could not have created Bashville. Such romances, by the bye, are probably common enough in real life. One of my own relations, an elderly lady, was, in her teens, cautiously approached by her father's gardener with honorable overtures on the part of his son, who was enamoured of the young lady of the house. Unlike Lydia Carew, however, she did not take a democratic view of the offer: she regarded it rather as an act of insane presumption on the part of a being of another and inferior order. And though she has long since been to a great extent cured of this crude class feeling, and has even speculated once or twice as to whether she did not then throw away a more valuable opportunity than that of which she subsequently availed herself, she has not quite lost the old sense that the proposal was, relatively to the ideas of the current epoch, somewhat too Radical. Pauline Deschapelles, and not Lydia Carew, is still the representative of the common feeling among the footman-keeping classes on the subject of matrimonial overtures from the kitchen to the drawing-room.

This brings me to another point. Lydia's reply to Bashville's declaration is superhumanly reasonable. But Lydia is superhuman all through. On the high authority of William Morris (privately imparted) she is a "prig-ess." Other critics, of a more rationalistic turn, revere her as one of the noblest creations of modern fiction. I have no doubt that the latter view is defensible; but I must admit that, for a man of Morris's turn, her intellectual perfections are rather too obviously machine-made. If Babbage's calculator is ever finished, I believe it will be found quite possible, by putting an extra wheel or two in, to extend its uses to the manufacture of heroines of the Lydia Carew type. Doubtless the superior mechanical accuracy of Lydia's ratiocinative action is calculated to strike awe into the average superstitious bungler, just as the unfinished machine of Babbage strikes awe into me—awe born of my own incapacity for numerical calculation, which is so marked that I reached my fourteenth year before I solved the problem of how many herrings one could buy for elevenpence in a market where a herring and a half fetched three halfpence. Babbage seems to have been even worse off in that respect than I, since he could not get on at all without a machine; and of course I, too, fall far short of Lydia Carew in the reasonableness of my private conduct. Let me not deny, then, without at all wishing to go back on my admirers and Lydia's, that a post-mortem examination by a capable critical anatomist—probably my biographer—will reveal the fact that her inside is full of wheels and springs. At the same time it must be distinctly understood that this is no disparagement to her. There is nothing one gets so tired of in fiction as what is called "flesh and blood." The business of a novelist is largely to provide working models of improved types of humanity; and I designed Lydia as a suggestion for a high-class modern woman, not to gratify my own taste in womanhood, but for purposes of general utility. And I still think she is a vast improvement on the current female type.

My first working model of this kind was the hero of my second novel ("Cashel Byron" was my fourth), a huge work called "The Irrational Knot." This was really an extraordinary book for a youth of twenty-four to write; but, from the point of view of the people who think that an author has nothing better to do with his genius than to amuse them, it was a failure, because the characters, though life-like, were a dreary company, all undesirable as personal acquaintances; whilst the scenes and incidents were of the most commonplace and sordid kind. My model man, named Conolly, was a skilled workman who became rich and famous by inventing an electro-motor. He married a woman whom I took no end of trouble to make as "nice" as the very nicest woman can be according to conventional ideas. The point of the story was that though Conolly was a model of sound sense, intelligence, reasonableness, good temper, and everything that a thoroughly nice woman could desire and deserve, the most hopeless incompatibility developed itself between them; and finally she ran away with a man whose deficiency in every desirable quality made him as unlike her husband as it is possible for one man to be unlike another. Eventually she got rid of her lover, and met her husband again; but after a survey of the situation, Conolly decided, like Nora in "A Doll's House," that the matrimonial relation between them had no prospect of success under the circumstances, and walked out of the house, his exit ending the book. This anticipation of Ibsen, of whom at that time I had never heard, seems to me to prove that he is a representative writer, marching with the world and not against it, or by himself, as some people suppose.

I hardly know anybody who has got through "The Irrational Knot."

Something was wanting in the book—perhaps a glovefight—which was not supplied even by the attraction of a subsidiary plot in which a fascinating but drunken actress threw a High Church clergyman into transports which he mistook for religious ecstasy. However, I suspect that the model Conolly was as incompatible with the public as with his wife. Long before I got to the writing of the last chapter I could hardly stand him myself.

A third novel, "Love Among the Artists," was written in 1881, and was interrupted by an attack of smallpox, my share of the epidemic of that year. Whether this enfeebled my intellectual convictions or not I cannot say; but it is a fact that the story exalts the wilful characters to the utter disparagement of the reasonable ones. As in most of my works, my aim throughout was to instruct rather than to entertain. I desired to shew our numerous amateurs of the fine arts, who would never have fallen in love with music or painting if they had not read books about them, the difference between their factitious enthusiasm and the creative energy of real genius. Some of the character studies are admirable, notably that of the musical composer Owen Jack, who is partly founded on Beethoven. I have a much higher opinion of this work than is as yet generally entertained; and, granting that it is perhaps hardly possible for an ordinary reader to persevere to the end without skipping, yet I think that he who reads as much of it as he finds he can bear, will be able to lay it down unfinished without any sense of having wasted his time, provided always that it is worth his while to read fiction at all.

After "Love among the Artists" came "Cashel Byron's Profession," which I confess I wrote mainly to amuse myself. The glove fight and the conventional lived-happily-ever-afterwards ending, to which I had never previously condescended, exposed me for the first time to the humiliation of extravagantly favorable reviewing, and of numbering my readers by some thousands. But long before this happened my self-respect took alarm at the contemplation of the things I had made. I resolved to give up mere character sketching and the construction of models for improved types of individual, and at once to produce a novel which should be a gigantic grapple with the whole social problem. But, alas! at twenty-seven one does not know everything. When I had finished two chapters of this enterprise—chapters of colossal length, but containing the merest preliminary matter—I broke down in sheer ignorance and incapacity. Few novelists would have had their perseverance shaken by a consideration of this nature; but it must be remembered that at this time all my works were in manuscript: the complete unanimity of the publishers in their conviction that there were more remunerative enterprises open to them than the publication of my works, had saved me from becoming pecuniarily dependent on fiction. Anyhow, I have written no more novels; and as, since then, eight years have passed, during which I have done enough gratuitous work to produce half a dozen novels had I been so minded, my abstention may be taken as perhaps the most significant of my criticisms on myself as a writer of fiction.

Eventually the two prodigious chapters of my aborted *magnum opus* were published as a complete novel, in two "books," under the title, "An Unsocial Socialist." Though to me they are a monument of my failure, I unhesitatingly challenge any living writer of fiction to produce anything comparable in vivacity and originality to the few early scenes in which the hero, Trefusis, introduces himself by masquerading as Jefferson Smilash at the girls' school. It is true that a moderately intelligent poodle, once started, could have done a good deal of the rest; but this is true of all works of art, more or less. The hero is remarkable because, without losing his pre-eminence as hero, he not only violates every canon of propriety, like Tom Jones or Des Grieux, but every canon of sentiment as well. In an age when the average man's character is rotted at the core by the lust to be a true gentleman, the moral value of such an example as Trefusis is incalculable.

On the whole, after having more than once considered the advisability of consigning the four novels I have mentioned to the oblivion which shrouds that desperate first attempt which has never seen the light, I have come to the conclusion, based on some experience as a reviewer of contemporary fiction, that Mr. Mudie's subscribers are very far from having reached that pitch of common sense at which they can decently pretend that my novels are not good enough for them. From their point of view the business of the fictionist is to tell lies for their amusement. Middle class respectability, out of the depths of the unspeakable dulness of its life, craves for scenes of love and adventure. Any book which conjures up some miserable ghost of either or both will go its circulating library round. Strenuous imaginings of muscle and pluck written by sedentary cowards for sedentary cowards and passionate descriptions beginning "Their lips met" which almost make one cry, so obvious is it that nothing but the most ghastly and widespread starvation of the affections could make such poor fare marketable: these form the staple of nine novels out of ten. But there are readers who have sufficient experience and sense of reality to require a much higher degree of verisimilitude from fiction if it is to produce any illusion for them. Others, especially in the numerous class of tolerably educated persons occupied daily in routine work which does not half employ their intellects, are speculative, restlessly cerebrative, and cannot be interested except by exhibitions of character or suggestions of social problems. To such I recommend the works of my youth, in spite of their occasional vulgarity, puerility and folly. Indeed, to the vulgar my vulgarity, to the puerile my puerility, and to the foolish my folly will be a delight instead of a drawback. For the merely inane there is twaddle about Art and even a certain vein of philandering and flirtation. As to the literary execution of the books, I suppose it will not now be questioned that I am no mere man of genius, but a conscientious workman as well. What could more reasonably be claimed?

The best way to procure copies of "The Irrational Knot," and "Love Among the Artists" is, I imagine, to advertise in the Sunday papers for old sets of the magazines which died of them, offering a suitable pecuniary inducement. "Cashel Byron's Profession" is still extant, and is retailed at ninepence by the London discount booksellers. An extraordinary increase in the popularity of "An Unsocial Socialist" is indicated by the fact that my royalties upon it in the year 1891 were 170 per cent. greater than those received in 1889. I doubt if any other living novelist can shew such a record. In fact 170 is an understatement; for the exact figures were two and tenpence for 1889 and seven and tenpence for the year 1891. If any publisher is in search of a novelist whose popularity is advancing by leaps and bounds, it is possible that a handsome offer might tempt me back to the branch of literature which I originally cultivated.

Editor's Notes

- The above review was first published in the *Novel Review* (with which is incorporated *Tinsley's Magazine*), n.s. 33 (February 1892): 236–42.
- On 4 January 1892 Shaw "worked all day at article for *The Novel Review* on my own works of fiction." The next day he reports "working at article; but not getting along quite so brilliantly as I had hoped. " However, on 6 January he "finished and sent off the article to Margaret Harkness" (*Diary* 783). Margaret E[lise] Harkness (1861?–1921), was a cousin of Beatrice Webb (see below, 199), and a Socialist, journalist, writer on the Middle East, and novelist (under the pseudonym of John Law), who owned the *Novel Review*. Weintraub reveals that next to his monthly summary of earnings at the end of the 1892 Diary,

Shaw wrote (in shorthand) "Cheque for £3, 13. 6 from *Novel Review* returned to Miss Harkness on the 13th. I did not care to take it from her, as she is presumably not making anything out of the review, which she has only just bought" (*Diary* 783). On 11 January, Shaw had noted in his *Diary,* "Article for *Novel Review* to be ready on the 15th" (and this is marked on the fifteenth, too). Later this year Shaw would be interviewed by "Miss Wilson" of the *Novel Review* about his first-performed play, *Widowers' Houses.*

▪ James Runciman (1852–91), English schoolmaster and journalist. While a schoolmaster, he contributed articles to the *Teacher* and *Vanity Fair,* on which journal he eventually took a permanent position, renouncing the teaching profession. He also contributed articles (some of which were reprinted) to the *Saint James's Gazette,* the *Standard* and the *Pall Mall Gazette,* plus essays on social and educational topics in the *Contemporary Review,* the *Fortnightly Review,* and the *Family Herald.* In 1901 Shaw himself turned *Cashel Byron's Profession* into a three-act play, writing it in a week, and calling it *The Admirable Bashville; or, Constancy Unrewarded.* In fact, he took his own advice, since the characters, though recognizably those of the novel, play out a script in blank verse to a plot that diverges greatly from the original. Perhaps it was in deference to his confessed dramatic indebtedness to *As You Like It* that Shaw wrote his play in blank verse. It was first performed professionally in 1903.

▪ Shaw seems to have been fond of Victor [Marie] Hugo (1802–85), and he went to see the Comédie Française perform *Ruy Blas* at Drury Lane on 27 June that year (*Diary* 912, 925, 950).

▪ [Edward George Earle Lytton] Bulwer-Lytton, first Baron Lytton (1803–73), English politician and author, in his parliamentary days supported himself financially by writing a series of novels, in addition to which he wrote plays. In *The Lady of Lyons; or, Love and Pride* (1838), Pauline Deschapelles, the proud daughter of a merchant of Lyons, is humbly loved by young Claude Melnotte, son of the Deschapelles' old gardener.

▪ Charles Babbage (1792–1871), British mathematician, and pioneer of computer science, one of whose machines, designed to solve complicated mathematical problems, was to be operated according to instructions punched in perforated cards. Inside his "analytical engine" there was to be a "store" where numbers were remembered, and a "mill" where arithmetical calculations were to be performed according to the instructions on the cards. Unfortunately, the machine was never built.

▪ William Archer, whose interest in the Norwegian dramatist Ibsen (1828–1906), began in the early 1870s, and who had translated and adapted *The Pillars of Society* for the first performance of an Ibsen play in England at the Gaiety Theatre, 15 December 1880, was the man who introduced Ibsen's work to Shaw. The earliest mention of Ibsen in Shaw's *Diary* is on 5 May 1885.

▪ Tom Jones, the foundling hero of Fielding's novel (1749), "violates every canon of propriety" by his affair with the gamekeeper's daughter Molly Seagrim, by falling in love with Sophia Western who is betrothed to another, and by his behavior toward the pedantic clergyman Thwackum and his philosopher colleague Square. Chevalier Des Grieux, the hero of the Abbé Prévost's *Manon Lescaut* (1731), has a passionate attachment to the young girl of the title, who is about to be made a nun against her will: they elope, and are reduced to the basest expedients, but both are redeemed by the power of their feelings. Shaw's hero, Sidney Trefusis, not only violates Victorian propriety; he also seems curiously devoid of feelings and preternaturally aware of economic issues: his scandalous behavior at his wife's funeral is enough to justify Shaw's original title for the book: *The Heartless Man;* see R. F. Dietrich, *Portrait of the Artist as a Young Superman. A Study of Shaw's Novels* (Gainesville: University of Florida Press, 1969), 155–58.

▪ "Mr. Mudie's subscribers" were those who paid a guinea subscription for new books to Charles Edward Mudie (1818–90) founder of a circulating library, whose name became a household word among the Victorian public. Mudie, a stationer and bookseller in Southampton Row, London, started to lend books in 1842. This was so successful a venture that ten years later he moved his "Select Library" into the big storehouse, which became such a familiar landmark in New Oxford Street. In 1860 these premises were enlarged and different branches established, and in 1864 "Mudie's" became a limited company. Its fortunes declined, however, and it finally closed its doors in the summer of 1937.

5 April 1892
INDIVIDUALISM REALISED* [C853]

"THE Outcome of Individualism," of which a third edition, revised and enlarged, has just come to hand, is Mr. J. H. Levy's contribution to the burning question of Socialism versus Individualism. Its effect, on the whole, is to confirm the growing opinion that the question will end by burning itself out, after duly singeing the fingers of most of the disputants. The signs of the times are for reconciliation—nay, for identification—of advanced Individualism with practical Socialism; and though political Impossibilists like Mr. Hyndman, and doctrinaire Impossibilists like Mr. Auberon Herbert, may still maintain the traditional feud, all those who, as Possibilists, come under the compulsion of common sense are being driven in the same direction.

---

* "The Outcome of Individualism." By J. H. Levy. 3d ed. (London: P. S. King and Son.)

Thus we find the Fabian Society now refusing to accept the antithesis between Socialism and Individualism; talking, in its later tracts, of "Unsocialism"; and recommending the public to read Mr. Levy and Schaeffle, not in scorn of their opposition, but evidently from a disposition to accept their practical proposals as very good Socialism, and their theoretical demonstrations as good propaganda in all but the name. This is a sensible tactic; but to Mr. Levy it means being "dished," a process to which he is not accustomed. An old dialectical hand is Mr. Levy—a trained intellect, a veteran platform fighter, a crafty debater, one who, as Rationalist, Freethinker, Malthusian, Republican, and, above all, as a hater of intellectual dishonesty in all its forms, has fought *contra mundum* long enough to be a past master in the art of such war, whether on the lines of his old master, Stuart Mill, or his old general, Bradlaugh. Now the Stuart Mill school is ingrainedly Individualist. All the true Millites got their bias in the struggle of Science and Freethought against the Church, and of the women against their exclusion from the professions and against the monstrous slavery in which the law held them before the Married Women's Property Act was passed. This struggle had the whole advanced Progressive battle-field to itself in the period which elapsed between 1850 and 1880, when Socialism had vanished with Chartism, and Mr. Henry George and Mr. Hyndman had not yet arrived. During that period the workers were busy with Co-operation and Trade Unionism, so that even the International, though Karl Marx was its president, went no further than International Unionism. The sort of culture which consists in reading all the most advanced books and small-talking about them afterwards, fastened, in those days, upon Matthew Arnold, Huxley, Tyndall, Darwin, and Herbert Spencer; whilst as to fiction it formulated the opinion that George Eliot was the greatest novelist that ever lived. It was not exactly Merrie England then; but it felt immensely intellectual; and Mr. John Morley wrote about Voltaire, spelt God with a small g, pointed out the inferiority of Macaulay's style, and made quite a reputation. It was all intensely anti-Socialist; and nothing is more natural than that the men who grew up in that atmosphere should now, in their middle age, be in full revolt against it, and using all the intellectual training they owe to it to devise schemes for the socialisation of the universe. When Mill's Autobiography came out, and was found to contain a confession of Socialism, his strongest partisans felt that they had received a stab in the back; and though Mr. Levy, who advocated Land Municipalisation here before Mr. Henry George was politically born, was far too well instructed to be taken aback as the smatterers in the movement were, yet it may be doubted whether so much of his present pamphlet would be devoted to criticisms of Mill if Mr. Levy had not some feeling that his old leader had deserted the flag. Here are the terms in which he introduces him:—

> When John Stuart Mill, who, in my opinion, has done more to propagate Socialism than any writer of our generation, Karl Marx not excepted—when John Stuart Mill included in the remarkable posthumous confessions which pained and astonished his most ardent admirers the statement that his views and those of his wife were such as would class them decidedly under the general designation of Socialists, he knew what he was saying.

This view is supported by Mr. William Morris, who once stated that he was converted to communism by Mill's chapter on it, the adverse verdict being so flagrantly against the evidence. Mill, like most conscientious men, always did give the verdict against the evidence, lest he should be led into doing an injustice by his bias in favour of his own opinion. Mr. Levy goes on to quote Mill repeatedly, each time only to gravel him on some economic point. The effect of this on the reader is to rouse in him the old Adam of disputatiousness, and to make him long to trip up Mill's victorious opponent. And, in truth, Mr. Levy does not always look to his own feet as heedfully as he might. For instance, in attacking Mr. Sidney Webb for proposing to socialise "rent of ability," Mr. Levy says:—

> Let it be clearly understood that the question at issue is one of politics not one of personal morals—not what it is the duty of a man *voluntarily* to devote to public uses of the fruits of his labours, but what his fellow men are justified in *forcing* him to yield up. A large portion of my life and energies have been given to work for which I have received no pecuniary reward. But I say plainly that, if any body of persons tried to exact this from me, they would find me made of stubborn material. Mr. Webb, in a lame sort of way, recognises this difficulty. The scheme, he says, "would effect its object, provided it were practicable;" to which I may add that the moon would make very good cream-cheese, provided that were practicable. The idea of stealing the chickens of genius before they are hatched ap-

pears to me as mad as it is unjustifiable. You may decree that the surplus of value over the wages of ordinary labour produced by a Landseer or a Millais, a Rubinstein or a Wagner, a Dickens or a Tennyson, an Erskine or a Burke, a Brassey or an Armstrong, shall be confiscated to public uses; but are you sure that, under these circumstances, it will be produced? If under such conditions it be produced, it is clear that Socialism must have forced an open door. It is much more likely to firmly close a partially open one. There is a great deal of "human nature" even in persons of ability.

This does not sound ill; but to say that if you want exceptional work you must pay extra wages—which is what it all comes to—not only begs the main question, but does nothing to settle how much extra wages you must pay. It is clearly one of the rights of the individual to pay no more for genius than enough to induce its possessor to exercise it. Now, Mr. Levy, though he has voluntarily given that large portion of his life and energies to the public "for nothing," has really been forced to do without payment by the fact that the public refuse to give for such work as his what they will give willingly for the work of Mr. Rider Haggard and Miss Lottie Collins. They have virtually said to him, "Either do it for nothing or let it alone"; and to his honour he has done it on those exacting terms. Miss Ellen Terry and Miss Ada Rehan would at present refuse to accept engagements at the salaries which satisfied Mrs. Siddons and Mrs. Jordan. Rubinstein would not play six bars in public for the sum which induced Mozart not only to play half a dozen concertos at as many different concerts, but to compose them into the bargain. Brassey and Armstrong would laugh at the considerations which prevailed upon Leonardo da Vinci to fortify Milan. Mr. Levy will not contend that the difference in terms in these cases is the measure of the difference in ability or exertion. It simply measures the increase of demand for the services of men and women of genius. It tells you what Mrs. Siddons and Mozart could get if they were alive now; and it also tells you what Miss Ada Rehan and Sir William Armstrong would have taken *faute de mieux,* if they had been alive then. Suppose it were possible to establish a state of things in which the highest salary obtainable by Miss Terry was one-tenth of what she now receives, which would be handsome pay for an average educated woman, nobody can suppose either that she would act only one-tenth as well as at present, or that she would refuse to act at all, and turn factory inspector. She would take what she could get, and earn it in the way most congenial to her—that is, by acting as well as she possibly could. Circumstances beyond her own control offer her at present six times what she would do her present work for rather than do anything else—that is all. In what way, then, could the cutting off of five-sixths of her salary (assuming that it were practicable) be described as the forcing of an open door? A system of equal remuneration, whatever else it might do, would certainly not put a premium on the common work which brings no social distinction with it: on the contrary, it would obviously put a premium on the work which brings fame and popular idolatry. The real difficulty would be, not to get actors and virtuosos and captains of industry under such a system, but to get sewermen and dustmen and shoe-blacks. What scavenger would do for the money paid for "Paradise Lost" as much work as Milton did?

One or two of Mr. Levy's points are ambiguously stated. Either they do not mean what the general reader will take them to mean, or they cannot be sustained. For instance, in dealing with the land question, he says:—

> I quite agree with Mill that "what is wanted is permanent possession on fixed terms."

Now if there is any Utopian aspiration which Political Economy has signally left for dead it is permanent possession of land on fixed terms. Mr. Levy and Mill might just as well have said, "What is wanted is a fixed margin of cultivation"—that is, a stationary population and stationary methods of production. If every increase of population lowers the margin of cultivation and raises rent, and every improvement in methods of production raises the margin and lowers rent, how is the rent to be secured to the community (as Individualism, through Mr. Levy, demands) if the land is to be held on fixed terms? —unless, indeed, Mr. Levy only means terms which vary on a fixed principle, which is by no means what the general reader understands by his phrase. Mr. Levy drops the rent question there, and says nothing of the pet contention of the Socialists that if we socialise rent we socialise the fund out of which capital accumulates, and upon which a huge mass of workers—servants, tradesmen, "luxury" manufacturers, and what not—depend for their living. If all this is to be seized and placed in the public treasury, how will Mr. Levy's Individualism provide for its restoration to general circulation if the State is neither to farm it out as capital, nor lend it to our municipalities for use in their socialised industries, nor administer it directly? Mr. Levy is silent on this crucial point, whilst complaining somewhat that the Socialists are silent as to his pamphlet.

Again, in dealing with the question of compensation to the land-lords, Mr. Levy puts the case in a way which will comfort the Duke of Westminster exactly as a dentist, forceps in hand, comforts a shrink-ing little girl in his chair by the bland assurance that he is not going to hurt her.

> Mr. Henry George would wipe out the National Debt by means of a sponge, and would "nationalise" land by seizing—by taxa-tion or otherwise—the whole of the rental of the country. To this I could not for a moment agree. However lacking in moral justification private property in land may have been originally, it has been recognized by the State; innocent persons have been induced to make investments in it; the transfers have been made according to forms prescribed by the State, which has also received a commission on each such transaction in the shape of a stamp duty. Under such circumstances, if we resolve—as I hope and believe we will—that private property in land shall cease to be, the cost of the change—so far as there is any—must be borne by the whole nation, as in the case of slave emancipation, and not by those only who happen to be in the possession of land when it is determined that this change must be made.

It certainly sounds reassuring—to the landed interest. But later on we learn that—

> The permanent fiscal burthens on land—which are really a reserve rental belonging to the State—would be jealously maintained.

This is to take place after the landlord's interests have been pur-chased at the public expense. Now it cannot be worth the nation's while to pay the landords a full equivalent for their interest in the land unless the nation collectively can administer the land more profitably than the landlords—a view which Mr. Levy cannot adopt without giving up his whole position of the superiority of "Individual-ist" to Socialist administration. Consequently, if the nation is to have any economic motive for buying out the landlords, it will have to manipulate those "fiscal burthens" (including, we presume, income tax) so as to contrive that the landlords shall be paid at least partly out of their own pockets—say to the extent of a ten per cent. discount. And if that succeeds, the nation might equally on Mr. Levy's principles and on Mr. George's raise the discount to 100 per cent. What, then, is the use of trying to persuade the landlords that it is possible to take away the economic advantage conferred on them by their property in land and yet leave them no poorer than before? If "compensation," "equitable terms," and so forth, mean only painless expropriation, why not call them so, instead of implying, as Mr. Levy seems to do, that it means indemnification?

Leaving the Individualist Tweedledum to argue these matters out at leisure with the Socialist Tweedledee, let us look at a couple of the more general views expressed by Mr. Levy as an Individualist.

> We seem to have come upon a time of utter infidelity to general principles, except that most vicious one that there are no general principles. There is always a large section of the British public ready to give a willing ear to this doctrine. It is one of those consecrations of empiricism which delight the heart of the British Philistine; for there is nothing on which he so much prides himself as his superiority to the shallow people who have not acquired his proficiency in the art of sitting between two stools—of gracefully taking a seat with an air of conscious superiority, between two contradictory propositions.

Compare this with what we are told by the new Individualists of the Norwegian school, which assures us that fidelity to general principles—in other words, the worship of "ideals"—is the whole secret of human slavery and baffled individuality. It is quintessential, we are told, that we should rather, like Ibsen's Ulric Brendel, become the wilful slaves of whisky than the rational slaves of principle, if Fate forces that crude alternative on us. And here, curiously enough, is Mr. Levy coming out, in apparent contradiction to himself, with the following Cassandra cry:—

> Our lives are getting to be more and more regulated from without, with the effects that we are becoming drained of our individuality and drilled into mere machines. The passive attitude of mind induced by this régime will, if that régime grow in intensity, be fatal to all manliness of thought and manliness of conduct.

In this melancholy forecast we miss Mr. Levy's normal elasticity of mind and vigilance of outlook; for whether we consider the Lancashire cotton operative rescued from his slavery by socialistic factory legislation, or the daughter of a county family enabled by the fight for Individualism to choose between Merton and Newnham as freely as her brother chooses between Kings and Christ Church, we see everywhere a growth of individual liberty which scandalises our grandmothers. If this has involved "utter infidelity to general principles," so much the worse for the general principles. Why should Mr. Levy, who has braved so many prophecies as to the doom of "utter infidelity" to one thing and another, at last lay down his liberty of thought at the feet of Individualism or any other "ism," and threaten the advocates of the opposition "ism" with damnation? Doctrinaire Individualism and doctrinaire Socialism have both had their day; and the successful propagandist henceforth will be, in a new and wider sense, what Mr. Levy has always been proud to proclaim himself—a free thinker.

Editor's Notes

- The above review was first published in the *Daily Chronicle*, 5 April 1892, 3:2–3.
- On 25 March 1892, Shaw traveled to Leek, in Staffordshire, to lecture to the Trades Council there. Shaw's *Diary* tells us that he "read for review in the train: J. H. Levy's *Individualism*." The following day he "wrote review of Levy's *Outcome of Individualism* in the train coming up" [to London from his Staffordshire engagement.] On 27 March Shaw "sent off review of Levy's book to the *Chronicle*" (*Diary* 807–8).
- J[oseph] H[iam] Levy (1838–1913), English academic, journalist and writer. After a forty-year career in the Board of Education, where he became examiner of school accounts and registers, he became in 1902 professor of logic and economics at Birkbeck College, and the City of London College, at both of which institutions he initiated the study of these subjects. Levy was leader writer of the *Examiner* from 1869 to 1875, and of the *National Reformer* from 1877 to 1890. In 1881 he became editor of the *Shield* (a post he held for five years, after which he edited the *Individualist*). He founded the London Dialectical Society, to which Shaw also belonged, and Shaw debated with him there. Levy was a Liberal in politics, and editor of *A Symposium on Value* to which Shaw, Wicksteed, Bax, and Hyndman contributed. The titles of some of his books and published lectures reveal his interests: *The Economics of Labour Remuneration* (1894),*Vivisection and Moral Evolution* (1902), *Freedom, the fundamental condition of morality* (1912), and *The Enfranchisement of Women* (1912).

- Hyndman (see above, 20).
- Auberon Herbert (see above, 83–84).
- Malthusians were followers of Thomas Robert Malthus (1766–1834), English economist. His *Essay on the Principle of Population* (1798) argued that population increases faster than the means of its subsistence, depressing living standards to a bare minimum. Whenever there is a relative gain in production over population growth, Malthus argued, it merely stimulates the latter; whereas if population overtakes production, its growth is checked by famine, disease, or war. Malthus's theories received support from many who were opposed to bettering the conditions of the poor, or who embraced Malthus's solution of "moral restraint" to keep down the population. His theories influenced Ricardo (see above, 56),while for [Charles Robert] Darwin (1809–82), the originator of the theory of evolution by natural selection, Malthus's phrase "the struggle for existence" found an echo in his own discoveries and, when applied to all organic life, provided the numerical surplus necessary for natural selection. Shaw gave a lecture on 20 June 1886, entitled "Socialism and Malthusianism," in which he found the two beliefs incompatible.
- The Married Women's Property Acts of 1870, 1874, and 1882 (the last of which repealed and consolidated the previous two acts) enormously improved the position of women unprotected by marriage settlement. Briefly, the Act of 1882 decreed that a married woman is capable of acquiring, holding, and disposing of by will or otherwise, any real or personal property in the same manner as if she were a *feme sole*. The act also contained provisions as to stock, investment, insurance, evidence, and other matters.
- Shaw's summation of "culture" 1850–80 begins with Matthew Arnold (1822–88), English poet and critic, who was the first to claim that the spiritual health of society depended upon there being sufficient people dedicated to the spread of "Culture," which he defined as "the acquainting ourselves with the best that has been known and said in the world." It also includes T[homas] H[enry] Huxley (1825–95), English pioneer biologist, who was the foremost and most lucid supporter in England of Darwin, whose evolutionary theories set the world on its ears when they were published in 1859. For Tyndall see above, 87. Herbert Spencer (1820–1903), English philosopher, had espoused evolutionary principles four years earlier, in *Principles of Psychology* (1855), and welcomed Darwin's findings as reinforcement of his own beliefs, which he applied to ethics and sociology. His notion that societies evolve in competition for resources for many justified morally the "survival of the fittest." For Shaw's review of Hugh Elliott's biography of Spencer, see below, 357.
- Elsewhere, Shaw called George Eliot the novelist of the movement that "may be said to have begun with Hobbes, and to have made its way in England as a sort of negative philosophy, materialistic, empirical, and utilitarian, up to 1880 or thereabout; but it was always far less a school of philosophy than a campaign against Church and State for free thought and free contract;" (Bernard Shaw, review of Moncure Conway's novel *Pine and Palm*, *Pall Mall Gazette* [13 March 1888], in *Bernard Shaw's Book Reviews*, 393).

- John [Viscount] Morley [of Blackburn] (1838–1923), English author and politician. In 1866 he became editor of the *Fortnightly Review,* which, under his anticlerical influence, became the voice of the English Positivists, and increased its circulation to some 30,000 readers. In 1880 he became editor of the *Pall Mall Gazette,* switching that paper's politics from conservatism to liberalism. In 1883 he was elected M.P. for Newcastle-upon-Tyne. He remained in politics until 1914 when he resigned from Asquith's cabinet in protest against the country's drift toward war. He also wrote about ten biographies, including in 1872 one of [François Marie Arouet de] Voltaire (1694–1778), French satirical author.
- John Stuart Mill (1806–73), British political scientist. He is probably most famous for his "Essay on Liberty" (1859); but had published *Principles of Political Economy* in 1848. In political economy he advocated policies he believed most consistent with individual liberty, believing that this could be threatened as much by social as by political tyranny. Shaw "read up Mill about money" in preparation for his paper on "Money" read to the Fabian Society, 20 February 1885 (*Diary* 62).
- The work of Landseer (see above, 64), English animal painter, and Millais (see below, 525–26), portrait artist, was enormously popular at this date. They were both sufficiently famous to be buried in Saint Paul's Cathedral.
- [Anton] Rubinstein (1829–94), Russian pianist and composer was also famous at this time particularly for his mastery of technique on the piano, while [Wilhelm Richard] Wagner (1813–83) was just beginning to supplant Brahms and Schumann in the minds of the concertgoing public. [Charles] Dickens (1812–70) and [Alfred, first Baron] Tennyson (1809–92) remained literary institutions. The great Scottish jurist [Thomas] Erskine (1750–1823) whose forensic skills defended many "Friends of the People" (including Thomas Paine), and the famous Irish statesman and philosopher [Edmund] Burke (1729–97) are given as examples of the highest in their professions. Thomas Brassey (1805–70), English engineer, is paired with [William George Baron] Armstrong (1810–1900), English inventor and industrialist, both of whose inventions, railway viaducts in the case of Brassey, and hydraulic engines and cranes in the case of Armstrong, made valuable contributions to their society.
- Shaw balances the popularity of J. H. Levy's work against that of [Sir Henry] Rider Haggard (1856–1925), whose novel *King Solomon's Mines* (1885) had made him famous; and an English music-hall entertainer Lottie Collins (1866–1910), whose enormous success was due entirely to one song, *Ta-Ra-Ra-Boom-De-Ay,* and the dance that went with it, which she first performed in 1891.
- Ellen Terry (see below, 526) was, in 1892, in the fourteenth year of her partnership with the famous actor manager Henry Irving (1838–1905) at the Lyceum. Shaw's interest in her also dated from 1878, just before her Lyceum contract, when he had seen her in *New Men and Old Acres* at the Court Theatre. The American actress Ada Rehan (1860–1916) had become famous in England playing Katherina in Augustin Daly's production of *The Taming of the Shrew* which, in 1888 he brought to England. Shaw hated Daly's version of

Shakespeare's play, but came to respect the ability of Ada Rehan, describing her in 1897 as "an actress of genius as well as of extraordinary technical accomplishment." Mrs. [Sarah] Siddons (1755–1831), English actress, and Mrs.[Dorothy] Jordan (1761–1816), Irish actress, were both very successful at London's Drury Lane Theatre in the late eighteenth century.

- The first evidence of the employment at Milan of the Italian painter, sculptor, architect, and engineer, Leonardo da Vinci (1452–1519) dates from 1487. Ludovico Sforza [il Moro], who had recently usurped the state from his nephew Gian Galeazzo, employed Leonardo to help to beautify and strengthen the *Castello,* the great stronghold of the ruling power in the state, against possible attack.
- Ulric Brendel is the penniless liberal in Ibsen's *Rosmersholm* (1886), who is nevertheless happy until he is disillusioned by the actions of his fellow liberals.
- By "Merton and Newnham" Shaw probably means to say Girton (founded 1869) and Newnham (founded 1871), both women's colleges at Cambridge University. Merton, still for men only in 1892, is an Oxford College (founded 1264). King's College is at Cambridge and Christ Church at Oxford. A year or so later Shaw would choose Newnham for his character Vivie Warren.

14 April 1892

THE PICKWICK PANTOMIME* [C856]

THE most curious passage in this reprint occurs in a letter which Dickens wrote in 1866, twenty-nine years after the publication of *Pickwick,* asking his son to obtain Mrs. Dickens's written testimony to the fact that Seymour, the artist, had nothing to do with the invention of the book. The last paragraph runs thus:

It seems a superfluous precaution, but I take it for the sake of our descendants long after you.

These words leave no reasonable doubt that the *Pickwick Papers,* in Dickens's maturest judgment, were good enough to be described, in the current literary slang, as "immortal." And certainly there is no

---

* "The Posthumous Papers of the Pickwick Club." By Charles Dickens. Reprint of the first edition, with an Introduction by Charles Dickens the Younger. (London: Macmillan, 1892.)

denying that when a book which was unprecedentedly popular half a century ago is at present more popular than ever it is waste of time to argue against its claim to rank as an English classic. But there are pages upon pages of *Pickwick* which explain the coldness with which it was received by literary experts at first, which make you lay the book down, and say to yourself: "Supposing I had not been a child when this first fell into my hands—supposing I had been an educated critic, and had formed my taste upon *Jonathan Wild* and *A Tale of a Tub,* in which the Pickwickian literary style is to be found in the full strength of its original purity and artistic integrity, would I not have been revolted by Dickens's conscious and insistent facetiousness, by his lapses into journalistic carelessness and commonplace, by the melodramatic vulgarity of his tragic episodes? Would it not have seemed an inept, juvenile, unappreciative imitation—an adulteration, in short—of Swift and Fielding?" Then comes the still more puzzling question, How long would that critical attitude have lasted? Macaulay, as we know, gave in when he came to Jingle's anecdotes on the Rochester coach, having held out for only twelve pages—just up to the point at which it becomes apparent that whatever the author's style may be he is working a mine of whimsical invention which no writer could possess and be poor in the essential qualities of a humourist. A deeper critic would probably have succumbed sooner rather than later. We fail to appreciate the power of observation displayed in the opening chapter, with its report of the meeting of the Pickwick Club, not at all because it is barefaced and overdone, but because either we have not seen as much of learned societies' meetings as Dickens did in his early reporting days, or else we have been more successfully imposed upon than he by the seriousness with which such bodies take themselves.

The general public, all innocence and reverent faith in public institutions, can never, indeed, be persuaded that Dickens was not a caricaturist. He has never been reproached with cynicism: all his ridiculous pictures of political and academic life pass as jocose exaggerations; and the real secret of the pre-eminence of *Pickwick* in point of popularity over all his other books is that it is the only one which can be read without an occasional uncomfortable suspicion that the author was in downright earnest after all. When he wrote it he had observed accurately enough, but he had not taken to heart what he had observed. His view of politics in it is often that of a rowdy undergraduate; and it is not too much to say that his view of humanity is sometimes that of a street arab. The Eatanswill election, though it is a faithful picture of what a country election would be to-day if the Corrupt Practices Act and Vote by Ballot were abolished, is described in all possible lightness of heart as a rare lark; whilst as to the characters, although they, too, are hit off accurately enough, he does nothing in chapter after chapter but laugh at Tupman for being fat, at the spinster aunt for being an old maid, at Tony Weller for being an apoplectic coachman, and at Winkle for being a duffer; whilst Jingle, Job [Trotter], Sam Weller and the Fat Boy form a harlequinade pure and simple, in which Mr. Pickwick himself, in spite of the affection which Dickens conceived for him as he warmed to his work, and as success encouraged him to take himself seriously, figures as the king of pantaloons. Our love and esteem for the "angel in tights and gaiters" must not blind us to the fact that Mr. Pickwick repeatedly gets drunk, and is tumbled head over heels, knocked about with fire-shovels and carpet bags, cuffed, cheated, mulcted, duped, haled before the magistrate, put in the pound, and pelted with turnips and rotten eggs, not to mention his mistaking a lady's bed for his own and getting into serious trouble in consequence. But it must be confessed that the Pickwickian harlequinade, as a harlequinade, is incomparable. As Gounod said of *Don Giovanni*, it is a summit in art beyond which no man can go without precipitous descent to the Albert Smith level. The old women in it, Mrs. Cluppins, Mrs. Sanders, Mrs. Bardell, Mrs. Weller, and the incomparable Mrs. Raddle, though they are treated with remorseless inhumanity, are none the less horribly and squalidly funny. Grummer, with his six special constables, eclipses all the stage policemen that Drury Lane has ever seen. In fact the whole entertainment is raised by its very intensity to the keenness of high comedy, and the glow and vigour of melodrama. Jingle, impossible as he is, seems almost like the truth about Mercadet and Robert Macaire; and Sam Weller has more of Sganarelle than of Joey in him. Indeed, Molière might have written a *Pickwick* had he been let run wild from all artistic tradition and provided with a British middle-class audience. The only figure of the conventional harlequinade which Dickens left as he found it—and the failure is significant of his cardinal disability as a novelist—is the columbine. There are several attempts at her—Arabella Allen, the pretty housemaid, Emily Wardle, &c.; but each seems the most hopeless doll in the set until we turn to the other and pronounce her worse. Still, who cares about the columbine being a doll when she has such a brother as Ben Allen and such an unsuccessful wooer as Bob Sawyer?

Later on, when Dickens realized that the people who so tickled his sense of the ridiculous were human beings like himself, and that the merry Eatanswill game was being played not for fun, but for solid plunder, the cost of which in human life and happiness no man could calculate, his humour came to be much less appreciated than before. For example, no figure in the *Pickwick* collection is funnier than the fatuous Mr. Sparkler in *Little Dorrit;* and the conferring of a public appointment on Mr. Sparkler is at the same time more farcical and more deeply observed and scrupulously and knowledge-ably described than the return of the Honourable Samuel Slumkey as the "representative" in Parliament of the unsoaped of Eatanswill. But in *Little Dorrit* the jobbery of Mr. Sparkler's sinecure, however sardonically laughable its details may be, leaves the reader much more uneasy than the death of the Chancery prisoner in the Fleet Prison in *Pickwick*. Again, in *Great Expectations,* the transactions of the club of rich young men called "The Finches of the Grove" are far more ludicrous and more convincing than the debate on Mr. Pick-wick's theory of tittlebats, or his learned interpretation of BILST UM PHSHI S.M. ARK; but they form part of a tragedy for all that—the tragedy of the miserable emptiness and shiftlessness of the life which society offers to such young men; and you laugh with the wrong side of your mouth.

After all, one can quite understand how it was that though *Little Dorrit* and *Great Expectations* are immeasurably the greatest works of their kind which the century has produced in England, *Pickwick* being mere schoolboy tomfoolery in comparison, yet the public cling to *Pickwick,* and there is quite a school of critics who feel that Dickens took an essentially ungentlemanly view of things, and try to believe that poor Thackeray, though a shocking cynic, was much the deeper of the two. The thought of setting up Thackeray against a novelist so prodigiously and obviously his superior as Dickens must have been fathered by a very bitter wish. It shows how very hard Dickens suc-ceeded in hitting the conscience of Society after that remarkable shat-tering of his complacent domestic ideals, and awakening to the broader social issues, which were marked in his career by the break up of his family life and the writing of *Hard Times*. No wonder we fly from our consciences to the careless humours of Nupkins and the homely but pungent satires of the long gamekeeper [in chapter 19] upon Mr. Winkle's shooting. And it may well be that long after those terrible cases of conscience which are thrust on us in *Great Expecta-tions* and *Little Dorrit* have been settled and happily forgotten, we shall still enjoy our thoughtless heehaw over *Pickwick,* which may consequently survive the other two, not as the greatest, but as the fittest. Let us hope so, at any rate.

It is only necessary to say concerning this new edition of the *Pickwick Papers* that it is the latest number of Messrs. Macmillan's 3s. 6d. series of works by popular authors; that all the old illustrations by Seymour and Phiz, with the design for the wrapper of the original monthly parts, have been reproduced, presumably by photographic process, from a set of good impressions from the plates, and that an introduction has been contributed by Mr. Charles Dickens[the Younger], whose conduct will, perhaps, strike Messrs. Chapman and Hall, the holders of the recently-expired copyright, as "wery far from fillal."

Editor's Notes

▪ This review was first published in the *Daily Chronicle* 14 April 1892, 3:1–2. It was reprinted in *Shaw on Dickens*, ed. Dan Laurence and Martin Quinn (New York: Frederick Ungar, 1985), 22–26.

▪ There is no mention in Shaw's *Diary* of when he began writing the above; but on 12 April 1892, he "finally revised and sent off *Pickwick* review" (*Diary* 812).

▪ Shaw's awareness and admiration of the work of Dickens and its influence upon him have been much documented, initially by Shaw himself: "When I first read *Great Expectations* I was not much older than Pip was when the convict turned him upside down in the churchyard; in fact I was so young that I was astonished beyond measure when it came out that the convict was the author of Pip's mysterious fortune, although Dickens took care to make the fact obvious to every reader of adult capacity. My first acquaintance with the French Revolution was acquired at the same age from *A Tale of Two Cities;* and I also struggled with *Little Dorrit* at this time. I say struggled; for the books oppressed my imagination most fearfully, so real were they to me. It was not until I became a cynical blasé person of twelve or thirteen that I read *Pickwick, Bleak House,* and the intervening works" (Bernard Shaw, the *World,* 19 October 1887). Shaw's *Diaries* reveal that, even in the 1880s Dickens still "oppressed his imagination." For example (11 November 1886): "Began review of *Phantasms of the Living,* and unfortunately got *Great Expectations* at the Museum to quote from with the result that I wasted nearly all the day reading it"; (28 March 1887) "Stayed at Museum until 20 and then came home intending to work at the paper; but it ended in my reading *Barnaby Rudge*"; (17 April 1887): "Up late idling and reading *Bleak House*." And as recently as 20 October 1892 Shaw had paid 6d for "*David Copperfield* to read in train." In fact, he was so familiar with Dickens that, in a review of "*Wellerisms*" *from* "*Pickwick*" *and* "*Master Humphrey's Clock*," by C. F.

Rideal and Charles Kent, published in the *Pall Mall Gazette* on 15 April 1887, Shaw actually assumed the persona of the son of one of Dickens's characters in the book, producing a humorous firsthand account of the Wellers! (see *Bernard Shaw's Book Reviews,* 267–69).

▪ Charles [Culliford Boz] Dickens Jr. (1837–96), English editor and compiler. The first child, and eldest son, of Charles and Catharine Dickens. Educated first at King's College, then at Eton, in 1853 he went to Leipzig for two years to acquire German. Returning to England, he worked briefly and without much interest in Baring's bank. After more travel in preparation to become an eastern merchant, he returned to England again and married the daughter of a partner in the publishing firm of Bradbury and Evans, and set up in business in the City, without much success. Charles Dickens had quarrelled with the firm, disapproved of the match, and did not attend his son's wedding. In 1869 Charles Jr. became subeditor of his father's periodical *All the Year Round,* and, on his father's death in 1870, became (under a codicil to his will) sole proprietor of that journal, with which he was connected until two or three years from his own death. He also became chief partner in the printing firm of Dickens and Evans, but again without much success; though he did launch a series of dictionary-guides to London, the Thames, Paris, and so on, that became popular. He later became a reader for Macmillan, and it was at this time that he edited for Macmillan a new edition of his father's novels, beginning with *The Pickwick Papers.*

▪ Robert Seymour (1800–1836), English sporting artist and illustrator. At the time of his collaboration with Dickens, Seymour was an established illustrator, with *Figaro in London, Humorous Sketches,* and the *Book of Christmas* to his credit. In 1835 his idea for the "Nimrod Club," a series of comic plates showing cockneys coming to grief at various sports, was embraced by the new firm of Chapman and Hall, who were looking for something to publish. Seymour suggested Charles Whitehead for the letterpress, and the latter suggested Dickens. Dickens's suggestions changed the whole enterprise: the subject was switched from sport to travel, and, most significant, the plates were to illustrate the text and not the other way round. Seymour was still the chosen artist; but Dickens grumbled at his work in a letter on 14 April 1836 (his design for *The Stroller's Tale,* "The Dying Clown," was not to Dickens's liking) and six days later, after producing only seven plates, Seymour shot himself. Long after his death, his widow claimed that he had had a larger share in originating the novel than Dickens had admitted, and c.1854 she published a pamphlet entitled *Account of the Origin of the Pickwick Papers.* Dickens repudiated her claim in a letter to the *Athenaeum,* and in his preface to the Charles Dickens Edition of the novel (1867), saying that Seymour "never originated or suggested an incident, a phrase, or a word, to be found in the book."

▪ *The Life of Jonathan Wild the Great* is a satirical novel by Henry Fielding, published in 1743 and *A Tale of a Tub* is [Jonathan] Swift's (1667–1745) first major prose satire, published in 1704.

▪ [Thomas Babington, first Baron] Macaulay (1800–1859), English author. His biographer confirms and clarifies Shaw's remark about Macaulay, who apparently read *Pickwick*. while sailing home from India: "Macaulay turned over with indifference, and something of distaste, the earlier chapters of that modern Odyssey. The first touch which came home to him was Jingle's "Handsome Englishman!" In that phrase he recognised a master; and, by the time that he landed in England, he knew his Pickwick almost as intimately as his Grandison." See Sir George Otto Trevelyan, *The Life and Letters of Macaulay* (London: Longmans, 1959 [reprint of the 1908 ed.]), 334.

▪ The first Corrupt Practices Prevention Act was passed in 1854 and contained comprehensive definitions of bribery, undue influence and intimidation, and fairly mild penalties for such misdemeanours. It was superseded in 1883 by the Corrupt and Illegal Practices Act, which effectively lowered election expenditures and made the penalties for corrupt practices more severe.

▪ The Ballot Act (1872) introduced voting by secret ballot, increased the number of polling places, and abolished public nominations.

▪ "Harlequin," "Pantaloon," and "Columbine" are three figures originating in the Italian improvised comedy known as the "commedia dell'arte." Arlecchino was one of the *zanni,* or servants; Pantalone, a miserly Venetian merchant; and Columbina, a female servant. John Rich (c. 1692–1761), who popularized and anglicized the harlequinade and the pantomime during his long term as manager of Drury Lane Theatre, London, played Harlequin as an acrobatic mime, who was enabled to win his lover, Columbine, through magic.

▪ [Charles François] Gounod (1818–93), French composer, who enjoyed great popularity in the Victorian period with light operas such as *Le Médecin Malgré Lui* (based on Molière's comedy) (1858), and with serious ones such as *Faust* (1859). In all he wrote twelve operas. His opinion of [Wolfgang Amadeus] Mozart's (1756–91) celebrated opera *Don Giovanni* (1787) is described by Shaw four months previously as an "authoritative utterance" (see Bernard Shaw, "The Mozart Centenary," in the *Illustrated London News,* 12 December 1891); but elsewhere he accuses Gounod of "maudlin Mozart idolatry."

▪ Albert [Richard] Smith (1816–60), English humorist, was a writer of burlesques and pantomimes, and a contributor to *Punch.*

▪ Mrs. [Martha] Bardell is Mr. Pickwick's landlady in Goswell Street, who is convinced that Mr. Pickwick has offered to marry her; Mrs. [Betsey] Cluppins and Mrs. [Susannah] Sanders are her bosom friends, Mrs. [Susan] Weller, is the wife of Tony Weller, the old coachman, and "the incomparable Mrs. [Mary Ann] Raddle," is Mr. Bob Sawyer's landlady, and a thorough shrew. [Daniel] Grummer is a constable in attendance at the Mayor's Court in Ipswich.

▪ [Alfred] Jingle is the impudent strolling actor in *The Pickwick Papers* who pretends to be a gentleman of consequence; Mercadet is a speculator in Honoré de Balzac's (1799–1850) *Le Faiseur* (1830), later adapted by Adolphe Philippe d'Ennery into the successful drama *Mercadet* (1840); Robert Macaire is a character—a clever and audacious rogue—in Benjamin Antiers' *L'Auberge des Adrets* (1832), and also in R. L. Stevenson and W. E. Henley's *Macaire* published in the same year as this review, but a copy of which Shaw borrowed from William Archer on 3 June 1888.

▪ Sganarelle is the name given to characters in several of Molière's comedies, but in this case Shaw refers to the cowardly servant in *Dom Juan; ou Le Festin de Pierre* (1665). Joey was the colloquial English term for a clown in Shaw's day, deriving from the nickname of Joseph Grimaldi (1779–1837), the most famous clown in the history of pantomime.

▪ Arabella Allen is the sister of Benjamin Allen and later wife of Mr. Winkle; the pretty housemaid is Emma, the servant girl at Mr. Wardle's; and Emily Wardle is the daughter of Pickwick's friend Mr. Wardle of Manor Farm, Dingley Dell, in *The Pickwick Papers*.

▪ The "original monthly parts" of *The Posthumous Papers of the Pickwick Club* were in green covers, a form of publication which Dickens adopted in all his subsequent monthly serials. They began in March 1836, with four illustrations by Robert Seymour. After Seymour's suicide, R. W. Buss was selected to succeed him, but his drawings were so inferior that he was dismissed and Hablôt Knight Browne (1815–52) was selected, furnishing two plates for issue no.4. In no. 5 he used the pseudonym "Phiz" for the first time, and retained it thereafter, illustrating all of Dickens's novels up to *A Tale of Two Cities* (1859).

23 April 1892

A GOSPEL FOR SPENDTHRIFTS* [C858]

MR JOHN ROBERTSON is never so thoroughly in his element as when he is putting somebody or everybody in the wrong. He is much more an iconoclast than even his predecessor in command of the *National Reformer;* for Mr. Bradlaugh had a distinct preference for victims in holy orders, whereas Mr. Robertson knows no distinction of age, sex, or belief. The least suspicion of idolization attaching to any teacher is enough to bring him out in his most implacable form. His writings are invaluable as correctives to hero-worship. It is not too much to say that his "Modern Humanists" renders it for the first time possible to put Carlyle and Ruskin into inexperienced hands without being at a loss for an antidote to the effects of immoderate indulgence in those authors. But Mr. Robertson naturally has the faults of his qualities; and when the business he takes in hand is the exposition of a scientific theory, he cannot be restrained from bringing to book all the writers who have gone wrong on the subject, and—if we may so flippantly

* "The Fallacy of Saving. A Study in Economics." By John Robertson. (London: Swan Sonnenschein.)

express ourselves—"giving them beans." This method has two disadvantages: it rakes up all the confusion that has ever existed on the subject in hand for the mere sake of proving that it is confusion, which is by no means always the same thing as dispelling it; and it lashes the author into so violent a reaction against the heresies he is rooting out that he is apt to recoil to the extreme verge of the opposite errors.

The fallacy which Mr. Robertson has attacked in this book is the common doctrine that saving is the whole economic duty of man, and that there is no limit to its practicability or advisability except that set by the self-indulgence of our fallen nature. It is evident, to begin with, that since human life depends on perishable products—since food, for instance, consists for the most part of substances which, when quite ready for consumption, become stale or putrid in a few days—there is no such thing nationally possible as saving in the sense of hoarding. Men must in the nature of things always live from hand to mouth, though the mouth may be the Duke of Westminster's and the hand that of his tenant. How, then, are men to provide food for their old age? Obviously the only possible way is for the child to be fed by the man, and, when it grows up, to repay the debt by supporting both the children and the aged, each individual consuming less than he produces during his working years, in order that he may consume without producing at all in his two childhoods—first and second. Thus all saving, in this sense, consists in getting people into one another's debt; and no man can possibly save except by a bargain with a "spendthrift" who wants, for the moment, to consume without producing, and so incur a debt to be paid in kind later on. This being so, it is clear that saving is impossible without spending; that the number of savers is limited by the number of spendthrifts; that the extent of the savers' savings is limited by the demand of the spendthrifts; that "universal" saving is impossible; and that if saving is a public virtue, the spendthrifts take as essential a part in it as the savers. This is Mr. Robertson's point; and the common implication that we can all save simultaneously if we will, and that we all ought to do it to the extreme of human endurance, is the fallacy which he attacks.

There is, however, another sense of the word "saving." It is very commonly used to indicate the production of things designed to make future production more efficient—roads, tools and machinery, for instance. In this sense saving is universally possible, but not to an unlimited extent. Every Robinson Crusoe can spend part of his day in making a spade, a plough, a palisade, a boat, or a cart, in order that he may make his work easier later on. But if he spends the whole day in such provision for the future, producing nothing for immediate consumption, he must speedily starve amidst his unfinished spades, ploughs, and boats. Thus here again the possibility of enhancing future gain is limited by the need for present consumption. And no conceivable accumulation of aids to production can ever enable Robinson Crusoe to discontinue working altogether except, as aforesaid, by virtue of a bargain with another man. He may equip himself so completely as to be able to produce more in an hour than he formerly did in a day; but whilst he remains dependent on perishable goods and immediate services he can only be superannuated by being fed and looked after by active workers. However, if he can find a thriftless man with no equipment of plough, &c., he will find that man willing to provide for him on condition of being allowed the use of his implements. But if every other person he can find has been thrifty too, and is as well equipped for production as himself, he will find his tools worth nothing to anybody, and will have either to go on working or else lie down and die, unless he can persuade people to support him out of mere charity. As surely as economic rent would vanish if all land were made equally fertile, just so surely would economic interest vanish if all men were made equally thrifty; and the popular economic notion that if we all saved money we might all stop working and live on dividends is as absurd as a proposal to nationalise the land in order to allow every Englishman to live ever after as an idle landlord on his share of the economic rent of it. And this fallacy is again Mr. Robertson's point in dealing with that sort of saving which consists of the production of aids to future production, and in advocating a system of national pensions as the inevitable final solution of the difficulty of provision for old age.

And now comes the question, Has Mr. Robertson fallen into any fallacies himself? It is hard to say, because he has so exhausted his energies in slaying the thrice-slain "fundamental propositions concerning capital" of John Stuart Mill that he ends by leaving his own position anything but clear. But most readers will put down the book with an impression that his statement that universal saving is impossible includes not only the acquisition by savers of claims on spendthrifts, but also the provision of aids to future production. Now there is nothing whatever in the nature of things to prevent everyone, under a suitable social system, from spending a part of his time in such provision; and though, as we have seen, the final result would be the extinction of economic interest and the consequent alteration of "independent incomes" into public pensions, yet this prospect is no *reductio ad absurdum* of universal thrift, but rather a high recommendation of it, since the labour of the community would be lightened to the utmost possible extent. All that needs to be urged *per contra* is that universal spending is absolutely necessary; that universal provision of increased facilities for future production, though possible to a certain extent, is only so in the hours which can be spared from production for immediate consumption; and that no degree of saving can enable any individual, under any circumstances, to cease working altogether except by quartering himself upon some active producer. All these considerations are present throughout Mr. Robertson's argument except that which affirms the possibility, within limits, of universal provision of aids to future production. The criticism of Cairnes on page 61 implies that such provision cannot be universal, because if everybody practised it equally there would be no demand for its products. But this only means that the products (tools for example) would not be saleable, which would no more detract from their utility than the non-saleability of a man's brains could deprive him of the benefit of keeping them in his own head. The ultimate product of a supply of the best instruments of production, carried to saturation point, would be the utmost possible lightening of toil or increase of output; and to secure this advantage in the future, men are quite willing to put in a certain quantity of work without any present return, whenever their appetite for work is not exhausted by the labour of supplying their more pressing present needs. In this sense "universal saving with gain all round" is undoubtedly a possible and highly beneficial employment for spare time and spare subsistence, whether for a single man on a desert island or for 40,000,000 of people in our own country. It may be remarked here that Jevons's passing definition of capital as "spare subsistence" is quite as near the point as Macleod's "Any economic quantity used for profit," which Mr. Robertson declares to be the "one truly philosophical one," though it is simply Mill over again, since it provokes all the old questions as to whether beefsteaks, ice puddings, education, &c., are capital or not. To the ambiguity created by the various senses in which the word saving is used must be added that which comes from Mr. Robertson's double mission as an abstract economist and a critic of existing society. Sometimes his ground is clear enough as in the following passage:—

> Mr. Loch quotes former Poor-law Committee-men as pointing out that certain forms of poor relief are "premiums upon indolence and vice." If there be any meaning in words, our systems

of land accumulation and free bequest of money-capital are premiums upon indolence and vice, fostering both in the highest degree; yet it never occurs to the critics in question to say so. On the other hand the relatively much smaller risk of promoting indolence and vice by a national pension system can be guarded against, and will be increasingly so in practice, by public interest inspiring public criticism.

Here Mr. Robertson is obviously the critic of existing institutions. But in the following passage a criticism of the same kind is put forward as "the final sociological truth."

> The economic truth is accurately put by Ruskin in the formula that riches are "a power like that of electricity, acting only through inequalities or negations of itself. The force of the guinea you have in your pocket depends wholly on the default of a guinea in your neighbour's pocket." And the final sociological truth is that "savings" do in the last resort represent a power to extort the labour of those who have been unable to "save" from having to toil for their life from their childhood, or being ill-fitted for a life of struggle.

This is certainly the truth about our present system; but it is surely not *the* final sociological truth. For example, it would not be the truth about a national pension scheme, which would nevertheless be maintained out of "savings" in a very common sense of that word-of-all-work.

One more criticism is suggested by Mr. Robertson's earnest declaration that "the line of upward progress can only be through an ideal of increasing and refining consumption." This, of course, is unassailable; but it is equally true that the line of upward progress at present lies through a considerable reduction in the hours of labour for the poor in much less and much plainer eating and drinking for the rich, not to mention that general simplification of life which comes with higher thinking. If we continue to progress, the man of the twenty-first century will come cheaper instead of dearer than the man of the nineteenth.

The most immediately salutary part of Mr. Robertson's book is that which insists on the fact that the possibility of enhancing future gain is remorselessly limited by the need for present consumption. It is by persistently ignoring this limitation that our public men so often exasperate the poor and shock all who realize the condition of the working classes by preaching saving to people whose trouble is that they have not enough to spend. When a rich man starves himself, wears foul clothes, and lives in a miserable room in order that he may save the more, we brand him as a miser, and denounce what he calls his "thrift" as indecent folly. We then turn round to people who are already starving in rags and filthy tenements, not from choice but from necessity, and recommend them to save—presumably by ceasing to eat altogether, and exchanging their rags for nakedness and their rooms for a dry arch of Waterloo Bridge. Such inconsiderate preachments rise readily to the lips of men who are rich enough to spend the incomes of twenty working class families, and yet have as much again left to save from; but their only effect on the masses is to bring the word "thrift" into such odium as discredits all providence whatever, reasonable as well as unreasonable. And this, no doubt, is why Mr. Robertson, like most other Socialists, has been forced to concentrate all his power on the arguments for more spending and to leave the monstrously overstated arguments for more saving to take care of themselves.

On the very important application of his theory to the population question, Mr. Robertson is more consistent than those Socialists who, like Mr. Henry George, assume that because there are not enough people in the world to develop its productivity to the highest possible degree—since, to put it another way, the more people we have the more wealth we produce per head—therefore the more children we have the better. But here the "fallacy of saving" has crept in again. A colonial settler or Far West backwoodsman may see plainly that since, in his circumstances, the way to be rich is to have as many hands to help him as possible, he would be better off with thirty strong sons and daughters than with none. But if he proceeds towards that end recklessly enough to bring half a dozen hungry and (as yet) unproductive children upon his hands before he can produce food enough for three, he will soon curse all those unlimited general propositions as to the desirability of an increase of population with which we have been familiar since the publication of "Progress and Poverty."

The cases of population and capital are not merely analogous: they are at bottom identical; and all general propositions as to the desirability of an increase of capital must be limited by a statement of the rate of increase before they can have any practical value. Most political economists have assumed that because we want more capital we cannot possibly save too much or spend too little. The opposite fallacy is, of course, that we cannot possibly spend too much or save too little. Mr.

Robertson exposes the first of these two fallacies, and leaves the second alone, having concluded (page 111) too hastily, as we think, that the course of action indicated is nationally impossible, which it certainly is not, as the Italian Government found when it nearly financed its railways out of existence by spending all the receipts and letting the plant and rolling-stock wear out, a piece of mischief which might be played by a Socialistic State upon the whole industrial plant of the country. As to his own position on the question it is, we repeat, not quite clear. In so far as it means that saving and spending, in the sense which identifies them with borrowing and lending, are in substance one and the same thing, and therefore cannot outstrip one another, he is indubitably right; and the truism is one that needed insisting on, since it is so commonly denied by implication. But if in his proposition that there can be no lending without simultaneous borrowing, Mr. Robertson includes the quite distinct proposition that there can be no production without simultaneous consumption, then his recoil from Mill has landed him in a fallacy as grave as that which he refutes. And if he wishes to escape being strongly suspected of having been so landed, he will have to rewrite several pages of his book, which, for the rest, and especially in those parts which are occupied with his own ideas and not those of Mill and Messrs. Mummery and Hobson, is a notable addition to the Social Science Series, by a writer who bids fair to make himself an English twentieth century Proudhon.

Editor's Notes

- The above review was first published in the *Daily Chronicle* on 23 April 1892, 3:1–2.
- On 14 April 1892, Shaw, together with Sidney Webb, Graham Wallas, and Beatrice Potter, went down to Arundel in West Sussex for a brief holiday, staying at the Bridge Hotel. (Later this year, Sidney Webb and Beatrice Potter would marry, see below, 199) Shaw's *Diary* for 17 April records "worked at the review of Robertson's *Fallacy of Saving* all the morning at the hotel" (*Diary* 813).
- John [MacKinnon] Robertson (1856–1933), Scottish journalist, politician, and scholar. His first journalistic work was on the staff of the *Edinburgh Evening News,* which he joined as a leader writer in 1878. Robertson's articles were interesting enough for him to be invited down to London by Charles Bradlaugh with whom, from 1884, he worked on the *National Reformer,* which he later edited, from Bradlaugh's death in 1891 to 1893. Then he started the *Free Review,* which he edited until 1895. Subsequently

he made his living by writing and lecturing, having a particularly successful tour of the United States in 1897–98. Shaw, who met Robertson frequently at the British Museum, and dined with him on numerous occasions, seems to have been initially impressed by Robertson's mind. However, the two quarreled later. Robertson had boarded with Annie Besant in the 1880s (he was her editorial assistant on *Our Corner*), and seems at that time to have been jealous of Shaw's relationship with her; and, apart from an early flattering notice of Shaw's novel *An Unsocial Socialist,* spent a deal of critical spleen on Shaw and his work. In 1906 Robertson was returned to Parliament as a Liberal for the Tyneside division. From 1911 to 1915 he was parliamentary secretary to the Board of Trade (in Asquith's government). Robertson was defeated in the election of 1918, and devoted himself thereafter to writing on a wide variety of subjects. Among his numerous publications are *Shakespeare and Chapman* (1917), *The Problem of Hamlet* (1919), *The Political Economy of Free Trade* (1928), and *History of Free Thought in the Nineteenth Century* (1929).

▪ Bradlaugh (see above, 83).

▪ [Thomas] Carlyle (1795–1881), Scottish historian, essayist, and sage, was enormously influential in Victorian thought: Shaw himself, who shows familiarity with Carlyle's work, may have been influenced by the latter's interest in German literature, ideas about the impermanence of human institutions, as seen, for example in Carlyle's *Sartor Resartus* 1833–34), and as expressed in *On Heroes, Hero Worship and the Heroic in History* (1841), the need for rule, not by the popularly elected representative, but by the strong, just man—who resembles somewhat the "men of destiny" with whom Shaw's plays abound.

▪ [John] Ruskin (see above, 65) was another seminal mind: by the early 1860s, deploring the profit-motive and the increasing industrialization of Britain, he became interested in politics; and in such books as *Unto This Last* (1862) and *Munera Pulveris* ten years later, advocated the organization of labor and other reforms.

▪ John Stuart Mill (see above, 113).

▪ [John Elliott] Cairnes (1823–75), Irish economist. In 1859 he was appointed professor of political economy and jurisprudence at Queen's College, Galway, at which time he became a close friend of John Stuart Mill. From 1866 to 1872 he was professor of political economy at University College, London. His first work *The Character and Logical Method of Political Economy* (1857) is regarded as the definitive statement of the English classical school of economics, stressing the deductive method of reasoning, the hypothetical nature of the discipline, and its independence from specific political or social systems.

▪ The population of Great Britain in 1892 was 37,732,922 (1891 census).

▪ [William Stanley] Jevons (1835–82), English economist and logician. In 1866 he took up a professorship at Owen's College, Manchester. Jevons introduced mathematical methods to economics, and was one of the first to use the concept of final or marginal utility (as opposed to the classical cost-of-production theories.) His work was enormously important to Shaw, who used it to refute parts of Marx's theory. In addition to his *Theory of Political Economy* (1871), Jevons's *Principles of Economics* was published posthumously in 1905.

▪ [Henry Dunning] Macleod (1821–1902), Scottish economist who regarded value as consisting in exchangeability (and did not regard it as dependent on utility or the cost of production), was the first writer to give prominence to the notion of credit and to the exchanges in which it plays a part. He added the phrase "Gresham's Law" to the economist's vocabulary to describe the idea that "where two media come into circulation at the same time, the more valuable will tend to disappear." (He erroneously supposed that Sir Thomas Gresham had reached this conclusion in the time of Elizabeth I.) Macleod was not regarded very highly in economic circles: he failed to obtain the chairs of political economy at both Oxford and Cambridge. He did, however, write a number of books, including *The Elements of Economics* (1881–86), *Elements of Banking* (1876), *The Theory of Credit* (1893–97), and *The History of Economics* (1896).

▪ Shaw's comment that "our public men so often exasperate the poor and shock all who realize the condition of the working classes by preaching saving to people whose trouble is that they have not enough to spend," was dramatized a year later in *Mrs. Warren's Profession,* when Vivie Warren indignantly enquires why her mother chose prostitution as her profession:

VIVIE [*intensely interested by this time*] No; but why did you choose that
    business? Saving money and good management will succeed in any
    business.
MRS. WARREN. Yes, saving money. But where can a woman get money to save
    in any other business? Could you save out of four shillings a week and
    keep yourself dressed as well? Not you . . .

▪ "Underneath the arches" of Waterloo Bridge was a famous place for down-and-outs to sleep. From the bridge itself many a suicide leaped into the Thames. Mrs. Warren tells how the clergyman was always warning her that her sister Lizzie would end by jumping off Waterloo Bridge.

▪ [Albert Frederick] Mummery (1855–95), English political economist and alpine climber. In 1889 he published the book to which Shaw refers: *The Physiology of Industry: being an exposure of certain fallacies in existing theories of economics,* in collaboration with [John Atkinson] Hobson (1858–1940), English economist and publicist. The latter devoted much of his time to economic and social studies, on which he published about thirty-five works. Much influenced by Ruskin (on whom he published a study), he approached economics as a humanist, but with an original view: an opponent of orthodox economic theories, he believed that "under-consumption" was the main cause of unemployment.

▪ [Pierre Joseph] Proudhon (1809–65), French journalist and Socialist, whose most original work, in which he can be seen as a forerunner of Marx, was *Qu'est-ce que la propriété?* in which he propounded the paradox that "property is theft." In 1842 he was tried for his revolutionary opinions, but acquitted; and in 1846 published his greatest work, the *Système des contradictions économiques*. During the Revolution of 1848 he attempted to establish a bank that would pave the way for Socialism by giving interest-free credit, but this failed utterly. The violence of his views finally led to three years' imprisonment; although he was released in June 1852, he was again condemned to three years' imprisonment in 1858, at which point he fled to Belgium, obtaining an amnesty in 1860.

29 April 1892

A DERELICT PLEA*
[C859]

THERE is something pathetic in the spectacle of a number of gentlemen gravely setting to work to prove that "the inherent incapacity of compulsory collectivism must play havoc with human progress," and that the ultimate result of our socialistic tendencies must be "a society like that of ancient Peru, dreadful to contemplate, in which the mass of the people, elaborately regimented in groups of 10, 50, 100, 500, and 1,000, ruled by officers of corresponding grades and tied to their districts, were superintended in their private lives as well as in their industries, and toiled hopelessly for the support of the governmental organisation." Englishmen always listen to such sermons with respect, and then, having solemnly vowed that nothing shall ever induce them to exchange British liberty for Peruvian bondage, proceed to municipalize the gasworks or take any other step that may strike them as being convenient, without the smallest regard to whether their action is socialistic or not. One can therefore afford to take this book calmly, knowing that not a single Progressively-minded person in the country will be scared by it into voting for the Moderates at the next County Council election.

Mr. Herbert Spencer's contribution to the volume may be judged from the following passage:—

---

* "A Plea for Liberty: an Argument against Socialism and Socialistic Legislation, consisting of Introduction by Herbert Spencer and Essays by Various Writers." Ed. Thomas Mackay. New and Revised Edition. (London: John Murray.)

> How [under Socialism] will the individual worker fare if he is dissatisfied with his treatment—thinks that he has not an adequate share of the products, or has more to do than can rightly be demanded, or wishes to undertake a function for which he feels fitted, but which is not thought proper for him by his superiors, or desires to make an independent career for himself? This dissatisfied unit in the immense machine will be told that he must submit or go.

Surely Mr. Spencer must by this time be the only sociologist in the world who does not know that the working classes would never have troubled their heads about Socialism if they had not found themselves landed, by what he pleads for as "liberty, " in the exact predicament which he describes in the words just quoted. He has left the enemy unread, and so missed the point of the controversy. The Socialists, rightly or wrongly, assert that the system of handing over a country to private proprietors to make what they can out of [it] in unrestrained competition with one another leads to a monopoly of land, then of capital, then of education and opportunity, and finally of government, the coercive forces of which are used by the monopolists to maintain their privileges by force, under the pretext of maintaining "order." This they attempt to demonstrate by an elaborate argument from abstract economics and from history. Any opponent of Socialism who prefers the *status quo* must either explode their demonstration or prove that, bad as the *status quo* is, every advance in the direction of Socialism would make bad worse. The chief authors of the "Plea for Liberty," since they are not advocates of the *status quo,* do not take this course. Being more insubordinate, more revolutionary than the Socialists themselves, they demand, as an alternative preferable to both Socialism and the *status quo,* a system freer than either. Mr. Donisthorpe or Mr. Auberon Herbert would run a greater risk of being burnt alive in a democratic persecution than Mr. Sidney Webb, or even Mr. Hyndman. Unfortunately for the clearness of their position, they get hampered, as opponents of Socialism, with the co-operation of the defenders of the *status quo*—including professional advocates, who are to the monopolist what the Christian Evidence man is to the Bishop, and who lecture for the Liberty and Property Defence League instead of the Fabian Society because the League pays its lecturers whilst the Fabians apparently dun theirs for subscriptions. Such advocacy is of course quite as honourable as that of a Queen's Counsellor; but it grievously confuses the argument, since the retained advocates are not really pleading for liberty at all, but simply for the incomes of their employers. When their pleadings are swept up along with essays on Utilitarian Individualism, Toryism, and Anarchism, with an audacious *jeu d'esprit* proving that all the colonies that have legislated socialistically are stone broke, a Friendly Society protest against national pensions, a string of prospectuses of Continental building societies, and a miscellaneous collection of criticisms of human nature with all the illustrations confined to instances of State action, the result is not a plea for liberty or for anything else, but simply a faggot of very ill-sorted sticks to beat Socialism with.

It is therefore impossible to deal with "A Plea for Liberty" as if it were a homogeneous book. In "Fabian Essays," to which it is supposed to be a counterblast, we had a historic basis, an economic basis, an industrial basis, and so on, each set forth in a separate essay, but accepted in all the rest. In "A Plea" there is no common ground, except dislike and mistrust of State action. The writers cannot even be likened to a scratch crew: every man is in a different boat, though for the moment they are all struggling to tow this island out of what they regard as the maëlstrom of Socialism. Perhaps the most disappointing essay in the collection is Mr. Auberon Herbert's "True Line of Deliverance." It begins with an argument against what is called the New Unionism, the example given being as follows:—

> The effect of the Dockers' monopoly is to lessen for all the other trades the advantage of Free Trade. Imported articles will be dearer in price, and the labour of other trades will exchange for less.

This means, in effect, that if the Dockers had not made a union their labour would have cost the shareholders only 5d. an hour instead of 6d. Mr. Herbert, not exactly catching the Dockers' point of view, has only found a new way to make an old observation. It does not matter one rap to the trades of the country as a whole whether the extra penny in dispute is spent by a shareholder or by a worker. But to the community as a whole it is decidedly an advantage that it should be spent by the man who wants it most.

Over the prospect of a federation of unions opposing a federation of employers Mr. Herbert waxes eloquent:—

> I ask unionists if they are willing to help forward such an organisation of society into these two hostile camps. I ask them

to think of the tremendous power that must be lodged in a few hands; of all the countless struggles and intrigues to obtain that power; of the worthless men who will succeed in obtaining it; of the fatal mistakes that will be made even by good and true men holding this power in their hands; and of the harsh, unscrupulous use that will be made of this power to destroy all individual resistance that is convenient.

This sounds precisely like an exhortation to the capitalists of America to refrain from organising pools and trusts; and it will probably meet with quite as much attention as if it had been. As one reads on it is impossible not to like Mr. Herbert for the simplicity with which he mentions the arguments against himself whenever they occur to him, even when he has no reason on earth to advance against them. For instance, he says that the advance of the Dockers' wages was "taken from the pockets of their fellow labourers." But on the previous page he says:—

Of course a trade unionist might reply that the advance of wages may be taken, without raising prices, from the profits of the employers. But that is in itself unlikely to happen, and not permanently profitable to the men when it does happen.

Mr. Herbert does not make even an attempt to substantiate the unlikeliness, or to explain why a temporary advantage should not be preferred to no advantage at all. Neither does he mention the fact that there is a rent and interest fund, as well as a profit fund, which can be drawn on, as the workers well know, for the enlargement of the wages fund. In recommending the worker not to obtain a rise of wages when trade becomes bad by demanding it through a union, but simply to wait patiently until the masters offer it, he is momentarily at a loss to find out anything to the disadvantage of the former method. Here is how he gets out of the difficulty:—

This time the union, on the alert, has insisted on a rise of wages. This rise of wages, *perhaps slightly in excess of what the rise in prices justifies,* may check the enterprise of the employer.

The italics are our own. What would Mr. Herbert say to a trade unionist who should try to arrive at the opposite conclusion by simply saying:—

This time the union, on the alert, has insisted on a rise of wages. This rise of wages, perhaps slightly under what the rise in prices justifies, may stimulate the enterprise of the employer.

Soon after this point, Mr. Herbert fairly outstrips criticism. He declares that capital demands a larger return in interest as unionism advances, in order to compensate it for the aggravation and risk of dealing with such bodies; he fixes the just price of labour at what the highest bidder would give for it at a general auction of the whole human race; he urges trade unionists to form what is practically a blackleg party within the unions; he paints a rosy picture of capital, "relieved of all attacks and misgivings" and encouraged by "a sense of complete security," becoming "intensely active," whilst as for the unions themselves—but here are Mr. Herbert's own words:—

Making investments for their members will be a leading function of the new unions. By means of the weekly subscriptions they will be always buying shares in the industries of the district, in gas, water, omnibus, tramcar, dock and railway companies, in the great industrial concerns where their members work, and then passing these shares on to the individual members as the small weekly payment comes up to the required amount. So also with land and houses. The unions would act as house-building societies. . . . More than this, every union of workers would have its farm in the country—held in good fee-simple and not under any imperfect land nationalisation tenure—which would provide pleasant and healthful change for its members in turn. Members would erect their own wooden rooms for the summer; there would be a sanatorium, and possibly certain articles, like eggs and milk, &c., &c., &c.

What can a merely mortal reviewer say to such a Utopia? since it is no longer considered polite to exclaim *Sancta simplicitas!* The working classes are to be all elevated on one another's backs; the landlords are to live on the interest on the price of their land purchased "in good fee-simple" by the working class out of wages kept down to 5d. an hour in order not "to lessen for all other trades the advantage of Free Trade"; and the capitalists, no longer dismayed by trade union demands for high wages, will multiply capital until interest disappears. The feeling of general security, in fact, will be as perfect as may be compatible with leaving Mr. Auberon Herbert still at large. One is half ashamed of chaffing a gentleman whose quaint mixture of Anarchism, Toryism, Republicanism, and invincible economic ignorance is yet made respectable by the most attractively simple sincerity and disinterestedness; but, after all, one must treat him as a responsible being to the extent of making it quite clear that he has not grasped the rudiments of industrial sociology.

A very different writer is Mr. Wordsworth Donisthorpe. He also is sincere and disinterested, but not altogether simply or attractively so. Instead of painting pretty portraits of his own amiable ideal of Truth, he snatches away the veil from the real goddess with a certain sardonic relish for the scandalizing effect on you of the indecorum of the spectacle. He has style, wit, instinct for reality, and is thoroughly alive. His essay is the only flash of literature in the volume; and a very brilliant flash it is, too. After Mr. Herbert Spencer's scrupulously accurate deductions from Peruvian premises, it is exhilarating to find Mr. Donisthorpe ruthlessly sweeping away all scientific frontiers between the province of the State and the "field sacred to individual freedom" by affirming that "a people might utterly abolish and extirpate the State and yet remain steeped to the lips in socialism of the most revolting type." On abstract Truth and Justice, two of the safest cards known in playing with the British public, Mr. Donisthorpe must be quoted rather than described:—

> Where is the harm in saying that two and two make five? Either you are believed or you are disbelieved. If disbelieved, you are a failure. One does not talk for the music of the thing, but to convey a belief. If you are believed, you have given away false coin or a sham article. The recipient thinks he can buy with it or work with it, and lo! it breaks in his hand. He hates the cause of his disappointment. "Well, what of that?" you say; "if I had been strong enough or plucky enough I would have broken his head, and he would have hated me for that. Then why should I be ashamed to tell a lie to a man whom I deliberately wish to hurt?" Here we come nearly to the end of our tether. Experience tells us that it is mean and self-wounding to lie, and we believe it. Those who try it find it out in the end.

Even this concession is not made with regard to lying in the abstract; for Mr. Donisthorpe proceeds to show that there are departments of lying which raise no scruples and incur no reproach.

> Justice has no meaning at all; that is, it conveys no definite meaning to the general understanding. Here is a flat race about to be run between a strong healthy boy of sixteen and a

delicate lad of twelve. What says Justice? Are we to handicap them, or are we not? It is a very simple question, and the absolutist ought to furnish us with a simple answer. If he says Yes, he will have half the world down on him as a Socialist leveller. If he says No, then he will have the other half down on him as a selfish brute. But he must choose. Lower yet; —even supposing that Justice has a distinct connotation, and further-more that it connotes something sublime; even then, why should I conform to its dictates? Because it is a virtue? Non-sense; because it is expedient. Why should I tell the truth? There is no reason why, except that it is expedient for me, as I know from experience. There is no baser form of lying than fly-fishing. Is it wrong? No. Why not? Because I do not ask the fishes to trust me in future. That is why.

We feel the liar in us protesting, in an agony of apprehension, that such things are subversive and ought not to be mentioned; but the honest man in us approves and confesses humbly that Mr. Donisthorpe is right. The rest of his essay makes hay, in the same spirited fashion, of our legal categories, by taking a series of piquant instances of the acts which we penalise in certain forms, and showing that we encourage and even enforce them in other forms. The literary art with which these instances are arranged makes the essay as readable as the least industri-ous student can desire; and the upshot of the whole is to establish Mr. Donisthorpe's contention that the State cannot legislate on general principles, but must settle each case on its separate merits, and accord-ing to its special circumstances. Of these circumstances and merits, the individuals interested are better judges than the State can be, and therefore the State should leave the settlement to them, subject only to such general conditions as may be needed to prevent them from set-tling it by bloodshed or in any way clearly barred by the common weal. "In short," says Mr. Donisthorpe, "what we have to do is to find the Least Common Bond in politics, as a mathematician finds the least common multiple in the field of numbers." With the question whether the least common bond must, as the Socialists contend, include the common ownership of the material sources of production Mr. Donis-thorpe does not meddle; so that his essay, though a brilliant and indeed unanswerable Individualist document, leaves the Socialist controversy practically untouched.

This is unfortunate; for Mr. Edward Stanley Robertson,who leads off the attack on the Socialists with a demonstration of "T h e Impracticability of Socialism," is a foeman much less formidable, his essay, to describe it frankly, being nothing more or less than the Noodle's Oration brought up to date. The Socialists will make him a handsome present of his criticisms of the ideal Collectivist State, the "monster workhouse" constructed by Schaeffle on conclusions drawn from the expressions of Karl Marx. When our perplexity is as to whether we are to vote for extending or crippling the powers of the County Council we are hardly in a humour to be enlightened in the following manner:—

> How could any public department undertake to say how many suits of clothes a given population will wear out in a given season? . . . When clothing has to be served out to soldiers, the soldiers are put under strict regulations as to its use. It is all the same pattern, and there is no personal choice about it. This is what makes the clothing of an army difficult, but practicable. But in civil life the conditions are wholly different. When did women ever submit to a uniform, unless it were for religious reasons? . . . It may suffice to say for the present that if Socialism does not cover this contingency, then collective production breaks down over the article of clothing. And, of course, to break down in one point is to break down in all. A chain is no stronger than its weakest link.

The last two sentences are a sufficient testimonial to Mr. Stanley Robertson's capacity as a sociologist. Here is another sample:—

> The letter-carrying department of the Post Office is very well managed, on the whole, in country places; but in London, and in large towns generally, the delivery of letters within the town leaves much to be desired. In this connection I cannot refrain from noticing the breakdown of letter-delivery arrangements which has taken place every Christmas since the Christmas card came into fashion.

It is at pages like these that the book wears out the reader's patience. Mr. Robertson's harping on difficulties which are as common to all possible systems, present or future, as old age and death; Mr. Howell's apprehensions about excessive interference with private affairs, as if any democratic community were likely to persist in regulating matters which it would obviously cost more to regulate than to let alone; Mr.

Mackay's attempt to generalize against any legal enforcement of contracts from the fact that "there are probably no debts more regularly paid than gambling debts"; and such merely rhetorical statements as that "there is in State monopoly no force making for progress unless we so term the blind sentimental agitation which is now assailing the Post Office in favour of an Anglo-Saxon penny post": all this might be turned inside out like a glove by any Socialist who wished to use it to attack the shortcomings of private enterprise, its failures, its mechanical rigidity, its social tyranny, its litigiousness, its venality and obstructiveness, &c., &c., after which private enterprise would not be a penny the worse unless it could be shown as well that the Socialist pill would cure the earthquake. The public wants no more of such idle recrimination. It sees that the working classes are going to capture the House of Commons, and so gain the power of doing what they please with the country. It sees also that the program of municipalisation, financed by the progressive taxation of unearned wealth, has lodged itself firmly in the political vacuum, and is being adopted on all sides by Radical politicians to-day, not because they are Socialists, but because there is no other program available. There is nothing for it now but to urge Spencer, Donisthorpe and Co. to follow the example of their rivals. They can hardly believe that Mr. Auberon Herbert's "True Line of Deliverance" will ever turn a vote for or against any party. At the County Council election there was not a single contest in which the publication of "A Plea for Liberty" had a feather's weight; whilst Mr. Webb's London program largely carried the whole election, simply because it was better than nothing, which was the alternative proposed by the Moderates. That was and is the political situation as between "Liberty and Property" and practicable Socialism; and so long as the one remains Conservative and negative, and the other Progressive and positive, Socialism will walk over the course, even if the mass of Englishmen continues to distrust it as deeply as Mr. Auberon Herbert does. It remains to be seen whether the authors of this "Plea" will complete their work by supplying the Moderates with a program for 1895.

Editor's Notes

- The above review was first published in the *Daily Chronicle*, April 29, 1892, 3:3–5. There is no indication in Shaw's *Diary* of when or where it was written. The volume reviewed is a "New and Revised Edition" of the book first published the previous year, consisting of the following essays: "From Freedom to Bondage," by Herbert Spencer; "The Impracticability of Socialism," by Edward Stanley Robertson; "The Limits of Liberty," by Wordsworth Donisthorpe; "Liberty for Labour," by George Howell; "State Socialism in the Antipodes," by Charles Fairfield; "The Discontent of the Working Classes," by Edmund Vincent; "Investment," by Thomas Mackay; "Free Education," by B. H. Alford; "The Housing of the Working Classes and of the Poor," by Arthur Raffalovich; "The Evils of State Trading, as Illustrated by the Post Office," by Frederick Millar; "Free Libraries," by M. D. O'Brien; "The State and Electrical Distribution," by F. W. Beauchamp Gordon; and "The True Line of Deliverance," by Auberon Herbert.

▪ Thomas Mackay, LL.D. (1849–1912), English writer on political economy. In addition to editing the above, Mackay wrote *The English Poor*, and also a third volume to *The History of the Poor Law*, supplementary to the standard work by Sir G. Nicholls and covering the period from 1834 to 1899. He was also the author of a biography of Sir John Fowler (the civil engineer), and was a frequent contributor on economic subjects to quarterly and other periodicals. In later life he received an honorary degree from Saint Andrews University.

▪ Herbert Spencer (see above, 112).

▪ Wordsworth Donisthorpe (see above, 82–83).

▪ Auberon Herbert (see above, 83–84).

▪ Sidney [James] Webb [Baron Passfield] (1859–1947), English social reformer, historian, and economist. In 1878 he entered the Civil Service (by open competition), becoming a clerk in the War Office. The following year, again by open competition, he gained a place in the Surveyor of Taxes' Office; and in 1881 he obtained a first-division clerkship in the Colonial Office. He was called to the Bar by Gray's Inn in 1885. Shaw had met Sidney Webb about 1879 at the Zetetical Society, and introduced him to the Fabian Society, which he joined in 1885. In the 1880s Webb taught Shaw German (using Marx and Goethe), and Shaw revised Webb's prose. Webb's talent for organization was put to good use with the Fabians, for whom he prepared such tracts as *Facts for Socialists* (1887), and *Facts for Londoners* (1889). In 1891, Webb resigned from the Civil Service in order to take a leading part in the Progressive campaign for the London County Council, to which he was elected in 1892 with a large majority (as a member for Deptford). With a bequest from a deceased Fabian, Sidney Webb was instrumental in establishing the London School of Economics and Political Science in 1895, where he was a professor of public administration from 1912 to 1927. He was an active member of the Labour Party, elected to the House of Commons in 1922, and held several administrative posts between 1924 and 1931. Sidney Webb was appointed to the Order of Merit in 1944, and received honorary degrees from the Universities of London, Wales and Munich. Shaw and the Webbs were close friends throughout their lives.

▪ H. M. Hyndman (see above, 20).

▪ The Christian Evidence Society—established in 1870, in recognition of the fact that atheism had become a problem in Victorian society—consisted not only of evangelical and moderate churchmen (Richard Whately, Archbishop of Dublin and Charles Dickinson, Bishop of Meath, both spoke on the Christian Evidence platform), but also of respected scientists, such as John Hall Gladstone and William Henry Dallinger. It viewed itself as an educational force, providing formal classroom opportunities through such organizations as the Y.M.C.A., and church institutes. It also sponsored publications, including the *Christian Evidence Journal* (which began in 1874); but perhaps its most significant work was R. A. Redford's *The Christian's Plea Against Modern Unbelief* (1883).

▪ A "scratch crew" refers to a boat-crew hastily assembled at the last minute to take part in a regatta.

▪ Edward Stanley Robertson (n.d.) was a member of the Liberty and Property Defence League, for whom he wrote *Communism,* and *The State and the Slums,* both in 1884.

▪ [George] Howell (1833–1910), English labor leader and writer. In 1864 he ceased working as a bricklayer to join the body of men who were bringing trade unionism into politics. His finest service to the trade union movement was as a parliamentary lobbyist, and he was instrumental in the passing of the Trade Union Acts of 1871 and 1876. From 1885 to 1895 he served as M.P. for Bethnal Green. Interestingly, however, he remained a liberal, opposing the notion of creating a new political party to represent labor. His other written works were numerous and include *A Handy Book of the Labour Laws* (1876), and *The Conflicts of Capital and Labour, historically and economically considered, being a history of the Trade Unions of Great Britain* (1878).

1 September 1892

SOCIALISM, UTOPIAN AND SCIENTIFIC* [C886]

IT is quite like old times to receive a book by one of those two doughty free companions, Karl Marx and Frederick Engels, the famous joint authors of the Communist manifesto of 1848, still the classic model for all Social Democrats in the manifesting stage, which, to tell the truth, is seldom a very active one, except in the literary sense. As usual, the world greatly softened towards Karl Marx after his death, in 1883. Nowadays, when a student wishes to "get up" the development

---

* "Socialism, Utopian and Scientific." By Frederick Engels. Trans. Edward Aveling. Social Science Series. (London: Swan Sonnenschein.)

of our modern industrial organisation from the phase marked by Adam Smith's well-worn account of the wonders of division of labour in pin-making by hand to that of the miracles of machinery about which the artisan reads in the articles on "Great Manufacture of Little Things," in *Cassell's Technical Educator*, with, of course, the institution and growth of our great factory code, his tutor sends him to Marx as the leading authority on the subject, albeit a most dangerous master-spirit of Socialism. This is already a considerable advance on the days when Marx and Engels—for the two are inseparable—were Ishmaelites under a European ban. Both of them were superior men in the best sense: in spite of certain aberrations which were the faults of their qualities, they saw through modern society right out to the other side of it and into the future; and things, on the whole, have since gone as they foretold. Marx was a Jew of the Jews, able and witty, but implacable and jealous. Engels, devoted to his friend, took up all his vendettas and was jealous for his sake, though his writing shows a Laboucherian easiness of temper and a flippancy of humour which differentiates it from that of Marx. They were both men of ardent imagination: the mere smell of a philosophic or economic treatise fired them with vast conceptions of themselves as economists and philosophers. Marx as the king of economists is a dramatic fiction, invented by himself and Engels, who believed implicitly in the quaint baby-house of bits and scraps about abstract human labour, wares, money, circulation, exchange, and the like, which Marx fondly constructed as an economic foundation for his great work "Capital." The baby-house was offered to the world in the shape of a new and infallible theory of value, forming a touchstone for all other economic treatises whatsoever; and as Marx applied the touchstone persistently, and as, unluckily, the theory of value was an unsound one, the result of the touchstone process was that all the other treatises were found wanting, and denounced as "bourgeois," which was the fellest epithet in the Marxian vocabulary. In fact, Marx, who was the greatest clinical lecturer on the diseases of capitalism that capitalism has yet produced, was, like many other brilliant clinical lecturers, a bad theorist, though theorising was his hobby. Into every economic treatise in the British Museum he seems to have dipped far enough to discover that the author was heterodox on the great value theory. He then contemptuously dismissed him, and incidentally got credit for having read him, by means of one of those pungent footnotes which occur so frequently in "Das Kapital." Entertaining as these footnotes are, they invariably miss the charac-

teristic economic point, weak or strong, of the author criticised, or
rather assaulted; and they are ominously peppered with those exultant little discoveries of plagiarism which are the sure sign of a bad
critic in all departments of the critic's art. In the end, the ostentation
of omnivorous economic reading wearies us, the more so as we are
driven to conclude that no man with the true economic instinct
could possibly have endured to wade through all the secondhand
trash quoted in the book. Even Macaulay, badly as he suffered from
the same disease, did not read political economy.

A certain irony is given to this aborted value theory by its vulnerabil-
ity to the line of philosophical criticism affected by Marx and Engels.
Though they both undertook to set Hegel right, as they set everybody
else right, on the subject of his Ideaism (after Ibsen one dares no
longer call it Idealism), they were nevertheless ardent champions of
the Hegelian dialectic as opposed to the old-fashioned metaphysics of
Bacon and Locke. Yet Marx broke down over the theory of value
because he could not catch the dialectic of it, and could only work
with the crudely positive Lockian theory which regards value as labour crystallised in commodities, and measurable by units of time.
This, however, was a great simplification of the subject for the working man and the ordinary citizen, who as a rule can understand nothing that is not put to them in the absolute Lockian manner; and to this
day the modern and essentially dialectical value theory of Jevons and
the Austrian school eludes the proletarian student, who gets on capi-
tally with Marx's rule of thumb.

This digression on Marx is compulsory here because, in dealing
with any work by Engels, we must put up with the great value theory
as we put up with any other foible of a great man or a good fellow. Also
it is necessary to admit, for the sake of a quiet life, that all other
authorities on social questions are either nincompoops or plagiarists,
and that Marx read their works, found them wanting, and set them
right finally and unquestionably. To any ordinary men such indul-
gences would be indignantly refused; but to these twain one cheerfully accords them. There is so much to be learned from them; they
are so confident and wholehearted, so dramatic in their demonstrations, so tremendously down on all that we instinctively dislike in
civilisation, so full of interesting information that has always been
kept from us lest it should turn our heads with revolutionary ideas,
that we allow them the most unreasonable privileges, and are not
surprised to find Engels boasting that "Das Kapital" is "the Bible of the
working classes" in Germany. Even in England its admirers are apt to

wax fanatical and to denounce the Wellhausens and Matthew Arnolds of Socialism as downright infidels.

The volume which has provoked these remarks is a translation of three chapters of Engels' "Herrn Eugen Dühring's Umwälzung der Wissenschaft," originally published about sixteen years ago. The three chapters, translated into English by Dr. Aveling, and arranged for separate publication under the title "Utopian and Scientific Socialism," will be new to English readers, although they have circulated in Germany to the extent of 20,000 copies, and have been translated into French, Italian, Spanish, Dutch, Danish, Russian, Polish, and Roumanian. Dr. Aveling's translation is introduced by a characteristic preface, dated April of this year, by Engels himself. It had better be judged by samples than criticised, especially as the samples will make better reading than any possible criticism. It begins with a chanticleer crow of heterodoxy to wake up the British bourgeois. Then, after a quotation from the inevitable Marx showing that England is the birthplace of Materialism, Engels goes on:—

> About the middle of this century what struck every cultivated foreigner who set up his residence in England was what he was then bound to consider the religious bigotry and stupidity of the English respectable middle class. We, at that time, were all Materialists, or, at least, very advanced Freethinkers; and to us it appeared inconceivable that almost all educated people in England should believe in all sorts of impossible miracles, and that even geologists like Buckland and Mantell should contort the facts of their science so as not to clash too much with the myths of the Book of Genesis; while, in order to find people who dared to use their own intellectual faculties with regard to religious matters, you had to go among the uneducated, the "great unwashed" as they were then called, the working people, especially the Owenite Socialists.

But England has been "civilised" since then.

> The Exhibition of 1851 sounded the knell of British exclusiveness. England became gradually internationalised in diet, in manners, in ideas, so much so that I begin to wish that some English manners and customs had made as much way on the Continent as other Continental habits have made here. Any-

how, the introduction and spread of salad oil (before 1851 known only to the aristocracy) has been accompanied by a fatal spread of Continental scepticism in matters religious; and it has come to this, that Agnosticism, though not yet considered "the thing" quite as much as the Church of England, is yet very nearly on a par, as far as respectability goes, with Baptism, and decidedly ranks above the Salvation Army. And I cannot help believing that under these circumstances it will be consoling to many who sincerely regret and condemn this progress of infidelity, to learn that these "new-fangled" notions are not of foreign origin, are not "made in Germany," like so many other articles of daily use, but are undoubtedly old English, and that their British originators 200 years ago went a good deal further than their descendants now dare to venture.

Then follows a rapid sketch of the religious developments evolved by Capitalism, all tending to the characteristic conclusion that the bourgeoisie, for their own purposes, encourage working-class piety.

Regardless of the sneers of his Continental compeers, the British bourgeois continued to spend thousands and tens of thousands year after year upon the evangelisation of the lower orders. Not content with his own native religious machinery, he appealed to Brother Jonathan, the greatest organiser in existence of religion as a trade, and imported from America revivalism, Moody and Sankey and the like. Finally, he accepted the dangerous aid of the Salvation Army, which revives the propaganda of early Christianity, appeals to the poor as the elect, and thus fosters an element of early Christian class antagonism which one day may become troublesome to the well-to-do people who now find the ready money for it.

Here is another prime morsel, all the better for not being too palpably made to fit any Marxian theory.

In England the bourgeoisie never held undivided sway. Even the victory of 1832 left the landed aristocracy in almost exclusive possession of all the leading Government offices. The meekness with which the wealthy middle class submitted to this remained inconceivable to me until the great Liberal manufacturer Mr. W. E. Forster, in a public speech, implored the young men of Bradford to learn French as a means to get on in the world, and quoted from his own experience how sheepish he looked when, as a Cabinet Minister, he had to move in society where French was at least as necessary as English. The fact was, the English middle class of that time were, as a rule, quite uneducated upstarts, and could not help leaving to the aristocracy those superior Government places where other qualifications were required than mere insular narrowness and insular conceit, seasoned by business sharpness. Even now the endless newspaper debates about middle-class education show that the English middle class does not yet consider itself good enough for the best education, and looks to something more modest. Thus, even after the Repeal of the Corn Laws it appeared a matter of course that the men who carried the day, the Cobdens, Brights, Forsters, &c., should remain excluded from a share in the official government of the country, until, twenty years afterwards, a new Reform Act opened to them the door of the Cabinet. The English bourgeoisie are, up to the present day, so deeply penetrated by a sense of their social inferiority, that they keep up, at their own expense and that of the nation, an ornamental caste of drones to represent the nation worthily at all State functions; and they consider themselves highly honoured whenever one of themselves is found worthy of admission into this select privileged body, manufactured, so to speak, by themselves.

A footnote to the above is also worth quoting.

Even in business matters the conceit of national Chauvinism is but a sorry adviser. Up to quite recently, the average English manufacturer considered it derogatory for an Englishman to speak any language but his own, and felt rather proud than otherwise of the fact that "poor devils" of foreigners settled in England and took off his hands the trouble of disposing of his products abroad. He never noticed that these foreigners, mostly Germans, thus got command of a very large part of British foreign trade, and that the direct foreign trade of Englishmen became limited almost entirely to the Colonies, China, the United States, and South America. Nor did he notice that these Germans traded with other Germans abroad, who gradually organised a complete network of commercial colonies all over the world. But when Germany, about forty years ago, seriously began manufacturing for export, this network served her admirably in her transformation in so short a time, from a corn-exporting into a first-rate manufacturing country. Then, about ten years ago, the British manufacturer got frightened, and asked his ambassadors and consuls how it was that he could no longer keep his customers together. The unanimous answer was: (1) You don't learn your customer's language, but expect him to speak your own; (2) You don't even try to suit your customer's wants, habits, and tastes, but expect him to conform to your English ones.

The preface concludes with a denunciation of the German middle class as "lamentably deficient in political capacity, discipline, courage, energy, and perseverance," whilst the German working class is credited with having made an extraordinary display of these qualities during the last twenty-five years. "Four hundred years ago," says Mr. Engels, by way of peroration, "Germany was the starting-point of the first upheaval of the European middle class. As things are now, is it outside the limits of possibility that Germany will be the scene, too, of the first great victory of the European proletariat?"

The body of the book is still fresh and striking in its presentation of the sketch of the socialisation of production in the workshop and factory by our modern Capitalism, whilst unquestioned appropriation of the product by the owner of the means of production still prevails as in the old days of the spinning-wheel and handloom. Some of the Marxian rhetoric, however, is getting old-fashioned: for instance, the iterated and reiterated "revolt of the form of production against the form of exchange"—a phrase which was from the first more dramatic than accurate—should be dropped now that banks and clearing-houses have carried the socialisation of exchange far beyond the socialisation of production. Much harder to bear than this is the Marxian "historic Materialism," which insists that all history is fundamentally an economic development. Certainly the economic conditions of existence impose themselves on us with enormous power; and the extraordinary effect which Buckle produced on his few readers was due to his making them for the first time conscious of that power. That is also the secret of Marx's influence, concerning which it is interesting to note that "Capital" never produces as imposing an effect on students who have been already through the "History of Civilisation" as upon those to whom the whole subject is fresh. Historic Materialism, indeed, seemed to change our minds as completely as natural selection. But the truth is that it was the change in our minds that opened our eyes to both. Every puppy thinks, when it first opens its eyes, that it has created the world; and it takes some time to convince it that it has only opened its eyes. Mr. Engels' share of this sort of illusion, common to us all, has too often led him to write as if the mere mechanism of business had created Socialism and were dragging Man into it willy-nilly. As a matter of fact the whole mechanism and material of Collectivism—factory steam engine, bank clearing-house, huge population, joint-stock company, Trust organisation and all, were just as available 1,000 years ago as they are to-day. There was plenty of steam in British kettles before Julius Cæsar landed; and if Julius had brought the islanders a power-loom they would probably have understood it, after a word of explanation, quite as well as most modern islanders. But if he had shown them a copy of *The Daily Chronicle* calling for the abolition of the buckhounds, he would have totally confounded them. When Mr. Engels writes as if the change from slavery to Capitalism were a material change and not a spiritual one; when he implies that Robert Owen's Socialism failed solely because he came before the development of the Ring and the Trust, he is, with all respect, giving us, not "scientific Socialism," not even Utopian Socialism, but obsolete mid-century materialism. Owen failed simply because the other people were not Owens. If they had been, our social conditions would have changed without the intervention of a single Whisky Pool or Lumber Trust. Mr. Engels, too, knows this as well as anybody. He is precisely like Marx in his fancy for elaborating huge toy theories; abusing everybody else for not adopting them; and then happily forgetting them all in his earnest moments. Listen to his conclusion:—

> State ownership of the productive forces is not the solution of the conflict; but concealed within it are the technical conditions that form the elements of that solution.
> This solution can only consist in the practical recognition of the social nature of the modern forces of production, and therefore in the harmonising the modes of production, appropriation, and exchange with the socialised character of the means of production. And this can only come about by society openly and directly taking possession of the productive forces which have outgrown all control except that of society as a whole. The social character of the means of production, and of the products, to-day

reacts against the producers, periodically disrupts all production and exchange, acts only like a law of nature working blindly, forcibly, destructively. But with the taking over by society of the productive forces, the social character of the means of production and of the products will be utilised by the producers with a perfect understanding of its nature, and instead of being a source of disturbance and periodical collapse, will become the most powerful lever of production itself. Active social forces work exactly like natural forces: blindly, forcibly, destructively, so long as we do not understand and reckon with them. But when once we understand them, when once we grasp their action, their direction, their effects, it depends only on ourselves to subject them more and more to our own will, and by means of them to reach our own ends.

All of which, with its stress on recognition, comprehension, and will, practically means that no set of material conditions is more socialistic than any other, and that not until the bias towards Socialism gets hold of us, and stimulates us to recognise and comprehend our economic conditions with a view to adapting them to Socialism, can there be any historical development in that direction. Mr. Engels, in fact, may be said to pitch Historical Materialism out of the window after first maintaining that Historical Materialism is "scientific Socialism." And so "scientific Socialism" goes the way of the great value theory and the rest of the Marxian aberrations. But it was inevitable that Marx and Engels should have overdone their position just as Darwin overdid Natural Selection and Malthus overdid the population question. They carry us past the truth; but they leave us nearer to it than they found us. That being so, we can say with all sincerity that we are glad to see the Marx-Engels literature getting into the hands of English readers; and we hope that every fresh translation will have a fresh preface, no less vivacious and suggestive than this latest utterance of the sage of Regent's Park.

Editor's Notes

- This review was first published in the *Daily Chronicle*, 1 September 1892, 3:1–3.
- At 1.00 P.M. on 23 August 1892 Shaw paid a visit to his playwright friend

Edward Rose (1849–1904). "Found that he had forgotten all about the appointment and had gone out. As he was expected back to lunch at 14, I sat on the ground outside and began review of Engels' *Utopian and Scientific Socialism* for *The Chronicle*." The next day he resumed work on the review ("Worked at the Engels' review as well as I recollect"); and on 25 August, "I believe I worked at the Engels' review; for I now remember traveling first class to Hammersmith so as to work comfortably at it." On the thirtieth he "finished and sent off review of Engels to *The Chronicle*. A heavy job" (*Diary* 847, 849).

• Frederick [Friedrich] Engels (1820–95), German Socialist, with Marx cofounder of "scientific Socialism." Born in Barmen, from 1842 he lived chiefly in England, though he met Marx in Brussels in 1844. With him he wrote *The Communist Manifesto* (1848), and with him returned to Germany to participate in the unsuccessful revolution of that year. After Marx's death in 1883, Engels spent the remainder of his life translating and editing Marx's writings.

• Edward [Bibbins] Aveling (1849–98), British scientist and Socialist reformer. He studied medicine and science, and taught anatomy at the London Hospital, but was dismissed as a "freethinker" (he had lost his religious faith on his mother's death in 1877.) For some time he, Annie Besant, and Charles Bradlaugh formed a sort of unholy trinity controlling the National Secular Society, and Aveling became very close to Annie Besant. However in 1884 he abandoned her for Eleanor, the attractive and talented youngest daughter of Karl Marx, whose legacy of £9,000 from Friedrich Engels he proceeded to spend. With her he shared an apartment in Great Russell Street, and made a little money by writing for journals like the *National Reformer*, and *Progress*, and by lecturing. Shaw was a frequent visitor to his home in the early 1880s, more for the company of Eleanor Marx, who had aspirations to become an actress, and who confided in him her unhappiness over Aveling's infidelities. With Aveling, Shaw was more circumspect. They attended concerts together and debated, often fiercely, over Marxian matters. Aveling, like Shaw, was a lecturer on Socialism (though later blackballed by the Fabian Society), and a member of and speaker at the Shelley Society, and the Communist and Playgoer's Clubs. Finally, Edward secretly married Eva Frye in June 1897. Eleanor Marx's response to this betrayal was suicide by poison on 31 March 1898. Four months later, Aveling himself died. In addition to the book reviewed here, Aveling also translated Haeckel's *The Pedigree of Man, and Other Essays* (1893); and under the pseudonym "Alec Nelson" he wrote a number of plays. Shaw allegedly modelled Dubedat, the artist in his own play *The Doctor's Dilemma* (1906) in part on Edward Aveling.

• For more than seventy years, Cassell and Co. published an enormous range of anthologies, self-help manuals, educational encyclopedias and children's annuals. *Cassell's Technical Educator* (an encyclopedia of technical education in four volumes) was published by Petter and Galpin (London, 1870–72).

- Macaulay (see above, 119–20).
- Hegel (see above, 56–57).
- [Francis] Bacon [first Baron Verulam and Viscount St. Albans] (1561–1626), English philosopher and statesman. His philosophy emphasized the belief that man is the servant and interpreter of nature; his logical method is known as ampliative inference, in which he inferred by use of analogy, from the characteristics of the larger group to which the datum belonged. Later experience, he believed, would correct evident errors. Such a method improved significantly scientific hypotheses, and is thought to have been fundamental to the scientific method. [John] Locke (1632–1704), English philosopher, considered to be the founder of empiricism, which emphasized the importance of the experience of the senses in pursuit of knowledge, rather than intuitive speculation or deduction. He thus developed Bacon's earlier approach (of reasoning from the particular to the general), giving it systematic expression in his *Essay Concerning the Human Understanding* (1690.)
- Jevons (see above, 63).
- [Julius] Wellhausen (1844–1918), German biblical scholar.
- "Herrn Eugen Dühring's Umwälzung der Wissenschaft" [*Herr Eugen Dühring's revolution in science*] was published in 1878.
- [William] Buckland (1784–1856), English geologist and clergyman who attempted to relate geology to the biblical description of the Creation; and [Gideon Algernon] Mantell (1790–1852), English paleontologist who wrote *The Wonders of Geology* (1838).
- "Brother Jonathan" is Engels's derisive reference to the famous American Congregational clergyman and theologian Jonathan Edwards (1703–58), whose hellfire preaching galvanized his parishes, and later, through his publications, much of the Christian world.
- [Dwight Lyman] Moody (1837–99), American evangelist, who worked on a farm and as a clerk in a shoestore until 1856, when he joined the Congregational Church, and went to Chicago to engage in missionary work. He was joined in his evangelistic work by [Ira David] Sankey (1840–1908), another evangelist and singer, who became president of the Y.M.C.A. in Indianapolis, and met Moody there at the Y.M.C.A. International Convention in 1870. Together Moody and Sankey held revival meetings all over the United States and Great Britain. Sankey travelled with Moody as solo singer, and compiled *Gospel Hymns* (1875–95), and *Sacred Songs and Solos* (1873), which was published in England and, it is claimed, had a circulation of more than 50,000,000 copies! It is an oft-repeated story that the visit to Dublin of Moody and Sankey provoked Shaw's first appearance in print in his secularist letter to *Public Opinion* on 3 April 1875.
- As to the Salvation Army one day becoming "troublesome to the well-to-do people who now find the ready money for it," in *Major Barbara* (1905), Shaw puts Capitalism's answer to this threat in the mouth of Undershaft, the millionaire arms-manufacturer, whose daughter Barbara has become a Major in the Salvation Army:

CUSINS: Well, I can only say that if you think you will get her away from the Salvation Army by talking to her as you have been talking to me, you don't know Barbara.

UNDERSHAFT: My friend: I never ask for what I can buy.

CUSINS [*in a white fury*] Do I understand you to imply that you can buy Barbara?

UNDERSHAFT: No; but I can buy the Salvation Army.

- [Richard] Cobden (1804–65) spent his time and energy lecturing and preaching Free Trade, and [John] Bright (1811–89), Radical politician, was closely associated with the Reform Act of 1867. W[illiam] E[dward] Forster (1819–96), English Liberal statesman, in 1870 was responsible for the Elementary Education Act.
- [Henry Thomas] Buckle (1821–62), English historian, whose major (unfinished) work *History of Civilization in England* (vol. 1, 1857; vol. 2, 1861) was highly acclaimed. Buckle attempted to treat history as an exact science, maintaining that climate, soil, food, and so forth form the character of a people. Not surprisingly, he discovered that only the English climate was conducive to a high level of civilized life!
- A buckhound is a smaller version of a staghound.

27 October 1892
BASSETTO ON LOGROLLER* [C898]

I wonder why I, of all *Star* reviewers, should have been asked to deal with this book—I, di Bassetto, most prosaic of critics. For I do not enthuse readily over the smaller fancy wares of art: the builder, not the jeweller, is the man for my money; and your miniatures and fan paintings, your ballads and *morceaux de salon* make but a finicking appeal to the Bassettian spirit, nursed upon cathedrals, frescoes, and giant Wagnerian music-epics. Besides, it is against my vow to let any man off cheaply in the arts. I am no smirking verger to let all comers who look good for a tip into the choir and among the tombs of the mighty dead, there to pose and scratch their names until Time, Death, and Judgment come down out of Mr. Watts's picture, and inexorably eject them. Rather let me stand at the gate I guard, fell, grim, and

* English Poems. By Richard Le Gallienne. Price 5s. net. (London: Elkin Mathews, 1892.)

venomous, not to say downright unpopular, holding it against all who are not strong enough to make a doormat of me. And yet Mr. Le Gallienne is such an uncommonly likely young man, and so easily able to do me a good turn some day—for is he not a professed logroller?—that I am half tempted to do what so many of the other vergers do, and make a pretty exhibition of tact and good nature by passing him quietly in after a little coquetry with his claims. But in England this cannot safely be done without a careful investigation of the applicant's moral character; and I regret to say that the most cursory examination of Mr. Le Gallienne's hymn-book is enough to convince any verger that a more abandoned youth has seldom presented himself at the choir gates of an English cathedral. Just listen to this, for instance—p.91,the first and third verse (the second is too awful for quotation).

"Let me take thy hair down, sweetheart,
    loosen little pin by pin,
Let me feel it tumbling o'er me,
    drinking all its fragrance in.
Let me wrap thee all within it,
    kiss thee through its golden thread—
O I shall go mad with kissing,
    kissing, kissing thy dear head.

O thy body, sweet, sweet body,
    let me drink and drink and drink!
Canst thou let me, like the minstrel,
    die upon the fountain's brink?
Love, O love, what *art* Thou? tell me
    is this heaven, hell, or where?
All I know is that I kiss thee,
    lying in thy yellow hair."

Now I ask, is this proper? Is it moral? The answer depends, obviously, on whether Mr. Le Gallienne is legally married to the lady. On this subject I proceed to collect the evidence. Let me admit at once that I find none to justify me in doubting that the above was addressed to the same lady as "Hesperides," which I pass unquoted with a blush, merely observing for the reader's convenience that it is to be found on page 72. But what about the following lines from the poem beginning, "Dear desk, farewell!" on pp. 115–116?

"How many queens have ruled and passed
Since first we met; how thick and fast
The letters used to come at first, how thin at last;
Then ceased, and winter for a space!
Until another hand
Brought spring into the land,"

&c., &c.

Can any man of experience believe that the author of this passage is a strict monogamist? Further evidence is to be found in the series of poems called "Love Platonic" (Platonic indeed!) in which Mr. Le Gallienne, after betraying the fact that the heroines are several and not one by little discrepancies which cannot be detailed here for lack of space, gets so confused by their multiplicity that he forgets which is which, and exclaims-

"Who is the lady I sing?
Ah, how can I tell thee her praise?
For whom all my life's but the string
Of a rosary painful of days."

But the worst is to come. One of the ladies is unquestionably a married woman. The poem entitled "Why Did She Marry Him?" will set a good many of Mr. Le Gallienne's domesticated friends speculating rather dubiously as to which of them is the subject of it. At any rate, since she did marry him, Mr. Le Gallienne's duty was plain. Instead of doing it he persevered in his addresses in the following fashion:—

"Yea, let me be 'thy bachelere,'
'Tis sweeter than thy lord,
[*note this preference*]
How should I envy him, my dear,
The lamp upon his board.
Still make his little circle bright,
With boon of dear domestic light,
While I afar,
Watching his windows in the night,
Worship a star
For which he hath no bolt or bar,
Yea, dear,
Thy 'bachelere.' "

I wonder what people would say of me if I wrote such things! It is all very well for Mr. Le Gallienne to call his poems "Platonic," and to pitch into the "Decadent poets" in his virtuous intervals; but if he came round watching my windows in that fashion, I should have a serious talk with Madame di Bassetto on the head of it.

Apart from these considerations of personal morality, which must ever come first with me, my chief quarrel with Mr. Le Gallienne arises out of a certain commonplaceness and banality of material, which is not altogether compensated by his dainty workmanship. For example, in the poem beginning "God gave us an hour for our tears," the question as to what use was made of that precious hour is answered in a way entirely worthy of the excellent Dr. Watts:—

> "Nay, this is all we did with our hour—
> We tore it to pieces, that precious flower;
> Like any daisy, with listless mirth,
> We shed its petals upon the earth;
> And, children like when it all was done,
> We cried unto God for another one."

Listen to this, addressed "To a Dead Friend":—

> "And is it true indeed, and must you go,
>   Set out alone across that moorland track,
> No love avail, though we have loved you so,
>   No voice have any power to call you back?
> And losing hands stretch after you in vain,
>   And all our eyes grow empty for your lack,
> Nor hands, nor eyes, know aught of you again."

That is the worst of knowing a poet: he is always longing for you to die, in order that he may have an opportunity of mourning you in verse. Oh, this eternal leakage of "idle tears," that have lost their novelty as completely as Prince Rupert's drops! You might have spared your dead friend, Mr. Le Gallienne. Here is another prime commonplace:—

> "A poet prayed, and the answer came—
> 'Thou shalt sing, and thy song shall bring thee fame;
> But this must thou give for thy silver tongue,
> Thrice three sorrows for each new song.' "

If Mr. Le Gallienne thinks this verse fresh enough for me, he greatly underestimates my literary experience. Now for a much prettier commonplace:—

> "O life is sweet, but nought so sweet
>   As this in morning weather,
> A man and maid with mouths that meet
>   And hearts that beat together.
>
> O life is sad, but nought so sad
>   As when the sun is setting
> That one forgets the joy they had,
>   And one has no forgetting."

One more arrant commonplace, entitled "Time Flies":—

> "On drives the road—another mile! and still
> Time's horses gallop down the lessening hill.
> O why such haste, with nothing at the end!
> Fain are we all, grim driver, to descend
> And stretch with lingering feet the little way
> That yet is ours—O stop thy horses, pray."

The commonplaceness is due to the usual cause—unconscious insincerity; leading to a preference for secondhand ideas. Mr. Le Gallienne ought to know that a writer should never read anything but the book of life. Yet he is not ashamed to call himself a "passionate reader," and to hail a mortal man of his own trade in this fashion:—

> "Doth it not thrill thee, Poet,
>   Dead and dust though thou art,
> To feel how I press thy singing
>   Close to my heart?—
>
> Take it at night to my pillow,
>   Kiss it before I sleep,
> And again when the delicate morning
>   Beginneth to peep?"

This dusty infatuation comes out again in some lines inspired by a remark of Mr. Gosse's. They are called "A Library in a Garden":—

"A world of books amid a world of green,
Sweet song without, sweet song again within;
Flowers in the garden, in the folios too:
O happy Bookman, let me live with you!"

After these comes a clever but idiotic rhymed epistle to Mr. Andrew
Lang, declaring it to be sufficient honor for a volume of verse to line the
shelves of that eminent book-fancier. Mr. Le Gallienne should remember the fate of the enthusiast who helped the Duke of Wellington to
cross Piccadilly, and received his thanks by vowing, with a flourish of
his hat, that to have been the slightest service to the greatest of warriors
and statesmen was an honor that rendered all thanks superfluous. The
Duke said simply, "Sir, don't be a damned fool," and stalked away into
Apsley House. Mr. Le Gallienne's compliment to Mr. Lang is certainly
prettier and more becoming than the poor *flaneur*'s compliment to the
Iron Duke; and yet somehow—well, I will not press the point, since it
was only a joke. The joke jars a little: that is all.

When Mr. Le Gallienne is sincere as well as fanciful, this is the way
he writes:—

"Some days there be when the loom is still
And my soul is sad as an autumn hill,
But how to tell the blessed time
When my heart is one glowing prayer of rhyme!
Think on the humming afternoon
Within some busy wood in June,
When nettle patches, drunk with the sun,
Are fiery outposts of the shade;
While gnats keep up a dizzy reel,
And the grasshopper, perched upon his blade,
Loud drones his fairy threshing wheel:—
Hour when some poet-wit might feign
The drowsy tune of the throbbing air
The weaving of the gossamer
In secret nooks of wood and lane—
    The gossamer, silk night robes of the flowers,
    Fluttered apart by amorous morning hours.
    Yea, as the weaving of the gossamer,
    If truly that the mystic golden boom,
    Is the strange rapture of my hidden loom,
As I sit in the light of the thought of—"

The next word being, needless to say, "her," breaks the spell, and makes you wish that the inevitable "my lady" was at the bottom of the sea. If Mr. Le Gallienne only knew how tired I am of "my lady." She has been the mistress of all the minor poets I ever knew; and not one of them ever found anything new to say about her. Here is a stanza which has escaped her:—

> "For all the silver morning is a-glimmer
> With gleaming spears of great Apollo's host,
> And the night fadeth like a spent out swimmer
> Hurled from the headlands of some shining coast.
> O happy soul, thy mouth at last is singing
> Drunken with wine of morning's azure deep,
> Sing on, my soul, the world beneath thee swinging,
> A bough of song above a sea of sleep."

The verse before this starts with "My lady," and is led by her into "pearly queendom," "dumb darkness," and all manner of disasters. But I have quoted enough. Mr. Le Gallienne's estimate of himself I rather like. He boldly says in an apostrophe to Song that his verses are

> "Stars that may linger yet
> When I, thy master, shall have come to die."

My own opinion is that immortality is not so cheap. It really does take a most tremendous equipment to survive oneself as a poet. In fact, the demand is so unreasonable that I do not myself consider immortality worth having at the price. For you must not only make good verses, but you must write poetry which the very cleverest poets of succeeding generations shall not be able to renew and replace. Looking at Mr. Le Gallienne's valentines and rhymed love letters and dedications, his prayers and pleas and songs, I can appreciate his delicate ear and fine literary taste, and feel in his work a charm of character that even his cleverness and wit have not been able to spoil; but I think, nevertheless, that there will always be three or four men in England able to do as well as he in poesy, especially when they fall in love; and these three or four, by renewing and replacing his poems (so far), will rob them of immortality. But then, what a ridiculous criticism that is, after all! It is as if I had been asked my opinion of a diamond bracelet, and had replied that its weight fell far short of a ton. However, I declared honestly at the outset that I was not the man for the job. If Mr. Le Gallienne will send me along something in five acts and in blank verse, or in thirty cantos or so, then I shall be in my element. In the meantime, my overtrial of him may amuse him; whilst my quotations, though they are by no means the plums of the book, may help the reader to form his own more sympathetic judgment.

C. DI B.

Editor's Notes

- The above review was first published in the *Star*, 27 October 1892, 4:1–2. It was reprinted in Richard Whittington-Egan and Geoffrey Smerdon, *The Quest of the Golden Boy: The Life and Letters of Richard Le Gallienne* (London: Unicorn, 1960).
- Shaw's *Diary* for 5 October 1892 reports that he "wrote review of Le Gallienne's *English Poems* for *The Star*" (*Diary*, 858). Shaw had been writing musical criticism for the *Star* since July 1888, when he covered musical events that conflicted with performances given by a fellow Socialist, Ernest Belfort Bax (see below, 229), who wrote under the pseudonym "Musigena." This necessitated differentiating between their copy, and Shaw adopted the pseudonym "Corno di Bassetto" (basset-horn), which he maintained when he took over completely from Bax in February 1889.
- Richard Le Gallienne (see above, 86–87). On 3 November 1892, Le Gallienne replied to Shaw's review with the following verse:—

> Poor little book, that only yesterday
> Fluttered new born in delicate array,
> How bruised and broken in the mud you lie;
> Surely some elephant was passing by;
> Or those mad herds of Galilean swine
> Have hoofed across that pretty page of thine.
> A nightingale the Minotaur hath torn,
> So seems my little murdered book this morn.
> Bury it gently where no eye may see,
> And for its epitaph write "C. di B."

Shaw wrote to Pakenham Beatty on 4 January 1893: "Why all this fury against a poor little sensitive plant like Richard? Why, his fighting weight is not two and a half ounces: a rough word would drive him to suicide. You do not suppose that he is a rough knuckled, thick skinned ruffian of the Trelawney type, do you? He was horribly hurt when I took his valentines and love letters, over every one of which I have no doubt he dropped a tear of quivering sensibility, and crumpled them up in my horny fist; and I shouldnt have done it if I had not thought that he was getting spoiled. As it was, I wrote the review in such a way as to sell his book; and sure enough his publisher tells me that after my review & the one in the St. James's Gazette, he sold 1250 copies! What do you think of that for a volume of minimus poetry? I know he complains of me; and his little poem in the Star was pathetic in its squeak of pain. I would willingly make him some amends for having hurt his feelings if there were any opening for doing so; but as there is none, I leave him to grow older & stronger" (*Collected Letters, 1874–1897*, 375). Perhaps Shaw was unaware of Le Gallienne's guilt over his infidelity to Mildred, his first wife, at this time. For even though Le Gallienne also heard at Hatchard's bookshop in Piccadilly that Shaw's review had done the book's sales a deal of good, he told his mother, "I don't care. . . . he is a vulgar-minded man"; see Whittington-Egan and Geoffrey Smerdon, *The Quest of the Golden Boy*, 202.

- G. F. Watts (see below, 524–25).
- Prince Rupert's drops were pear-shaped pieces of glass, made by dropping molten glass into water, which burst into fragments if the slender tail is broken. They were introduced into England from Germany by Prince Rupert, Duke of Bavaria (1619–82).
- Andrew Lang (1844–1912), Scottish poet, scholar, historian, folklorist, and man of letters, deserved Le Gallienne's praise. One of the most versatile writers of his day, he wrote poetry, works on the folklore and mythology of many nations, fairy tales for children; and, as a historian he wrote the monumental four-volume *History of Scotland* (1900–1907). He was also a distinguished classical scholar, producing with Samuel Henry Butcher (1850–1910) one of the best translations of Homer's *Odyssey*.
- Apsley House, which stands on the site of the old lodge of Hyde Park, was designed by Robert Adam for Baron Apsley in 1817. Wellington bought the house some forty years later, and, with his architect, Benjamin Wyatt, redesigned it, adding the pedimented portico outside and refacing the walls with Bath stone; adding (in 1828) a west extension. In 1947 the seventh duke presented Apsley House to the nation. In 1982 the house was redecorated, and the public rooms re-created to the original designs. It now houses the Wellington Museum.
- Shaw's request for Mr. Le Gallienne to "send . . . something in five acts and in blank verse" is surprising in view of his comments on the efforts of David Graham and W. W. Aldred in a review entitled "In Five Acts and in Blank Verse," in the *Pall Mall Gazette* (14 July 1887); see *Bernard Shaw's Book Reviews* 295–99).

13 February 1893

MR. WILLIAM MORRIS AND THE MIDDLE AGES* [C927]

IF anyone wants an amusing author whose style is not in the least *fin de siècle*, Bartholomew Anglicus is his man. That is, Bartholomew as edited by a Mediævalist like Mr. Steele, with a nice sense of how much of him modern readers are likely to stand. For one has to discriminate. Take theology for example. Bartholomew was immense in it; but our modern theological works are hard enough to bear without adding the burden of the thirteenth century to our load. Again, we do not want too much of thirteenth-century medicine in a book intended mainly for our amusement. Regarded as a joke, mediæval pathology and therapeutics are far flatter than the uproarious science of to-day. Later ages may smile over Bartholomew's careful explanation of madness as "infection of the foremost cell of the head, with privation of imagination, like as melancholy is the infection of the middle cell of the head, with privation of reason"; but to us, who are familiar with the experiments of Ferrier in "the cells of the head," and with the feat of cutting a hole in the pate—otherwise "trephining"—for the relief of brain disorders, Bartholomew's notions are the dullest common-sense. Here is a sample of them:—

> The medicine is that in the beginning the patient's head be shaven and washed in lukewarm vinegar, and that he be well kept or bound in a dark place.

Turn we now to Bartholomew's *materia medica:*—

> To heal *or to hide* leprosy, best is an adder red with a white womb, if the venom be away, and the tail and the head smitten off, and the body sod with leeks, if it be oft taken and eaten.

Observe here the brutally unprofessional candour of the phrase "to heal or to hide." Would any respectable modern practitioner betray

---

* "Mediaeval Lore: An Epitome of the Science, Geography, Animal and Plant Folk-lore and Myth of the Middle Age. From the encyclopaedia of Bartholomew Anglicus." Edited by Robert Steele, with a Preface by William Morris. (London: Elliot Stock.)

the cardinal secret of his profession like this? There is a certain feeble humour about the variegated adder; but will anyone contend that it is worth laughing at in an age which has seen the rare pranks that have been played, and are still at their maddest, with mercury, salicylic acid, atropine, bromide of potassium, hasheesh, opium, chloral, and a dozen other drugs? Let us at once leave Bartholomew's medicine aside with the contempt it merits, and pass to his remarks on foodstuffs. And as a warning to vegetarians, and an exquisite example of the occasional occurrence of strikingly modern phrases in Bartholomew's prose, let us first take his account of the bean:—

> Beans be damned by Pythagoras' sentence, for it is said that by oft use thereof the wits are dulled and cause many dreams. Or else, as other men mean, for dead men's souls be therein. Therefore Varro saith that the bishop should not eat beans. And many medley beans with bread corn to make the bread more heavy.

Bartholomew's natural history is not to be described by mortal pen other than his own: every sentence in it is more appetising than the one before. Would there were space here to quote the whole of it! Mr. Henley's sketch of "the rakehell cat" was much bepraised the other day; but could the art of Henley and the science of Darwin combined improve on the following?—

> He is a full lecherous beast in youth, swift, pliant, and merry, and leapeth and reseth on everything that is to fore him; and is led by a straw and playeth therewith, and is a right heavy beast in age and full sleepy and lieth slyly in wait for mice, and is aware where they be more by smell than by sight, and hunteth and reseth on them in privy places; and when he taketh a mouse he playeth therewith and eateth him after the play. In time of love is hard fighting for wives, and one scratcheth and rendeth the other grievously with biting and with claws; and he maketh a ruthful noise and ghastful when one proffereth to fight with another, and hardly is he hurt when he is thrown down off an high place. And when he hath a fair skin he is, as it were, proud thereof, and goeth fast about; and when his skin is burnt then he bideth at home, and is oft for his fair skin taken of the skinner and slain and flayed.

This is the language of a close and accurate observer. Bartholomew knew cats as few men know them, but his observation was necessarily limited to the fauna of his own country, and the public will be much misled if they attach equal authority to the statements which he confessedly derived from the accounts of the Stanleys and Emins of his day. It is doubtful, for instance, whether the following very interesting details concerning the elephant can be accepted as strictly scientific:—

> Also there is another thing said that is full wonderful. Among the Ethiopians in some countries elephants be hunted in this wise. There go in the desert two maidens all naked and bare, with open hair of the head; and one of them beareth a vessel and the other a sword. And these maidens begin to sing alone; and the beast hath liking when he heareth their song, and cometh to them and licketh their teats, and falleth asleep anon for liking of the song; and then the one maid sticketh him in the throat or in the side with a sword, and the other taketh his blood in the vessel, and with that blood the people of the same country dye cloth, and done colour it therewith.

It is hard to have to leave quite unquoted the section on birds and fishes; but there would be no ending if the sampling process were once begun. Nor may we linger over the men of Ireland, who "be singularly clothed and unseemly arrayed and scarcely fed; they be cruel of heart, fierce of cheer, angry of speech, and sharp natheless: they be freehearted and fair of speech, and goodly to their own nation"; nor even over the Scots, who "despise some deal the usage of other men in comparison to their own usage. And so each laboreth to be above: they detract and blame all other and envy all other; they deride all other and blame all other men's manners: they be not ashamed to lie, and they repute no man, of what nation, blood, or puissance so-ever he be, to be hardy and valiant but themselves. They delight in their own: they love not peace." For it is time to pass on from the fun the general reader will get from the book to its interest for the literary student.

Take the following sentence from the end of the section on the human body—

> For by the spleen we are moved to laugh; by the gall we are wroth; by the heart we are wise; by the brain we feel; by the liver we love.

Every section of this sentence is an incandescent light thrown on dozens of odd passages not only in mediæval poetry but in the Elizabethan drama. As Mr. Steele says in his preface, "our author affords us perhaps the simplest way of learning what Chaucer and Shakespeare knew and believed of their surroundings." The quality wanted to guide a modern editor in selecting from the whole encyclopædia is the instinct which recognizes the bits which struck the popular imagination, and so got woven into the art of the time. How successful Mr. Steele has been in this is proved by the fact that he has drawn a preface from Mr. William Morris, a thing not compassable by the vulgar arguments which publishers address successfully to professional editors. Here is what Mr. Morris says of the book:—

> To my mind no excuse is needful for the attempt made in the following pages to familiarise the reading public with what was once a famous knowledge-book of the Middle Ages. But the reader, before he can enjoy it, must cast away the exploded theory of the invincible and wilful ignorance of the days when it was written. The people of that time were eagerly desirous for knowledge, and their teachers were mostly single-hearted and intelligent men, of a diligence and laboriousness almost past belief. This "Properties of Things" of Bartholomew the Englishman is but one of the huge encyclopædias written in the early Middle Age for the instruction of those who wished to learn; and the reputation of it and its fellows shows how much the science of the day was appreciated by the public at large, how many there were who wished to learn. Even apart from its interest as showing the tendency of men's minds in days when science did actually tell them fairy tales, the book is a delightful one in its English garb; for the language is as simple as if the author were speaking by word of mouth, and not lacking a certain quaint floweriness which makes it all the easier to retain the subject-matter of the book.

Upon which the only comment we will venture to make is to express a hope that Mr. Morris does not fall into the great error of supposing that because Science has lost her fairy fancy, she has at all lost her mendacity. Your modern scientific encyclopædia contains more delusions and superstitions than Bartholomew, but fortunately it is so much duller reading that the delusions have twenty times less spreading power than Bartholomew's.

There is a chapter on Mediæval Manners—all too short—containing two charming paragraphs, entitled respectively "Of a Child" and "Of a Nurse." But it also contains the following, which show the seamy side of the ordered inequality, domestic and political, of that age:—

> Also a bond servant suffereth many wrongs, and is beat with rods, and constrained and held low with diverse and contrary charges, and travails among wretchedness and woe. Hardly he is suffered to rest and take breath. And therefore among all wretchedness and woe the condition of bondage and thraldom is most wretched. Dread maketh bond men and women meek and low; and goodly love maketh them proud and stout and despiteful.
>
> A man is bound to rule his wife, as the head hath charge and rule of the body.
>
> The father showeth his son no glad cheer, lest he wax proud. The more the father loveth his child the more busily he teacheth and chastiseth him and holdeth him the more strait under chastising and lore; and when the child is most loved of the father it seemeth that he loveth him not; for he beateth and grieveth him oft lest he draw to evil manners and tatches; and the more the child is like to the father the better the father loveth him.
>
> The birch hath many hard twigs and branches with knots, and therewith often children are chastised and beaten on the bare buttocks and loins.

These features of mediæval life are not quite so cheerful as the art side of it; but when the history students of the coming age rake up in the British Museum Library our "Death in the Workshop" articles, and the reports of the Society for the Prevention of Cruelty to Children, it is not at all certain that they will compare the nineteenth century with the middle age with the complacent sense of improvement which we miss so much in Mr. William Morris.

Editor's Notes

▪ The above review was first published in the *Daily Chronicle*, 13 February 1893, 3:1–2.

- According to Shaw's *Diary,* he "began, finished and sent off review of *Medieval Lore*" on 1 February 1893. Perhaps it was a coincidence that Robert R. Steele, its compiler, spent the evening with Shaw a month before (on 7 January); but it is tempting to think that there was discussion of the book on that occasion.

- Robert R[eynolds] Steele (1860–1944), English medieval scholar, who was by profession a schoolteacher, but by avocation a student of medieval literature, producing a steady stream of editions and translations of works by Democritus, Huon of Bordeaux, Alexander de Villa Dei, Roger Bacon, Francis of Assisi, and Bartholomew Anglicus (see below). He was a member of the Fabian Society, and friend of William Morris, whose *Defence of Guinevere, and other Poems* he edited in 1904. Shaw knew both Steele and his wife.

- Bartholomew [Bartholomæus] Anglicus (fl. 1230–50), English Franciscan encyclopedist. He studied at Oxford and Paris, and lectured at the Franciscan house of studies at Magdeburg. His great work—the one reviewed above— *De Proprietatibus Rerum,* completed c. 1240–50 and in wide use in the Middle Ages, was a treatise on the natural sciences designed for theologians and preachers. It was largely based on the works of others, such as Isidore of Seville and Robert Grosseteste.

- [William] Morris (1834–96), English poet, Socialist, and craftsman. Morris was a leading figure in the Socialist movement of the day, financing the journal *Commonweal* to disseminate his views. Politically Morris was an idealist, seeking to inculcate Socialist principles rather than promoting allegiance to political parties; but in matters of art he was a man of action, and single-handedly set about to reform Victorian styles by the manufacture of furniture, wallpaper, and fabrics. He set up his dyeing and weaving works at Merton Abbey in 1881, and, with Emery Walker, began the Kelmscott Press early in 1891, using his own designs for the type and ornamental letters. In the late 1880s Morris set up his own Hammersmith Socialist Society, which met in a converted stable at Kelmscott house at Hammersmith. Shaw was a regular speaker at the Sunday meetings, where he strengthened his friendship with Morris's younger daughter May, and increased his admiration for her father.

- [Sir David] Ferrier (1843–1928), Scottish neurologist, whose most significant work began in 1873 on the localization of brain functions: it formed the subject of his Croonian Lectures at the Royal Society in 1874 and 1875, and grew into his treatise *The Functions of the Brain* (1876, 2d ed. 1886), which was translated into several languages. Shaw's acknowledgment of Ferrier's contribution to brain surgery is interesting in view of his persistent belief in antivivisection; for Ferrier was an inveterate vivisector; and his experiments on apes (inducing in them cerebral strokes, for example), might have been expected to arouse Shaw's wrath.

- Pythagoras (sixth century B.C.) Greek philosopher, and [Marcus Terentius] Varro (116–27 B.C.), Roman scholar and author who allegedly composed 74 different works comprising about 620 books. Pythagoreanism was more a way

of life than a philosophy, involving moral asceticism and ritual rules of abstinence (of which the one quoted and reinforced by Varro is, perhaps, the most
famous.)

- "reseth on" means "rushes upon," from the OE verb *ræsan*.
- The "rakehell cat" was presumably drawn by the London-born painter of
domestic scenes Lionel-Charles Henley (c. 1843–93), who from 1862 had
exhibited at the Royal Academy and elsewhere.
- [Sir Henry Morton] Stanley (1841–1904), Welsh explorer and journalist.
His famous trip to Africa to "find Livingstone" is better known than his more
dangerous expedition in 1886 for the relief of Mehmed Emin Pasha (originally Eduard Schnitzer) (1840–92), German explorer. After landing at the
mouth of the Congo with 650 men, he marched into the forest with half his
force, and although disaster overtook his rear column, he met Emin Pasha on
the shores of Lake Albert in April 1888. Emin Pasha was a skillful linguist
who added much to the knowledge of African languages, as well as sending
back to Europe valuable collections of plants and animals. The year before
this review was written, Emin Pasha was murdered by Arabs in the Manyema
country.

18 February 1893

WAGNER—AT LAST!* [C929]

WAGNER has come at last ! Never was there a greater mistake than to
suppose that our intimacy with "Lohengrin," our growing familiarity
with "Die Meistersinger," and the distant acquaintance we have
scraped with "Tristan" and "The Nibelungs' Ring," not to mention the
silly caricature of "Tannhäuser" which has occasionally appeared at our
opera houses, have introduced us to Wagner. We might just as well
claim to have made the acquaintance of Ruskin on the strength of a
stroll through the Turners in the National Gallery. It is greatly to be
suspected that the majority of our Ruskinites have no turn for pictures;
and it is certainly quite possible to be a Wagnerite and to be no more
susceptible to musical impressions than an adder. Mr. Whistler is said
to have once enthusiastically poured out a list of the many accomplishments of Sir Frederic Leighton. "Paints, too," he added as an after-

* "Richard Wagner's Prose Works." Trans. William Ashton Ellis. Vol. 1. (London: Kegan
Paul.)

thought. Had Wagner been his theme he might have made an equally imposing list without forestalling his opportunity of adding, "Composes, too." Wagner was poet, metaphysician, sociologist, politician, revolutionary convoy officer and tocsin ringer, journalist, orator, conductor, theatrical manager, and the greatest musical critic in the world. And about all this the British public knows practically nothing. Mr. Dannreuther's translation of "On Conducting" and "Beethoven" are never taken up except by musicians; and the old translations of "Opera and Drama" in the *Musical World* and other papers, made by men who turned Wagner's German into the most outrageous English nonsense, were altogether unreadable. His dramatic poems are known to opera-goers, of course; but his essays as a writer and thinker are now opened up to English readers for the first time by Mr. Ashton Ellis, whose enterprise, if the remaining volumes keep up to the standard set in the present one, will hold the field as the standard English translation of one of the most famous European authors of the century. A comparison of Mr. Ellis's work with any of the attempts to be found in our old musical magazines will show that an adequate translation of Wagner is almost a work of re-creation. In so far as former translators have been unable to get on Wagner's plane; to interpret his illustrations and allusions in the light of a culture as broad as his own; in short, to think his thoughts if not to originate them, in just that degree have they been able to extract from Wagner's books and their own dictionaries nothing but flagrant balderdash, which has served many a time to verify the professional opinion that Wagner was a fool because his ideas and his style of composition were so extremely unlike those of, for instance, the late Sir George Macfarren. Nobody will derive from Mr. Ellis's translation any other impression of the author's capacity than they would derive from the original if they were able to read it; and no higher compliment than this could be paid to any translator. Possibly the man who will translate Wagner himself into a cheap edition of a popular Englishman (much as Puck "translated" Bottom), may push his book into regions where Mr. Ellis's twelve-shilling translation of Wagner's own language and method of exposition from German into English will hardly penetrate; but it will never be worth any man's while to attempt to beat Mr. Ellis on his own ground.

It is not possible to give here any adequate notice of a volume containing half a dozen works which might each be made the subject of an elaborate criticism. All that can be done is to explain the peculiarity which their standpoint will have in England. First, then, let it [be] admitted that, in spite of our Puritanism, we take a great interest in

Art here. If a man walks into a drawing-room and causes it to be known that he can play the pianoforte, there is an extraordinary curiosity to see him do it. We run after pictures, give much mouth-honour to the classic drama, and are absolutely agreed that Art is a first-rate element in culture. Books about painting and music, and analytic programs of concerts, are the means of extracting hard British cash from our pockets to a handsome tune every year. But what we read about Art affects us as the allusions to champagne in Ouida's novels affect an imaginative factory girl. She becomes curious about it, associates a lavish supply of it with the splendours and joys of life, will go some distance to look at a bottle of it in a shop window, will feel that she has her foot on the social ladder the first time she finds herself seated in a café where the woman at the next table is actually drinking it, will long to taste it, and will finally, perhaps, allow the glorified liquor to turn the scale the wrong way. Then comes the ecstatic experience of raising the first glass to her lips, followed by the horrible discovery that she does not like it—the heartbreaking self-conviction of vulgarity with which she hides her guilty secret that she would rather have beer or lemonade. Just so does the Britisher read his "Stones of Venice" until he trembles and thrills with enthusiasm for Carpaccio and Tintoretto, counting himself not happy before the day when he books with Cook or Gaze to Venice, where he hastens, suffocating with emotion, to San Giorgio Schiavone, only to stand chapfallen in a dirty little church, seeing nothing around him that he likes half so well as the chromo-lithograph he bought with the last Christmas number of the *Illustrated London News*. Just so, again, will the devotee of music read Sir George Grove on Schubert, or Otto Jahn on Mozart, or Wagner on Beethoven, and everybody on Wagner, until he can scarce contain his impatience for the next performance of the Ninth Symphony at the last Richter concert of the season, into which he will squeeze though it cost him four hours waiting for the opening of the doors. And then the terrible dulness of the masterpiece, the weariness of sitting it out, the insufferable heat, the impossibility of attending after the first thirty bars—worst of all, the shameful consciousness of hankering after the Christy Minstrels downstairs—of wishing that he could sleep out the immortal setting of Schiller's "Ode to Joy," and dream all through it of Marie Lloyd singing "Oh, Mister Porter, what shall I do?"

But it is the glory of an Englishman never to know when he is beaten. Since he knows that he *ought* to like Art, his first care is to go on doggedly swallowing it with a Spartan air of relish; his next, to try to regain his self-respect by acquiring a genuine taste for it. And he soon finds out that though Art itself be unpalatable, it has innumerable points in which any intelligent man can become a connoisseur. The diligent Venetian tourist soon discovers all manner of intellectual interests and ingenious exercises in the galleries. To study the evolution of style and technique[,] to spot this picture as a Bellini and that as a Giorgione before looking at his catalogue; to distinguish an early manner from a late manner; to reconstruct the Renascence in the pictures it produced; to trace the influence of a historic event in this corner of a picture, and of a passage from Dante in the other: these and a thousand other diversions may make our Philistine come to love Art as passionately as an entomologist loves beetles. And the same salvation comes to the would-be *fanatico per la musica*. The Ninth Symphony is not half dull when you are tracing the sonata form in its construction, and watching for the difficult passage in A flat for the horn in the slow movement, or chuckling over the humour of tuning the drum in octaves in the scherzo, or comparing the Schiller theme with Beethoven's first attempts at it as revealed in the sketch-books edited by Nottebohm, not to mention over again the evolutionary and other interests which music has in common with painting and the other arts. And when our Philistine is an expert in all this, and has fortified himself further with a true palatal taste for the qualities which Mozart had in common with Offenbach, or Carpaccio with Mr. Burton Barber, he considers himself a lover of Art and an authority on it, although obviously he may remain, as on the day of his first disappointment, as blind as a bat and as deaf as a post to that beauty and eloquence of form, colour, and sound which the true artist loves and seeks to create, and which alone are entitled to the name of Art. However much a man may know *about* paintings or symphonies, he can never know Art unless he has a primitive appetite in him which is satisfied and delighted by the sight or sound of works of Art. He alone who understands this distinction can understand the difference between the Art criticism of such men as Wagner in Germany and Morris in England, both creative artists of the first rank themselves, and the books and notices about pictures and concerts, often learned, ingenious, able, and interesting, but always hopelessly beside the point, which are poured forth every year to console and flatter our deafness and blindness.

In this light, perhaps, the following quotations from one of Wagner's prefaces may not lose their significance by their isolation from the context:—

> It would be interesting if the verdict upon Art should fall back into the hands of those who understand Art; whereas the peculiarity of our present course of education has brought round the view that the judgment on a thing must come from a quite different domain to that of the thing itself; forsooth, from "the absolute Reason," or mayhap from "the self-thinking thought." . . . Whoever will permit himself to be led by the hand of one who has become clear on this point—not on the path of abstract speculation, but guided by the impulse of *direct artistic need*—will not, I trust, be vexed to wander with me over the path on which I reached that outlook.

It is noteworthy that this vital distinction between Art and the conditions, professional, technical and physical, under which Art operates, should have apparently helped Schopenhauer to his mastery of the cognate distinction between the will of man and the contriving faculties and executive activities which it sets in operation for its own satisfaction. Schopenhauer, it will be remembered, was highly sensitive to music. And Wagner seized with enthusiasm on Schopenhauer's point when he took up his great work for the first time. We find him, in the preface to the 1872 reissue of "Art and Revolution," describing as "an unspeakable benefit" the enlightenment of "those who have learnt from Schopenhauer the true meaning and significance of the Will." It is necessary, however, to assure the unfortunate English reader that he need not fear being pestered by Wagner with what one must really call the cackle about pessimism and misogyny which passes here for Schopenhauerism.

The hope that the hour has come for the success of Wagner in England as an author is strengthened by the extent to which the leading spirits of our democratic movement are beginning to talk Wagner without knowing it. Formerly nobody could see why a writer on Art should drag in Democracy and Woman, and the Working Classes and the Jerry Builder, instead of confining himself to "the *morbidezza* of Andrea del Sarto" and the "marvellous foreshortening of the Carracci" or the three styles of Beethoven. Ruskin's first experiments in this direction were regarded as petulant aberrations. But nowadays all important popular writers on Art find themselves driven into the same path; and what is more, they would not be read if they did not. And this is because we are at last coming to see that Art is not merely a fashion, but an organic part of life, not a dispensable, unneedful luxury, but a need so deep that no abundance of bread and butter can keep us fully alive whilst it is starved. Good luck, therefore, to Wagner in English. He could not have arrived at a happier moment.

Editor's Notes

- The above review was first published in the *Daily Chronicle*, 18 February 1893.
- On 8 February 1893, Shaw "began review of Wagner's prose works vol. 1, for the *Chronicle*." These were very busy days for Shaw, and it was a week before he got round to Ellis's translation again, during which time he made a draft letter to defaulting members of the Fabian Society, attended a musical concert, wrote his article for the *World*, and another for the *Workman's Times*, attended two meetings of the Fabians, corrected the proof of his own biographical notice for *Cassell's Cabinet Portrait Gallery*, lectured twice on Liberalism, drafted an agreement for the publication of his first (and recently produced) play *Widowers' Houses*, and wrote a dozen letters. On 14 February, he notes "worked away at the review of Wagner," and the following day, "finished and sent off review of the first volume of Ellis's translation of Wagner's prose works" (*Diary* 904–7).
- [William] Ashton Ellis (1853–1919), English physician and translator. He was a pioneer in English Wagnerian studies, editing A. Smolian's *Themes of Tannhäuser* (1891), and factually refuting Ferdinand Praeger's allegation that Wagner was a red-handed revolutionary who had fought on the barricades in 1849 (made in *Wagner as I Knew Him* [1892]) in a book entitled *1849: A Vindication*, published in the same year. After the publication of the *Prose Works* reviewed above, Ellis also published *The Correspondence of Wagner and Liszt* (1897), followed by a great deal more of Wagner's correspondence, and the "authorized version" of C. F. Glasenapp's *Life of Richard Wagner* (1900). Shaw was acquainted with Ellis through the latter's lectures, and in 1907 tried to exert his influence with R. B. Haldane (then secretary of state for war, but touted as a possible successor to Campbell-Bannerman, the Liberal prime minister, who died the following year) to obtain a Civil List pension for Ellis, "who" (he claimed) was "pawning his spare scarf-pins."
- Shaw's interest in Wagner was lifelong, but his proselytizing on Wagner's behalf was most intense in these early journalistic days, culminating in his famous critical essay *The Perfect Wagnerite* (1898).
- In 1843 the first volume of Ruskin's *Modern Painters* was published, in part a successful defense of the then controversial English painter [Joseph

Mallord William] Turner (1775–1851), whom he had met shortly after graduating from Oxford. Turner's work foreshadowed that of the Impressionist painters.
- The National Gallery, founded in 1824, was moved from its original home in Pall Mall to its present site on the north side of Trafalgar Square (constructed from 1832 to 1838), and the gallery's first director, Sir Charles Eastlake, enriched the collection with 139 pictures, many from the Italian Renaissance, and raised the gallery to a position of high rank among the galleries of Europe. By 1870 there were significant works of Rubens and Rembrandt on display, and numbers of British painters were represented, including Hogarth, Gainsborough, and Constable. Some of Turner's paintings (see above) are still to be found at the National Gallery; however, four years after the above article was published, many of Turner's works that had remained in his possession at his death in 1851, were moved to the newly opened Tate Gallery, in Millbank. Here the Clore Gallery (designed by James Stirling) for the Turner collection opened in 1987.
- Adders were traditionally, but incorrectly, thought to be deaf.
- James [Abbott McNeill] Whistler (see above, 65).
- Frederic [first Baron] Leighton [of Stretton] (1830–96), English painter and sculptor, who rose to immediate recognition in 1855, when his painting *Cimabue's Madonna carried in Procession through Florence* was purchased by Queen Victoria. He was made an Academician in 1868 and at the time of the above review was president of the Royal Academy. Shaw was respectful (sometimes tongue-in-cheek) of his presidency and his technical expertise as an artist; but his final judgment on him was given a year after the painter's death: "Madox Brown was a man; Watts is at least an artist and poet; Leighton was only a gentleman"; see Stanley Weintraub, *Bernard Shaw on the London Art Scene, 1885–1950* (University Park: Pennsylvania State University Press, 1989), 404.
- Shaw reviewed Edward Dannreuther's (1844–1904) translation of Wagner's *On Conducting [Über das Dirigiren]*, for the *Pall Mall Gazette* on 28 May 1887; see *Bernard Shaw's Book Reviews*, 272–77.
- Sir George [Alexander] Macfarren (1813–87), English conductor and composer. His great ambition was to write an opera that would somehow reflect the spirit of England (he much admired the operas of Weber, with their roots in Germanic folklore). In this endeavor he failed, though he wrote four operas, nine symphonies, three concertos, a quantity of chamber music, and many vocal works. In 1875 Macfarren was appointed Sterndale Bennett's successor as professor of music at Cambridge. In 1883 he was knighted. In this review, Shaw contrasts the pedantic "academician" with Wagner.
- "Ouida" [Marie Louise de la Ramée] (1839–1908), English novelist who wrote forty-five novels, most of which deal with fashionable life and exhibit a rebellion against the moral ideals displayed in much contemporary fiction. Shaw, reviewing *Othmar* (1885) for the *Pall Mall Gazette,* summed up the typical Ouida novel as "diffuse, overloaded with worthless mock sociology, perceptibly tainted by a pervasion of the sexual impulses, egotistical and tiresome,

and yet imaginative, full of vivid and glowing pictures, and not without a considerable moral stiffening of enthusiasm—half-reasoned but real—for truth and simplicity, and of protest against social evils which is not the less vehement because certain emotional and material aspects of it have a fascination which the writer has not wholly escaped" (*Bernard Shaw's Book Reviews* 107).

▪ Thomas Cook (1808–92), English travel agent and temperance reformer. It was a temperance gathering which led to Cook's most famous occupation, when he arranged with the Midland Council Railway Company to run a special train from Leicester to the meeting. On 5 July 1841, some 570 passengers were carried from Leicester to Loughborough and back at a shilling a head. This, believed to be the first publicly advertised excursion train ever run in England, was so successful that Cook gave up his other work to concentrate on running pleasure-trips, a venture that was given impetus by the Great Exhibition of 1851 (which Cook helped 165,000 visitors attend). In 1855 Cook expanded his tours to include the Continent. The extension to the United States was made in 1866. Three years later Cook's Tours reached as far as Palestine; and his son John Mason Cook (1834–99) was appointed agent for passenger travel on the Nile. The firm took the name Thomas Cook and Son in 1872. Henry Gaze and Sons, though modeled on the line of Cook even to the system of issuing tickets, appears to have operated on a smaller scale. They began in the 1860s, their advertisements always stressing the "high-class" quality of their conducted tours, whether "four-in-hand carriage drives," which started every day to visit the sights of Paris and Versailles, their "Nile tours," or their "teachers' vacation excursions to Europe."

▪ *The Stones of Venice* by John Ruskin was published in three volumes (1851–53).

▪ [Vittore] Carpaccio (1455?–1526?), Italian painter. Born in Venice, and much influenced by the Venetian painters Gentile and Giovanni Bellini, Carpaccio executed four cycles of narrative paintings, the second of which, depicting nine scenes mainly from the lives of Saint George and Saint Jerome, is to be found in Scuola San Giorgio degli Schiavoni in Venice.

▪ Tintoretto (see above, 65).

▪ Shaw himself had made his first trip to Italy with members of the Art Workers Guild in September 1891, and his views of the tourist-ridden cities, where "churches are used in such a way that priceless pictures become smeared with filthy tallow soot," found in his letter from Venice to William Morris of 23 September 1891, and in his later article "On Going to Church," in the *Savoy*, January 1896, sound a note of sympathy for the disappointed visitor characterized in the above review.

▪ Sir George Grove (1820–1900), English music critic, best known for having projected and edited the *Dictionary of Music and Musicians*, which remains a standard reference in music. It was published from 1878 to 1889, and volume 21 was reviewed by Shaw in the *Pall Mall Gazette* on 15 January 1886 (see *Bernard Shaw's Book Reviews* 85–88). Among Grove's many services to music were (with Arthur Sullivan) the rescuing of the instrumental music of Schubert's *Rosamunde* in 1867 and, on 26 October 1880, the discovery of a letter revealing that the true author of the *Deutsches Requiem* was not in fact Schubert's brother but Schubert himself, a fact he revealed in his famous article on the composer (to which Shaw refers) in the first edition of his *Dictionary*.

- The mid-nineteenth century's growing interest in Mozart reflected a general growth of interest in music of the past. Otto Jahn's (1813–69) four volume *W. A. Mozart*—the first scholarly biography that embodied new research—was published in the centenary year, 1856; while Wagner's important monograph on Beethoven was published in his centenary year, 1870.

- Hans Richter (1843–1916), German conductor. His meeting with Wagner at Triebschen in 1866 revolutionized his career: he became one of Wagner's favorite conductors, chosen by the composer to conduct the entire *Ring des Nibelungen* at the Bayreuth Festival in 1876. Accompanying Wagner to London in 1877, he conducted several Wagner Festival concerts at the Royal Albert Hall, and in May 1879 these became annual events later called simply the "Richter Concerts," which he continued to conduct until 1897, in which year he became conductor of Manchester's Hallé Orchestra.

- Edwin Pearce Christy (1815–62), American entertainer, born in Philadelphia, and the creator of the Christy Minstrels, a black-faced troupe of singers, successful in New York and London.

- Marie Lloyd [born Matilda Alice Victoria Wood] (1870–1922), English music hall entertainer. She had made her first appearance at the Royal Eagle Music Hall [later the Grecian] in 1885. Her first great success, "The Boy I Love Sits Up in the Gallery," was followed by many famous songs including the song mentioned here, "Oh, Mr. Porter, what shall I do?" She went on to become one of the best-known figures in the Edwardian heyday of the music hall, performing in America, South Africa, and Australia.

- Giovanni Bellini (c. 1430–1516), Italian painter. Arguably the greatest Venetian artist of his time, he was instrumental in making Venice as prominent an artistic center as Florence. Famous for his treatment of light, and his ability to integrate figures successfully in landscapes, he is perhaps best known for a long series of very human Madonnas. He exerted a powerful influence upon talented young artists of the day, including Giorgione [Barbarelli] (c.1478–1511).

- [Martin] Gustav Nottebohm (1817–82), German musicologist, who made a comprehensive survey of and commentary on Beethoven's sketches [*Ein Skizzenbuch von Beethoven*, 1865], which produced remarkable insights into the inner workings of the music. [Jacques] Offenbach (1819–90), German composer of a great many light operettas that were extremely popular in the late nineteenth century.

- [Charles] Burton Barber (1854–94), English artist, who worked entirely in London as a sporting and animal painter, specializing in portraits of dogs, often with children. He painted Queen Victoria with her favorite dogs (and her grandchildren); he also painted "Fozzy," the Prince of Wales's dog. He exhibited regularly at the Royal Academy from 1866 to 1893.

- [Arthur] Schopenhauer (1788–1860), German philosopher. Wagner refers to Schopenhauer's notion that all the experienced activity of self is Will, including unconscious physiological functionings, this Will being the inner nature of each experiencing being. The popular "cackle about pessimism" resulted from the negative implications: since, according to Schopenhauer, the Will constantly pushes the individual toward achieving successive goals, none of which can provide lasting satisfaction for the infinite activity of the life force, or Will, the latter inevitably leads man to pain, suffering, and death in an endless cycle, and can only be tolerated through an attitude of resignation.

- The term "Jerry Builder" dates from 1881 (OED), the "Jerry" in question being short for Jeremiah, in reference to his Lamentations in the Old Testament.
- "the *morbidezza* of Andrea Del Sarto" [properly d'Agnolo] (1486–1531) means the "softness" or "mellowness" of this Italian painter's work
- The Carracci were a family of Bolognese painters, among the most important in the Italian sixteenth century. Lodovico (1555–1619); his cousin Annibale (1560–1609); Agostino (1557–1602), Annibale's older brother; and Antonio (c. 1583–1618), Agostino's illegitimate son. There is a strongly naturalistic element in their work, and the "marvellous foreshortening" referred to describes a familiar positioning of the human figure in their canvases, in which the subject's legs are stretched toward the viewer.
- A nineteenth century notion, popularized by Lenz in his *Beethoven et ses trois styles* (1852), was that the "three styles" of [Ludwig van] Beethoven (1770–1827) correspond roughly to three periods of his writing life: a formative period, finishing about 1802, a second period lasting until 1812, and a transcendent third period, lasting from 1813 to 1827. Recent scholarship has tended, if not to scrap this rather simple schema, at least to refine it by the addition of subperiods.

4 April 1893

NATIONALISATION, RESTORATION, TAXATION* [C939]

WHEN Mr. Henry George gave new life to the land reform movement at the beginning of the last decade by his "Progress and Poverty," he insisted strongly on the distinction between land and capital, not only as economic categories, but as practical sources of income. Thus he stated that when the Duke of Westminster takes, say, £1,500 out of the earnings of London for one day's rent of his landed property

* *Land Nationalisation.* By Harold Cox. Social Questions of To-day. (London: Methuen.)

therein, the sum should be confiscated by taxation. But if the duke contrives to invest his money in a joint-stock enterprise before the visit of the tax collector, and so transforms his rent into interest, then, said Mr. George, it has become sacred and must go untouched as the just reward of the Duke's industrial enterprise, thrift and foresight. It did not take much sagacity to see that if we ran the community on these principles we should have industrial millionaires exempted from taxation, and working-class proprietors of houses erected by building societies paying through the nose. The Georgian "single tax" in short, is nothing but old Mirabeau's *Impôt unique* over again; and it needs no Voltaire come from the dead to laugh it away with a new edition of "L'Homme à Quarante Ecus" [*sic*]. Practical men knew from the first that Mr. George's theoretic distinctions were of no value as a basis for practical legislation, and that when the time was ripe for action the Chancellor of the Exchequer would have to discriminate, not between land and capital in the academic manner, but between unearned and earned incomes, between drones and workers, between the savings of veterans or widows and the inheritances of children who only need a healthy incentive to work to save them from becoming Jubilee Plungers and useless men about town. Mr George, pressed on these matters, added to the confusion of his doctrine by attempting some further theoretic distinctions between monopolies and non-monopolies; and so the Progressive movement swept on and forgot him. Nevertheless, there are still plenty of Georgeites among our political propagandists, encouraging their Radical friends to clamour for the special taxation of "ground values," and the exemption of dividends from liability on the ground that "to tax interest is to tax industry, whereas to tax rent is only to tax the landlord"—as if the idle proprietor of an urban site purchased by his grandfather stood in any different relation to the community from the idle shareholder in a gas company started by capital subscribed by *his* grandfather.

It is on this confusion of ideas and on its spurious economic basis that Mr. Cox has come down like several thousand of brick. With exasperating cocksureness he smashes the single tax, pulverises the resuscitated land tax of 1692, and scatters the partialities of the English Land Restoration League. He is right in the main; but he is coldly barbarous in establishing his rightness; and in view of the invaluable work done by the red vans of the E. L. R. L. in waking up the country districts on the land question, and of the fact that Georgeism, in spite of its errors, makes excellent converts to Progressivism, one feels that Mr. Cox, to say the least, might have been more sympathetic. However, his view clearly is that it is not his business to spare the feelings of blunderers; and it may be that he is right there too, the question at issue being one of the most serious we have to deal with. At any rate it is a relief to be taken by him outside the prevalence of that reciprocal admiration which makes the atmosphere of progress occasionally rather stuffy.

If the land restorers want to retort on Mr. Cox, they will find their opportunity in his chapter on the theory of rent, in which he unexpectedly exhibits a fanatical attachment to the ultra-historical school in economics, by this time much more out of date than Georgeism. He attacks Ricardo in the style of Carey, and goes the length of declaring that "perhaps the most sweeping condemnation of the Ricardian theory is to be found in the fact that Ricardian theorists invariably argue as if the only crop obtainable from the soil were a crop of wheat." Now by "the Ricardian theorists" Mr. Cox would ordinarily be understood to mean General Walker, Professor Marshall, and Mr. Sidney Webb and his Socialist friends. From these writers we have had elaborate demonstrations of the application of the Ricardian law to personal ability and to industrial capital—demonstrations that have taken us long past the crop-of-wheat phase of the theory. And all these demonstrations have widened and confirmed the Ricardian law, not abrogated it. If Mr. Cox wishes to verify its daily reality he has only to compare rents at the Marble Arch with rents at Kilburn, or the rent of any two farms in Kent, and he will get all the evidence he can reasonably require. Indeed, the Ricardian law is very clearly at the root of his own main contention that taxation falls on the landlord, and not on the occupier. Apparently, what Mr. Cox really means is not, as he begins by saying, that the Ricardian law is not borne out by facts, but, as he finally says, that it is a platitude, which is quite another matter, and one which need not be disputed here. One or two of his criticisms, aimed nominally at the theory of rent, are really only fatal to the Ricardian theory of value, which is admittedly exploded. On the whole, the chapter on economic theory must be pronounced the weak link in an otherwise sound and strong chain of reasoning.

On the question of the incidence of taxation, Mr. Cox opens fire as follows:—

Local rates are a charge upon real property, payable in the first instance by the occupier. Is he also the final payer? That is the whole matter in a nutshell. But the answer to this apparently straightforward question seems to vary with the shifting mood of the person who undertakes to deal with it. When, for example, a proposal is made in the House of Commons by a Tory Government that local rates should be relieved by contributions from the imperial exchequer, Liberal and Radical Members will denounce the proposal as a bribe to the landowning classes; while the Tories will contend that it is the poor distressed occupier whom they wish to relieve. A few months later the Liberals will be demanding that the rates shall be divided equally between owner and occupier in order to relieve the *latter,* and the Tories will reply that the owner already pays the whole rate.

This is no fancy picture. It is a matter-of-fact description of discussions that have taken place in the House of Commons more than once within the last half-dozen years.

Here Mr. Cox certainly scores off the House of Commons. His solution is the orthodox Ricardian one that "in every case the landlord ultimately pays the taxes on land." But this is just the point where we want an application of the historical method which Mr. Cox was so bent on in the previous chapter. By owner and occupier in this connection, the economists mean landlord and *rackrented* tenant. When the tenant is not rackrented, then the occupier in the eye of the economist is the owner also to the extent to which his rent falls short of the rackrent. Suppose such a tenant, though only paying £50 a year rent, would, if pressed, pay £55 sooner than move, then, clearly, if a rate amounting to £5 a year were newly imposed and collected from him, he would not be able to shift it on to the landlord, since he himself would be, economically speaking, a beneficiary landlord to the tune of the annual £5. The whole practical difficulty which the London County Council finds in acting on Mr. Cox's perfectly sound economic theory is that London is not fully rackrented, and that therefore fresh taxation collected from the occupiers would not always be recovered by them from the landlords. Mr. Cox, in a very able chapter on taxation, however, practically makes a clean sweep of the rates altogether, including betterment and improvement rates, the highly popular arguments for which he attacks with Satanic glee, advocating in thoroughgoing fashion the compulsory purchase of the improved areas by the municipality as a preliminary to the carrying out of the improvement. Finally, he holds that the only logically and practically defensible methods of raising public funds are death duties (without distinction between personalty and realty) and poll taxation including graduated income tax.

Everyone who likes the country will appreciate Mr. Cox's claim for "the right to roam," which relieves the book from the reproach of being unsympathetic, as the Georgeites will probably accuse it of being. The historical sketches of the decay of our manorial system and the growth of our fiscal systems are capital: most readers will find in them just what they want to know, free of all encumbrance. As has already been intimated, the style is cool, but it is none the less readable; whilst the matter is useful, and the force and relevance to current politics of most of the criticism are undeniable.

Editor's Notes

- The above review was first published in the *Daily Chronicle*, 4 April 1893, 3:2–3.
- On 29 January 1893, Shaw lectured in Croydon, and "Took Cox's book on *Land Nationalisation* to read in the train." On 2 February, "At about 13 [Shaw] began review of Harold Cox's book on *Land Nationalisation* and worked away at it until 17.30 when it was ready to send off" (*Diary* 900–901).
- Harold Cox (1859–1936), English economist and journalist. Under the influence of Edward Carpenter (see below, 229) he spent a year working as an agricultural laborer in Kent and Sussex, where he applied scientific methods to agriculture. From 1885 to 1887 he taught mathematics in the Mohammedan Anglo-Oriental College at Aligarh in India. Returning to England in 1887, he first read for the Bar, but finally turned to journalism and authorship. Brother-in-law of Sydney Olivier, and initially, like Shaw, a Fabian, he had been friendly with Sidney Webb, with whom he had collaborated on *The Eight Hours Day* (1891). However, he finally abandoned Socialism, and from 1906 to 1909 he was Liberal M.P. for Preston. In 1920 he wrote an anti-Socialist pamphlet, *Economic Liberty*. Shaw knew Cox well, frequently dined with him, and attended his Fabian lectures. Indeed, on 6 January 1893, Shaw had attended Cox's lecture on "Socialism applied to Land," which might have been *l'idée mère* for this review.
- Henry George (see above, 21).
- [Victor Riqueti, Marquis de] Mirabeau (1715–89), French author and political economist, father of the revolutionary politician and orator. In his *Théorie de l'impôt* (1760), he attacked with all the energy of his son the inefficient system of the Farmers General of the taxes and the complex administration of taxation under the Old Regime, and proposed a single tax ["l'impôt unique"], levied on land alone. This caused his imprisonment at Vincennes, and then exile to his country estate at Bignon, where the "school of the physiocrats" was established; in 1765 Mirabeau bought the *Journal de l'agriculture, du commerce, et des finances*, which became its official voice.
- Voltaire's *L'homme aux quarante écus* (1768) was more than a rebuttal of Mirabeau; it was a devastating blow to Mercier de La Rivière (1720?–93), whose *L'Ordre naturel et essential des sociétés politiques* (1767) was the manifesto of the Physiocratic school. Shaw, writing to the American million-

aire Joseph Fels on 23 March 1909, said "I have always wanted to have Voltaire's Homme aux Quarante Ecus—the tract in which he smashed old Mirabeau's Single Tax panacea (*l'impôt unique*)—translated & reprinted as a Fabian tract" (*Collected Letters 1898–1910*, 839).

▪ The slang expression Jubilee Plungers appears to mean "high-spirited gamblers"; "jubilee" implied a carefree spirit, and a "plunger" was a reckless better or speculator (c. 1876).

▪ The English Land Restoration League had begun in 1883 (as the Land Reform Union) to propagate the Land Nationalization ideas of Henry George (see above, 21).

▪ David Ricardo (see above, 56).

▪ [Henry Charles] Carey (1793–1879), American economist. His three volumes of *Principles of Political Economy* were published from 1837 to 1840.

▪ [Francis Amasa] Walker (1840–1897), American educator, economist, and statistician. In 1869 Walker was appointed chief of the Bureau of Statistics, which he reorganized and improved. The wealth of information on the economic and social situation of the United States he obtained assisted in his becoming professor of political economy and history in the Sheffield Scientific School of Yale (1873 to 1881), and president of the Massachusetts Institute of Technology from 1881 until his death. He was a firm believer in competition, yet he advocated reduced working hours for labor; he was a free trader and an internationalist, and this may have made him better known and respected as a theoretical economist in England than at home. He wrote *The Wages Question* (1876), *Money* (1878), *Land and its Rent,* and *Political Economy* (1883). Shaw reviewed Walker's article "The Source of Business Profits," in the first volume of the *Quarterly Journal of Economics* in the *Pall Mall Gazette* on 18 October 1887.

▪ [Sidney] Webb (see above, 139). One of Sidney Webb's closest Socialist friends was, of course, Bernard Shaw.

▪ A "rackrented" tenant is one who is charged a rent equal, or very nearly equal, to the full annual value of the land.

22 February 1896
THE NEW FACTORY ACT* [C1121]

THIS book is dedicated to "Herberto Henrico Asquith, magna assecuto, majora desiderantes." I am informed by friends of mine who have not

---

* "The Law relating to Factories and Workshops." By May E. Abraham (one of Her Majesty's Inspectors of Factories) and Arthur Llewellyn Davies. (London: Eyre and Spottiswoode, 1896.)

forgotten their Latin so completely as I have that this means "To Mr. Asquith, who, however much he has done, ought to do a good deal more," which appears to me to be exactly what an Inspector of Factories should say on such an occasion. But there are always heavy difficulties in the way of factory legislation. The average English journalist or politician is, on industrial questions, merely a pompous ass, intimidated by political economy. At the mention of factory legislation he distends himself with weary ignorances, naïve misconceptions, and exploded foreign competition scares, all of them as dead as Nassau Senior, until finally the Factory Inspectors and a few energetic people who know what they are talking about seize the Home Secretary by one coat-tail, whilst the manufacturers who stand to lose by the threatened legislation hold on to the other; and the result is according to the balance of political brute force between public spirit on the one side and private interest on the other.

The effect of factory legislation is perfectly clear. It raises the standard of civilization among the protected workers; and it raises the standard of capacity needed for success in the competitive struggle between the employers. That is why able employers like it, and dull ones dread it and raise the cry of ruin to their industry. In the absence of effective factory legislation any greedy rascal with a turn for business can crowd an ordinary dwelling-house with starving wretches, knowing that such sanitary accommodation as there is will break down in a week. He can let it break down; he can slave-drive his employees to the limits of human endurance and beyond it; he need not clean the place nor ventilate it; he can let matters come to typhus-fever point, and then send out his infected goods to be worn or consumed by innocent people who order them through a respectable tradesman and know nothing of such horrors. This is the old theoretic "liberty of the individual," "freedom of contract," and so forth, still trotted out, whenever a Factory Bill is in hand, by the belated Whig, the old-fashioned editor whose strong point is a grasp of imaginary foreign politics, the academic prig-politician, and the ladies of the Women's Employment Defence League, all of them officiously ready catspaws for the bottom layer of sweaters whose narrow margin of profit is sure to be knocked off by the least additional instalment of decency, humanity, and public safety. Every time we insist on another coat of limewash, another cubic foot of space per head, another drain-pipe, another half-hour off the working day, we submerge a batch of anxious, narrow, barely competent "manufacturers," and throw their business into the hands of men of superior ability and education. That this process of the elimination of the unfittest is a beneficial and inevitable one need not be treated as an open question. The advocate of factory legislation does not now engage its opponents in dialectical fencing matches on abstract principles: he simply bludgeons them with the unanswerable results of a century of experience. The practical problem that now confronts every successive Government is how far it can venture at any given moment to raise the legal standard of treatment for our factory population without demanding too much from our "captains of industry." For instance, if we were to compel factory owners to provide Turkey carpets, Chippendale chairs, Kelmscott Press books, and first-rate orchestral concerts for the comfort and cultivation of their employees, even the ablest employers might find it impossible to cope with such conditions—in which case the industry would simply stop. The reasonable line of opposition to any Factory Bill is, therefore, not to attack factory legislation on principle, or to talk obsolete nonsense about freedom of contract, but to argue that the standard of comfort for employees and of ability for employers has already been raised as high as the produce of the industry in question, or the supply of organizing ability in the ranks of the governing classes, will permit.

How miserably far we are from having approached any such limit in the last Factory Act may be judged by the defeat of Mr. Asquith's attempt to include laundries under the heading of factories. Why the sort of man who wears fourteen shirts a week should be anxious to maintain a state of things in which the chances of getting fever in his starch are appallingly high is not apparent; but there can be no question that he helped energetically to snatch the laundries from the rescuing hands of Mr. Asquith, and fling them back into the abyss, in spite of all that the Factory Inspectors, especially the women, could urge to save them. In a typical petty laundry you get the work crowded each week into two or three days of from fourteen to seventeen hours each, wages from two to three shillings a day, a demoralizing truck in gin against which the law is powerless, and—as likely as not—a case of scarlet fever in the next room. One would have supposed that these abuses would find no friends outside the ranks of the poor and influenceless women who conduct such establishments. But not a bit of it. A number of middle-class ladies who have done excellent work in securing for women of their own class the right to compete for University degrees and professional diplomas, and with whom, accordingly, the freedom of women from all prescriptive legislation is a fixed idea, rallied to the defence of overtime, gin, and starvation wages, on the ground that if laundry work were done decently and soberly, it would fall into the hands of men. And as they made themselves very disagreeable, and nobody cared particularly for the unfortunate laundrywomen, our linen is still morally dirty. Fortunately common sense forced itself even into the intellectual confusion which ranged Mr. Gerald Balfour shoulder to shoulder and brain to brain with Mr. Jesse Collings against the right of the community to insist on its industries being decently and humanely conducted. The battle for the exclusion of the laundries from the Factory Acts had no sooner been won than the victors grew uneasy; and a number of the Factory Act provisions were hastily slipped back again in Committee, even to the extent of an ineffective restriction of overtime, and a fine of £10 for specially resolute and barefaced attempts to give customers scarlet fever or small-pox.

An evil which touches the general public even more nearly than the condition of the laundries is the condition of the bakehouses. Though the Act of '83 prohibited the unmentionable nastinesses that were once common, a good deal of our daily bread would still not be eaten if the consumers saw it made. We cling to our existing underground bakeries; but the '95 Act at least forbids the establishment of any new ones.

The most disappointing section of the Act is that dealing with outworking, or the giving out of work by the large employer to be done, not in the factory under his own supervision and on his own responsibility, but in the worker's home, or in the sweater's den. Here again we find the worst conditions in the trades which most nearly touch our own persons—our bread treated worse than our underclothing, and our overclothing treated worse than our bread. Take this typical utterance on the subject: —"Going into some workshops," says Mr. Factory Inspector Lakeman, "you find a filthy bed upon which the garments which are made are laid; little children, perfectly naked little things, are lying about the floor and on the beds; frying pans and all sorts of dirty utensils, with food of various descriptions, on the bed, over the bed, everywhere; clothes hanging on a line . . . ashes all flying about, and the atmosphere so dense that you get ill after a night's work there." After the Factory Inspector comes the doctor, with his experience of finding persons in the workshops dying of phthisis, or getting through scarlet fever, small-pox, or measles, with their bedcovering always reinforced by the garments—*our* garments—on which the workers are engaged. It may be supposed that this squalid system at least secures cheapness. But it does nothing of the sort—quite the contrary. The great clothing factories of Leeds, capably managed, with their steam power and machinery, and their enormously better conditions of life for the workers employed, can turn out goods as cheaply as the most abjectly ferocious sweater can. The truth is, the domestic sweater is about as competent to manage an industry as a bargee is to command an ironclad; and the danger to the country of his incompetence is infinitely greater. Experience has by this time placed the remedy beyond all reasonable doubt. Compel the giver-out of work to supply the Factory Inspector with the addresses of the places where the work is done, and to produce a sanitary certificate of their fitness for use as workshops. Make the landlord heavily responsible if his premises are used as workshops without proper sanitary accommodation for such a purpose. If this were effectively done, the sweating game would not be worth the candle. The employer, no longer able to evade his responsibility, would meet it by getting the work done in his own factory. The landlord would not allow his room to be used for purposes which would involve him in the provision of sanitary accommodation on the scale of a railway station. And the tailoring trade, the boot and shoe, slipper and fur, nail and chain trades, would develop in the same beneficial way as the spinning and weaving trades have done, from centres of misery, demoralization, and infection, into great regulated industries.

The effort made by the '95 Act in this direction is a deplorably lame one. Following up the '91 Act, the Home Secretary may specify an area within which the employers in certain specified trades must keep a list of the places at which their given-out work is done, and send a copy of it twice a year to the Factory Inspector. "If," says Miss Abraham, "an Inspector finds that any place where outworkers are employed is injurious or dangerous to their health, he may give notice to the occupier of the factory or workshop or other place from which the work is given out, or to a contractor employed by the occupier, that the place is so injurious or dangerous. Then if, *after a month from the receipt of the notice,* the occupier or contractor gives out work to be done in the same place, the Inspector may proceed against him; and if the Court finds that the place is in fact injurious or dangerous, the occupier or contractor is liable to a penalty not exceeding £10." That is to say, the employer, by simply changing his sweater once a month, can evade the Act altogether; and this in the face of the fact that the whole history of factory legislation is the history of a conflict between ingenious evasion on the one hand and tightening-up to baffle evasion on the other.

Although the Home Secretary gains under the new Act a certain power of prohibiting the employment of any class of persons whatever in the dangerous trades, it is so jealously circumscribed that it is not likely to have much practical effect. Nothing has been done to secure a real half-holiday in the non-textile trades. As might have been expected, a faithless party, a weak Government, and a moribund Ministry gave us an Act just made better than nothing by the bare necessities of the case, and by the efforts of the handful of people, including the author of this book, who did what they could to get something real done, and, for once in a way, were not obstructed and snubbed by the Minister whom they were helping. But what does that matter now? Mr. Asquith, having the choice of being the next Liberal Prime Minister or going back to the Bar, has gone back to the Bar, and negotiates compromises for noble families whose offspring rashly offer their hands to actresses. It is a fine stroke of irony; but it does not promise well for our authors' "majora desiderantes."

I must not conclude without testifying that "hoc opusculum," which costs five shillings, is an excellent practical guide to the Acts now in force and their administration. I have had to refer to it several times for the purposes of this article, and have each time found the information I required concisely and intelligibly given in the handiest form and the likeliest place.

BERNARD SHAW

Editor's Notes

- The above review was first published in the *Saturday Review* 81 (22 February 1896): 192–93.
- This book's full title is *The Law Relating to Factories and Workshops (including Laundries and Docks) Part I: A Practical Guide to the Law and its Administration* by May E. Abraham (One of Her Majesty's Inspectors of Factories). *Part II: The Acts with Notes, containing The Factory and Workshop Acts 1878 to 1895; the Shop Hours Acts, 1892 to 1895; the Truck Acts, 1831 and 1887; Parts of Other Acts Relating to Factories and Workshops; All Orders Made by the Secretary of State under the Factory and Workshop Acts; with Explanatory Notes* by Arthur Llewellyn Davies, Of the Inner Temple, Barrister-at-Law, *With an Appendix containing a full list of Special*

Rules made for Dangerous Employments, and a Complete Index to Both Parts. It is not mentioned in Shaw's *Diary;* nor is its review. During January and February 1896, Shaw was much taken up with the drama, writing *You Never Can Tell,* and reading the finished *Arms and the Man* (1893–94), *Candida* (1894), and *The Man of Destiny* (1895) to groups of friends; while many of his nights were spent visiting other authors' plays, which he now regularly reviewed for the *Saturday Review.* Nevertheless, he still had time for politics. On 10 January 1896, Mrs. Sidney Webb lectured at the Fabian Society on "Women and Factory Legislation," and on 5 February Shaw dined with R. B. Haldane and met Asquith and Arthur Balfour. Either of those events could have provided him with May Abraham's book, or at least the impulse to review it.

- May E. Abraham (1869–1946), Anglo-Irish factory inspector. In 1887 May Abraham came to London to seek her fortune, bringing with her from Ireland an introduction to Emilia [Lady] Dilke, a reformer and member of the Women's Trade Union League, of which May Abraham became treasurer. She later formed an organization of unskilled women to spearhead agitation in an attempt to have laundries included in the upcoming Factory Act, then before the Commons. So much public attention was focused on the poor conditions in which working women existed that a Royal Commission on Labour was set up, and May Abraham was appointed as one of the four female assistant commissioners whose job was to undertake field enquiries for the commission. Following the recommendations of the report, Asquith, home secretary in Gladstone's government, decided to appoint two women to the Inspectorate (of the Factory Department of the Home Office), and in 1893 May Abraham became the first female factory inspector in England. She conducted numerous prosecutions for violations of Factory Act legislation, and pushed for further reforms, particularly the reduction of child labor. Her marriage to Liberal M.P. "Jack" Tennant in 1896 finished her life as a factory inspector, but she still contrived to exert great influence over the consolidating Factory Act of 1901. She later took part in the Royal Commission on Divorce (1909), the Central Committee on Women's Employment (1914), and chaired the Maternal Morality Committee (1928), which supervised the Maternity and Child Welfare Act of 1918.

- Arthur Llewellyn Davies (n.d.). Apart from his collaboration with May Abrahams on the above book, little is known about him, except that he won the Le Bas prize at Cambridge University in 1884 with his essay *Usury in India, with special reference to the condition of the ryots in the Deccan.*

- Herbert Henry [first earl of Oxford and] Asquith (1852–1928), English Liberal statesman. He was Liberal M.P. for East Fife (in Scotland) from 1886 to 1918. He was made home secretary in the Liberal administration of 1892, and remained so during May Abraham's tenure as factory inspector (until 1895). He became prime minister in 1908. His tenure was stormy: he had to cope with the suffragette movement, the threat of civil war over Home Rule for Ireland, and the international crises that precipitated World War I, for the first two years of which he remained prime minister of a coalition government. In 1916 he was ousted by Lloyd George and a group of Conservatives who thought him not aggressive enough in time of war.

- Nassau [William] Senior (1790–1864), English economist, and in 1825 the first holder of the professorship of political economy at Oxford. He was the author of a report upon which was founded the Poor Law of 1834. Senior was particularly influenced by Malthus (see above, 112), whose theory he applied to the reform of the poor laws. He also opposed the trade unions.

- William Morris (see above, 165). The famous *Kelmscott Chaucer* was issued in this very year.

- Shaw in *Major Barbara* (1905) gives dramatic voice to the argument that factory legislation raises the standard of civilization among the protected workers, which, in turn, raises the standard of capacity needed for success in the competitive struggle between the employers. Barbara, who had always thought of her father's armaments factory as a "sort of pit where lost creatures with blackened faces stirred up smoky fires and were driven and tormented," is reassured by Undershaft: "My dear, it is a spotlessly clean and beautiful hillside town." It is Stephen Undershaft who indirectly touches on the problem raised by Shaw in this review of whether it is possible to overdo the benefits.

- Gerald [William, second earl of] Balfour (1853–1945), Scottish politician. Brother of Arthur Balfour (1848–1930), Scottish statesman and philosopher (see below, 425). He was chief secretary for Ireland from 1895 to 1896, president of the Board of Trade from 1900 to 1908, and the local government board from 1905 to 1906.

- Jesse Collings (1831–1920), English politician. He was elected Radical for Ipswich in 1880, was a Unionist from 1868 to 1918; at the time of the above review he was undersecretary for the Home Office.

- The Factory and Workshop Act of 1883 subjected bakehouses to special requirements, but only *newly erected* bakehouses! The remainder were extremely unsanitary.

- The Factory and Workshop Act of 1895, in brief, dealt with overcrowding, the sanitary conditions for outworkers (that is, those who take work home to complete it), provision of lavatories, ventilation, fencing off of dangerous machinery, and took within its purview premises omitted from previous acts, such as laundries, docks, wharves, and quays. It also made the owner of a tenement factory (that is, a building containing several factories) liable for prosecution if the above standards were not met, extended its coverage to *all* bakehouses, and prohibited the construction of underground bakehouses for the future; though it still allowed existing underground bakehouses to operate.

- A "bargee" was a man who worked on a sailing barge, and an "ironclad" was an armor-plated vessel, therefore a warship.

- The Liberal defeat in 1895 left Asquith out of office for eleven years and, as Asquith himself remarked, "it was necessary to find *de quoi vivre*." He had no independent means, and the loss of his ministerial salary was a blow. In consequence, Asquith decided to return to his work as a barrister; and this excited much comment (besides that of Shaw) because it was unprecedented that a minister who had exercised judicial functions in the capacity of home secretary should resume the position of an advocate.

11 April 1896

NIETZSCHE IN ENGLISH* [C1131]

IT is with a most opportune consideration for my Easter holiday that Messrs. Henry & Co. have just issued the first volume of their translation of the works of Friedrich Nietzsche. And such a volume, too! containing everything that he wrote just before he reached the point at which Germany made up its mind that he was mad, and shut him up, both figuratively and actually. Whilst I am still at large I may as well explain that Nietzsche is a philosopher—that is to say, something unintelligible to an Englishman. To make my readers realize what a philosopher is, I can only say that I am a philosopher. If you ask incredulously, "How, then, are your articles so interesting?" I reply that there is nothing so interesting as philosophy, provided its materials are not spurious. For instance, take my own materials—humanity and the fine arts. Any studious, timorously ambitious bookworm can run away from the world with a few shelvesful of history, essays, descriptions, and criticisms, and, having pieced an illusory humanity and art out of the effects produced by his library on his imagination, build some silly systematization of his worthless ideas over the abyss of his own nescience. Such a philosopher is as dull and dry as you please: it is he who brings his profession into disrepute, especially when he talks much about art, and so persuades people to read him. Without having looked at more than fifty pictures in his life, or made up his mind on the smallest point about one of the fifty, he will audaciously take it upon himself to explain the development of painting from Zeuxis and Apelles to Raphael and Michael Angelo. As to the

---

* *Nietzsche contra Wagner, &c.* Vol. 1. of the *Collected Works of Friedrich Nietzsche.* Trans. Thomas Common. (London: Henry, 1896.)

way he will go on about music, of which he always has an awe-stricken conceit, it spoils my temper to think of it, especially when one remembers that musical composition is taught (a monstrous pretension) in this country by people who *read* scores, and never by any chance listen to performances. Now, the right way to go to work—strange as it may appear—is to look at pictures until you have acquired the power of seeing them. If you look at several thousand good pictures every year, and form some sort of practical judgment about every one of them—were it only that it is not worth troubling over—then at the end of five years or so you will, if you have a wise eye, be able to see what is actually in a picture, and not what you think is in it. Similarly, if you listen critically to music every day for a number of years, you will, if you have a wise ear, acquire the power of hearing music. And so on with all the arts. When we come to humanity it is still the same: only by intercourse with men and women can we learn anything about it. This involves an active life, not a contemplative one; for unless you do something in the world, you can have no real business to transact with men; and unless you love and are loved, you can have no intimate relations with them. And you must transact business, wirepull politics, discuss religion, give and receive hate, love and friendship with all sorts of people before you can acquire the sense of humanity. If you are to acquire the sense sufficiently to be a philosopher, you must do all these things unconditionally. You must not say that you will be a gentleman and limit your intercourse to this class or that class; or that you will be a virtuous person and generalize about the affections from a single instance—unless, indeed, you have the rare happiness to stumble at first upon an all-enlightening instance. You must have no convictions, because, as Nietzsche puts it, "convictions are prisons." Thus, I blush to add, you cannot be a philosopher and a good man, though you may be a philosopher and a great one. You will say, perhaps, that if this be so, there should be no philosophers; and perhaps you are right; but though I make you this handsome concession, I do not defer to you to the extent of ceasing to exist. After all, if you insist on the hangman, whose pursuits are far from elevating, you may very well tolerate the philosopher, even if philosophy involves philandering; or, to put it another way, if, in spite of your hangman, you tolerate murder within the sphere of war, it may be necessary to tolerate comparatively venial irregularities within the sphere of philosophy. It is the price of progress; and, after all, it is the philosopher, and not you, who will burn for it.

These are shocking sentiments, I know; but I assure you you will think them mere Sunday School commonplaces when you have read a little of Nietzsche. Nietzsche is worse than shocking, he is simply awful: his epigrams are written with phosphorus on brimstone. The only excuse for reading them is that before long you must be prepared either to talk about Nietzsche or else retire from society, especially from aristocratically minded society (not the same thing, by the way, as aristocratic society), since Nietzsche is the champion of privilege, of power, and of inequality. Famous as Nietzsche has become—he has had a great *succès de scandale* to advertise his penetrating wit—I never heard of him until a few years ago, when, on the occasion of my contributing to the literature of philosophy a minute treatise entitled "The Quintessence of Ibsenism," I was asked whether I had not been inspired by a book called "Out at the other side of Good and Evil," by Nietzsche. The title seemed to me promising; and in fact Nietzsche's criticism of morality and idealism is essentially that demonstrated in my book as at the bottom of Ibsen's plays. His pungency; his power of putting the merest platitudes of his position in rousing, startling paradoxes; his way of getting underneath moral precepts which are so unquestionable to us that common decency seems to compel unhesitating assent to them, and upsetting them with a scornful laugh: all this is easy to a witty man who has once well learnt Schopenhauer's lesson, that the intellect by itself is a mere dead piece of brain machinery, and our ethical and moral systems merely the pierced cards you stick into it when you want it to play a certain tune. So far I am on common ground with Nietzsche. But not for a moment will I suffer any one to compare me to him as a critic. Never was there a deafer, blinder, socially and politically inepter academician. He has fancies concerning different periods of history, idealizing the Romans and the Renascence, and deducing from his idealization no end of excellences in their works. When have I ever been guilty of such professorial folly? I simply go and look at their works, and after that you may talk to me until you go black in the face about their being such wonderful fellows: I know by my senses that they were as bad artists, and as arrant intellect-mongers, as need be. And what can you say to a man who, after pitting his philosophy against Wagner's with refreshing ingenuity and force, proceeds to hold up as the masterpiece of modern dramatic music, blazing with the merits which the Wagnerian music dramas lack—guess what! "Don Giovanni," perhaps, or "Orfeo," or "Fidelio"? Not at all: "Carmen," no less. Yes, as I live by bread, as I made that bread for many a year by listening to music, Georges Bizet's "Carmen." After this one is not surprised to find Nietzsche blundering over politics, and social organization and administration in a way that would be impossible to a man who had ever served on a genuine working committee long enough—say ten minutes—to find out how very little attention the exigencies of practical action can be made to pay to our theories when we have to get things done, one way or another. To him modern Democracy, Pauline Christianity, Socialism, and so on are deliberate plots hatched by malignant philosophers to frustrate the evolution of the human race and mass the stupidity and brute force of the many weak against the beneficial tyranny of the few strong. This is not even a point of view: it is an absolutely fictitious hypothesis: it would not be worth reading were it not that there is almost as much evidence for it as if it were true, and that it leads Nietzsche to produce some new and very striking and suggestive combinations of ideas. In short, his sallies, petulant and impossible as some of them are, are the work of a rare spirit and are pregnant with its vitality. It is notable that Nietzsche does not write in chapters or treatises: he writes leading articles, leaderettes, occasional notes, and epigrams. He recognizes that humanity, having tasted the art of the journalist, will no longer suffer men to inflict books on it. And he simplifies matters, quite in the manner of the leading article writer, by ignoring things as they are, and dealing with things as it is easiest, with our prejudices and training, to think they are, except that he supplies the training and instils the prejudices himself as he goes along, instead of picking up those that lie about the street as one does in writing leaders for the daily press.

There are two reasons why I can say no more than this about Nietzsche. The first is that I am lying on a hillside in the sun, basking, not working. The second is that I must reserve some space for Miss Clo Graves's "Mother of Three" at the Comedy, which has plucked me up from that hillside by the roots . . .

G.B.S.

Editor's Notes

- The above review was first published in the *Saturday Review* 81 (11 April 1896): 373–74. The original article also contained a notice of a play entitled *A Mother of Three. A New and Original Farce in Three Acts*. By Clo. Graves, which Shaw saw at the Comedy Theatre, 8 April 1896. Extracts of the review were reprinted in *Nietzsche, Friedrich, Thus Spake Zarathustra,* trans. Thomas Common (London: William Reeves, 1902), and the whole article was reprinted in Bernard Shaw, *Dramatic Opinions and Essays* (1906), and in *Our Theatres in the Nineties* (1932), ii, 92–98.

▪ There is no reference in Shaw's *Diary* as to when Shaw wrote the above review; however, its last paragraph suggests that it was finished on 8 April 1896, while Shaw was staying at Stocks Cottage, Aldbury, near Tring in Hertfordshire with Graham Wallas. That day he came back to London by the 4:51 P.M. train to attend the first night of Clo Graves's play (see below).

▪ Friedrich [Wilhelm] Nietzsche (1844–1900) German philosopher. At first influenced by both Schopenhauer (see above, 174–75), and Wagner (see above, 230–37), the rationale of whose music drama he expounded in his essay *Die Geburt der Tragödie aus dem Geiste der Musik [The birth of tragedy from the spirit of music]* (1872), as Nietzsche developed his own philosophy, he began to believe that the pessimism in Schopenhauer negated the life impulse and that Wagner's music was primarily a narcotic for a decadent age. After bouts of illness, Nietzsche was forced to resign his post at the University of Basel in 1878, and spent the next decade writing at various French and Swiss health resorts. Finally, in 1889, after producing some of his most powerful writings, *Menschliches-Allzu Menschliches [Human, all too human]* (1878–80); *Also Sprach Zarathustra [Thus spake Zarathustra]* (1883–84); *Jenseits von Gut und Böse [Beyond good and evil]* (1886); *Zur Genealogie der Moral [On the genealogy of morality]* (1887), Nietzsche suffered a mental breakdown. He retired to Weimar (to his mother's home) where his sister Elizabeth cared for him until he died. Nietzsche is best remembered in the popular imagination for having glorified the *Übermensch* ["overman" or "superman"], and the latter's ruthless will to power. When Shaw published *Man and Superman* in 1903 many critics (among them Shaw's friends William Archer and G. K. Chesterton) saw it as a dramatization of Nietzschean theory. Shaw, however, in a letter to Archibald Henderson (and elsewhere) makes it clear that his view of the superman/slave question was more political than psychological; that is, more akin to that of the Scot Stuart Glennie, who saw the supermen as white races exploiting other nations, than Nietzsche's view that weaknesses idealized as "virtues" constituted a self-imposed "morality" imposed by the second-rate on themselves.

▪ Thomas Common. Unidentified translator.

▪ In Shaw's play *The Philanderer,* written three years before this review but as yet unperformed, the leading character Charteris, a thinly veiled portrait of Shaw himself, describes himself as a philosopher; and in 1902, Shaw would write to Siegfried Trebitsch (his German translator): "I want the Germans to know me as a philosopher, as an English [or Irish] Nietzsche [only ten times cleverer]" (*Collected Letters 1898–1910,* 298).

▪ Zeuxis was a fifth century B.C. Greek painter who excelled in representing natural objects (allegedly painting a bunch of grapes so realistically that birds tried to eat them), and Apelles was a fourth-century B.C. Greek painter, whose work is also known only through ancient writings.

- Schopenhauer (see above, 174–75).
- *Don Giovanni* (1787) is by Wolfgang Amadeus Mozart, *Orfeo* (1607) is by Claudio Monteverdi, and *Fidelio* (1805) is by Ludwig van Beethoven.
- Clo[tilde Inez Mary] Graves (1863–1932), Irish short story writer, novelist, and dramatist. *A Mother of Three* was her second attempt at drama, in which—as Shaw observed—"struck . . . by the success of Charley's Aunt and The Strange Adventures of Miss Brown, in which the main joke is the dressing up of a man as a woman, [Miss Graves] has tried the effect of dressing up a woman as a man." Shaw found that there was "plenty of fun in it; and in that fun there lurks occasionally a certain sense of the humour of indecency which drives me to conclude that Miss Clo Graves is an Irish lady." Clo Graves wrote twenty novels and volumes of stories; and from 1911 began to publish large historical novels under the pseudonym "Richard Dehan."

1 July 1896
OUR BOOK-SHELF:
"THE ECONOMICS OF SOCIALISM"*
[C1144]

THIS book is announced as "intended to supply a want, frequently expressed by opponents of Social-Democracy, namely, that there is no standard work on Economics from the Socialist standpoint." The Twentieth Century Press, in inviting the Fabian Society to review it, places us in a position of some difficulty. Mr. Hyndman, speaking of the economics of "Fabian Essays," says, "It would be mere waste of time to call attention to such nonsense, but that I believe it still has some influence with the ignorant." Now, if we praise our genial comrade, he will, on hearing applause from such a quarter, exclaim, with the Greek orator, "What foolish thing have I said?" On the other hand, if we venture to express a modest disagreement with him, we shall be taxed with resentful spite. For Mr. Hyndman is very severe with his

---

* "The Economics of Socialism." By H. M. Hyndman. (Twentieth Century Press, 1896.) Price 3s.

critics. "Seeing," he declares, "that a well-known Professor actually argued with me at a public meeting against the social labor value theory on the ground that crinolines when out of fashion were of little value and were disposed of for next to nothing, thus omitting to consider that, when first in fashion, they sold for many times their labor value—Seeing, I say, that such crass mental carelessness as this passes muster for controversy even among the intelligent, it is almost impossible to set a limit to the ignorance of the learned." Apparently the poor Professor's only sin was in omitting to point out that "the social labor value theory" was wrong both ways; and yet how unmercifully Mr. Hyndman lashes him for him his considerateness! We shall take warning by his fate and leave this terrible Marxist alone, merely whispering to our readers that the recently published third volume of Marx's "Capital" flatly contradicts—as the Fabians always said it would—Mr. Hyndman's repeated assertions that "all commodities which appear on the market of the world for exchange are estimated relatively to one another as portions of the amount of necessary social labor exerted by human beings to produce them—aliquot parts of the social labor day, or week, or month—measured by time." Finally, we give Mr. Hyndman's summing up of the rent question for the delight of the Anarchists, who, to do them justice, have always been exactly of his opinion in the matter. "When private property ceases, when human beings cease to strive against one another, and antagonistic classes cease to be, rent will cease too. Rent, in short, will no more exist under the Communism of the future than it existed under the Communism of the past; and the very idea of rent being exacted under Socialism in order to stop a fight for a dwelling on Richmond Hill [see Fabian Tract No. 45, "The Impossibilities of Anarchism," for the explanation of this friendly remark] will be regarded by coming generations, if they ever hear of that absurd figment of the imagination, as conclusive evidence of the narrowminded prejudices of the educated middle class of the nineteenth century." On the whole, we can but congratulate the Twentieth Century Press on the completeness with which it has carried out its intention of providing "a work on Economics from the Socialist standpoint" which shall "supply a want frequently expressed by the opponents of Social-Democracy." An author better equipped for that mission than Mr. Hyndman could not have been found.

To the friends of Social-Democracy we recommend Mr. Hyndman's portrait-frontispiece, and the many pages in which, forgetting the obstinate heresy of the Fabian Society, he is entertainingly loquacious in his own buoyant fashion. A cheap edition of the book, with all the economics left out, would be welcome to most of us.

G. B. S.

Editor's Notes

- The above review first appeared in *Fabian News* 6 (July 1896): 21–22, but there is no reference to it in Shaw's *Diary*.
- H. M. Hyndman (see above, 20).
- Shaw had contributed the Economic essay in *Fabian Essays* (1889), which, like the other essays in the book, was a revision of public lectures delivered the previous year.
- The "Greek orator" was Phocion, by common consent the most honest statesman of his time; one who so despised the Assembly, that when it applauded him he asked a friend "What foolish thing have I said?" (or, in some translations "Have I not unconsciously said something bad?")
- The explanation of the "friendly remark" about fighting "for a dwelling in Richmond Hill" is to be found on page 8 of Fabian Tract No. 45, *The Impossibilities of Anarchism,* a paper by Shaw himself, read to the Fabian Society on 16 October 1891, and published in 1893. In it, he ridicules the American anarchist Benjamin Tucker's notion that the occupier—the actual worker—in a business should also be its owner. What would happen, queried Shaw, when his retirement from his place of business would still leave the worker in possession, as occupying owner, of his private residence? particularly since "this might be of exceptional or even unique desirability in point of situation. It might, for instance, be built on Richmond Hill, and command from its windows the beautiful view of the Thames valley to be obtained from that spot. Now it is clear that Richmond Hill will not accommodate all the people who would rather live there than in the Essex marshes. It is easy to say, Let the owner be the occupier; but the question is, Who is the occupier? Suppose it were settled by drawing lots, what would prevent the winner from selling his privilege for its full (unearned) value under free exchange and omnipresent competition?" (Bernard Shaw,*The Impossibilities of Anarchism* [London: Fabian Society, 1893], 8–9).
- The tone of this review reveals the relationship that existed between Shaw and Hyndman at this date. The mannerisms of the expostulatory Hyndman had already been satirized dramatically by Shaw in *The Philanderer* (1893) in the person of Craven. Hyndman, for his part, three months later (on 20 October) in the *Saint James's Gazette* attacked Shaw over the latter's article on the death of Morris; and this, in turn led to a rebuttal from Shaw.

8 January 1898

THE WISDOM OF THE WEBBS* [C1246]

[PUBLISHED THIS WEEK]

IT is an ill wind that blows nobody any good. The luck that follows ability and energy has come to Mr. and Mrs. Sidney Webb in the shape of an industrial dispute which makes the subject of their magnum opus all-important at the moment of its publication. "Industrial Democracy" is one of those books before which the candid reviewer throws up the sponge. When one of our cleverest politicians and most successful administrators takes to wife a trained investigator of equally conspicuous enterprise and ingenuity, and the twain devote six years' time and trouble, and a sum running into four figures for special out-of-pocket expenses alone, to an industrial inquiry mainly concerning districts in which it is easier to find an auk or a dodo than a man of letters, the academician who does not wish to make himself ridiculous will frankly leave the responsibility for nine-tenths of their report with its authors, and admit that the only verdict that can decide its value is the verdict of history. All that can be said is that if the startling group, or rather crowd, of novel and illuminating conclusions here put forward with a mass of apparently unanswerable evidence, stands the test of the industrial development of the next fifty years, "Industrial Democracy" will be the "Wealth of Nations" of the twentieth century.

Let us make a dash at a few of the points likely to be pounced on at the present moment. How, for instance, does the new Webb wisdom bear on the Engineers' Lock-out? Very enlighteningly and very trenchantly indeed, though we doubt whether either the engineers or their employers will be clever or studious enough to piece together the passages that concern them, and construct their case accordingly. If they do, they will learn many things. First, that the authors regard the aspiration of the more extreme section of the employers to demolish Trade Unionism as precisely on a par, in point of ignorance and unsanctified simplicity, with the resistance of the greener sort of trade-unionist to machinery. Second, that the employers could state a con-

---

* "Industrial Democracy." By Sidney and Beatrice Webb. 2 vols. (London: Longmans.)

vincing case on many points, not against Trade Unionism, but against the Amalgamated Society of Engineers. Third, that the constitution of the A.S.E., allowing of unauthorized and unconcerted local strikes at the expense of the whole union, and aiming at the amalgamation of trades which should be federated instead, makes it intolerable, not only to the employers, but to the other unions, thus explaining why the document which the employers took as their brief at the late conference was actually the manifesto of one of the most important trade-unionists in the kingdom, Mr. Robert Knight, the generalissimo of the Boilermakers. Fourth, that the employers would have won hands down if they had known what they were about, and not suffered their Hotspurs to betray them into the mere class folly of a London clubman's attack on Trade Unionism. All this might have been turned to good account by the masters had it been put into their hands a few months ago. But it is here associated with so well marshalled a case in favour of collective bargaining that, as things now stand, the likelihood is that the general body of trade-unionists, who would undoubtedly, and for good reasons, have been by no means sorry to see the A.S.E. get a sound drubbing on any issue peculiar to itself, will now come to the rescue. The same want of science in industrial policy that led the employers to attack collective bargaining unintentionally in the confusion of the struggle will equally prevent them from effectively disclaiming their blunder.

Mr. and Mrs. Webb appear in their well-known character of Fabian Collectivists in their preference for legal enactment before collective bargain, and, above all, in their uncompromising demand, supported by a most formidable mass of illustration and argument, for the legal establishment of a minimum standard of subsistence, including wages as well as sanitation and hours of labour, in all industries. In this connexion it is impossible not to be struck by their adroit contrast between the decay of British agriculture as an unregulated industry with a consequent abjectly low standard of wage for its employees and of ability for its farmer-organizers, and the immense advances made in our factory industries in direct proportion to the stress of regulation imposed on them by the Factory Acts, with the consequent forcing up of the condition of the workers, and of the degree and quality of the ability indispensable to a successful employer. This may be taken as an example of the effective special pleading in which the book abounds— a special pleading which will probably carry the verdict of a heavy majority of the national jury in the end unless counsel on the other side wake up very considerably from their self-satisfied academic lethargy.

Neo-Protectionists will find the lines of defence for Free Trade puz-zlingly shifted. According to Mr. and Mrs. Webb, foreign competition is not, as it is always assumed to be, international competition. Given a certain demand for exports to pay for imports,the real competition is between the various English trades to decide what the exports shall consist of. Thus Lancashire cotton competes for its share of our foreign trade, not with Bombay cotton, but with Cleveland minerals, Northamp-ton boots, Sheffield saws, and matches and sweated clothes from Bow and Stepney. In this competition excellence counts for a good deal; but, unfortunately, cheapness counts for more. Consequently the foreign trade falls into the hands of the best and worst trades, especially the worst. Now, it is contended, all the worst trades are what the authors call "parasitic trades:" that is, instead of paying their way by supporting their own labour, they employ women living partly at the expense of their families on wages earned by their fathers in other trades, which are thus made to subsidise the "parasitic trades." Mr. and Mrs. Webb advocate, with unapologetic directness, and with a cogency appalling to the laissez-faire school, the screwing up of these parasitic industries to self-supporting point by an iron law of minimum, and are prompt with their demonstration that if such stress of regulation screws any industry out of existence we shall be well rid of it.

On the Malthusian problem the authors do not mince matters as regards its change of aspect during the last twenty years. In the seventies the population question, meaning always the inevitability of an increase of children following an increase of wages, was the unan-swerable objection to all Collectivist schemes of Social reform. Henry George's vehement attack on Mill's statement of it shows how impor-tant it seemed. To-day that attack is the idlest of library curiosities. The population is at present deliberately restricted artificially except in those sections of the labouring class where poverty and reckless-ness make even the least expensive providential measures impossible. To old-fashioned readers the most disquieting pages in "Industrial Democracy" will be those statistical charts which prove, apparently beyond question, that an advance in wages is now-a-days followed with the utmost certainty by a decrease in the rate of multiplication of the class earning it.

There is a highly entertaining and novel chapter on a very dry and hackneyed subject: to wit, the higgling of the market. Even the econo-mists will be tickled by the unexpectedness with which the familiar Socialist exposition of the disadvantages at which the workman higgles with the manufacturer is followed by a demonstration that the manufacturer himself is similarly oppressed by the wholesale trader, the trader by the shopkeeper, and the shopkeeper by the customer. In fact, there is no subject, however often it has been threshed out academically, on which the authors' first-hand investigations and thoroughly concrete and contemporary methods have not led them to conclusions, or at least pregnant observations, which make it very dangerous for the doctrinaire reviewer to glance at the heading, skip the chapter, and jump to the conclusion.

There is nothing more to be said. The book is either the most remarkable economic treatise of the nineteenth century, or else the most plausible of its pseudo-scientific delusions.

Editor's Notes

- The above review was first published in the *Saturday Review* 85 (8 January, 1898): 51–52. It was reprinted in the *American Fabian* (New York) 4 (February 1898): 14.
- On 23 July 1892, Sidney Webb (see above, 139) married [Martha] Beatrice Potter (1858–1943), who, though from a wealthy background, had become equally active in social reform under the influence of Joseph Chamberlain (whom she almost married). She studied economics and philosophy (one of her earlier mentors had been Herbert Spencer), and worked in the East End of London among the poor. She met Sidney Webb in 1890, in which year he introduced her to Shaw at a Fabian meeting. Shaw regularly had Sunday lunch with them during the 1890s, forming a friendship with Beatrice who allegedly provided the stimulus for Shaw's writing *Mrs. Warren's Profession* (1893); in the late summer of 1895, Shaw finished writing *The Man of Destiny* while staying with the Webbs. Their ashes were buried in Westminster Abbey.
- From July 1897 to January 1898 there was a national lockout in the engineering industry, and the unions were forced to reduce their demands.
- Shaw refers to the two large flightless extinct birds, the dodo, which formerly inhabited Mauritius and was last observed in 1681, and the great auk, which was hunted till about 1850.
- Adam Smith (1723–90), Scottish philosopher and economist. His celebrated treatise on political economy *An Inquiry into the Nature and Causes of the Wealth of Nations* (1776), to which Shaw refers, was the first comprehensive treatment of political economy. It sets out with the doctrine that the labor of the nation (and not land, as claimed by the French Physiocrats) is the source of its means of life. Shaw had favorably reviewed Bohn's Standard Library edition of this work (with an introduction by E. Belfort Bax) for the *Pall Mall Gazette* on 16 September 1887, and also wrote a note for the *Com-*

monweal Calendar on the anniversary of Smith's death in June 1888, in which he found the treatise not "old-fashioned."
▪ Malthus (see above, 112).

10 September 1898

TOLSTOY ON ART* [C1289]

LIKE all Tolstoy's didactic writings, this book is a most effective boobytrap. It is written with so utter a contempt for the objections which the routine critic is sure to allege against it, that many a dilletantist reviewer has already accepted it as a butt set up by Providence to show off his own brilliant marksmanship. It seems so easy to dispose of a naif who moralises on the Trojan war as if it were a historical event!

Yet Tolstoy will be better understood in this volume than in his Christian epistles, because art is at present a more fashionable subject than Christianity. Most people have a loose impression that Tolstoy as a Christian represents Evangelicalism gone mad. As a matter of fact, Tolstoy's position, as explained by himself, is, from the Evangelical point of view, as novel as it is blasphemous. What Evangelicalism calls revelation, vouchsafed to man's incapacity by Divine wisdom, Tolstoy declares to be a piece of common sense so obvious as to make its statement in the gospels superfluous. "I will go further," he says. "This truth [resist not evil] appears to me so simple and so clear that I am persuaded I should have found it out by myself, even if Christ and His doctrine had never existed." Blasphemy can go no further than this from the point of view of the Bible-worshipper. Again he says, "I beg you, in the name of the God of truth whom you adore, not to fly out at me, nor to begin looking for arguments to oppose me with, before you have meditated, not on what I am going to write to you, but on the gospel; and not on the gospel as the word of God or of Christ, but on the gospel considered as the neatest, simplest, most comprehensible and most practical doctrine on the way in which men ought to live."

---

* "What is Art?" By Leo Tolstoy. Translation from the Russian original by Aylmer Maude, embodying the Author's last alterations and revisions. (London: The Brotherhood.)

What makes this attitude of Tolstoy's so formidable to Christians who feel that it condemns their own systematic resistance to evil, is the fact that he is a man with a long, varied and by no means exclusively pious experience of worldly life. In vain do we spend hours in a highly superior manner in proving that Tolstoy's notions are unpractical, visionary: in short, cranky; we cannot get the sting and the startle out of his flat challenge as to how much we have done and where we have landed ourselves by the opposite policy. No doubt the challenge does not make all of us uneasy. But may not that be because he sees the world from behind the scenes of politics and society, whilst most of us are sitting to be gulled in the pit? For, alas! nothing is plainer to the dupe of all the illusions of civilisation than the folly of the seer who penetrates them.

If Tolstoy has made himself so very disquieting by criticising the world as a man of the world, he has hardly made himself more agreeable by criticising art as an artist of the first rank. Among the minor gods of the amateur he kindles a devastating fire. Naturally, the very extensive literary output of delirium tremens in our century receives no quarter from him: he has no patience with nonsense, especially drunken nonsense, however laboriously or lusciously it may be rhymed or alliterated. But he spares nobody wholly, dealing unmercifully with himself, sweeping away Mr. Rudyard Kipling with the French decadents, and heaping derision on Wagner. Clearly, this book of his will not be valued for its specific criticisms, some of which, if the truth must be told, represent nothing but the inevitable obsolescence of an old man's taste in art. To justify them, Tolstoy applies a test highly characteristic of the Russian aristocrat. A true work of art, he maintains, will always be recognized by the unsophisticated perception of the peasant folk. Hence, Beethoven's Ninth Symphony, not being popular among the Russian peasantry, is not a true work of art!

Leaving the Ninth Symphony to take care of itself, one cannot help being struck by the fact that Russian revolutionists of noble birth invariably display what appears to us a boundless credulity concerning the virtues of the poor. No English county magnate has any doubt as to which way an English agricultural laborer would choose between Tolstoy's favorite Chopin nocturne (admitted by him to be true art) and the latest music-hall tune. We know perfectly well that the simplicity of our peasants' lives is forced on them by their poverty, and could be dispelled at any moment by a sufficient legacy. We know that the equality which seems to the rich man to be accepted among laborers (because he himself makes no distinction among them) is an illusion, and that social distinctions are more pitifully cherished by our poor than by any other class until we get down to the residuum which has not self-respect enough even for snobbery. Now, whether it is that the Russian peasantry, being illiterate and outlandish, has never been absorbed by European civilisation as ours has been, or else that the distance between peasant and noble in Russia is so great that the two classes do not know one another, and fill up the void in their knowledge by millennial romancing, certain it is that the Russian nobles Kropotkin and Tolstoy, who have come into our counsels on the side of the people, seem to assume that the laboring classes have entirely escaped the class vices, follies and prejudices of the bourgeoisie.

If it were not for this unmistakeable error in Tolstoy's premisses, it would be very difficult to dissent from any of his judgments on works of art without feeling in danger of merely providing him with an additional example of the corruption of taste which he deplores. But when his objection to a masterpiece is based solely on the incapacity of a peasant to enjoy it or understand it, the misgiving vanishes. Everything that he says in condemnation of modern society is richly deserved by it; but if it were true that the working classes, numbering, say, four-fifths of the population, had entirely escaped the penalties of civilisation, and were in a state so wholesomely natural and benevolent that Beethoven must stand condemned by their coldness towards his symphonies, then his whole case against civilisation must fall to the ground, since such a majority for good would justify any social system. In England, at least, one cannot help believing that if Tolstoy were reincarnated as a peasant he would find that the proletarian morality in which he has so much faith is nothing but the morality of his own class, modified, mostly for the worse, by ignorance, drudgery, insufficient food, and bad sanitary conditions of all kinds. It is true that the absolutely idle class has a peculiar and exasperating nonentity and futility, and that this class wastes a great deal of money in false art; but it is not numerically a very large class. The demand of the professional and mercantile classes is quite sufficient to maintain a considerable body of art, the defects of which cannot be ascribed to the idleness of its patrons.

If due allowance be made for those considerations which, be it remembered, weaken society's defence and not Tolstoy's attack, this book will be found extraordinarily interesting and enlightening. We must agree with him when he says, "To thoughtful and sincere people there can be no doubt that the art of the upper classes can never be the art of the whole people." Only, we must make the same reservation with regard to the art of the lower classes. And we must not forget that there is nothing whatever to choose between the average country gentleman and the gamekeeper in respect of distaste for the Ninth Symphony.

Tolstoy's main point, however, is the establishment of his definition of art. It is, he says, "an activity by means of which one man, having experienced a feeling, intentionally transmits it to others." This is the simple truth: the moment it is uttered, whoever is really conversant with art recognizes in it the voice of the master. None the less is Tolstoy perfectly aware that this is not the usual definition of art, which amateurs delight to hear described as that which produces beauty. Tolstoy's own Christian view of how he should treat the professors of this or any other heresy is clearly laid down in those articles of faith, already quoted above, which conclude his "Plaisirs Cruels." "To dispute with those who are in error is to waste labor and spoil our exposition of the truth. It provokes us to say things that we do not mean, to formulate paradoxes, to exaggerate our thought, and, leaving on one side the essential part of our doctrine, play off tricks of logic on the slips which have provoked us." Fortunately for the entertainment of the readers of "What is Art?" Tolstoy does not carry out his own precepts in it. Backsliding without the slightest compunction into the character of a first rate fighting man, he challenges all the authorities, great and small, who have committed themselves to the beauty theory, and never quits them till he has left them for dead. There is always something especially exhilarating in the spectacle of a Quaker fighting; and Tolstoy's performance in this kind will not soon be forgotten. Our generation has not seen a heartier bout of literary fisticuffs, or one in which the challenger has been more brilliantly victorious.

Since no man, however indefatigable a reader he may be, can make himself acquainted with all that Europe has to say on any subject of general interest, it seldom happens that any great champion meets the opponent we would most like to see him join issue with. For this reason we hear nothing from Tolstoy of William Morris's definition of art as the expression of pleasure in work. This is not exactly the beauty doctrine: it recognizes, as Tolstoy's definition does, that art is the expression of feeling; but it covers a good deal of art work which, whilst proving the artist's need for expression, does not convince us that the artist wanted to convey his feeling to others. There have been many artists who have taken great pains to express themselves to themselves in works of art, but whose action, as regards the circulation of those works, has very evidently been dictated by love of fame or money rather than by any yearning for emotional intercourse with their fellow creatures. It is, of course, easy to say that the works of such men are not true art; but if they convey feeling to others, sometimes more successfully and keenly than some of the works which fall within Tolstoy's definition, the distinction is clearly not a practical one. The truth is that definitions which are applied on the principle that whatever is not white is black never are quite practical. The only safe plan is to ascertain the opposite extremes of artistic motive, determine which end of the scale between them is the higher and which the lower, and place each work in question in its right position on the scale. There are plenty of passages in this very book of Tolstoy's—itself a work of art according to its own definition—which have quite clearly been written to relieve the craving for expression of the author's own combativeness, or fun, or devotion, or even cleverness, and would probably have been written equally had he been the most sardonic pessimist that ever regarded his fellow creatures as beyond redemption.

Tolstoy's justification in ignoring these obvious objections to the accuracy and universality of his treatise is plain enough. Art is socially important—that is, worth writing a book about—only in so far as it wields that power of propagating feeling which he adopts as his criterion of true art. It is hard to knock this truth into the heads of the English nation. We admit the importance of public opinion, which, in a country without intellectual habits (our own, for example), depends altogether on public feeling. Yet, instead of perceiving the gigantic importance which this gives to the theatre, the concert room, and the bookshop as forcing houses of feeling, we slight them as mere places of amusement, and blunder along upon the assumption that the House of Commons, and the platitudes of a few old-fashioned leader writers, are the chief fountains of English sentiment. Tolstoy knows better than that.

> Look carefully [he says] into the causes of the ignorance of the masses, and you may see that the chief cause does not at all lie in the lack of schools and libraries, as we are accustomed to suppose, but in those superstitions, both ecclesiastical and patriotic, with which the people are saturated, and which are unceasingly generated by all the methods of art. Church superstitions are supported and produced by the poetry of prayers, hymns, painting; by the sculpture of images and of statues; by singing, by organs, by music, by architecture, and even by dramatic art in religious ceremonies. Patriotic superstitions are

supported and produced by verses and stories, which are supplied even in schools; by music, by songs, by triumphal processions, by royal meetings, by martial pictures, and by monuments. Were it not for this continual activity in all departments of art, perpetuating the ecclesiastical and patriotic intoxication and embitterment of the people, the masses would long ere this have attained to true enlightenment.

It does not at all detract from the value of Tolstoy's thesis that what he denounces as superstitions may appear to many to be wholesome enthusiasms and fruitful convictions. Still less does it matter that his opinions of individual artists are often those of a rather petulant veteran who neither knows nor wants to know much of works that are too new to please him. The valid point is that our artistic institutions are vital social organs, and that the advance of civilisation tends constantly to make them, especially in the presence of democratic institutions and compulsory schooling, more important than the political and ecclesiastical institutions whose traditional prestige is so much greater. We are too stupid to learn from epigrams; otherwise Fletcher of Saltoun's offer to let whoever wished make the laws of the nation provided he made its songs, would have saved Tolstoy the trouble of telling us the same thing in twenty chapters. At all events, we cannot now complain of want of instruction. With Mr. Ashton Ellis's translation of Wagner's Prose to put on the shelves of our libraries beside the works of Ruskin, and this pregnant and trenchant little volume of Tolstoy's to drive the moral home, we shall have ourselves to thank if we do not take greater care of our art in the future than of any other psychological factor in the destiny of the nation.

G. B. S.

Editor's Notes

- The above review first appeared in the *Daily Chronicle*, 10 September 1898, 3:1–2, and was reprinted in Aylmer Maude's edition of *Tolstoy on Art and Its Critics* (1925).
- Shaw had ceased keeping a diary the previous year, no doubt because he had better things to write. The above review, however, must have been written during his long convalescence from a foot disorder which had begun in April 1898, and continued into the next year. Four months earlier Shaw had written to the playwright Henry Arthur Jones enthusiastically recommending

Tolstoy's book, calling it "the best treatise on art that has been done by a literary man (I bar Wagner) in these times" (see *Collected Letters 1898–1910* 44). Shaw's use of the journalistic "we" in this article is uncharacteristic of him (and unrelated to his recent marriage to Charlotte Payne-Townshend on 1 June 1898). Four years previously, in G. B. Burgin's Symposium "Some Literary Critics" (*The Idler* 5 [June 1884]: 514), he had stated:

> The critic is bound to give the fullest exhibition of his likes and dislikes as such, so as to make clear, in the course of his notices, the degree of prejudice under which he is writing, and to keep the public in mind of the fact that he is a single person. Need I add that I don't believe in the journalistic "we" in the case of a verdict delivered by one man on the work of another.

Shaw was one of many people asked by the editor of the *Surrey Times* at the beginning of February 1899 what books he would recommend for a cottager or artisan's library that could be purchased for the sum of £2. "Tolstoi's 'Essay on Art' " is recommended by Shaw, for the "cottager with a turn for thinking" (see the *Surrey Times*, 18 February 1899, 7:4–5); and he was still sufficiently impressed with Aylmer Maude as a translator of Tolstoy to defend him vigorously seven years later, when Max Beerbohm attacked Maude's translation of *The Power of Darkness* in the *Saturday Review*. Shaw's riposte, in the form of a letter to the editor, stated that "Tolstoy himself has appealed to Europe to judge What is Art by Mr. Maude's translation, and not by the censored and mutilated Russian version. And nobody can read it and suppose that Mr. Maude is not either a highly competent translator or else a man of original genius who is writing under the pseudonym of Leo Tolstoy" (Bernard Shaw, letter to editor of the *Saturday Review* 14 [January 1905]).

▪ [Count Lev Nikolaevich] Tolstoy [or Tolstoi] (1828–1910), Russian novelist, moral philosopher, and social reformer. His prose epic *War and Peace* was completed in 1869, and its publication, and that of *Anna Karenina* which appeared in installments from 1875 to 1877, ensured Tolstoy's place as a truly great writer. After 1876 Tolstoy became deeply absorbed in matters moral and religious, studied the Gospels and, dismissing the ritual and dogma of the Russian Orthodox Church, established his own variant of Christianity, epitomized in the words of Matthew, "resist not evil"; in short, a nonviolent creed similar to that advocated by Mohandes Gandhi in the next century. Indeed, "Tolstoyism," as it was called, became an established sect around 1884, acquiring many converts. Tolstoy's new faith found its expression in a series of remarkable works, such as *A Confession* (1879), *The Memoirs of a Madman* (1884), *The Death of Ivan Ilyich* (1886), the play *The Powers of Darkness* (1889), the novel *The Kreutzer Sonata* (1889), the above-reviewed treatise, which first appeared in 1896, and the long novel *Resurrection* (1899–1900.) Two years before Tolstoy's death Shaw sent him a gift of an inscribed copy of *Man and Superman* (1901–3). Tolstoy replied that he was pleased with Shaw's "attitude toward civilization and progress," but he also felt that people who possessed both the understanding of the evils of life and the literary talent of Shaw should not jest about such a subject as the purpose of human life. Shaw wrote to Tolstoy again in the year of the latter's death, this time enclosing a copy of *The Shewing-up of Blanco Posnet* (1909), explaining in the accompanying letter his own religious views. Again Tolstoy read the play with pleasure; but he disagreed with Shaw's theology, and again he criticized Shaw's tendency to make a jest about sacred subjects.

▪ Aylmer Maude (1858–1938), English translator and expounder of the works of Count Leo Tolstoy. In 1874 Maude went to the Moscow Lyceum for two years, after which he became a tutor, and married (in 1884) the daughter of a British businessman living in Moscow. Maude himself was employed as a manager (and later director) of a large Russian carpet factory until 1897, when he and his wife returned to England. Before leaving Russia, Maude had become friends with Tolstoy, and in England he and his wife devoted their lives almost entirely to the translation of Tolstoy's works into English. Jointly they translated *Anna Karenina, War and Peace,* and *A Confession;* but Maude himself translated the works on religion and art. After visiting Tolstoy in 1902, he was authorized to write *The Life of Tolstoy* (see below, 254 et seq.), which was completed shortly before Tolstoy died.

▪ Rudyard Kipling (1865–1936), English writer. To this point (1898) his reputation had been established largely by the short story collection *Plain Tales from the Hills* (1888), *Soldiers Three* (1889), and *The* [two] *Jungle Book* [s (1894 and 1895), although he had also published two successful collections of verse. In 1907 he would become the first English writer to receive the Nobel Prize for literature. Tolstoy, extraordinarily, includes Kipling alongside Zola, Bourget, and Huysmans, as authors handling "harrowing subjects" who do not even conceal the trick by which they intend to take the reader in!

▪ [Prince Petr Alekseevich] Kropotkin (1842–1921), Russian geographer, revolutionary, and nihilist. In 1872 he adopted the socialist revolutionary views of the extremist section of the International Workingman's Association, and later became an anarchist. He was imprisoned in Russia in 1874, escaped to England in 1876; in France in 1883 he was sentenced to five years' imprisonment for anarchism, but was released in 1886, and settled again in England until the revolution of 1917 took him back to Russia. His writings (which were in both French and English) include *Paroles d'un Révolté* (1885, translated into English in 1899), *Fields, Factories and Workshops* (1899), *Terror in Russia* (1909), and *Ethics, Origin and Development* (1924).

▪ William Morris (see above, 165).

▪ It was not [Andrew] Fletcher of Saltoun (1655–1716) who offered to make the songs; but in a letter to the marquis of Montrose he wrote: "I knew a very wise man so much of Sir Chr—'s sentiment, that he believed if a man were permitted to make all the ballads, he need not care who should make the laws of a nation."

▪ Ashton Ellis's translation of Wagner's Prose (see above, 166 et seq.).

▪ [John] Ruskin (see above, 65).

30 May 1902

BRITAIN FOR THE BRITISH* [C1398]

HOPE springs eternal in the human breast. Here is Nunquam again explaining to John Smith what an ass he (Smith) is, and what an excellent thing Socialism is. Nunquam does it very well: he sticks to John Smith and Socialism all through with an unfailing dramatic grip of the situation. He does not digress for a moment to grind any axe of his own, or to hit any other Socialist with it, or to play ping-pong with theories of value: he has one hand on the scruff of John Smith's neck and the other on the facts of our civilization all the time. There are very few men who can write as Nunquam does, with conscience and strong feeling; and yet without malice. We have plenty of political essayists who write without malice; but it is easy to be polite when you are indifferent to your subject, and are really concerned about nothing but your own manners and style. We have a few who write with conscience and strong feeling; but they begin with virtuous indignation and culminate in venom. Nunquam keeps his temper, and treats the heathen as fellow men to be converted, not as reptiles to be scotched. He does not think much of the British; but that only sets him upon making more of them. Above all, he has that power of getting at other people's points of view which enables him, when he is not writing persuasives to Socialism, to follow the trade of Shakespear and Dickens. This gives him an immense advantage as a pleader. Even Ruskin and Carlyle could only impose on the world, with extraordinary intensity and ingenious eloquence, their own view of our civilization. They were perfectly successful in convincing John Smith (when he read them) that things were wrong from their point of view; and they enlarged his mind by making him conscious of that point of view. But they did not shew him that anything was wrong from his own point of view; and since he was neither a Carlyle nor a Ruskin, and so could not get away from his own point of view to theirs, they still needed a Nunquam to make the matter plain to them by transposing the tune from their eternal magnificent D flat major (good for the trombones) into the plain G and B flat of their favourite songs and cornet marches, and then shewing them how much better they might play it if they chose.

---

* "Britain for the British." By Robert Blatchford. Editor of the *Clarion*. (London. Clarion Press, 1902.) 2s.6d.

The book has only one serious fault: the price is not plainly marked on the cover. It is a book for poor men, and poor men are often shy men. The other day I saw a book in a shop window in Holborn which I thought likely to be useful to me in my profession. The price did not matter, as my buying it was a matter of business. I expected it to cost about seven and sixpence, the usual Holborn translation of seven francs fifty (it was French). But when I said "How much?" the answer was "Twenty-four shillings net," which I accordingly forked out. Now suppose my countenance had fallen, and I had been compelled by mere poverty to apologize to the bookseller for troubling him, and retire shamefully without the book! Well, there are many sensitive souls among the very cream of the class for whom Nunquam writes who will look wistfully at the cover of "Britain for the British" and not dare to ask for it lest the price should be prohibitive. A mean sort of shame, you will say; but would such books be needed if such mean shames were not in the very air of our civilization? Comrades: I no longer worry you to Educate, Agitate, Organize. I am tired of shouting at the Proletarians of all lands to Unite; but I do ask you to mark your goods in plain figures. I havnt the remotest notion of the price of this book. It may be a shilling (if so it is very cheap); it may be half-a-crown; it may be six shillings less threepence in the shilling for cash. It gives the price of every other Socialist book in the world, and says nothing about its own. This is carrying self-sacrifice to the verge of suicide.

"Britain for the British" is dedicated to A. M. Thompson and the Clarion Fellowship. I think it is a mistake to drag in Thompson. His is a ruined mind. The sooner Nunquam faces the fact that when he tells off a writer, however gifted, to do the theatres for a paper, that writer's reason will be overthrown and his emotions debauched, the better. Thompson was once an able and earnest man: he is now only a dramatic critic, and a reactionary one at that. He is no longer a Socialist: he is only a false-pathosticator, a snivelling sentimentalist. Away with Thompson! Down with Thompson! Thompson be blowed! The book should be dedicated to the memory of Dangle, who was a good man.

In reading the book I have made a few notes, in the manner of reviewers, on certain passages; but I shall not trouble the *Clarion* with many of them. The first concerns the quotations from the Litany, which, alas! appeal more movingly to Nunquam's literary instinct than they will to John Smith's Philistinism. But I suggest there is a use for that Litany even for John Smith. Instead of dulling his senses to it by having it gabbled to him every week by a curate with an Oxford accent from the time he is too young to understand it to the later time when he is too anxious for public-house opening time to attend to it, how would it do to keep it from him until he is of an age to feel and think, and then take him into church, seat him solemnly in the bishop's chair, and say the Litany *to him.*

> That it may please Thee to strengthen such as do stand; and to comfort and help the weak-hearted; and to raise up them that fall; and finally to beat down Mammon under our feet.
> We beseech thee to hear us, John Smith.

At all events, if you dont do it John Smith, nobody else will.

On minor points, I think Nunquam is occasionally over scrupulous in his care not to overstate his case. He seems generally to knock a certain percentage off his figures as a concession to his opponents (for instance, he takes 6,000,000 as the number of adult working men instead of 8,000,000); but as all the independent statistical investigations made since we began to sling figures (Booth's and Rowntree's, for example) have shewn that the facts were worse than we dared to estimate, or could afford to ascertain, there is no need for so much modesty.

Again, why is Nunquam shy of calling profits "rent of ability"? Is it because some of our thistle-eaters hee-hawed at the term when the Fabians first used it? Nunquam speaks of "wages of ability"; but you might as well call the rent of a farm "wages of land," or dividends "wages of capital." A borough engineer gets wages for his ability; but the exploiter of a private engineering firm gets the full rent of it.

Nunquam's *reductio-ad-absurdum* of "overproduction" is the only passage in which he is more witty than convincing. Overproduction is a quite possible operation: even the members of a Socialist community might catch more turbot than they could eat before it went rotten, and might run themselves short of egg sauce in the meantime. Consequently, though Nunquam is quite right in his exposure of the folly of saying that people are hungry because they produce too much food, there is nothing foolish in saying that people are out of eggs because they produce too many fish. Overproduction is inevitable under competition, because when John Smith wants one pair of boots the three nearest bootmakers each produce a pair to sell to him, so that three pairs are produced where only one is wanted. Therefore John Smith comes to suspect in a muddled way that however idiotic overproduction may seem when it is handled in print by a genius like Nunquam, it does occur somehow. A line or two of extra explanation would save John much doubt and brain worry on this point.

There is a sentence on page 116 which makes me restive, though it is perfectly reasonable and correct in its context. "Suppose we organize our out-of-works under skilled farmers, &c." I implore Nunquam to suppose nothing of the sort, even for the sake of the most telling argument ever devised. As long as Socialists make their experiments with out-of-works and Capitalists make theirs with picked in-works, we shall have no lack of object lessons in the folly and impracticability of Socialism and the prudence and efficiency of Capitalism. Nunquam knows this as well as I do; but books are sometimes read and reviewed by fools who will spread themselves on any detached phrase that offers a clothes-line for the noodle's oration.

On page 170 I notice a claim for "the Initiative and Referendum." Here I recognize the baleful influence of Thompson. It certainly is a great pity that whilst the House of Commons was wasting night after night in wrangling over its new procedure rules, the nation had not the power to Initiate a proposal in Parliament of the one thing needful, a limitation of speeches to ten minutes for private members, and, say, an hour for the front bench to share between them as they please. But Thompson thinks that legislation without discussion, and divisions taken by counting 12,000,000 postcards or so, are the right things; and therefore I should say that nothing is more certain to mislead John Smith at present than a recommendation of the Referendum and Initiative without a whole book by Nunquam to explain how utterly impracticable the current popular conceptions of them are. And the book must be addressed not to John Smith, but to Alexander Thompson, late Dangle deceased. That is what comes of fashionable theatre-going!

This exhausts my cavillings. I have picked some four and a half tiny holes in the mere wording of as many inessential phrases in a book of 173 pages—say 60, 000 words. Not much of a cavil, is it? "Britain for the British" is an invaluable book; and John Smith will be the better for it if there is any betterment in him. Meanwhile, at him again Robert Blatchford: at him again!

Editor's Notes

- This review was first published in the *Clarion,* Friday 30 May 1902, 1:3–5, a newspaper founded in December 1891 by the Socialist journalist Robert Blatchford, who became its editor. It was, perhaps, the first working-class paper (since the *Northern Star*) to gain a mass circulation and be self-supporting. There even developed a "Clarion Fellowship," the name given to various clubs that sprang up round the newspaper (notably the Clarion Cycling Clubs); and the newspaper's influence was at its peak at the time of the above review. Thereafter its popularity waned, largely because Blatchford failed to realize the significance of the workers' struggles in the early part of the new century. It was, it is said, the only newspaper not to mention the General Election in 1910, when forty Labour members were elected to Parliament! Although it was still read by the troops in the trenches in 1914, its jingoistic tendencies made it increasingly less popular. By the end of 1916 it had vanished.

- Again there is no specific information as to when or where the above review was written. The first months of 1902 saw Shaw involved in casting, attending rehearsals, and writing "The Author's Apology," for *Mrs. Warren's Profession* (1893) (which was to be performed at last by the Stage Society), and in the revival of *Captain Brassbound's Conversion* (first produced at the Strand Theatre, London in 1900) at the Queen's Theatre Manchester, with Janet Achurch, herself a Mancunian, playing Lady Cicely Waynflete. At the same time Shaw was corresponding with Lillie Langtry who wanted to play the part of Lady Cicely in London, while privately exhorting Ellen Terry to try the same venture. During much of this time the Shaws lived at Piccards Cottage, Guildford, Surrey, which, however, they sold in April 1902. At the time of the review's publication, Shaw was staying at the Royal Hotel, Sandgate, Kent.

- Robert Blatchford (1851–1943), English journalist and author. After various occupations, including brushmaking and a five-year stint in the army, Blatchford turned to journalism in the early 1880s, working first on the *Manchester Sporting Chronicle,* and then the *Sunday Chronicle.* He was converted to Socialism by reading William Morris, and joined the Fabian Society. In spite of the right-wing politics of the *Sunday Chronicle,* Blatchford managed to use the newspaper to support the workers in the great strike in Manningham Mills in Bradford, which led to the founding of the Bradford Labour Union; but also his dismissal from the *Chronicle.* This in turn led to the founding (by Blatchford, A. M. Thompson and others) of the weekly newspaper the *Clarion,* which had attracted sufficient readers by 1895 for them to move from Manchester to London. Blatchford, one of those self-educated Socialists of the 1890s who were impatient with the middle-class intellectualizing of the mostly university-educated London Fabians, felt that the gap between the working classes and Socialist ideals should be bridged by simple straightforward, but impassioned communication, after the style of the revivalist preacher. Indeed, in the *Clarion* on 25 April 1896, he wrote, "If Socialism is to live and conquer, it must be a religion." "Nunquam" ["Never"] carried this missionary zeal and everyday speech into the writing of several books of popular Socialism and several novels and stories. Shaw's relationship with the editor of the *Clarion* was never very warm. Initially, Blatchford had refused to print Shaw's letters, which were critical of him; and Shaw's first article in the *Clarion* (on South Africa) appeared in May 1900. Thereafter he frequently contributed articles. But Blatchford was one of many who were to turn violently against Shaw on the publication of his *Common Sense About the War* (1914). Shaw took a humorous view of Blatchford's attitude (see below, 289).

▪ Shaw, in referring to Macbeth's veiled comment to his wife about the need to murder Banquo, uses Theobald's emendation, "We have scotch'd the snake not kill'd it," an unnecessary change according to Kenneth Muir, who points out in the Arden Shakespeare that the original "We have scorch'd the snake" ("scorch'd" meaning "slash'd, as with a knife—*OED*") makes perfect sense.

▪ Shaw's cavilling over the visibility of the book's price was answered by an editorial note at the end of his review that reads: "The edition of 'Britain for the British' submitted to Mr. Shaw was the cloth issue at 2s. 6d.; the price of the paper edition—3d—is plainly marked on the cover."

▪ Alexander [M.] Thompson (1861–1948), English dramatic author and journalist. He became drama critic to the *Sunday Chronicle,* and founded the *Clarion* (with Blatchford) in 1891(see above), becoming part proprietor and acting editor, contributing articles to this and to numerous other publications under the pseudonym of "Dangle"; work that was also published in book form with such titles as *Dangle's Mixture, Dangle's Rough-Cut,* and *Dangle's Guide to Paris.* His stage work included a number of pantomimes for Robert Courtneidge and libretti for numerous comic operas and musical plays. His autobiography *Here I Lie* was published in 1937.

▪ Shaw's humorous attack upon Thompson's "ruined mind" is a reminder that he himself was a theatrical reviewer for the *Saturday Review* from January 1895 to May 1898.

▪ [Charles] Booth (1840–1916), English shipowner, social reformer, and statistician, devoted eighteen years to the writing of his monumental *Life and Labour of the People in London* (17 vols., 1891–1903), which contained many firsthand surveys and original statistics, and [Benjamin Seebohm] Rowntree (1871–1954), English manufacturer and philanthropist wrote books such as *Poverty: a Study of Town Life* (1901).

▪ The paragraph on page 116 reads in full: "Suppose we organize our out-of-works under skilled farmers, and give them the best machinery. Suppose they only produce one-half the American product. They will still be earning more than their keep."

▪ The "procedural wrangling" of the House of Commons, which was trying to make itself more efficient and responsible and to strengthen its rules for maintaining order, took place during the early part of 1902, occupying weeks of debate, and filling columns of the *Times* newspaper.

1 May 1905

A NEW BOOK FOR AUTHORS AND PRINTERS* [C1482]

MR. HOWARD Collins has certainly done this job extraordinarily well—so well, that there is really nothing to be said about it except to recommend his book unconditionally to all authors and printers, journalists and typists, proof-readers and compositors. In the matter of technical treatises authors have been half spoiled and half starved. Dictionaries, encyclopædias and gazetteers have been heaped on them; impertinences about style and grammar come in a constant stream from people who cannot write to people who can; but a codification of typographic usage has hitherto been lacking, except in Mr. Hart's little pamphlet, which was not in the general market. As to the ordinary school textbooks of English composition (some of them actually in use at the universities), and the catchpenny guides to correct punctuation and the like, most of them would set every purchaser ridiculously and disastrously wrong if it were humanly possible to remember—or indeed in any real sense to read—their ignorant and arid lessons. What was wanted was a man with literary faculty enough to write a bearable book, with judgment and common sense enough to hold the balance between usage and logic, with that rather special technical sense which enables a man to see the importance of apparently little and dry tidinesses, with an enlightened appetite for socially useful work, and with means and leisure to devote himself to it. In short, a man in a million. Fortunately, he has been found; and his name is Howard Collins.

---

* "Author and Printer: A Guide for Authors, Editors, Printers, Correctors of the Press, Compositors, and Typists. With full list of abbreviations. An attempt to codify the best typographical practices of the present day." By F. Howard Collins, author of "An Epitome of the Synthetic Philosophy of Herbert Spencer." (London: Henry Frowde, 1905.)

The book is well planned technically. It is not a heavy shelf book of reference, useless to nomadic authors. It weighs only fifteen ounces, fits in the jacket pocket, and yet contains over four hundred well packed pages, more legible without spectacles than most dictionaries. In form it is a dictionary and literary encyclopædia, set in double columns. If you write "beleiveable," and it strikes you as not looking all you expected, you turn the word up and find "believable-*not* able" [*sic*]. If you are in a difficulty about punctuation, or do not know how to mark corrections in your proof, you turn up Proofs or Punctuation, as the case may be, and find as many rules on these subjects as anyone can safely claim authority for. There are blank pages at the end of each letter to supply new references, or make good omissions, if you can find any. The price is five shillings.

It is impossible to give a complete list of all the headings under which the references fall, for Mr. Collins has employed that elusive gift of the born indexer, an imaginative divination, often apparently whimsical, of the puzzles presented by the preparation of books for the press, so that he helps you not only in your rational difficulties (which experience soon provides for), but in those addleheadednesses which often paralyze an author without rhyme or reason. Just as Roget's Thesaurus is valuable because Roget was an oddity, so is Mr. Collins, too, in that sense, an oddity who knows that the right station for a lifebuoy is not always the most obvious place for falling into the water.

As I began writing for the printer thirty years ago, I have not approached Mr. Collins's book in the spirit of a learner; yet the first thing my eye lit on was something I had never noticed before: namely, that I have never in my life spelt M'Gregor according to usage, always using the apostrophe instead of the turned comma, which, it appears, is right in O' Neill. I say "according to usage", because in this, as in many other matters, there is neither right nor wrong. If there were, I could have argued the case out for myself. Usage in printing is like etiquette: it is mostly a matter of usage, not of morals or manners. The thing to be done is not important; but it is highly important that everybody should do it, and be able to depend on everybody else doing it in the same way. In matters where reason enters, Mr. Collins does not hesitate to vote with the reasonable minority against the thoughtless majority. Take for example the usage as to whether inverted commas should follow or precede stops. In a sentence in which a quotation occurs there can be no question that it is simply a logical error to place stops belonging to the main sentence within the quotation marks instead of after them. But the contrary usage is so common that I have hardly ever had my copy accurately followed in this respect. Mr. Collins prescribes the correct way, following the careful usage of the few and not the thoughtless usage of the many.

I do not praise Mr. Collins's rules because they are invariably my own. They are not. Every writer of dramatic dialogue soon finds that usages founded on the art of the essayist and historian defeat his attempts to convey a vivid impression of excited speech: for instance, that a torrent of questions and explanations cannot be represented by the stately series of separate sentences into which an inquiry into the characteristics of Marcus Aurelius can be broken. Yet even here I find that on the points at issue, Mr. Collins qualifies his rule so as to provide for me. Then again, every author with an eye for the appearance of a page of type (if any such there be) must by this time have several artistic quarrels with usages which have grown up during the period of desolating Philistinism which separates Caslon from Morris.

Ever since Morris awakened our artistic conscience to the fact that a book has to be looked at as well as read, and that the most enchanting poem or absorbing story in the world may be made into a disgusting spectacle by vile manufacture and base materials, or, even more effectually, by elaborate and costly snobbishness, certain typographical practices which are rational enough (however unnecessary), have become less and less bearable. For instance, inverted commas and apostrophes are so ruinous to the appearance of a printed page that people with cultivated eyes will finally refuse to buy editions in which The Merchant of Venice is printed "The Merchant of Venice"; and don'ts and won'ts and haven'ts and didn'ts (all quite harmless, pretty, and characteristic without the apostrophe) are peppered all over the page. Since Morris's death the finest books produced in England, as far as I know, are the Ashendene Press books of Mr. Hornby, and the Doves Press books of Cobden Sanderson and Emery Walker. But why did the Doves Press begin with a Latin Text to shew the noble type it designed on the lines of Jensen? And why did it go on to the Doves Bible now in progress? No doubt because Latin and Scripture do not require the pepper pot.

Mr. Collins leaves all this out of account. He even prints his title page in at least six different types, an outrage for which Morris would have slain him where he stood. But whilst I note the omission I do not blame it: on the contrary, I highly applaud the judgment and resolution with which Mr. Collins has resisted the enormous temptation to give a helping hand to pet reforms under the pretext of codifying usage. But he has not made the necessary rule an excuse for countenancing the slipshod abandonment of old usages, which are both handsome and correct. He insists on the use of z instead of s in the termination ize. He points out that £ should follow the pounds figure instead of preceding it. Both these usages are traditional as well as correct.

Yet Mr. Collins is human enough to commit one crime. The blood-curdling vulgarism of programme for program is expressly prescribed by him. I must really send him a telegramme containing an appropriate epigramme on the point.

G.B.S.

Editor's Notes

- The above review was first published in the *Author* (the monthly organ of the Incorporated Society of Authors) 15, no. 8 (1 May 1905): 246–48. This journal was founded (and originally edited) in May 1890 by Sir Walter Besant (1836–1901), first chairman of the Society (1884). Shaw had first contributed to this periodical in 1901 ("How to Make Plays Readable" [C1377]), and had written two more articles, in 1902 and 1903, before the present one.
- There is no indication of when or where Shaw wrote the above review, but it is surprising that he had time to write it at all. The previous year, 1904, had seen the beginning of Shaw's busiest decade, and the start of his enormous reputation as a dramatist through the first professional public performances of his plays in London. Shaw still found time to help his first biographer Archibald Henderson by writing voluminous reminiscences. More important, on 22 March 1905, he began writing *Major Barbara,* a play he would not finish until October.
- F[rederick] Howard Collins (1857–1910), English writer. He also wrote *An Epitome of the Synthetic Philosophy of Herbert Spencer* (in 2 parts, 1889, 94); a pamphlet *The Diminution of the Jaw in the Civilized Races as an Effect of Disuse* (a criticism of W. Platt's "Are the effects of use and disuse inherited?"1891); and *Twelve Charts of the Tidal Streams near the Channel Islands and neighbouring French Coast* (1897).
- Mr. Hart's "little pamphlet" was [Horace] Hart's *Rules for Compositors and Readers at the University Press, Oxford* (revised by J. A. H. Murray and H. Bradley), which had been through eighteen editions by 1904!
- [Peter Mark] Roget (1779–1869) was perhaps "an oddity" in Shaw's words, because he was eclectic in his interests. He was the son of a Huguenot

minister, a physician, secretary of the Royal Society, Fullerian professor of physiology at the Royal Institution, and yet wrote his famous *Thesaurus of English Words and Phrases* (1852), which went through twenty-eight editions in his lifetime, and is still a standard reference work.

▪ Marcus Aurelius [Antoninus], originally Marcus Annius Verus (121 B.C.–80 B.C.), Roman emperor. One of the most respected Roman emperors, he is also one of the few whose writings have survived: his *Meditations,* twelve books recording (in Greek) his moral precepts, and his innermost thoughts, which include periods of loneliness, but stoical fortitude in the face of death and disasters, and a belief in the virtues of wisdom, justice, and moderation.

▪ [William] Caslon (1692–1766), English type-founder. He began as a gun engraver and toolmaker in London in 1716, but soon began cutting type for printers. His delicate "old face" Caslon types were widely used both in Europe and the United States until the close of the eighteenth century. However, in the 1850s they were revived, and retain their popularity today.

▪ [William] Morris (see above, 165).

▪ The above acknowledgment that Morris's medievalism "awakened our artistic conscience to the fact that a book has to be looked at as well as read," had led already to Shaw's dislike of unnecessary apostrophes ("senseless disfigurements that have destroyed all the old sense of beauty in printing"), and years later in *Saint Joan,* to Warwick's declaration: "There is nothing on earth more exquisite than a bonny book, with well-placed columns of rich black writing in beautiful borders, and illuminated pictures cunningly inset. But nowadays, instead of looking at books, people read them . . ."

▪ [Thomas James] Cobden-Sanderson (1840–1922), a leader of the nineteenth-century revival of artistic typography, worked with William Morris, and in 1900 founded the Doves Press at Hammersmith. In 1916 the press closed, and Cobden-Sanderson threw the type into the Thames.

▪ Emery Walker (see below, 395).

▪ Shaw's applause for "the judgment and resolution with which Mr. Collins has resisted the enormous temptation to give a helping hand to pet reforms under the pretext of codifying usage" did not prevent him forty-five years later from his own efforts in the direction of spelling reform in clause 35 of his will, where he bequeathed a sum of money to investigate the possibility of a forty-letter British alphabet [additional to the Roman one], and to publish in it and distribute a transliterated copy of *Androcles and the Lion.* After some dispute in the courts, a prize of £500 was offered in 1958 in a contest to select a "Proposed British Alphabet" of forty symbols, and four contestants (out of 467) were declared the winners. Accordingly, a transliteration of *Androcles* was made by Peter MacCarthy of Leeds University, and 3500 copies distributed to "every public library in the English-speaking world and every national library in every other country," as required by Shaw's bequest.

1 July 1905

CONFESSIONS OF A BENEVOLENT AND HIGH-MINDED SHARK* [C1483]

THIS book has the double charm of infinite comedy and obvious authenticity. Most confessions are spurious. Blameless wives of country clergymen have a mania for writing memoirs of improper females: city missionaries write autobiographies of convicted cracksmen: the penitent forms of the Salvation Army are crowded with amiable creatures confessing the imaginary brutalities they did not commit before they were converted. Confessions, in short, as Dickens succinctly put it, are "all lies." But this confession is genuine. The author is a real publisher from his bootsoles to his probably bald crown. There never was such a publishery publisher. The experienced author will read his book with many chuckles, and put it down without malice. The inexperienced author will learn from it exactly what he has to face when he meets that most dangerous of all publishers, the thoroughly respectable publisher.

Need I add that the confession is not a confession at all? It contains only one admission: that publishers do not know how to advertize, and can do nothing more for a book than the book can do for itself. This, so far as it is true (and it is not wholly nor exactly true) is so obvious that there is no merit in confessing it. And the rest of the book is quite the reverse of a confession. It is an advertisement, an apology (in the classical sense), occasionally almost a dithyramb; and its tune throughout is the old tune "Wont you walk into my parlour?"

A few simple principles furnish our professing penitent with a solid moral basis. Of these the chief is that Nature ordains ten per cent. as the proper royalty for an author.[1] He makes no qualification as to the price of the book. It may be published at a shilling, or six shillings, or twelve shillings, or twenty-four. That does not matter. Nature does not fix the price of a book, though a dollar and a half is suggested as a desirable figure. She *does* fix the author's percentage—at ten. The penitent admits with shame that there are reckless publishers who

---

* "A Publisher's Confession." By Walter Hines Page. (New York: Doubleday, Page, 1905.)
1. This view is strenuously combated by theatrical managers, to whom the Voice of Nature whispers five per cent. as seemly and sufficient.

offer more, and avaricious and shortsighted authors who are seduced by their offers. But bankruptcy awaits the former; and remorse and ruin are the doom of the latter. The book itself must needs be starved by cheap manufacture. The goose that lays the golden eggs (that is: the ten per cent. publisher) is slain by that thriftless and insatiable grasper, the twenty per cent. author.

I shuddered as I read. For I too have a confession to make. I have not only exacted twenty per cent. royalties; but I have actually forced the unfortunate publisher to adorn the dollar-and-a-half book with photogravures. It is quite true that the particular publisher whom I used thus barbarously actually did become bankrupt. But he broke, not because he paid too high royalties, but because his profits were so large that he acquired the habits of a Monte Cristo, and the ambitions of an Alexander. Far be it from me to blame him or bear malice. I still believe in his star. Three or four more bankruptcies, and he will settle down and become a steady millionaire.

But the exaction of twenty per cent. is not the blackest crime of which an author can be guilty. Our penitent is, in the main, kind to authors. I handsomely admit that authors are not angels—at least not all of them. Without going so far as to say that some authors are rascals, I yet believe that authors have been known to practise on the vanity, the credulity, the literary ignorance, and the business flabbiness of publishers to get advances from them on books that remain unwritten to this day. Every season brings its budget of scamped, faked, and worthless books, feverishly pushed, to prove that those eminent and typical publishers Alnaschar & Co., have again had their belly filled with the east wind by some duffer whose pretensions would not take in an ordinarily sharp bookstall boy. There are authors who make the poor publisher pay through the nose for nothing but their names in his list. For all these deceits and failures and oppressions our penitent has not a word of reproach. He forgives us everything, except DISLOYALTY. That is to him the one unpardonable and abominable sin. Loyalty, loyalty, loyalty, is what he asks before everything. To change your publisher is to become "a stray dog"—his own words, I assure you. To bite the hand that fed you; to turn on the man who raised you from obscurity to publicity; to prefer another's twenty per cent. to his ten: this is human nature at its worst. The pages of the confession almost blush as they record the shameful fact that there are viper-authors who do this thing, and blackleg-publishers who tempt them to do it.

Here is a powerful pen-picture of the polyecdotous author. "That man now has books on five publishers' lists. Not one of the publishers

counts him as his particular client. In a sense his books are all neglected. One has never helped another. He has got no cumulative
result of his work. He has become a sort of stray dog in the publishing
world. He has cordial relations with no publisher; and his literary
product has really declined. He scattered his influence; and he is
paying the penalty."

What an awful warning!

Yet, now that I come to think of it, I have done this very thing my
very self. Dare I add that I would do it again to-morrow without the
slightest compunction if I thought I could better myself that way. My
publisher's consolation is that though I have no bowels, at least I do
not pose as his benefactor, nor accuse him of disloyalty because he
publishes books by other authors. Granted that an author with two or
three publishers may seem (in America) as abandoned a creature as a
woman with two or three husbands, what about a Solomonic publisher with half a hundred authors!

"Every *really* successful publisher" says our penitent (who is rather
given to dark hints that the other publishers are not all they seem),
"could make more money by going into some other business. I think
that there is not a man of them who could not greatly increase his
income by giving the same energy and ability to the management of a
bank, or of some sort of industrial enterprise." May I point out that this
is true not only of publishers but of all criminals, as many a judge has
remarked before passing sentence. Whenever I meet a burglar, I always ask him why he runs such fearful risks, and performs such
prodigies of skill and enterprise in opening other people's safes, when
he might turn publisher and be just as dishonest and ten times as rich
for half the trouble. As to authors, I never yet met an author who was
not convinced that if he put into business half the talent and industry
he puts into literature, he could in ten years time buy up the Steel
Trust that bought up Mr. Carnegie.

The truth is, I suspect, that a publisher is an infatuated book fancier
who cannot write, and an author is an infatuated book fancier who can.
But the Confession does not urge this view, nor even mention it. According to it "from one point of view the publisher is a manufacturer and a
salesman. From another point of view he is the personal friend and
sympathetic adviser of authors—a man who has a knowledge of literature and whose judgment is worth having." Yes: I know that other point
of view: the publisher's own point of view. I have had tons of his sympathetic advice; and I owe all my literary success to the fact that I have
known my own business well enough never to take it. Whenever a

publisher gives me literary advice, I take an instant and hideous revenge on him. I give him business advice. I pose as an economist, a financier, and a man of affairs. I explain what I would do if I were a publisher; and I urge him to double his profits by adopting my methods. I do so as his personal friend and wellwisher, as his patron, his counsellor, his guardian, his second father. I strive to purify the atmosphere from every taint of a "degrading commercialism" (that is how the Confession puts it), and to speak as man to man. And it always makes the stupid creature quite furious. Thus do men misunderstand one another. Thus will the amateur, to the end of the world, try to mix the paints of the professional.

I think I will give up the attempt to review this book. I cannot stand its moral pose. If the man would write like a human being I could treat him as a human being. But when he keeps intoning a moral diapason to his bland and fatherly harmonies about the eternal fitness of his ten per cent. on six shillings; his actuarial demonstrations that higher royalties must leave his children crying in vain to him for bread; his loudly virtuous denunciation of the outside publisher who publishes at the author's expense (compare this with his cautious avoidance of any mention of the commission system used by Ruskin, Spencer and all authors who can afford the advance of capital); his claim that all the losses caused by his endless errors of judgment are to be reckoned by authors as inevitable and legitimate expenses of his business; and his plea that his authors should take him for better for worse until death do them part: all this provokes me so that it is hard for me to refrain from describing him to himself bluntly in terms of his own moral affectations.

However, I will be magnanimous, and content myself with the harmless remark that the writer of the Confession is a very typical publisher. Publishers of a certain age always do go on exactly like that. The author's business is not to mind them, and to be infinitely patient with their literary vanity, their business imbecility, their seignorial sentiments and tradesmanlike little grabbings and cheapenings, their immeasurable incompetence, their wounded recollections of Besant, their stupendously unreadable new book that is coming out the week after their timid refusal of the latest thing that does not reflect the chaos of secondhand impressions which they call their own minds; and the dislike of steady industry, the love of gambling, the furtive Bohemianism that induced them to choose their strange and questionable occupation.

As for me, all I ask on the royalty system at six shillings is a modest twenty per cent. or so, a three year's trial, an agreement drafted by myself, and an unaffected bookseller. I dont want a compulsory partner for life. I dont want a patron. I dont want an amateur collaborator. I dont want a moralist. I dont want a Telemachus. I dont want a pompous humbug, nor a pious humbug, nor a literary humbug. I can dispense with a restatement of the expenses, disappointments, trials, and ingratitudes that pave the publisher's weary path to a destitute old age in a country house, with nothing to relieve its monotony but three horses, a Mercedes automobile, and a flat in London. I have heard it so often! I dont expect absolute truth, being myself a professional manufacturer of fiction: indeed I should not recognize perfect truth if it were offered to me. I dont demand entire honesty, being only moderately honest myself. What I want is a businesslike gambler in books, who will give me the market odds when we bet on the success of my latest work. No doubt this is a matter of individual taste. Some authors like the bland and baldheaded commercial Mæcenas who loathes a degraded commercialism; tenders a helping hand to the young; and is happy if he can give an impulse to the march of humanity. I can only say that these benefactors do not seem to get on with me. They are too sensitive, too thinskinned, too unpractical for me. The moment they discover that I am a capable man of business they retreat, chilled and disillusioned. Not long ago one of these affectionate friends of struggling authors, representing a first-class American firm, proposed to bind me to him for life, not by the ties of reciprocal esteem, but by legal contract. Naturally I said, "Suppose you go mad! Suppose you take to drink! Suppose you make a mess of my business!" The wounded dignity and forgiving sweetness with which he retired, remarking that it would be better for the permanence of our agreeable relations if we let the matter drop, are among my most cherished recollections.

I hope I have not conveyed an unfavorable impression of what is— to an author at least—quite a readable, and not an unamiable little book. There are scraps of good sense and even of real as distinguished from merely intended candor in it, mixed up with some frightful nonsense about "literary" books, our penitent being firmly persuaded, like most publishers, that a really literary book is one in which the word "singularly" occurs in every third line, and in which "I dont know where he went to" is always written "I know not whither he is gone." But perhaps the best feature of the little book is the testimony it bears between the lines to the continued and urgent need for an Authors' Society.

G. BERNARD SHAW

Editor's Notes

- The above review was first published in the *Author,* 15, no. 10 (1 July 1905). An extract of this appeared in 1978 in Victor Bonham-Carter's *Authors by Profession.*
- Shaw wrote this review in June 1905 (see note below), although, as he told James Huneker, he was still "too busy rehearsing and producing to attend to any publishing business for the moment." Moreover, the Shaws were leaving their country house (the Old House, Harmer Green, Hertfordshire) at the end of June, so there was much packing up to do; and then they were going to Ireland for three months to rest and give Shaw a chance to finish *Major Barbara.* However, as Shaw told Forbes Robertson: "in that three months I have to write a new play and to revise half a dozen French and German translations of my old ones. I have to see an old novel [*The Irrational Knot*] through the American press, and write a preface for it. I have to prepare John Bull's Other Island for publication. I have to do half a dozen articles now months in arrear. The translators are howling, pressed by the Berlin & Viennese theatres for prompt copies. The publishers are howling, because the public are red hot for Shaw books. Everybody's fame and future is staked in my attending to him before the end of the week. How much holiday do you see for me in this?" (*Collected Letters 1898–1910,* 534).
- Walter Hines Page (1855–1918), American journalist, publisher, and diplomat. After working on the *Forum* and the *Atlantic Monthly,* in 1899, together with the American publisher Frank Nelson Doubleday (1862–1934), he founded the publishing house of Doubleday, Page. In 1900 their firm established a general information magazine, *The World's Work,* which Page edited until, in 1913, President Woodrow Wilson appointed him ambassador to Great Britain. After the outbreak of the First World War in 1914, Page opposed President Wilson's neutrality stance, threatening resignation before America joined the war in April 1917. In addition to the above book, Page also wrote *The Rebuilding of Old Commonwealths* (1902), and a novel *The Southerner* (1909) under the pseudonym of Nicholas Worth.
- The reference to "the penitent forms of the Salvation Army . . . crowded with amiable creatures confessing the imaginary brutalities they did not commit before they were converted," reminds one that Shaw at this very time was slowly writing *Major Barbara,* in whose second act, at the Salvation Army shelter, amiable creatures like Snobby Price and Rummy Mitchens discuss their "conversions."

RUMMY: Who saved you, Mr. Price? Was it Major Barbara?
PRICE: No: I come here on my own. I'm going to be Bronterre O'Brien Price, the converted painter. I know wot they like. I'll tell em how I blasphemed and gambled and wopped my poor old mother—

RUMMY [*shocked*] Used you to beat your mother?

PRICE: Not likely. She used to beat me. No matter: you come and listen to the converted painter, and you'll hear how she was a pious woman that taught me me prayers at er knee, an how I used to come home drunk and drag her out o bed be er snow white airs, an lam into er with the poker.

- It is Mr. Wemmick (in *Great Expectations*), showing Pip his "collection of curiosities," which includes "several manuscript confessions written under condemnation," who declares, "every one of 'em Lies, sir."
- "The Spider and the Fly," by Mary Howitt (1799–1888), begins:

> "Will you walk into my parlour?" said a spider to a fly:
> "'Tis the prettiest little parlour that ever you did spy."

- The publishing firm begun in 1897 by Grant Richards (1872–1948) published several early works of Shaw, including *The Perfect Wagnerite*, a commentary on the *Ring of the Nibelungs*, and also *Plays Pleasant and Unpleasant* in 1898; the last-named containing photogravures of Shaw himself as frontispiece. The firm of Grant Richards became bankrupt in January 1905, Shaw's correspondence providing a lively commentary on its collapse.
- Alnaschar, in *The Arabian Nights*, was "The Barber's Fifth Brother" who, having inherited one hundred pieces of silver, invested them in a basket of glassware, and then fantasized about the fame and fortune that would derive from successive trading ventures. His final daydream, in which he had married the daughter of the chief vizier and spurned her with his foot, "Thus!" led to his kicking the basket, smashing his wares.
- Shaw's word for an author with many publishers ("polyecdotous") was presented to him by Gilbert Murray. While writing the above review Shaw wrote a letter to Murray (17 June 1905), asking for an adjective to denote an author with several publishers. "I have used publygamous;" he wrote: "but this suggests the 'hippos a river & potamos a horse' style of derivation." Murray replied the following day: "A publisher is Ekdotês; so that 'monecdotous' and 'polyecdotous' would seem to be correct words. (the o short; the accent on the ec.) I should avoid 'publygamous'; it would be Graeco-latin for a prostitute, unless you could show by the context that it meant 'married to a poplar tree!" (*Collected Letters 1898–1910*, 530–31).
- [Andrew] Carnegie (1835–1919), American industrialist and philanthropist, was one of the earliest users of the Bessemer process of making steel in the United States, and controlled about a quarter of America's iron and steel production. In 1901 he sold his company to the United States Steel Corporation for $250,000,00 and retired from business.
- [Sir Walter] Besant (see above, 217).
- In Greek mythology Telemachus was the son of Odysseus and Penelope, appearing in the *Odyssey* where, from being an inexperienced youth in the

first part, he develops into a most resourceful man in the second. He is an intelligent and enterprising helper and astonishes his mother by taking command of the house.

- Gaius Cilnius Mæcenas (fl. c. 70–8 B.C.) A Roman famous for his literary patronage in the time of Augustus, whose friend and advisor he also became.

1 April 1907

OUR BOOK-SHELF: "FRIEDRICH NIETZSCHE: THE DIONYSIAN SPIRIT OF THE AGE"* [C 1582]

THIS little book on Nietzsche by a competent Fabian is badly wanted in England. There is not space enough to spare in FABIAN NEWS to consider why modern capitalistic civilization meets every plain statement of an obvious truth with a passionate denial (usually accompanied by a threat of legal proceedings), and every appearance of an original genius with an outburst of silly uppish abuse and ignorant misrepresentation: all that can be said here is that if half the energy that has been wantonly devoted to persuading England that Wagner was neither a passable musician nor a decent man; that Ibsen was a vicious and morbid dullard; and that Nietzsche was the unscrupulous apologist of every selfish bully in Europe, had been employed in keeping English culture reasonably up to date, our generation would have gained at least thirty years in comparative enlightenment. It is old-fashioned now to dispute about Wagner and Ibsen; but on Nietzsche folly and ignorance are still busy. The journalists have read in one another's paragraphs a certain sentence about "the big blonde beast"; and from this misunderstood sample they construct an imaginary Nietzsche of impossible mental and moral inferiority to themselves. If they ever asked themselves how this depraved and imbecile phantom succeeded in making an impression on Europe which they, with all their superiority, cannot make even on Fleet Street, they would proba-

---

* "Friedrich Nietzsche: the Dionysian Spirit of the Age." By A. R. Orage. (T. N. Foulis, London and Edinburgh; 1906.) 1s. n.

bly reply that the Kopenick captain did no less, and that Nietzsche was the Kopenick captain of philosophy.

Anyone who will take the trouble to read Mr. Orage's very interesting and readable little book will pay no attention in future to this sort of journalistic anti-Nietzscheanism. His selection from Nietzsche's aphorisms and his statement of Nietzsche's position are just what is needed: that is, they give the characteristic and differential features of Nietzsche's philosophy and influence, and make quite clear those categories of Apollan and Dionysian which are not only useful as instruments of thought, but indispensable conversationally as the catchwords of Nietzschean controversy. This is no small critical feat; for, like all mortal men, the actual Nietzsche was to a great extent the child of his age, a German professor like any other German professor of the Wagnerian-Darwinian half of the nineteenth century, afflicted with conventional and sometimes very Philistine delusions as to the glory of the Renaissance, the nobility of the ancient Romans, the importance and permanent validity of the mere fashions of his day in erudition, the scientific character of physics and biology as opposed to the anti-scientific character of religion, the fundamentality of love and beauty as the subject and object of art, the supremacy of classical architecture: in short, the whole intellectual bag of tricks of his generation. I have seldom read ten pages of Nietzsche without coming upon some historic or artistic illustration in which the conventionality and shallowness of the view he accepts is not in striking contrast to his ingenious, original and suggestive application of it. The most original writer in the world can no more avoid the common thought of his age and species than he can avoid the common features which make all white men seem alike to a negro; but this did not prevent Nietzsche from producing, in "Also Sprach Zarathustra," the first modern book that can be set above the Psalms of David at every point on their own ground. Mr. Orage, more Nietzschean than Nietzsche himself—as he ought to be—shews his competence and his advantage over mediocrity by omitting the common form, and giving the distinctive features by which Nietzsche stands out from the mob of Europeans as a man of genius.

If Mr. Orage ever writes an essay on the collision between Nietzscheanism and Socialism in England, he might, I suggest, find some interesting material in the early essays of Belfort Bax, who in the eighties did really startle the generation of Socialists represented by Carpenter, Hyndman, Morris, and the founders of the Fabian Society, by the "transvaluation of values" in his criticisms of capitalist morality, and in Stuart Glennie's theory of Christianity as a slave morality, which is in some ways more convincing, as it is apparently more erudite historically, than Nietzsche's.

G. B. S.

Editor's Notes

▪ The above review was first published in *Fabian News* 17 (April 1907).

▪ Again, no specific information exists as to when or where Shaw wrote the above review; but as usual it was sandwiched between playwriting, play production, and politics. *The Doctor's Dilemma* (1906), written the previous August–September, had had its opening night at the Court Theatre on 20 November, less than a month after the Shaws had moved into the rectory at Ayot St. Lawrence in Hertfordshire, the house which they were to purchase in 1920, and live in until they died. In the winter of 1906 Shaw was still busy with the Fabian Society, too, which now was increasing in numbers and included the fiery H. G. Wells (see below, 346–47), with whom Shaw quarreled both in print and in debate. Early in 1907 Shaw told the young playwright Erica Cotteril that he was "years behindhand with pressing work." We may be sure, however, that Shaw finished the above review before he and Charlotte left for France on 30 March 1907, returning on 11 April.

▪ A[lfred] R[ichard, originally James] Orage (1873–1934), English editor, and exponent of social credit. In 1893 he became an elementary school teacher at Leeds, but soon developed an interest in guild Socialism, claiming that his socialism "was an anthology of the mediaeval stained glass of Morris, the sandals of Carpenter, Keir Hardie's cloth cap and red tie, and Shaw's jingling bells and cap"; (see Norman and Jeanne MacKenzie, *The Fabians* (New York: Simon and Schuster, 1977), 344. In the spring of 1907, Orage and another young Fabian, Holbrook Jackson (with help from Shaw and others) purchased a small weekly journal, *The New Age,* which rapidly became the champion of every kind of dissent from the convention in matters of art and politics, and was particularly useful as a platform for feminist politics. Orage, however, left the Fabian Society; and in 1918 he met Major Clifford Douglas who convinced him that social credit was a sound economic scheme; thereafter Orage became a strong advocate of it. But after the First World War he also came under the influence of the occultist P. D. Ouspensky and the Russian mystic George Gurdjieff, with the result that in 1922 Orage relinquished the editorship of the *New Age,* and spent more than a year at Gurdjieff's institute (at Fontainebleau), studying the latter's philosophy. He spent from 1923 to 1930 in the United States, giving lectures to raise funds for the institute. In 1930 he returned to England and began the *New English Weekly,* which became the mouthpiece for social credit.

• The Kopenick captain was Wilhelm Voigt, an uneducated middle-aged Prussian with quite a long criminal record, who, in the previous October (1906), had dressed himself in an officer's uniform bought from an old-clothes shop, commandeered a squad of soldiers, and taken over the town hall in Köpenick, near Berlin, arresting the mayor, and obtaining control of the municipal treasury. Twenty-five years later the German playwright Carl Zuckmayer (1896–1977) made the incident into a satirical play *Der Hauptmann von Köpenick,* which was banned by the Nazis, presumably because its laughter at the worship of military uniform was too much for them.

• Ernest Belfort Bax (1854–1926), English philosophical author and lawyer, and one of the founders of the English socialist movement. Bax was a prolific writer of books on Socialism, the French Revolution, Germany, and the philosophy of Kant, and Shaw reviewed his *A Handbook of the History of Philosophy* for the *Pall Mall Gazette* on 26 September 1887. Bax also edited the journals *Time* and *To-Day* with James Leigh Joynes and Hubert Bland (1856–1914), the last of which publications serialized two of Shaw's novels (see above, 33, 96). Bax and Shaw were close friends in the 1880s, sharing interests in Socialism and music. Bax was also Shaw's predecessor as musical critic of the *Star* (see above, 158).

• [Edward] Carpenter (1844–1929), English poet and social reformer. Born in Brighton, he became an Anglican clergyman, but left the church and visited America where he met Walt Whitman, who influenced him considerably. Returning to England he became a Socialist and a craftsman, inspired by William Morris. He was one of the Fellowship of the New Life, a rustic group of Socialists who withdrew from nineteenth century civilization to pursue the "Simple Life," described as "the abandonment of superfluous luxury . . . needless trifles . . . meaningless literature . . . wearisome ornaments . . . useless servants . . . toilsome calls, condolences, congratulations, Xmas cards, and crinkum-crankum in general, which feed neither the body nor the soul" (Anon., *Seed-Time* [July 1889]; quoted in Norman and Jeanne MacKenzie, *The Fabians* [New York: Simon and Schuster, 1977], 180). Carpenter himself made sandals as well as poems, and managed a prodigious output of books, including *Towards Democracy* (1883), *Civilization, its Cause and Cure* (1889), and an autobiography *My Days and Dreams* (1916). Shaw's essay "The Illusions of Socialism" appeared in Carpenter's *Forecasts of the Coming Century* (1897).

• [H. M.] Hyndman (see above, 20).

• [William] Morris (see above, 165).

• [John S[tuart] Stuart-Glennie (1832–1909?), Scottish historian and folklore specialist. He published numerous books on history, criticism and translations, such as *In the Morning Land; or, the Law of the Origin and Transformation of Christianity* (1873), *Pilgrim Memories; or, Travel and Discussion in the Birth-Countries of Christianity with the Late Henry Thomas Buckle* (1875), and *The Romance of the Youth of Arthur* (1880). He also founded the Celtic League, to which Shaw briefly belonged. Shaw attended several of his lectures at the Fabian and Royal Historical Societies in the 1880s, and no doubt read his books. In a letter to Archibald Henderson in 1905, Shaw, repudiating the claim that his works were influenced by Nietzsche, said "Both Stuart Glennie and Belfort Bax were (and are) Socialists and strenuous opponents of Christianity, basing their views on a philosophy of history. As I am notoriously a Socialist, the first authors whose influence might have been traced in my works by English critics are Stuart Glennie and Bax. But no. Our critics must run to Strindberg and Nietzsche" (*Collected Letters 1898–1910*, 554).

21 November 1909

BERNARD SHAW ON SHAMS OF RULE AND OF RELIGION* [C1714]

THE fact that a book dealing with political conditions is a romance is a guarantee of its political importance, because romances are the only documents that are now free to tell the truth and sure to be read.

Sooner or later, the grosser follies and falsehoods get exposed. The fools and liars convict themselves boastfully out of their own mouths because they conceive their folly as wisdom and patriotism, believe their own lies and know that their intentions are good. But who is it that detests the exposure and drives its lesson home to the public? Usually the man of letters. Across the channel, when the officers and gentlemen who represented the old nobility and the old religion of France had with most patriotic and pious intentions perjured and forged their way through the Dreyfus affair, it was a novelist, Zola, who smashed their conspiracy up and brought the nation to its senses. In Egypt it was a poet, Mr. Wilfrid Scawen Blunt, who released the survivors of Denshawai and reduced the apologists who had certified it as "just and necessary" to giving equally credulous and well-meant and equally mistaken certificates to the vivisectors of dogs and rabbits in England. And it is again a man of letters, Hall Caine, who has gone deeper in his new book, "The White Prophet," and has put his finger on the real reason why British pro-consuls get stuffed periodically with the silly romance of a murderous conspiracy of Islam against Christendom.

---

* "The White Prophet." By Hall Caine. Illustrated by R. Caton Woodville. Heinemann: London, 1909.

That reason is that the situation of Pontius Pilate and Caiaphas is constantly and inevitably reproduced whenever we seize a foreign territory, as Rome seized Judea. Pontius Pilate becomes the catspaw of Caiaphas exactly as in Hall Caine's romance the consul general becomes the catspaw of the Grand Cadi. When an original religious genius arises, Jesus, Mahomet, Savonarola, St. Francis or St. Clare, his first attack is on the Temple, and while the people make him the leader of their eternal revolt against priestly tyranny and corruption, the priests accuse him of political conspiracy, and incite the military authorities to put him down with fire and sword. Thus they made Pontius Pilate crucify Jesus. Mahomet escapes them by the skin of his teeth, and, seeing that he must smash or be smashed, comes back in arms and conquers both priest and soldier. Savonarola is burnt by the cardinals. St. Francis dies young, before it becomes expedient to burn him, and St. Clare, who survives him, fights the pope to the last because she wants her Clares to be poor Clares and he wants them to be women of property. This situation, with its explanation of the cry of smash the Mahdi, and of the cock-and-bull story of the conspiracy of Islam, which the Egyptian Caiaphases planted in Lord Cromer and Sir Edward Grey, is the one which Hall Caine has presented in the form of a romance. In no other form would our credulous, pleasure-loving, intellectually lazy, governing classes read it. Since romance is to carry the day, Hall Caine has used it on the right side, and beaten Caiaphas at his own game.

Hall Caine has also seen what none of our officials and foreign office ministers have ever dreamt of. I mean the coming reconciliation between the best Christians and the best Mahometans. The greatest thing that the empire has done is to knock out of us Britons the insular and insolent bigotry that used to assume that our share of inspiration and revelation was the whole, and that other people's prophets were imposters and other people's creeds damnable errors. Whilst Arab children were taught to respect Jesus in the name of Mahomet, English children were taught to despise and slander Mahomet in the name of Jesus. This is a heavy score to the credit of Mahomet; but the same fate finally overtook both prophets: the cults established on their teachings ended by claiming their authority for most of the errors they strove against. Christianity has already undergone one reformation, and it is very badly in want of another. Mahometanism is in the same predicament; and since the essential religious ideas by which both sects (they are only sects, big as they are), will be reformed are the same, the opportunity for a reconciliation is a golden one, and Hall

Caine, in seeing and understanding it, has risen to the height of his profession. Mahometanism has, from the point of view of the sceptical educated Englishman of the Darwinian period (that is, of the governing class of today), the advantage that whereas many such Englishmen do not believe that Jesus ever existed, and those who do despise Him because He was not "fit" to survive in the struggle for life, Mahomet's existence is as unquestionable as Henry the Eighth's, and his success was as solid as Mr. Carnegie's. Also when his followers persisted in trying to degrade him from the rank of prophet to that of a vulgar wizard (exactly as in the case of Jesus) he honestly and impatiently told them again and again that he was only a man, and could not perform miracles. Thus he appeals to men who are by temperament anti-Christian, just as he appealed to Napoleon who said at St. Helena that he thought Mahometanism was, on the whole, the most useful of the religions.

Now as to the definite charges made against Hall Caine for his new book, "The White Prophet," I leave out of the question the hackneyed literary attack. Hall Caine sells a thousand copies where most of the rest of us either sell a hundred or cannot escape from journalism into books at all. We console ourselves by privately observing that his style is different from ours, and publicly saying that he has no style at all. And when he does a stroke of important public work as in the present instance, we disloyally join the official hue and cry against him. For which we ought to be shot as traitors to our profession. However, that matters to nobody but our petty selves. The public charges against the novelist are the important ones.

First, he is charged with using Lord Cromer as a model for one of his figures. Well, why should he not? He had to present a type of which Lord Cromer has been held up as the ideal representative. He has given his figure a private history that completely detaches it from Lord Cromer as a private man. And he has taken Lord Cromer's public traits at the highest valuation of Lord Cromer's most devoted flatterers. He has certainly not said an unfavorable word for which he has not Lord Cromer's own warrant in published official documents. It is true that the figure he draws is a character in a romance; but are the innumerable newspaper articles that told the tale of the conspiracy of Islam, and the strong stern Englishman who stamped it out by hanging and flogging helpless unarmed, unorganized peasants any the less romances, and very vile and silly romances, too? If we refuse to read bluebooks, and insist on having romances, let us at least have them written by a master hand, with some knowledge and conscience behind it.

The next charge is that Hall Caine's picture of the British occupation is not in accord with the facts. This is true. Hall Caine has neither the cynicism nor the specific talent for extravagant farce to paint the official occupation as it really is. When I did it—when I told the story of how the officials demanded the suppression of the Egyptian newspapers and "a considerable increase in the army of occupation" because three thieves knocked a soldier off a donkey everybody laughed, but nobody believed me. I quoted the official letters and gave the official references in vain; the facts are too absurd, too grotesquely comic to be credible. There are truths too ridiculous to be thinkable except as jokes, just as there are truths too shameful to be mentioned by decent writers. Hall Caine has throughout represented occupation officialism as public-spirited, high-minded and earnestly patriotic even when misled and mistaken. There is no evidence that it deserves any such compliment. On its own showing, it is mostly snobbish, uppish, buffish, narrow, ignorant, conceited, and subject to paroxysms of panic in which it is capable of the vilest cruelty and injustice. But it is protected from exposure by the idolatry of officialism which has lately taken possession of England. Only the other day Mr. Walkley, an upper division civil servant, and one of the most brilliant critical essayists in the country, told the select committee on stage plays, in effect, that he had no faith in the power of decency, honor, virtue, the grace of God, or the common law to keep the English theater from debauchery, but that all those forces could not do could be done infallibly, omnisciently and omnipotently—in short, divinely—by an official. And the speaker of the house of commons indorsed his opinion. Both gentlemen naively added that the theater had become so corrupt under official despotism that they could not take their daughters to see officially licensed plays without careful inquiry beforehand as to their decency. What is to be done in the face of such idolatrous infatuation?

The next charge—a well-worn one—is that "The White Prophet" has inflamed sedition and provoked riot and insurrections. The curt reply that it hasn't is too trite to be interesting; besides it is a mere fact, and facts are not popular in this country. Why does the official world always make this charge? For exactly the same reason that the lion tamers at the music-halls always put up strong railings and carry terrible whips and iron bars when they enter the den and stand dauntlessly in the midst of twenty lions. If they revealed the fact that the lions had been carefully fed to such an extent that the offer of a nice plump baby would simply nauseate them—if they reminded the audience that African travelers testify that it takes several days' starvation to induce a lion to attack a man—people would not pay to see the performance. But it is more romantic to believe that the performer is facing a frightful danger with iron nerve. Even when the lady (it is more effective when a lady does it) has openly to slash a lion across the eyes with a whip before it can be persuaded even to growl at her, the audience still loves to think that she is taking her life in her hand. Now this is a very favorite official performance in Egypt, except that as our officials go through it with sheep instead of lions, more sensational steps have to be taken to persuade the public that the Egyptian sheep is the most savage of man-eaters. It is lucky for the officials that the English are not logical; for the first half of the official story is that the Egyptians are such abject slaves and cowards that England had to rescue them from the most horrible oppression by Ismail, and could make soldiers of them only by giving them English officers; and the second half is that they are so desperately ferocious, bloody-minded and implacable, that at a word of encouragement from an English novelist, they will rise and sweep the Occupation into the Nile after ravishing all the white women and massacreing [sic] all the white men. But nobody sees the incoherence. As the first half shows the Englishman as magnificently superior, and the second as dauntlessly brave, he does not notice that they flatly contradict one another.

The truth is that any novelist who could really make tyranny dangerous would be the greatest living benefactor of the human race. Men, whether white or red, yellow or black, are not too insurrectionary, but too docile, too sheepish, too cowardly, to keep the world decent. That is why their condition is so miserable and their history so dishonorable. If we could depend on a sanguinary revolution in England once a month until the crooked were made straight, and the rough places plain, we should presently be a happy and prosperous nation. The real objection to Hall Caine's novel is that it may make the Egyptians too patient and confiding by persuading them that all Englishmen are as sympathetic and as high-minded as the author.

Finally there is the objection that Hall Caine's hero, an Arab, has a "creeping" resemblance to Jesus, who, as we all know, was a thorough English gentleman. Worse still, he has, in doing so, suggested that Jesus was a reality instead of a picture by Holman Hunt. Mr. Gilbert Chesterton has just said very truly and forcibly that the one thing you must not assume in England is that God is something real "like a tiger." If we keep a god at all, we keep Him as we keep a watchdog; he may bite everybody else—indeed, that is what he is for—but he must not bite us. Hall Caine's prophet does not wag his tail at the door of the British consulate and bark and bite at the door of the mosque. He is a humane and honorable preacher, who appears superhuman in England only because he is neither a snob nor a sensualist. But suppose he were a reincarnation of Jesus! Does any Christian who has the faintest notion of what his religion means doubt that the spirit of Jesus is alive among us by continual reincarnation, and cannot be kept alive in any other way? What are we coming to when even professional writers are ignorant of this commonplace? The illiteracy which would forbid a man of letters to write an imitation of Christ might be forgiven to the Irish peasant, who is afraid to mention the fabrics, and tremblingly alludes to them as "themselves" when the terrifying subject is forced on him; but that London journalists should have sunk to such an abyss of tribal ignorance is enough to make us ask, with a gasp, how long it will be before the civilized nations of Europe and Asia will come and conquer us for our own good, as Caesar conquered us in the comparatively enlightened age of Boadicea.

Fortunately the novelist represents English feeling far more than the press or the governing class. He is comparatively a free man and can speak out. The English press is not free. Its notion of foreign policy is to hold up as the masterpiece of diplomacy such contemptible documents as the Anglo-Saxon agreement, in which the speculators of England and Russia, conspiring to tempt capital out of their own countries into Persia, have made a "keep-off-the-grass" compact for dividing the spoils. When our government class loses the power of remembering yesterday and foreseeing tomorrow, and spends today in talking manifest folly, it is time for the man of letters to take the instruction of public opinion out of its hands. And it is extremely reassuring to find that there is at least one man of letters who is not shirking that duty. In shouldering it, Hall Caine deserves well of his countrymen, and though it is perhaps too much to hope that they will have the political sagacity to appreciate his public spirit as a citizen, they may have imagination enough to come under his spell as a romancer.

Editor's Notes

- The above review was originally printed as a pamphlet on 11 October 1909; and subsequently in the *Atlanta Constitution,* 21 November 1909,

2B:2, on the occasion of the first American publication of *The White Prophet*, by Grosset and Dunlap of New York (in August 1909); and by D. Appleton, New York. The newspaper familiarized its readers with the furor over the book in the following headnote to Shaw's article: "(Note—The publication of a recent novel by Hall Caine has precipitated a tremendous literary controversy in England. The discussion involves the question of literary censorship, of a novelist's right to portray sacred characters or public men in his books, or to criticise his country's political policy in connection with what is admittedly a fictitious narrative. Mr. Caine deals severely with the British method of governing dependent peoples and especially with English administration in Egypt, where the scene of the story is laid. As a result he has been bitterly arraigned by the ardent imperialists, and a dramatization of his book by Beerbohm Tree has been interdicted by the government's theatrical censor. These developments have led Mr. George Bernard Shaw to take up the cudgels in defense of literary freedom and to ridicule the official attitude on the question in his usual brilliant fashion.)" Under this, in bold type, it repeats "By George Bernard Shaw."

▪ Shaw had this year been bedeviled by censorship problems of his own. *The Shewing-up of Blanco Posnet* (written between 16 February and 8 March 1909 also for Beerbohm Tree, who had repeatedly asked Shaw for a play) horrified Tree and was rejected by the censor on the grounds that it was blasphemous. The resulting letters by Shaw to the *Times* prompted the prime minister to appoint a select committee of both houses of Parliament to investigate the whole question of censorship. In the meantime, Dublin being outside the jurisdiction of the Lord Chamberlain, Shaw gave the play to Lady Gregory for the Abbey Theatre, and this gave rise to another flurry of official activity as the British government pressured the Lord Lieutenant of Ireland to have the play stopped, and the Viceroy's undersecretary actually threatened to revoke the patent of the Abbey Theatre if Shaw's play was performed there. Yeats and Lady Gregory, encouraged by a fusillade of letters from Shaw, stood their ground, making minor cuts as concessions to good taste, and the play began its run on 25 August 1909, to a huge expectant audience, which remained amused but puzzled by the censor's outrage at what seemed to them a mild satire. Hall Caine's novel *The White Prophet* had been published on 12 August 1909, two days before Shaw set out on his holiday to Ireland. He reached the Parknasilla Hotel, Sneem, Co. Kerry on the nineteenth, and on 29 August, he wrote to Gilbert Murray: "There is a case which interests me personally . . . and that is the case of Hall Caine's White Prophet. I think H.C. should be backed up. Egypt is a leading case on which we shall have to fight the whole question of coercive Imperialism versus federated commonwealths. . . . I have read half through The White Prophet & seen some of the Aspects of the East articles in the Daily Telegraph; and I have no doubt that H. C. is in earnest and on the right tack. I hear Heinemann is getting up some sort of testimonial preface or manifesto as a counterblast to the Imperialist attacks on the book and to the snobbish shame that prevents the men who privately sympathize with H.C. from letting him use their names. I am quite game to contribute (much good that will do him, I fear!); and I also want him to go before the Select Committee & tell the story of how the censorship stopped The White Prophet at His Majesty's—that is, if it really was the Censor, and not Tree, who stopped it" (*Collected Letters 1898–1910*, 865–66). Shaw wrote his response on 6 September 1909 as a preface to the second edition of Hall Caine's book, but Heinemann issued it in October as a pamphlet, and it subsequently appeared (with numerous typographical errors) as the above review in the *Atlanta Constitution*.

- [Sir Thomas Henry] Hall Caine (1853–1931), English novelist. Born in the Isle of Man, he was resident in Liverpool when the articles he contributed to the *Builder* and *Building News* brought him to the attention of Ruskin. He also joined the "Notes and Queries" Society, and made many other useful friendships in the late 1870s, most notably that of Dante Gabriel Rossetti (1828–82), who, after Hall Caine's lecture on the poet in 1879, invited him to stay in his home. After Rossetti's death, Hall Caine married and worked for a while on the staff of the *Liverpool Mercury*, in which his first novel, *The Shadow of a Crime* was serialized in 1885. Two years later his novel *The Deemster* was enormously popular. In the same year Shaw reviewed *A Son of Hagar* very unfavorably for the *Pall Mall Gazette*. In spite of Shaw's opinion, however, Hall Caine became extremely popular producing a score of novels that were translated into many languages, one of which, *The Eternal City* (1901) sold over a million copies, and several of which, including *The Manxman* (1894) were adapted to the stage. Shaw reviewed this last in the *Saturday Review* on 23 November 1895, and was just as unimpressed by Hall Caine's play as he had been with his novel.

- [Sir Herbert] Beerbohm Tree (1853–1917), English actor-manager, who became manager of the Haymarket Theatre in London in 1887, and in 1897 of His Majesty's Theatre (which he had built out of the box-office success of George du Maurier's *Trilby* in 1895, in which he played Svengali). Tree and the censor rarely saw eye to eye. In 1892, when the Shelley Society, of which Shaw was a member, was trying to stage a production of *The Cenci* (which deals with the theme of incest), for a time it appeared that Tree would lend them the Haymarket Theatre for the production; but an interview with E. F. S. Pigott, the then licenser of plays, changed his mind. And seven years after this review, when Tree produced Shaw's *Pygmalion*, his own publicity campaign sparked such sensationalism (even before the performance) over the phrase "Not bloody likely," that Shaw, according to Richard Huggett, "fled from London": "He had just seen a set of photographs taken after the première which made him look like an old dog who'd been caught in a fight and got the worst of it. He was so appalled that he refused to allow them to be published but he did send a set to Tree and Mrs. Pat with a brief inscription:'This is *your* doing!' "; see Richard Huggett, *The Truth about Pygmalion* (London: William Heinemann, 1969), 156.

- [Captain Alfred] Dreyfus (1859–1935), a French army officer, was convicted on a charge of treason in 1894. Found guilty of planning to smuggle a list of secret military documents to the German Embassy in Paris, Dreyfus was reduced in rank and transported to Devil's Island for the rest of his life. Two years later, however, Lt. Col. George Picquart, then head of military intelligence, discovered evidence that convicted another man [Major Esterhazy] of writing the treasonous document, but the evidence was suppressed and Picquart dismissed. The same evidence was presented by the relatives of Dreyfus, and the army had no choice but to court-martial Esterhazy. However, he was acquitted early in 1898. At this time the novelist Emile Zola (1840–1902) wrote an impassioned letter to *L'Aurore* under the heading *J'accuse,* which denounced the cover-up by both the military and civil authorities. Zola himself was tried for libel, fined, and sentenced to a year in prison; but he escaped and spent a brief exile in England, causing the Dreyfus case to become a worldwide scandal. Meanwhile, in August 1898, Picquart's successor (Col. Hubert-Joseph Henry), confessed that he had forged documents to implicate Dreyfus, was arrested and committed suicide in his cell. A retrial of Dreyfus was announced, but it merely produced a second conviction—which verdict was so unpopular that it unseated the French government in 1899, and drastically reduced the power of the military in France. Dreyfus himself, reinstated as a major, was decorated with the *legion d'honneure,* and served in World War I.

▪ Wilfrid Scawen Blunt (1840–1922), English poet. In the diplomatic corps, he championed the cause of Ahmed Arabi Pasha and Egyptian nationalism in the early 1880s. Blunt's book *The Secret History of the English Occupation of Egypt* (in two volumes, 1907) deals with Arabi Pasha's uprising in 1881, crushed by British forces in 1882, and the subsequent occupation army that ruled there. Denshawai was a little village in the Nile Delta, scene of an altercation on 13 June 1906 over British officers, who were shooting the villagers' pigeons. The resultant fracas, which wounded the Egyptians and bruised the Britishers, led to brutal retribution by the British military authorities, who issued sentences of death, hanged men before their wives and children, and condemned others to penal servitude for life. Shaw describes these atrocities in detail in his "Preface for Politicians" in *John Bull's Other Island* (1907). Blunt encouraged opposition to what he considered to be "a judicial crime of the largest dimensions committed by our representative in Egypt" by compiling an article ("Atrocities of Justice under British Rule in Egypt") that was a fierce denunciation of Lord Cromer (see below), and Sir Edward Grey's weakness in concealing the truth of the Denshawai affair in reports to Parliament. Cromer resigned as a result. Blunt (who met Shaw in 1906) admired Shaw's own hatred of injustice.

▪ Shaw's opposition to vivisection, and to those who issue "equally credulous and well-meant and equally mistaken certificates to the vivisectors of dogs" was lifelong. On 10 June this year he had delivered an address to the British Union for the Abolition of Vivisection, which was published shortly thereafter.

▪ Pontius Pilate (?–c. 36) was Roman procurator of Judæa and Samaria, and

Caiaphas the high priest in Jerusalem, at the time of Jesus Christ's crucifix-ion (Matt. 26).

▪ Mahomet (Turkish pronunciation of Muhammad, or Mohammed, c. 570–632), founder of Islam.

▪ Girolamo [Jerome] Savonarola (1452–96), Italian preacher, reformer, and ascetic who denounced abuses in the church, assumed the mantle of prophet, and antagonized Pope Alexander VI, who finally excommunicated him for seditious teaching. Savonarola declared this judgment invalid, was tried as a heretic and burned.

▪ Saint Francis [of Assisi; originally Giovanni Francesco Bernadone] (1182–1226), Italian monk, preacher, founder of the Franciscan Order. Born into a wealthy family, he later renounced riches, and one day heard a call to go out into the world, possess nothing, and do good everywhere. He gathered around him twelve disciples who elected Francis to be their supe-rior. In 1212 he received into the fellowship a young well-born nun of Assisi [later Saint] Clare, who established the Order of the Poor Ladies [the "Poor Clares"].

▪ [Evelyn Baring, Earl] Cromer (1841–1917), English colonial administra-tor, was British controller-general of Egyptian finance from 1879 to 1880, and agent and consul-general in Egypt from 1883 to 1907. For Sir Edward Grey, who had been the latter's private secretary in 1884, see below, 285).

▪ [Andrew] Carnegie (see above, 225).

▪ A[rthur] B[ingham] Walkley (1855–1926), English drama and literary critic. A brilliant scholar at Oxford, he rose to high rank in the Civil Service, but under the influence of William Archer began writing theatrical reviews. When the *Star* newspaper was founded in 1888 he became its drama critic, a post he held until 1900, calling himself 'Spectator.' He also contributed periodical articles on the theater and drama in general, and so began his career as a critical essayist. Collections of his criticisms appeared in volume form, *Playhouse Impressions* (1892), and *Frames of Mind* (1899), in which year he began contributing drama criticism to the *Times,* whose full-time drama critic he became the following year. Not surprisingly then, he was asked to address the Joint Select Committee of the House of Lords and the House of Commons on the Stage Plays (Censorship), whose 375-page re-port, weighing more than two pounds, contains the evidence of some re-markable writers, including (among many others) Bernard Shaw and Hall Caine. Unfortunately, instead of allowing the writers to read an initial state-ment of their views, the committee proceeded entirely by cross-examination, which prevented coherent arguments from being presented. However, Shaw's censure of Walkley is just. Walkley's main point concerned the psy-chology of crowds, which, he maintained, made a censorship of plays neces-sary, whereas books did not produce the same effect on the individual. Logically, this led Walkley (under cross-examination by Herbert Samuel) to admit that, if his argument held true, one should also censor political meet-ings, lectures, and sermons.

▪ In his "crooked were made straight, and the rough places plain," Shaw paraphrases Isaiah 40:3: "Every valley shall be exalted, and every mountain and hill shall be made low: and the crooked shall be made straight, and the rough places plain."

- [William] Holman Hunt (1827–1910), English painter, whose famous didactic picture of Christ, "The Light of the World" made an enormous impression when first exhibited at the Academy Exhibition of 1854; subsequently its replica toured the world. The original now resides in Keble College, Oxford.
- Gilbert [Keith] Chesterton (see below, 331–32).
- [Gaius Julius] Caesar (100 or 102–44 B.C.) Roman general and statesman, invaded Britain in 55 and 54 B.C., but was not contemporary with Boadicea [or Boudicca], the warrior-queen who lived in the first century A.D.
- The "Anglo-Saxon agreement," in which "the speculators of England and Russia . . . have made a 'keep-off-the-grass' compact for dividing the spoils" was the Russo-British Convention of 1907, engineered in part by Sir Edward Grey (see below, 285). Its chief provisions in regard to Persia were that Britain undertook to seek no political or commercial concessions north of Kasr-i-Shirin, Isfahan, Yezd, and Kakh; Russia undertook the same south of the Afghan frontier to Gazik, Birjend, Kerman, and Bander Abbasi; both agreed that the area between should be neutral, and that all previous concessions should be respected; and finally that should Persia fail to meet its liabilities in respect of loans contracted, Britain and Russia reserved the right to assume control over Persian revenues.

24 December 1910

MR. FRANK HARRIS'S SHAKESPEAR*
[C1756]

I must not affect an impersonal style when reviewing a book in which I am introduced so very personally as in the preface to this play by Frank Harris. He accuses me flatly of cribbing from him, which I do not deny, as I possess in a marked degree that characteristic of Shakespear, Molière, and Handel, which is described as picking up a good thing where you find it. After all, what did Mr. Harris mean me to do? He published certain views about Shakespear, just as Darwin published certain views about the origin of species. But whereas Dar-

---

* "Shakespeare and His Love." By Frank Harris. F. T. Palmer. 2s. 6d. net.

win did not expect biologists to continue writing as if Chambers's Vestiges of Creation were still the latest thing in their science, Mr. Harris seems seriously to believe that I ought to have treated the history of Shakespear exactly as the Cowden Clarkes left it, and to have regarded his observations as non-existent. The mischief of such literary ethics is shewn in Mr. Harris's own work. It is impoverished by his determination not to crib from me, just as my work is enriched by my determination to crib from him. Nothing that he ever said or wrote about Shakespear was lost on me. Everything that I ever said or wrote about Shakespear seems to have been lost on him. Consequently, my Shakespear has everything that is good in Harris and Shaw. His Shakespear has only what is good in Harris. I respectfully invite my friends and patrons to walk up to *my* booth, as offering, on his own shewing, the superior exhibition.

I doubt, however, if our plays would have differed by as much as three words if we had never heard of or met one another. I should not dwell on Mr. Harris's complaint (which has been so valuable an advertisement for both of us) if it were not that I want to crush Mr. Harris on certain points on which I have a real quarrel with him. I say nothing of his picture of me as a successful and triumphant plunderer of other men's discoveries and picker of other men's brains. But I have a word to say as to Mr. Harris's latest picture of himself during this bay-tree-flourishing of mine. Here it is, in his own words:—

"Whoever will be one of 'God's spies,' as Shakespeare called them, must spend years in some waste place, some solitude of desert and mountain, resolutely stripping himself of the time-garment of his own paltry *ego,* alone with the stars and night winds, giving himself to thoughts that torture, to a wrestling with the Angel that baffles and exhausts. But at length the travail of his soul is rewarded; suddenly, without warning, the spirit that made the world uses him as a mouthpiece and speaks through him. In an ecstasy of humility and pride—'a reed shaken by the wind'—he takes down the Message. Years later, when he gives the gospel to the world, he finds that men mock and jeer him, and tell him he's crazy, or, worse still, declare they know the fellow, and ascribe to him their own lusts and knaveries. No one believes him or will listen, and when he realises his loneliness his heart turns to water within him, and he himself begins to doubt his inspiration. That is the lowest hell. Then in his misery and despair comes one man who accepts his message as authentic-true; one man who shows in the very words of his praise that he, too, has seen the Beatific Vision, has listened to the Divine Voice. At once the prophet is saved; the sun irradiates his icy dungeon; the desert blossoms like a rose; his solitude sings with choirs invisible. Such a disciple is spoken of ever afterwards as the belovéd, and set apart above all others." [Mr. Harris goes on to say that I am not such a disciple.]

This remarkable portrait has every merit except that of resemblance to any Frank Harris known to me or to financial and journalistic London. I say not a word against finance and the founding of weekly journals; but if a man chooses to devote to them what was meant for literature, let him not blame me for his neglected opportunities. Mr. Harris reviles me for not rolling his log; but I protest there was no log to roll. The book called "The Man Shakespeare," and this play flung in my venerable face with a preface accusing me of having trodden a struggling saint into darkness so that I might batten on his achievements, might just as well have been published fifteen years ago. If they have been suppressed, it has been by Mr. Harris's own preoccupation with pursuits which, however energetic and honorable, can hardly be described as wrestling with angels in the desert in the capacity of one of "God's spies." I have never disparaged his activities, knowing very little about them except that they seemed to me to be ultra-mundane; but I feel ill-used when a gentleman who has been warming both hands at the fire of life, and enjoying himself so vigorously that he has not had time to publish his plays and essays, suddenly seizes the occasion of a little *jeu d'esprit* of my own on the same subject (for I, too, claim my share in the common Shakespearean heritage) to hurl them, not only into the market, but at my head. If he has been neglected, he has himself to thank. If he really wishes to keep in the middle of the stream of insult which constitutes fame for fine artists to-day, he must give us plenty of masterpieces to abuse, instead of one volume of criticism fifteen years late, a few short stories of the kind that our Philistine critics and advertisement managers do not understand even the need of reviewing, and a play which has been kept from the stage by obvious unsuitability to the resources and limitations of our commercial theatres.

Coming to the play itself, the first thing one looks for in it is Shakespear; and that is just what one does not find. You get "the melancholy Dane" of Kemble and Mr. Wopsle; but the melancholy Dane was not even Hamlet, much less Shakespear. Mr. Harris's theory of Shakespear as a man with his heart broken by a love affair will not wash. That Shakespear's soul was damned (I really know no other way of expressing it) by a barren pessimism is undeniable; but even when it drove him to the blasphemous despair of Lear and the Nihilism of Macbeth, it did not break him. He was not crushed by it: he wielded it Titanically, and made it a sublime quality in his plays. He almost delighted in it: it never made him bitter: to the end there was mighty music in him, and outrageous gaiety. To represent him as a snivelling, broken-hearted swain, dying because he was jilted, is not only an intolerable and wanton belittlement of a great spirit, but a flat contradiction of Mr. Harris's own practice of treating the plays as autobiography. Nobody has carried that practice to wilder extremes than he; and far be it from me to blame him, because nobody has discovered, or divined, more interesting and suggestive references. But why does he throw it over when he attempts to put Shakespear on the stage for us? He says that Hamlet is Shakespear. Well, what is Hamlet's attitude towards women? He is in love with Ophelia. He writes her eloquent love letters; and when he has fascinated her, he bullies her and overwhelms her with bitter taunts, reviles her painted face, bids her to get her to a nunnery, and tells her she was a fool to believe him, speaking with even more savage contempt of his own love than of her susceptibility to it. When he finds that he has unintentionally killed her father with a sword thrust, the one thing that never troubles him is the effect on her and on his relations with her. He thinks no more of her until he accidentally finds himself at her funeral, and learns that she has been driven to madness and suicide by his treatment and his slaying of her father. He exhibits rather less of human concern than any ordinary stranger might, until her brother, a man of conventional character and habits, breaks down in the usual way and bursts into melodramatic exclamations of personal grief and vindictive rage against the man who has killed his father and broken his sister's heart. Hamlet's artistic sense is revolted by such rant. He ridicules it fiercely; tells the brother that his own philosophic humanity is worth the "love" of forty thousand brothers; and expresses himself as surprised and hurt at the young man's evident ill-feeling towards him. And with that he puts poor Ophelia clean out of his mind. Half-an-hour later he is "sorry he forgot himself" with her brother; but for her he has no word or thought: with the clay from her grave still on his boots, he jumps at the proposal of a fencing match, and thinks he shall win at the odds.

If Hamlet is Shakespear, then Mr. Harris's hero is not Shakespear, but, in the words of Dickens, whom Mr. Harris despises, "So far from it, on the contrary, quite the reverse." "Men have died from time to time; and worms have eaten them; but not for love," says Shakespear. And again, "I am not so young, sir, to love a woman for her singing"— the only thing, by the way, that could move him. "Her voice was ever soft, gentle, and low" is his tenderest praise.

Add to this the evidence of the sonnets. Shakespear treated the dark lady as Hamlet treated Ophelia, only worse. He could not forgive himself for being in love with her; and he took the greatest care to make it clear that he was not duped—that there was not a bad point in her personal appearance that was lost on him even in his most amorous moments. He gives her a list of her blemishes: wiry hair, bad complexion, and so on (he does not even spare her an allusion to the "reek" of her breath); and his description of his "lust," and his revulsion from it, is the most merciless passage in English literature. Why Mr. Harris, who insists again and again that in the sonnets and in Hamlet you have the man Shakespear, should deliberately ignore them in his dramatic portrait of Shakespear, and make him an old-fashioned schoolgirl's hero with a secret sorrow and a broken heart and a romantic melancholy—rather like Mr. Jingle cutting out Mr. Tupman with the maiden aunt—is a question I leave him to answer as best he may.

However, I must not pretend not to know the answer. Mr. Harris says that his Shakespear is not Mr. Jingle, but Orsino, in Twelfth Night, and Antonio, the "tainted wether of the flock."

Now, even if we allow this—if we throw over Hamlet, Berowne, Mercutio, and those sprite-like projections of Shakespear's impish gaiety, Richard III. (Act I.) and Iago, the fact remains that Orsino throws over his dark lady with a promptitude which convinces us that the only thing he really cares about is music. And Antonio does not care about women at all. Even Posthumus, another of Mr. Harris's pet prototypes, is much more disgusted at his own folly, and at the wreck of his own life and the unsatisfactoriness of the world in general, than sentimentally heartbroken about the supposed death of Imogen. Macbeth, when his wife's death is announced, says it is a pity she should die at a moment when he has more important matters to attend to. In every case where the Shakespearean man is untrammeled by the catastrophe of a borrowed story, and is touched by sexual sorrow, he is moved, not, like Laertes, to agonized personal grief, but to self-forgetfulness in a deeper gravity of reflection on human destiny. In short, the authority cited by

Mr. Harris for the authenticity of his heartbroken Shakespear is flatly against him instead of for him.

One crowning intrusion of commonplace sentiment is the exhibition of Shakespear as sentimentally devoted to his mother. I ask Mr. Harris, in some desperation, what evidence he has for this. Even if we assume with him that Shakespear was a perfect monster of conventional sentiment, filial sentimentality is not an English convention, but a French one. Englishmen mostly quarrel with their families, especially with their mothers. Shakespear has drawn for us one beautiful and wonderful mother; but she shews all her maternal tenderness and wisdom for an orphan who is no kin to her, whilst to her son she is shrewd, critical, and without illusions. I mean, of course, the Countess of Rousillon in All's Well that Ends Well; and here I will make Mr. Harris a present of a guess quite in his line. Mr. Harris, following Tyler and several of his predecessors, identifies Mr. W. H. of the sonnets as the Earl of Pembroke. Now, in the sonnets we find Shakespear suddenly beginning to press Mr. W. H. to marry for the purpose of begetting an heir. Nothing could be more unnatural as from one young man to another. And nothing could be more natural if Mr. W. H.'s mother asked Shakespear to do it. If Mr. W. H. was Pembroke, his mother very likely wanted him to marry. Now, "Sidney's sister, Pembroke's mother," the subject of Jonson's famous epitaph, was by all accounts a perfect model for the noble and touching portrait which Shakespear called the Countess of Rousillon. So there you are, with an original for the only sympathetic mother except Hermione (a replica), in Shakespear's plays, without resorting to the French convention of "ma mère," and flying in the face of all the other plays! Yet Mr. Harris will have it that Shakespear idolized his mother, and that this comes out repeatedly in his plays. In the names of all the mothers that ever were adored by their sons, where? Hamlet, for instance? Are his relations with his mother a case in point? Or Falconbridge's, or Richard the Third's, or Cloten's, or Juliet's? The list is becoming thin, because, out of thirty-eight plays, only ten have mothers in them; and of the ten five may be struck out of the argument as histories. Nobody but Mr. Harris would cite the story of Volumnia and Coriolanus as Shakespearean autobiography; and nobody at all would cite Margaret of Anjou, the Duchess of York, or Constance. There are, for the purposes of Mr. Harris's argument, just two sympathetic mothers in the whole range of the plays. One is the Countess of Rousillon and the other is Hermione. Both of them are idealized noblewomen of the same type, which is not likely to

have been the type of Mrs. John Shakespear. Both of them are ten-
derer as daughter's mothers than as son's mothers. The great Shakespearean heroes are all motherless, except Hamlet, whose scene
with his mother is almost unbearably shameful: we endure it only
because it is "Shakespear" to us instead of an affective illusion of
reality. Never do we get from Shakespear, as between son and
mother, that unmistakable tenderness that touches us as between
Lear and Cordelia and between Prospero and Miranda. Mr. Harris
insists on Prospero and Miranda in his book; but in his play, Shakespear's daughter is a Puritan Gorgon who bullies him. This may be
good drama; but it is not good history if Mr. Harris's own historical
tests are worth anything.

The identification of the dark lady, of which Mr. Harris has made so
much, is of no consequence. Mr. Harris's play would be none the
worse if the heroine were called Mary Jones or Mary Muggins. But
since he insists on it, it may as well be said that in spite of the brave
fight made for the Fitton theory by Thomas Tyler the weight of evidence is against it. I have myself called the Dark Lady Mary Fitton
because one name is as good as another; and for stage purposes I
wanted a name that would remind Elizabeth of Mary Queen of Scots.
But what does the Fitton case come to? If it were certain that Mr. W.
H. were the Earl of Pembroke, and if the portraits of Mary Fitton were
those of a wonderful and fascinating dark woman like Mrs. Patrick
Campbell or Miss Mona Limerick, then, no doubt, the case would be a
fairly probable one. But Pembroke is not even the favorite among the
many guesses at the identity of Mr. W. H.; and the portraits are not the
portraits of a dark woman. This latter fact would smash the Fitton
hypothesis, even though Pembroke were Mr. W. H., as, in my opinion,
he may have been; for the only weighty argument against him—that a
bookseller would not have dared to call an earl plain Mister for fear of
the Star Chamber—altogether leaves out of account the likelihood
that Pembroke himself, though not averse to being known to an inner
circle as "the onlie begetter" of so famous a collection of sonnets, could
hardly have allowed himself to be published to all the world as the
wicked earl in the little drama of the faithful poet, the wanton lady,
and the false friend.

And now, what does all this matter? What has it to do with the
merits of Mr. Harris's play? Really very little; for though it would be
highly interesting and relevant if it explained why Mr. Harris has
substituted for Shakespear quite another sort of hero, it explains
nothing of the sort. Mr. Harris's changeling is not Shakespear: he is

Guy de Maupassant. And this is not surprising; for it happens that when De Maupassant's short stories were almost the foremost phenomenon in European fiction, Frank Harris was the only writer of short stories in England for whom we could claim anything of the like quality. So that by depicting himself on his best behaviour, Mr. Harris has achieved a very good De Maupassant, and called him Shakespear.

What has kept the play from the stage is, no doubt, partly the fact that the pioneer enterprises can neither afford spectacular costume plays nor act them very well (modern realism is their strongest ground), and partly because there is not material enough in the Fitton episode for a big production at, say, His Majesty's. Nor does the melancholy, low-toned, sentimental Maupassant-Shakespear come out with the brilliancy, humor, and majesty that both the public and the actor look for in a part with so famous a name. Yet it is a noble and tender part; and the real difficulty is the slenderness of the material, and the brute fact that the dark lady episode came to no more than an *amourette.* Everything we know about Shakespear can be got into a half-hour sketch. He was a very civil gentleman who got round men of all classes; he was extremely susceptible to word-music and to graces of speech; he picked up all sorts of odds and ends from books and from the street talk of his day, and welded them into his work; he was so full of witty sallies of all kinds, decorous and indecorous, that he had to be checked even at the Mermaid suppers; he was idolized by his admirers to an extent which nauseated his most enthusiastic and affectionate friends; and he got into trouble by treating women in the way already described. Add to this that he was, like all highly intelligent and conscientious people, business-like about money and appreciative of the value of respectability and the discomfort and discredit of Bohemianism; also that he stood on his social position and desired to have it affirmed by the grant of a coat-of-arms, and you have all we know of Shakespear beyond what we gather from his plays. And it does not carry us to a tragedy.

Now Mr. Harris's play begins by suggesting that it is going to be a Shakespearean tragedy. It leads up to the brink of a tragedy, and then perforce suddenly stops and skips to the year 1616, when the poet is depressingly ill and presently dies a depressing death as a beaten man. Jonson and Drayton are duly introduced; but instead of having the traditional roaring time with them and killing himself with a final debauch of wit and wine, he allows them to be driven ignominiously from the house by his pious daughter whilst he is in the depths of his next-morning repentance. De Maupassant dies of exhaustion, in fact; and that is not the Shakespearean way of dying. All Shakespear's heroes died game. The spectacle of Shakespear dying craven, with rare Ben and Drayton slinking off before the sour and stern piety of Puritan Mistress Hall, is bitterly masterly, but masterly in the modern iconoclastic vein, not in the heroic Shakespearean one.

Nevertheless, the play must be performed; for like everything that Mr. Harris writes carefully, it is a work of high and peculiar literary quality. It is also truly Shakespearean in its character drawing: everybody on the stage, brief as his or her part may be, gives some hint, however trifling, of a marked temperament of some recognizable kind. Mary Fitton is quite modern, and *amoureuse* and a *revoltée*. She would be quite in place in a play by Sudermann, and is therefore not credible as the daughter of an Elizabethan squire; but she is vivid in her courage and generosity, and not unworthy of Shakespear's regard. Pembroke, the handsome, daring young gallant, whose number is nevertheless very distinctly number one, is excellent. The attempt to reproduce Falstaff as Chettle is a literary *tour de force;* and though Mr. Harris, with his sombre, sardonic, almost macabre touch, takes the fun out of the poor old Bohemian drunkard, and makes him a saddening rather than an amusing spectacle, this very modern and serious turn to an old joke is unquestionably the right turn. The idea of making the prudent Shakespear lend Chettle money from a feeling that he ought to pay him for his unconscious services as a model, is a shrewd one.

Scene after scene in the Fitton episode is interesting and full of literary distinction and tenderness and fancy. The treatment is neither modern nor Elizabethan—or, rather, it is both by turns. Shakespear sometimes quotes himself and sometimes says such things as "What wine of life you pour!" which comes right dramatically, but is impossible historically (Shakespear only once makes a metaphor of wine, when Macbeth, pretending to be horrified at the discovery of Duncan's bleeding corpse, says "The wine of life is drawn; and the mere lees is left this vault to brag of"). Generally speaking, Mr. Harris's style, short, mordant, rather grim when it is not almost timidly delicate, excludes Shakespear's. At first we miss the extravagance, the swing, the impetuous periods, the gay rhetoric of the immortal William. But as an attempt to reproduce them could be at best only second-hand Shakespear, we soon admit that original Harris is not only fresher, but better. The curious mixture of eighteenth-century sentiment and modern culture and freethinking (in the literal sense) recalls Oscar Wilde, and perhaps explains an absurd tradition current ten years ago, that Mr. Harris was Oscar's "ghost": a tradition that shewed the most desolating lack of literary perception and sense of character. The thumbnail sketch of Elizabeth is brutal; but it bites effectively.

And now, by how many of us could as much success be achieved if we attempted to handle such a subject? I could say a good deal more; but I have already gone beyond all reasonable limits of space—Mr. Harris's own fault for wasting so much on an idle controversy. I heartily recommend the play to our theatrical reformers. As a full-sized tragedy, it might bewilder, disappoint, and fail, because there was no tragedy in the historic facts. But, as an exquisite episode, it will delight all genuine connoisseurs, if any such exist in England—which I am sometimes tempted to doubt.

G. B. S.

Editor's Notes

- The above review was first published in the *Nation*, 8, (24 December 1910): 542–44, and reprinted in Bernard Shaw, *Pen Portraits and Reviews* (1931), the text of which is substantially the same, the only alterations being the omission of the period [.] after Mr., the modernizing of "to-day" as "today," and the addition of the first accent on *révoltée*, which had been omitted in the original.
- Shaw and his wife were outward bound from Bristol on board the *S. S. Port Antonio,* to visit Sydney Olivier in Jamaica on the day when this review was published. It was the final salvo in a battle of words between Frank Harris and Shaw that had begun innocently enough on 13 November 1910, when Shaw spoke in the *Observer* about his forthcoming play, *The Dark Lady of the Sonnets.* Ten days later, Harris's play appeared in print, and its author gave a long interview to W. R. Titterton of the *Daily News,* in which he began by disparaging Shaw's knowledge of Shakespeare, and went on to accuse Shaw of appropriating to himself Harris's "discovery" that "Hamlet Macbeth Shakespeare lives behind the masks of the heroes of his plays." He complained that his own play on Shakespeare had been rejected because "Tree couldn't stomach [Harris's unheroic] Shakespeare." And now, concluded the indignant Harris, Shaw's own play *The Dark Lady of the Sonnets* was about to be performed in which (as appeared from Shaw's interview in the *Observer*) Shaw had annexed "the whole of the theory I have built up during the past fifteen years, and [acknowledges] the annexation with a

contemptuous pat on the head" ("G.B.S. and the Dark Lady," *Daily News,* 23 November 1910). Shaw's play, written in three days as a fundraiser for a national theater in memory of Shakespeare, had its premiere the following day exactly a month before this review was published, on 24 November 1910 at the Theatre Royal, Haymarket, starring Granville Barker as Shakespeare, and Mona Limerick (see below) as the Dark Lady. Although he had been denounced by Frank Harris as a plagiarist, Shaw shared the author's box that night with Harris and his wife; no doubt because his written response to Harris had been printed in the *Daily News* on the day of the performance. It also took the form of an interview with W. R. Titterton, in which Shaw correctly gives Thomas Tyler (see below) credit for the Mary Fitton theory; and afterwards is amusing at Harris's expense. The above review gave Shaw a chance to put Harris's play into perspective, and liberate his own knowledge of Shakespeare.

▪ Frank Harris (1856–1931), Irish-American journalist and author. Born James Thomas Harris in Galway, Ireland, (or, according to his later account, at Tenby, in Wales), he left school in 1870 and went to the United States, where his occupations ranged from bootblack to law student. He returned to Europe about 1876, and entered Fleet Street, becoming a most colorful character in journalistic circles. He was successively editor of the *Evening News* (1882–86), the *Fortnightly Review* (1886–94), the *Saturday Review* (1894–98)—while Shaw was its dramatic reviewer—and *Vanity Fair.* Shaw said that Harris "had no quality of editorship except the supreme one of knowing good work from bad, and not being afraid of it." Harris wrote two other plays: *Mr. and Mrs. Daventry* (1900), which he had planned with Oscar Wilde, and to which Shaw suggested a scenario sequel, and *Women of Shakespeare* (1911). He also wrote volumes of short stories, *The Man Shakespeare* (1909) which, Harris claimed, Shaw reviewed in "forty folios" that no one would publish, books on Oscar Wilde and other contemporaries, and the four-volume *My Life and Loves* (1922–27), a boastful account of his early intellectual and sexual exploits, which was initially banned as pornography. Harris's last book was *Bernard Shaw,* which was seen through the press by Shaw himself, and published posthumously in 1931.

▪ Robert Chambers (1802–71), English publisher who wrote about the evolution of the species in his book *Vestiges of Creation* (1844).

▪ [Charles] Cowden Clarke (1787–1877), English Shakespearean scholar, who, with his wife Mary Victoria Novello (1809–98), produced an annotated edition of Shakespeare's works in 1869.

▪ [John Philip] Kemble (1757–1823), English actor, whose Hamlet exemplified the "classic style," characterized by a careful analysis of the role to discover in it a single all-pervasive quality.

▪ Mr. Wopsle was a friend of Joe Gargery's in Dickens's *Great Expectations.* At first parish clerk, he afterward becomes an actor in London under the stage-name of Mr. Waldengarver. Pip and Herbert go to a small theatre to witness his impersonation of Hamlet. It is not a success: "Whenever that undecided Prince had to ask a question or state a doubt, the public helped him out with it. As for example; on the question whether 'twas nobler in the mind to suffer, some roared yes, and some no, and some inclining to both opinions said 'toss up for it.' "

- "Men have died from time to time and worms have eaten them, but not for love," says Rosalind in *As You Like It.*
- It is Kent in *King Lear* who, in answer to Lear's question "How old art thou?" replies, "Not so young, Sir, to love a woman for her singing."
- "Her voice was ever soft, / gentle, and low," is said of Cordelia by King Lear.
- Shaw quotes the anti-Petrarchan Sonnet 130 ("My mistress' eyes are nothing like the sun"), which is a satire not on the lady herself but upon the conventional hyperboles used by poets in describing ladies.
- The sonnet on lust is 129 ("Th' expense of spirit in a waste of shame / Is lust in action . . .").
- Mr. Jingle is the strolling actor in *The Pickwick Papers* who insinuates himself into the travelling Pickwick Club and, when Tracy Tupman has fallen in love with Miss Rachael Wardle, a maiden aunt of doubtful age, steals her affections away from him and elopes with her.
- Antonio is the melancholy friend and sponsor of Bassanio in *The Merchant of Venice,* whose pound of flesh is forfeit to Shylock; Berowne [or Biron] is one of the three lords attending on the King of Navarre in *Love's Labour's Lost;* Mercutio, the hotheaded friend of Romeo in *Romeo and Juliet,* and Iago (to whom the noun gaiety could never apply) is, in Coleridge's famous phrase, the "motive-hunting malignity" from *Othello.*
- In Shakespeare's First Folio (1623), our only authority for *All's Well that Ends Well,* the Countess was of Rosillion, not Rousillon, which is what the place became in the emendations of Rowe and Theobald. There was no Dramatis Personae in the First Folio.
- Thomas Tyler (1826–1902), English scholar. At the British Museum, where he was a frequenter of the Reading Room, he made the acquaintance of Shaw in the early 1880s. Shaw attended lectures by Tyler, and with him was a member of the New Shakspere Society, founded by F. J. Furnivall in 1873. On 7 January 1886, Shaw reviewed for the *Pall Mall Gazette* Tyler's photo-lithographic facsimile of *Shakspere's Sonnets,* in the introduction to which Tyler first broached the "Mistress Fitton theory." (see *Bernard Shaw's Book Reviews* 79–83). Shaw tells the story of this review, and gives a sketch of Tyler's character in the Preface to *The Dark Lady of the Sonnets.*
- Shakespeare's *Sonnets* (1609), four-fifths of which were apparently dedicated to a "fair youth," and the rest to a "dark lady," were prefaced on their first publication by a mysterious dedication signed T.T. (Thomas Thorpe, a publisher who owned the original copy) which read:—

TO THE ONLIE BEGETTER OF
THESE INSVING SONNETS
MR. W. H. ALL HAPPINESS
AND THAT ETERNITIE

PROMISED BY
OUR EVER-LIVING POET
WISHETH
THE WELL-WISHING
ADVENTURER
IN SETTING FORTH

Seas of critical ink have been spilled in endeavors to identify the "Mr. W. H." of the dedication, William Herbert, Earl of Pembroke being a claimant first advanced by James Boaden in 1832 to counter the popular Earl of Southampton [Henry Wriothesley] theory begun by Nathan Drake in 1817. Thomas Tyler (see above) was a Herbert advocate in his 1890 edition of *The Sonnets*. The first seventeen sonnets urge the young man to marry and procreate an heir.

▪ The epitaph on the Countess of Pembroke ascribed to Ben Jonson (1573–1634) is more probably by William Browne of Tavistock. Whalley first printed the poem as Jonson's, claiming that it was "universally assigned" to him. However, it is not to be found in any Jonson manuscript, and the autograph copy is—according to Herford and Simpson—"decisive for Browne's authorship." The epitaph reads as follows:

Underneath this sable Herse
Lyes the subject of all verse,
Sydneyes Sister: Pembrokes mother.
Death, ere thou hast slaine another
ffaire & Learn'd & good as she,
Tyme shall throw a Dart at thee.
Marble Pyles let no man raise
To her Name for after dayes.
Some kind woman borne as she,
Reading this, like Niobe
Shall turne Marble & become
Both her Mourner & her Tombe.

According to Shaw (in his Preface to *The Dark Lady of the Sonnets*) the idea that the Countess of Pembroke urged Shakespeare to induce her son to marry was Tyler's, not Shaw's own.

▪ Hermione is the long-suffering Queen in *The Winter's Tale,* mother of Mamillius and Perdita; [Philip] Falconbridge [known as the Bastard] is the half-brother of Robert Falconbridge in *King John,* and the natural son of Richard I. He compels his mother, Lady Falconbridge, to reveal his true identity in the first scene of the play; Cloten is the doltish son of the conniving Queen in *Cymbeline;* Volumnia is the mother of Coriolanus in the play of that name: in her pleading scene with her angry son (V.iii) she wins peace for Rome; Margaret of Anjou is the fierce, revengeful wife of Henry VI in *Henry VI* (scenes i–iii), and in *Richard III*, with a contempt for her husband; the Duchess of York is the mother of Richard in *Richard III* (Richard instructs Buckingham to throw a slur upon her character); and Constance is the distraught mother of the murdered Prince Arthur in *King John*.

- In Shaw's day, Shakespeare was credited with thirty-seven plays, not thirty-eight. Today, with the addition of such plays from the apocrypha as *The Two Noble Kinsmen*, the number may be higher.
- Mrs. Patrick Campbell [née Beatrice Stella Tanner] (1865–1940), English actress, who married Patrick Campbell in 1884 and made her début on the stage in Liverpool in 1888 in a play called *Bachelors*. From 1891 to 1893 she played unsuccessfully in melodramas at the Adelphi; but the artist Graham Robertson suggested her to George Alexander for the lead in Pinero's new drama, *The Second Mrs. Tanqueray*, in which she played a "woman with a past." Her success in this role was tremendous. Subsequently she played other strong roles in plays by Pinero, Henry Arthur Jones, and Ibsen. Her Ophelia (to Forbes Robertson's Hamlet) was not so lavishly praised, though Shaw defended her performance in the *Saturday Review*. In 1914 she created the role of Eliza Doolittle in Shaw's *Pygmalion*. At the time of writing the above review, however, Shaw was still two years away from the sexual infatuation for her that dominated his private life from 1912 to 1914. In those years Shaw spent long hours with her (as she was convalescing from an illness), wrote copious letters to her and distressed his wife Charlotte. The unconsummated "affair" finished when "Stella" married her second husband, Major George Frederick Myddleton Cornwallis-West.
- Miss Mona Limerick [Mary Charlotte Louise Gadney] (n.d.). Born in South America, her acting début was at Bristol, in May 1902, as Cynthia Doone in *A Touch of Nature*. She married Ben Iden Payne, and with him was prominently associated with Miss Horniman's Repertory scheme in the Gaiety Theatre, Manchester, where, among many other roles she played Blanche in Shaw's *Widowers' Houses;* a part she played again in 1909 at His Majesty's Theatre, London. In fact she played a great deal of Shaw in her short acting career: she created the title role [Mary Fitton] in the first production of Shaw's *The Dark Lady of the Sonnets* in 1910; and in February 1911 she toured as Ann Whitefield in *Man and Superman*. In 1914 she played at the Lyceum, Edinburgh, with Esmé Percy, again managing to include a deal of Shaw in the repertoire: she appeared in *Man and Superman, Candida,* and *The Philanderer.* Subsequently, an American tour with Esmé Percy in 1916 included appearances in *Overruled* (1912) and *Man and Superman.*
- The Star Chamber was "A court, chiefly of criminal jurisdiction, developed in the 15th c. from the judicial sittings of the King's Council in the Star Chamber at Westminster and abolished by the Long Parliament in 1641" (*OED*).
- Guy de Maupassant (1850–93) French fiction writer who wrote novels, but is best known for his nearly three hundred short stories, which are written with mordant humor and satire.

- The Mermaid tavern, where Shakespeare and Jonson habitually caroused, was celebrated by Francis Beaumont in the following lines:

> What things have we seen
> Done at the Mermaid! heard words that have been
> So nimble, and so full of subtle flame,
> As if that every one from whence they came
> Had meant to put his whole wit in a jest,
> And had resolved to live a fool the rest
> Of his dull life.

- Michael Drayton (1563–1631), English poet. He lived in Warwickshire and is traditionally supposed to have been with Shakespeare on the day of the latter's death.
- Shakespeare's eldest child, Susannah (1583–1649), in 1607 married the fashionable physician John Hall, one of whose patients was Michael Drayton. Whatever his wife's beliefs, Hall was certainly of Puritan sympathies.
- [Hermann] Sudermann (1857–1928), German dramatist and novelist. He wrote a number of realistic plays. Shaw had been reading his novel *Song of Songs* (1908) as he prepared a preface for volume 1 of his own *Dramatische Werke*, translated into German by Siegfried Trebitsch, which would be published in Berlin in 1911.
- [Henry] Chettle (?–c. 1607), English dramatist and pamphlet writer. He published a pamphlet, *Kind Heart's Dream* (1593) apologizing for Greene's celebrated attack on Shakespeare, which certainly gives warrant for his knowing the latter; and from 1598 he wrote plays for the Rose Theatre on the Bankside, most notably *The Tragedy of Hoffman* (1602). He also collaborated on many other plays, and wrote an elegy on the death of Queen Elizabeth, *England's Mourning Garment* (1603).

1 May 1911

OUR BOOK-SHELF: "THE LIFE OF TOLSTOY: LATER YEARS"* [C1772]

THIS book has a special interest for Fabians in two ways. First, being written by a Fabian, it instinctively answers the particular questions about Tolstoy's life a Fabian would ask. Second, it is an

---

* "The Life of Tolstoy: The Later Years." By Aylmer Maude. (Constable. 10s. 6d. n.)

admirable book to put into the hands of those converts to Socialism who imagine that the way to be a Socialist is to begin at once acting as if Socialism were already established: that is, acting like a lunatic. There are such people still in spite of Fabian propaganda. The lady who suddenly drags her servants into the drawingroom; introduces them to her friends; and tells them virtually that unless they consent to be treated as friends and fellow-citizens they will be discharged without a character, is still quite a possible phenomenon; for there is hardly any limit to the childishness and want of social sense which our system makes possible in genteel "independent" private life.

The most astonishing part of Aylmer Maude's book is its revelation of the extent to which this sort of folly was carried by Tolstoy. He was a man of genius in the very first flight of that rare species. He had the penetrating common sense characteristic of that first flight. And yet no English old maid of county family, living in a cathedral town on £300 a year, could have made more absurd attempts to start an ideal social system by private misconduct than he. He put on the dress of a moujik exactly as Don Quixote put on a suit of armor. He tried to ignore money as Don Quixote did. He left his own skilled work to build houses that could hardly be induced to stand, and to make boots that an army contractor would have been ashamed of. He let his property drift to the verge of insolvency and ruin like the laziest Irish squire because he disapproved of property as an institution. And he was neither honest nor respectable in his follies. He connived at all sorts of evasions. He would not take money on a journey; but he would take a companion who would buy railway tickets and pay hotel bills behind his back. He would not own property or copyrights; but he would make them over to his wife and children, and live in their country house in Yasnaya and their town house in Moscow very comfortably, only occasionally easing his conscience by making things as difficult and unpleasant for them as possible. He insisted on celibacy as the first condition of a worthy life; and his wife became sixteen times a mother, and found him an uxorious husband at seventy. In the ordinary affairs of life he shirked every uncongenial responsibility whilst availing himself of every luxury he really cared for. And he railed at his wife and family for enabling him to do it, treating his wife as ethically inferior because she insisted on saving the family from ruin until at last she gave him up as impossible and managed for him without saying anything harsher than her Russian formula "Nothing matters so long as the baby is not crying."

Probably many of Tolstoy's admirers dismissed these facts during

his lifetime as silly legends invented by people who did not understand him. But it seems clear now that they were quite true. Not, of
course, that Tolstoy was factproof. He soon found out by experience
that his follies were tiresome; and he never did anything when he
was once tired of it, though he did not always cease to recommend
others to do it. But one is none the less left asking why he did not
foresee the inevitable breakdown of his attempts to behave like a
disciple in Jerusalem 1900 years ago. After reading Aylmer Maude's
book I was tempted to answer that he never foresaw anything, and
learnt what he did learn by the simple process of knocking his head
against it. The Fabian reader may here lose patience and say that if I
have nothing more sensible to say than that Tolstoy was a fool, I had
better drop the subject and leave this review to more competent
hands. Others may say that we all learn things by knocking our
heads against them. Others, again, may say that Tolstoy had been
through all ordinary reasoning and come out on the other side of it
with the knowledge that we can only extend the range of possibility
in human conduct, as in other things, by continually attempting the
impossible. I said all these things to myself as I read. But take a
single incident from the book. Tolstoy writes The Kreutzer Sonata. It
is suggested that it should be read to the family and their guests at
Yasnaya. Tolstoy, assenting, hands the MS. to a gentleman to read.
The gentleman begins confidently; presently grows doubtful; finally
tells the Countess that he really cannot go on reading in the presence of the younger girls. Tolstoy, on being asked whether the book
is fit for their ears, replies calmly that they had better go to bed,
which they do before the reading is proceeded with. Now to say that
Tolstoy could not have foreseen this is to say that he had not intelligence enough to know that if he went out into the rain without an
umbrella he would get wet. Yet it is clear from the narrative that he
did not foresee it; and this must mean that he was so continually
preoccupied with his ideas and his imagination that he seldom gave
his mind to more immediate practical considerations—including the
consideration of other people's feelings and convenience—until his
neglect produced its inevitable consequences. No wonder the Countess was often near the end of her patience! Indeed there is one
occasion recorded by Maude when Tolstoy's preoccupation with his
own conscience carried him into inhuman callousness. His trick of
suddenly leaving the house and declaring he could no longer endure
to live in such a fashion has been brought into prominence since
Maude's book was published by his death on one of these occasions.

But when we read that he once did so when his wife was actually in the pains of childbirth, and that when, having kept her whilst in this condition in mortal anxiety about him for many hours, during which she refused to go to bed or even to leave the garden, he at last returned, he proceeded to pursue the subject of his grievances to her without regard to her travail, we are amazed at the extent to which a man who was boundlessly sympathetic on paper with imaginary beings could be so outrageously inconsiderate to real people in his own home. When we go on to ask why people stood all this from him, the reply must be partly that the Countess did not stand it, but took into her own hands the affairs he neglected, besides giving him pieces of her mind on occasion. She must be a woman of remarkable strength of character to have borne her burden without breaking down completely. If it be true that the effects of the strain on her had their share in the circumstances of that final flight from Yasnaya which ended in Tolstoy's death, no one can blame her.

So much for that part of the social burden which Tolstoy flatly refused to shoulder. After all, we cannot quarrel very deeply with him for his refusal: if a man does more than his share of extraordinary work for the world, we can hardly complain because he refuses to do the ordinary tasks which society offers him, and which are calculated for quite another sort of man. But it must be said that his own peculiar work would have been much better done in some respects if he had managed his estates and administered and exploited his copyrights instead of leaving all this instructive drudgery to his wife. It ended in his wife knowing a great deal more, in some respects, than he did of men and affairs, and in his using his powers and influence to set men on impracticable and mischievous enterprises. No doubt these had their value: Aylmer Maude himself exposes and confutes the Tolystoyan Anarchism with much more effect and conviction after his actual experience of a Tolstoyan community and of the Doukhobor affair than if he had been steered clear of such adventures by Tolstoy instead of being misled into them. But if this were held to justify Tolstoy for misleading him, any sort of bad advice would be justified. What one does not gather from the book is whether Tolstoy remained in a condition of invincible ignorance (for he went on giving the bad advice just as if it had worked perfectly) or whether he simply would not take the trouble to change his mind. He was most unfortunately incapable of laughing at himself, though he had a keen sense of the irony of wasted philanthropic effort: for example, whilst he was organizing famine relief as practically as the Fabian Society itself could have organized it, he ridiculed the whole business steadily all through as a ghastly futility. Yet when a Tolstoyan colony was making itself a spectacle for gods and men, not by organizing relief for starving people, but by reducing well-fed ones to destitution, his irony was never aroused: he persuaded himself—and sometimes even persuaded the colonists—that all that was wrong was that they had not been quite foolish enough. On the whole we must conclude that it was a grave and incurable defect in Tolstoy's training that he had never been obliged to do a real job of real work, and do it for his living. His spell of soldiering was of no use to him in that way: a man learns nothing of affairs from being cooped up in a battery and fed like an artillery horse whilst he fires cannons at the French and English and is fired at by them. Everything else that he did he played at and soon got tired of, except literature. In that he was a giant: in business and practical politics he was so inferior to his biographer that the book is a combination of eulogy and apology: Aylmer Maude has to say, in effect, "This man was so great—so impressive—that he made me accept him as my leader in matters in which he was, compared to me, a baby. And I still accept that position, though I am bound to shew you how mischievously impractical he was."

Everybody else was forced into the same position. Whether it was Tchertkoff caricaturing his absurdities, or Maude carefully testing them by experiment, or the Countess rescuing him from them with a strong practical hand, the result was always the same: nothing mattered provided the baby was not crying. If you have a baby who can speak with Tzars in the gate, who can make Europe and America stop and listen when he opens his mouth, who can smite with unerring aim straight at the sorest spots in the world's conscience, who can break through all censorships and all barriers of language, who can thunder on the gates of the most terrible prisons in the world and place his neck under the keenest and bloodiest axes only to find that for him the gates dare not open and the axes dare not fall, then indeed you have a baby that must be nursed and coddled and petted and let go his own way in spite of all the wisdom of governesses and schoolmasters. And the reviewer is as helpless as anyone else. Tolstoy is not even *à prendre ou à laisser.* You have to take him whether you like him or not, and take him as he is. Maude's book, which will stand, I think, among the big biographies of our literature, *must* be read, no matter what you may try to think of its hero.

G. B. S.

Editor's Notes

- This was first published in the *Fabian News* 22 (May 1911): 45–46. Abridged accounts of it were reprinted in the *Pittsburgh Gazette Times*, 4 June 1911, and *Current Literature* (New York), July 1911, and in the 1929 edition of *The Life of Tolstoy: The First Fifty Years*. There is no indication of when or where it was written. The book was the second of two volumes on Tolstoy's life. *The First Fifty Years* appeared in 1908; *The Later Years* in 1910.

- The Shaws arrived back from Jamaica on 26 January 1911, and Shaw instantly plunged into literary and political activity, seeing plays through the press, being elected to the Academic Committee of the Royal Society of Literature, and finishing his latest drama *Fanny's First Play* on 5 March. Holroyd is undoubtedly correct when he says, "In hasty intervals he reviewed Aylmer Maude's biography of Tolstoy"; see Michael Holroyd, *Bernard Shaw: Volume II: 1898–1918. The Pursuit of Power* (Chatto and Windus, London, 1989), 279.

- Aylmer Maude (see above, 207). Maude was on the Fabian Executive from 1907 to 1912.

- A "moujik, " or "muzhik," is a Russian peasant.

- The "Doukhobor affair" refers to Aylmer Maude's part in arranging the Doukhobor emigration to Canada in January 1899. At that time various parties of this persecuted religious sect (totaling approximately 7500) found sanctuary when the Canadian government granted them territory in what is now the province of Saskatchewan. Tolstoy's public prominence prevented the Russian government from attacking him, but his disciples suffered (see below).

- [Vladimir Grigorevich] Chertkov (1854–1936), Russian journalist, editor, publisher, and prominent Tolstoyan. A captain in the Imperial Guards, he resigned his commission in 1881 to espouse a life of utter spiritual and material simplicity. Two years later, a meeting with Tolstoy confirmed him in his spiritual path. Unfortunately, his bellicose attitude and cavalry-officer manners (which caused Tolstoy's daughter to describe him as "the tsar of the Tolstoyans") made his support for Christian pacifism incongruous. In 1884 Chertkov founded a publishing house to proclaim the new faith, providing the poor with inexpensive books (many by Tolstoy), beautifully illustrated. Chertkov's championing of the persecuted Dukhobor sect led to his exile in England from 1897 to 1905, where he published Tolstoy's works, condemned the Tsarist regime, and labored like Aylmer Maude to help the Dukhobors migrate to Canada. Returning from exile in 1905, Chertkov again involved himself in the affairs of Tolstoy, who came increasingly to rely on him. This caused at first friction and finally open hostility between Tolstoy's wife Sophia and Chertkov, who tried to gain control over Tolstoy's diaries and conspired to have himself appointed literary executor in Tolstoy's will. In July 1910 Sophia suffered a mental breakdown, threatening to murder Chertkov and take her own life. Undoubtedly the quarreling and stress, in such contrast to the qualities of gentleness and long-suffering beloved of Tolstoy, contributed to the latter's final flight from Yasnaya Polyana and his death at Astapova Station in November 1910. The fight over Tolstoy's archives that followed was settled in 1917 by the Revolution when they were nationalized.

1 June 1911

OUR BOOK-SHELF: "THE FOUNDATIONS OF THE NINETEENTH CENTURY"* [C1775]

THIS very notable book should be read by all good Fabians. In spite of its length and the stiffness of those metaphysical sections which go [to] the heart of the differences between Thomas Aquinas and Luther, Aristotle and Goethe, Ezekiel and Christ, it is really a magnificent manifesto of Greek art, of Roman Republicanism, of Christianity, of Protestantism, of Nationalism, of Individualism, of Aristocracy, of Freethought, of the great white north, of man's unbounded inner freedom and infinity confronting the limited mechanism of nature outside him, flung in the teeth of Catholicism, Fraternity, Imperialism, Judaism, Jesuitism, Cosmopolitanism, Mongrelism, the Unholy Roman Empire and all the powers of darkness. Most of us, reading this list of the battalions of the two opposing armies, will ask whether there is not some confusion. It sounds as if a Napoleonic historian had mixed up the battle of Waterloo, and got Ney and Picton fighting D'Erlon and Brunswick, with Blucher commanding the French against the English under the command of Wellington and Napoleon. That is just why the book should be read; for it is a masterpiece of really scientific history. It does not make confusion: it clears it away. It will shew many Fabians what side they are really on, lifting them out of mere newspaper and propaganda categories into their right camp.

---

* "The Foundations of the Nineteenth Century." By Houston Stewart Chamberlain. 2 vols. (John Lane; 32s. n.)

Needless to add, it is a book which any fool can pick little holes in: in fact, several fools have already wasted many review columns in doing so. A writer who, like Houston Chamberlain, knows enough about the higher mathematics to understand that they are the science, not of accuracy, but of the inaccuracy that does not matter, and that it was just the limits of accuracy which for so long prevented mathematics from coming to anything but a little simple arithmetic, does not attempt to write a great historical conspectus and a philosophy of civilization within the limits imposed by the demand for complete "explanations" and unquestionable proofs. His test of evidence, and even of the character of historical persons, is really the test of repugnance or congeniality: he cross-examines a repugnant witness and hurls him from the box disgraced and per-jured, and the next moment accepts without demur a congenial witness who has not a whit more external authority for his state-ments; but he knows quite well what he is about all the time, and makes no pretence of impartiality, seeing clearly that impartiality may and often does lame and sterilize minds that are feeble enough to be imposed on by it, and achieves nothing because it is, after all, an inhuman sham, the real check on falsehood being the desire for knowledge, the instinct for truth, the hatred of being deceived, without which no man can meddle successfully with history or philosophy, or indeed be anything but in the long run an enemy of mankind. He is thus a great generalizer, a surveyor of world-wide tides and currents, an organizer of thought as distinguished from the crowd of our mere specialists, naturalists, catalogue makers, and accumulators of hard dead data.

The criticism of the experienced Fabian, of the practical demo-crat, will be, probably, that the opposition of a great Germanic stock to the chaos of mongrels which finally captured the Holy Roman Empire in the XIII century or thereabouts, no longer exists in a form which admits of the one element ostracizing or offering pitched battle to the other. Mr. Houston Chamberlain is right in protesting against the lumping together under the general name of "humanity" of people who have different souls; and our hearts go out to his contention that the Renascence was no Rebirth at all, but the entry of a new race upon the stage of history. All the same, no political segregation of that race seems now practicable. What Mr. Houston Chamberlain calls the Chaos (meaning the population of mongrels produced by the Roman Pontifical Empire and controlled by the real Judaic Ezekielite Jew who still believes in the dedication of the whole earth by Jehovah to the domination of his chosen people) is an accomplished fact; and the enemy who confronts the Fabian at every election is not a mongrel, a Basque, or a Jew, but a British greengrocer, in whose short round skull all the superstitions of Egypt, all the national conceit and lust for universal domination of the English, and all the militarism and fanaticism of Ignatius Loyola find a comfortable lodging. What are Immanuel Kant and Richard Wagner to do with this respectable man but vote against him in a continual minority?

Perhaps the question will be answered when Mr. Houston Chamberlain comes to deal, not with the foundations of the wicked century, as we Fabians may take leave to call it, but with that century itself and its present successor. Meanwhile, as this book has produced a great effect in Germany, where 60, 000 copies are in circulation, and is certain to stir up thought here, whoever has not read it will be rather out of it in political and sociological discussions for some time to come.

G.B.S.

Editor's Notes

▪ This review was first published in the *Fabian News* 22 (June 1911): 52–53.

▪ We have it on the authority of Gilbert Murray that Shaw read this book on the long rough voyage home from the West Indies between 12 January and 26 January 1911. Since he reported to Granville Barker that he had done "quite a lot of reading & writing" on the voyage out, one may guess that he also wrote the review on the voyage home. In the "Preface on Children" in *Misalliance* Shaw makes the astonishing claim that "the greatest Protestant Manifesto ever written, as far as I know, is Houston Chamberlain's Foundations of the Nineteenth Century: everybody capable of it should read it." One must remember that *Misalliance* (in Siegfried Trebitsch's translation) was first published in Germany.

▪ Houston Stewart Chamberlain (1855–1927), English-born German author. Born in Southsea, he was educated in France and Vienna before emigrating to Germany in 1885. In 1908 he married Eva Wagner (1867–1942), the younger daughter of the composer Richard Wagner (see above, 113), and became a German citizen in 1916. The above-reviewed book is his most notable work; and it is hardly surprising that it was popular in Germany, proclaiming, as it does, the superiority of the German people, who were descended—according to Chamberlain—from superior Teutonic [or "Aryan"] stock. Chamberlain's anti-Semitism and general racism encouraged greatly the racist doctrines of Adolf Hitler (1889–1945) and his Nazi party.

- The Battle of Waterloo, the final and decisive struggle in the long Napoleonic Wars, was fought on 18 June 1815, near Waterloo, Belgium. In reality, it presented the Duke of Wellington (see above, 75–76), together with the Prussian Field Marshal Gebhard Leberecht von Blucher (1742–1819), fighting Napoleon Bonaparte (1769–1821) and Michel Ney, Duc d'Elchingen, Prince de la Moskova (1769–1815) Marshal of France. When Napoleon had escaped from Elba and returned to France in 1815, Ney was sent to oppose Napoleon's advance. Instead he joined forces with the emperor. Ney killed Frederick William Brunswick (1771–1815) at Quatre Bras, and led the center at Waterloo. After the defeat, however, he was condemned for high treason and shot. General Jean-Baptiste Drouet D'Erlon (1765–1844) was the First Corps Commander of Napoleon's army, which managed to miss the entire battle. A courier bringing an order (intended for D'Erlon) bypassed Marshal Ney (thus violating protocol) so that, although D'Erlon reached Ligny according to the order, it was rescinded, and he and his troops withdrew again. Sir Thomas Picton (1758–1815), by contrast, was seriously wounded at Quatre Bras, and died leading his men to the charge at Waterloo.

- Thomas Aquinas (see below, 381).

- [Saint] Ignatius [of] Loyola [or in Spanish Íñigo de Oñez y Loyola] (1491–1556), Spanish ecclesiastic and founder of the Society of Jesus. Recovering from wounds received as a soldier at the siege of Pampeluna in 1521, he read a book on the lives of the saints, and determined to devote himself to a spiritual life. Accordingly, he undertook a pilgrimage to Jerusalem followed by a rigorous formal education, beginning with grammar school in Barcelona, and studying at the universities of Alcalá de Henares, Salamanca, and Paris, from which he graduated in 1528. It was also there that he formed the pious brotherhood that became the Society of Jesus. Pope Paul III officially confirmed the Order in 1540. Loyola was canonized by Pope Gregory XV in 1622.

- Immanuel Kant (1724–1804), German philosopher. Kant believed in the fundamental freedom of the individual to obey the laws of the universe consciously, as revealed by reason. His philosophical views, contained in his *Critique of Pure Reason* (1781), espouse what is called "transcendentalism," which regards the objects of the material world as fundamentally unknowable, serving merely as the raw material that produces sensations. Thus objects, of themselves, have no existence, and space and time, too, are really only part of the mind, "intuitions" by which we measure and judge perceptions; and in the *Metaphysics of Ethics* (1797). Kant's ethical system is based on his belief that reason is the final moral authority, and his influence is probably greater than any other philosopher of the modern period.

21 October 1911

HYNDMAN* [C1785]

NOT many men living have impressed themselves on the consciousness of the political world in such a fashion that, in a political and
literary review of picked circulation, one can drop the Mister in
heading an article about them. We say Hyndman as who should say
Bismarck, or Cagliostro, or Garibaldi, or Savonarola, or Aristotle, or
Columbus. A mysterious quality this, when it exists in anyone but a
poet. Poets are entitled to it in all the arts: there is nothing in calling
Raphael Raphael instead of Messer Sanzio, or Beethoven Beethoven,
or Shakespear Shakespear. But why should Hyndman be Hyndman
and not Mr. Hyndman; or, still worse, a Mr. Hyndman? Though he
is a remarkable person—one would say brilliant if that adjective
were not for some reason appropriated by comparatively young
men—he has done nothing that has not been done equally well by
men who cannot be identified without at least a Christian name, not
to mention those who carry their Misters with them to the grave. It
is clearly a matter of faith and conviction, not of works, this indefin-
able quality of personal style that has maintained Hyndman as the
figure-head of a great revolutionary movement, even when there
was really no movement behind the figure-head. It is not a triumph
of tact: no man has done more unpardonable things, or done them
so often (within the limits of the pardonable, if you will excuse the
contradiction). It is not a triumph of sagacious leadership overcom-
ing all defects of manner: on the contrary, Hyndman has charming
manners and is the worst leader that ever drove his followers into
every other camp—even into the Cabinet—to escape from his leadership. It is not any item from the catalogue of accomplishments and
powers Macaulay kept for advertizing his heroes. Hyndman is accomplished; but his accomplishments are not unique. It is really the
man himself that imposes, Heaven knows why! Samuel Foote is said
to have stopped a man of striking carriage in the street with the
inquiry, "May I ask, sir, are you anybody in particular?" Had he met
Hyndman, he would have had the same curiosity; but he would not
have dared to ask.

Hyndman has now given us an autobiography that does not do him

* "The Record of an Adventurous Life." By Henry Mayers Hyndman. (Macmillan.)

justice; and yet you can say of it, as you can say of so few volumes of reminiscences, that he is his own hero. He tells you much about people he has met; but he does not hide behind them. And yet he has, to an extraordinary degree, the art of telling you nothing, either about himself or anyone else. Here, for instance, is an account of George Augustus Sala's quarrel with George Meredith in Hyndman's presence. He tells it with an air of telling you everything, and yet at the end you know absolutely nothing that you did not know from the index: namely, that Sala and Meredith quarrelled. You do not know what it was about, or what was said, or how they took it. What you do know is that Hyndman was there; and this, somehow, suffices. Do not hastily conclude that the narrative is so egotistical that Hyndman has insisted on playing the two others off the stage. On the contrary, Hyndman is more reticent about himself than about the others. This is no book of confessions. Confession is not a Hyndmanesque attitude. Not only is it true that, save for a hitherto unpublished fact or two, there is nothing in this book about Meredith, Mazzini, Disraeli, Clemenceau, Morris, and Randolph Churchill (all of whom have chapters to themselves) that could not have been compiled by a clever writer who had never met them; there is actually nothing about Hyndman himself that could not have been written, and even considerably amplified, by a constant companion. It is not a revelation of the man: it simply lets you know Who's Who. And yet it is frank to recklessness. Never was there a book where there was less need to read between the lines. Except a few harmless little chuckles over successes that were quite genuine, there is no boasting; indeed, Hyndman does not cut anything like so imposing a figure in these pages as he did in the public eye on several occasions. In the expression of his dislikes he is abusive and positively spiteful without the smallest affectation: his collection of *bêtes noires,* headed by Mr. John Burns, is reviled without mercy or justice, and, what is much less common, without hypocrisy or any pretence of superiority to hearty ill-will; whilst, on the other hand, his more congenial friends and faithful followers are praised with equally unscrupulous generosity. Consequently, some of his swans are geese, and some of his geese are swans; but no great harm is done: you can always make allowances for the temper of a man who shews his temper fearlessly, whereas your man of good taste, who is afraid to praise and stabs only in the back, would mislead you seriously if he could lead you at all. And yet, in spite of all this openness, and of a vivacity that never flags and a touch on the pen that never bores, the fact remains that at the end of the book you see no deeper into Hyndman or his friends and contemporaries than you did at the beginning, though you have had a long and entertaining conversation about them. That is, if you already know your Marx and have got over the great Marxian change of mind—the great conversion which made a Socialist of Hyndman. If not, the book may be the beginning of a revelation to you. But if you know all that beforehand, the book will be to you a book of adventures and incidents, not a book of characters.

This will not surprise anyone who knows that there is a specific genius for politics, just as there is a specific genius for mathematics or dramatics. Hyndman is a born politician in the higher sense: that is, he is not really interested in individuals, but in societies, states, and their destinies. Apparently he did not care a rap for his own father; and it may be doubted whether he would care a rap for his own son if he had one; but he can see no faults in the Social-Democratic Federation, the ugly duckling which has well-nigh ruined him. He vituperates Mr. John Burns, from whom he got no new political ideas, quite callously; but there is enthusiasm, almost tenderness, in his account of Marx, though Marx quarrelled with him, and strove far harder to injure and discredit him than Mr. Burns did, even under the strongest provocation. The explanation is that Marx widened his political horizon as no other man. Hyndman began with the nationalism of Cavour and Mazzini: he ended with the internationalism of Marx. After Marx there was nothing to discover in the sphere of pure politics except methods; and for methods Hyndman has no patience, no aptitude, and no qualifying official experience. He never went on from the industrial revolution to the next things—to the revolution in morals, and to the formulation and establishment of a credible and effective indigenous Western religion. There is not a word in this book to indicate that the contemporary of Cavour and Marx was also the contemporary of Wagner the artist-revolutionary, of Nietzsche the ethical revolutionary, of Sidney Webb the pathfinder in revolutionary methods, or of Samuel Butler the founder of the religion of Evolution. Hyndman played the flute and played duets with Mrs. Meredith without troubling himself about Wagner; dismissed popular religion as superstition and fraud, and was too glad to be rid of it to see any need for replacing it; and found the current morality quite good enough to furnish him with invectives against the injustice and cruelty for which he honorably loathed capitalistic society. His book, though nominally brought up to 1889, really stops with the enlargement of his political conception of the world by Marx, and with his founding of the

Democratic Federation. He half promises to bring his history up to date in a future volume; but what has he to add, except a record of his own impatience with the Fabian Society, the Independent Labor Party, and the other bodies and movements which took the tactics of Socialism out of his hands, complicating and obscuring his splendid Marxist vision with all sorts of uncongenial details, and elbowing out his poor but devoted disciples with—as he considered them—all sorts of uncongenial, lower-middle-class snobs and heretics?

It is not easy to reduce so exuberant a personality as Hyndman's to a type; but, roughly, we may class him with the freethinking English gentlemen-republicans of the last half of the nineteenth century: with Dilke, Burton, Auberon Herbert, Wilfrid Scawen Blunt, Laurence Oliphant: great globe-trotters, writers, *frondeurs,* brilliant and accomplished cosmopolitans as far as their various abilities permitted, all more interested in the world than in themselves, and in themselves than in official decorations; consequently unpurchasable, their price being too high for any modern commercial Government to pay. On their worst side they were petulant rich men, with perhaps a touch of the romantic vanity of the operatic tenor; and, as the combination of petulant rich man with ignorant poor one is perhaps the most desperately unworkable on the political chess-board, none of their attempts to found revolutionary societies for the advancement of their views came to much. One of the things Hyndman has never understood is the enormous advantage the founders of the Fabian Society had in their homogeneity of class and age. There were no illiterate working-men among them; there were no born rich men among them; there were no born poor men; there was not five years' difference between the oldest and the youngest. To Hyndman the acceptance and maintenance of such homogeneity still seems mere snobbery. He took up the democratic burden (as he regarded it) of working with men and women not of his generation, not of his class, not of his speed of mind and educational equipment. When the Fabians refused to involve themselves in that hopeless mess, he despised them. He even says, wildly, that they killed Morris by their refusal, just as the Unionists say Mr. Asquith killed Edward VII. The Labor men knew better. They did not join the Fabian Society; but they made good use of it.

Still, the struggle with incongruity and impossibility on which Hyndman entered in 1881, though it has involved a fearful waste of his talent and energy, had something generous and heroic in it. In the Labor movement the experienced men will allow Hyndman no public virtue save this, that he has kept the flag flying—the red flag. And there are so many men who have every public virtue except this, that the exception suffices. Hyndman is still Hyndman, still, head aloft and beard abroad, carrying that flag with such high conviction that the smallest and silliest rabble at his heels becomes "the revolution." And outside that rabble there are still some friends, though he himself cares for nobody and nothing but the last act of the tragedy of capitalism.

G. B. S.

Editor's Notes

- This review was first printed in the *Nation* 10 (21 October 1911): 135–36, and reprinted in Rosalind Travers Hyndman's *The Last Years of H. M. Hyndman* (London: Grant Richards; New York: Brentano's) 1924, and in *Pen Portraits and Reviews* (1931). There is no clear indication when Shaw wrote the review.

- On 19 June 1911, the Shaws left England for a tour of Continental Europe, "motor-mountaineering," in Shaw's words, through France, Switzerland, Germany, Austria, and Italy, and returning to London at the beginning of October. The letters Shaw fired off during this holiday were mostly negative responses to proposals of one kind or another: he was extremely insulting to Arnold Daly (over a failed production of *Arms and the Man* at the Criterion Theatre), brusque with F. C. Whitney, offhand with Janet Achurch, and ridiculed Galsworthy's proposal for a moratorium on the manufacture of airplanes. The tone of the above review of Hyndman's book suggests Shaw wrote it at the same time.

- Bismarck (see above, 30 and 56).

- Giuseppe Balsamo, known as Count Alessandro di Cagliostro (1743–95), Italian adventurer and charlatan, who went round Europe selling drugs and potions, and became a well-known figure at the court of Louis XVI. Alexandre Dumas *père* wrote a romance about him, *Joseph Balsamo; or Memoirs of a Physician* (1846–48).

- Giuseppe Garibaldi (1807–82), Italian nationalist, who devoted his revolutionary zeal to Italian unification and freedom. In 1848, he organized a corps of about three thousand volunteers in an unsuccessful fight against the Austrians in Lombardy—as a young man, Hyndman assisted Garibaldi's forces in this struggle. In 1860, with the support of Conte Camillo Benso di Cavour (1810–61), Garibaldi led an expedition of one thousand men from Genoa to Sicily, then governed by the king of Naples. His men were distinctively dressed in red shirts and became known as the "Red Shirts" or "The Thousand." He defeated the Neapolitans decisively on the banks of the River Volturno on 26 October 1860.

- Savonarola (see above, 239).

- Aristotle (384–322 B.C.), Greek philosopher.
- [Christopher] Columbus [or in Italian Cristoforo Colombo; or, in Spanish Cristóbal Colón (1451–1506), Italian-Spanish explorer, known as the discoverer of America.
- The name of the great Renaissance painter Raphael—in Italian Raffaello—is in full Raffaello Santi, or Raffaello Sanzio (1483–1520).
- Samuel Foote (1720–77), English wit, actor, and playwright. His lifelike mimicry of prominent people caused litigation on several occasions. His plays were principally political satires.
- The quarrel between George Augustus [Henry] Sala (1828–95), English journalist and novelist, and Meredith, in Hyndman's presence must remain a mystery. In his letter of 17 September 1866 to Frederic Chapman, Meredith (see above, 94) reports meeting Sala in Venice, but does not refer to the unpleasant scene mentioned on page 75 of Hyndman's book.
- [Giuseppe] Mazzini (1805–72), Italian revolutionary. From exile to election to office, and from prosecution to pardon, Mazzini was in the forefront of the struggle for Italian unification and the republican movement throughout Europe.
- Disraeli (see above, 56).
- [Georges] Clemenceau (1841–1929), French statesman. He rose to become leader of the Radical Party in 1876. He was opposed to colonialism, resisted monarchists of all groups, and favored the separation of church and state. He extended his influence through journalism, in *La Justice* (a journal he had founded in 1880), *L'Aurore,* which became a vehicle for anticlericalism, and was instrumental in defending Alfred Dreyfus (see above, 237–38), and *Le Bloc* (1900–1902). In October 1906 he became premier of France, establishing close relations with Great Britain. In 1909 his ministry fell, and in the year of this review, he was again in the Senate, where until the outbreak of World War I he urged French military preparedness against the growing German menace. Premier again in 1917, he earned the nickname "the Tiger" for the ruthlessness of his administration: he made Ferdinand Foch marshal of France, organizing the nation for an all-out war effort. He was still as violently anti-German after the armistice of 1918, declaring that the Germans should be rendered incapable of further warfare.
- Morris (see above, 165).
- [Lord] Randolph [Henry Spencer] Churchill (1849–95), English politician, father of Sir Winston Churchill, third son of the seventh duke of Marlborough. He was secretary for India in Lord Salisbury's first ministry; and, during his early years in Parliament, developed a special interest in the affairs of Ireland (where his father, the duke of Marlborough, was lord-lieutenant). He attacked the alliance between Gladstone and the "Parnellites" in 1883–84; and he took a prominent part in the heated debate on the Home Rule Bill (which he called a "desperate and insane measure"), which dominated the spring and summer of 1886, seeking to unite those who were opposed to it. In the ensuing general election on 22 July 1886, which defeated Gladstone and brought Salisbury back as prime minister, he was re-elected, and accepted the second place in the

ministry, the chancellorship of the Exchequer and the leadership of the House of Commons. However, he resigned the chancellorship five months later, over a dispute, and thereafter his political energy declined.

- John Burns (1858–1943), British Labour politician. He led the Social Democratic Federation demonstration of 8 February 1886; as "The Man with the Red Flag" he resisted (and was battered by) the police on "Bloody Sunday," 13 November 1887; he represented Battersea on the London County Council, led the great Dock Strike of 1889, and was elected M.P. for Battersea in 1892. Shaw, whose acquaintance with Burns went back to 1885, frequently lectured in Battersea, because it was John Burns's "stronghold." Burns became president of the Local Government Board in 1905, and of the Board of Trade in 1914, resigning, as a pacifist, on the outbreak of World War I. He was the first Cabinet minister from the working classes in Britain. Ten years before this review was written, Shaw in a letter to Beatrice Webb had referred to Hyndman "keeping up a feud with John Burns and the Fabian Society."
- Wagner (see above, 113, 166, et seq.)
- Nietzsche (see above, 192).
- Sidney Webb (see above, 139).
- Samuel Butler (see below, 306–7). His interest in the theory of evolution (which had germinated in New Zealand, where he first read Darwin), resulted in a series of books on the subject, including *Life and Habit* (1877), *Evolution, Old and New* (1879), *Unconscious Memory* (1880), and *Luck, or Cunning as the Main Means of Organic Modification?* (1887). Shaw reviewed this last book enthusiastically for the *Pall Mall Gazette* on 31 May 1887, under the heading "Darwin Denounced." His description above of Butler as "the founder of the religion of Evolution" reveals the extent of Butler's influence on Shaw. In fact, Butler preferred the views of the French biologist and botanist Jean Baptiste [Chevalier de] Lamarck (1744–1829), some of whose notions of "creative evolution" where "needs create new organs" Shaw adopted and expounded in his works, notably *Man and Superman* (1903) and *Back to Methuselah* (1922).
- [Sir Charles Wentworth] Dilke (1843–1911), English radical politician, whose travels in Canada, Australia, the United States, and New Zealand are chronicled in *Greater Britain* (1868).
- [Sir Richard Francis] Burton (1821–90), English orientalist and explorer. Expelled from Oxford, he joined the army in 1842 and, during seven years in India, mastered a number of Eastern languages in preparation for a series of explorations. In 1853, disguised as an Afghan he made the pilgrimage to Medina and Mecca (being one of the few white men to enter those cities); he explored Somaliland with John Hanning Speke (1827–64), served in the Crimean War, returned to Africa with Speke, and discovered Lake Tanganyika. He also amassed a huge collection of notes on matters sociological, anthropological, and erotological, the publication of which in a series of books and translations made him extremely wealthy in his last years.
- Auberon Herbert (see above, 83–84).
- Wilfrid Scawen Blunt (see above, 238).

■ Laurence Oliphant (1829–88), South African novelist and travel writer. At nineteen he began those wanderings that continued all his life, traveling widely in India, Russia, the United States, and Canada, often in war zones, frequently putting his life in danger. He is supposed to have plotted with Garibaldi, was certainly Secretary to Lord Elgin in Washington, Canada, China, and India (when the mutiny was at its height). He was the *Times* correspondent during the Polish insurrection of 1863, and saw the war in Schleswig-Holstein the following year. In 1865 he returned to England and obtained a seat in Parliament, but resigned to become a full-time writer.

18 October 1913
SIR ALMROTH WRIGHT'S POLEMIC*
[C1910]

THIS book, looked forward to with ecstasy since its author addressed to *The Times* the wildest letter ever published on a subject which might, in view of the antiquity of his view of it, almost be defined as Lovely Woman, could be described as "unexpurgated" only by a particularly innocent and, at bottom, rather chivalrous Irishman. The word is no more than Sir Almroth Wright's apology for not accepting women as angels. The book may be left on the drawing-room table in country house and parsonage without misgiving.

The advocates of Votes for Women, confronted with it, will find themselves in the unhappy position of the journalists in Rudyard Kipling's story. They, it will be remembered, saw the sea serpent. At first they thought they had the chance of their lives; then, over-whelmed by the hugeness of the chance, they dropped their pens and were silent. Their luck was overdone: the real sea serpent was incredible. Sir Almroth Wright is too easy a victim. He offers the Suffragist so many openings that she will, like Achilles surveying Hector, be unable to make up her mind as to which particular spot she will stab. Finally, she will be disarmed by the manifest inhumanity of hitting a defenceless antagonist at all.

---

* "The Unexpurgated Case Against Woman Suffrage." By Sir Almroth E. Wright, M.D., F.R.S. Constable. 2s. 6d. net.

Fortunately, it is easy to land Sir Almroth on the flat of his back without doing him any vital harm. He is an intellectual man; and intellect is still so new a toy in evolution that those who possess it are often more interested in their intellectual processes than in their conclusions. Sir Almroth loves to show off his intellectual method, to explain it, to find new names for its stages. If he makes a mistake, he makes it definitely, precisely, and consequently detectably. He does not, as an English writer would, get into a muddle from sheer dread of finding himself out or giving himself away. With admirable honesty and splendid lucidity, he gives himself away on toast done to a turn and buttered with opsonin. He positively guides your finger to the spot at which a flick of your nail will bring down his house of cards in irretrievable ruin.

For example:

"My reasonings have the sanction which attaches to them as based upon premisses arrived at by the method of *diacritical judgment*. . . . When I venture to attempt a generalisation about Woman, I endeavour to recall to mind without distinction all the different women I have encountered, and to extricate from my impressions what was common to all—omitting from consideration (except only when I am dealing specifically with these) all plainly abnormal women."

And here is what Sir Almroth extricates as the specifically Feminine, as Woman, Lovely Woman:

"Woman's mind in appraising a statement attends primarily to the mental images which it evokes, and only secondarily—and sometimes not at all—to what is predicated in the statement. It is over-influenced by individual instances; arrives at conclusions on incomplete evidence; has a very imperfect sense of proportion; accepts the congenial as true, and rejects the uncongenial as false; takes the imaginary which is desired for the reality, and treats the undesired reality which is out of sight as non-existent—building up for itself in this way, when biased by predilections and aversions, a very unreal picture of the external world."

In short, exactly like Man's mind, which is just the fact that Sir Almroth, this time not sufficiently diacritical, thought he was going to disprove. And the criticism is only the echo of that which the most serious woman in Shakespeare's human comedy levels at "Man, proud man, drest in a little brief authority."

There is something staggering in the fact that a writer of Sir Almroth Wright's quality, capable of that penetrating clinical description of the political disabilities of mankind—penetrating almost to the heights of rhetoric and poetry—should be so ludicrously blind to the sex of the patient. Shakespeare, speaking of himself and Sir Almroth and me and the rest of us as "this glassy essence, this angry ape," is bitter, but within his rights and entitled, alas! to the verdict; but what sort of figure would Shakespeare have cut had he added: "You must understand, gentlemen, that these remarks are confined strictly to Ann Hathaway, and that I, the Masculine Male Manly Man, am obviously purely intellectual and aniconic in appraising statements; am never over-influenced by individual instances; never arrive at conclusions on incomplete evidence; have an absolutely perfect sense of proportion; cannot be tricked into accepting the congenial as true or denying the uncongenial as false; do not believe in things merely because I wish they were true, or ignore things because I wish they did not exist; but live, godlike, in full consciousness of the external world as it really is, unbiased by predilections and aversions; for such, gentlemen, is the happy effect of the physiological attachments of Man's mind"?

Witness it, ye pages of masculine history, ye halfpenny popular men's papers, ye twopenny and sixpenny unpopular men's papers, ye *Church Timeses* and lay *Timeses* and *Spectators* and *Lancets,* ye general elections and by-elections, ye wars and rumours of wars, ye Lords and Commons, ye man-made Cases, expurgated and unexpurgated, for and against Woman's Suffrage and all other earthly controversies! Witness it, above all, the reviews which are even now appearing in our most respectable organs applauding all this blazing absurdity, the familiar symptom of ordinary sex-conceit, as a serious contribution to a serious question!

The truth is it is not a contribution to the question of Woman Suffrage at all; but as a criticism of the political competence of mankind it has its points. It is impossible, in the face of history and contemporary facts, to deny that Man as he exists at present is what Sir Almroth Wright calls Woman, and that even when you give him a liberal education and a scientific profession, and he distinguishes himself in it by exceptional ability, his political and social views are not only womanish in Sir Almroth's most invidious use of the term, but often flatly childish. The case is, indeed, more serious than he thinks, for he is happy in the delusion that we have in the specifically masculine intellect and character a refuge from the follies and errors of the specifically feminine character, whereas there is no evidence that the qualities of intellect and character needed for political organisation are any more specifically sexual than digestion or blood circulation or cell structure. Sir Almroth Wright explaining that his mother and his wife are inferior to himself is only the pot calling the kettle black. The utmost that real science can allow him is that there are specifically human qualities of intellect and character; and in conceding this it must not be forgotten that so able and politically experienced a genius as Swift ended by declaring that the evolutionary progress from horse to man was all to the bad. The discovery of evolution has completely knocked on the head the grandfatherly conceit, which Sir Almroth would call grandmotherly, that Man and Brute are essentially and totally different, and that Man differs always in the superior direction.

Perhaps the quaintest thing Sir Almroth sets down is his jibe at the man whom he calls "the complemental male," who "solemnly draws himself up and asks, 'Are you aware, sir, that you are insulting my wife?' " Now, it may be conceded that any man who draws himself solemnly up deserves to be let ludicrously down; but he may have a just grievance for all that. Doctors and divines are much given to drawing themselves up solemnly when laymen question their omniscience and infallibility, but this does not prove that the layman is always in the right on the point at issue. As a matter of fact, Sir Almroth Wright does insult everyman's wife and everyman's mother, including his own; and "the unexpurgated case" in his title means simply the frankly insulting case. If a man tells a woman that she is relatively to himself an inferior beast, he insults her. Mr. Sandow can, without insulting me, tell me that he is stronger than I am muscularly; but if he tells me that I am a fool—and this is, in one word, what Sir Almroth Wright calls every woman—he insults me, and can only put himself right by evidence as incontrovertible as that of a spring grip or a set of heavy weights in the muscular instance. Sir Almroth attempts no proof; he simply points to the common experience of the world that we are all fools. Woman will not be satisfied with that. She will ask "Am I a bigger fool than you?" If he answers "No," his case falls to the ground; if "Yes," a flatter insult cannot be conceived.

Lack of space makes it impossible to deal with Sir Almroth's elaboration of his case. So much the better, perhaps; for a great deal of it only shows how incredibly thoughtless and unobservant an exceptionally gifted man can be. In his worst pages the Breadwinner struts unashamed, claiming that his wife does nothing and he everything, because he intercepts her wages and can spend them in drink with impunity. Sir Almroth firmly believes that when the landlord pays the taxes the tenant escapes them; that the supertaxed Nut maintains a State on which the charwoman is an ungrateful parasite; that one of the triumphs of the Male intellect was the discovery that the way to deal with sweating is to Let It Alone (alas! for my sex, he is right there, only it was hardly a triumph, was it?); that John Stuart Mill was an uxorious gaby who invented the Economic Man; that nobody should have a vote unless they have sufficient physical force to take what they want, and thereby make the vote superfluous; and heaven knows what other worn-out reach-me-downs of the like quality. It is all quite amazing from a man so interesting, so stimulating, so original in his own department.

It is noteworthy that in his criticism of the modern expensive woman and his formulation of the claim for the seclusion of woman on the ground that men are so susceptible that they cannot work when there is a woman within sight, he has been anticipated by Mr. Granville Barker in *The Madras House* and Mr. H. G. Wells in *Marriage;* and that whilst the playwright and the romancer are saturated with the scientific spirit, Sir Almroth Wright is romantic, fact-proof, whimsical, quarrelsome, and jealous to an extent that will certainly provoke Mrs. Fawcett to quiet scorn and Mrs. Pankhurst to withering contempt. My own conviction is that Sir Almroth Wright comes to grief on this subject because he had several brothers and no sisters. He is still afraid of women, still unable to conceive that they belong to his own species, still by turns irritated and attracted by these strange monsters. This theory of his attitude may be erroneous, but at least it is strictly scientific, and the facts are beyond dispute.

The book may do some good, after all. John Stuart Mill certainly was a little uxorious; and it is as well to remind the uxorious that women have all the faults of men, and that Votes for Women will no more achieve the millennium than Votes for Manufacturers did in 1832 or Votes for Working Men in 1867 and 1885. Above all, it may help to effect a reduction to absurdity of Sex Recrimination, that Duel of Sex in which Ibsen and Strindberg were such mighty opposites. It was an inevitable phase; let us hope that it will end over Sir Almroth Wright's book in frank confession and good-humoured laughter.

G. B. S.

Editor's Notes

• This review was first published in the *New Statesman* 2 (18 October 1913): 45–47; and reprinted by the Irishwomen's Suffrage Federation in

1913; and again in *The Fabian Feminist,* ed. Rodelle Weintraub in 1977. *The New Statesman,* first published on 12 April 1913, was the brainchild of the Webbs, and Shaw was one of its original proprietors, directors, and regular (anonymous) contributors. But he was temperamentally out of step with its editor Clifford Sharp, with whom (at least) Beatrice Webb agreed. She confided to her diary in July 1913 that Shaw had injured the *New Statesman,* saying "we have the disadvantage of his eccentric and iconoclastic stuff without the advantage of his name." Shaw soon ceased to be a regular contributor. On 5 October 1916 he complained about Sharp's editorial support for Asquith; and he finally severed his connection with the *New Statesman* on 13 October that year. It is significant that this and subsequent reviews in that journal are signed G.B.S.

▪ Shaw maintained that he was "as sound a feminist as Mary Wollstonecraft;" and certainly (like the review above) his articles and letters to the *Times* and the *New Statesman* were frequently reprinted in feminist papers such as *Suffragette.* In 1913 the women's movement was going through a troubled time: their members were being arrested, imprisoned, and tortured by being forcibly fed. At the behest of Winifred Holiday, Shaw gave an impassioned speech against this at Kingsway Hall on 18 March; a speech that made a powerful impression and was reported in full in the *London Budget* on 23 March. Among other things, Shaw said: "I contend that forcible feeding is illegal. I contend that if you are tried in a public court and sentenced to imprisonment you are sentenced to imprisonment, and not to torture, except insofar as imprisonment may be torture. . . . I contend that if the Government wants to break people's teeth with chisels, and force food into the lungs, and run the risk of killing them, to inflict what is unquestionably torture on them, their business is to bring in a bill legalising these operations. There is no reason why they should hold back. They have no shame in doing it without the law. Why should they be ashamed of doing it with the law?"

▪ Sir Almroth E[dward] Wright (1861–1947), English bacteriologist. After employment at the Universities of Cambridge and Sydney, and the Army Medical School at Netley, Wright became pathologist to Saint Mary's Hospital. There in 1908, with the help of others, Wright founded the Inoculation Department as a separate financial entity, and remained its director until a year before his death. His pioneer work on immunization began in 1896, and he made numerous important discoveries on the protective power of blood against bacteria. In 1904, Wright published his *Short Treatise on Antityphoid Inoculation, Containing an Exposition of the Principles of the Method, and a Summary of the Results Achieved by its Application,* the first, and perhaps the most important of the books he wrote; though another important work was his *Principles of Microscopy* (1906), in which year he was knighted and made a Fellow of the Royal Society. Shaw's forty-year association with Wright began in 1905 when Wright sent him his pamphlet on tuberculosis inoculation and an invitation for Shaw to visit his laboratory at Saint Mary's Hospital. This led to Shaw's presence at numerous medical debates there, and to the birth of *The Doctor's Dilemma* on the occasion when a team of medical men were discussing which patients to accept for a new experimental treatment, since they had too many cases to cope with. (However, Edith Finch, in *Wilfrid Scawen Blunt 1840–1922* [London: Jonathan Cape, 1938], 394, claims that "Blunt . . . gave Shaw the suggestion for *The Doctor's Dilemma*.)

▪ In March 1912 Almroth Wright unburdened himself to the *Times* on the topic of woman suffrage. The letter, captioned "Sir Almroth Wright on Militant Hysteria," claims (among other things) that "no doctor can ever lose sight of the fact that the mind of woman is always threatened with danger from the reverberations of her physiological emergencies"! After several columns of print, in which he puts women into different types, describes as "fatuous" the idea that women should be paid the same wage as a man for the same work, claims that the methods used by the suffragists are "immoral" (in their use of violence, particularly), and insists that women would be voters "quite incompetent to adjudicate upon political issues," he concludes that if woman suffrage comes to England "it will have come as a surrender to a very violent feminist agitation . . . which we have traced back to our excess female population and the associated abnormal physiological conditions." The response from women readers was remarkably restrained; an "Anti-Militant Suffragist" (a wife and mother) on 2 April summing up the general opinion that Wright was to be deeply pitied.

▪ The title of Kipling's story is "A Matter of Fact," and it appeared in *Many Inventions* (1893).

▪ "With admirable honesty and splendid lucidity, he gives himself away on toast done to a turn and buttered with opsonin." The buttering with opsonin reference is straight from *The Doctor's Dilemma,* a play submitted to Sir A. Wright to check its medical credentials.

▪ It is Isabella, the noble nun in *Measure for Measure* who repudiates Angelo's lust, yet whose purity is "unaccompanied by any Pharisaic harshness toward the follies of others," who says:

> But man, proud man,
> Dress'd in a little brief authority,
> Most ignorant of what he's most assur'd—
> His glassy essence—like an angry ape
> Plays such fantastic tricks before high heaven
> As makes the angels weep.

▪ *The Lancet* was (and is) the journal of the British Medical Association.

▪ In the fourth part of Jonathan Swift's (1667–1745) *Gulliver's Travels* (1726), Gulliver visits the country of the Houyhnhnms, or horses endowed with reason. Their simplicity and virtue are contrasted with the disgusting brutality of the Yahoos, which are beasts shaped like men.

▪ [Eugene] Sandow (1867–1925), German-born American strongman, born in Königsberg of Russian parents. He had been exhibited by Florenz Ziegfeld at the Chicago Fair in 1893, and opened a health institute in Saint James's

Street, London. According to Hesketh Pearson, "Sandow tried to entice [Shaw] as a pupil and develop him physically. Shaw said, 'You misunderstand my case. I have seen you supporting on your magnificent chest twenty men, two grand pianos, and a couple of elephants; and I have no doubt you could train me to do the same. But my object as to pianos and elephants and crowds is to keep them off my chest, not to heap them on to it' "; see Hesketh Pearson, *Bernard Shaw. His Life and Personality* (1942), Reprint Society Edition (London: Collins, 1948), 331.

- John Stuart Mill (see above, 113).
- A "gaby" is a simpleton (*OED*).
- Granville Barker's play *The Madras House* (1910) concerns the selling of a long-established drapery business to an American investor; but the play derives its force from the juxtaposition of the household of the firm's manager (with his six unmarried and frustrated daughters) and the male-dominated boardroom and offices of his Bond Street firm. As Desmond MacCarthy remarks: "Difference of sex at once makes for intimacy and disturbs the detachment, that impersonal detachment in intimacy, which for Philip Madras is the intensest form of living. The Man-Woman problem has been the subject of countless plays in which the psychology of relations between the sexes has been the theme, but I think it may be claimed for *The Madras House* that the peculiar aspect of it (an important one), which Philip Madras is the means of throwing into relief, has never been so curiously and delicately treated on the stage"; see Desmond MacCarthy, *Theatre* (London: MacGibbon and Kee, 1954), 114–15.
- H. G. Wells's novel *Marriage* (1912) also illustrates that aspect of the Man-Woman question:

> "It's been horrible waiting," said Marjorie, without moving; "horrible! Where have you been?"
> "I've been working. I got excited by my work. I've been at the laboratory. I've had the best spell of work I've ever had since our marriage."
> "But I have been up all night!" she cried, with her face and voice softening to tears. "How *could* you? How *could* you?"
> He was surprised by her weeping. He was still more surprised by the self-abandonment that allowed her to continue. "I've been working," he repeated, and then looked about with a man's helplessness for the tea apparatus.

- [Dame Millicent Garret] Fawcett (1847–1929), English suffragette and educational reformer. In 1867 she married Henry Fawcett (1833–84), the blind professor of political economy at Cambridge. She opposed the militancy of the Pankhursts, but campaigned for women's suffrage and higher education for women. She was a founder of Newnham College, Cambridge (1871), and was president of the National Union of Women's Suffrage Societies from 1879 to 1919. Among other works she wrote *Political Economy for Beginners*

(1870), a novel *Janet Doncaster* (1875), and *The Women's Victory—and After* (1920). She was created Dame in 1925.

- [Emmeline "Emily" Goulden] Pankhurst (1857–1928), English suffragette. In 1879 she married Richard Marsden Pankhurst, a radical barrister who had been the author of the first women's suffrage bill in Britain, and of the Married Woman's Property Acts of 1870 and 1882. In 1889 Mrs. Pankhurst founded the Women's Franchise League. Although she disagreed philosophically with Shaw's approach to social questions, Mrs. Pankhurst had declared that Ann Whitefield (in *Man and Superman*) "strengthened her purpose and fortified her courage." In 1903, with her daughter Christabel Harriette (1880–1958) she founded the Women's Social and Political Union, an extremely militant organization that fought bitterly for the franchise. She was frequently imprisoned, and underwent hunger strikes and the torture of forcible feeding (see above). She wrote her autobiography *My Own Story* (1914).
- The Whig Bill of 1832 enfranchised the middle class; the Tory Bill of 1867 enfranchised householders; the Liberal Bill of 1885 enfranchised the agricultural laborer.
- [Henrik] Ibsen (1828–1906), the founder of modern prose drama, was much in favor of the emancipation of women, and wrote *A Doll's House* (1879) to protest the social imprisonment of women in nineteenth-century society; (Johan August) Strindberg (1849–1912), victim of three broken marriages, saw the relationship between the sexes as adversarial, and wrote plays like *The Father* (1887), *Miss Julie* (1888) and *The Dance of Death* (1900), in which the savagery of such relationships is mercilessly examined.

4 February 1915

IS ENGLAND BLAMELESS?* [C1983]

THE time will come when this will seem an extraordinary [*sic*] silly question. When all is said that possibly can be said for the war, it is a monstrous crime against civilization and humanity; and the notion that any of the parties voluntarily engaged in it can be blameless is absurd. It is impossible to discuss war practically without a suspension of all ordinary morals and all normal religious and humanitarian pretensions. Even that is not enough: it is necessary to set up,

---

* "Is Britain Blameless?" By A. Fenner Brockway. (National Labour Press.) 1d.

alongside of martial law (which, as the Duke of Wellington remarked, is no law at all), an outrageous special morality and religion, in which murder becomes duty and patriotism, and in which
our glory lies, not in doing the will of God, but in indulging Lord
Roberts's "will to conquer," which is our more accurate English
version of the "will to power" that shocks us so in the pages of
Nietzsche. Under such circumstances common sense is turned
topsy turvey; "frightfulness" becomes "the truest mercy"; and the
world goes mad.

That is a pretty complication to begin with. But here in England
our party system has complicated even this insane complication. The
war has been declared on our part nominally by a Liberal Government supported by a Liberal majority in the House of Commons, but
really by a secret coalition (since revealed) between the Imperialist
section of the Cabinet and the Imperialist Opposition, the price paid
being the suspension of Liberal legislation during the war, and consequently the political paralysis of the nation, with the scandalous
result (among others) that the House of Commons is actually shut
up and its members practically disbanded at the moment when the
conduct of an appalling war depends on their vigilance and criticism.
And this situation has been brought about not merely by pressure of
circumstances, but by the deliberate and positive hoodwinking by
the Prime Minister and the Secretary of State for Foreign Affairs of
their own party by assurances which will figure in constitutional
history as the boldest and most successful prevarications to which
the official conscience has ever been reconciled by its conception of
patriotism.

Consider now the predicament in which this places the ordinary
Liberal partisan, whose seat in Parliament, and with it all his political
and social ambitions, depends on his sticking to Mr. Asquith and Sir
Edward Grey, no matter how contemptuously they may disregard his
feelings and his desire to keep up a pretence of having political principles as well as a side in the party conflict. He cannot act like the men
who really have principles, and are in politics for the sake of them.
The position is quite simple for such men: when they find that they
have been played with, duped, and betrayed, they simply walk out,
like Lord Morley, Mr. Burns, and Mr. Trevelyan, or, if they have no
office to walk out of, denounce their leaders, like Mr. Ponsonby. But
the poor Partisan, the mere barnacle on the party ship who must sink
to the bottom if he is detached from it, has to pocket his betrayal and
save his face as best he may.

It is easily done, after all. If a man kicks you, and you cannot knock him down, the best plan is to walk on as if nothing had happened, and speak with enthusiasm of him as your best friend for ever after. When America the other day told us flatly that we had been guilty of repeated breaches of international law, and that she was not going to stand it, we all burst into a chorus of appreciation of her cordial tone and shook her hand warmly until we felt it safe to let go. And the Liberals, having been completely sold by their leaders, have made up their minds not to notice it, and to stand by one another in backing up a fairy tale of two noble Liberal apostles of peace suddenly and treacherously surprised by a monstrous and totally unforeseen and unprovoked attack on Belgium by a nation of Odin-worshipping Huns headed by a fiend with upturned moustaches. And they will brazen that out without the least thought of the mischievous effect it may have on neutral opinion or even on the direct fortunes of the war. The French and British Foreign Offices may overwhelm us, as they have done, with White Papers and Orange Books and Blue Books contradicting the Liberal fable in every letter and on every page; and the Germans may flood America with facsimiles of the documents they found in Brussels proving that the violation of Belgium was foreseen and has been provided against (very properly) by us for eight years past: that is, from the moment when the Liberal Party came into power in 1906 and let Sir Edward Grey loose on foreign affairs; but the Liberal papers will still hail every document (knowing that the public will not read it) with brazen assurances that it proves the precise opposite of what it says, and that the Huns have now indeed been exposed and Peace once more justified in her friend the Foreign Secretary.

And now comes the question: Why should not the Labour Party accept this convenient fiction, and patriotically help to save the face of the Liberal leaders? Why need Mr. Fenner Brockway come along with his pamphlet, "Is Britain Blameless?" to give the Liberal show away and set the Kaiser chuckling? Does not patriotism consist mainly in covering your own country with fictitious whitewash, and the enemy with fictitious soot?

The answer is that it is impossible to hide the proceedings of Mr. Asquith and Sir Edward Grey. They are now avowed by themselves and completely published and documented before the whole world; and as the world has not the Liberal partisan reason for shutting its eyes and ears, it is silly to repeat stories that nobody believes. Even at home there is, outside the Liberal Party, no future for the Liberal fable. The Unionists, who are Imperialists almost to a man, glory in the war as an

Imperialist war, and will go to the country on the proud plea that it was the support they pledged to Mr. Asquith that saved England when he could not trust his Liberals to stand by him when the hour struck for executing the great Imperialist plan to prevent Germany from mastering Europe and reducing us to a third-rate Power.

Among the Labour members the fable is vehemently denounced except by those who are mere Liberal partisans; and the voices of these are practically inaudible because nobody will listen to a man who is neither an official Liberal nor an interesting (because original and independent) Labour champion. In short, the fable is not only incredible but contemptible; for everyone despises the fabulist (to put it politely) who does not tell a good one when he is about it.

Now for the harm the fable does. Unless the neutral nations can be persuaded to believe it, it must seem to them the most paltry hypocrisy; and as the Germans have nothing to do but quote our own official documents and the speeches of the two ministers concerned to knock it into a cocked hat, they will steadily gain on us if we are not as bluntly candid as Bethmann Holweg himself. If it were not that most of the pro-Germans in America have been as childish as the pro-British with their pleas of Injured Innocence,they would have damaged us seriously in American eyes, though the Americans have been so strongly biassed against Germany by their horror at the devastation of Belgium that Sir Edward Grey might quite safely have replied to the American note by: "My Dear Wilson: You may tell your Copper Kings to go to Jericho, for the American people will never let you turn on us until we have shifted the Huns out of Belgium." But we can wear down even that sympathy if we persist in talking hypocritical nonsense with so clever an advocate as Dr. Bernhard Dernburg there to take advantage of every lapse we make from the popular line of the bluffest, frankest, bravest candour. The writers who nag, and snivel, and recriminate, and self-righteously proclaim our moral superiority to our enemies would do us less harm if they put on pickelhaubes and served in the German trenches against us.

That is why we had better know the worst of ourselves and admit it before we open our own case, which is quite presentable as an Imperialist case, and overwhelming as a democratic case. Every litigant who brings a case to a solicitor is convinced that the strong points in his favour are those which make him out to be a saint and his opponent a mean sneak. And every lawyer has to break gently to his client that these cherished points would only set the judge and jury against him, and that the case as it must go into court is much less flattering to himself. And the litigant thinks his lawyer grossly unjust and inappreciative [sic], and submits with a very bad grace. Just so in this international case, all the belligerent nations kick hard against the impartial unflattering truth as it must be put to the neutral nations, and think it infamously unpatriotic of the Fenner Brockways and other sane spokesmen not to concentrate themselves wholly on their client's blamelessness and their opponents' wickedness. Nevertheless, the counsel who resolutely clears his brief of unsound claims is the one who gets a verdict on the sound ones.

At all events whoever reads this pamphlet will not fall into the mistake of arguing with the pro-Germans like a pettish governess scolding a dirty little boy. He will know that our diplomacy has been no better and no worse than that of our neighbours, though, as we outwitted the Germans on the point of our intentions, we may perhaps claim to have played the game more cunningly. And he will not force the point about the Scrap of Paper when he understands what very pretty play Dr. Dernburg could make with the Act of Algeciras which we tore up in the face of Germany when she was piously defending the guaranteed independence of Morocco.

It is only too easy to trump up a moral case against all these manœuvres of our aristocratic secret diplomacy; for aristocracy, in England as in Germany, has no middle-class morals, and only gets itself and us into trouble when it pretends to have them for the sake of the middle-class vote. When the vote at stake is not the middle-class vote, but that of the neutral nations, the Foreign Office must take its proper aristocratic, supermoral Imperialist ground. On that it can shew to considerable advantage to its natural Jingo supporters, especially when it is successful in the field; but to the rest of us it can appeal only by being brave and frank and chivalrous, and not pretending to be better than its own caste abroad, at war or in peace.

Editor's Notes

- This review was first published in the *Labour Leader*, 12, (4 February 1915), 5:1–4, and reprinted in the pamphlet's second edition in the same year 1915. Again no verifiable date exists as to when or where Shaw wrote the review.
- At the outbreak of World War I, on 4 August 1914, Shaw and his wife were at a hotel in Salcombe, Devon, where, shortly afterward, Shaw drafted his highly contentious pamphlet *Common Sense About the War*,

which first appeared as a supplement to the *New Statesman* on 14 November 1914. It was so outspoken in what Henderson calls its "disloyalty to loyalty" that many of Shaw's friends and admirers turned against him, there was an outcry in the press, and the pamphlet itself was used by the Germans for propaganda purposes. Shaw spent much of the war explaining what he had meant; and in a sense the above review continues the debate, as a sort of "apologia pro suae sententiae." With the hindsight of history there is little doubt that Shaw's version of the events that led to World War I was closer to the truth than the "fairy tales" purveyed by much of the contemporary press.

- The Act of Algeciras (see below, 318).
- [Baron] A[rchibald] Fenner Brockway (1888–1988), English politician and author. He became the subeditor of the *Christian Commonwealth* in 1909; and subeditor of *the Labour Leader* two years later; and then its editor from 1912 to 1917 (and thus was its editor at the time of this review.) He was the secretary of the No Conscription Fellowship from 1912 to 1917. Imprisoned three times in the First World War, he became as a result of his experiences joint secretary of the Prison System Enquiry Committee in 1920, which produced the influential report *English Prisons Today*. He became organizing secretary of the Independent Labor Party in 1922; its general secretary in 1928, and also from 1933 to 1939. In 1929 Brockway was Labour M.P. for East Leyton. His pacifism began to change with the approaching menace of Fascism, and he resigned from the No More War movement in 1936 at the time of the Spanish civil war. He claimed to be the last Socialist to speak publicly in Germany before Hitler came to power in 1933. He also claimed to be the first to speak after the war, when 100,000 Germans heard him speak in Hamburg. He managed to found a movement for a United Socialist States of Europe, and its conference in 1948 was attended by African and Asian delegates who asked Brockway to chair their Congress of Peoples Against Imperialism. In 1950 he was returned to Parliament as Labour M.P. for Eton and Slough, which he represented until 1964. In that year he moved to the House of Lords, where he continued to campaign for another forty years on behalf of the liberation of colonial people in Africa and Asia. In 1954 Brockway was in at the beginning of the antinuclear movement, and he continued to attend disarmament conferences well into his nineties. He wrote more than twenty books, including *Inside the Left* (1942), *Outside the Right* (1963), *Towards Tomorrow* (1977), and *98 Not Out* (1986).
- Frederick Sleigh [first Earl] Roberts of Kandahar, Pretoria, and Waterford (1832–1914), English soldier. In 1880, in the Second Afghan War, he led a march through difficult terrain to relieve the siege of Kandahar, and there he involved the Afghan army in a defeat that ended the war. In 1900, as supreme commander of the British forces in South Africa, he defeated the Boer army, occupied the Boer Republics of Orange Free State and Transvaal and announced their annexation to the British Empire. He returned to England, having handed over command to Kitchener, and in 1901 was

created an earl and appointed commander-in-chief of the British army. He
retired in 1904.

- Sir Edward Grey, [third baronet and Viscount Grey of Fallodon] (1862–
1933), English statesman and bird-lover. In 1905, when the Liberals came to
power under Campbell-Bannerman, Grey took over the Foreign Office, at the
head of which he remained until December 1916. He was much criticized as
foreign minister, chiefly for the secret 'military conversations' he engaged in
with France as to how to answer a German threat should it occur; conversations that were not reported to the Cabinet. While seeking to ensure that
Britain would not be without friends in the event of war, he was still trying to
maintain peace by making concessions to German expansionism, allowing
Germany (in 1913) to extend her influence in Asiatic Turkey, and granting
her a large share of the Portuguese colonies in Africa (particularly Angola). In
1914 Grey made helpless attempts to refer the assassination of the Archduke
Francis Ferdinand to European arbitrament. His wartime policy in the Bal-
kans was ill-informed and indefinite. Elsewhere, too, his policies were criticized, particularly the secret Treaty of London (26 April 1915) made with
Italy as the price of her entering the war on the Allied side. This consisted of
bribing Italy with large sections of the Dalmatian coast, inhabited by Yugo-
Slavs, which caused enormous trouble after the war. Grey's release came
when Asquith's government collapsed, to be reconstructed under Lloyd
George. Grey's health was also failing: he began to go blind; and turned (no
doubt with relief) from foreign affairs to the more predictable and less critical
birds he had learned to love so much as a boy on his father's estate in
Fallodon, Northumberland. Shaw's incessant attacks on this particular minister had formed part of a groundswell of irritation in the press. As G. M.
Trevelyan puts it in the *Dictionary of National Biography*: "The way for the
change of ministry had indeed been prepared by a campaign of abuse of
which he had had his share, but which fell off him like water from the back of
one of his Fallodon ducks; he did not waste his small ration of eyesight in
studying the productions of the gutter press." In his declining years Grey
wrote the story of his public career in two volumes *Twenty-five Years, 1892–
1916*; while the *Fallodon Papers* (1926), and *The Charm of Birds* (1927)
earned him the respect of a wider public.

- Morley (see above, 113), whose entry into politics (and thus replacement
as editor of the *Pall Mall Gazette*) in 1883 had paved the way for Shaw's
regular contributions to that journal, had resigned from the post of Lord Privy
Seal and from public life on the outbreak of war in 1914, as a protest against
the Allied intervention; John Burns (see above, 270) had resigned his chair-
manship of the Board of Trade; while Mr.[later Sir Charles Philips, third
Baronet] Trevelyan (1870–1958) had also resigned as Liberal parliamentary
secretary to the Board of Education.

- [Arthur Augustus William Harry, first Baron] Ponsonby [of Shulbrede]
(1871–1946), Liberal M.P. for Stirling Burghs, which he represented from
1908 to 1918. On the eve of the First World War, his speech in the House of
Commons, reported in the *Times* on 4 August 1914, began to cheers as he

spoke of the great war that was about to begin; but the cheering turned to cries of dissent when Ponsonby went on to describe the waving and cheering of drunks in the streets he had seen the previous night, which he said "was called patriotism"; and when he regretted the tone of the foreign secretary's speech, which he likened to the cries of the half-drunken youths. He concluded by trusting that "the Foreign Secretary would use every endeavour to the very last moment, looking to the great central interests of humanity and civilization to keep this country in a state of peace."

- The British had a blockade policy to stop all German imports (including those from the still neutral United States). Discussions between the British foreign secretary, Grey, and the American ambassador in London, Walter Hines Page (see above, 224) continued throughout autumn 1914. On 2 November 1914, Britain declared the entire North Sea a military area, saying that neutral ships would cross it at their own risk. British ships routinely stopped vessels from neutral countries suspected of carrying contraband cargoes (though Britain paid for such goods when seized). On 26 December, the United States protested against British interference with American merchant ships at sea. However, Shaw's reference to "America the other day [telling] us flatly that we had been guilty of repeated breaches of international law, and that she was not going to stand it," refers particularly to the crises which occurred in January and February 1915, notably to the transfer to American ownership of the German vessel *Dacia*, whose new owner then proposed to dispatch her to Bremen with a cargo of cotton! After grim discussions with Page, Grey (on 20 January 1915) declared that the *Dacia* was a test case, and would be refused passage. Finally, however, direct confrontation was averted by allowing the French navy to capture the *Dacia* and apply the rules of the French Prize Court.

- [Theobald von] Bethmann Hollweg (1856–1921), German statesman. In 1909 he succeeded Prince Bernhard von Bülow as Chancellor of the German Empire. Shaw refers to Bethmann Hollweg's 1914 blunt declaration that the 1839 Treaty guaranteeing the neutrality of Belgium (see above) was a "scrap of paper." In 1917 Bethmann Hollweg was forced to resign his chancellorship because he disagreed with Germany's policy of unlimited submarine warfare.

- Dr. Bernhard Dernburg (1865–1937), had been German colonial secretary since 1907. He was one of the moderates in Germany, advocating a mid-Europe solution, as opposed to the Pan-Germans, who were in favor of wholesale annexations and Germanization. In *Deutsche Politik* in 1917 he blamed the British for initiating the propaganda war, saying: "When we make experiments in lies and deceptions, intrigue and low cunning, we suffer hopeless and brutal failure. Our lies are coarse and improbable, our ambiguity is pitiful simplicity. The history of the War proves this by a hundred examples. When our enemies poured all these things upon us like a hailstorm and we convinced ourselves of the effectiveness of such tactics, we tried to imitate them. But these tactics will not fit the German. We are rough but moral, we are credulous but honest." In response to this last comment, Mr. Punch re-

marked: "Before this touching picture of the German Innocents very much abroad, the Machiavellian Briton can only take refuge in silent amazement."
- "Die Pickelhaube" means "the spiked helmet."

13 March 1915

THE GERMAN WAR BOOK AND THE BRITISH LIMIT* [C1996]

I must really, as an honest reviewer, warn the public against the pretences on which this book has been placed on the market. I opened it with eager anticipations of having my blood raised to boiling point by a manual of such cynical perfidy and cruelty as only the stony heart and brazen forehead of the Prussian enemy could set down in print for the horror and execration of all good Britons. The publishers promised me, on the very jacket of the book, to make my flesh creep. Professor Morgan has padded the volume with fifty pages of expatiation on its infamy. Thus primed, I skipped large and quite interesting chunks of the Professor so as to get to the Prussian monstrosity as fast as possible. And what did I find?

Suppose a policeman were to wake you up at night to tell you that he had found a burglar of the most repulsive appearance, crime-stained, cross-eyed, bullmouthed, crouching in your coal cellar. And suppose on hastening downstairs to give the loathsome ruffian in charge, you found the Dean of Westminster, irreproachably dressed, waiting for you in your drawing room. That will give you an idea of how completely sold I was when I read the German War Book. I declare before heaven and earth that it might be one of the publications of the S. P. C. K. It would be perfectly in its place in the *Encyclopaedia Britannica*. Offered to a Parish Magazine it would be rejected as not lively enough. My favourite writer on military subjects is Sir Mark Sykes; but I find Colonel Maude and Major Stewart-Murray stimulating and entertaining; and the eulogistic notices in which the

---

* "The German War Book, being 'The Usages of War on Land' issued by the Great General Staff of the German Army." Translated, with a critical Introduction, by J. H. Morgan, M.A., Professor of Constitutional Law at University College, London. (John Murray.)

Daily Mail used to praise Major Stewart-Murray as a disciple of "the great Clausewitz" have lately taken on a fresh delight for me. I can imagine the scorn with which these British militarists will receive the Prussian War Book—the ribald but manly laughter with which they will dispose of its anxious correctness, its namby-pamby sentimentality, its careful respect for civilian and pacifist opinion, its scrupulous piety, and its constant appeals to chivalry. Do not the following passages almost call for an organ accompaniment?

> "Chivalrous feelings, Christian thought, higher civilization and, by no means least of all, the recognition of one's own advantage, have led to a voluntary and self-imposed limitation, the necessity of which is to-day tacitly recognized by all States and their armies."
>
> "Wide limits are set to the subjective freedom and arbitrary judgment of the commanding officer: the precepts of civilization, freedom and honour will have to guide his decisions."
>
> "As regards the personal position of the inhabitants of the occupied territory, neither in life nor in limb, in honour nor in freedom, are they to be injured; and every bodily injury due to fraud or negligence, every insult, every disturbance of domestic peace, every attack on family honour and on morality, and, generally, every unlawful and outrageous attack or act of violence are just as strictly punishable as though they had been committed against the inhabitants of one's own land."

Could any gentleman say more? I will not quote the passages which deal with prisoners of war: let it suffice that no Englishman can read them without sincerely envying the lot of the soldier who falls into the hands of the enemy. Free postage, free carriage of presents, a committee to look after him, and an absolute exemption from lodgment in a prison or penal establishment of any sort are but drops in the brimming cup of his comforts and privileges. The book is open to one criticism, and one only. It is that until we have armies of angels officered by saints and commanded by prophets and martyrs, the chances of its pious injunctions ever receiving much attention in actual warfare are hardly worth considering. They will most certainly not be carried out by us; and the Germans themselves have had to give them up as a bad job. Take for instance the following passage: "A prohibition by international law of the bombardment of open towns and villages which are not occupied by the enemy, or defended, was, indeed, put into words by The Hague Regulations, but appears superfluous, since modern military history knows of hardly any such case." Alas! it is but a few weeks since these good resolutions ended in a rain barrel in the innocent village of Heacham. The Germans dropped an incendiary bomb into it. In this they showed a double want of judgment. In the first place a rain barrel is the last spot on earth that lends itself to the successful operation of an incendiary bomb. In the second, the bomb did effectually explode the notion that the Germans have a perfect system of espionage on our East Coast. If they had, they would have known that Mr. Robert Blatchford lived just round the corner from that rain barrel, and that he is the sort of man to make more noise about a single bomb dropped in his own village than about a hundred dropped in Dunkirk, Düsseldorf, Freiburg and other towns where the women and children, being foreign, are conventionally assumed by us to be naturally bomb-proof. The bombarders of Heacham can only plead that a village occupied by Mr. Blatchford can hardly be described as "not occupied by the enemy."

And here I would suggest to the authors of the German War Book that since the extension of war to the air has made an end of the notion that any place can now be considered undefended, it would be well to restate the case for civilian immunity from the modern point of view, which is, I take it, that whereas a bombardment of Woolwich, with its crowded streets of working people and their closely packed families, would be a horrible business, and could have no effect in inducing the governing classes, none of whom live in Woolwich or ever intend to live there, to make an end of the war and avoid wars in future, a single bomb neatly dropped into the grand stand at Goodwood at a suitable moment, and the systematic demolition of our country houses (not, of course, the Red Cross ones, where there are only common people and soldiers and middle-class professionals like nurses and doctors), of expensive pleasure resorts, and generally of all places in which two or three of our governing classes are likely to be gathered together, would produce more effect than the destruction of a thousand poor suburbs and the slaughter of all their unconsidered denizens. The hint need not be lost on our own commanders. Bomb-dropping on Essen and Cuxhaven leaves Germany cold: it does no harm that cannot be repaired by making the poor work overtime. But Homburg now—? I will not press the point: still, if we are really making war on Junkerdom, is it not common sense to aim our bombs at the Junkers?

But the indiscretion of these remarks shows how much more prudent it is not to write war books, however pious. For it is impossible to give any sort of practical advice to an army or to codify the usages of war without either dishonesty or atrocity. The German War Book pleads for chivalry and generosity to the verge of making itself ridiculous. It forces us to ask the authors bluntly whether the Germans suppose that omelettes can be made without breaking eggs. Yet what does its anxious chivalry come to after all? The authors, being honest according to their lights, are compelled to admit that though they are bound to declare that the inhabitants of an invaded country should not be compelled to give information serviceable to the invaders, yet it is hopeless to expect that any mortal army will refrain from such compulsion. They say frankly that anything may, or at least will, be threatened or done if it promises to attain its military object; and Belgium be their witness that they were entirely right in their estimate of human nature under the test of war. Finally, they sum the whole position up in what they call the double rule, which is that though "no harm must be done, not even the very slightest, which is not dictated by military considerations (Hear, hear! Fine Fellows!), every kind of harm may be done, even the very utmost, which the conduct of war requires, or which comes in the natural course of it" (Yah! Huns! Pirates! Child Killers! Shame!).

Before endorsing these execrations, please read the following quotations from British authorities quoted in the February supplement to the *Berliner Tageblatt*. They refer to something that happened in 1807; but that was the last time our national independence was at stake in a European war; and its further relevance to the present situation is established by the fact that Major Stewart-Murray, in a war book—nominally a peace book, by the way—published in the present century with a preface by Lord Roberts, selects this very incident to shew that pacifist sentimentalities about international law are not war, and that when we suddenly bombarded and plundered the capital of a neutral country (Denmark) without declaring war, we were thoroughly justified by what the German Chancellor calls "a state of necessity," the plain implication at the time when Major Stewart-Murray's book was issued being that we should be acting strictly according to British precedent if we suddenly attacked and sank the German fleet without notice or declaration of war, as, from the militarist point of view, we no doubt ought to have done if public opinion would have stood it. The situation in 1807 was that Britain, being at war with France and Russia, suddenly discovered that these two countries had secretly agreed to seize the fleets of the three neutral States of Denmark, Sweden, and Portugal, and with them to make good the losses suffered by the French navy in the battle of Trafalgar. The only way to prevent Napoleon doing this was to be beforehand with him; and accordingly Canning promptly sent out a fleet under General Gambier and an army under General Cathcart to seize the Danish fleet before Napoleon could lay hands on it. The Danes naturally objected to surrender their fleet; and their objection was overcome by bombarding Copenhagen for three days. The *Berliner Tageblatt* quotes our official justifications of this *coup de main*, from the King's proclamation downwards. Here they are:

ROYAL PROCLAMATION. While he [the King] laments the cruel necessity which has obliged him to have recourse to acts of hostility against a nation with which it was His Majesty's most earnest desire to have established the relations of common interest and alliance, His Majesty feels confident that in the eyes of Europe and the world the justification of his conduct will be found in the commanding and indispensable duty, paramount to all others among the obligations of a sovereign, of providing, while there was yet time, for the immediate security of his people.

MR. LUSHINGTON. The first law of nature, the foundation of the law of nations, is the preservation of man. It is on the knowledge of his nature that the science of his duty must be founded. When his feelings point out to him a mighty danger, and his reason suggests the means of avoiding it, he must despise the sophistical trifler who tells him it is a moral duty he owes to others to wait till the danger break upon his foolish head, lest he should hurt the meditated instrument of his destruction. Upon this general principle of the law of nature and of nations I maintain the morality and certainly the necessity of the expedition against Copenhagen.

MR. MILNES. He maintained that no law of nature could be violated by the measures taken by us to insure our own safety. It was the most flagitious of all descriptions of morality that would allow the opportunity of self-preservation to pass by unimproved.

LORD PALMERSTON. Much had been said by a right honourable gentleman on the law of nations, on right and policy: he [Lord P.] was as ready and willing as any man to pay his tribute of respect to them, and to recommend their application whenever circumstances would permit it: he was afraid, however, that although much talked of, they were little understood: the consequence was that many people abused the terms and took one for the other. In the present instance he was glad to observe that we did not suspend them without necessity, or, in other words, that we used them in conformity to the law of nature, which dictated and commanded self-preservation.

FOREIGN SECRETARY GEORGE CANNING. Was it to be contended that in a moment of imminent danger and impending necessity we should have abstained from that course which prudence and policy dictated, in order to meet and avert those calamities that threatened our security and existence, because, if we sank under the pressure, we should have the consolation of having the authority of Puffendorf to plead?

MR. PONSONBY (Opposition). No writer on the law of nations, or on any other law, or on common justice, had ever maintained that one Power could be justified in taking from another what belonged to it, unless a third Power meant and was able to take the same thing.

The *Berliner Tageblatt* simply adds: "Eines Kommentars werden diese Zitate nicht bedürfen." It cannot condemn Britain and Canning without condemning Germany and Bethmann-Hollweg. But it can and does put us in the same predicament. We cannot condemn Germany and Bethmann-Hollweg without condemning Britain and Canning. Let Mr. Podsnap, at present distracting us from the serious work of beating the Germans by his blatant trumpetings of his own moral superiorities, take heedful note, and, in the happy phrase of Mr. H. G. Wells, cease flapping his mouth on the foe.

The truth is, war, as between the belligerents, is a suspension of morality and religion and ethics and all the social commandments, just as it is a suspension of law and constitutional government within the belligerent countries; and this German War Book makes the best of it without dishonestly attempting to conceal the worst of it. The shrieks it has provoked only prove that many of our journalists have not the least notion of what war really is, and conceive it quite simply as a state in which it is glorious and heroic for Englishmen to shoot foreigners, but dastardly and murderous for foreigners to shoot Englishmen. They are very much in the mental condition of the late Duke of Cambridge, who is said to have had all his doubts as to the wisdom of the Crimean War swept away, and replaced by a furious hatred of the Russians, when he saw them firing at the Guards as callously as they were wont to fire at mere line regiments with whose messes the Duke did not dine. Even my glorious compatriot Sergeant O'Leary, whose portrait shews the remarkable forehead which enabled him to keep that long head of his whilst other men were losing theirs, and to attend to them dispassionately with a magazine rifle, seems from his letters to his family to be under the impression that "the Huns" behaved most reprehensibly in trying to slay the Irish Guards. Perhaps they did; but the reproach comes oddly from the slayer of a whole trenchful of them. A regiment of O'Learies would wipe out a German army corps: let us therefore applaud the heroism of the German troops who still confront the Irish Guards so devotedly. I dare say it is unpatriotic and pro-German of me; but I do think it a rotten thing to call men opprobrious names when they are fighting for their country for all they are worth.

I will not say that I wish the belligerents could learn to fight like gentlemen; for if we fight like gentlemen and sportsmen we shall be beaten by any nation which makes a serious business of killing us. That is how the French were beaten at Creçy and Poitiers. We are at present being driven to the last and meanest atrocity of war: the atrocity of starving our enemy. And we have driven the enemy to the villainy of hiding in the depths of the sea and torpedoing every keel that passes above. When it comes to that, we have both got pretty well down on the raw of necessity and self-preservation. But at least I can express a wish that the civilians on both sides would fight with their pens as cleanly and good-humoredly and bravely as the soldiers do with their guns and bayonets. When Mr. St. John Ervine let fly the other day about "our cowardly press and our contemptible parliament" he gave a good many of our journalists and politicians no more than they deserved. To me and to many others not the least of the horrors of this war has been the degradation of that national literary staff whose duty it is to keep our public character up to the mark in emergencies. It is pitiable to see how some of us have succumbed to the strain. We have run about screaming with panic when the example of a stout countenance was of all things required from us. We have changed from humane, humorously self-possessed gentlemen to vituperative hysterical cads. Whatever standards we may have borne in the endless strife for civil liberty and justice, we have thrown them away and fallen on our knees in abject surrender at the first roar of the German cannon. Too many of the clergy have become a mere rabble of apostates, shrieking for blood. Professors, unnerved and overstrained, have lacked even the lusty brutality of the Jingo clergy. Decent poets have scribbled hymns of hate, and tried to score music hall claptrap for the cornet and banjo. Responsible editors have written as if there were a mafficking mob under their windows ready to hang them at the first calm and masterful word, instead of a rather disgusted public—especially the enlisted public— wishing that somebody would talk a little sense. A thousand German spies and ten army corps within sight of London could not have dismayed us as much as the more terrified of our own compatriots have dismayed us. But there is no reason to suppose that these nerve cases are representative of the nation. Nobody is a penny the worse for their shrieking: the men who keep their heads also keep the attention of the people and come through the test of public meetings and press publicity triumphantly. The panic mongers are, so far, nowhere. In France the mobbing of Anatole France and the blacklisting of Puccini (we beat the French there by our good sense about German music) were despicable enough; but at least there is Clemenceau to hold the fort for free thought and free speech and Gustave Hervé, the most readable of the French journalists, to chaff himself and his friends in *La Guerre Sociale*, and, always debonair, to snap his fingers at the enemy instead of throwing mud that never reaches them. In Germany there is Maximilian Harden, whose common sense about the war, by forcing us to admit that the German spirit is still elate and formidable, frightens us more than the gibberings and clawings of all the delirious German professors and parsons and journalists who reassure us by going on like some of ours. What is happening in Russia I do not know, though there was some hope in the old joke, now stale, about England being resolved to fight to the last drop of Russian blood. You can always rally a nation while it has some wit left. America, to judge by some of its papers, is mad with British patriotism, Polish nationality, and Belgian freedom; but it is not for us to quarrel with them for this. More power to their elbows, say I, even though, like the young lady in *Fanny's First Play*, I can't help smiling.

But the fact that others are as bad as we is not a brave man's consolation. I call on the scared fugitives from my profession to pull themselves together and quit themselves as manfully as the soldiers. It is useless for romantic literary men to tell me that I am incapable of understanding that war has ennobled them. I quite understand how easily our vanity persuades us that excitement is ennoblement. Patriotism, Love, and Drink are potent producers of that flattering illusion. I am not taken in, though I admit that a frightened man's anxiety for his skin may be sincerer and therefore better for him than a dilettante's anxiety about his soul and about the fine arts. It is not noble to rave abusively at your enemy (not to mention your friend) instead of "covering him steady" with the pen as Sergeant O' Leary did with the magazine rifle.The men who wrote this German War Book are more formidable than the men who have tried to tear it to pieces; and we should be in a bad way indeed if our own General Staff had not more sense and pluck than most of the book's reviewers. It is a quite useful, interesting, instructive, well written, honest book, telling the truth exactly as our soldiers would tell it; and the sooner we learn to look facts in the face as its authors do, the sooner we shall be able to convince them that peace with us is better for them and the world than war.

G.B S.

Editor's Notes

- This review was first published in the *New Statesman* 4 (13 March 1915): 559–61.
- There is no indication in Shaw's correspondence as to when the above review was written; but he was at this time still so overwhelmed by letters about his *Common Sense about the War* that he had given up the attempt to answer them separately. Inevitably, then, his public utterances possess an explicatory function.
- [Brigadier-General J[ohn] H[artman] Morgan (1876–1955), Welsh military journalist, soldier, and professor of constitutional law. From 1901 to 1903 he was on the literary staff of the *Daily Chronicle*, and from 1904 to 1905 was a leader-writer on the *Manchester Guardian*. In 1908 he was appointed to the chair of constitutional law and legal history at University College, London, and in 1910 published *The House of Lords and the Constitution*. In 1913 he was appointed Rhodes Lecturer in the University of London in the Law of the Empire. When World War I broke out, Morgan offered himself for active service, but was attached to the adjutant-general's staff as Home Office representative with the British Expeditionary Force to inquire into the conduct of the Germans in the field. His report, published by the Parliamentary Recruiting Committee, was much in demand. In addition to the above-reviewed book, Morgan published *War: Its Conduct and Legal Results* (1916), and in the same year *Leaves from a Field Note Book*. After the war, Morgan represented the Adjutant-General at the peace conference, was British military representative on the Prisoner of War Commission, and finally retired from the army in 1923. In 1926 he was appointed reader in constitutional law to the Inns of Court, and took silk. Between the wars he studied the disarmament and rearmament of Germany, and revealed how the German officer

corps had avoided the provisions of the Treaty of Versailles in his book *Assize of Arms* (1945). From 1942 to 1945 he acted in a counselling capacity to the parliamentary postwar policy group, and later to the American commission at the Nuremberg Trials (of Nazi war criminals), which he witnessed.

▪ The S.P.C.K. was the Society for Promoting Christian Knowledge.

▪ Sir Mark [sixth baronet] Sykes (1879–1919), English traveler, soldier, and politician. During the South African War he served with the Yorkshire militia; and in 1911 he was returned as the Conservative candidate for Central Hull. He soon became a well-known speaker in the House of Commons, with a turn for satirical mimicry. This last he put to good use in collaboration with Edmund T. Sandars in a parody of the *Infantry Drill Book* entitled *Tactics and Military Training by Major-General D'Ordel* (1902). To underline the reformist intent of the authors, the following statement was printed at the beginning of the book: "This book is by no means merely a joke at the expense of an imaginary personality; it bears also a serious lesson. Major General D'Ordel impersonates characteristics but too common among those who, at all events until lately, directed the policy and administrations of the War Office." Sykes soon had the opportunity of influencing such policy himself: receiving the rank of lieutenant colonel in 1914, he was given orders to go to Serbia, Bulgaria, Egypt, and India, and, in 1915, when France objected to the proposed action of the British in Syria, Sykes, because of his fluent French and firsthand knowledge of the area, was despatched by the Foreign Office to hold formal conversations with the French about the future of the Near East. Throughout the remainder of the war, Sykes continued to advise the Foreign Office, and to mediate between Zionist and Arab claims in Palestine. There seems little doubt that the physical and mental stress caused by this led to his weakened resistance to the influenza which he died of in the postwar epidemic.

▪ Colonel Frederic [Natusch] Maude (1854–1933), and Major Stewart Lygon Murray (1863–?), were both military strategists. Shaw refers specifically to the latter's book *The Future Peace of the Anglo-Saxons* (1905), which contained a preface by Field-Marshal Earl Roberts. Both Maude and Murray studied von Clausewitz (see below), Maude bringing out an edition of his *On War* in 1908, and Murray producing an Introduction to Clausewitz's *On War* the following year, which was reprinted in a popular edition in 1914.

▪ [Karl von] Clausewitz (1780–1831), German soldier and military theorist. Clausewitz fought against Napoleon at Waterloo; in 1818 became a major general; and from 1818 to 1830 was director of the German War School. Clausewitz's fame as a military theorist came from his posthumously published masterpiece *Vom Krieg [On war]*, 3 vols., 1833; translated into English, 1873. His books, which greatly influenced military men of many countries, considered war as a political act to be directed by the political leadership of a nation, and military operations themselves as a strategic science.

▪ The Germans bombed the east coast, concentrating upon King's Lynn, on the night of 19 January 1915. *The Times* reported tersely, "An airship passed over Hunstanton (being described by one who saw it as "the size of a church") about 10 o'clock and followed the Great Eastern Railway track by way of Heacham" (where lived Robert Blatchford (see above, 212–13)). "Here a bomb was dropped. It fell several hundred yards from some cottages, and, beyond tearing up the ground, did no damage. The explosion of the bomb was very loud, and alarmed the whole district; in the quietness of the night the report was heard between four or five miles away." The airship also passed directly over Sandringham which was the Norfolk home of King George V.

- The Hague Regulations (or Conventions) to ameliorate the conditions of warfare were drawn up at the two Hague Conferences of 1899 and 1907.
- In *Heartbreak House*, the play he would begin the following year, Shaw himself arranges the demolition of at least one country house by aerial bombardment.
- Lord Roberts (see above, 284–85).
- [James] Gambier, first Baron Gambier (1756–1833), English naval commander, was not a general but an admiral when he commanded the British fleet at the bombardment of Copenhagen in 1807. In fact he was made Admiral of the Fleet in 1830.
- [Sir William Schaw, first Earl] Cathcart (1755–1843), Scottish soldier and diplomat who commanded the land forces at the bombardment of Copenhagen.
- [Henry John Temple, third Viscount] Palmerston (1784–1865), English politician. In 1807 he was elected member for Newport [Wight] Two years later he was junior lord of the Admiralty and secretary at war. He would be prime minister in 1855.
- George Canning (1770–1827), English statesman. In 1807 he was minister for foreign affairs in the mixed (largely Tory) government under the leadership of the Duke of Portland.
- [Stephen] Lushington (1782–1873), English politician who was returned as a Whig for the borough of Great Yarmouth in the general election of 1806.
- [Robert Pemberton] Milnes (1784–1858) [known as "Single-speech Milnes"], English politician, is best remembered for refusing both the Chancellorship of the Exchequer and a peerage.
- [Samuel, Freiherr von] Puffendorf (1632–94), German writer on jurisprudence. His great book *De Jure Naturae et Gentium* was published in 1672.
- [William, Viscount Duncannon] Ponsonby [afterward fourth earl of Bessborough] (1781–1847), English politician. In 1805 he entered Parliament as Whig member for Knaresborough, but was "an unready speaker and held aloof from debate."
- "Eines Kommentars werden diese Zitate nicht bedürfen," means "A commentary regarding these quotations won't be necessary."
- Mr. Podsnap was the pompous, self-satisfied "member of society," in Dickens's *Our Mutual Friend*, swelling with patronage of his friends and acquaintances: "Mr. Podsnap was well to do, and stood very high in Mr. Podsnap's opinion."
- Bethmann Hollweg (see above, 286).

- [Major Michael J.] O'Leary (1888–1961), Irish soldier and building contractor. Born at Kilbarry Lodge, Macroom, County Cork, he was a lance corporal with the first Irish Guards when he won his Victoria Cross on 1 February 1915. He had been promoted to the rank of sergeant by the time he was presented to the king (on 22 June 1915) to receive his Victoria Cross: "For conspicuous bravery at Ouinchy. . . . When forming one of the storming party which advanced against the enemy's barricades he rushed to the front and himself killed five Germans who were holding the first barricade, after which he attacked a second barricade, about sixty yards further on, which he captured, after killing three of the enemy and making prisoners of two more." He was given a commission in the first Batallion Connaught Rangers, and served with distinction throughout the war, being mentioned in dispatches and receiving a Russian Cross of Saint George to go with his V.C. He rejoined the army in 1939 as a captain, and served in the Middlesex Regiment from 1940 to 1944, when he joined the Pioneer Corps. He was discharged on medical grounds in 1945. Shaw's principal character in *O'Flaherty V.C.* (1915) is based very loosely on O'Leary. He too was born in the lodge of a great Irish estate (his mother believes Shakespeare was born in County Cork!), has killed six Germans, the papers are full of his shaking hands with the English king at Buckingham Palace, and he too goes back to the war.
- St John [Greer] Ervine (1883–1971), Irish playwright and author. Born in Belfast, in 1900 he, like Shaw, emigrated to London where he also wrote novels and plays. At the time of this review he was manager of the Abbey Theatre, Dublin, where his first plays *Mixed Marriage* (1911), and *Jane Clegg* (1914) were produced. He served in the First World War with the Dublin Fusiliers and lost a leg; and after the war he continued to write successful plays. Indeed, in the 1930s Shaw befriended him, and even collaborated with him in his three-act comedy *People of Our Class* in 1936. Five years after Shaw's death Ervine wrote *Bernard Shaw: His Life, Work and Friends*.
- "A *mafficking* mob"; the word is from the place-name Mafeking, treated jocularly as a present participle: a journalistic word used to designate the extravagant behavior of the London crowds on the Relief of Mafeking (17 May 1900) (*OED*).
- Anatole France [pen-name of Jacques Anatole François Tibault] (1844–1924), French novelist. He was one of the French intellectuals who, under the leadership of Emile Zola, fought successfully for the exoneration of Dreyfus, the French army captain convicted of treason (see above, 237–38). Thereafter Anatole France became an outspoken humanitarian who attacked with brilliant satire the political and social abuses of his time. In December 1913 he had traveled to London, and made a speech to the Fabian Society (at the Suffolk Galleries), with Shaw in the Chair. On that occasion: "When Anatole France rose to make his speech, he began with the customary 'Mesdames et Messieurs,' and then, turning to Bernard Shaw, he added with a bow and a smile, 'et le Molière d'Angleterre!' " (James Lewis May, *Anatole France. The Man and his Work. An Essay in Critical Biography* [1924; repr. London: Kennikat, 1970], 102). However, as an antimilitarist, Anatole France joined

the "Union Sacrée" after the war broke out, optimistically believing that Socialists of all nationalities would band together to stop the conflict. Late in
August 1914 he published a message hoping for a reconciliation with the
Germans; this provoked a violent reaction from French nationalists, who
threatened Anatole France with bodily harm. His response was to volunteer
for military service (at the age of 70!), and to write the unfortunate patriotic
series *Sur la Voie glorieuse*.

- [Giacomo] Puccini (1858–1924), Italian composer. At the outbreak of hostilities in 1914, Italy was still neutral, but public opinion was divided between
the Germanophiles and the pro-Allied sympathizers. Puccini inclined to the
Central Powers: he did not care for the French who had also attacked his
operas, while in Germany he had had more success. He was reported as
having said that so far as he was concerned, the Germans could not capture
Paris too soon, and this caused a rift between himself and Toscanini. But the
real trouble began in 1915 when a German newspaper announced that
Puccini was one of those artists and composers who had signed a manifesto
condemning Germany's invasion of Belgium, no doubt referring to the so-
called *King Albert's Book*, in which notable men and women throughout the
world paid tribute to the heroic Belgian king. Puccini, however, had not been
asked. Following the German report, then, Puccini published a denial, assert-
ing that he had never signed such a declaration; indeed, he added, he had
never been anti-German, and he entertained feelings of friendship and gratitude toward any country where his music was performed. His statement
caused a violent reaction in the French press, an attack led by Léon Daudet
(son of Alphonse), who, after Italy had entered the war on the side of the
Allies, attacked Puccini's operetta *La rondine* (produced in Monte Carlo in
1917) for lack of patriotism in his nationalist newspaper *L'action française*.
This led to the temporary banning of Puccini's music in France, though he
made amends by publishing in April 1917 another long refutation protesting
that his life and art proved him a patriot, and further instructing the Paris
Opéra-Comique to donate an entire year's royalties from the performances of
his works to a fund for wounded soldiers.
- Clemenceau (see above, 269).
- Gustave Hervé (1871–1944), French journalist. In 1897, at the beginning
of the Dreyfus affair, he started his political career by publishing a sensational
letter (in advance of Zola's *J'Accuse*), that cost him his professorship at Rodez
in the south of France. Later, he managed to exchange posts with a professor
at Sens (in Burgundy). In April 1900 the Federation de l'Yvonne branch of
the French Socialist Party founded the *Travailleur Socialiste* newspaper, in
which Hervé began publishing antimilitarist articles (under the *nom de
plume* "Un Sans-Patrie,"), one of which was so inflammatory that the Government took proceedings against Hervé, and again he lost his job. For four years
Hervé lived with the French peasantry, expounding, in simple language, his
Socialistic and pacifist principles. His anti-recruitment pamphlets to con-
scripts led to his prosecution and a five-year prison sentence. However, he
was released after about six months; and immediately set about studying law.

In the teeth of opposition from other barristers he was called to the Paris Bar in 1906. In 1908, he founded his own Socialist journal *La Guerre Sociale*, and, for insulting the French army in it, was sentenced to a year's imprisonment and expelled from the Paris Bar, However, he left the Socialist Party shortly after the outbreak of the war in 1914. Later he changed the name of his journal to *La Victoire,* and supported the policies of Clemenceau (see above, 269).

▪   Maximilian Harden [real surname Witkowski] (1861–1927), German journalist. Born in Berlin, he founded in 1892 a political weekly journal *Die Zukunft,* in which he aroused the hostility of the government. His attacks finally brought a charge of criminal libel, but he was exonerated, and some of the leading figures in the government were driven from public life in 1906 and 1907. During World War I, Harden retained his freedom to criticize government policy, urging a negotiated peace, and warning the German government that it had seriously underestimated the military strength of the United States.

▪   The "young lady" in *Fanny's First Play* (1911), which was at the time of this review in revival at the Kingsway Theatre, directed by Shaw, was Dora Delaney, a stranger who turns up at the Gilbey residence in act 1 to explain that their son Bobby is in jail in consequence of a "bit of fun" they both had with a policeman's helmet. Mr. Gilbey is furious. Mrs. Gilbey is astonished that her son is keeping company with Dora:

MRS. GILBEY . . . The things people do! I cant understand them. Bobby never told me he was keeping company with you. His own mother!
DORA [*overcome*] Excuse me: I cant help smiling.

8 May 1915

MR. GILBERT CANNAN ON SAMUEL BUTLER* [C2002]

IN choosing Mr. Gilbert Cannan to write on Butler for his critical series, Mr. Martin Secker has shown either luck or cunning; for the book has style and wit, and does its work in a highly readable manner up to the point at which Butler must be left to speak for himself. Its presentation of Butler as a Character, with an engaging literary talent

---

* "Samuel Butler. A Critical Study." By Gilbert Cannan. (Martin Secker). 7s. 6d.

and a racy vein of eccentric humor is complete and elegant. It does not present Butler as a man of genius, because Mr. Cannan does not consider Butler a man of genius. I do. And I may as well explain the difference.

A man of genius is not a man who can do more things, or who knows more things, than ordinary men: there has never been a man of genius yet who has not been surpassed in both respects in his own generation by quite a large number of hopeless fools. He is simply a man who sees the importance of things. Otherwise every schoolmaster would be greater than Christ. Mr. Cannan says that the nearest in spirit to Butler of any man of his time was W. S. Gilbert. This is a staggering statement, because on Butler's plane one does not think of Gilbert; and when we are reminded of him there we feel that Butler mattered enormously more than Gilbert, who in such a comparison seems not to have mattered at all. Yet, on reflection, one has to admit that they have something in common. The particular vein of wit which leads some men to take familiar and unquestioned propositions and turn them inside out so neatly as to convince you that they are just as presentable one way as the other, or even that the sides so unexpectedly and quaintly turned out are the right sides, is one in which Butler and Gilbert were natural adepts. But Gilbert never saw anything in the operation but a funny trick. He deliberately separated its exercise from his serious work, and took it off as a man takes off his hat in church when he attempted serious drama. Whenever Butler performed it he presently realised that the seeming trick was an inspired revelation. His very hoaxes were truths which Providence tempted him to entertain for fun until they made themselves indispensable. "Every jest is an earnest in the womb of time." That womb was incarnated in Butler's head, not in Gilbert's. Butler saw the importance of what he had hit on, and developed it into a message for his age. Gilbert saw it as a quip and left it at that: he could hardly develop a string of quips as far as a second act without petering out. Gilbert was a belittler: he jeered at old women like a street boy with a bad mother. Butler tore off the mask and tripped up the cothurnus of many a pretentious pigmy, thereby postponing public recognition of him until the PPs of his generation had died or doddered out; but he was a man of heroic admirations whereas the people whom Gilbert admired have yet to be discovered. Mr. Cannan himself points out appreciatively that Butler made a Sybil of Mrs. Jupp, which may in the books of the recording angel balance his make a booby of Sir Benjamin Layard. There is stuff enough in *Trial by Jury* and *The Pirates of Penzance* to set up an Ibsen in his business; but Gilbert, though he could penetrate to the facts, and saw the fun of their incongruity with the glamor through which most of us see them, could not see their importance. Thus Butler forged his jests into a weapon which smashed the nineteenth century, whilst Gilbert only made it laugh. No two men could have been more widely disparate in the scope of their spirit, though their specific humor reacted to the stimulus of human folly in the same manner. Gilbert with the word Chesterton added can turn things inside out and write amusing phrases as well as Gilbert; but he does it to high purpose. Oscar Wilde at his best knew that his gift was divine in its nature. In this they both stood far nearer to Butler than Gilbert did. Gilbert, in short, is an excellent illustration of how useless Butler's specific turn of humor would have been to him had he not been a man of genius; and in this capacity only has he the right to appear in a book about Butler.

Butler's great achievement was his perception, after six weeks of hasty triumph in Darwin's deathblow to the old Paleyan assumption that any organ perfectly adapted to its function must be the work of a designer, of the unspeakable horror of the mindless purposeless world presented to us by Natural Selection. Even with Butler's guidance those of us who are not geniuses hardly see that yet; and we babble about Nietzsche and Treitschke with Darwin's name written all over the Prussian struggle for the survival of the fittest. Mr. Cannan, exquisitely appreciative of Butler as a British Worthy, and enamoured of Mrs. Jupp (who is, by the way, a reincarnation of Mrs. Quickly), does not see it in the least, and thereby wholly misses Butler's greatness, being indeed rather ignominiously driven at the end, in spite of the evidence of the earlier chapters to which Butler has stimulated him, to deliver a half-hearted verdict of Spoiled Artist, and Failure, and to dismiss Butler's great vision as the effect of the terror inspired in the ex-evangelical by Darwin, "the greatest figure of the time." Here the word Figure seems well chosen to avoid calling Darwin the greatest man of his time (he *was* the greatest naturalist of his time, and a very amiable person to boot); but the phrase may be a mere *cliché*; for Mr. Cannan does not follow up the distinction it implies. "It became a passion with Butler," he continues, "to tell others not to be afraid; and this passion, as fear died down, was congealed into an obsession which is responsible for the tiresome reiteration of the evolution books." This is a settler. Mr. Cannan has grasped neither the point at issue nor its importance. That is why he fails to see how Butler was a great man, and invents a silly-clever explanation of his quarrel with Darwin. Nothing that I have read in Butler, or gathered from his conversation, conveys the very faintest suggestion of terror or of the "who's afraid" attitude. On the contrary, he was distinguished by his derisive insensibility to the awe which conventional and pious reputations inspire; and as to Darwin, though it was considered very wicked in Butler's time to countenance Darwin in any way, Butler's attitude towards him was one of strenuous championship until he foresaw how the Darwinians, in their revolt against crude Bible worship, would empty the baby out with the bath and degrade the whole conception of Evolution by levelling it down to Natural Selection, which, though a potent method of adaptation, is not true Evolution at all. As a young man, Butler said, in *Life and Habit*, that Darwin had "banished mind from the Universe." As an old man, he said the same thing to me in private conversation with an intensity that flatly violated his advice to all of us to hold convictions lightly and cultivate Laodiceanism. Until Mr. Cannan grasps the importance of that simple statement through an intuition that the difference between Butler's view of the universe and the Darwinian view of it as a product of Natural Selection is the difference between heaven and hell, he will not begin to imagine what Butler's life was about, though he may write very pleasantly and wittily about Butler's talents and accomplishments and foibles. Nor will he appreciate the grimly humorous satisfaction with which Butler on that occasion added "My grandfather quarrelled with Darwin's grandfather; my father quarrelled with Darwin's father; I quarrelled with Darwin; and my only regret in not having a son is that he cannot quarrel with Darwin's son."

But Mr. Cannan's book is the better in some respects for leaving Butler's message to be taken from Butler himself, especially as it will send people to Butler instead of scaring them off, as mere paraphrases of great writers do. To write a book about a man who has written books about himself is an impertinence which only an irresistible charm of manner can carry off. The unpardonable way of doing it, and the commonest, is to undertake to tell the public what a writer has already told them himself, and to tell it worse or tell it all wrong. Mr. Cannan has not committed this outrage. Indeed he interferes too little: for instance, he says not a word of Butler's epochmaking suggestion that poverty and ugliness should be attacked as crimes instead of petted and coddled like diseases. He just allows his mind to play round Butler, and thus makes him the attractive occasion of a book rather than its subject. Here are some samples of his play. "Butler could never respect Darwin when he found humor lacking in *The Origin of Species*. That was really the beginning and the end of Darwin's offence; and because of it Butler at last could not take anything Charles Darwin said or did seriously." Now this, though quite wrong—for Butler was the only contemporary of Darwin who took him really seriously—is much better than saying that Butler was terrified by Darwin; and it is amusing, anyhow. Again, "In Butler's world there is no freedom except freedom from humbug. He knows nothing of the proud insistence that volition shall proceed contaminated by desire. His view was that volition was in all probability contaminated by the interests of ancestors and posterity, and that there was no help for it." This is better still. And such literary frivolities as "I cannot believe in Butler's God, simply because he does not write about his God with style," have the merits of frivolity; for frivolity has merits: for instance, it is often pleasant. Besides, the laugh here is with Butler, who had the supreme sort of style that never smells of the lamp, and therefore seems to the kerosene stylist to be no style at all. I do not offer these quotations as at bottom more relevant to Butler than to Boccaccio; but a writer who can go on so is readable on his own account, Butler or no Butler; and if the samples encourage my readers to try the whole book, they can judge for themselves its stupendous demerits as a criticism of Butler the Great as distinguished from Butler the Character.

I am disposed to reproach Mr. Cannan a little for saying in effect that Butler was no use except as a literary artist, and then giving him away to the so-called scientific people because he was an artist. If Mr. Cannan chooses to allow himself to be humbugged by these ridiculous distinctions, he might at least give his own side the benefit of them. But he would do still better if he would revise his book in the light of a serious consultation with himself as to whether he really believes that a naturalist is always, and a thinker never, a man of science; and if so, why? Butler told us a great deal about life and habit, luck and cunning, that nobody had ever told us before, having an extraordinary talent for observing and interpreting both. Darwin told us a great deal about pigeons and worms that nobody had ever told us before, having a remarkable turn for watching pigeons and worms. Why is Darwin classed as a man of science and Butler as an artist of no science? Leonardo da Vinci remarked that the sun did not go round the earth. Galileo made the same remark. Why did nobody believe Leonardo or regard him as a man of science; and why does everybody applaud Galileo as the great scientific discoverer of the fact that it is the earth that goes round the sun? Does anyone seriously suggest that these Galileos and

Harveys and Darwins had greater minds than Leonardo or Goethe or Kant or Butler or any of the great artists and philosophers who have grasped the importance of science and applied their wits to its problems? Even Weismann, who was so much more speculative than Darwin that he developed Darwinism into an extravagant lunacy, and made some brilliant hits in the process, describes how the "discovery" of the cellular structure of living organisms was anticipated fully by a pure mystic whose very name nobody can recollect without referring to Weismann's History of Evolution. Why should Mr. Cannan do less justice to the scientific importance of poets and prophets than a naturalist like Weismann?

The real distinction between the two classes is clear enough. The so-called discoverers have been the collectors of evidence and the demonstrators (by put-up jobs called experiments) of facts and forces already divined by men with brains enough not to be wholly dependent on material demonstration. St. Thomas, with Christ staring him in the face, refused to believe that he was there until he had put his fingers into his wounds, thereby establishing himself as the prototype and patron saint of all the "discoverers" who, as the Irish say, "would guess eggs if they saw the shells." Darwin's was an exceptionally exasperating case, because he not only got the credit of having discovered Evolution, which had been promulgated and thoroughly established in the period of Goethe and Darwin's grandfather (1790–1830), but had actually substituted for this great general conception an elaborate study of that pseudo-evolution which is produced by external accident (as if a tree could be properly said to have been "evolved" into firewood by the storm which blew it down). This was not Darwin's fault: he did not call the process he demonstrated Evolution, but Natural Selection; still, Darwinism was none the less irritating and disastrous because Darwin was not a Darwinist. The intelligent people jumped wildly at Natural Selection because it knocked Paley and the Book of Genesis clean out. The stupid people took it up because, like St. Thomas, they could understand a soulless mechanical process, but could not conceive a vital process like Evolution. The result was half a century of bedevilment, folly, pessimism, despair and cowardice, of which we are now reaping the fruits in Flanders; and against this Butler stood for years alone; for one cannot count the belated pietists who wanted to go back to the Garden of Eden. In a word, Butler stood alone for science against the purblind naturalists and biologists, with their following of miracle mongers, experiment jobbers, and witch doctors, all absurdly claiming to be *the* men of science. And I contend that Mr. Cannan, belonging as he does to Butler's camp, should stand to his guns and defend the apprehensive mind and the intuitive imagination against the peering eyes and the groping fingers. Besides, Butler has won. Why does Mr. Cannan, like Frederick at Molwitz, throw up the sponge for him?

G. B. S.

Editor's Notes

▪ The above review was first published in the *New Statesman* 5 (8 May 1915): 109–10, and subsequently reprinted in Bernard Shaw, *Pen Portraits and Reviews* (London: Constable, 1931 and 1932), the text of which is substantially the same, the only alterations being the omission of the period [.] after Mr., the de-italicizing of book titles, and the addition of commas before Shaw's direct quote 'Butler on that occasion added[,] "My grandfather quarrelled with Darwin's grandfather . . . [etc.],' and in the list in the last paragraph 'half a century of bedevilment, folly, pessimism, despair[,] and cowardice, . . . (etc.), which had been omitted in the original.

▪ In the first months of 1915 Shaw was still busy with war work in England. However, on 31 March the Shaws went to Ireland for a few months and when this review appeared were staying with Lady Gregory while Shaw worked on a sequel to *Common Sense about the War*, originally entitled *Uncommon Sense about the War*, which was never published.

▪ Gilbert Cannan (1884–1955), English novelist and dramatist. Born in Manchester and educated there and at King's College, Cambridge, Cannan was called to the bar in 1908. The following year he became drama critic on the *Star* (for a year), and thereafter authored a series of books such as *Peter Homunculus* (1909), *The Joy of the Theatre* (1913), *Adventurous Love, and other verses* (1915), *Pugs and Peacocks* (1921), *Annette and Bennett* (a novel, 1922); and plays, such as *Miles Dixon* (1910), *Everybody's Husband* (1917), and *The Release of the Soul* (1920); and translations of Heine, Aleksinkaya, and Chekhov.

▪ Samuel Butler (1835–1902), English philosophical author. Graduating from St. John's College, Cambridge in 1858, he dashed his family's hopes that he would proceed to ordination in the Church of England (like his father), by proposing to study art. In consequence he was banished to New Zealand, and early in 1860 became a highly successful sheep-farmer on Canterbury Island. Returning to London, he settled down to painting, writing, and music. Though considering himself a painter, he began to weave certain articles and sketches into a sustained satirical narrative entitled *Erewhon: or Over the Range* (1872), which was published anonymously at his own expense. This account of the discovery of a country wherein manners are the opposite of those in England, where poverty and ill health are crimes, and where theft results in hospital treatment, achieved wide acclaim. In 1873, he published a rationalist satire on religion *The Fair Haven* (under the pseudonym of John Pickard Owen), and the same year began his novel *The Way of All Flesh*. In his opening sentence Shaw puns on the title of Butler's *Luck, or Cunning as the Main Means of Organic Modification?* which he reviewed for the *Pall Mall Gazette* on 31 May 1887. Shaw met and dined with Butler on several later occasions, and corresponded with him. The last book published in Butler's lifetime was *Erewhon Revisited* (1901), showing how a religious cult can grow from a supposed miracle. Shaw was instrumental in getting this book published by his own publisher (Grant Richards) after Longman's had refused to publish it, even at Butler's own expense. After Butler's death, there were numerous annual "Erewhon" dinners held, and Shaw occasionally attended and spoke at these functions.

▪ [Sir] W[illiam] S[chwenck] Gilbert (1836–1911), English playwright, librettist, and lyricist. He was an unsuccessful barrister, who began his literary career by joining the staff of *Fun* as a regular contributor. He also contributed humorous verse to *Punch* (under the pseudonym of "Bab"). In 1869 these verses were collected as *The Bab Ballads*. In the 1860's Gilbert contributed numerous farces and plays at the Royalty and Haymarket Theatres, many of which were performed but never published. From the 1870s such plays as *The Palace of Truth* (1870), *Randall's Thumb* (1871), and *Pygmalion and Galatea* (1871) were played successfully, and established Gilbert's reputation as a playwright. However, it is as the librettist and partner of Sir Arthur Sullivan (1842–1900), that he is best remembered in the series of light operas associated with their name. Shaw's dislike of Gilbert (evident in this review) was no doubt intensified by the fact that his friend William Archer, who had credited Gilbert with fathering the "problem play," saw other similarities between Shaw and the older dramatist; similarities that Shaw indignantly repudiated, for example, in his letter to William Archer on 23 April 1894 (see *Collected Letters 1874–1897*, 425–428). Nevertheless, Gilbert no doubt had been a formative influence on Shaw in his first years as a playwright (see my article "One Man and His Dog: A Study of a Deleted Draft of Bernard Shaw's *The Philanderer*," in *Modern Drama* [May 1967]: 69–78).

▪ Oscar [Fingal O'Flahertie Wills] Wilde (1854–1900), Irish playwright, novelist, essayist, poet, and critic. Wilde's early published works included two collections of fairy stories *The Happy Prince and Other Tales* (1888), and *A House of Pomegranates* (1892) and a group of short stories, *Lord Arthur Savile's Crime* (1891). His only novel *The Picture of Dorian Gray*, a melodramatic tale of moral decadence, appeared in the same year. Wilde's dramatic reputation rests on the four comedies *Lady Windermere's Fan* (1892), *A Woman of No Importance* (1893), *An Ideal Husband* (1895), and *The Importance of Being Earnest* (1895), plays characterized by clever plots and remarkably witty dialogue. In the same year that the last of these was produced, and at the height of his literary career, Wilde was prosecuted for sodomy in one of the most sensational trials of the nineteenth century. He was sentenced to two years' hard labor in prison, where he also wrote the confessional *De*

Profundis; and, on his release *The Ballad of Reading Gaol* (1898). Wilde died in Paris. Shaw, who through the intermediary of his sister Lucy had first met Wilde at one of Lady Wilde's *soirées musicales* in the 1880s, clearly admired his fellow citizen's artistry in the early 1890s, as is revealed by their exchange of correspondence at that time, and Shaw's reviews of Wilde's theatrical work in the *Saturday Review*.

▪ William Paley (1743–1805), English theologian. His most original work, published in 1790 (*Horae Paulinae*) was designed to disprove the hypothesis that the New Testament was a cunningly devised fable, and this led to his famous *Evidences of Christianity* (1794). However, his most widely popular work was *Natural Theology, or Evidences of the Existence and Attributes of the Deity* (1802).

▪ Heinrich von Treitschke (1834–96), German historian. His chief work, *The History of Germany in the Nineteenth Century* written from 1879 to 1894, and translated into English during the First World War, expressed his ardent belief in a powerful Germany with a powerful empire, and suggested the necessity of waging war to maintain such power.

▪ "Mrs. Jupp" is the curate Ernest Pontifex's worldly, garrulous landlady in Samuel Butler's *The Way of All Flesh*. Gilbert Cannan does dwell on her somewhat in his *Samuel Butler. A Critical Study.* (London: Martin Secker, 1915): "The figure of Mrs. Jupp brings a·rich flavour of reality into what might so easily have been mere intellectual irony, like that of *The Fair Haven.* This old bawd, 'an old whore's body with a young whore's mind,' is of the gallery of John Donne. . . . Mrs. Jupp is Butler's trump card, and he plays her exactly at the right moment. . . . She is the *dea ex machina*, whose job it is to deliver Ernest from his parents" (122–24).

▪ Mistress Quickly is the equally garrulous hostess of the Boar's Head tavern in Eastcheap in Shakespeare's *Henry IV* and *Henry V*, in which last play she is represented as married to Pistol, who speaks of her death in act V, scene i.

▪ Shaw in his 1907 Preface to *Major Barbara* echoes Butler, declaring that the "greatest of evils and the worst of crimes is poverty"—an idea which he expresses in the play through the mouth of Undershaft.

▪ As a scientist Leonardo da Vinci (see above, 114) towered above all his contemporaries; had his notebooks been published they would have revolutionized the science of his day. His manuscripts, however, were not easily decipherable, and much of his accomplishment was neither revealed nor understood until the twentieth century. It is interesting in this connection that, in addition to his astronomical observations, Leonardo made anatomical ones, which included studying the circulation of the blood, thus anticipating William Harvey (see below).

▪ Galileo Galilei (1564–1642), Italian astronomer and physicist, was also multi-talented, making discoveries in mathematics and hydrostatics as well as astronomy. His heliocentric theory proved the theory of Nicolaus Copernicus [also known as Mikolaj Kopernik, and Niklas Koppernigk (1473–1543), the Polish astronomer, whose system, explained in his book *De Revolutionibus*

Orbium Coelestium [*On the revolutions of heavenly bodies*], published shortly
after his death in 1543, refuted the geocentric Ptolemaic System.
▪ William Harvey (1578–1657), English physician and discoverer of the
circulation of the blood, which discovery was first published in his *Exercitatio Anatomica de Motu Cordis et Sanguinis* (1628).
▪ August Weismann (1834–1914), German biologist, best known as the
originator of the germ-plasm theory of heredity, which states that a special
hereditary substance (germ-plasm) constitutes the only organic continuity
between one generation and the next. He assumed that the primary constituents in germ-plasm were minute particles (which he called biophores), similar to the modern conception of genes.
▪ Frederick II of Germany [Frederick the Great] (see below, 318).

17 July 1915

PROFESSOR GILBERT MURRAY'S DEFENCE OF SIR EDWARD GREY* [C2009]

WHEN this book was announced, my first impulse was to congratulate Sir Edward Grey on the distinction of his advocate. Professor
Gilbert Murray has won a position in literature by his translations of
Euripides, and in modern thought by his essays, which cannot be
compromised even by his Oxford professorship. Lucky Sir Edward
Grey!

And yet I am not so sure of it. If I were Sir Edward Grey, I think I
should have preferred Serjeant Buzfuz. It is not always wise to indulge in the luxury of a Judicial Committee barrister when the case is
to be tried at the Old Bailey. Buzfuz would have piled on the greatness
of Sir Edward Grey's cause, and then piled on the greatness of Sir
Edward Grey until he was as big as his Cause. He would not have
been stopped by the need for stretching his client a bit. And he might
have got his verdict.

Professor Murray is not free to stretch eminent persons in this

---

* "The Foreign Policy of Sir Edward Grey, 1906–1915." By Gilbert Murray. (Clarendon
Press.) 1s.6d.net.

manner. He is under the tyranny of his intellect and his conscience. His intellect perceived a discrepancy between the Cause and the Man. To conceal that discrepancy it was necessary either to deal with the Man in terms of the Cause: that is, to magnify the Man until he was as big as the Cause, like Buzfuz, or to deal with the Cause in terms of the Man: that is, to reduce it to the dimensions of a trivial embarrassment calling for the exercise of a little gentlemanly feeling and thoroughly amiable intentions.

My regard for Professor Murray, like that of Mr. Tupman for Mr. Pickwick, must not seduce me into ignoring the obvious question as to which of these two courses involves the more flagrant intellectual misdemeanour. But I deliver no verdict: neither course is defensible, though Professor Murray's is, as might have been expected, the more chivalrous. Let me, however, explain to him why he took it, apart from his good nature. To falsify Sir Edward Grey by making him up as Bismarck would have coarsely violated the veracity of his dramatic instinct. The modern Euripides could not have done it: his hand would have refused the task in spite of him, had he attempted it. On the other hand, to dwarf that monstrous triviality, European diplomacy, must have been the constant impulse of the Euripidean irony within him. Grey was never ruffian enough to be a bully. Murray was never fool enough to be a Jingo. Was it not natural that he should say to Grey, "Let us help one another out of this wretched mess." To be a really energetic Imperialist you must have illusions about the Empire; and you must know Greece as a piffling little kingdom with pro-German leanings in its high places, never as Hellas. Professor Murray has no illusions about the Empire (he was born in Australia); and Hellas is the motherland of his soul, something to him that Holloway can never be. And Sir Edward Grey, though considerably stupider, perhaps, has much the same feeling towards the Empire. It is to him a worry and not a citadel. He has intellect without cupidity; and his idealism utterly refuses to flow in the channels which serve for totally unintellectual energies like those of, say, the late Joseph Chamberlain.

I approach the actual contents of the book with reluctance. I ask myself will Murray ever forgive me if I turn on my own share of the Euripidean irony, and, so to speak, seethe the kid in its mother's milk. I have marked passage after passage that seems to be the work of the sub-conscious translator of The Trojan Women rather than of the champion of the Foreign Office. The italics might have been underscored here and there by Mephistopheles. The record of the Twelve Days before the war spares Grey nothing.

Just think of it. Here was England, with Continents for colonies, with her mighty fleet, her stirring tradition, her unbeaten record, her millions of men spoiling for a fight, her thousands of millions of money gaping for $4\frac{1}{2}$ per cent., towering, in spite of all Germany's laurels, as the most formidable single-handed Power on this earth. Her sword was in Sir Edward Grey's hand, her purse in his pocket, her men at his back. There was no need to shout: England's whisper was the thunder of Europe. In 1911, Mr. Lloyd George had shaken his mailed fist just once at the threat of war, and the sky cleared obsequiously in a moment.

Hear now the voice of the Lion, as it was raised during that twelve days when the fate of Europe was in the balance that England held. "England can play the part of mediator better if she is not committed." "If Russia takes the view which any Power interested in Serbia will naturally take, England will be helpless, owing to the time limit and the terms of the ultimatum." "The only chance of peace is for Germany, France, Italy and Great Britain to keep together and join in asking Austria and Russia not to cross the frontier until we have time to try and arrange matters." "Grey proposes conference" and "presses that Serbian reply should be treated as a basis of discussion" (that is, that the conference should talk about pretexts and side issues). "We might ask Germany to suggest the lines on which she would consent to work with us." "If Germany will suggest any method to which she does not object—since mine is inacceptable—France, Italy, and Great Britain are ready to follow her." "Great Britain cannot promise to intervene, but will not necessarily stand aside." "British ambassador presses German Government for an answer to Grey's appeal to them to suggest some method by which the Four Powers could use their mediating influence." "If Germany will get any reasonable proposal put forward." "The observation of the neutrality of Belgium may be, if not a decisive, an important factor in determining our action." And during all these ifs and ans, and appeals to Germany and everyone else to suggest something, the allies were positively shouting to Sir Edward to say straight out whether he was going to fight or not: in other words, what England would stand and what she would not. And he could not even bring himself to say positively that he would fight if Belgian neutrality were violated!

I had to refer Professor Murray's comment to my secretary to make sure that I was not dreaming it. "Whether Grey's policy was right or wrong, it was from the beginning *quite definite* ." Those are the very words: "quite definite." But the explanation is clear enough. On the ninth of this month Professor Murray, delivering his presidential address to the Society for Psychical Research, confessed to the possession of telepathic powers. It must have been by the exercise of these powers that he divined, from the utterances quoted above, that Sir Edward Grey had warned Europe definitely that we were unalterably resolved to defend Antwerp as if it were Portsmouth, and the Pas de Calais as if it were Kent; that as surely as Germany struck at France, we should strike at Germany, Belgium or no Belgium; that our navy was ready, our expeditionary force ready, our honor pledged, our interest clear; that Mr. Lloyd George's threat of 1911 still held good; and that Germany and Austria must choose between the peace of Europe with the friendship of England and a European war with England in it against them to her last man and last farthing.

Alas! the Prussian war party does not consist of telepathists. They read nothing but what was on the surface: the evasions of an embarrassed diplomatist, bound to peace at any price by a Pacifist parliamentary majority and an India and Ireland on the brink of revolt. The minister who would not even commit himself unequivocally to stand by Belgium—virtually to defend Dover—was clearly not going to fight. Their chance had come at last to wipe out the humiliation of 1911 and to smash the Franco-Russian peril. And when the lion suddenly threw off his sheepskin and sprang on them, they very naturally gave Sir Edward Grey credit for a masterly feint of which the great Frederick himself might have been proud.

Those who believe "it was bound to come" must congratulate themselves on the way in which Sir Edward's earnest desire for peace drowned Europe in blood. His popularity with our own war party shews how thoroughly they appreciate his exploits as L'Etourdi. To them he largely owes his reputation as, above all, a man of character. The truth is, Sir Edward Grey has quite a busy intellect; but, for purposes so highhanded and exacting, and occasionally so bluntly menacing, as those of our diplomacy, he has something much worse than no character at all: he has the wrong character for the job. The proof of his intellect is to be found in the remarkable dispatch (No. 101, p. 55, in the White Paper) quoted by Professor Murray on page 24. "If the peace of Europe can be preserved, and the present crisis safely passed, my own endeavour will be to promote some arrangement to which Germany could be a party, by which she can be assured that no aggressive or hostile policy would be pursued against her or her allies by France, Russia, and ourselves, jointly or separately. I have desired this and worked for it, etc., etc." Here the fatal "If," the helpless "some arrangement," shew how unable Sir Edward is to drive nations to carry out his intellectual conclusion. But the intellectual conclusion is sound. What was needed to save the situation was not merely England's threat, but England's guarantee. Sir Edward saw that at last as an intellectual proposition—had, in fact, as he says, seen it for years past, but had been unable either to utter the threat (except when Mr. Lloyd George helped him out) or give the guarantee.

After swallowing the twelve days and the war, Professor Murray has a comparatively easy time over Morocco and Persia. He has no difficulty in shewing that our engagement to maintain the integrity and independence of Morocco was impossible, and that if Europe was to have any rights of way or rights of trade in Persia, some western Power must take her by the scruff of the neck and reorganize and police her. But who deniges of it, Betsy? We were quite right to tear up the Algeciras scrap of paper; but was it quite playing the game after that to take so high a tone when Germany did the same thing under pressure of a far more tremendous peril? Why not have said frankly "We care no more for the 1839 treaty than we did for the Act of Algeciras; but we will not have you in Flanders or on the Scheldt; and if you take a step in that direction off go our guns: we have arranged it all with Belgium"?

As to Persia, there is no denying that it was necessary to take her by the scruff of the neck; but there was a very thorny question as to who was to do it. There was England; there was Russia; and there was Mr. Shuster, calling himself the Persian nation. Professor Murray explains that Mr. Shuster was an arbitrary gent, and that the Russians drifted to and fro between mere easygoing slummocking and fits of savage fury in which they sawed the Persians in two and marched between the pieces. After Denshawai Sir Edward could hardly say much about the sawing; but still the issue was a fairly clear one between Democracy and Autocracy; and it was emphasized, as Professor Murray points out, by the American's outspoken abhorrence of Russian political institutions and his indifference to the sacred etiquette of paying calls. Sir Edward, as an English country gentleman and a baronet, naturally came down on the side of the Russian autocracy against the American Nationalist and Republican. No doubt there was very little choice in the matter: the Russians had the bigger stake in Persia, and had the advantage of being on the frontier; and Sir Edward may have been simply facing inexorable facts when he concluded that if he did not like the Russian view of Mr. Shuster he would have to lump it. But what annoyed the Democrats was their suspicion that Sir Edward really did like the Russian view because it was the autocratic and antinationalist: in short, the country house view. Professor Murray shews, I think successfully, that Sir Edward simply took the course dictated by circumstances. He always does. But Sir Edward forgets that England is a circumstance, and should do some of the dictation. And that is the whole case against Grey: the case that Murray, with the friendliest intentions, has proved up to the hilt.

There is a fine passage on page 9 of Professor Murray's book in which he confesses he was wrong instead of Sir Edward Grey. The conclusion leaves me incredulous, though it is very handsome of him to have written it. He adds, "I also felt, with some impatience, that though, as an outsider, I could not tell exactly what the Government ought to do, they surely could produce good relations between Great Britain and Germany if only they had the determination and will." Here, to the great danger of my own character, I have the advantage of Professor Murray. I wish I could truthfully shield myself in his modesty. But I am in the insufferable position of having known exactly what the Government should have done, of having told them exactly what to do, and of having proved right at every point. It is almost too much for human nature to bear. But the fact must be faced. Only, too much must not be built on it. I protest I am not a great diplomatist. Like other Socialists, I have been too much preoccupied with the atrocities of peace and the problems they raise to pay due attention to the atrocities of war. But I have not been unconscious of the European question; and I have made a few shots at solutions from time to time. None of these have been received with the smallest approval; but at least I may be permitted to point out that they have all come out right. I steadily ridiculed the anti-armament agitation, and urged that our armaments should be doubled, trebled, quadrupled, as they might have been without costing the country one farthing that we were not wasting in the most mischievous manner. I said that the only policy which would secure the peace of Europe was the policy of using a powerful armament to guarantee France against Germany, and Germany against Russia, aiming finally at a great Peace Insurance League of the whole northwest of Europe with the United States of America in defence of western democratic civilisation against the menace of the east, and possible crusades from primitive black Christians in Africa. I did not say all this after the mischief was done and the war in progress, nor in the twelve days during which the lives of millions of men were muddled away by the diplomatists. I said it to the British public whilst there was still time. I said it to the German ambassador whilst there was still time (his reply, in effect, was that Sir Edward Grey was the greatest statesman, the nicest man, and the truest friend to Germany that ever lived). I can now indulge in the mean luxury of saying "I told you so." Sir Edward, who finally came round to my opinion, apparently thought so, but did not tell us so until it was too late. When the war broke out I said some more things which were frantically contradicted, and which have all turned out to be precisely true. I set an example of sharp criticism of the Government and the War Office which was denounced as treasonable, and which now proves to be the only way of saving our army from annihilation, the Government having meanwhile collapsed and vanished, as every ordinarily self-possessed person foresaw that it must.

One fact seems established by this beyond a doubt: to wit, that I am the gravest public danger that confronts England, because I have the strange power of turning the nation passionately away from the truth by the simple act of uttering it. The necessity for contradicting me— for charging heroically in the opposite direction to that pointed out by me—is part of the delirium of the war fever. Sir Edward Grey, on the other hand, is spoken well of by all men. But he too is the victim of a mysterious fate. He is, as Professor Murray repeatedly testifies, the most truthful of men. Yet he never opens his mouth without deceiving us. He is the most loyal of simple manly souls; yet he is accused of betraying every country and every diplomatist who trusted him. He is the kindest of men; and yet he has implicated us in the tortures of Denshawai and brought upon us the slaughters of Armageddon. Clearly there are two men in England who must be sent into permanent retirement. Depend on it, there is something fundamentally wrong with them. It is a pity; for they are stuffed with the rarest virtues, though I say it who should not. One of them is Sir Edward Grey; and the other is

G. B. S.

Editor's Notes

- This review was first printed in the *New Statesman* 5 (17 July 1915): 349–51. It was probably written in early July 1915, at the same time that Shaw was concluding his never-to-be-published pamphlet called "More Common Sense About the War," scraps and fragments of which appeared in "Notes of the

Week" in the *New Statesman*. On 14 July 1915, Shaw wrote to Gilbert Murray: "I have done you in (the Grey book) for this week's New Statesman. I thought it better to slaughter you myself than leave you to some young butcher with no respect for his elders. And you have done Grey in. What ironic fiend possessed you? The horrid cruelty with which you put all his footle in italics would revolt Euripides. . . . The knock-out is perfection. He was always guided by circumstances. Not like Napoleon, who said 'I make circumstances' or like me, who, going one better than Nap, say '*I* am a circumstance.' Youve really handled the man barbarously in your dramatic delirium." (*Collected Letters 1911–1925*, 300–301).

▪ [George] Gilbert [Aimé] Murray (1866–1957), Australian classical scholar and writer. Born in Sydney, New South Wales, he arrived in England at the age of eleven and attended Merchant Taylors' School and Saint John's College, Oxford. He was professor of Greek at the University of Glasgow from 1889 to 1899, and Regius Professor of Greek at Oxford from 1908 to 1936. He was thought to be the foremost Greek scholar of his time, publishing works on the Greek epic, Greek religion, and the classical tradition in poetry. He also made many celebrated verse translations of Greek plays, notably critical editions of the works of Euripides (3 vols., 1901, 1904, and 1910) and of Aeschylus (1937). Some of his translations were performed at London's Court Theatre in the first decade of this century. Shaw's lifelong friendship with Gilbert Murray began ten years before that. He called upon Murray's classical knowledge for his plays, modifying *Caesar and Cleopatra* (1898), for example, in accordance with Murray's comments; and Murray himself was the original for Adolphus Cusins in *Major Barbara* (1905), just as his wife Lady Mary was for Major Barbara herself, and his mother-in-law the Honourable Rosalind Frances Stanley [Lady Carlisle] was the model for Lady Britomart Undershaft. Moreover, Shaw's *Geneva* (1936–38) was in both form and content influenced by Murray, whose work for the cause of the League of Nations after World War I interested Shaw, and whose study of Aristophanes in 1933 prompted Shaw to cast his play in the form of an Aristophanic lampoon.

▪ Sir Edward Grey (see above, 285).

▪ Serjeant Buzfuz is Mrs. Bardell's counsel in Dickens's *The Pickwick Papers*, remarkable for his bullying insolence to the witnesses on Mr. Pickwick's side.

▪ The Old Bailey is the Central Criminal Court in London, so called from the ancient *bailey* of the city wall between Lud Gate and New Gate, within which it lay (*OED*).

▪ Tracy Tupman is a member of the Corresponding Society of the Pickwick Club in *The Pickwick Papers*, who accompanies Mr. Pickwick on his travels.

▪ Bismarck (see above, 56).

▪ Joseph [Austen] Chamberlain (1836–1914), English statesman. Born in London and educated at University College School, in 1854 he migrated to Birmingham where he worked in a screw factory, became mayor in 1873, and retired the following year, having made a fortune. He was a strong radical at this time, and Birmingham rapidly became a pattern of improvement for the whole country. In 1876 he was returned unopposed for Birmingham, and soon made his presence felt in Parliament, advocating free schools and the creation of allotments by compulsory purchase. (In Shaw's *John Bull's Other Island* [1904], Broadbent is still smarting under Mr. Chamberlain's economic heresy). When the Liberals were returned to power in 1880, Gladstone appointed Chamberlain president of the board of trade with a seat in the Cabinet (though he had held no previous office). In 1886 he was president of the local government board; but his opposition to the Home Rule bill caused him to resign his post. This split the Liberal Party, and at the next general election Chamberlain was returned as the leader of seventy-eight Liberal Unionists. He became colonial secretary in Lord Salisbury's third administration in 1895, and was held responsible by many for the South African War in 1899, but his other foreign efforts on the whole strengthened the British Empire in Australia and South Africa, and he is credited with cementing Anglo-American relations.

▪ Shaw employs irony in his remark about Murray's italics "which might have been underscored by Mephistopheles," since, in *Major Barbara*, Mephistopheles is the name that Adolphus Cusins (based on Gilbert Murray) constantly calls Undershaft, the millionaire arms-manufacturer.

▪ [David] Lloyd George, first Earl Lloyd-George of Dwyfor (1863–1945), Welsh Liberal statesman. Though he began his political career in 1890 when he was elected Liberal for Carnarvon Boroughs, it was in his capacity as chancellor of the exchequer from 1908 to 1915 that he reached his height as a social reformer, with the Old Age Pensions Act in 1908, and the National Insurance Act in 1911. It was also in that year that Lloyd George raised the "mailed fist" to prevent war, when Germany laid territorial claim to Morocco, and despatched a cruiser to the port of Agadir on the Moroccan coast. On 21 July, Sir Edward Grey sent for the German ambassador in order to impress upon him that the British government would not remain passive if Germany tried to establish herself at Agadir. That night Lloyd George was due to speak at the annual banquet of bankers and merchants of London, at the Mansion House; and it was suggested that no reference to this incident might send Germany the wrong signal about the British government's determination. Accordingly, though he did not mention Germany by name, Lloyd George gave a fine fighting speech about Britain maintaining her prestige among the Great Powers: a speech that created a sensation in the Continental press, and led to long complaints from Germany, who, however, refrained from exacerbating the situation.

▪ The Society for Psychical Research was formally constituted on 20 February 1882, with the philosopher Henry Sidgwick (1838–1900), as its first president. In addition to its interest in apparitions and supernatural manifestations, the Society concerned itself with thought-transference, hypnotism, and extra-sensory perception; thus, its investigations, though unorthodox by today's standards, bordered on more orthodox and novel branches of study, such as psychology. Shaw, though humorously skeptical, took the Society seriously until about 1887, and reviewed books written by its members. How-

ever, Shaw thought Gilbert Murray unsuited for the post of president of the
Society for Psychical Research ("It needs a hardy liar: nobody else is of any
use." See Shaw's letter to Gilbert Murray, quoted above.)
▪ "The great Frederick" was Frederick II [known as Frederick the Great]
(1712–86), the cultured King of Prussia (1740–86) whose able military leadership and brilliance during the Seven Years' War established Prussia as a
rival to Austria in her domination of the German states.
▪ "L'Etourdi," literally the "Scatterbrain." Molière's first comedy was called
L'Etourdi (1655), in which Lélie—a perfect bungler—is the protagonist.
▪ In Dickens's Martin Chuzzlewit, Betsey Prig, a nurse from Saint Bartholomew's Hospital who takes turns nursing with Mrs. Sarah Gamp, the midwife
and nurse, accuses her of dropping her snuff in patients' food:

> "Why Betsey Prig!" cried Mrs. Gamp, "how can you talk so?"
> "Why, ain't your patients, wotever their diseases is, always a sneezin'
> their wery heads off, along of your snuff?" said Mrs. Prig.
> "And wot if they are?" said Mrs. Gamp.
> "Nothing if they are," said Mrs. Prig. "But don't deny it Sairah."
> "Who deniges of it?" Mrs. Gamp inquired.
> Mrs. Prig returned no answer.
> "Who deniges of it, Betsey?" Mrs. Gamp inquired again. Then Mrs.
> Gamp, by reversing the question, imparted a deeper and more awful
> character of solemnity to the same. "Betsey, who deniges of it?"

▪ German intervention in 1905 to support Moroccan independence against
French economic and political interference in that region caused France to
threaten war; but the crisis was settled by the international conference at
Algeciras in Spain in 1906 which led to the Act of Algeciras (to which Shaw
refers).
▪ On 2 August 1914 Germany informed the Belgian government of its intention to march on France through Belgium to forestall a French attack from the
same quarter. Belgium refused to allow them, invoking the London Treaty of
1839 which promised neutrality to Belgium in the event of a conflict between
the other powers. Britain, one of the signatories of the Treaty, sent an ultimatum to Germany on 4 August demanding that Belgian neutrality be respected.
When this ultimatum was rejected, Britain declared war on Germany.
▪ In the nineteenth and early twentieth centuries Britain and Russia struggled for hegemony in Persia (see above, 240). This foreign influence in Persia
led to a nationalist movement and the demand for a constitutional government. In 1906 Shah Muzaffar-ed-Din was forced by popular pressure to
convoke a national assembly, which drew up a liberal constitution. His successor Mohammed Ali attempted to destroy the constitutional movement by
force, but was defeated and deposed, and his twelve-year old son placed on
the throne as Ahmed Shah, and a regency was set up. In 1911 the American
financier William Morgan Shuster (1877–1960) arrived in Persia, invited by
the national assembly to reorganize the finances of the country. His reforms,

however, were frustrated by the hostility of the Russians. He was dismissed, and Russian power became predominant in Persia.

- Denshawai (see above, 238).

13 May 1916

THE CASE AGAINST CHESTERTON*
[C2062]

IN Russia the intelligent are a class with a name. In England they are nameless and despised, or, when that is impossible owing to their bumptiousness, mistrusted. Our plan has the advantage that every Englishman passes as possibly intelligent until he opens his mouth or takes up his pen, just as he passes for an intrepid pugilist until some- one assaults him. And as in practice nobody ever does assault him, he has only to avoid the pen and confine his remarks to simple meteoro- logical observations and demands for beer to keep up the national character of Britain as the mother of strong silent men, all able to use their fists.

Mr. Julius West is of Allied extraction. I have never been able to decide exactly what Mr. Gilbert Chesterton's nationality is, except that he is certainly not an Englishman: at least, I take it that an English- man would not in England seem extraordinary and even unique. When he is not writing he is talking; and he is often doing both: yet he has not compromised himself. And Mr. Julius West has written a book about Mr. Chesterton, which book I am supposed to be reviewing. It is distinguished from most books of the kind by the circumstance that Mr. West has apparently read Mr. Chesterton's works, which is con- trary to all precedent, and also by a command of our language which is a very agreeable change from our own mere habit of it. His English, like Mr. Conrad's English, has a quality seldom attained by purely British writers. No doubt this is because English words have to mean something to a foreigner before he can use them at all, whereas to an Englishman they are only noises to express his high spirits or his ill-

---

* "G. K. Chesterton. A Critical Study." By Julius West. (Martin Secker.) 7s. 6d. net.

humour as the case may be. Anyhow, Mr. West contrives to be very readable on a subject on which most unmitigatedly English writers are mere petulant nuisances.

Once in his book Mr. West has failed in tact. To declare that all attempts to parody Mr. Chesterton have been failures, and then to dedicate the book containing the declaration to Mr. J. C. Squire, is excusable only by absence of mind. Also I would warn Mr. West and all whom it may concern not to be misled by the younger generation of British penmen (those under fifty or thereabouts) who believe that their grandfathers all read Mill, and all belonged to a period called Early Victorian, in which the dull dogs had their day. Mill was the inspirer, not, as Mr. West implies, of the Socialist reaction of the eighties, but of the rearguard actions fought against it by Benthamite Individualism under such captains as Bradlaugh and Herbert Spencer. Mill's final conversion to Socialism, though claimed for the Fabian side by Mr. Sidney Webb, was ignored as completely as Solomon's final conversion to the worship of Ashtaroth; and the statement lately slipped into currency that the Fabian Society was, like its strongly Individualist and Malthusian predecessor the Dialectical Society, founded on Mill, is not merely wide of the mark: it actually hits the back of the target. Mr. West has been led by it to say that I hold all Mill's beliefs. There was a time when all the Intelligent held Mill's disbeliefs; and this lasted until his disbeliefs became so general that they were no longer perceptible, like the disbelief in the flatness of the earth. But very few people knew that Mill had any beliefs at all, except perhaps in peasant proprietorship, which was anathema to the Socialists.

Mr. West has also heard that I am "an avowed and utter Puritan," and that Mr. Chesterton is a Catholic Tory. I do not object to being called a Puritan, because it means only that I do not drive through the town with a painted Monte Carlo countess; and Mr. Chesterton probably does not object to have it intimated in the same excessive way that he is neither a Methodist nor a Manchester doctrinaire. But both statements are overdone: they are the literary equivalents of burning down the house to roast the pig. I should roughly class John Knox among the famous fools of history, and Calvin among its famous scoundrels; and the spectacle of Mr. Chesterton on his knees every Easter before a creature of like passions (in homœopathic dilution) with himself and much less brains, confessing his sins and receiving absolution, is one which the world has not yet seen; nor does Mr. Chesterton's outlook on politics resemble that of Sir Leicester Dedlock. I suggest, therefore, that this use of Puritan and Catholic and Tory as abusive epithets, though exhilarating, is apt to mislead those who are not in the family joke.

But it has its uses when applied to Mr. Chesterton; for there is no man alive who more needs being driven by mere stress of misunderstanding to a serious definition and determination of his own views and destiny. Being an artist of almost magical dexterity in language and casuistry, he indulges in art for art's sake quite recklessly. Compared to him, poor Whistler, whom he despises, was a bigoted missionary, devoting his whole life to the steadfast propaganda of certain qualities in design and painting. No doubt if Whistler had been Rubens, with the Chestertonian power and exuberance of that painter, he might have been as unscrupulous as Rubens with his brush or Chesterton with his pen. But be that as it may, he had a definite faith and stuck to it: you always knew where to have him and what he stood for. Does anyone know where to have Chesterton and what he stands for? In the world of romantic ideals, yes: he is as popular as a film drama, though not so vulgar. But in the world of things as they are, who can depend on him? Take, for example, his attitude towards the public-house. If I confessed to him that I helped to build The Fox and Pelican at Grayshott he would scorn me, because it was a reformed public-house, and is now, I think, a People's Refreshment House. My teetotal friends were horrified at my endowing the accursed thing. The local drunkards were even more disgusted by the substitution of stunning good beer, which made them drunk cheaply and precipitately, for the unreformed stuff which spread the process over a whole evening and went to their livers rather than to their heads. I do not defend my reformed public-house; but still less can I defend Mr. Chesterton's still more extravagantly reformed sort: the romantic imaginary public-house, the public-house that never was on sea or land, the public-house that has the sign of The Flying Inn, the public-house in which you may drink draughts of beer and rum that would empty the horn of Odin, and grow more splendid and strong and uproariously poetic with every mouthful, the public-house where you can drink without squandering the money you should take home to your wife and children because there is nothing but paper money to pay, where you do not stagger to the sewer trap to be sick in the face of heaven, where—to mention no more unpleasant things—drink is not drink but a dream, and the worship of Dionysos does not turn into a sick headache. Now I say that there is no such public-house: it is an idealistic mask for the real public-house. I doubt whether Mr. Chesterton has ever been in a real public-house: I think he ekes out the taproom stories of Dickens and Jacobs with memories of one or two reluctant visits to saloon bars in the Strand to avoid hurting the feelings of humble admirers insistent on treating him. I began public life by being trotted about the streets of Dublin by Irish nursemaids whom amorous carmen treated, not forgetting a sip of ginger beer for the childher. I spring from a very large family; and every large family has its percentage of drunkards. I have lived in the house with tipplers. I have tested in my own person the alleged inspiration to be derived from what Mr. Chesterton will not let me call alcohol and yet honourably shrinks from calling booze; and I can bear witness to its enchanting reduction of my critical faculty as evidenced by the manuscripts which I read over and tore up next day. I have watched the difference between driving a car before lunch and after, and have learnt to insist on taking the wheel myself if even a spoonful of *vin compris* has formed part of the driver's lunch. And I remain incurably convinced that there is no future for Dutch courage or Dutch inspiration or Dutch poetry: alcohol is useful only in parliaments where the boredom is so intolerable that it cannot be endured without narcotising the critical faculty, and incidentally the conscience, at the bar or at dinner.

I therefore take Mr. Chesterton's glorification of the rum bottle and the beer barrel as art for art's sake, pure Anacreontic playboyishness in a hearty popular disguise; and I shall some day organise a presentation to him of a proof impression of Cruikshank's Bottle. He may frame it as a frightful example of what comes of being serious; but it will glare at him as a reminder of what comes of cutting one's appetite in two and throwing away the better half of it. I have suffered from both halves myself, having been defeated in an election because the drunkards on the register objected to my being a teetotaler, and the teetotalers objected still more to my refusal to cut off the liquor not only of the drunkards but of everyone else as well. They preferred the success of the publican's candidate to that of a man who refused to vilify publicans, having found very capable colleagues and good friends among them; and I daresay Mr. Chesterton hails their choice (not as to my person, but on principle) with three times three.

I dwell on the Drink Question because it illustrates the quarrel which the rising generation is fastening—and fastening successfully—on Mr. Chesterton. Mr. Julius West begins his book by an evidently sincere announcement that he is going to show that Mr. Chesterton is a writer of the highest quality and the deepest importance. And yet, whenever he gets away from Mr. Chesterton's literary *tours de force*, he finds himself complaining of inconsistency, reaction, obsolescence, aimlessness, and, when science is concerned, something which he would obviously call stupidity if he did not attribute it (rashly, I think) to ignorance. The only conclusion that comes out of it all is that Mr. West has no use for Mr. Chesterton except as a literary artist and a rhapsode who occasionally contradicts himself by some inspired utterance which he never follows up, and forgets five minutes afterwards as Morris accused Ruskin of doing habitually.

I do not see what else Mr. Chesterton can expect at the hands of intellectually conscientious youth. It is his delight on a shiny night in the season of the year to *épater* not *le bourgeois*, but the extreme left, the revolutionists, the agnostics, the Dwellers on the Threshold of the millennium. This is a pious and necessary work. I have always protested against the devil having all the good tunes of criticism, irony, ridicule and all the other tonics. I well remember the beneficial effect of the scandalised dismay, the sense of unheard-of outrage, which spread through the solemn ranks of Marxism when I first treated an International Socialist Congress to several columns of descriptive reporting in the capitalist press of just that sidesplitting kind which its absurdities deserved; and I have no objection whatever to Mr. Chesterton pitching into the teetotalers, the Protestants, the Agnostics, the Scientists, Christian and anti-Christian, the Jews, the Pacificos, the Eugenicans, the Suffragists, the Socialists, and, when the feeble-minded and the children are in question, into all the tribe of Mr. Honeythunder, with every weapon that can put the fear of God into them and keep it there.

All the same, when things have to be done, and people to be endured and dealt with, the man who gets his way is the positive man and not the negative or derisive one. It is unnecessary to urge that there are feeble-minded people in the world; for the war has just now brought out the fact that there are hardly any other people. But there are people so feeble-minded that unless they are kept in tutelage they cannot live at all. And everybody is feeble-minded in one department or another. Mr. Chesterton probably needs the tutelage of a solicitor, a doctor, and a stockbroker; and each of these three tutors of his may be feeble-minded to the last degree about golf, on the merits of which Mr. Chesterton is, I fancy, supremely sane. My own gorgeous abilities do not exclude pitiable imbecilities in directions which, in self-defence, I abstain from indicating. Samuel Pepys was an able man; but he was weak as water among the wives of the dockyard artificers, and even in the kitchen. I have known people in both sexes who combined extraordinary talent with a ruinous incapacity for living within their incomes. The French institution of a Council of Prudent Persons to look after people who are unable, on one point or another, to look after themselves, is a very reasonable and necessary one; and both I and Mr. Chesterton—clever as we are—would probably be the better for one, though I should not envy the prudent ones their job.

However, let me come down from what is desirable to what is already recognised as necessary. We have masses of feeble-minded people who can no more be left to themselves without gross cruelty than a newly-blinded soldier from the front can be left to negotiate the Mansion House crossings without a guide. What does Mr. Chesterton propose to do with them? Let us take it that he has kicked Mr. Honeythunder into the horse-pond. Let us assume that he has snatched from the hands of Mrs. Sidney Webb all those perfectly sane and responsible cases whom, merely because they are poor and she is an interfering woman, she has sequestrated from their ordinary avocations and enslaved in a fiendish craze for subjugating her impecunious fellow creatures (I hope I am not understating the Chestertonian and Wellsian view of that unquestionably very active and inquisitive lady). He will still have a residuum on his hands. What will he do with them? That is what Mr. Julius West and some others evidently want to know. They surmise that he would call them the Little Sisters and Brothers of Jesus, and pack them into a convent or monastery where the Factory Acts do not run. They even suggest that his soul would be so completely satisfied with the kicking and ducking of Honeythunder and the discomfiting of Mrs. Sidney Webb, that he would forget all about the feeble-minded and leave them to be resumed by his two victims the moment his back was turned. But they don't *know*. Why? Because Mr. Chesterton has never told them.

Take again the children of the poor. Mr. Chesterton is, to his honour, a sound Dickensian, and does not think any child ought to be like Jo in *Bleak House*. Well, the practical alternative, until poverty is abolished, is to spend money enough on Jo to bring him up decently. Who is to have the spending of that money and the responsibility for Jo? Clearly, answers the feeling heart, Jo's mother. Now that may solve the problem for Jo A (pardon the official classification), whose mother is a mother in a thousand, or, to be roughly accurate, one of from 25 to 33 per cent. of our impecunious motherhood. But Jo B has no mother. Jo C has a mother who can be trusted with the money if she is inspected a little. Jo D has a gloriously drunken mother who will not only drink Jo's endowment but force him to add to it as a thief, and force his sister to add to it as a child-prostitute. It is no use shrieking that this is a libel on motherhood. If the thistle of poverty bore nothing but grapes we should not want to uproot it. The objection to poverty is precisely that it inevitably produces such results. What would Mr. Chesterton do with Jo C and Jo D? Will he say, like the bold bishop, that he had rather see Jo free (as in *Bleak House*) than inspected or torn from his mother's arms? Not without denying his master, Dickens, who was always himself Honeythundering at "my lords and gentlemen and right honourables and wrong honourables of every degree" to officiously make Jo their business; to demolish Tom-All-Alone's; to endow and inspect and clean up; and to replace Mrs. Pardiggle and Bumble and Gradgrind, not by beer and jollity and the fighting part of knight-errantry and mediæval religion, but by the sworn enemy and vowed destroyer of the accursed Poor Law: in short, by Mrs. Sidney Webb. He no sooner showed how Mrs. Pardiggle, fool and snob and self-elected irresponsible uninspected inspector, made the miserable savages she inspected worse, than he went on to show how the two decent ladies she brought with her made them better. The bond of sympathy between Mr. Sidney Webb and myself is that we were both brought up on *Little Dorrit*. No use coming Dickens over us. What would Mr. Chesterton do with Jo? His reply would make an excellent subject for an article in the *New Witness*, which really ought now to be called the Three Witnesses: meaning, not those whom some Trinitarian forger foisted on St. Jerome's Vulgate for so many centuries, but St. Gilbert, St. Cecil, and St. Hilary.

Then, as to the Jews. We cannot massacre the Jews without carting them all to Russia, which is hardly feasible. We must put up with the Jews, just as we must put up with the Irish in spite of the alarming consequences of allowing young men to be imported from Dublin to London, as Lord Northcliffe was, and as I was. Considering that it is with the greatest difficulty that Englishmen can be induced to put up with one another, it is too much to expect them to love the Jews; but they must let them live, and there's an end on't. Macaulay showed, years before I was born, that the case trumped up by our Jew-baiters could just as easily be trumped up against men with red hair or any other distinctive mark. That demonstration remains unrefuted and indeed irrefutable. Now, since Macaulay's time it has become apparent to all the world that the Jews are the only people in Britain who combine culture and intellectual activity and susceptibility with commonsense and practical business ability. When you speak of the selfish, greedy, pushing plutocrat who makes money and spends it in getting a great deal more of what a navvy likes, you are never thinking of a Jew. And when you speak of the unpractical dreamer, full of books and pictures and noble ideals, but hopeless when it comes to business, and convinced that politics and economics and mathematics are the dry pursuits of soulless and sexless men and women, you are again not thinking of a Jew. If all the portfolios of the Cabinet were strictly reserved for Jews, and the proceedings of the House of Commons conducted in Yiddish, we have every reason to expect that the country would be governed much more intelligently than it is at present, and with a steady regard to the value of intellectual training, knowledge of languages and literature, and artistic culture, instead of our present implacable and boorish contempt for them. These hard facts—for such they are, to our shame—will not yield to jibes at "the Infant Samuel" and implications that no Christian would have behaved as the Lord Chief Justice did about his Marconi shares. If the German Junkers were to drop their silly and snobbish prejudice against the Jews, and admit them to their imperial councils, as our Junkers have done, I should be seriously alarmed; for our tolerance of the Jews is one of the advantages we have over Germany in the war. Does Mr. Chesterton, like Mr. Houston Chamberlain, really think that a Jew, *qua* Jew, is a worse man than himself? Mr. West has clearly a right to know.

The Suffragists can afford to forgive Mr. Chesterton a good deal in consideration of his having given us the best and finest masculine statement yet made of the worth of women. Why he finished by denying them a vote without at the same time disclaiming one for himself is just one of the matters he ought to explain. The highwayman who robbed Squire Western's sister of her jewels at least gave a reason for it; and curiously enough, it was essentially if not verbally the very reason Mr. Chesterton gives for robbing women of their political rights. For my part I cannot work up much enthusiasm for the vote (having one myself); but I think, on Mr. Chesterton's own grounds, that it is monstrous that any public authority should sit without the counsel and presence of women, no matter how they are chosen; and until women concentrate their claims on this immovable human truth, and recognize that Votes for Women is by itself only a *reductio ad absurdum* of Votes for Men, they will not corner Mr. Chesterton, much less the people who are stupider than he, of whom the number is considerable.

Mr. Chesterton, as an anti-Modernist, compromises himself perhaps more vitally than as an anti-Socialist. His notion that he is an anti-Socialist is founded on the erroneous superstition that he was once a Socialist. An early fancy for Socialism no more makes a man a Socialist than an early fancy for the architecture of St. Sophia's makes him a Moslem. In the spirit of the schoolmaster who offered Coleridge a little essay on method to cure his discursiveness, I recommend my own tracts to Mr. Chesterton to cure his delusion that social salvation is attainable by a combination of personal righteousness with private property in the form of a picturesque allotment. When Mr. Chesterton combines a knowledge of the law of rent with his regard for the law of God, he will become a Socialist for the first time; and his Socialism will stick.

But anti-Modernism is another matter. The law of rent and the law of value are, unfortunately, still in the technical sphere: they are not in the air: they are known only to those who have cared enough about the intellectual soundness of their politics to make a special study of economics. Diners-out do not talk of Gresham's law, or Ricardo's law, or Jevons's law, any more to-day than they did when they dined with Shakespeare at the Mermaid, with Johnson at the Literary Club, or with Dickens at Tavistock House. But they do talk about Evolution and Natural Selection (often, alas! confusing them damnably) and about Eugenics, about Darwin and Mendel, Bergson and Butler, Herz and Marconi, aeroplanes and trinitrotoluene. Now it is not conceivable that Mr. Chesterton is as ignorant of these matters as Shakespear, Johnson and Dickens. He cannot believe that Marconi is a bookmaker with whom certain politicians had shady dealings; that Galton was a prurient blackguard who invented the word eugenics as a mask for disgusting improprieties; that Evolution is a silly and blasphemous attempt to discredit the Garden of Eden; that motor-cars are nuisances, aeroplanes toys to which Chinese kites are far superior, and war still an affair of battle-axes mightily wielded by armour-plated athletic giants. Yet Mr. Chesterton has written a good many sentences which seem to mean either these things or nothing. I will even go so far as to say that it will serve him right if future professors, specialising in the literature of the Capitalistic Era, explain to their students that they must not rely on traditional dates, as it is clear from internal evidence that though Wells and Bennett and Chesterton are dated as contemporaries, Chesterton must have died before the middle of the nineteenth century, and may perhaps be placed as early as the fifteenth or sixteenth as a master of the School of Rabelais. Wells and Bennett, on the other hand, could not possibly have come earlier than the post-Ibsen. "As against this," we may conceive the future professor lecturing, "it is alleged that one of Chesterton's best books is a monograph on Shaw, who is dated as a contemporary of Wells. But the best authorities are agreed that this extraordinarily enlightened author was one of the pioneers of the twenty-fifth century, and that the allusions to him in the books of the nineteenth and twentieth centuries are later interpolations, the pseudo-Chesterton book being probably by Shaw himself, a hypothesis which fully accounts for its heartfelt eulogy. It has been objected that the writer does not seem to have read Shaw's works; but this is clearly an intentional mystification, very characteristic of the freakish founder of the Shavians."

Not to labour the point further, Mr. Chesterton does unquestionably affect to throw back to the grandfathers of Mr. Bennett, Mr. Wells, and Dr. Saleeby rather than forward to the Democracy of Walt Whitman and Edward Carpenter. Like Morris, he goes back to the Middle Ages, but does not, like Morris, finally admit that we are in the Dark Ages and that the Middle Ages are still far ahead of us, and that our news about them is as yet news from nowhere. Nietzsche's appeal to him to be a good European does not move him. His Radicalism is not that of Cobden but of Charles James Fox, including his enthusiasm for the French Revolution, so heavily blown on by Marx and his school.

In the end we are left in doubt whether Chesterton is a man who has swallowed all the formulas, and decided that the older ones are on the whole the least absurd, or a man who has never swallowed any modern formulas at all, though he has smelt plenty of them. The difference is important; for though a Modernist may trust a man who, having read the story of Jonah and the Great Fish side by side with a volume of the Higher Criticism, prefers Jonah as not only more amusing but more probable and less far-fetched, yet he will shrink from the guidance of one who does not know what the Higher Critics have to say. Criticisms by mentally deficient people are sometimes extraordinarily enlightening. For example, Mr. Chesterton, who has both delicacy and common-sense in a very high degree, could never have done the work of Freud, who has neither delicacy nor common-sense. When Mr. Chesterton broke his arm, I deplored it as an accident; but Freud, if he had heard about it, would have concluded that Mr. Chesterton had subconsciously done it on purpose to punish himself for some frightful secret crime. Nobody but a fool would have thought of such a thing; but then wise men are always overlooking things that are visible to fools; and though I once broke my own arm and therefore most vehemently reject the Freudian psychoanalysis of Mr. Chesterton's mishap, I pay a serious if disrespectful attention to Freud. For I have never forgotten Vasari's story of Michael Angelo laughing at the stonemason's statue because it had no knees. The stonemason took his statue away; sawed through the legs; inserted a pair of knees; and brought it back to his illustrious critic to ask was it right now? "I should never have thought of that," said Michael. Precisely. When will Mr. Chesterton take off his hat to Freud, or, say, to Dr. Saleeby (who is very far from being mentally deficient except when the Great Inoculation Swindle is in question) as Michael Angelo took off his hat to the stonemason?

However, in all this I am not conducting my own case: I am holding a brief for Mr. Julius West and the Modernists. For my own part I would not have Mr. Chesterton other than he is. It is just as important that Mr. Chesterton should object to our modern education as that Mr. Wells and Mr. Bennett should object to our want of it. The knight-errant who turns up everywhere because he has no destination sometimes does more than the man who is too busy to attend to anything or see anybody. And though the knight-errant who seeks for giants and cuts their heads off is out of date, nothing can be more modern than Sir Chesterton of Overroads, who seeks for convictions and turns them inside out. Convictions are prisons, says someone (it sounds like Nietszche), and all that can be said in their defence is that the spirit of man is like steam or petrol vapour: it will not do any work until you put it in a strong prison, even at the risk of its bursting the prison and destroying you. Mr. Chesterton's spirit is so extremely explosive that it bursts every strong modern prison; so for the present he uses any old, patched, leaky and elastic gasbag that may be lying ready to his hand on the dustheap of history, and uses it less as a cylinder than as a jester's bladder to belabour painlessly the people he thinks ridiculous and shallow. The result is very entertaining to the bystanders, and often highly suggestive and instructive. The thing is done with a peculiar art which combines the intellectual strategy of Butler: "Be Laodicean: hold your convictions lightly," with an energetic determination to fight for every halfpenny as if it were a million, or, as Shakespear put it," greatly to find quarrel in a straw." He contrives to be as sympathetic as Hamlet and as rumbustious as Fortinbras at the same time. He neither fights principles nor defends them; but he faces opponents gleefully, and indeed invents them and imposes monstrous opinions and fantastic legends on them for the sake of leading a crusade against them, like Don Quixote with the sheep and the windmills. I love to see quiet Quakers like Mr. Grubb and conscientious reasoners like Mr. J. A. Hobson suddenly transmogrified into Judases and Lucifers and Antichrists, and assailed with a thundering charge as of all the hosts of heaven, led by the giant figure of Mr. Chesterton, who seems always to leave millions of dead in his ensanguined track as he sweeps on. It is pleasant, too, to hear Mr. Grubb and Mr. Hobson, neither dismembered nor even dusty, indignantly exclaiming, "What the devil do you mean, Mr. Chesterton, by knocking off our hats like that?" This apparent exaggerativeness, however, is not necessarily a defective sense of proportion. An error of a millimetre at the cannon's mouth may mean an error of a mile when the shell explodes; and it is the way of big men to think of the mile rather than of the millimetre, and to swear at the gunner with proportionate vehemence. I must not allow this explanation to reflect on Mr. Hobson; for Mr. Hobson is generally dead on his target whilst Mr. Chesterton, in a magnificent frenzy, is all over the shop. But that is in wartime, when all the imaginative people are in a more or less pathological condition, and will tolerate no aim except at the German target.

I agree very heartily with Mr. West as to Mr. Chesterton's success in his single essay as a playwright. I shirk the theatre so lazily that I have lost the right to call myself a playgoer; but circumstances led to my seeing *Magic* performed several times, and I enjoyed it more and more every time. Mr. Chesterton was born with not only brains enough to see something more in the world than sexual intrigue, but with all the essential tricks of the stage at his fingers' ends; and it was delightful to find that the characters which seem so fantastic and even ragdolly (stage characters are usually waxdolly) in his romances became credible and solid behind the footlights, just the opposite of what his critics expected. The test is a searching one: an exposure to it of many moving and popular scenes in novels would reveal the fact that they are physically impossible and morally absurd. Mr. Chesterton is in the English tradition of Shakespear and Fielding and Scott and Dickens, in which you must grip your character so masterfully that you can play with it in the most extravagant fashion. Until you can present an archbishop wielding a red-hot poker and buttering slides for policemen, and yet becoming more and more essentially archiepiscopal at every roar of laughter, you are not really a master in that tradition. The Duke in *Magic* is much better than Micawber or Mrs. Wilfer, neither of whom can bear the footlights because, like piping bullfinches, they have only one tune, whilst the Duke sets everything in the universe to his ridiculous music. That is the Shakespearian touch. Is it grateful to ask for more?

G. B. S.

Editor's Notes

- This review was first published in the *New Statesman* 7 (13 May 1916): 133–36. Also in the *Metropolitan Magazine* (New York) 44 (June 1916). There is no indication of when Shaw actually wrote it.
- Julius West (1891–1918), Fabian author and journalist. Born in Saint Petersburg of Jewish parents, at the age of two months he removed to London with his father [Semon Rappoport] who was correspondent for various Russian newspapers. He left school in 1906 and became first a temporary clerk at the Board of Trade, then a junior clerk in the office of the Fabian Society and secretary to the Fabian Research Committee. In 1913 he published *Atlantis, and other poems* (a book ignored by both public and critics), and Fabian Tract No. 168, *John Stuart Mill*. In the same year he became the company secretary of the *New Statesman*. When the First World War broke out he tried to join the army; and in spite of his parlous health, he was declared physically fit; but since he was not a naturalized British subject he could not have a commission. Eventually he was allowed to join the ambulance corps in London. In 1914 he had made his way to Saint Petersburg as a war correspondent; thence to Moscow and Warsaw. The year following this review, West would make his way to Saint Petersburg again, in the early months of the Bolshevik regime, although he, Ramsay MacDonald, and F. W. Jowettt were refused passports and were prevented by the Seaman's Union from sailing. In February 1918 he left Saint Petersburg to attend the Stockholm Conference. From there he traveled back to London, where it was clear that he was unwell. Nevertheless he was asked to go to Switzerland (which was then a place of political intrigue), and did so; but returned seriously ill with tuberculosis, going first to a hotel in Surrey, and then to a sanatorium. He died shortly after the end of the war, of a complication of influenza and pneumonia. With William Foss he wrote *The Social Worker and Modern Charity* (1914). He also published translations of Chekhov's plays, and wrote *The Fountain; or, the De Pootkius Family at home and abroad. An initiation into the secrets of the literary trade* (1916).
- G[ilbert] K[eith] Chesterton (1874–1936), English critic, novelist, playwright, and poet. His first writing was in periodicals and much of his best work is to be found in essays and articles in the *Bookman*, the *Speaker*, the *Illustrated London News* , and his own journal *G. K.'s Weekly* , which grew

from the *New Witness*, which, in turn, he had taken over from from his younger brother, Cecil Edward Chesterton (1879–1918), when the latter went to France. Cecil joined the Fabian Society in 1905, and shortly thereafter G. K. Chesterton himself was attracted to the meetings, particularly those of the Arts Group. But by 1910, both Chestertons had moved away from Fabian thinking, and G. K. toward a neo-medievalist "distributivist" theory. Interesting, in view of Shaw's amused imaginary picture above of Chesterton at confession, is the latter's conversion to Roman Catholicism in 1922, following a long process of soul-searching. Chesterton's first two books were collections of poetry, *The Wild Knight*, and *Greybeards at Play* (1900). Although his most important writings are polemics and critical studies of other writers including Shaw himself (1910) he is, perhaps, best remembered for his fiction, particularly the novels *The Napoleon of Notting Hill* (1904), and *The Man Who Was Thursday* (1908), and for the detective stories relating the adventures of a mild-mannered Roman Catholic sleuth, Father Brown. In 1909 Shaw sent Chesterton a fantastic scenario of a play he wanted him to write. The play was never written; though in 1913 (again encouraged by Shaw) Chesterton did write the play called *Magic*, much admired by Shaw (see above), but a stage failure. Shaw first debated with Chesterton publicly in 1911, when, on 29 May, Shaw addressed the Heretics' Society on "The Religion of the Future," to which Chesterton replied with a speech entitled "Orthodoxy" on 17 November, at the Guildhall in Cambridge. The tone of both lectures was genial and fair-minded, and Shaw, having lunched with Chesterton shortly after the latter's speech, arranged the first of their famous debates at the Memorial Hall in London on 30 November. Chesterton became not only a brilliant debater, but a legendary figure: very stout, dressed in a cloak and a wide-brimmed hat, untidy and absent-minded. Shaw and Chesterton debated regularly to a growing audience and, for the final time, at the Kingsway Hall in the last week of October 1927, when enormous crowds burst into the building, Hilaire Belloc chaired the debate, and the BBC relayed their voices throughout the country. In spite of their differing philosophies, Chesterton said of Shaw that "the responsibility in him rang like steel;" and Shaw, for his part, used Chesterton as a model for the character Immenso Champernoon in *Back to Methuselah*: "a man of colossal mould, with the head of a cherub on the body of a Falstaff."

▪ [Joseph] Conrad [born Jozef Teodor Konrad Korzeniowski] (1857–1924), Novelist, born in Podolia in the Ukraine, whose sea career formed the basis for his numerous fictions, the first example of which was *Almayer's Folly* (1895), published with the help of Edward Garnett (see above, 65–66). By this time he had settled in England, having been adopted, as he said, by the genius of the English language, of which he remains one of the great stylists.

▪ The work of [Sir] J[ohn] C[ollings] Squire (1884–1958), English author, is composed of light verse and parody as in *Steps to Parnassus* (1913) and *Tricks of the Trade* (1917). His writings also include anthologies, criticisms, and short stories.

- Mill (see above, 113).
- Jeremy Bentham (1748–1832), English philosopher, jurist, and social reformer, chiefly remembered for his doctrine of "utilitarianism," derived from his *Fragment on Government* (1776), and *Introduction to Principles of Morals and Legislation* (1789), which, in essence, contends that an action is moral to the degree that it is useful, the usefulness in question being its capacity to give pleasure, or prevent pain. This leads to the notion that the end of all legislation should be "the greatest happiness of the greatest number."
- Bradlaugh (see above, 83).
- Spencer (see above, 112).
- In *the Bible* (1 Kings 11:4–5), we are told:

> For it came to pass, when Solomon was old, that his wives turned away his heart after other gods: and his heart was not perfect with the Lord his God, as was the heart of David his father.
>
> For Solomon went after Ashtoreth the goddess of the Zidonians, and after Milcom the abomination of the Ammonites.

- Malthus (see above, 112).
- For Shaw, no doubt, the folly of John Knox (c. 1513–72), Scottish Protestant reformer, was his single-minded intransigence and hostility to every aspect of life that did not advance his cause; while Shaw no doubt regarded John Calvin [Jean Chauvin, or Caulvin] (1509–1564), the French theologian and reformer, as a scoundrel because, to the "folly" of his extreme dogmatism and severe discipline, which in fact split the evangelical churches into the two great Lutheran and Reformed groups, he added a ferocity that resulted, among other things, in the burning at the stake of Spanish theologian Michael Servetus in 1553, and the expulsion from Geneva in 1555 of his political foes, the Libertines (who were in reaction against the extreme moral severity of the Calvinists).
- Sir Leicester Dedlock, in Dickens's *Bleak House*, is a representative of one of the great "county" families of England: "Sir Leicester Dedlock is only a baronet, but there is no mightier baronet than he. His family is as old as the hills, and infinitely more respectable. He has a general opinion that the world might get on without hills, but would be done up without Dedlocks."
- Whistler (see above, 65), an economical worker, is contrasted with [Peter Paul] Rubens (1577–1640), famous Flemish painter, whose delight in the color, shape, and texture of the visible world gave rise to flamboyant, action-filled paintings.
- Grayshott, a village near Hindhead in Surrey, was without a public house in 1898, when the Shaws were living at Pitfold, two or three miles away. To prevent one of the major breweries from establishing a pub there, the local villagers, headed by the Reverend J. M. Jeakes, decided to open an inn of their own which, in the words of Dan Laurence, "would be designed to discourage inebriety" (see *Collected Letters 1898–1910*, 59). In 1899, therefore, was established "The Fox and Pelican," a public house that offered hot

meals, social evenings, dominoes, and draughts. The villagers had bought shares in the pub, which was operated under the aegis of the People's Refreshment House Association, managed by local residents and supervised jointly by the wife of the local doctor and that of the rector. Charlotte Shaw had bought shares in the enterprise from the beginning, and Shaw made his own investment later.

- W[illiam] W[ymark] Jacobs (1863–1943), English short story writer. Born in Wapping, London, he wrote mostly humorous stories of sailormen and dockside taverns, in collections like *Many Cargoes* (1896), *The Skipper's Wooing* (1897), and *Deep Waters* (1919).
- There was alcohol abuse on both sides of Shaw's family: his father, George Carr Shaw was certainly an alcoholic, as were his father's brothers Uncle Barny [William Bernard], and Uncle Fred [Richard Frederick]; while, on his mother's side, Shaw's Rabelaisian Uncle Walter [Gurly] was also a tippler.
- [George] Cruikshank (1792–1878), English caricaturist and illustrator, who made his name as a political cartoonist with *The Scourge* (1811–16) and *The Meteor* (1813–14). He was an illustrator of many famous books including Dickens's *Sketches by Boz* (1836) and *Oliver Twist* (1838); but in his later years he devoted a great deal of his work to the cause of temperance, with a series of works entitled *The Bottle* (1847) to which Shaw here refers, *The Drunkard's Children* (1848), and the cartoon *Worship of Bacchus* (1862).
- Morris (see above, 165).
- Ruskin (see above, 65).
- The chorus of the old English folksong "The Lincolnshire Poacher" is: "Oh, 'tis my delight on a shining night in the season of the year."
- Luke Honeythunder, in Dickens's unfinished *The Mystery of Edwin Druid* (1870), is chairman of the Convened Chief Composite Committee of Central and District Philanthropists, and guardian of Neville and Helena Landless. He is a large man, with a tremendous voice, and an appearance of being constantly engaged in crowding everybody to the wall: "Though it was not literally true, as was facetiously charged against him by public unbelievers, that he called aloud to his fellow-creatures: 'Curse your souls and bodies, come here and be blessed!' still his philanthropy was of that gunpowderous sort that the difference between it and animosity was hard to determine."
- Samuel Pepys (1633–1703), English diarist and admiralty official, whose celebrated *Diary* runs from 1 January 1660 to 31 May 1669, in which year his wife died and his eyesight failed him. His *Diary* reveals indeed, as Shaw contends, that Pepys was susceptible to feminine charms.
- Beatrice [Mrs. Sidney] Webb (see above, 199).
- Jo, also known as "Toughey," is a young boy, a street crossing sweeper in *Bleak House*, very muddy, very hoarse, very ragged. A stranger who has died suddenly had given him once the price of a supper and a night's lodging and had been seen speaking with him. Thus Jo becomes accidentally possessed

of information that involves Lady Dedlock's secret, and is driven away from London by officers in the service of Mr. Tulkinghorn, always being told to "move on," no matter where he seeks a resting place. He is finally befriended by a kindly physician, and in his fatal illness is properly cared for. He desires to be laid in the strangers' burying ground, near his unknown friend.

- Tom-All-Alone's, in *Bleak House*, is the fever house slum where Jo habitually sleeps. It is in "a villainous street, undrained, unventilated, deep in black mud and corrupt water—though the roads are dry elsewhere—and reeking with such smells and sights that [Mr. Snagsby], who has lived in London all his life, can scarce believe his senses."
- Mrs. Pardiggle, also from *Bleak House*, is one of those charitable people who do little and make a great deal of noise; Mr. Bumble is the beadle in the workhouse where Oliver Twist is born, in the novel of that name; and Thomas Gradgrind of Stone Lodge, Coketown, is the retired mill-owner in *Hard Times*, who is obsessed with the doctrine of facts and neglects normal human feelings.
- [Alfred Charles William Harmsworth, first Viscount] Northcliffe (1865–1922), Irish journalist and newspaper magnate. Lord Northcliffe was one of the pioneers of mass-circulation journalism. In 1894 he took over the *London Evening News*. He also published a number of Sunday magazine papers; and in 1896 started the *Daily Mail*, considered in its day American in style and news presentation. With his brother Harold Sydney Harmsworth [later Lord Rothermere] (1868–1940), he bought up the *Sunday Dispatch*, and numerous smaller papers; in 1903 started the first newspaper for women, the *Daily Mirror*; founded the Amalgamated Press for periodical and popular educational literature, and obtained the rights to vast forests in Newfoundland for newsprint. In 1908 Northcliffe became proprietor of the *Times*, restored its sagging circulation in 1914 by reducing its price, and made its editorial policy a mouthpiece for his political ambitions.
- Macaulay (see above, 119–20).
- Chesterton's "implications that no Christian would have behaved as the Lord Chief Justice did about his Marconi shares," refers to the scandal involving several members of the Liberal government including Lloyd George and Sir Rufus Isaacs (1860–1935), who had speculated in the shares of a company associated with the Marconi company, which had received a government contract. Cecil Chesterton (see above) and Hilaire Belloc had made allegations of corruption, with hints of anti-Semitism, in their journal *Eye-Witness*. Godfrey Isaacs [brother of Sir Rufus] brought an action for criminal libel against the two in 1913.
- Houston Chamberlain (see above, 262–63).
- Shaw appears to be referring to the ruffian in *Tom Jones* who robbed Mrs. Waters (not Mrs. Western), and who thought that he had murdered her: "As he concluded, therefore, that his only safety lay in flight, he thought the possessing himself of this poor woman's money and ring would make him amends for the additional burthen he was to lay upon his conscience."

- Saint Sophia or Santa Sophia, the museum of Byzantine art in Istanbul, Turkey, itself perhaps the greatest achievement of Byzantine art, formerly a mosque and originally the Christian church of the Divine Wisdom, built between 532 and 537 at the command of the Emperor Justinian.
- Shaw's list of "modern thinkers" includes Darwin (see above, 112); [Gregor Johann] Mendel (1822–84), Austrian biologist and botanist, the discoverer of inheritance characteristics and hybridity in plants, which led to the formulation of Mendel's Law of Segregation, his Law of Independent Assortment, his principle of Factorial Inheritance and his quantitative investigation of single characters, which have become the basis of modern genetics; Henri Bergson (1859–1941), French philosopher, who contrasted the fundamental reality of the flux of human consciousness with the inert world of physical objects, chosen by Shaw (as was Samuel Butler) because he modified the Darwinian idea of a deterministic natural selection by positing an *élan vital*, or creative impulse at the heart of evolution; Heinrich Rudolf Hertz (1857–94), the German physicist who in 1887 discovered electromagnetic waves, which, excepting wavelength, behave like light waves, a discovery that fascinated [Guilelmo, Marchese] Marconi (1874–1937), the Italian physicist and inventor who experimented with a device to convert those electromagnetic waves into electricity, making his first successful experiments in wireless telegraphy in 1895. Trinitrotoluene, in this case symmetrical or 2, 4, 6-trinitrotoluene, commonly known as T.N.T., is the best known of the nitro-substitution compounds produced by substituting three nitro groups for three hydrogen atoms in toluene, the low melting point of which allows it to be poured into artillery shells and other explosive devices.
- [Sir Francis] Galton (1822–1911), English scientist. He was a cousin of Charles Darwin, traveled in Africa, and is best known for his work in anthropology and heredity, and his pioneer work in eugenics seen in *Hereditary Genius* (1869) and other works.
- [Enoch Arnold] Bennett (1867–1931), English novelist and critic, who, in addition to such novels as *Anna of the Five Towns* (1902), *The Old Wives' Tale* (1908), and the Clayhanger series, all of which feature the pottery industry, between 1908 and 1911 contributed shrewd and pungent reviews to A. R. Orage's weekly *New Age*, under the pseudonym of Jacob Tonson.
- Dr. C[aleb] W[illiams] Saleeby (1878–1940), English eugenist, was resident physician in the Maternity Hospital and in the Royal Infirmary, Edinburgh, and assistant to Sir Jonathan Hutchinson at the Polyclinic, London, but was also most active in social organizations, a member of the National Birthright Commission from 1913 to 1916, and its chairman from 1918 to 1920. After the war and throughout the 1920s he lectured all over the world on public health. Among his publications are *The Cycle of Life* (1904), *Parenthood and Race Culture, an Outline of Eugenics* (1909), *Woman and Womanhood* (1912), *The Progress of Eugenics* (1914), *The Whole Armour of Man* (1919), and *Sunlight and Health* (1923). In 1924 he was the founder and chairman of the Sunlight League, and edited their journal *Sunlight*.

Five months after this review, on 27 October 1916, Shaw would give the lecture "Life" (in the Fabian series "The World in Chains,") and explain his theories of biology and creative evolution before "the amazed Saleeby" who was in the chair.

- Walt Whitman (1819–92), American poet, best known for the twelve poems that made up his *Leaves of Grass* (1855). It may, however, be his prose work *Democratic Vistas* (1871), to which Shaw refers: a fearless scrutiny of the corruption that had defaced democracy in the Reconstruction era. Even shorter pieces like "Democracy in the New World" and "In Memory of Thomas Paine" reveal his concern for the principles that had first animated the Union.
- Edward Carpenter (see above, 229).
- Nietzsche (see above, 192).
- Richard Cobden (1804–65), English economist and politician. His public career was launched after a visit to the United States by the publication in 1835–36 of two pamphlets advocating free trade and a foreign policy of peace and non-intervention. He entered Parliament in 1841 and was instrumental in the repeal of the Corn Laws. He was opposed to factory legislation, believing in a laissez-faire policy.
- Charles James Fox (1749–1806), English liberal politician. Undoubtedly Shaw is thinking of Fox's famous oratorical contests with Pitt, whom he fought over the regency, the trial of Warren Hastings, and the French Revolution.
- Sigmund Freud (1856–1939), Austrian neurologist and founder of psychoanalysis. After studying medicine at Vienna, in 1855 he went to Paris to study under Jean Martin Charcot and his field of study changed from neurology to psychopathology. Back in Vienna he developed the technique of conversational "free association" and refined psychoanalysis as a method of treatment. Despite opposition from friends, patients, and colleagues he developed this revolutionary thinking, and in 1900 published his important work *Die Traumdeutung* [*The interpretation of dreams*]. Weekly seminars in his home with kindred minds like Alfred Adler and Carl Jung—though these two later broke with Freud to develop their own theories—led to the formation of the International Psychoanalytical Association, and more important books, the most recent of which at the time of the above review was *Totem and Tabu* (1913.)
- Vasari (see above, 64–65).
- In the Preface to *The Doctor's Dilemma* (1906) Shaw had inveighed against the perils of inoculation, believing it dangerous to disregard a patient's "opsonic index" at the moment of inoculation; a belief that derived from the work of Sir Almroth Wright, who had "proved" that if you inoculated patients with pathogenic germs at the moment when their phagocytes were at the weakest, the consequences could be fatal. Shaw's views on the subject had changed by the time he came to write the Preface to *Saint Joan* in 1924, where he even comments favorably on compulsory inoculation.
- "Convictions are prisons," (see above, 189).
- Hamlet tells us in act IV, scene iv:

> Rightly to be great
> Is not to stir without great argument,
> But greatly to find quarrel in a straw
> When honour's at the stake.

- Hobson (see above, 129).
- Wilkins Micawber is an agent for Murdstone and Grinby's with whom David Copperfield lodges when he is working at the firm's warehouse. Micawber is always living beyond his income, and always waiting for something to "turn up." His debts at one point land him in the King's Bench Debtors' Prison. Finally, however, he emigrates *en famille* to Australia, where he becomes a successful magistrate.
- Mrs. Wilfer is a tall angular woman, much given to tying up her head in a pocket handkerchief knotted under the chin. She is the wife of Reginald Wilfer (a clerk who works in the drug-house of Chicksey Veneering and Stobbles in Dickens's *Our Mutual Friend*), and makes her husband and family generally uncomfortable.

22 July 1916

WHAT MR. WELLS THINKS IS COMING*
[C2083]

MR. WELLS is not one of those writers on whom reviewers can sit in judgment without risk of making themselves ridiculous. Many attempts at that adventure have produced the effect of a pickpocket trying the Lord Chief Justice; and though one would dearly like to see this happen, the difficulty in the way is that a pickpocket clever enough to do it would be too clever to be a pickpocket. Therefore I hasten to announce that I am here not to admonish and reprove Mr. Wells in the customary fashion, but to discuss one of his suggestive propositions.

He says that if Germany would give us the guarantee of good intentions involved in her becoming a republic, we should take her to our hearts at once. He repeats this in another place, declaring emphatically that public opinion would not in that case allow any Government

---

* "What is Coming?" By H. G. Wells. (Cassell 6s. net.)

to go on with the war. I hope this is true, and therefore think it a wise saying; but let us see how it looks from the other end. Suppose Germany gave the guarantee, and the Hohenzollerns and Hapsburgs, crowns, thrones, and all, vanished for ever into the blind cave of eternal night! Suppose we said "Good boys: we forgive you. Cease firing there at once."

How if the Germans were to keep on firing, and, on receiving a scandalized demand for explanations of this ungrateful and implacable conduct, were to reply, "It is true that we have become a republic; but you have not; and Russia has not. We did not remove Hohenzollern and Hapsburg to make Romanoff cock of the walk; to leave your Greys and Milners the power they have wrested from the Crown without giving it to the people of England; and to leave the United States in a naval nutcracker between the British and Japanese monarchies. It is our turn now to ask for guarantees. Make Mr. Wells Foreign Secretary, and we will take you to our hearts fast enough in spite of his proclamation of a personal vendetta (which will evaporate in a week), and even invite you to join us in putting pressure on Russia to get rid of Peter the Great as effectually as we have got rid of Frederick the Great. But while your Junkers remain in the saddle, all you can claim is that the boot is now on the other leg. We cheerfully admit that our militarist *régime* was a nuisance: that is why we have got rid of it. But your Mr. Wells has admitted, and even volunteered the statement, that your own militarist empire was the Hohenzollern model; and if all we hear of your dealings with conscientious objectors be true, the British sergeant and the British colonel can still give lessons in brutality to their Prussian imitators. Therefore the establishment of a German Republic is not the establishment of peace between it and the Anglo-Russian Alliance: on the contrary, you and Russia are the last foes to be overcome. Lord Grey and Mr. Wells, in calling for a revolution in Germany, are simply calling for a monopoly of militarist empire in Europe for England and Russia, and for Japan in the East, unless they accompany their demand with an offer of a revolution at home. The foreign policy of the new German Republic is to detach the French Republic from its unnatural alliance with the barbarous monarchs of Britain, Japan, and Muscovy, thus establishing an overwhelming claim on American sympathy; to swing round Scandinavia, Holland, and Belgium to the German side; to buy the support of Italy with the Trentino; to carry out Roger Casement's suggestion of an independent Ireland guaranteed by the Continental Powers as a citadel of the freedom of the seas; and so enable the peoples of Europe to snap their fingers at the militarist and navalist British Junkers and at the Prussianized bureaucracy and Grand Dukery of Petrograd."

Now if we merely gasped helplessly at these unfamiliar views, and exclaimed "This is infamous. You actually refuse to take our good intentions for granted!" every foreigner would laugh; and we should not be strong enough to make him laugh on the wrong side of his mouth, though that would be our first indignant impulse. Mr. Wells must therefore work out the counter-guarantees the Germans are entitled to ask for. If Lord Grey, instead of merely saying, through a Chicago paper, "Will you make a revolution?" had said, "Will you make a revolution if we do?" the Germans might conceivably have replied, "Now you're talking." But surely the gander who recommends to the goose a sauce which he shews no disposition to partake of himself is in rather an equivocal position. If we will not face a domestic political split in the face of the enemy,we can hardly expect the Germans to face one, especially as our theory is that their situation is more dangerous than ours.

Mr. Wells is, happily, free from the illusion of "a just and lasting peace." The people who are in favor of a just and lasting peace are not in favor of peace at all, because under existing political arrangements no peace can be lasting; and no peace can under any circumstances be just. The usual recipe for a lasting peace seems to be "Exterminate the Hun." If we exterminated the Hun, we should probably have to fight our Allies on the question whether Britain, France, or Russia should repopulate and govern Hunland. Enormous questions would be opened by the extinction of any European Power: that is why Turkey, the Sick Man of Europe, has lived to claim the two sensational victories of the present war over the British Empire. Even the enfeeblement of Germany to a point at which her power would be negligible would create a vacuum in the middle of Europe which would certainly produce a devastating cyclone. We really must begin to consider something beyond the immediate satisfaction of our pugnacity. Nobody has yet the slightest idea of what is to happen in Mesopotamia if the Allies clear out the Turks. And none of these questions admit of a "just" solution: you may place a frontier here or there because it is convenient, or because it is insisted on by someone strong enough to hold it against all encroachers, but not because it is just. I remember an old Irish inscription, "A line drawn from this lamp post through the one diagonally opposite is the true meridian," patriotically implying that the meridian at Greenwich is an imposture; and I know that men say similarly silly things about the Rhine and the Carpathians; but Justice is catholic, and knows nothing of frontiers or of treaties brought about by war. Heaven itself could not make a just treaty between the present belligerents; and those who expect mortal diplomatists to do it are crying for the moon.

Besides, only cravens demand an eternal peace. Unless we drop the military attitude altogether, and admit that fighting, far from being the breath of our snorting nostrils and the salvation of our souls, is a most unpleasant and terrifying obligation, we are bound in honor to make peace only on the understanding that we shall be ready to begin fighting again the very next day, and yet again and again without a moment's hesitation to all eternity, if our honor and interest demand it. The shameless way in which our funksters cry aloud that we must kick our enemy to death when we get him down, and that to allow him to recover his breath and have another go at us is madness and ruin, robs war of all its decencies and our traditions of all their glory. No doubt the clamor for security—for making this the last war—is natural, because, as Mark Twain put it tersely, "the average man is a coward." But cowardice, like seasickness, has to be left out of account whilst war remains as inevitable as travelling; and, however our knees may knock, we must always be prepared to take our cowardice in both hands and fight. A nation which gives up saying, "We always are ready, Steady, boys, steady," and begins to shriek that, at all costs, it must never have to fight again, is evidently a nation that can be bullied. Yet what is this war for except to prove that it is no use bullying us?

As, nevertheless, all the big civilized communities, however loudly they may shout "Who's afraid?" and "*Jusqu'au bout*," are verging hard on this inglorious frame of mind, and their only sincere prayer is "Give us peace in our time, O Lord," the great need of the hour is a statesman with character enough to point out that all the cards are on the table and all the bluffs blown on, and with ability enough to take seriously in hand what Mr. Wells and President Wilson are urging: to wit, the institution of a Supernational Tribunal and Legislature. For that is the only alternative to war. The Fabian Society's specifications for this structure are, as far as I know, more complete, and more carefully discussed and thought out than any others that have yet been published; and as they do not differ from the numerous American and English plans that have been sketched except in respect of their greater elaboration, and their fuller information and documentation as to what has already been done, it will not be necessary this time to send Mr. Lloyd George to Germany to ask what we should do to be saved.

The real difficulty is the first step, which must be the proposal of a judicial decision. For that we need at the Foreign Office a spokesman of the British Empire who will face the situation and can make the nation and the world face it. We have not got that spokesman. Lord Grey scolds and recriminates, and cannot forget or forgive the omission of Germany to allow him to repeat his little success with a conference during the Balkan crisis. When the Imperial Chancellor pays him an apparently undeserved compliment as to his attitude when the Treaty of Berlin was violated by Austria, he shouts, "That is a first-class lie." When the Turks declare war, he calls them degenerate. Now there is undoubtedly a popular demand for this sort of thing. But there is also a somewhat superabundant supply of it from the press and platform. If Lord Grey would edit a paper, or take the boards alongside Mr. Horatio Bottomley, his scoldings, his recriminations, and his wounded diplomatic susceptibilities would enter into the vulgar currency of patriotism fitly enough. But they will never end a war or inaugurate an organization of supernational law. They may stoke up a meeting of the Anti-Gentleman League; but they will not raise a nation to the plane of high and nationally disinterested thinking on which the destiny of European civilization should be discussed.

We must not forget that the Germans have already a striking advantage in the frankness of the Bismarck tradition. That frankness by no means departed from the diplomatic tradition of disingenuousness to the extent of excluding lies; but its lies were real lies, meant to deceive, and not absurd attempts to whitewash blood and iron, nor governess's lectures on virtuous behavior addressed by the pot to the kettle. The Imperial Chancellor, unlike our statesmen, catches the ear of Europe and America because, with all his concessions to German patriotism, he talks far more about real things than we do, and calls a scrap of paper a scrap of paper. In doing this he may be compared to a French *savate* player opposed to an English pugilist. The pugilist despises a man who kicks, and thinks that the simple counter is to seize the uplifted foot, and throw the dastardly kicker violently on his back. The *savate* player proffers his toe cheerfully, and when it is duly seized, turns his back on the pugilist, drops on both his palms, and kicks him decisively in the frontal sinus with the free foot, the pugilist obligingly supporting the other during the operation. Just so does Lord Grey snatch at the frankness of Bethmann-Hollweg to claim some trumpery moral superiority, and thereby not only wastes a great deal of time, but presently finds our own military necessities (in

Greece, for example) enabling his opponent to return his moral kick with crushing effect.

What we want is a spokesman who will never deny, never excuse us, never accept a seat in the dock even to secure a verdict, never bandy abuse, never waste time trumping up moral cases, never call his opponent a liar with or without an epithet, and never blench before a mob, however patriotic: one who will ungrudgingly make our enemies a present of all the information they already possess and all the credit they obviously deserve, and who will make the gallery play to him instead of allowing it to make him play to it, whilst compelling the attention of Europe and educating both neutral and belligerent opinion by keeping hard down all the time on the realities of the situation, and writing across the heavens those large issues between Democracy and Autocracy without which the war, bulky and destructive as it is, has no importance and no dignity; for if we are engaged in a mere Junker dog-fight, it matters nothing to mankind whether the bulldog or the dachshund be top dog.

Lord Grey is not this kind of man: that much has been evident to all the world, not merely since 1914, but since 1906. His very virtues are a disqualification for his office: he has been the round man in the square hole all through. Two first-rate defences of him have been published: one by Gilbert Murray, the other by William Archer: Murray defending him against the accusation of being a man of war, and Archer against that of being a man of peace; and both have succeeded so completely that the two have together proved how impossible it has been for the Powers to find out what England really meant to stand for, or to feel sure that she meant to stand for anything.

Yet I cannot console Mr. Wells by any hopes that we shall put the right man in the right place. It is the misfortune of England that she is still far richer and stronger than she need be to hold her own. An unsuitable Minister does not necessarily mean defeat to her: he is only a handicap. Two hundred years ago she won the prototype of this war, although every word of Swift's indictment of the conduct of the Allies was true. Only, she dragged it on, from sheer incapacity of her politicians to end it, for four years after she was offered the terms on which she finally sheathed the sword. And we are likely to do the same again; for Lord Grey and his colleagues seem as little able to end this or any other war as they were to prevent it. We gave them a mighty sword; and they had not the nerve to throw it into the scale when the beam was still balancing between peace and war. When Germany kicked the beam, they could not help themselves; and now they are brainlessly awaiting the upshot of the trial of brute force without, as far as any of us can see, the faintest prevision of the dangerous situation in which we shall be placed by a victorious demonstration that we hold the key of the world's cupboard and are too lazy to do anything with it but leave it to the party politicians as mere spoil, to be scrambled for by the winners in the demoralizing toss-up of a general election on our system—which one is glad to find Mr. Wells denouncing. They cannot even control their generals, whose caprices are now worth more than the pledges of the Premier. When one recalls the wars of the French Revolution, when Members of Parliament went single-handed into camp to arrest generals in the presence of their troops, and send them to the guillotine for insubordinations and failures which would secure them baronies in England to-day, one realizes how hopelessly our governors have failed to educate the rank and file to the pitch of democracy at which an army of six millions is a guarantee of liberty instead of a bodyguard of military tyranny; and how many millions will have to perish uselessly because we have such hazy notions of the difference between government and golf. "War," wrote an officer from the front the other day, "is a game played by children and directed by idiots." He was wrong as to the idiots; for the truth is, it is not politically directed at all. It is a fire burning itself out as best it may, because the poker is too big for party politicians to wield.

Meanwhile, it will unfortunately always be popular for our Front Benches to declare that it is traitorous to talk of peace, and that they are heroically determined to fight to a finish. I say unfortunately, because any fool as strong as England can fight to a finish. Indeed he must fight to a finish whether he likes it or not. He can also declare that the peace to follow a finish must be dictated by him, though there is clearly no must about it, even if he wins, since he cannot win singlehanded, and will certainly be outwitted in the division of the spoils if he cannot hold his own in cunning with his Allies. All such declarations are great signs of folly; for nobody with any ideas of what to dictate, or any sense of the neutral and circumstantial pressure under which the peace must be dictated, would condescend to such empty claptraps. I cannot recall a single Front-Bench utterance on the subject of the war that has left us with an idea that we might not have picked up at any recruiting meeting and thrown away as already in stock and considerably shopsoiled. If the whole German army were to throw its weapons down and its hands up to-morrow, and Mr. Joseph King were to ask, in his reckless manner, "What are we going to do now?" I should expect Mr. Asquith to say, "I hope to make a statement next March," and to *think* "God knows!" and Lord Grey to urge that Germany could not now refuse that conference. Assume no more than that the Allies drive the Turks out of Mesopotamia; yet I will give sixpence to anyone who will tell me who is to have the Bagdad Railway and who the Garden of Eden. Men are saying desperately that if they must go on fighting until the Government begins thinking they will have to fight for ever. For consolation they must turn to Napoleon, who said that if you only go on fighting long enough the other fellow will stop. Let us hope that the Hun will be the other fellow in this case, and that things will tumble into shape afterwards by mere gravitation. Our Ministers can at least be trusted in that case to look as like Sir Isaac Newton as possible.

Under such circumstances I must not say, in the Front-Bench manner, that Mr. Wells's book is worthy of his high reputation. I am silenced by a doubt as to whether he has a high reputation. I do not often see a review of his prophetic works which shews anything like an adequate sense of his extraordinary powers; and I sometimes see reviews that are not even commonly generous. For our politicians, whom his books most immediately concern, they do not seem to exist: hardly a Minister opens his mouth without betraying an abysmal ignorance not only of Mr. Wells's prophecies, but of the popular text-books which he must have mastered before he was ten years old, if indeed he was not born with the knowledge they impart to duller men, just as he was born with a knowledge of the nutritive value of milk. It is safe to guess that Mr. Wells read Macaulay's Essays before he was sixteen: it is extremely doubtful whether any member of the Cabinet has yet got so far as Little Arthur's History of England. Mr. Wells's conclusions represent the integration and ratiocination of a mass of historical and scientific facts, much of it necessarily the common inheritance of all thoughtful educated men, which , if it has ever been planted in the heads of our party leaders, has either been sterilized by the aridity or excessive sentimental moisture of the soil, or after some faint sprouting has withered and perished; for neither in our official counsels as to war economy nor our attempts at emergency legislation does Parliament think or act in the least as Mr. Wells thinks or would have it act, or indeed at all otherwise than as a very average guild of tinkers might be expected to set about saving the country. There is hardly a problem that has not been worked out and solved for Parliament by persons of the general type of Mr. Wells, if not of his individual genius; but it invariably proceeds as if every member were Adam the day after his expulsion from Paradise. And thus, however much genius England produces, she never gets any further than she can fight. The pilots who weather the storm never look at the stars and have never heard of the mariner's compass. Infatuated with the skill with which they can handle the little fleet of party canoes in Election Dock, they tackle the ocean with a great contempt for faddists (*parteilos* [*sic*] *Gesellen*), and like the Irish Pilot cry, "I know every rock on this coast [*crash*]—and that's one of them."

If the greatness of a nation be measured by the blindness of its rulers it survives, Britain may transfer her idolatrous worship of German organization, German infallibility, German profundity, German philosophic integrity, German self-esteem, as expressed by that thoroughgoing Englishman Mr. Houston Chamberlain, to her own self. If we can win in the field, there will be nothing new about that, happily; but if our present political leaders can handle the victory to our permanent advantage, I owe them an apology.

G. B. S.

Editor's Notes

▪ The above review was first published in the *Nation* 19 (22 July 1916): 506–8, with the following disclaimer: "[Mr. Shaw's view of the large issues of diplomacy and personality with which he deals is, of course, his own. —ED., THE NATION]." It was also published as "Bernard Shaw Ridicules Great Britain's Plan of Crushing Germany," in the *New York American* 2 (10 September 1916): 7–8, 2:1–2. Shaw's correspondence gives no clue as to when he wrote it.

▪ H[erbert] George] Wells (1866–1946), English novelist, short story writer, and popular historian. Wells was restlessly interested in such contemporary issues as free love, Fabianism, progressive education, scientific theory "world government" and human rights. His reputation as the author of *The Time Machine* (1895), *The Island of Doctor Moreau* (1896), *The Invisible Man* (1897), and *The War of the Worlds* (1898), was already well established when he met the Webbs in 1902, in the wake of his best-selling book *Anticipations* (1901), which explored the scientific possibilities of the new century. Wells's view of a collectivist society run by a managerial elite appealed to the Fabians, and Wells (sponsored by Shaw and Wallas) joined the Society in February 1903. His novel *A Modern Utopia* (1905) fictionalized Fabianism, and by 1906 he was sufficiently flattered as a prophet to set about reforming the Fabian Society. Wells, however, hotheaded and confrontational by nature, rapidly alienated the membership. He attacked Shaw for reducing the "high business of Socialism" to "an idiotic middle-class joke," and in the ensuing confrontation was outdebated by Shaw, taking refuge in the public acclaim brought by his writing. Indeed, after further rancorous exchanges with the Webbs and others, he finally resigned from the Fabian Society on 16 September 1908. Wells's major novels, such as *Love and Mr. Lewisham* (1900), *Kipps* (1905), *Tono-Bungay* (1909), and *The History of Mr. Polly* (1910) are works of social realism, drawing heavily on his own experiences among the lower middle class. Given to writing prophetically as in the book reviewed above, Wells continued to see himself as an educator, producing *The Outline of History* (1920). At his last home in Regent's Park, which he refused to leave during the air-raids of World War II, he wrote the interesting *Experiment in Autobiography* (1934), as well as the suddenly pessimistic *Mind at the End of Its Tether* (1945), which expressed doubts about the future survival of the human race.

- Shaw quotes Shakespeare's Richard III, who, in act V, scene iii of that play admonishes Catesby to

> Send out a pursuivant-at-arms
> To Stanley's regiment; bid him bring his power
> Before sunrising, lest his son George fall
> Into the blind cave of eternal night.

- [Lord] Grey (see above, 285).
- [Alfred, first Viscount] Milner (1854–1925), English statesman. From 1892 to 1897 he was chairman of the Board of Inland Revenue. From 1897 to 1905 he was high commissioner in South Africa, receiving a baronetcy in 1901, and a viscountcy in 1902 for his services before and during the Boer War. In the December following Shaw's review he would enter the War Cabinet. From 1918 to 1919 he was secretary for war, and from 1919 to 1921 colonial secretary.
- The territory of Trentino-Alto Adige was part of the Austrian Tirol until the end of World War I, when it was ceded to Italy. In 1948 Trentino-Alto Adige was established as an autonomous region.
- Shaw was very fond of Mark Twain [pseudonym for Samuel Langhorn Clemens] (1835–1910), whom he met on 17 June 1907, frequently referring to such works as *The Innocents Abroad; or The New Pilgrim's Progress* (1869), *A Connecticut Yankee in King Arthur's Court* (1889), *The Tragedy of Pudd'nhead Wilson* (1894), and *Personal Recollections of Joan of Arc, by the Sieur Louis de Conte* (1896).
- Shaw quotes from the song "Heart of Oak," by David Garrick (1717–79), set to music by William Boyce (1711–79), the full chorus of which reads:

> Heart of oak are our ships,
> Heart of oak are our men;
> We always are ready;
> Steady, boys, steady;
> We'll fight and we'll conquer again and again.

- *Jusqu'au bout,* "On to the end."
- "Give [us] peace in our time, O Lord," is a line from the Book of Common

Prayer that seven years later Shaw will most tellingly give to De Stogumber, the English chaplain in the Epilogue to *Saint Joan*: "Oh, do not come back: you must not come back. I must die in peace. Give us peace in our time, O Lord!"

- Thomas Woodrow Wilson (1856–1924), twenty-eighth president of the United States. He became governor of New Jersey in 1911, and the following year (and again in 1916) was elected president of the United States. Wilson's administration, which ended unfortunately in his physical breakdown, was memorable for Prohibition and Women's Suffrage amendments to the Constitution, America's involvement in World War I, and his important part in the peace process. However, in a conversation with Archibald Henderson, Shaw later claimed that Wilson should have stuck to his guns in initiating the Tribunal (mentioned above); but unfortunately he caught "war fever, and, to the utter consternation of his admirers, began to talk of German guilt and so forth. . . . The purely pathological nature of this disastrous change was proved by the breakdown in Mr. Wilson's health which followed. It was a tragic calamity. Whether history will ever forgive him for his apostasy at a moment when all the remaining hopes of the half-despairing goodwill of the world were centred on him I cannot tell. I do not feel bitter about it myself, because I saw too much of that brain fever that was so sudden in its attack and so complete in its transformation of reasonable men into raging lunatics" (G. B. Shaw, from *Table-Talk of G.B.S. Conversations on Things in General between Bernard Shaw and his biographer*. By Archibald Henderson [London: Chapman and Hall, 1925], 178–79).

- Lloyd George (see above, 317).

- Horatio William Bottomley (1860–1933), English journalist, entrepreneur, and politician. A persuasive speaker and a brilliant journalist, he also revealed a talent for making money: by 1900 he had promoted almost fifty companies, whose total capital was £20,000,000. However, he was twice charged with fraud (though acquitted); and between 1901 and 1905, had sixty-seven bankruptcy petitions and writs filed against him. The following year he founded the weekly journal *John Bull*, and became M.P. for South Hackney, a position he held until 1912. During the period that Shaw is writing about, Bottomley was still receiving subscriptions for various enterprises (up to the sum of £900,000). By 1918 he had been discharged from his bankruptcy, and again became an M.P. for another four years. Finally, in 1922, he was found guilty of fraudulent conversion, and sent to prison. He died in poverty.

- Savate is a French form of kick-boxing, popular in the 1860s, the word deriving from the Old French *çabot* [sabot], or *savate*, which means an old shoe.

- Bethmann-Hollweg (see above, 286).

- For Shaw's review of Murray's *The Foreign Policy of Sir Edward Grey 1906–1915*, see above, 309.

- William Archer (1856–1924), Scottish dramatic critic and author, and translator of Ibsen's plays (he published the complete works in 1906–7), became Shaw's mentor, guide, and friend while the latter was "devilling in London," and, in 1884, Shaw's collaborator on his first dramatic effort "Rheingold," later finished as *Widowers' Houses* (1892). Archer also wrote numerous books about the drama, including *Masks or Faces?* (1888) and *Play-making* (1912), besides editing the works of Congreve, and writing four plays himself, the most successful of which was *The Green Goddess* (1923). Here, however, Shaw refers to Archer's book *The Thirteen Days* (1915), which attempted to make sense out of the chaotic two weeks leading up to the outbreak of war in 1914. In it Archer is impressed with Grey: "I went into the investigation believing, in a general way, in Sir Edward Grey's ability and good sense; I came out of it with an enthusiastic admiration for the skill, the tact, the temper, the foresight, the unwearied diligence and the unfailing greatness of spirit with which he ensued and strove for peace" (William Archer, *The Thirteen Days. July 23—August 4, 1914. A Chronicle and Interpretation* [Oxford: Clarendon Press, 1915], 4).

▪ During the Spanish War of Succession in the early years of the eighteenth century, secret peace negotiations were in progress, and Jonathan Swift (1667–1745) abandoned his editorship of the Tory journal the *Examiner* in June 1711 in order to write *The Conduct of the Allies*, an outstanding political pamphlet in support of the proposals for peace in the Continental campaign.

▪ Mr. Asquith (see above, 186–87).

▪ Joseph King (1860–1943), English politician, at this time was Liberal M.P. for North Somerset.

▪ The first collected edition of Macaulay's (see above, 119–20), *Critical and Historical Essays* was published in 1843.

▪ *Little Arthur's History of England*, by M.C. [Maria Graham, later Lady Callcott] in two volumes, printed by Murray of London in 1835, was a popular children's history. The book went through ten editions, culminating in the anniversary edition of 1936.

▪ *parteilos* [should be *parteilose*] *Gesellen* means "non–party members."

▪ "The pilots who weather the storm never look at the stars and have never heard of the mariner's compass." In this line we have one of the central metaphors of *Heartbreak House*, Shaw's yet unfinished play, which dramatizes the paralysis of politicians and the general helplessness of the British ruling class in the face of a crisis, and which Shaw had begun writing a month before at Wyndham Croft. The character of Dunn [the Burglar] was Captain Shotover's ex-boatswain, who had also been a pirate in China. Shaw substitutes "Election Dock" for the "Execution Dock" of the River Thames, where pirates were put to death; and his joke about the Irish pilot is rendered more seriously in the play by Shotover, who declares, "Every drunken skipper trusts to Providence. But one of the ways of Providence with drunken skippers is to run them on the rocks." The connection between England and the metaphor of the drifting ship is made clear in the following exchange:

HECTOR. And this ship we are all in? This soul's prison we call England?
CAPTAIN SHOTOVER. The captain is in his bunk, drinking bottled ditch-water; and the crew is gambling in the forecastle. She will strike and sink and split. Do you think the laws of God will be suspended in favor of England because you were born in it?

HECTOR. Well, I dont mean to be drowned like a rat in a trap. I still have the will to live. What am I to do?

CAPTAIN SHOTOVER. Do? Nothing simpler. Learn your business as an Englishman.

HECTOR. And what may my business as an Englishman be, pray?

CAPTAIN SHOTOVER. Navigation. Learn it and live; or leave it and be damned.

- Houston Chamberlain (see above, 262–63).

17 February 1917

THE ARTSTRUCK ENGLISHMAN*
[C2109]

To an Irishman there is always something indecent in the way an Englishman takes to art, when he does take to it. He worships it; exalts its artifices above its inspirations; makes gods of its frail and ridiculous human instruments; pontificates and persecutes in its name; and ends in delirium and drunkenness, which seem to him the raptures of a saint's vigil. Swinburne's article on Victor Hugo in the Encyclopædia Britannica is quite a mild example, though it repeats the word "deathless" as often as a Jingo war editor repeats the word "unflinching." The idolatry of the Bible, which has played such a curious part in British history, is really a worship of literary art: no other nation speaks of "The Book of Books" as if the phrase were in the Athanasian Creed, just as no other nation stands up in the concert room when the Hallelujah chorus is sung. There are moments when a sober man wants to shake the idolator and talk to him like a Dutch uncle, or like Lady Macbeth when she said to her blithering, ghost-ridden spouse: "When all's said, you look but on a stool."

I am myself a literary artist, and have made larger claims for literature—or, at any rate, put them forward more explicitly—than any writer of my generation as far as I know, claiming a continuous inspiration for modern literature of precisely the same character as that con-

---

* "Men of Letters." By Dixon Scott. With an Introduction by Max Beerbohm. (Hodder & Stoughton. 6s. net.)

ceded to the ancient Hebrew Scriptures, and maintaining that the man of letters, when he is more than a mere confectioner, is a prophet or nothing. But to listen for a writer's message, even when the fellow is a fool, is one thing: to worship his tools and his tricks; his pose and his style, is an abomination. Admire them by all means, just as you admire the craft of the masons and the carpenters and sculptors who built your cathedral; but don't go inside and sing Te Deums to them.

Dixon Scott was an exceedingly clever young man, with a most remarkable specific literary talent. Reading his criticisms is like watching revolver practice by a crack shot: the explosiveness of the style and the swiftness of the devastation hide the monotony of the mood and method. His longest and most deeply-felt effort was an essay on William Morris; his most elaborate, an essay on me. When it first appeared in The Bookman, I read it with the chuckle of the old hand whose professional tricks have landed a young one in a transport of innocent enthusiasm. But I was finally shocked by his preposterous reversal of the natural relative importance of manner and matter. He quoted a long sentence of mine, which derived a certain cumulative intensity from the fact that it was an indictment of civilization, as a specimen of style, and then, with an amazingly callous indifference to the fact that he, like the rest of us, was guilty on all its counts, simply asked, with eager curiosity, and a joyous sense of being the very man to answer the question, "Now what pose is this?" It was very much as if I had told him the house was on fire, and he had said, "How admirably monosyllabic!" and left the nursery stairs burning unheeded. My impulse was to exclaim, "Do you suppose, you conceited young whelp, that I have taken all that trouble, and developed all that literary craft to gratify your appetite for style? Get up at once and fetch a bucket of water; or, at least, raise an alarm, unless you wish me to take you by the scruff of the neck and make you do it. You call yourself a critic: you are a mere fancier."

This, I think, is what, in Touchstone's phrase, obliges me to disable Scott's judgment. It comes out extravagantly in his essay on Morris, which is a long and sincerely felt protest against the author of "The Defence of Guinevere" maturing into the author of "Sigurd," of "A Dream of John Ball," and of "News from Nowhere." It is like a man complaining that his wife does not remain a girl: a sort of lèse humanité against which human honor revolts. The excuse is, of course, the writer's youth.

That maturity involves quite poignant losses to set against its consummations is only too true. Mozart's "Abduction from the Seraglio" is monotonous and resourceless compared to his Don Juan; but it has a charm and freshness that Mozart could not recapture, young as he was when he died. To ask Morris to give Sigurd the charm of Guinevere—a charm of helplessness, weakness, innocence, boyish romance—was like asking any poet of fifty to give us an Alastor: he could not if he would, and what is perhaps more to the point, he would not if he could, because no man will go back on a good bargain merely because one of the coins he had to pay away was a sixpence he had once tried to break with a girl sweetheart. We must put up with these inevitables; and Dixon Scott's complaint that Morris did not spend his whole life in defending Guinevere is no more sensible than a complaint that General Douglas Haig can no longer cut a figure as a sprinter. But when the youth takes it so seriously that he must needs set up the most laboriously ingenious explanations of why Morris and the rest of us deliberately stifled our instincts; corrupted our natures; and perverted our talents instead of going on writing Guineveres and Alastors for him: in short, of why we grew up expressly to spite him, he goes over the edge of silly-cleverness into the abyss of folly. One has a startled sense of the artist conceived as a pet lap dog for the dilettanti, having his growth stunted by a diet of gin that he may be a more amusing monster than Nature made him.

I should not quarrel with this folly if it were recognized as such; for a good deal of new country is discovered by simply going astray. The straight and narrow path has been so often explored that we all go a little way down the paths of danger and destruction merely to see what they are like; and even the paths of tomfoolery may lead to a view or two. Dixon Scott had qualifications for such ramblings which made him a very agreeable critic, and sometimes a very useful one. Chief among these was his knowledge of the natural history of the artist, which preserved him from many current journalistic sillinesses. To take a personal example, the fact that I am an Irish Protestant, and that I published a volume called "Three Plays for Puritans," has created a legend about the gloomy, sour, Sabbath-ridden, Ulster-Covenanting home in which I was brought up, and in which my remarkable resemblance to St. Paul, St. Anthony, and John Knox was stamped on me. To Dixon Scott this was as patently absurd as an assumption that the polar bear owes its black fur to its negro parents. He at once picked out the truth and packed it into the statement that I am the son of Donizetti's Lucrezia Borgia (as a matter of fact I was brought up in an atmosphere of which two of the main constituents were Italian opera and complete freedom of thought; and my attitude to conventional British life ever since has been that of a missionary striving to understand the superstitions of the natives in order to make himself intelligible to them). All through this book, in dealing with me, with Wells, with Kipling, with Houghton, he is saved again and again by his knowledge of the sort of animal the artist is in his nonage. Unfortunately his knowledge stops there. He does not understand the artists' manhood; protests with all his soul against the inevitable development; and always, however ridiculously, sets up the same theory that the shy romantic dreamer has put on a mask, which, as he wittily says, gets so hard pressed upon his face by popular applause that it moulds his very features to its shape. Shaw, Kipling, Wells and Co. are timid children desperately playing at being strong but by no means silent men; and he tries to strip our masks off, and show our real faces, which, however, are all the same face, and a very obvious doll's face at that. His mistake is in taking the method of nature, which is a dramatic method, for a theatrical pose. No doubt every man has a shy child in him, artist or no artist. But every man whose business it is to work directly upon other men, whether as artist, politician, advocate, propagandist, organizer, teacher or what not, must dramatize himself and play his part. To the laborer who merely digs and vegetates, to the squire who merely hunts and eats, to the mathematician and physicist, the men of the orchestra and the tribune may seem affected and theatrical; but when they themselves desire to impress their needs or views on their fellows they find that they, too, must find a pose or else remain paralyzed and dumb. In short, what is called a pose is simply a technical condition of certain activities. It is offensive only when out of place: he who brings his public pose to the dinner table is like the general who brings his sword there, or the dentist who puts his forceps beside his plate, just to shew that he has one. He cannot, however, always leave it behind him. Queen Victoria complained that Gladstone talked to her as if she were a public meeting; but surely that is the way in which a Prime Minister should address a queen when affairs of State are on the carpet. Lord Melbourne's pose may have been more genial and human; but so it was when he addressed a public meeting. Dixon Scott takes this very simple natural phenomenon, and, guessing at once that he can be very clever about it if he begins by being very stupid, pays that price for being clever. It is monstrously stupid to try to foist Morris, Wells, and Kipling (to say nothing of myself) on the reader as creatures with guilty secrets, all their secrets being the same secret: to whit, that they are not Morris, Wells, and Kipling at all, but sensitive plants of quite another species. Still, on that stupid assumption he writes very cleverly, sometimes with penetrating subtlety. But as he remains the Fancier, he is never sound, and is only quite satisfactory when dealing with pure virtuosity, which he finds only in Max Beerbohm's "Zuleika." And then he has to leave you in ignorance of the fact that Max is the most savage Radical caricaturist since Gillray, and that "Zuleika" is only his play, not his work.

It was a kind and devoted act of Mr. St. John Adcock to collect and edit these reviews, and very modest of him to allow Max to take the stage as their introducer. They are the best monument the untimely-slain author could have desired. I have no space here to do more than point out the limitations of Dixon Scott's view of art, and how the young literary voluptuary flourished at the expense of the critic of life. But I can guarantee the book as being not only frightfully smart in the wrong places, but, in the best of the right ones, as good as it is in the nature of the best journalistic criticism to be.

G. B. S.

Editor's Notes

- The above review was first published in the *Nation* 20 (17 February 1917): 682, 684. Also in the *New Republic* (New York) 37 (February 1917). Reprinted in Bernard Shaw, *Pen Portraits and Reviews* (London: Constable, 1931 and 1932), the only changes being the removal of inverted commas around titles and the italicizing of the word *dilettanti*.
- In 1917 Shaw elected to keep a diary for a year "as a sample slice of my life," but only managed to keep it up for ten days. However, the few days that Shaw did keep enable us to conjecture that the above article was written before the turn of the new year, and to be certain that the proofs were read on 9 January 1917: "After dinner I corrected the proof of my review of Dixon Scott's book for *The Nation*, and played for awhile with the pianola: Elgar's *Carillon*, the *Marche au Supplice* from Berlioz's *Fantastic Symphony*, Schumann's *Traumerei* etc." (*Diary* 1178).
- Dixon Scott (1881–1915), English journalist and author. Resolved to be a journalist, he lived with his parents near Market Harborough writing a weekly article for the *Liverpool Courier*, whose editor, Macleay, was one of the first to appreciate Scott's talent. He also contributed many signed reviews to the *Manchester Guardian*, and became friends with many of that celebrated journal's

writers. Sir William Robertson Nicoll, the influential Scottish critic, editor of the *Expositor* and the *British Weekly,* and founder in 1891 of the *Bookman,* spotted Scott's work, and soon the latter was contributing critical essays to the *Bookman.* His friends pressed him to publish some of these articles as a book, a task interrupted by the outbreak of the First World War. Dixon Scott became a lieutenant in the Royal Field Artillery and sailed for Gallipoli, arriving there on 2 October 1914. Three weeks later (on 23 October) he died of dysentery on board a hospital ship. It was felt by his surviving friends that his plan to publish a collection of his essays should be carried through as a tribute to his memory. Accordingly the essays were edited for the press by A. St. John Adcock. Scott's article "The Innocence of Bernard Shaw," reproduced in the book, was originally published in the *Bookman* in 1913.

▪ [Sir Henry] Max[imilian] Beerbohm (1872–1956), English writer and caricaturist. His first volume of essays, some of which had appeared in the *Yellow Book,* appeared under the ironic title *The Works of Max Beerbohm* (1896). He succeeded Shaw as drama critic on the *Saturday Review* and remained its drama critic until 1910, when he married and went to live in Rapallo, Italy. His brilliant, delicate caricatures were collected in various volumes including *Twenty-five Gentlemen* (1896) and *Poet's Corner* (1904). His humorous essays were also published, but his best-known work was his single novel *Zuleika Dobson, or, An Oxford Love Story* (1911), a witty romance.

▪ [Algernon Charles] Swinburne (1837–1909), English poet, playwright, novelist, and critic. Swinburne was born in London, but spent his childhood on the Isle of Wight. He was educated in France, and at Eton, and Balliol College, Oxford, though he did not graduate from the latter. Fluent in French, he did indeed find Victor Hugo one of his literary and revolutionary influences. Swinburne produced a vast amount of poetry. He also wrote verse plays, and a deal of criticism on Baudelaire, Blake, Webster, Shakespeare, Byron, Dickens and, of course, Victor Hugo. Shaw was introduced to Swinburne by Theodore Watts [later Watts-Dunton], who had become the alcoholic Swinburne's nurse and legal and financial adviser, at "The Pines," Putney, on 22 May 1890, where he had lunch. Five years later, asked by the *Idler* magazine to recommend the next poet laureate (Tennyson had died in 1892), he recommended Swinburne, saying: "Mr. Swinburne is a born Poet Laureate: he has always been worshipping somebody; and he would soon get used to the substitution of the Prince of Wales for Victor Hugo"; (see Bernard Shaw, *Idler* (February–July 1895): 418. In fact Alfred Austin was given the post in 1896.

▪ It is in act III, scene iv of Shakespeare's play, when Macbeth is publicly shaken by the arrival of the ghost of Banquo at the feast, that he is rebuked by his wife.

▪ Touchstone's "Reply Churlish" disables his judgment. In *As You Like It* the jester explains to Duke Senior the Lie Seven Times Removed: "As thus sir. I did dislike the cut of a certain courtier's beard; he sent me word, if I said his beard was not well cut, he was in the mind it was; this is called the Retort Courteous. If I sent him word again, it was not well cut, he would send me word he cut it to please himself; this is called the Quip Modest. If again it was not well cut, he disabled my judgment; this is called the Reply Churlish . . . " (V.iv).

- William Morris (see above, 165).
- [Joseph Chrysostom Wolfgang Amadeus] Mozart (1756–91) wrote *The Abduction from the Seraglio* in 1782, the year he married. His *Don Giovanni* was first performed in Prague in 1787.
- *Alastor, or, the Spirit of Solitude*, a poem by Percy Bysshe Shelley, was published in 1816, when the poet was twenty four. The poem concerns the contemplative idealist and laments the conditions of the real world even while it condemns the self-centered attitude of the idealist.
- Douglas [first Earl] Haig [of Bemersyde] (1861–1928), Scottish soldier and field-marshal. It was he who, in August 1914, took the First Corps of the British Expeditionary Force to France and succeeded Sir John French as commander-in-chief in December 1915. Through Lt. Col. Hutton Wilson, press chief for the British Expeditionary Force, Haig had recently invited Shaw to the front which is why, no doubt, Shaw used him as an example. At fifty-six General Haig was beyond sprinting. Subsequent ages have also found fault with him as a tactician. He was forced to wage a costly war of attrition in the trenches, hampered by the distrust and interference of Lloyd George. However, Haig was still in charge when the army's successful offensive of August 1918 led to the German plea for an armistice. After the war Haig organized the Royal British Legion for the care of ex-servicemen.
- Saint Anthony [more properly Antony] called "The Great" or Antony of Thebes (251–356) was an Egyptian ascetic, founder of Christian monasticism, who spent twenty years in rigorous seclusion in an old ruin at the top of a hill before being persuaded by the prayers of numerous anchorites to leave his retreat and found a monastery near Memphis and Arsinoë.
- Saint Paul (first century) born Jewish and trained as a rabbi, persecuted Christians, including Saint Stephen, until his own conversion to Christianity on the road to Damascus, after which he was known as the Apostle of the Gentiles. He is famous for his mission journeys and also for over a dozen New Testament Epistles.
- John Knox (see above, 333).
- [Gaetano] Donizetti (1797–1848), Italian operatic composer, who produced no fewer than twenty-three operas from 1822 to 1829, including *Lucrezia Borgia*, first performed at La Scala, Milan, in 1833. In the opera, a banquet is held at Ferrara, interrupted by the sound of monks singing a dirge in an adjoining room. The doors open to admit Lucrezia Borgia. The banqueters are her enemies. She has poisoned their wine. The dirge is for them. But among them, unbeknown to her, is Gennaro, her illegitimate son whom she loves dearly. She offers him an antidote, but he refuses to save his own life while his friends are dying. She then tells him she is his mother; but instead of accepting the antidote, he repulses her. Lucrezia herself then drinks from the poisoned cup he used, and dies upon his lifeless body. Further approval of Dixon Scott's remark is illustrated by Shaw's acknowledgment to Ernest

Newman of 25 October 1917: "I was brought up on Donizetti to some extent (Dixon Scott made an extraordinarily good shot when he said that I was the son of Donizetti's Lucrezia Borgia)"; (see *Collected Letters 1911–1925*, 512).
- H. G. Wells (see above, 346–47).
- Rudyard Kipling (see above, 207).
- [William Stanley] Houghton (1881–1913), British dramatist. When Annie Horniman founded the Manchester Repertory Company, which took up its quarters in the Gaiety Theatre in 1908, Houghton's one-act play *The Dear Departed* was performed as a curtain raiser to Shaw's *Widowers' Houses*. Houghton wrote a dozen plays, the best known of which are *The Younger Generation* (1910) and *Hindle Wakes* (1912). In the last years of his short life, illness prevented Houghton from enjoying his growing fame.
- William Lamb, second Viscount Melbourne (1779–1848), English statesman. He was the prime minister in office at the accession of Queen Victoria in 1837, advising the young queen on her duties with much tact. Even during the coronation ceremony she glanced toward him and reported that he gave her "such a kind" and "fatherly look."
- [James] Gillray (1757–1815), English caricaturist. Born in Chelsea, the son of a soldier from Lanark, he first made his name as an engraver about 1784, and from 1779 to 1811 produced fifteen hundred caricatures aimed at the French, Napoleon, George III, and the leading politicians and social follies of his day. He went insane in the last four years of his life.

17 March 1917

HAS HERBERT SPENCER REALLY TRIUMPHED?* [C2115]

IN a way, Mr. Havelock Ellis's celebration of "The Triumph of Herbert Spencer" is very pleasant to me. As a Socialist, I have been in full reaction against Herbert Spencer's senile politics (not those of his prime) for nearly forty years; and I see in the experience of the war, not their triumph, but the *coup de grâce* that puts them out of their lingering pain. But I have always been revolted by that mean belittlement of the hero which in our unmannerly community is the received method of questioning his influence. Herbert Spencer quite naturally

---

* "Herbert Spencer" By Hugh Elliot. (Constable. 6s. net.) In the series "Makers of the Nineteenth Century (1915–1928), ed. [Arthur Frederick] Basil Williams.

and unaffectedly lived the life of a great man, and played the great game all through; and whoever does not see this and take off his hat to him, does not know a gentleman when he meets one. When Mr. Havelock Ellis faces an ungrateful and ungenerous posterity, and calls for three cheers for Herbert Spencer, I cannot believe that any decent soul will refuse to hail his name with three times three if he really knows what Spencer did and how much the world owed to it in his time. Even those who take no interest in his philosophy will feel a quaint affection for the man who, when he was not faithfully straightening out the tangled thought of his century, was inspiring himself with Meyerbeer's music; giving up his horse because, on its discovery of his intense dislike to coerce any living creature, it went slower than he walked, and finally grazed by the roadside without respect for the philosopher's pressing appointments; refusing the proffered affection of George Eliot because she was not as beautiful as the Venus of Milo; and, when his landlady objected to his describing her in the census paper as "the lady with whom Mr. Herbert Spencer lives," pondered on her unaccountable recalcitrance for an hour, and then altered the entry to "the lady who lives with Mr. Herbert Spencer." Speculative criticism may yet conjecture that he must have been the original of Wagner's Parsifal, *"der reine Thor durch Mitleid wissend."* All the horses in paradise are probably now struggling for the honor of carrying him at full gallop to whatever destination he may be seeking uncoercively.

Mr. Havelock Ellis inevitably salutes him as "the essential Englishman, pure and unmitigated, the complete middle-class Englishman of the straitest sect, the naked, typical Englishman." That is what we always say of a man who disagrees with his contemporaries on every subject on which it is possible for a man to disagree with the majority without being stark mad, and who would have been lynched if the common Englishman of his day had been intelligent or erudite enough to find out what he really believed and disbelieved—especially what he disbelieved. It is like saying that St. Sophia's is a typical church. Mr. Havelock Ellis offers as evidence the fact that Spencer was a member of the committee of the Athenæum Club, which is hardly a general English characteristic, and that he did not know German, in which respect he might be described as a typical Chinaman. I am afraid the statement that Spencer was a typical Englishman will not wash. But it may be said fairly and significantly that he was one of those men of whom Englishmen say that he was typically English: a thing they never say of Shelley. And when the proposition is narrowed down to his being a typical middle-class Englishman, it may be interpreted as meaning that as he had never been broken in to communal life either by slavery, by graduation at a university, by State service, or by belonging to a social circle so exclusive that everybody in it is supposed to know everybody else, he was an inveterate anarchist. Being also a man of vigorous mind, a freethinker in the best sense, he was, within the limits imposed by his humanity and common sense, a great Anti, or Conscientious Objector.

Mr. Havelock Ellis says that "the war has put the final seal on Herbert Spencerism." But I have heard another man say that the war has put the kybosh on Herbert Spencer. I cannot find the word "kybosh" in the dictionary: it may be Hebrew for the final seal, for all I know. Perhaps the editor will invite philologers to open a correspondence on the subject. But I think the gentleman I have just quoted meant that the war had made Spencer's Unsocialism ridiculous. And the only demurrer that can be put in is that war is not a fair test of anything. You cannot reasonably say that war has put the kybosh on domestic architecture or on cities that do not see the sky through steel nets, merely because our houses will not resist the impact of nine-inch shells, and the atmosphere is not proof against the droppings from Zeppelins. I should admit that if Spencerism had made good in peace, it could not be discredited because it had broken down with a crash in war. But the truth is that Spencerism was such a disastrous failure in peace that war actually produced comparative prosperity and social sanity by a better distribution of wealth and a more patriotic employment of men. The fact that the evils of Unsocialism had created vested interests in waste, in poverty, in dishonesty, in drunkenness, in prostitution, in incompetence, snobbery and imposture, so huge that they resisted everything short of Armageddon, may be the explanation of Armageddon; but it is no justification of Unsocialism, and no triumph for the philosopher who opposed both Socialism and Militarism.

The mischief of the present situation is that we have been too lazy to accept the teachings either of the Socialists or of Herbert Spencer and his disciple, Hilaire Belloc. From Turgot and Adam Smith to Cobden, Bastiat, and Herbert Spencer, economists and philosophers have preached freedom of contract and of everything else; and from Robert Owen and Fourier to Morris and the Sidney Webbs, they have preached the common rule, the collective bargain, the communal life, and the doctrine that Robinson Crusoe, monarch of all he surveys, is far more a slave than the man who carries the weight of a thousand laws and works for something bigger than himself. But bless you! the British people have not taken the slightest notice of these intellectual and imaginative exercises. When the slaughter of children's bodies and souls in the cotton factories became unbearable, they drifted into sham factory legislation for fifty years, and then, all the shams being exposed, made the legislation real. They drifted into Free Trade because there was money in it; and when, later on, the Midlands concluded that there was money for them in Protection and tried to revive it under the title of Tariff Reform, the ensuing debates proved nothing except that our political Free Traders did not know the A B C of Free Trade. We have drifted down stream in the current, and up stream in the eddy, without the least notion whither we are going. No statesman has lost a vote by talking the crassest Little Englandism to the working classes, and the crudest bellicose Imperialism to the non-working classes, in the same breath.

Things came to a pitch at last at which the governing classes found the British people out as the helpless drudges they are, and the British people found the governing classes out as the voluptuous and amiably incapable ignoramuses *they* are. What is more, both sides found themselves out at the same moment. Thus, bereft of the reciprocal idolatry which both of them once tried to live up to, they fell into mere cynical opportunism, neither knowing nor caring whether the particular measure at which they happened to be snatching or railing was Socialism or Unsocialism, or what deluge it might bring down or stave off next year. In those days statesmen committed themselves to gigantic wars, and lied about them instead of preparing for them, lest they should split their half-Pacifist party. When the war came, they amused the people by discussing the colossal indemnities they intended to exact from the Powers before whose troops their own were in headlong flight; and these same Powers, who had been terrifying the world (to their own undoing) for years by their boasts of an irresistibly perfect military organization and devotion to the State, were unable to follow up their outnumbered and half-equipped foes because their military nonpareils proved to be tacticians of the school of Offenbach's General Boum, and tried to reduce fortresses without siege guns, and to dash to Paris without provisions. The really big part of the business of government, both in Germany and England, has been too silly for words. To suggest, even in an epithalamium, that the crash in which it has ended has any reference to political science or philosophy, or can be either a triumph or a defeat for anybody who ever gave five minutes' thought to its problems, is to become an accomplice in the welter of humbug and intellectual confusion in which great names are current only as advertisements for the party intrigues of commonplace men.

The mess we are in just now is due to the fact that, though war on the present scale promptly reduces private capitalism and *laisser-faire* to absurdity, it cannot improvise the trained public service required by Socialism. Mr. Lloyd George's attempt to repeat Cromwell's Reign of the Saints with a Reign of Practical Business Men provokes Mr. Gilbert Chesterton's scepticism as to its underlying theory that, as he concisely puts it, "every man who desires to make a great deal out of the community will also ardently desire the community to make a great deal out of him." Mr. Chesterton might have gone further, and pointed out that even if the war has saved the souls of the great exploiters, and made them genuinely anxious to do the very reverse of what they have made their fortunes by doing, they are still much less qualified to begin than the novices who have nothing to unlearn, or even than the old bureaucracy, which has, at least, the tradition of public service. What has already actually happened is that they have begun doing the thing they are accustomed to do and know how to do, like the acrobat who became a monk, and, finding himself too illiterate to pray to the Blessed Virgin, turned double somersaults on the steps of her altar. Our Lady, no doubt, took the will for the deed, being in no very pressing need of a few extra prayers; but we shall not beat the Germans on the strength of the well-intended somersaults of our ex-provision merchants, railway directors, and family solicitors. Cromwell's experiment ended in a dictatorship and government by major-generals. Fortunately for himself, Cromwell was equal to the job, which was then a comparatively small one. It is now enormously bigger and more complex. Thus, Mr. Lloyd George has, in fact, backed himself to have an enormously bigger and more complex brain than Cromwell.

Also, it is to be observed that the powers he wields are stupendously more dangerous and destructive than any within Cromwell's reach. Shakespeare warned us that

"Could great men thunder
As God Himself does, God would ne'er be quiet;
For every pelting petty officer
Would use his heaven for thunder, nothing but thunder."

Well, Mr. Lloyd George, like the Kaiser, can thunder, and worse. No calamity yet attributed to God has laid the earth waste, and strewn it with mangled and poisoned and strangled men as the policies of modern statesmen have laid waste our battle fronts. No natural famine and pestilence in civilized Europe has left behind it a region as vast as Poland drily reporting that in all its borders no child under seven is left alive. Lucky had it been for the inhabitants of these desolate places had our pelting petty officers wielded "nothing but thunder." Heroic, indeed, must be the confidence of Mr. Lloyd George and Lord Northcliffe and the Practical Men of Business, who are prepared to handle these plagues and save their country and everybody else's country without knowing what Herbert Spencer knew, by their mother wit alone. And they had better be as good as their word; for such is the nature of these plagues that if you do not handle them pretty masterfully, they tear you to pieces. Any fool can set them raging; but it takes a very considerable statesman to control and finally stop them.

The Ottoman Empire, in the days of its glory, recognized this, and did not trust to casual commercialists turning their hands to keeping an empire on the strength of having spent their prime in keeping a shop. It deliberately selected the most promising Christian children, and educated and trained them as a governing caste. Thereby it procured an Imperial service which enabled it for centuries to walk over its less thoughtful neighbors as a tank walks over a machine gun. There was no resisting it until this Imperial service, corrupted by its own power, connived at its own corruption, and became the sham that made Turkey the Sick Man of Europe. It is the inevitability of this corruption, in civilizations otherwise commercial, that has produced democracy, which begins as a sham, and ends (let us hope) as a reality, instead of beginning, like the Ottoman Empire and the feudal system, as a reality, and ending as a sham.

The peril of the present juncture is that we are at the sham end of feudalism and the sham beginning of democracy, each baffling and muddling the other, and neither having any real grasp of the situation. The Kaiser's nobles have no more real statesmanship than our own upstarts. They are all empirics attacking symptoms, and incapable of discovering or contriving causes. A statesman should be able to produce a result at ten removes: the rulers of Europe cannot do it at one, and are tumbling back helplessly into every exploded crudity, like mutineers who throw the captain overboard, because they think that the art of navigation is only his tyranny.

Just as literature is produced by teaching everyone to read and write, and letting who can produce "Hamlet" and "Prometheus Unbound," so democracy must be produced by giving everyone a careful political education, and letting who can govern by consent. At present our most carefully educated people know the difference (until they forget it) between a spondee and a dactyl, and do not know the difference between a trade unionist and a Thug. We cover up the deplorable result by an idolatry of the voter more impudent than any idolatry of kings and icons has ever been, and call it democracy. We cling to property and Unsocialism until nine-tenths of the people have no property and are not "in Society"; and when we try Socialism, we are so ignorant of how to do it that we throw our liberties after our property, guaranteeing the dividends of our remaining proprietors, and making ourselves the slaves of their agents, the employers. Naturally, the ghost of Herbert Spencer rises and points to the title of his old pamphlet on "The Coming Slavery"; and Mr. Belloc says, "I told you so."

But that does not help very much. We have held it happier to be thriftless and imprudent, and to enjoy ourselves with the Bing Boys. And, whatever the British journalists and tub-thumpers who have never been in Germany may pretend, the Germans have been more thoroughly, scientifically, and beerily pleasure-loving and Bing-boyish than we. So let us drop all this nonsense about the triumph of the philosophers, and set to work cheerfully to muddle out as we muddled in, like jolly Britons with an ingrained contempt for spoilsports like Herbert Spencer. We have chucked Mr. Asquith and Viscount Grey because, having got us into this mess, it became clear that they could not get us out of it. And as it is thus made sufficiently probable that Mr. Lloyd George will be chucked also if *he* cannot get us out of it, we may as well give him a sporting chance, and let him rip. I use the language appropriate to the nature of the case.

G. B. S.

Editor's Notes

- The above review, which was first published in the *Nation* 20 (17 March 1917): 805–6, purports to be of Hugh Elliot's *Herbert Spencer*, but does not mention that book at all. The first three paragraphs concern themselves instead with Havelock Ellis's short essay "Herbert Spencer," (later printed in

The Philosophy of Conflict, and Other Essays in Wartime). The fact that Hugh Elliot's book is not mentioned seems to have gone unremarked and uncorrected by either the editor of the *Nation*, or by Shaw himself when he reprinted the essay in *Pen Portraits and Reviews* (London. Constable, 1931 and 1932), the only changes made being the dropping of the final "e" in "Shakespeare," and the omission of inverted commas around titles. It is not known when Shaw wrote the above review.

▪ Hugh [Samuel Roger] Elliot (1883–1930), English author, whose first reading of Spencer's work was carried out on active service in the South African War. In addition to *Herbert Spencer*, he translated Hagenbeck's *Beasts and Men* (1909) and Lamarck's *Zoological Philosophy* in 1914, edited the letters of John Stuart Mill in 1910, and the latter's essay on the protection of infant industries in 1911; in 1912 he published *Modern Science and the Illusions of Professor Bergson*; and in 1919 *Modern Science and Materialism*, and in 1922 he published *Human Character*.

▪ Herbert Spencer (see above, 112).

▪ [Henry] Havelock Ellis (1859–1939), English physician and author. After completing his medical education he devoted himself chiefly to research and writing. From 1887 to 1889 he was general editor of the "Mermaid Series," of early English dramatists, and from 1889 to 1914 he edited the "Contemporary Science" series. During World War I Ellis published his *Essays in Wartime*, two collections of short essays on various subjects, from Luther to the politics of women. Ellis was a pioneer researcher into the psychology and sociology of sex, and is perhaps best remembered for his six-volume *Studies in the Psychology of Sex*, which had enormous influence on all subsequent writers on the subject. His autobiography *My Life* was published in 1940.

▪ Giacomo Meyerbeer [Jakob Liebmann Beer] (1791–1864), German operatic composer. From 1834 he lived permanently in Paris, where his successful opera *Les Huguenots* was first performed in 1836. Shaw claimed that the part of Raoul in that opera "affords every possible opportunity to an artist, both vocally and histrionically"; and Meyerbeer's next two operas *Le Prophète* (1849), and *L'Africaine* (performed after his death in 1865), established him as an operatic composer of the first rank.

▪ George Eliot (see above, 96, 112).

▪ "*Der reine Thor durch Mitleid wissend*," means the "pure fool grown in wisdom through compassion."

▪ Saint Sophia's (see above, 336).

▪ Shaw's inability to find the word "kybosh" in the dictionary may have been because he was looking in the wrong place. *Kibosh* is certainly in the *OED*, listed as *slang*, first recorded in 1836 in Shaw's very phrase "to put the kibosh on," meaning "to finish off," or " do for." In 1873 the word was extended to mean "nonsense," later shortened to "bosh." Shaw's guess as to its Hebrew beginnings is perhaps not a bad one; for though it is described as being of obscure origin, the *OED* thinks it is Yiddish.

▪ Hilaire Belloc (see below, 379).

▪ [Anne Robert Jacques] Turgot (1727–81), French economist and statesman. As comptroller-general of finance under Louis XVI, he began to introduce wide sweeping reforms, breaking down the trade barriers within the French provinces, reducing expenditure and increasing revenue without introducing new taxes. When he sought to break down the immunity from taxation enjoyed by the aristocracy, they pressed for his dismissal. After only twenty months Turgot was removed from office, and France drifted towards the Revolution of 1789. As Shaw said in his own review of Léon Say's *Turgot* (12 August 1888): "Turgot is known to the general reader as a man of heavy qualities, but wise withal, who might have averted the French revolution if he had been given his own way in 1776" (see *Bernard Shaw's Book Reviews* 431–34).

- Adam Smith (see above, 199–200).
- Cobden (see above, 337).
- Bastiat (see above, 83).
- Robert Owen (see above, 20–21).
- [François Marie Charles] Fourier (1772–1837), French social theorist, who published a number of utopian Socialist works such as *Le Nouveau Monde industriel et sociétaire* (1829) containing his plans for a reorganization of society based upon a principle of harmony among the material universe, and organic, animal, and human life. Fourier planned to divide society into cooperative communities (each of about sixteen hundred people) that would inhabit a vast communal building [a "phalanstery"] in the centre of an agricultural area. Elaborate rules would control the conduct of the inhabitants, whose notions of marriage and property ownership were to be completely redesigned. Fourier's attempts to interest wealthy speculators in his scheme failed, but by 1832 his followers had begun practical experimentation, and though all of the more than forty "phalanxes" founded in France and the United States failed, Fourierism claimed many adherents.
- The poet William Cowper (1731–1800) wrote *Verses Supposed to Be Written by Alexander Selkirk* (the model for Defoe's Robinson Crusoe) which begin: "I am monarch of all I survey."
- Morris (see above, 165).
- Sidney Webb (see above, 139).
- General Boum is the old fire-eating soldier found in Offenbach's *La Grande Duchesse de Gérolstein* (1867). The Grand Duchess, inspecting the troops on the eve of battle, is much taken by a young Private Fritz (General Boum's rival for the attentions of a local peasant girl), and promotes him to the rank of captain. He ridicules General Boum's plan of campaign and, when the old General objects to so young an officer sitting at the conference table, the Grand Duchess promotes Fritz to the rank of general, and makes him commander-in-chief of the army, in which post he is so successful that the old General determines to fight a duel with him; but is too cowardly to turn up.
- Lloyd George (see above, 317).
- Chesterton (see above, 331–32).
- Shaw quotes Isabella, the nun in *Measure for Measure,* pleading for her

brother's life with Angelo, the Deputy; though in both Quarto and Folio texts, the word "Jove" is substituted for "God."

▪ "The rulers of Europe . . . are . . . like mutineers who throw the captain overboard, because they think that the art of navigation is only his tyranny." The nautical simile reminds one again of *Heartbreak House*, which Shaw was still writing.

▪ A spondee [- -] as in *they think*, and a dactyl [-uu] as in *nautical*, are prosodical terms.

▪ *Thug* is given an upper-case "T" because Shaw remembers its Hindi origin, referring to the professional bands of murderers in India who strangled their victims.

▪ "The Bing Boys" were Alfred Lester and George Robey, who, with Violet Loraine, were playing in the show of that name by George Grossmith and Fred Thompson (lyrics by Clifford Grey, music by Nat Ayer) at the Alhambra Palace. The show cheered many a tired soldier back from the trenches, and its hit songs "If You Were the Only Girl in the World," and "Another Little Drink Won't Do Us Any Harm" were popular for years.

4 November 1917

SOMETHING LIKE A HISTORY OF ENGLAND AT LAST* [C2150]

THIS book, and Mr. Maurice Hewlett's "Hodgiad," raise hopes that the next generation may learn something of what it needs to know about the history of its own country. Hitherto historians have laid hands on the schoolboy, and assumed that their business was to qualify him as a professional historian, just as the classical pedants assumed that their business was to make him a professional grammarian. In my time they always began their histories by saying that true history is not a record of reigns and battles, but of peoples. They then proceeded to give ten times as much information about the reigns and the battles as the older historians, like Robertson, who, in his history of Mary Queen of Scots, introduced an unavoidable allusion to Rizzio with an elaborate apology for mentioning a thing so abysmally beneath "the dignity of history" as an Italian who was only

---

* "A Short History of England." By G. K. Chesterton. (Chatto and Windus. 5 s.)

a professional man. Every page of Mr. Hewlett's "Queen's Quair" would have made Robertson blush all over. But I think Robertson had more sense than Macaulay, because he recognized that history, as he understood it, was not a common man's business. Macaulay knew that modern democracy was making history a very important part of a common man's business; but he does not seem to have considered that our common democrats must, if they are to vote with any intelligence and exercise any real power, know not only the history of their own country, but that of all the other countries as well. Otherwise he would have bethought him that it is utterly impossible for common men to learn all these histories in such detail as he gives of his little parliamentary corner of the reigns of Charles II., James II., and William III., whose alliance with the Pope shot forward a gleam of humour (which Macaulay rather missed) over so much subsequent chalked-up polemic in Ulster. Even if you find Macaulay so very readable that you waste on his history the time you should spend on more pregnant documents, the one thing that you do not learn from him is English history.

Mac (if I may thus familiarly abbreviate him) did not improve matters by pointing out how unimportant were kings and queens compared with Hodge and Tom, Dick and Harry. It was not that when he came to the point he had nothing particular to say about Hodge and the rest, and became obsessed with the insignificant proceedings of a parliamentary dodger entitled Halifax, who, though too intelligent to be a good party man, was much less interesting than his merry monarch. It was rather that Hodge and the rest are not really a bit more important than their masters. The notion that the village champion metabolist, who for a wager consumes a leg of mutton, a gallon of beer, and a hundred oysters at one sitting, is any more important than the king who ate too many lampreys and was never seen to smile again, is much stupider than the contrary notion that what the king does matters a great deal and what the peasant does matters not at all. England's kings and cardinals were the most important people in England until they were supplanted by England's capitalists: the only wonder about the peasants is that they so helplessly let the kings and cardinals and capitalists do what they liked with them.

*   *
*

No. What the common man wants is not a history of the kings or the priests, or the nobs or the snobs, or any other set, smart or slovenly, but a vigorously comprehended and concisely presented history of epochs. Nearly fifteen years ago, in a play called "John Bull's Other Island," I showed an inspired (and consequently silenced) Irish priest saying to a couple of predatory commercial adventurers that "for four wicked centuries the world has dreamed this foolish dream of efficiency; and the end is not yet. But the end will come." If anyone had asked me then why I fixed that date (to do the British public and the critics justice, nobody ever did), I should not have been able to refer them to any popular history for an explanation. In future I shall be able to refer them to Mr. Chesterton's. For Mr. Chesterton knows his epochs, and can tell you when the temple became a den of thieves, though he leaves out half the kings and gives never a date at all. Far from being discursive, as the critics are saying, he is at once the most concise and the fullest historian this distressful country has yet found.

*   *

*

I hope I am not expected to write a brilliant review of Mr. Chesterton: I might as well try to write a comic review of Mark Twain. There is nothing worth saying left to be said of his book, because he has said it all himself: he is too good a husbandman to leave much for the gleaners. Let me therefore ask him for another chapter in his next edition. I can even give him subjects for two chapters.

The first is the establishment of the party system in Parliament at the end of the seventeenth century. If Mr. Chesterton will discuss this with everyone he meets, from Cabinet Ministers to cobblers, he will discover that nobody has the least idea of what the party system is, and that nobody will take the trouble to find out, because everybody is convinced that he knows already. "You will always have the party system," they will say: "there will always be Conservatives and Progressives: it is human nature." This misunderstanding is the mask under which the system secures toleration. The party system is just two centuries old. Before it was established there were Whigs and Tories, Cavaliers and Roundheads, Papists and Lutherans, Lancastrians and Yorkists, barons and burgesses, Normans and Saxons, Romans and primitive Sinn Feiners; but there was no party system. And to this add that though our municipal councillors include Home Rulers and Unionists, Free Traders and Tariff Reformers, Churchmen and Dissenters, the party system does not exist in local government, and could not possibly establish itself there, because the constitution and procedure of the local authorities is less adapted to it than a lathe to churning butter. On a local public authority a man can vote on the merits of the measure before him and not on the question whether his party will remain in power or not, because his party is not in power: the public authority is in power. There is no Cabinet, no appeal to the country, no monopoly of administration by any one party. When the Chairman of a Committee brings forward a measure and is defeated, he does not resign: he only sulks; and his Committee goes on as before. The ablest members of the body are always in full activity side by side, no matter how furiously they may differ on politics, religion, or any other controversial subject.

*   *

*

To the wretched members of the House of Commons this seems too good to be true. There the ablest man in the House may be excluded from office and condemned to barren criticism for twenty years if he is in Opposition, and if the elections during that period produce "no change." He never votes on the merits of the measure before the House: he must vote against the very Bill he will himself presently introduce if he comes into office through defeating it; and he must vote for revolutionary measures which he will drop like hot potatoes if a defeat of the Government places him in a position to carry them out himself. He may be noted for the activity of his intellect outside the House, demonstrating it by the alertness with which he keeps up to date in philosophy, science, and art; yet inside the House he must, as a party man, appear a Philistine, an ignoramus, a reactionary, without character enough to rise to the selfish stability of an idiot. And unless he is a party man, he has not the faintest chance of ever taking part in any administration. If he is suspected of having any other price than a place in the Government when his side is in power—if he will once consent to the other side doing the right thing, or hesitate to support his own side when it is bent on doing the wrong thing, he is politically lost. He has, in that case, no more chance of office, or even of a party seat, than Mr. Chesterton, or Mr. Sidney Webb, or Mr. Maurice Hewlett, or than Ruskin or Carlyle had or than any other person who is public spirited instead of party spirited, who has less respect for the party game than for golf or skittles, and who, like Hamlet, "lacks ambition," and curses the divine spite that would lay on him the burden of straightening a world out of joint.

The introduction of this amazing system under the pressure of a European conflict prototypical of the present war was, in point of its effect in establishing the parliamentary power of the modern plutocratic oligarchy, epoch making; and as such it demands its place in Mr. Chesterton's history. It made Walpole possible; and it made any

other sort of man than Walpole impossible except in frightful emergencies: that is, too late. It was by far the most revolutionary act of
the glorious, pious, and immortal Dutchman to whom England was
nothing but a stick to beat Louis XIV., and who found that without
the party system the stick would break in his hand as fast as he
could splice it. It was invented and suggested to him by an English
nobleman educated abroad; and no English nobleman educated at
home has ever been able to understand it. Marlborough,who succeeded to William's throne under cover of Anne's petticoats, understood it so little that he tried to drop it until he was driven back to it,
still without understanding it, by the same pressure of the Roi
Soleil.

*   *

*

The second chapter which Mr. Chesterton's history lacks is a description of the establishment of the modern police by Peel, who thus
broke that weapon of the riot which the workers had often used much
more effectively than they have since used the vote. Without that new
force the nineteenth century, rightly perceived by Mr. Chesterton to
have been the most villainous and tyrannous period in recorded history, could never have consummated its villainy in the full conviction
that it was the proud climax of progress, liberty, and leaping and
bounding prosperity. When its attention was drawn by some sensational horror to the cruellest and most bigoted of its own laws, it called
them mediæval, and believed it. What a theme for Mr. Chesterton!

Editor's Notes

- This review first appeared in the *Observer*, 4 November 1917, 3:3–4 with
the subscription: "Reviewed by Bernard Shaw." There is no indication when
it was written. It was subsequently reprinted in Bernard Shaw, *Pen Portraits
and Reviews* (1931), the only alterations being the omission of inverted commas around titles, and the removal of periods after "Charles II.," and so forth.
- G. K. Chesterton (see above, 331–32).
- Maurice [Henry] Hewlett (1861–1923), English novelist, poet and essayist. He was writer of successful historical romances such as *Richard Yea and
Nay* (1900) and *The Queen's Quair* (1904); but Shaw also refers here to his
long narrative poem (in twelve books) published in 1916 as *The Song of the
Plow*, a mythic consideration of the lot of the agricultural laborer, which
celebrates

Hodge the plowman, ridging the crest
Under the stars with his oxen-team.

- Thomas Robertson D.D., minister of Dalmeny published *The History of Mary Queen of Scots, including an examination of the writings which were ascribed to her* in Edinburgh in 1793.
- [David] Rizzio (?1533–1566), Italian courtier and musician who, entering the service of Mary Queen of Scots in 1561, soon became her favorite, was appointed private foreign secretary in 1564, and negotiated her marriage with Darnley in 1565. The latter's jealousy over Rizzio's influence with Mary and his strong political power caused him to plot Rizzio's assassination in the palace of Holyrood.
- Macaulay (see above, 119–20).
- It was Henry I of England (1068–1135) who expired on 1 December 1135 from feasting on too many lampreys (eel-like fish) after a day of hunting.
- Shaw refers to the fourth act of *John Bull's Other Island* (1904), where Father Keegan speaks to Tom Broadbent and Larry Doyle.
- Sidney Webb (see above, 139).
- Ruskin (see above, 65).
- Carlyle (see above, 128).
- [Sir Robert] Walpole [earl of Orford] (1676–1745), English statesman. He became first lord of the treasury and chancellor of the exchequer in 1715. The recently-crowned King George I (who could not speak English) was bored by parliamentary proceedings, and left Walpole to chair a small group of ministers, which was the forerunner of today's Cabinet. Walpole is therefore regarded as England's first prime minister. He was on close terms with the Prince of Wales [later George II], and, in addition to his earldom was presented with 10 Downing Street, which has been the permanent London home of British prime ministers ever since. Shaw had no love for Walpole whom he described in his Preface to *Plays Unpleasant* as "unable to govern without corruption."
- The "glorious, pious, and immortal Dutchman" was William III (1650–1702), king of Great Britain and Ireland (with Mary) from 1689. Because of the lurking fear in the British mind of a resurgence of Catholicism in England, when James II began his policy of Catholicization in 1685, William was invited by seven British notables (the "Immortal Seven") to become king, and protect Protestant liberties in England. James fled to France, the throne was declared vacant, and William and Mary were proclaimed king and queen jointly in February 1689. As Shaw implies, William's primary concern thereafter was to mobilize British arms and money for the Continental war effort against Louis XIV, "Le Roi Soleil."
- [Sir Robert] Peel (see above, 77). Shaw's feeling comments on the breaking of the power of riots by the police force were no doubt reinforced by his own experiences thirty years earlier, when, on 13 November 1887 ("Bloody Sunday," as it came to be called), a mass meeting called in support of free speech in Trafalgar Square was brutally broken up by mounted police. Shaw,

who was one of the marchers, escaped in the confusion, but many demonstrators were injured, (one dying later), and Shaw attacked Sir Charles Warren (then commissioner of police) in the press.

9 February, 1918

HOW FREE IS THE PRESS?* [C2163]

"To release the truth against whatever odds, even if so doing can no longer help the Commonwealth, is a necessity for the soul," says Mr. Belloc. And again, "Those who prefer to sell themselves or be cowed, gain as a rule, not even that ephemeral security for which they betrayed their fellows; meanwhile they leave to us [journalists] the only permanent form of power, which is the gift of mastery through persuasion."

Now it is more than forty years since my first contribution to the press appeared in print; and I am not sure that this necessity of the soul to which Mr. Belloc testifies, thereby echoing Jeremiah (a Jew, I regret to say) who declared that the word was in his heart as a burning fire shut up in his bones, and he was weary with forbearing and could not stay, is really a necessity of *the* soul. I must ask whose soul? Certainly not that of your average journalist or of the man who swallows his articles as soothing syrup. The first necessity of such souls when truth is about, as it always is, is camouflage, or, better still, complete cover. I, like Mr. Belloc, and those heroes of the free press whom he celebrates in this book: Mr. Orage, the Chestertons, and himself, have conducted truth raids, and seen all England rush to the cellars every time. It takes a very hardy constitution to stand the truth. Is an evening with Ibsen as popular as an evening with Mary Pickford at the movies? A simple No is hardly emphatic enough. One feels the need of the French *Point!* so useful in similar emergencies to Molière.

Before I forget it—for I am going to wander considerably—let me say that Mr. Belloc's pamphlet is true enough within its own express limitations. It serves the press right, the parliament right, and our plutocratic humbugs right. But I think he lets the public off too easily;

* "The Free Press." By Hilaire Belloc. (Allen & Unwin. 2s. 6d. net.)

and as for the free press, by which he means specifically The New Age, The New Witness, and in general the coterie press, he is a bit of a flatterer. An amiable weakness; but still, a weakness.

The coterie press is no doubt a free press in a sense; and I have often availed myself of its freedom to say things I should not have been allowed to say elsewhere. When I want somebody to throw a stone at the Lord Mayor, or the Lord Chamberlain, or any other panjandrum, I do not offer six-and-eightpence to my solicitor to do it: I offer a shilling to a tramp. The tramp is free to throw the stone: the respectable solicitor is not. Similarly, when the missile is a literary one, I do not send it to The Times, I offer it to a coterie editor. He has the tramp's freedom. He is not afraid of the advertisers, because he has no advertisements. He is not afraid of the plutocrats, because he has no rich backers. He is not afraid of the lawyers, because he is not worth powder and shot. He is not afraid of losing his social position, because he is not in smart society, and would rather die than get into it. Sometimes he is not afraid of anything, because he has no sense.

In short, Mr. Belloc will say with some impatience, the coterie editor is free; and I do not alter that fact by explaining why he is free. *Parfaitement, cher Hilaire* (which I may translate as "Who deniges of it, Betsy?"); but does this freedom, this irresponsibility, carry with it any guarantee of liberality or veracity? Clearly not: all that it does is, within certain limits, to allow the coterie paper to be liberal and veracious if it likes. But if you come to that, do not Lord Northcliffe's millions set him free to attack and destroy people who could crush a coterie paper by a libel action or by setting Dora at it, if Lord Northcliffe liked? Let us not deceive ourselves: we are between the nether millstone of the press that is too poor to tell the truth and the upper one of the press that is too rich. Mr. Belloc says that the false-hood of the press operates more by suppression of truth than assertion of lies. Well, I am prepared to maintain that every coterie editor in the world suppresses more truth, according to his lights, than Lord Northcliffe. He perceives more. My fellow countryman, Lord North-cliffe, whom I do not know personally (otherwise how could I be free to be uncivil to him?) is not, for an Irishman, conspicuously intellec-tual, though he may pass in England; and it must be plain to everyone that his brother was far more completely and unreservedly sincere in his denunciation of the Germans as police-court murderers for actu-ally killing Englishmen in war, and in his conception of the British Museum as a comfortable place for his armchair and Turkey carpet, than any coterie paper has ever dared to be in any single sentence it has published. What happens is not that a certain born liar named Harmsworth publishes a paper to tell his lies in, and that a child of integrity named Belloc or Shaw publishes another to tell the utter truth. It is simply that Belloc and Harmsworth publish papers to say what they sincerely want to have said as far as the police will let them. Their success is according to the number of people who agree with them. Consequently, as Harmsworth's tastes are widespread, his paper catches on; the public rallies to him; he is made a peer; he makes and unmakes ministers and commanders as Warwick made and unmade kings; and he establishes his brother, in the middle of an epoch-making war, as chief of a national service on which our fate in the war will probably depend, without having to offer the public the smallest evidence that the said brother is capable of conducting a whelk-stall successfully. Belloc, on the other hand, having very select intellectual tastes, has presently to sell his paper as a coterie paper, and set up as a war prophet in the columns of the sort of paper he denounces as corrupt, in which employment his gains are like the stripes of Autolycus, mighty ones and millions.

That both Northcliffe and the coterie editor immediately find themselves entangled in the coils of their own circulation, and obliged, on pain of being unable to meet their engagements, to consult their readers' opinions as well as their own, does not leave the coterie editor with any advantage. I have belonged to too many coteries to have any illusions on this point. My correspondents frequently appeal to me to intervene in some public question on the ground that I am a fearless champion of the truth and have never hesitated to say what I think. I reply always, "Heaven save your innocence! If you only knew all the things I think and dare not say!"

Let us have a look at the general ethical character of Mr. Belloc's free press. His favorite example is The New Witness, *ci-devant* The Eye-Witness, founded by himself, and now edited by Mr. Gilbert K. Chesterton as *locum tenens* for Mr. Cecil Chesterton, who is in arms in defence of his country. Well, The New Witness is easily the wickedest paper in the world as far as my knowledge goes. G. K. C. as Antichrist has achieved a diabolical enormity which goes to the very verge of breaking down through over-acting. His policy is that of Count Reventlow (with the boot on the other leg, of course); but although Reventlow has a much stronger historical case (for what are the trumpery exploits of the new toy soldiers of the new toy kings of Prussia beside our terrific record of invasion, piracy, plunder, conquest, and arrogant claim to rule the waves as well as make Governor Generalships of all the earth for our younger sons?) he cannot touch Mr. Chesterton in skill as a pleader, or ferocity as a crusader. There is no "Vengeance is mine, saith the Lord" nonsense about Mr. Chesterton. For him, vengeance is the Napoleon of Notting Hill's. He calls on Kensington and Croydon and Tooting and Balham to wipe out the accursed races of Central Europe; to bind their kings in chains; to cast them into the abyss, as holy Michael cast Lucifer from Heaven. Not one chivalrous word escapes him when the Hun is his theme. We are to curse the Germans when they are up and kick them when they are down. To turn the page from Mr. Chesterton preaching hate against the Prussians to Mr. Ernest Newman extolling Beethoven and Bach is to turn from the blasphemies of a stage demon to the judgments of sanity and civilization.

Dare I ask Mr. Belloc why Mr. Chesterton tolerates Mr. Newman? He has almost boasted of his ignorance of and indifference to music. I have no inside knowledge of the matter; but I strongly suspect that The New Witness is as much in the hands of a moneyed interest as the Cocoa Press or the Northcliffe Press or any of the other journalistic ventures that grind the axes of the rich.

Let me hasten to add that, if my suspicion is well founded, the particular interest which supports Mr. Chesterton is as gloriously indifferent to his patriotic views on the war as he himself is to Mr. Newman's unpatriotic preference of Handel to Dr. Arne and of Mozart to Sir Henry Bishop. In fact, I drag the matter in expressly to show that Mr. Chesterton, by an extraordinary piece of luck, is really free to say what he likes about everything except music (which he does not want to say anything about); and this he would not be if the money behind the paper were political money or smart society money or commercial money. Therefore the diabolical element in Mr. Chesterton's gospel of murderous hate on a basis of our heavenly nature as opposed to the hellish nature of the Prussian, is quite wanton: he is as free to be bravely magnanimous, chivalrous, Christian, fair and reasonable before Europe, and contrite before history and Heaven, as he is to be just the opposite. Otherwise he would chuck The New Witness as he chucked The Daily News. What makes his choice frightfully wicked to me is that it is not natural choice but artistic virtuosity. He is not really a devil. He can no more hate the Kaiser than Shakespear could hate Iago or Richard. Mr. Belloc is a good hater: the proof is that though he is a humorist, there is not in this little book of his, launched as a torpedo at poor

Northcliffe, a single conscious joke. There are two unconscious ones. He speaks of "two dots arranged in a spiral" (let him arrange two dots in a spiral if he can); and he says that a newspaper report is less truthful than the thousand tongues of rumor because it tells the same thing simultaneously to a million people in the same words. And this is not a joke at all, because when all the witnesses tell the story in the same words, the case is sure to be a conspiracy. But Mr. Chesterton, in his wildest hymns of hate, will break into a joke on his top note, preferably some outrageous pun. He has actually written during the war a book called The Crimes of England, putting Reventlow's case ten times better than Reventlow could put it himself; and no Sinn Feiner alive can write on the oppression of Ireland as he does. Talk of his handling of the violated treaty of 1839, the scrap of paper! You should hear him on the Treaty of Limerick. To put it in the Irish way, his war articles are not devilry: they are pure devilment. To put it in the English way, they are art for art's sake: the political variety of Whistlerism.

So much for your free press at its freest. As Napoleon made war because he could do it so well, the brothers Chesterton write invective because they do it so well. Betrayed as they are at every step to connoisseurs, Gilbert by his humor, and Cecil by his good humor (his smile becomes sunnier at every epithet), they are taken at their word by readers who are not connoisseurs (if any such can read really artistic writing) and play The Corsican Brothers in the costume of The Christian Brothers. And in the strangest way, having no Northcliffe to forge chains for them, they forge chains for themselves, making rules for their artistic and intellectual games which finally leave them speechless on the most vital issues of the day. Take for example the case of the new Bishop of Hereford. Everybody knows the bishop's views on the Virgin Birth and the Resurrection. Everyone chuckled cynically over the solemn assurance of his ecclesiastical superior that there was no evidence that the postulant held any such views. Granted that "the capitalist press" had to allow its readers to gather the truth between the lines, still, it was bolder than The New Witness, which dared not print any lines to read between. The New Witness may not allude to Evolution, to the Virgin Birth, to the Resurrection, or even to the Garden of Eden, lest it should have to choose between modernism and patent bosh. It has laid on itself the fantastic bond that it must believe what Buffalmacco believed when he painted the walls of the Campo Santo in Pisa, and must forget what has been learnt since. When we are threatened, and indeed already oppressed, by a tyranny of pseudo-science worse than even the tyranny of pseudo-education, The New Witness must take the Inquisition's view of eugenics and welfare work, and dares not venture into argument because it would have to refer to later authorities than Aristotle and Thomas Aquinas, and thus get ahead of Buffalmacco. It has forbidden itself to talk a word of sense about Mr. Herbert Samuel, because Mr. Samuel is a Jew, and Buffalmacco must place him with Judas Iscariot in hell. The consequence is that it has to live on Buffalmacco's fat, so to speak, to an extent that may eventually make even the Chestertons unreadable. It is hard enough to keep up the interest of a journal even by the freest play upon the actual events of the current week in every department. But if you must ignore not only the current week, but the last three or four centuries, and dare not hint that the earth may be round, you are committing yourself to a literary *tour de force* which begins by being impossible and must end by being ridiculous.

The New Age, Mr. Belloc's other example of the free press, may be compared to the venture of a too clever painter who, finding the Academy and all the regular galleries closed to him, opens a Salon of the Rejected to provide an exhibition for himself. The experiment has been remarkably successful: Mr. Orage has secured a free pulpit for himself; and his contributors are often as readable as he. Even when he has to fill up with trash, it is not really worse than the average "middles" of his contemporaries, though it may be less plausible and trade-finished. But outside Mr. Orage's own notes the paper has no policy and no character. It is a hotch-potch, stimulating thought in general, but not prompting opinion like The Nation or The New Statesman, nor reflecting it like The Spectator. It cannot get things done any more than Notes and Queries can: it is probable that politicians pay much more attention to John Bull. Its freedom is the freedom of the explosive which is not confined in a cannon, spending itself incalculably in all directions.

Organized capital and Judaism do not trouble themselves much with The Freethinker, the organ of the atheists, or The War Cry, the organ of the Salvation Army. Yet the late editor of the Freethinker was not the same man in his private correspondence with Meredith as in his editorial columns. He knew quite well that the sort of atheist who called the Bethlehem stable The Pig and Whistle, not merely to change the atmosphere of the discussion, but with the quaintly snobbish notion that nothing miraculous could happen in a vulgar public house, was a danger to Secularism; yet he was not free to say so: too many of his subscribers would have suspected him of superstition, if not of downright Christianity, and abandoned him. The leaders of the Salvation Army know as well as old General Booth did that religion does not stand or fall with belief in the adventure of Jonah and the great fish, nor consist of a race for the prize of Heaven; but they dare not say so: they would be cast out as atheists by "some of our old folk." Those who pay the piper call the tune, unless the piper is a veritable Pied Piper whose tune no one can resist.

And here, I think, is the factor to which Mr. Belloc gives too little space in his book. There are no irresistible Pied Pipers; but the skill of the piper counts for what it is worth. No release from the pressure of capitalism can make an editor free if he lacks character and judgment. If he has them, he can make a capitalist paper as free as a coterie paper. When The Times makes a series of *gaffes* culminating in the rejection of the Lansdowne letter, it is not because advertizers or proprietors have dictated them, but because the editor, though he may be stuffed with all sorts of excellent qualities, does not know what to put in and what to leave out in his correspondence columns. Mr. Massingham, in the teeth of his proprietors and of all the vested interests, political and commercial, which controlled the daily papers he edited, succeeded in changing the politics and outlook of The Star and The Chronicle from the Whig-ridden Socialist Radicalism of the 'eighties to the Collectivist Progressivism of the 'nineties. Capital has neither a body to be kicked nor a soul to be damned: advertizers are only a mob, without sense enough, as Mr. Belloc points out, to use the opportunities offered them by the highly specialized coterie papers. An editor is a man: something much more formidable. Mr. Belloc himself has achieved the astounding and hardly sane feat of establishing, with other people's capital, a press organ of the Holy Roman Empire in London in the twentieth century. He is driven to conclude that the able-minded editor with convictions will finally beat the whole field, and destroy the forces that now make his strife so inhumanly hazardous.

My own most polemical writings are to be found in the files of The Times, The Morning Post, The Daily Express, The World, and The Saturday Review. I found out early in my career that a Conservative paper may steal a horse when a Radical paper dare not look over a hedge, and that the rich, though very determined that the poor shall read nothing unconventional, are equally determined not to be preached at themselves. In short, I found that only for the classes would I be allowed, and indeed tacitly required, to write on revolutionary assumptions. I filled their columns with sedition; and they filled my pockets (not very deep ones then) with money. In the press as in other departments the greatest freedom may be found where there is least talk about it.

G. B. S.

Editor's Notes

- The above review was first published in the *Nation* 22 (9 February 1918): 599–600, 602, and reprinted in *Pen Portraits and Reviews* (1931), the only alteration being the omissions of periods after "Mr." Again there is no indication of when the review was written.
- [Joseph] Hilaire [Pierre René] Belloc (1870–1953), French-born British poet, novelist, biographer, historian, and travel writer. In 1902 he became a naturalized British subject, and a Liberal M.P. for Salford in 1906, but did not run for re-election in 1910, having becoming disillusioned with the party system and what he considered the continual encroachment on individual liberty caused by social legislation. His books *The Party System* (1911) (written with Cecil Chesterton), and *The Servile State* (1912) speak to these issues. His first books, *Verses and Sonnets* and *The Bad Child's Book of Beasts* were published in 1896. He also wrote novels (many illustrated by G. K. Chesterton), nonsense stories, numerous travel books, and biographies. Belloc's meeting with G. K. Chesterton in 1900 led to a collaboration on a number of works that recorded their common beliefs and interests, and made Shaw (who in his time debated with both men) nickname the duo "The Chesterbelloc."
- Shaw ironically "regrets" to confess that Jeremiah was a Jew because of Belloc's anti-Semitism. In a 1925 letter to Augustin Hamon, Shaw accused both Chesterton and Belloc of professing anti-Semitism "as a sort of Catholic literary affectation."
- In Jeremiah 20:9, when the prophet has been put in the stocks by Pashur the chief priest, he vainly resolves not to proclaim the word of the Lord any more: "Then I said, I will not make mention of him, nor speak any more in his name. But *his word* was in mine heart as a burning fire shut up in my bones, and I was weary with forbearing, and I could not stay."
- Orage (see above, 228).
- Mary Pickford [stage name of Gladys Marie Smith] (1893–1979), American stage and motion-picture actress, and motion-picture producer. Born in Toronto, Canada, she began her movie career in 1913 (Shaw uses the American slang word "movie" which appeared at the same date), playing in *The Violin Maker of Cremona* for the Biograph Company (which became Paramount Pictures) under the direction of D. W. Griffith. At the time of Shaw's

remark, Mary Pickford's highly acclaimed performances in *Rebecca of Sunny-brook Farm* and *Poor Little Rich Girl* (both 1917) would be fresh in the minds of his readers. In fact, she became one of the most popular stars in the history of motion pictures, and was known by the nickname "America's Sweetheart." She retired from the screen in 1933, and her autobiography *Sunshine and Shadow* was published in 1955.

▪ Shaw had declined in humorous exasperation a request that he should contribute to the Socialist magazine *New Age* when it was first founded in October 1894 (see *Collected Letters 1874–1897*, 455). Subsequently, however, the journal was purchased by Orage and Holbrook Jackson (with Shaw's help: see above, 228), and published the work of Shaw, the Chestertons, Arnold Bennet, and so forth.

▪ *The New Witness* (see above, 332).

▪ "Who deniges of it, Betsy?" (see above, 318).

▪ Lord Northcliffe and his brother (see above, 335).

▪ "Dora" is the Defence Of the Realm Act.

▪ The "national service" of which Viscount Rothermere became chief (from 1917 to 1918) was the Air Ministry.

▪ Shaw's repudiation of himself as a truth-teller ("Heaven save your innocence! If you only knew all the things I think and dare not say!") is an echo of Professor Higgins in *Pygmalion:*

MISS EYNSFORD HILL. If people would only be frank and and say what they really think!
HIGGINS [*relapsing into gloom*] Lord forbid!
MRS. EYNSFORD HILL [*taking up her daughter's cue*] But why?
HIGGINS. What they think they ought to think is bad enough, Lord knows; but what they really think would break up the whole show. Do you suppose it would be really agreeable if I were to come out now with what *I* really think?

▪ Autolycus is the amusing, thievish, and witty peddler in Shakespeare's *The Winter's Tale*. When feigning distress upon the highway, he tells the foolish Clown (whose pocket he is later to pick) to help him pluck off his remaining rags:

CLO. Alack, poor soul! thou hast need of more rags to lay on thee, rather than have these off.
AUT. O, sir, the loathsomeness of them offends me more than the stripes I have received, which are mighty ones and millions.

▪ Count [Ernst zu] Reventlow (1869–1943) was an intensely chauvinistic German journalist on the staff of the *Deutsche Tagezeitung* during the First World War.

▪ Ernest Newman (1868–1959), English music critic. He contributed at this time musical criticism to the *New Witness* , but later became successively music critic of the *Manchester Guardian*, the *Birmingham Post*, and from 1920 of the *Sunday Times*. His work was witty, elegant, and factual. Shaw had disputed with Newman (over a work of Richard Strauss) three years previously in the pages of the *Nation*; but more recently had written him admiring letters. Perhaps Shaw's commendation was because of Newman's preference for the German-born composer [George Friederic] Handel (1685–1759) over the Englishman [Thomas Augustine] Arne (1710–78); or the Austrian genius Mozart (see above, 240) over the Londoner, Sir Henry [Rowley] Bishop (1786–1855); or perhaps it was because of Newman's deep insight into the works of Wagner, whose biography he published in four volumes from 1933 to 1937.

- The [London] Treaty of 1839 (see above, 285, 318).
- William III beat his rival James II in Ireland at the Battle of the Boyne in July 1690; but some Catholic soldiers held out, and the last major battle of the 1688–91 war was fought at Aughrim on 12 July 1691. The Treaty of Limerick was signed on 3 October 1691. It ostensibly gave Catholics the same liberties of religion as they had enjoyed under Charles II; but free exercise of religion was not specifically promised, nor were there any safeguards for Catholic property. Indeed, so badly drawn up was the treaty, and so much was altered in the ratification process that its terms were allowed to be distorted, which led to great bitterness between the English and the Irish.
- *The Corsican Brothers* was a melodrama translated from the French by Dion Boucicault and first produced in 1848. It contained a famous duel scene; and Charles Kean made a great showing at the Princess's Theatre playing both Louis dei Franchi and his twin, Fabien, who avenges Louis' death.
- The Right Reverend Herbert Hensley Henson (1863–1947) became the new bishop of Hereford on 1 January 1918. His controversial views on the Apostle's Creed led to a dialogue with "his ecclesiastical superior," Randall Thomas Davidson (1848–1930), the Archbishop of Canterbury, caused several prelates to protest in print, and a number, including the bishops of Winchester and Worcester to decline to take part in his confirmation.
- [Cristofani Buonamico, called] Buffalmacco (1262?–1351) is probably not the artist who "painted the walls of the Campo Santo in Pisa." The frescoes there (which represent landscape-rich scenes from the life of Job) were more probably the work of Taddeo Gaddi (active c. 1320–66). Buffalmacco is credited with the design for the windows of the chapel of Saint Louis in San Chiara, Assisi.
- The encyclopedic Greek philosopher Aristotle (384–322 B.C.) exerted an enormous influence on medieval theology, especially through the Italian Scholastic philosopher and theologian [Saint] Thomas Aquinas (1225–74), who published commentaries on him, thus making Aristotle's thought both available and acceptable to Christendom. In his philosophical writings Aquinas combined and reconciled Aristotle's scientific rationalism with the Christian doctrines of faith and revelation.
- Herbert Louis, first Viscount Samuel (1870–1963), English Liberal states-

man and philosophical writer. He entered parliament in 1902, and held a number of different offices, including postmaster general (1910 and 1915), and Home Secretary (1916, and 1931–32). He was high commissioner for Palestine from 1920 to 1925. He was also the author of a number of philosophical works, such as *Practical Ethics* (1935), *Belief and Action* (1937), and *In Search of Reality* (1957). At the time of writing the above review Shaw was of the opinion that Samuel should succeed Lloyd George as prime minister (see *Collected Letters 1911–1925*, 529–31).

▪ *Notes and Queries*, an academic journal for readers, writers, collectors, and librarians began in 1849, and still continues.

▪ *John Bull* (see above, 348).

▪ The "late editor of the Freethinker" was Charles Bradlaugh (see above, 83). As a persecuted atheist he sought and received sympathy from George Meredith (see above, 94–95), particularly after the De Rin case (with Bradlaugh as plaintiff), which toiled its way through the courts for three years (from 1867 to 1870.) As an atheist Bradlaugh was not allowed to take the oath, which meant that he couldn't testify; and although he won the case, it cost him enough financially to ruin his business, and turn him to lecturing and politics.

▪ "The Pig and Whistle" was the name given to numerous British public houses.

▪ [William] Booth (1829–1912), English religious leader. Converted to Christianity in 1844, he became a Methodist New Connexion minister on Tyneside; but his restlessness and desire to carry out more thoroughly his Christian witness caused him to begin his London's East End "Christian Mission" in 1865, which developed into the Salvation Army in 1878.

▪ The "Lansdowne letter" was written by [Henry Charles Keith Petty-Fitzmaurice], fifth marquis of Lansdowne (1845–1927) English statesman. From 1915 to 1916 he sat (without portfolio) in Asquith's coalition cabinet; but his letter published in the *Daily Telegraph* on 29 November 1917 advocating a negotiated peace, was denounced by Lloyd George as defeatist, and virtually concluded Lansdowne's political career. The *Times* justified its own rejection of the letter by publishing the contemptuous refusal of the government to discuss the document, and the adverse reports of individual members of Parliament, and of the National Party, which deplored "that any British journal should have published a document which was calculated to impair the unity of the nation." They also reported that the letter was regarded in Germany as a "sign that the Entente recognizes the struggle to be hopeless;" emphasized the hopes it raised in Austria, and described it as a weapon for the Italian pacifists (see the *Times*, 3 December 1917).

▪ [Henry William] Massingham (1860–1924), English journalist. In 1888 he joined the staff of the *Star* (recently founded by T. P. O'Connor). In spite of Shaw's claim that he was allowed to publish his views in the right-wing press, Massingham must have remembered differently. When the latter was assistant editor to T. P. O'Connor, he hired Shaw in 1888 as a political writer; but Shaw resigned because of O'Connor's objection to his socialistic attacks on

Tory figures! In 1890 Massingham became editor of the *Star*; a year later he became editor of the *Labour World*; he joined the *Daily Chronicle* in 1892, and became its editor from 1895 to 1899. At the time of the above review he was editor of the *Nation*, for which Shaw was writing, a task he had assumed in 1907, and which he held until a year before his death.

1 November 1919

SAMUEL BUTLER: THE NEW LIFE REVIEWED* [C2252]

In the great tradition of British criticism, a book to review is an occasion to improve. Even if it were not so, the life of Samuel Butler would be an irresistible temptation to any writer with an ounce of homily in him. It is a staggering object-lesson in the villainy (no milder expression is adequate) of our conventional clergyman schoolmaster education, and of the family and class life to which it belongs.

Mr. Festing Jones's memoir, though one of the most complete ever written, is nevertheless not quite complete. Butler told the story of his childhood so frightfully well in his novel, "The Way of All Flesh" that Mr. Festing Jones has recognised the hopelessness of attempting to do that work again and do it better. It cannot be done better: "The Way of All Flesh" is one of the summits of human achievement in that kind; and there is nothing for it but to require from the reader of the memoir as a preliminary qualification that he shall read the autobiography in the novel. Indeed a good deal of Mr. Jones's memoir will be only half intelligible to anyone who has not already come to know Butler's parents as the detestable Theobald and his Christina, whose very names proclaim that they had made their gods as hateful to their son as themselves. Butler is the only man known to history who has immortalized and actually endeared himself by parricide and matricide long drawn out. He slew the good name (and it was such a very good name!) of his father and mother so reasonably, so wittily, so humorously, and even in a ghastly way so charitably,

---

* "Samuel Butler: Author of Erewhon (1835–1902.) A Memoir." By Henry Festing Jones. (London: Macmillan) 2 vols. 42s. net.

that he convinced us that he was engaged in an execution and not in a murder.

But the moral of this memoir is that not even genius can come through such an education as Butler's with its mind unwounded and unlamed. It was his genius, always breaking through to the truth, that revealed to him whilst he was still a boy that this devoted father to whom he could never be too grateful, and this pious angel mother in whose watchful care he was so fortunate, were at best a pair of pitiably perverted and intimidated nobodies, and that he hated them, feared them, and despised them with all his soul. Unfortunately the matter could not stop there. Butler was naturally affectionate to the point of being gulled by heartless people with ridiculous ease. As a child he had sought for affection at home, only to have his feelings practised on by his mother to wheedle confidences from him and have him beaten by his father, who trained him exactly as if he were a performing animal, except that he did not teach him anything amusing. But the child went on assuming that he loved his dear parents, and that they were all happy together in their domestic affection, spotless respectability, and unchallenged social precedence. When he realized how he had been duped and how he had duped himself, he reacted to the opposite extreme with such violence that he set up as a rule in the art of life that the stupidest and most mischievous of mistakes is to force yourself or humbug yourself into liking things that are really repugnant or uninteresting to you. Accordingly, all through this memoir we find Butler "hating," on principle, everything that was not immediately congenial and easy to him at the very first taste. He "hated" Plato, Euripides, Dante, Raphael, Bach, Mozart, Beethoven, Blake, Rossetti, Tennyson, Browning, Wagner, Ibsen, and in fact everyone who did not appeal to his palate instantly as a lollypop appeals to the palate of a child. The exception was Handel, because he had learned to like Handel's music in the days of his childish illusion; but I suspect that if he had never heard Handel's music until after he had set up his rule he would have denounced him as a sanctimonious drum major, and classed him as one of The Seven Humbugs of Christendom. It is true that these repeated denunciations of great men as impostors and humbugs are made with a tart humour which betrays a subconscious sense of their folly, and saves Butler from being classed as a vulgar nil-admirarist; but the trick is none the less tiresome and even sinister, because it is plain that Butler did seriously narrow his mind and paralyze his critical powers by refusing to take any trouble to find out what our greatest teachers were driving at, or to face the drudgery of learning their peculiar idiom. For a man with his love of music to begin with gavottes and minuets and never get any further (for that is what it came to) was monstrous. I risk his rising from the grave to smite me when I add, as I must, that he never said a word about Handel worth reading; he liked the hailstones running along the ground and the sheep going astray, every one to his own way; but Handel could hardly have said more to him on that than "Thank you for nothing." It is flatly impossible to believe that a man who could see no greatness in Bach was really admiring what is great in Handel, however sincerely he may have relished Handel's more popular vein.

Then, again, Butler's public manners were atrocious. Privately, he was most courteous, most considerate, if anything too delicate in his conscientiousness. But if he did not like a man's public opinion and work, or the man did not like his: in a word, if he did not feel perfectly happy with him, he treated him as a moral delinquent, derided him, insulted him, and even cut him in the street. In other words, he behaved exactly as his father would have behaved if his father had had courage and wit as well as thoroughly bad civic manners. In the war of cliques which never ceases in London, he heaped scorn on the Darwin clique, and not only resented the shallow snobbery which led it to underrate him, and to persuade Darwin himself that it was beneath his dignity to clear up a very simple misunderstanding which had led Butler quite naturally to accuse him of controversial foul play, but retaliated in kind. For there was inevitably a Butler clique as well as a Darwin clique. Butler's bite was so powerful that he may be said to have been a clique in himself in so far as he acted in the clique spirit; but with Miss Savage, Festing Jones, Gogin, Pauli, not to mention Emery Walker, Sydney Cockerell, and the steadily growing outer ring of Butlerites of whom I was one, he was by no means alone *contra mundum*. As the best brains were always with Butler, Darwin, a simple-souled naturalist with no comprehension of the abyss of moral horror that separated his little speciality of Natural Selection from Butler's comprehensive philosophic conception of Evolution, may be pardoned for his foolish estimate of Butler as "a clever unscrupulous man," and for countenancing the belittling of him by Huxley and Romanes that now seems so ridiculous. They really did not know any better. But in the selfsame spirit, without the selfsame excuse, Butler and his clique belittled poor Grant Allen, one of the most amiably helpful men that ever lived, and one, moreover, who recognised Butler as a man of genius, and declared that he "bore its signet on his brow." Butler, with unconscious but colossal arrogance, simply damned his impudence, denying that there was any such thing as genius, and heaping scorn on Allen because he was not at once ready to declare that Butler was right about evolution, and Darwin a disingenuous sciolist. Miss Savage, pretending to forget Allen's name, wrote of him as Allen Grant; and Mr. Festing Jones leaves the readers of his memoir to infer that he was an unamiable and rather contemptible man. All the more annoying this because Grant Allen had the same grievance as Butler: he could not live by his serious scientific work, and had to write novels and stories to keep himself and his family alive.

BUTLER'S BIGOTRY.

The truth is, we all did that sort of thing in those days; and we are doing it still. Nine-tenths of English criticism to-day is either log-rolling or bad manners; and at the root of the evil are pure snobbery, bigotry, and intolerance. I will not say that Butler was as bad as his father, because, with his greater powers and opportunities, he was very much worse. Ardent Butlerite as I am, I cannot deny that Butler brought a great deal of his unpopularity on himself by his country-parsonage unsociability and evangelical bigotry. One does not get rid of that bigotry by merely discarding the Resurrection and making pious people laugh against their wills with such sallies as "Resist God and he will flee from you," or "Jesus: with all thy faults I love thee still." Bigotry in a parson is at least not unexpected and not unnatural if he is in earnest about the 39 articles; but in a rampant anti-clerical like Butler it tempts us to say that as he brought so much of the worst of the Church with him when he came out of it he might as well have stayed in it to please his father.

Still, when all is said that can be said against Butler, the fact remains that when he was important he was so vitally important, and when he was witty he was so pregnantly witty, that we are forced to extend an unlimited indulgence to his weaknesses, and finally to embrace them as attractions. His excessive and touchy self-consciousness; his childish belief that everything that happened to him, no matter how common and trivial, was interesting enough to be not only recorded for the sake of an authentic human document but sold to the public as *belles lettres*; his country parsonage conviction that foreigners with their quaint languages, and working-class people with their ungentleman-

like and unladylike dialects, were funny creatures, whose sayings were
to be quoted like those of clever children; his patronizing and petting of
his favorites and his snubbing and cutting of his aversions: all these,
with his petulant and perverse self-limitation and old-bachelorism,
would have damned fifty ordinary men; yet they were so effectually
redeemed by belonging to Butler, and in fact being Butler, that it never
occurs to Mr. Festing Jones to conceal, extenuate, or apologize for
them.

Those to whom Butler was a stranger did not forgive him so easily.
Take, for example, his "Alps and Sanctuaries." We have to read it to-
day, not only for the promise and beauty of its title, but for the sake of
the titbits it contains: in short, because it is by Butler. But barring
those titbits it is surely the silliest book ever written by a clever man.
Its placid descriptions of itineraries compared to which the voyages of
a motor 'bus from Charing Cross to Hyde Park Corner are chapters of
romance, and its promiscuous quotations from Handel, in which ele-
giac passages which might conceivably have been recalled by the
beauty of an Italian valley are not distinguished from toccata stuff that
reeks of the keyboard and of nothing else, explain only too fully why
the book was refused by the publisher who had rashly commissioned
it, and why its first sale did not reach 500 copies. No Butlerite was
surprised or offended when, buying a later book with a title which
suggested a pious pilgrimage, he had suddenly sprung on him a most
irreverent onslaught on Sir Benjamin Layard, whose only offence was
that he was a bigwig, and that to Butler a bigwig meant merely a silk-
stockinged calf to fix his teeth in; but Butlerites were few and strangers many; and strangers could not be expected to know that when you
bought a book by Butler you never got what you paid for. True, you got
something better; but then you did not want something better. A
bookseller who responded to an order for La Vie Parisienne by sending
The Methodist Times might establish a reputation as a humorist, but
he would hardly make a fortune in his business.

There were other ways in which Butler did not live up to his
professions. In Erewhon he would have been tried for the serious
offence of gullibility, and very severely punished. The Pauli case
would have put him quite beyond the pale of Erewhonian sympathy.
And Pauli would have been knighted for gulling Butler so successfully. It is all very well to call Butler's forbearance to Pauli delicacy;
but in any other man we should call it moral cowardice. I am not
sure that it was not something worse. The rectory-born lust for patronage and charity was in Butler's blood: he had absolutely no con-

science as to how he demoralised other people provided he could make them his pensioners. If Pauli, infamously pocketing his pension of £200 a year under pretence of penury when he was making £900 as a barrister and a mendicant whilst Butler was on the verge of bankruptcy, had avowed and asserted his independence, I verily believe Butler would have quarrelled with him at once. As it was, when death revealed the fraud, Butler's only regret was that Pauli was not alive to be forgiven. In that Butler was his father all over. Well might he make his prototype Ernest in "The Way of All Flesh," put his children out to nurse with a bargee on the ground that, if he kept them with him, an inexorable heredity would force him to treat them as badly as his father had treated him.

If these things are not firmly said about Butler, his example will corrupt the world. From idiotic underestimate and neglect of him we are already turning to deify him, in spite of his own warnings, as one who could do no wrong. The reviews of Mr. Jones's memoirs are as shameless in this matter as the memoir itself. Mr. Jones has, on principle, concealed nothing. He even gives the name of the witty and amiable French mistress whom Butler patronised incognito very faithfully but very cautiously for sixteen years, at the end of which he ventured to tell her who he was and where he lived, and admitted her to his circle (one gathers) for the four more years which elapsed before her death. Twenty years ago such a revelation might have pilloried Butler. To-day we steadily refuse to overhear Mr. Jones's communication. It is, by the way, a great pity that Butler did not carry out his intention of dealing with the question of marriage as he had dealt with evolution. His reiteration of the not very respectable old proverb that it is cheaper to buy the milk than to keep the cow did not, in spite of the French lady, do Butler justice, being obviously a relic of that shallow Hedonism which seemed to the mid-century Victorians to follow logically when they discovered that the book of Genesis is not a scientific account of the origin of species, and that the accounts given by the evangelists of the Resurrection do not tally so exactly as the depositions of police witnesses in Sinn Fein prosecutions. Instead of concluding that these things were not of the real substance of religion, and that it did not matter one straw to that real substance whether they believed or disbelieved this or that tradition or parable that had become connected with it, they still went on assuming that it mattered so tremendously that they could not get rid of the crudest and most utterly irrelevant miracle story without bringing down the whole ethical structure of religion with a crash. Those were the days when an army officer of my acquaintance said to me gravely, "I know for a fact that the rector's son behaved disgracefully with the house-maid; and you may tell me after that that the Bible is true if you like, but I shall not believe it." The alternative to believing silly things about God seemed to be blank materialist Hedonist atheism. Yet Rousseau had said a hundred years before, "Get rid of your miracles, and the whole world will fall at the feet of Christ." And there you have it. As Butler's education consisted in concealing Rousseau's religious discoveries from him, he imagined that he had lost his faith when he had only lost his superstitions, and that in getting rid of the miracles he had got rid of Christ, of God, of The Church, and of any obligations to pursue anything but his own pleasure. It was in this phase that he nicknamed his father Theobald and his mother Christina, and per-haps decided to buy his milk instead of keeping a cow. His mind was too powerful to be imposed on in that way for long: but it need not have been imposed on for five seconds if his University had treated Voltaire and Rousseau as classics and seers, instead of as "infidels." It was at Shrewsbury School and Cambridge that Canon Butler had been taught to pretend to his son that his mother was killed by "Ere-whon." That is, his public school and university education had incul-cated an ignorance more dense and dangerous than the ignorance of an illiterate ploughman. How silly it all seems now, except perhaps to the hundreds of Canon Butlers still corrupting their sons in our par-sonages, and probably beating them if they catch them reading Butler—Butler! who stood for the very roots of religion when Darwin was "banishing mind from the universe"!

DILETTANTE WEAKNESSES.

I cannot judge whether Mr. Festing Jones's exhaustive and very cleverly documented memoir is going to be one of the great British biographies or not. It interests me throughout; but then I knew Butler and many of the other persons with whom the two volumes deal. For strangers, possibly, the death of Miss Savage at the end of the first volume will make it hard for the second to be equally amusing. She was a most entertaining woman who had caught Butler's comedy style so well, and even assimilated his art of life so congenially, that but for her alert feminine touch Butler might be suspected of invent-ing her letters. Her stories and jokes are all first-rate. Butler is not at his brightest in his remorse for having been occupied with his own affairs instead of with hers: his affectionate feeling that he had treated her badly was, as he would probably have admitted if some robust person had taxed him with it, priggish and childish.

Besides, Butler's bolt is shot in the first volume. In the second he is no longer the great moralist of "Erewhon" and the forerunner of the present blessed reaction towards Creative Evolution, but a dryasdust dilettante fussing about Tabachetti and Gaudenzio di Ferrara, Shakespeare's Sonnets, and the authoress of the Odyssey. His shot about the Odyssey got home. All the pedants thought the attribution of the Odyssey to a woman monstrously improbable and paradoxical only because the Odyssey had always been thoughtlessly attributed to a man; but the moment the question was raised it became, to those who were really familiar with the two epics, not only probable but almost obvious that Butler had hit on the true secret of the radical and irreconcilable difference between the Odyssey and the Iliad. It was equally clear that he was right in his opinion that the first batch of Shakespeare's Sonnets was the work of a very young man. But who cared, outside the literary fancy? To the mass of people whose very souls' salvation depended on whether "Erewhon" and "Life and Habit" were sound or unsound it mattered not a dump who wrote the Odyssey, or whether Shakespeare was 17 or 70 when he wrote the Sonnets to Mr. W. H. And though Raphael's stocks were down heavily and Michael Angelo's not what they had been, yet the stocks of Tabachetti and Gaudenzio di Ferrara, whose works are not visible to us in England,were not sufficiently up to induce anyone to exchange. His other heroes, Giovanni Bellini and Handel, were very far from being overlooked or needing his assistance in any way, unless, indeed, he had struck a blow at the horrible festivals at which the scattered wheezings and roarings and screamings of four thousand Crystal Palace holiday-makers were making Handel's oratorios ridiculous. He missed that chance of a hook hit at the white chokers. He had nothing new to say about his two pets: he was only a Don Quixote with two Dulcineas. Meanwhile the intellectual and artistic world to which he was appealing was intensely interested in two new giants: Richard Wagner and Henrik Ibsen, the latter carrying on young Butler's battle against old Butler's ideals most mightily. And what had Butler to say about them? "Ibsen may be, and I dare say is, a very wonderful man, but what little I know of him repels me, and, what is worse, bores me." After not only saying this, but actually writing it, could Butler pretend that the worst we can conceive of his father the Canon or his grandfather the headmaster-Bishop in the way of dull arrogance, insolence, snobbery, pomposity, Podsnappery, ignorance half genuine, half wilful and malicious, were not squared and cubed in their gifted son and grandson? And again "Carlyle is for me too much like Wagner, of whom Rossini said that he has *des beaux moments mais des mauvais quarts d'heure*— my French is not to be trusted." Were we to be expected to listen to a man who had nothing better than that to say about the composer of The Ring twenty years after that super-homeric music epic had been given to the world? Surely we were entitled to reply that if Butler was too gross a Philistine or too insular an ignoramus to be civil to Wagner, he might at least have been just to Rossini, who, with unexpected and touching greatness of character, earnestly repudiated the silly anti-Wagner jibes attributed to him, and said to Wagner himself—Wagner being then the worst reviled musician in Europe, and Rossini classed as the greatest—that if it had been possible for serious music to exist in the Italian opera houses, he might have done something; for "*j'avais du talent.*" How disgraceful Butler's sneer appears in the light of such sublime self-judgment! No doubt Butler did not know of it; but he could have found it out in less time than it cost him to learn Shakespeare's Sonnets by heart. He could at least have held his tongue and concealed his ignorance and spite, which, please observe, was not provoked spite, but sheer gratuitous insular spite for spite's sake. His own experience should have warned him. Why did nobody say this to him, and produce that conviction of sin to which he was certainly accessible? Mr. Festing Jones, a serious and remarkable musician must have known that when Butler went on like this he was talking and writing vulgar and uppish nonsense. Perhaps he did venture occasionally; but he is too loyal a biographer to tell us about it.

Nothing more is needed to explain why Butler made no headway with his books about art and literature, and his records of his globe trottings. He accounted for it himself by saying that failure, like success, is cumulative, and that therefore it was inevitable that the longer he lived the less successful he should be. But the truth is that he spent the first half of his life saying all that he had to say that was important, and the second half dabbling in painting and music, and recording the thrills of "a week in lovely Lucerne" (much as the sisters he derided might have done), without getting beyond mediocrity in painting and slavish imitation in music, or gaining knowledge and sense of proportion in criticism. It is really appalling to learn that this man of genius, having received the very best education our most expensive and select institutions could give him, and having withal a strong natural taste for music and literature, turned from Bayreuth in mere ignorant contempt, and yet made every Christmas a pious pilgrimage to the Surrey pantomime, and wrote an anxiously careful account of its crude buffooneries to his musician friend. Is it to be wondered at that when an investment in house property obliged him to engage a man of the people as his clerk, this recruit, Mr. Alfred Emery Cathie, had to constitute himself his valet, his nurse, his keeper, and his Prime Minister and Executive all in one, and to treat him as the grown-up child his education had left him? Alfred is the real hero of the second volume, simply as a good-natured sensible Englishman who had been fortunate enough to escape the public schools and the university. To Butler he was a phenomenon to be quoted with patronising amazement and admiration whenever he exploded a piece of common sense in the Clifford's Inn lunatic asylum. What Butler was to Alfred (except a great man) will never be known. Probably a rare good old sort, quite cracked, and utterly incapable of taking care of himself. Butler was at least not ungrateful.

Throughout this later period we see Butler cramped and worried when he was poor, spoilt when he was rich, and all the time uneasy because he knew that there was something wrong, and yet could not quite find himself out, though his genius was always flashing through the fog and illuminating those wonderful notebooks with their queer strings of overrated trivialities, profound reflections, witty comments, humorous parables, and family jokes and jibes to please Gogin and Jones or annoy the Butlers.

THE FAULT OF EDUCATION.

Now why, it may be asked, do I, who said, and said truly, that Butler was "in his own department the greatest English writer of the latter half of the nineteenth century," now attack him in his grave by thus ruthlessly insisting on his failings? Well, I do so precisely because I want to carry on his work of demonstrating the falsehood and imposture of our "secondary education" and the mischief of treating children as wild beasts to be tamed and broken instead of as human beings to be let develop. Butler held up his father to ridicule and infamy, and exclaimed, "This is what your public school, your university, your Church, made of him." But the world replied, "Oh yes: that is all very well; but your father was a rotter and a weakling: all public school and university men are not like him." Now if, as is at last possible with this ruthlessly faithful memoir of him in our hands, we can say, "This is what your public school and your university and your country parsonage, made, not of a rotter and a weakling, but of a man of genius who was all his life fiercely on his guard against their influence," then we can go one better than Butler, and make his ghost cry "Splendid! Don't spare me. Rub it in; and more power to your elbow!"

For we must not deceive ourselves. England is still governed from Langar Rectory, from Shrewsbury School, from Cambridge, with their annexes of the Stock Exchange and the solicitors' offices. And even if the human products of these institutions were all geniuses, they would finally wreck any modern civilised country after maintaining themselves according to their own notions at the cost of the squalor and slavery of four-fifths of its inhabitants. Unless we plough up the moral foundations of these places and sow them with salt, we are lost. That is the moral of the great Butler biography.

G. B. S.

Editor's Notes

▪ The above review was first printed in the *Manchester Guardian* 1 November 1919, 7:1–7 followed in upper case letters by the phrase BY GEORGE BERNARD SHAW; and reprinted in Bernard Shaw, *Pen Portraits and Reviews* (1931), with the following alterations: quotations around titles disappear; the period is removed in the abbreviation "Mr."; "nil-admirarist" becomes "nil-admirerist"; the "yse" or "ise" endings take a "z" instead of an "s"; "to-day" becomes "today"; "country-parsonage" becomes "country parsonage"; "anti-clerical" becomes "anticlerical"; "motor 'bus" becomes "motor-bus"; and "Shakespeare" loses the final "e." P. N. Furbank began his review of Peter Raby's biography of Butler in the *Times Literary Supplement*, for 8 February 1991, by saying: "It gives one a pleasant feeling about the art of literary journalism that Bernard Shaw, reviewing Festing Jones's *Memoir* of Samuel Butler in 1919, for the *Manchester Guardian*, managed to say practically everything about Butler one could ever wish said—passionately, good-humouredly and beyond contradiction."

▪ When Shaw, who was busy writing *Back to Methuselah* and also involved in postwar politics, found time to write the above review is not clear; but that Butler was on his mind is proven by the fact that he invoked him in a letter to William Archer in the spring of 1919, and in October of that year, giving advice to T. D. O'Bolger who was writing a biography of Shaw to "work out the apparent inconsistencies" in Shaw's personal recollections, he said, "Read or re-read Butler's 'Way of All Flesh,' which is the authentic biography of a fated prophet" (*Collected Letters 1911–1925,* 637). It is precisely that injunction which is made at the beginning of the above review. In the light of his review, it is significant, too, that in the above letter Shaw cautioned O'Bolger to be kind to his parents, particularly George Carr Shaw, expressly telling his biographer, "I should like you to make a sympathetic figure of my father; but you will miss his character if you mention his drinking habit, and leave out his clinging to the notion that he was a teetotaller. He *was* a teetotaller morally: he had the deepest conviction of the misery and horror of drink of any man I ever met" (*Collected Letters 1911–1925,* 635).

▪ Henry Festing Jones (1851–1928), English lawyer, author, and composer. After graduating from Cambridge with a B.A. in 1873, he was articled to a solicitor, and qualified fully in 1876. On 10 January that year he made the acquaintance of Butler through another Cambridge man, and thereafter their friendship became close. They enjoyed concerts and traveled together and, under Butler's influence, Festing Jones tried his hand at composition, finally collaborating with Butler in *Gavottes, Minuets, Fugues & other short pieces for the piano* (1885). He also wrote about twenty-six songs (to the words of various poets) from 1886 to 1907; and in 1897 a comic opera for schools, *King Bulbous.* Festing Jones lived in Barnard's Inn and Staple Inn during Butler's lifetime. On the latter's death, he moved to Maida Vale and set up housekeeping with his sister. He edited *The Note Books of Samuel Butler* (1912), and was joint editor of the Shrewsbury Edition of Butler's complete works. Shaw recommends Festing Jones's *Samuel Butler, Author of Erewhon: a Memoir* in his preface to *Heartbreak House* (1921).

▪ Samuel Butler (see above, 306–7).

▪ It is ironic, and a tribute to Shaw's evenhandedness, that the list of Butler's "hates" includes many of Shaw's own loves, including Raphael, Bach, Mozart, Beethoven, Blake, Browning, Wagner, and Ibsen!

▪ [Eliza Mary Ann] Savage (1835?–85), English governess, needlewoman, and writer. After 1866, Eliza Savage lived with her parents at 22 Beaumont Street, London, and, during the early parts of that year and the next, she went daily as governess to the house of John Sumner, son of the archbishop of Canterbury, and uncle of Butler's friend Bertha Thomas. Introducing one of her pupils to a drawing-art class directed by a student from Thomas Heatherley's School of Art in Newman Street, she met Samuel Butler for the first time. According to him she knew him for some years before she conceived a liking for him; but in 1875 Butler believed that Eliza Savage wished to marry him (whereas he did not wish to marry her). She kept up a friendly, lively, and at times intimate correspondence with him until her death. Early in 1871 Butler submitted the MS of *Erewhon* to Miss Savage with a request that she read it and comment on it; and from this time until her death, Butler submitted everything he wrote to her scrutiny, and revised it in the light of her criticisms. She herself wrote only one book, *Art Needlework: a guide to embroidery in crewels, silks, appliqué; and a short history of the art of embroidery* (1877) under the pseudonym E. Masé. She also contributed articles to the *Drawing Room Gazette* and the *Woman's Gazette*.

- [Charles] Gogin (1844–1931), English painter and cartoonist, and friend of Samuel Butler. He first exhibited at the Royal Academy in 1871, but exhibited rarely; his last time being in 1893. His studio was in King Henry's Road, London, where Butler's burlesque opera *Narcissus* was rehearsed in 1888. In 1896 he painted Butler's portrait, which now hangs in the National Portrait Gallery. At one time he tried (without much success) to teach Butler to etch. He was Butler's companion on the latter's regular Sunday rambles in Surrey, and accompanied him to France.

- [Charles Paine] Pauli (?–1897), English lawyer and friend of Butler. Educated at Winchester School and Oxford, he went out to New Zealand and was helping on a sheep station near Christchurch in 1863 when he met Samuel Butler, and both men returned to England (Butler lending him his fare). Thereafter, Pauli became a lawyer and remained in London, lunching with Butler three times a week, never telling his friend where he lived, but always claiming that his law practice barely covered his expenses. In the winter of 1879 he contracted a severe cold, and died; after his death to Butler's indignation it transpired that Pauli had been quite wealthy, and had lived in a most fashionable part of London.

- [Sir] Emery Walker (1851–1933), English typographer and publisher. He founded (with Walter Boutall) the firm of Walker and Boutall which finally became Emery Walker Limited. Since its office was next door to the chambers of Samuel Butler, he formed a friendship with him; and since the works were at a Georgian house in Hammersmith, which was near Kelmscott House, the home of William Morris, he soon became friendly with him also; and their friendship developed into the famous business partnership, the Kelmscott Press (see above, 165). Shaw was also very friendly with Walker, and saw him once or twice a week for the last two decades of the nineteenth century, dining with him, going for walks with him, accompanying him to recitals, and visiting Italy with him and other friends in 1894. Emery Walker introduced Shaw to Samuel Butler on 15 November 1889. Stanley Weintraub records Butler's comment about that occasion, written in a notebook almost a decade later: "Emery Walker once brought [Shaw] up to see me, on the score that he was a great lover of Handel. He did nothing but cry down Handel and cry up Wagner. I did not like him and am sure that neither did he like me" (*Diary* 559).

- [Sir] Sydney [Carlyle] Cockerell (1867–1962), English director of the Fitzwilliam Museum and authority on illuminated manuscripts. His long connection with the fine arts began when he became secretary of the New Gallery and of the Arts and Crafts Society; after which he acted as secretary to William Morris and the Kelmscott Press (1892–1898), was a printing and engraving partner of Emery Walker (see above), and director of the Fitzwilliam Museum, Cambridge from 1908 to 1937. Under his directorship, the museum achieved a high standard of artistic display and was enormously enriched by gifts. Cockerell was best known as an authority on illuminated manuscripts, and published several scholarly works. His friendship with Shaw went back to before the turn of the century, and they traveled together in Italy, and frequently met and corresponded. Cockerell was also named literary executor in Shaw's (revised) will (3 August 1913). He introduced Shaw to both T. E. Lawrence [of Arabia] and Sister Laurentia [Maclachlan] in the early 1920s.

- Huxley (see above, 112).
- [George John] Romanes (1848–94), Canadian-born English naturalist. He was brought to England as a small child, became a close friend of Charles Darwin while at Cambridge, and supported his arguments in such works as *Animal Intelligence* (1881), and *Scientific Evidences of Organic Evolution* (1881).
- [Charles] Grant [Blairfindie] Allen (1848–99), Canadian-born novelist, philosopher and scientific writer. He completed his secondary and university education in England. In 1877 he published *Physiological Aesthetics* (he espoused an evolutionary theory of philosophy, based on the ideas of Herbert Spencer), and this was followed by a number of "popular" scientific works such as *Colin Clout's Calendar* (1883), a work praised by Darwin and Huxley. He had also begun to write fiction, often of a powerful kind, including *Strange Stories* (1884), *This Mortal Coil*, and *The White Man's Foot* (1888) (which last two Shaw reviewed for the *Pall Mall Gazette*: see *Bernard Shaw's Book Reviews*, 638) and *The Woman Who Did* (1895), which achieved a *succès de scandale*. He also published a volume of poetry, and a philosophical work, *Evolution of the Idea of God* (1897), and a number of essays and journalistic pieces. Shaw's generosity in this review toward Grant Allen is remarkable, considering that the latter had friends at the *Pall Mall Gazette* who removed the offensive portions of Shaw's reviews of his work before they were printed. Indeed, Shaw's entire review of Grant Allen's *Darwin* in October 1885 was rejected by Charles Morley, literary editor of the *Pall Mall Gazette*, on the dubious ground that he felt compelled to print a review of the book submitted by a "distinguished contributor" (*Diary* 120).
- Sir A[usten] H[enry] Layard (1817–94), whom Shaw unaccountably calls Benjamin, was attacked by Butler in the introduction to *Ex Voto* (1888). Here he ridicules Sir Henry Layard's description of Varallo (published in Kugler's *Handbook of Painting*), beginning, "Sir Henry Layard has evidently either never been to Varallo, or has so completely forgotten what he saw there that his visit no longer counts," and goes on to pour scorn on the unfortunate Sir Henry's artistic and historical ignorance, calling some of his comments "as fundamentally unsound as any I ever saw written, even by a professional art critic or by a director of a national collection."
- *La Vie Parisienne* (no doubt named after the Offenbach opera) was a French journal dealing in often highly erotic articles and illustrations with the social and cultural life of Paris. The journal began in 1836 and ended in 1939.
- The "witty and amiable French mistress whom Butler patronised incognito very faithfully but very cautiously for sixteen years," was Lucie Dumas [or

Dewattines, her mother's maiden name, to which she changed her own some years before her death] (1851–92). She was from Paris, but Butler met her somewhere near the Angel at Islington in 1872. Though she spoke some English, she and Butler conversed in French and, during the twenty years of her intimacy with him, according to Festing Jones, she had no rivals. Her summary of Butler is not unlike that of Shaw: "Il sait tout; il ne sait rien; il est poète." In March 1892 she died of tuberculosis, Butler arranging for her burial at Kensal Green. Festing Jones describes her as "an admirable woman, absolutely trustworthy, with considerable knowledge of the world, great natural intelligence, and what her brother, who was with her during the last years of her life, called 'un cœur d'or' "; (see Henry Festing Jones, *Samuel Butler: Author of Erewhon [1835–1902]. A Memoir* [London: Macmillan, 1919], 2:7 128).

- Jean-Jacques Rousseau (1712–78), French philosopher and social and political theorist, whose political writings helped prepare the ideological background for the French Revolution.
- Voltaire (see above, 113).
- [Jean Baptiste Tabaguet] or Tabachetti [really Jean de Wespin] (?–1615), Flemish sculptor. Born in Dinant, he went first to Crea and worked in the Paradiso Chapel in 1590 (where his brother Nicola Tabachetti also worked), and from there to Varallo, working there from 1598 until he died.
- Gaudenzio di Ferrara [or Gaudenzio Ferrari] (c. 1470–1546), Italian painter who was responsible not only for the painting and sculpture in the Chapel of the Holy Sepulcher on the Sacro Monte in Varallo, Sesia (notably the statue of Stefano Scotto),but probably also instrumental in the chapel's overall architectural design.
- Shaw himself chaired Butler's lecture entitled "Was *The Odyssey* written by a Woman?" in March 1893 and the following month attended both his lecture "*The Odyssey* and the Woman Question" and his lecture on Shakespeare's *Sonnets*.
- That "Raphael's stocks" *were* down in late Victorian England seems indicated by Shaw's lecture on art given on 10 December 1885 to the Bedford Debating Society, where, pointing out that the number of ideas in a painting is an indication of the greatness of the painter, Shaw said: "It would be easy to shew, on the same lines, that Mr. du Maurier is inferior to Raphael; but I shall not attempt it, as the majority of my audience probably prefer Mr. du Maurier to Raphael" (*Bernard Shaw on the London Art Scene 1885–1950*, 62).
- Giovanni Bellini (see above, 174).
- "A hook hit at the white chokers." The boxing metaphor came naturally to Shaw (see Introduction), and the white choker was a scarf (worn particularly by clergymen), symbolic of the middle classes in Shaw's day.
- Don Quixote, the hero of Cervantes's *Don Quixote de la Mancha* (1605–15), imagining himself called upon to pursue knightly quests, nominates a pretty girl from a neighboring village to be the mistress of his heart, calling her Dulcinea del Toboso, though she is unaware of this honor.
- Richard Wagner and Henrik Ibsen were the two most significant artistic influences in Shaw's developing life as a writer.

- The annual festival devoted to the work of Richard Wagner is held in the Festspielhaus in Bayreuth, a theater designed by Wagner and officially opened in 1876.
- The Surrey pantomime took place at the old Surrey Theatre at year's end, and was typically a dramatization of a traditional fairy tale with singing, dancing, acrobatics, clowning, topical jokes, a "transformation scene," and certain stock roles, especially the "principal boy" (that is, the protagonist) played by a woman, and the "dame" played by a man.
- Alfred Emery Cathie (1865–1947), English clerk, personal valet, and general attendant to Samuel Butler. In 1887 he started working for Butler, who undertook Cathie's education, giving him music lessons, and taking him on the Continent each Whitsuntide to show him foreign countries. In July 1894 Cathie married, which effectively put a stop to his "education," whose only result, in any case, seems to have been to afford Butler and Festing Jones amusement at Cathie's expense. Alfred Cathie had three children, but remained a close companion to the end of Butler's life. With the £2,000 bequeathed to him in Butler's will, Cathie bought a small general shop in Canal Street, Mile End, investing the remainder of the money, and living with his family on its dividends and the profits from the business.

22 November 1919

HOW IRELAND IMPRESSED MR. CHESTERTON* [C2257]

THESE Irish impressions are not, as the title page states, impressions by Mr. Chesterton. They are impressions by Ireland on Mr. Chesterton. I am tempted to recommend the book in which he has recorded them as a proof that an Englishman is a much pleasanter, jollier, kindlier human variety than an Irishman; and though I am checked by the reflection that all Englishmen are unfortunately not like Mr. Chesterton, and that he describes himself as a blend of Scotch, French, and Suffolk Dumpling, still, the net result is the sort of man that England can produce when she is doing her best. Like all such Englishmen he is a thoroughgoing Irish patriot, and will not hear of romantic Ireland being dead and gone. It exists still for him; and he

---

* "Irish Impressions." By G. K. Chesterton. Collins. 7s. 6d. net.

holds us in an esteem which would make us blush if so conceited a nation knew how to blush; for we are very far from deserving it. Our vices are so obvious that they have troubled him,though they have not estranged him. Of Dublin he tells us faithfully that though the inhabit- ants can dream they cannot sleep, having all the irritability of insomnia and all the meanness and jealousy of perpetual wideawakeness, and that they slander one another with an abominable ungenerousness. In Belfast he is staggered into laughter and horror at the mad pride and wicked selfishness of the purse proud commercial Irish Calvinist; and if he had travelled south instead of north, he would have discovered that the kindlier life and thought of Catholic Ireland does not save it from the infatuate and deadly-sinful conviction that it lives in a world of its natural inferiors. Mr. Chesterton is too kind, and too sensible of his position as an honoured guest in Ireland, to put it quite so bluntly; but I am an Irishman and need not mince matters. I know what he means, and that he has said too little instead of too much. I am not implying that he has been insincere, or that he has stooped for a moment to blarney; but when I recall those few impish but deadly-well-aimed pages in *Joan and Peter*, in which Mr. H. G. Wells described that stone corridor from Donnybrook to Stillorgan which in England would be an open country road; reduced some of the heroes of the 1916 rising to the dimensions of mischievous boys with catapults; and exposed the facile derision of Dublin as the ill-natured incontinence so much of it really is, I feel how enormously friendly Mr. Chesterton has been, even though he has spoken a more terrible word than any that fell from Mr. Wells, by frankly and gravely saying that he found every fine quality in Dublin except charity. If he could have said that he found nothing else, we could have held up our heads before him.

Mr. Chesterton begins with a fantasia on Browning's theme the Statue and the Bust. The statue is George II., in Stephen's Green; and the bust is Mangan. It is, like all Mr. Chesterton's fantasias, a very pretty one; but it is foreign to Dublin. It presents the brazen George as an insult to our nationality. I ask Mr. Chesterton to consider this a little more curiously. Human feeling is not rooted in mere politics. The fact that the man on the horse was meant to represent a foreign tyrant has no effect on the Dublin child—and it is as a little child that the Dubliner first sees George prancing in the eye of heaven. Lives there the child, Irish or English, who does not rejoice in a gigantic toy soldier, with horse and sword all complete, or who does not recoil in terror and loathing from that unnatural thing, a black metal head with the face of a schoolmaster and no body? Equestrian statues are always romances to those who are brought up in their shadow, however infamous the name on the pedestal. It is usually in Latin; and anyhow, who knows or cares more about George II. than that he risked his own skin in his battles; that the Irish brigade licked him at Fontenoy; and that he made a joke good enough to be made again by Abraham Lincoln? The only equestrian statue that has ever excited political feeling in Dublin is King William in College Green, who was not a German but a Dutchman, and was the Pope's ally to boot; and, curiously enough, the Irish Protestants have succeeded in making William so amusing that the most rabid Nationalists cannot feel really angry with him and the only attempt to blow up his statue was the work of the Protestant students of T. C. D. Could Mr. Chesterton take even the Kaiser seriously if he had heard him from childhood described as "glorious, pious and immortal," and seen him daily in the costume of Julius Cæsar on a horse engaged in demonstrating with his legs the geometrical heresy that two sides of a triangle are together equal to the third? No: in spite of Macaulay, William's glory will fade, and his piety become incomprehensible; but his immortality is assured as long as one stone of Dublin stands on another.

Besides, did not Mr. Chesterton notice that Dublin is a perfect museum of Georgian art, especially the art of domestic architecture; so that you can find streets upon streets in which the hall doors, the fanlights, the steps, and the placing of the windows fascinate observant English connoisseurs like the walls of a picture gallery? Any attempt to disparage Georgian art in Dublin must be sternly silenced by shouts of "No Politics."

There is one other passage in which Mr. Chesterton seems to write not only as an English stranger, but as one of our conquerors. It is perhaps the most surprising passage in the whole book. He speaks of "a horrible whisper which can scarcely now be stilled," of something "still too hideous to be easily believed." And what is this evil which blackens the sun for Mr. Chesterton? Nothing but this, that "it is said, with a dreadful plausibility, that the Unionists were deliberately trying to prevent a large Irish recruitment, which would certainly have meant reconciliation and reform. In plain words, it is said that they were *willing to be traitors to England* if they could only still be tyrants to Ireland." But bless your eyes, Mr. Chesterton, why not? The Belfast Unionists cannot be "traitors to England" simply because they are not Englishmen. Do you suppose that the use they make of the British army and the British fleet and the British Castle and the British Treasury and all the other weapons of the ascendancy is to serve England's ends, or that the intense scorn and self-righteousness, which you yourself felt to be infernal as it shows itself towards their own ragged townsmen no less than towards their Catholic fellow countrymen, changes to disinterested devotion when they turn their eyes to England? As far as they have any historical sense and self-denying fanaticism at all, their heroes are Gustavus Adolphus, William III. and Frederick the Great. King George, not having been born in Belfast, and having often shaken hands openly with black Papists, is to them nothing but a recreant Defender of the Faith, a mere English Ritualist who has no true Orange respect for his coronation oath. A readiness to kick the English crown into the Boyne on the slightest tolerance of the Pope is the first test of a good Orangeman. England's loyalty to Ulster they understand; but Ulster's loyalty to England! God help your innocence, Gilbert Chesterton!

However, let me confess that in what I have just said, I am, for educational purposes, dealing with what Mr. Chesterton says rather than what he means. He is not really thinking of loyalty to England, but of loyalty to Christendom, as he conceives it. He has a theory of the war which in Ireland will seem to be little more than a bee in his bonnet. To that I should say that it is and it is not. I think Mr. Chesterton is right in his generalization that in the war, though it was quite patently planned on both sides as an old-fashioned struggle for the Overbalance of Power, yet a triumph for the Hohenzollerns would have been a triumph for Dublin Castle and all that Dublin Castle stands for, a triumph of matter over spirit, of fact over faith, of despair over hope, of Caliban over Prospero. I myself took Mr. Chesterton's line almost exactly in the matter of Irish recruiting; and it may interest him to know that I was baffled by the determination of the authorities not only to stop recruiting by going the wrong way about it, but to stop every attempt to go the right way about it. My stifled appeals were in part almost paraphrases of Mr. Chesterton. But I cannot agree with him that the materialistic side of the Renaissance began in Berlin, or that Machiavelli was a Pomeranian grenadier. The utmost any Irishman can concede to an English guest is that the English governing classes are no worse than the Prussian governing classes; and even this civility can hardly be justified except on the ground that both were as unscrupulous, as aggressive, and as—shall we say acquisitive?—as their opportunities made possible. Belfast is in a position to say to Mr. Chesterton, "You want to hate the Germans? Look at home. And go down on your knees and pray that both German and Briton may escape justice and be saved by mercy." I cannot understand how a man of Mr. Chesterton's moral genius can mistake the filthy rags of anti-German righteousness for good sense, much less for a philosophy of European history.

This queer anti-Prussian, anti-Semitic, pseudo-historical theory is oddly mixed up with an economic Utopia which Mr. Chesterton and Mr. Belloc call the Distributive State. To me, who have a rival Utopia, it seems to consist of a pound of trite sense, and several tons of the most dangerous error and the most frightful nonsense. The pound of sense is that every man shall have his own vine and his own fig tree and that none shall make him afraid. The error is that proprietorship is good for the soul. And the nonsense is that a decent civilization could be made by a hoard [sic] of small proprietors each squatting jealously on his own dunghill. I have often told Mr. Chesterton that he would not believe all this if he were an Irishman. And now he has at last visited Ireland, and come back apparently without having exchanged a word with a peasant proprietor or with a priest. When at last he came up against his hobby, the Catholic Church, for which he has done everything except join it, he does not appear to have noticed it. He did find himself in a road with a big property in a neglected state on one side and several little properties well looked after (probably by co-operators) on the other. And he exclaims "I told you so." He assumes that the minds of the little proprietors are so well cultivated as their acres; but he does not seem to have put this assumption to the test of any personal intercourse with them. On that road he may have met, and I have no doubt did meet, certain men in black coats and clerical collars who had absolutely no property at all: men who, when the British Government paid them for acting as chaplains in the trenches, endorsed the cheque without taking the trouble to look at the amount; handed it over to the treasurer of their order; and never gave it another thought. To these destitute and miserable slaves—for such they must be if there is anything in Chesterbelloquacity— Mr. Chesterton might in charity have addressed a few exhortations, in the manner of Tennyson's northern farmer, to save their souls by acquiring a little property. He could have easily called out the nearest peasant proprietor to give the unpropertied man an object lesson in the magic of property in its effect on the mind and character. But perhaps he tried; and the peasant would not come. There is nothing like peasant property for teaching people to keep themselves *to* themselves. If the peasant had come, it might have proved that his prosperity was due to his having allowed the I.A.O.S. to corrupt his Robinson Crusoic independence of his neighbours. The I.A.O.S., I may inform Mr. Chesterton (though I suspect him of knowing it), is an order of pestilent fellows who preach that it is the greatest possible mistake to own your own threshing machine, or your churn, or your own horse, or your own steam engine. In my opinion it is a still greater mistake to own your own land, and the worst mistake of all to own your own soul. Anyhow it is a historical fact beyond all question that England ruined Ireland and India by destroying the character and wrecking the happiness of their villagers; and that the precise method by which she did it was the substitution of private for communal property in land. The truth is, private property in the earth is contrary to common sense and incompatible with human nature.

But all this affects only the first two little chapters of Mr. Chesterton's book. The rest is delightful, deep, and spiritually nutritious. Some of it is better fun than any Irishman could make: for example, the story of the Unionist who was shot by the British troops, and Mr. Chesterton's moralizing thereon. With a turn of the hand this extraordinarily skilful literary virtuoso, pretending all the time to be nothing but a carelessly jolly Englishman, misquotes Mr. Yeats to show that he can paraphrase him in as exquisite Irish English as Lady Gregory's, and makes us laugh, in the characteristic Irish manner, at some barbarous calamity that would make sane men grieve. He is enormously robust and exquisitely subtle (like Handel), as funny as a harlequinade and as serious as an epic, and doing it all with an immense good humour which prevents his prodigious cleverness from ever wearying or tiring you, and makes him a model guest because he is such a perfect host. The world is not half thankful enough for Chesterton; and I hope Ireland will not be among the ingrates; for no Irishman alive or dead has ever served her better and more faithfully with the pen than he.

BERNARD SHAW

Editor's Notes

■ The above was first published in the *Irish Statesman* (22 November 1919):530–33. There is no indication in Shaw's correspondence when he wrote the review, which was reprinted in *The Matter with Ireland*, ed. Dan H. Laurence and David H. Greene (1962).
■ G. K. Chesterton (see above, 331–32).

- H. G. Wells (see above, 346–47).
- In the twelfth chapter of *Joan and Peter* (1918), Wells describes the irritation of Peter towards the Irish as they drive through the "high walls" on the Donnybrook road, which he sees as symbolic of the "Fixed Ideas" of the Irish. A few lines later we have this significant comment:

> The automobile halted for a moment at crossroads, and the finger-post was in Erse characters.
> "Look at that! " said Peter with genuine exasperation. "And hardly a Dubliner knows fifty words of the language! It's foolery. If we were Irish I suppose we should smother London with black-letter. We should go on pretending that we, too, were still Catholics and Protestants. The pseudo-Protestants would hang Smithfield with black on account of the martyrs, and the pseudo-Catholics would come and throw the meat about on Fridays. Chesterton and Belloc would love it anyhow . . . ."

- "The Statue and the Bust" is a dramatic romance by Robert Browning. In it Duke Ferdinand and the bride of the head of the noble Riccardi house fall deeply in love with one another. Riccardi suspects, and has his new wife confined to a chamber for life. Duke Ferdinand rides past her palace and they see each other through the window; but in spite of plans for her to escape and join the Duke, years pass by, age creeps on, and it becomes evident that it will not happen. Perceiving that she looks older and greyer, the lady has her servants call the famous sculptor Della Robbia to fix the remains of her beauty so that it shall no more fade. Della Robbia makes her a face on the window, waiting, as ever, for her lover to pass by. Unknowingly, the Duke also commissions John of Douay to make an equestrian statue of him, and places it in the square outside the Riccardi Palace, the face of the figure looking forever at one of the windows.
- [James Clarence] Mangan (1803–49), Irish poet, whose life was a "tragedy of hapless love, poverty and intemperance." He worked variously as a lawyer's clerk and in the library of Trinity College, Dublin, and published, among other things, English versions of Irish poems in *The Poets and Poetry of Munster* (1849), including "My Dark Rosaleen" and "The Nameless One."
- The "joke" of George II (1683–1760) was his reply to one who complained that General Wolfe was a madman: "Oh! he is mad, is he? Then I wish he would *bite* some other of my generals." Abraham Lincoln expressed the same sentiment when told that General Grant was drinking too much whiskey: "Get me the brand, and I'll send a barrel to my other generals." Shaw himself thought the joke good enough to adapt, too. In *Saint Joan* (1923) we have the following exchange:

POULENGY. It is a certainty. Her words and her ardent faith in God have put fire into me.

ROBERT [*giving him up*] Whew! You are as mad as she is.

POULENGY [*obstinately*] We want a few mad people now. See where the sane ones have landed us!

- King William (see above, 371).
- T.C.D. is Trinity College, Dublin.
- Gustavus Adolphus [Gustav II Adolf] (1594–1632), king of Sweden, champion of Protestantism, known as the 'Lion of the North.' After defeating the Russians, and receiving a large part of Finland and Livonia through the Treaty of Stolbova (1617), he fought a long and successful war against Poland, which left him free to intervene directly in the Thirty Years' War (1618–48) on behalf of the Protestants against the Holy Roman Emperor, Ferdinand II. In the spring of 1632 he advanced into Bavaria, captured Augsburg and Munich, and in November of that year met the forces of the emperor in a tremendous battle at Lützen (near Leipzig). The Swedish army won, but Gustavus himself was killed. His heart was taken back to Stockholm in his blood-stained silken shirt.
- Frederick the Great (see above, 318).
- Hilaire Belloc (see above, 379).
- Chesterton did convert to Catholicism in July 1922.
- Tennyson's "Northern Farmer," speaking on his deathbed in an almost impenetrable Lincolnshire dialect, gives materialistic advice to his son, Sammy, advising him to "goä wheer munny is." He begins thus:

> Dosn't thou 'ear my 'erse's legs, as they canters awaäy?
> Proputty, proputty, proputty—that's what I 'ears 'em saäy . . .

- The I.A.O.S. was the Irish Agricultural Organization Society.
- [William Butler] Yeats (1865–1939), Irish poet and dramatist. In 1885 his first lyrics were published in the *Dublin University Review,* in which year he also published *The Island of Statues* (1885). In 1887 the family moved to Bedford Park, London, where Yeats's reputation as an anthologer and as a poet began to grow. Shaw had first met Yeats on 12 February 1888; but although they shared common acquaintances in William Morris, and later the actress Florence Farr (for whom they each wrote plays), the two men were poles apart artistically: Yeats interested in mysticism and the occult, and a philosophy of poetry that emphasized the associative power of the imagination very differently from the intellectual clarity and rhetorical force of Shaw. Like Shaw, however, Yeats, apart from his poetry, included in his work drama, criticism, essays, journalism, and novels, and both men won the Nobel Prize for Literature.
- Lady [Isabella Augusta] Gregory (1852–1932), Irish playwright. In 1880 she became an associate with W. B. Yeats in the foundation of the Abbey Theatre in Dublin, and wrote a number of excellent short plays, such as *Spreading the News* (1904) and *The Rising of the Moon* (1907).

22 November 1919

OUR GREAT DEAN* [C2256]

WILLIAM RALPH INGE is our most extraordinary Churchman, our most extraordinary writer, and in some very vital respects our most extraordinary man. He is a living paradox, a Churchman who does not stone the prophets, a prophet who is a high dignitary of the Church, and so many other contradictory things as well that we have to analyse and explain him before his existence becomes credible.

To begin with, he has had to struggle from his birth, and indeed for generations before his birth, with disadvantages that would have crushed any common spirit and sterilised any common mind. His heredity and environment are appalling. His father was the head of an Oxford College, and his mother the daughter of an archdeacon. And he met this black-coated destiny by that gamest sort of defiance which consists in embracing it; for he deliberately married the granddaughter of a bishop and the daughter of an archdeacon. I have not the privilege of knowing his sons; but if ever I meet them I shall regard them with anxious curiosity. If I had a son with such fearfully unfair antecedents I should bring him up as an ignoramus and an atheist, so as to give him at least half a chance of acquiring a mind of his own.

I need hardly add that Dr. Inge has been every sort of scholar and prizeman a Cambridge Don can be at his worst; that he has been an Eton master as well as an Eton boy; that he is a Doctor of Divinity and a Dean; and that he is allowed to say what he likes on the assumption (safe in ninety-nine per cent. of similar cases) that after going through such a mill he cannot possibly have anything new to say. But the miracle is that he has. By all human calculation he ought to be exactly like either Samuel Butler or Samuel Butler's father. He is like neither. Without one of the disreputable advantages enjoyed by Mr. H. G. Wells, Mr. Gilbert Chesterton, and myself, he is as complete a Freethinker as any of us, and has compelled us to take off our hats to his intellect, his character, his courage, and—speaking professionally, as one author to another—his technique. If you do not read these outspoken essays of his, you will be as hopelessly out of the movement as if you had not read my latest preface, or Mr. Chesterton's book on Ire-

---

* "Outspoken Essays." By William Ralph Inge, C.V.O., D.D., Dean of St. Paul's. (Longmans. 6s. net.)

land, or Mr. Wells's "Joan and Peter," or "The Undying Fire." For the truth is, the undying fire is in the Dean; and as it is a fire of such exceeding brightness that it blinds people with weak eyes instead of enlightening them, he is commonly called "The Gloomy Dean" by these poor ophthalmics.

The highest business of a critic is to proclaim the man: his next concern is to indulge the smaller self by nagging at the man's book. These essays, dazzling as they are, have done much to confirm me in a conviction which has been deepening in me for years, that what we call secondary education as practised at our public schools and universities is destructive to any but the strongest minds, and even to them it is disastrously confusing. I find in the minds of all able and original men and women who have been so educated, a puzzling want of homogeneity. They are full of chunks of unassimilated foreign bodies which are much more troublesome and dangerous than the vacancies I find in the minds of those who have not been educated at all. I prefer a cavity to a cancer or a calculus: it is capable of being filled with healthy tissue and is not malignant. In the mind of the Dean, which is quite unmistakably a splendid mind, I find the most ridiculous substances, as if, after the operation of educating him, the surgeon-pedagogue had forgotten to remove his sponges and instruments and sewn them up inside him. When a Dean has a rigid bearing, as Deans are apt to have, it is commonly said of him that he has swallowed a poker. Dean Inge, though not excessively stiff in his deportment, has swallowed a whole set of fire-irons; and it is too late now to extract them. There they are, and there they must remain until he extrudes them naturally, as he has extruded bits of them already.

I know how long such things stick. When I was a child I was told that a gentleman who had paid us a visit was a Unitarian. I asked my father what a Unitarian was; and he, being the victim of a sense of humour and a taste for anti-climax which I have to some extent inherited, thoughtlessly replied that the Unitarians are people who believe that our Lord was not really crucified at all, but was "seen running away down the other side of the Hill of Calvary." Childlike, I accepted this statement *au pied de la lettre*, and believed it devoutly until I was thirty-five or thereabouts, when, having occasion one day to make some reference to Unitarianism in print, and being led thereby to consider it more closely, I perceived that my father's account of the matter would not stand the fire of the Higher Criticism.

Now it is clear that somebody, perhaps the Dean's father, but more likely some benighted university tutor preparing him for an examination, told him (a) that the Rev. Thomas Malthus had satisfied himself that a single human pair could, with unlimited food, cover the habitable earth three deep with people in a thousand years or so; (b) that therefore if there were only one man in the world he could have all the food in it, but that if there were two he could only have half, or a third if there were three, (c) that the eternal law of life is the "law of diminishing return," (d) that the more people there are in the world the poorer they must be (except the upper class, who are exempt from nature's laws), (e) that it follows logically that an Englishman cannot spin cotton or weave carpets unless he eats less than a Hindu or a Parsee, (f) that anyone capable of a syllogism must conclude that the skilled laborer is the natural enemy of the professions, and that the commercial brigands who exploit him are their devoted patrons, (g) that without Capitalism the workers must perish, (h) that the Industrial Revolution impoverished England by producing an excessive population, (i)—I spare you the rest of the alphabet.

I hope, now that I have exposed this farrago of nonsense to the Dean in its nakedness he will recant his economic fatalism as I have recanted the much more plausible and pardonable error of my father on Unitarianism. Indeed, his own conclusions are a sufficient *reductio ad absurdum*. One of them is that both industrialism and population will disappear if we practice birth control, and will leave us as we were in the early eighteenth century, grouped in our proper stations round the squire and his relations, not forgetting, I hope, the country parsonage. Another—a real breath bereaver this—is that the best thing the Russians can do is to restore the monarchy!!!

If the Dean is unappalled by the hopelessness of the first conclusion and the wickedness of the second (he evidently does not realise how much better the worst we know of Lenin is than the best we know of Tsardom), I would ask him to contemplate the career of Mr. Asquith. Mr. Asquith came up from his university with his very lucid mind carefully furnished with the standard set of university excuses for robbing the poor, called by the Dean himself "the old political economy." Firm and calm in its entrenchment, he condescended to impart its synthesis of society to an audience, mainly of Socialists, at The Working Men's College. They listened, and awaited the ignobly easy task of wiping the floor with him. But he baffled them completely by simply refusing to debate or discuss the matter. One does not discuss the inexorable destiny of humanity: one abides it. One does not debate with persons so ignorant as to suppose that there is any room for debate on matters that were settled, and settled for ever, as long ago as the year 1830. He left the room haughtily, and proceeded, as front bench man and finally Prime Minister, to deal with Socialism and the Labour Movement on the assumption that Socialists are ignorant of political economy; that the Collectivism which was growing up under his nose was a tinker's Utopia; that employers are still competing with one another in the public interest instead of combining against it; and that the establishment of a minimum wage is contrary to the laws of nature. The Dean describes the social result in one of his unforgettable phrases as "a condition of septic dissolution."

The truth is that all this sham political economy has not been even academic since Mill, in the process of writing the treatise in which he began by accepting it all, was irresistibly driven to Socialism before he finished it. It is true that up to so late a period as the date of the Dean's birth it was still possible to admit that Capitalism, or the substitution on principle of Mammon for God, had, in spite of all its infamies, broken the shell for a rebirth of society and incidentally done more harm than good. But since that time the evil of its central sin of godless selfishness has been working itself out. God is not mocked after all. Capitalism is now hindering more than it ever helped; and it will be the ruin of our civilisation, as it has been the ruin of so many previous ones, if the Dean (among others) does not purge his education out of his system; go to his religion for his politics; and reconcile Christ Logos to Christ Communist. To put it shortly, the Dean's economics will not wash; and we are all by this time Marxist enough to fear that if we go wrong in our economics, we shall go wrong in everything.

I conclude that the secret of a genuine liberal education is to learn what you want to know for the sake of your own enlightenment, and not let anybody teach you anything whatever for the purpose of pulling you through an examination, especially one conducted by persons who have been taught in the same way. You may think you can discard it all when it has served its turn; but it sticks all the more treacherously because you have a theory that you have cleared it all out. Before you know where you are, you have tripped over a block of it.

Both Democracy and Socialism need continuous and fierce criticism; but unless the critic understands them and knows that their theory is impregnable, and that the shutters are up on The Manchester School, he will produce no more impression on them than Archbishop Ussher's ghost would on the Dean if it reproached him with his ignorance of the fact that the world is only 5,923 years old. In the Church Dr. Inge is like a refiner's fire: he puts it to its purgation and

purification as no atheist could. But when he turns to industrial politics he is worse than ineffectual: he discredits birth control by giving
the wrong reasons for it, because he has never drawn a curve of
production per head of population through time in the light of modern
economic science, and therefore never discovered that the curve begins as a curve of prodigiously increasing return, with diminishing
return so far ahead that the prospect of a world crowded right up to its
utmost resources in edible carbo-hydrates and nitrogen (or whatever
posterity will call its bread and butter) would appal the most sociable
man alive. If Malthus himself were with us now, he would be worry-
ing about the decline of population, not about its increase. For the
increase which startled him produced such leaping and bounding
prosperity, as Gladstone called it, that the classes benefited by it became too dainty and thoughtful to breed recklessly as they had done
before; and now we have the very poor pullulating, and the better
sorts sterilising themselves. The Dean sees the danger, and comes
down rightly and boldly on the side of control; but he imagines that we
produce less per head as we increase in numbers, whereas the fact is
that we produce more, though we are foolish enough to use the increase in supporting more idlers instead of making the labourers rich
enough to revolt against uncontrolled child bearing.

But it is exasperating to have to cavil at the Dean's economics when
there is so much to be said in praise of his divinity. In that sphere he is
beyond praise. I suppose I think so because he comes out at last as a
great Protestant; and I am so thorough an Irish Protestant myself that I
have all my life scandalised the Irish Protestant clergy, and made the
Irish priests chuckle, by declaring that a Protestant Church is a contradiction in terms. The true Protestant is a mystic, not an Institutionalist.
Those who do not understand this must read the Dean's superb essay on
Institutionalism and Mysticism, which contains an inspired page (232)
which ought to be included in the canon. His essay on St. Paul convicts
me of having taken too static a view of a developing spirit, and almost
persuades me that the Supplanter of Christ found his soul at last.

I shall not stand between the Dean and his readers by any attempt to
describe or paraphrase his doctrine: I simply agree and admire. Snobs
will be scandalised, and some timid souls terrified, by the passages that
suggested the epithet "outspoken," such as the curt dismissal of Bible
science as "a cosmology which has been definitely disproved," and the
declaration that if the bishops refuse to ordain all those postulants who
cannot swallow the creeds, the infallibility of the scriptures, the thirty-
nine articles, and the virgin birth in the old-fashioned way, the clergy

will consist of fools, bigots and liars. But it is now clear that the Church can be saved, if it is not past salvation, only by men with character and mental force enough to be able to say such things without conscious audacity. Whether the Dean will stay in it when he has saved it is not quite a foregone conclusion. He is so much more a prophet than a priest that one's first impulse on learning that he is Dean of St. Paul's is to cry *"Que diable allait il faire dans cette galère?"* As it is, he helps the lame dog over the style with a roughness that betrays the imperfection of his sympathy with Institutionalism. His treasure is in a wider region than The Church of England, or any other such local makeshift; and where his treasure is, there must his heart be also.

G. B. S.

Editor's Notes

▪ There is no indication when the above review was written. It appeared on the same day as the review of Chesterton's *Irish Impressions*, in *Everyman* 15, where it was headed "The Book of the Week," 160–62. It was reprinted in *Hearst's Magazine* (New York) 37 (March 1920); and again in Bernard Shaw, *Pen Portraits and Reviews* (1931), with the usual alterations of "ise" to "ize" and the omission of periods in "Mr." and "Rev." In 1939, when Hesketh Pearson, another biographer of Shaw, expressed surprise at Shaw's praise of Inge, Shaw wrote to him: "As to Inge, read his *Outspoken Essays*, and my review of it headed *Our Great Dean*. . . . And never mind his pre-Marxian political economy. Labor politics are not his job. When he is on his job he is easily one of the first minds in England. Remember: you have to account for my admiration of him"; (see Bernard Shaw, letter to Hesketh Pearson, 4 September 1939, published in Hesketh Pearson, *Bernard Shaw. His Life and Personality* (originally published 1942; published by the Reprint Society by arrangement with Wm. Collins, 1948), 439.

▪ William Ralph Inge (1860–1954), English theologian. After leaving Cambridge he taught at Eton for four years; then from 1889 to 1904 he was a fellow at Hertford College, University of Oxford. In 1905 he became vicar of All Saints, Ennismore Gardens, Kensington. In 1907 he was elected Lady Margaret's Professor of Divinity at Cambridge, a position he held until 1911. He was dean of Saint Paul's Cathedral, London, from 1911 to 1934. His criticism of the direction of modern life and his generally pessimistic outlook earned him the sobriquet of "the gloomy dean." Among his writings are *Personal Idealism and Mysticism* (1907), *Faith and its Psychology* (1909), *Personal Religion and the Life of Devotion* (1924), *The Platonic Tradition in English Religious Thought* (1926), and *The Diary of a Dean* (1949), the subject of one of Shaw's last book

reviews (see below, 536). It was, however, the above review that led to Shaw's friendship with Dean Inge, a friendship which continued until Shaw's death.
- Samuel Butler (see above, 306–7).
- Shaw's latest Preface was to *Heartbreak House*, published in September 1919. The press response (apart from a friendly review in the *New Witness*) had been generally unfavorable, and Shaw had actually written letters to J. C. Squire and Lena Ashwell (see above, 5) whose reviews were particularly vitriolic; Chesterton's *Irish Impressions* was reviewed by Shaw on this very date, and Wells's *Joan and Peter* is mentioned above on 399.
- H. G. Wells's *The Undying Fire* was published in 1919.
- Unitarians are members of a religious body that affirms the single personality of the Godhead, as opposed to believers in the Trinity. The English Unitarians date from Theophilus Lindsay's 1773 secession from the Anglican Church; and it was to some form of Unitarian Church that the English (as opposed to the Scottish) Presbyterians ultimately turned.
- Malthus (see above, 112).
- Asquith (see above, 186–87).
- Mill (see above, 113).
- The so-called Manchester School sprang from the Anti–Corn Law League founded by seven Manchester merchants in 1837, animated by the free trade principles of Richard Cobden (see above, 151).
- [James] Ussher (1581–1656), Irish prelate and archbishop of Armagh , the best-known of whose writings, the *Annales Veteris et Novi Testamenti* (1650–54), propounded a long-accepted chronology of Scripture that fixed the Creation precisely at 4004 B.C.
- *Que diable allait il faire dans cette galère?* [What the devil was he doing in that galley?]: from Molière's *Les Fourberies de Scapin*, act 2, scene 7.

8 August 1920

THE WEBB CONSTITUTION* [C2295]

I wonder how many eons will elapse before some historian startles England by a gorgeous rhetorical passage on the happiness of the twentieth century in enjoying the counsels of that extraordinary partnership known as Sidney and Beatrice Webb. Will nobody write a festival play entitled "The Fortunate Marriage" to celebrate the golden wedding of this amazing pair? I dare not face the clamour, as of a thousand

---

* "A Constitution for the Socialist Commonwealth of Great Britain." By Sidney and Beatrice Webb. (Longmans 12s. 6d. net.)

offended operatic tenors and prima donnas, that would arise if I said that Sidney and Beatrice were, obviously and easily, he the ablest man and she the ablest woman in England in their own very comprehensive line; but I may say without fear of contradiction that they are the ablest couple, and that the accident of their marrying one another was so impossible as a mere piece of luck that it has restored faith in Providence to a Darwinised world. With the Webbs as our champions we can challenge all the nations of the earth. Talk of German industry and thoroughness, French logic and lucidity, Dutch accomplishment and authority in law and finance, Russian freedom of thought and intellectual enterprise, Scandinavian steadiness, and Swiss independence! We answer triumphantly, The Webbs! and Europe, abashed, accepts a back seat. The Webbs are, in fact, spot-barred in the game of capping authorities; for their rivals, not having been sensible enough to intermarry, cannot single-handed face the Webb combination.

*   *

*

And yet among the many benevolent fairies who must have crowded to their christenings, there was one malignant elf who pretty nearly undid all the good done by the others by the masterstroke of damning the pair to be English. Of all tragedies of square pegs in round holes, can there be one more heartrending than that of a supreme genius for law and order condemned to live in an inveterately anarchist country, and to devise perfect schemes of government for a nation which has defied aristocracy, oligarchy, and democracy and all systems of government with equal success because nothing will induce it to consent to be governed at all? The first condition of stable government, say the Webbs with unquestionable truth, is that it shall be government by consent of the governed. Never, exclaims the ungovernable Briton. Death first! Starvation first! To hell with the Webbs and their schemes for regulating us! We will not be regulated. We will do what we like and die in the workhouse. This regulation business is stifling, disgusting, un-English. The women declare that if Beatrice had her way the railway companies would give every woman a ticket of the same colour instead of leaving her free to choose one suited to her complexion. The men complain that under Sidney's tyranny they would have to do whatever work was offered to them instead of being free to choose between a job at the docks and a house in Belgrave-square, a shooting box in Scotland, a villa on the Mediterranean, a country house with dower house attached, and a steam yacht. In vain does Beatrice, with her unruffled pleasant reasonableness, pat the mutinous lady on the head and say, "My dear child, your tickets are all the same colour at present; and each little girl cannot receive individual treatment at the booking office." In vain does the less complacent Sidney snap out: "Are you in the docks now by your own choice, pray?" The incorrigibly non-adult native of this island angrily replies: "That's just it: you want us to face facts. What sort of life would it be if we had to face facts? Leave us to our romance: we might be a bit hampered by the capitalist system now and then, and we grant you that prices and rents and rates and fares are a scandal and a disgrace; but at least our imaginations are free; and what is the matter with you two is that you have no imagination."

*   *

*

Thus are the Webbs not only England's glory, but also the most disparaged people within the narrow seas. Read the notices of this book of theirs: the most remarkable book of the year or of many years. Note how, when it is praised, it is praised with difficulty as of a Scot joking, and how the enforced acknowledgments, not so much of its merits as of the reviewer's hopeless inadequacy, are full of resentment. Why am I genuinely appreciative? Why have I always backed the Webbs, admired them, known their value? Because I am an Irishman and understand the vital necessity for government, for law and order, and know the horror of being governed by anarchists whose notion of keeping society together is to muddle their way into difficulties and bludgeon their way out. The Webbs should have been born in Skibbereen.

*   *

*

I shall, therefore, not waste time in recommending this book to the authors' countrymen; for all its best qualities will only repel them. The Russians, as soon as the foreign pressure which is giving complete coercive powers to their dictators relaxes and compels them to adopt a constitution, will find in it plans and specifications which they will certainly not find in the Communist Manifesto of Marx or in Das Kapital. Every country in the world in which the capitalist system has outgrown that parliamentary patch on feudalism and mediæval municipalism with which civilisation has been trying to make public and private ends meet for the last few centuries, will have either to take the Webb constitution intelligently as a basis of discussion with the view to constitutional reform, or else do as the English will do: that is, refuse to have anything to do with it until the present machinery breaks down altogether and lands them in chaos, and then submit to it because nature abhors a vacuum. No one else could have produced the book, because no one else has put in the lifetime of work, both in research and in practical administration, of which it is the climax. I have often had occasion to say to a university scholar who was determined not to write a book until he could write a good one that in that case he would never write a book at all, because you cannot write a good book until you have written twenty bad ones. The Webbs have bettered my counsel by writing twenty good ones. Their "Industrial Democracy," for example, is incomparably the greatest work of its kind produced in England since Adam Smith's "Wealth of Nations"; and only by writing that book and its companions, and by writing them not in the study, but in the field of actual affairs, could the Webbs have qualified themselves to write this comparatively short but pregnant essay.

*   *

*

I purposely refrain from dealing with its content in such a way as to make my readers imagine that they know all about the book when they have only read a review of it. It proposes, and, indeed proclaims, the inevitability of two main constitutional changes. First, the ruthless scrapping of our present contemptible-because-inadequate Parliament, and the establishment of two separate Parliaments, one of them dealing with general legal and cultural institutions, with international relations and finance; and the other with our industrial institutions, thus frankly making an end, once for all, of the tradition that government is not concerned with industry, though the nation is dependent upon it for its very existence. Second—and here we come to a notable stroke of the famous Webbian ingenuity—the staggering problem first propounded by Mr. H. G. Wells, of how to reconcile our local government not only with the overrunning and obliteration of old parish boundaries by the growth of modern urban districts, but with the simple fact that an area that is convenient and economical for one public service can for another only be described as outrageous, is solved by a proposal that the whole country shall be divided into Wards, and that the Ward representative, instead of being a member, as at present, of a single local body absurdly trying to combine such narrowly local functions as street sweeping with provincial services like electric power, water, and internal communication by tramway and so forth, shall sit on a parish assembly for one purpose, an urban district assembly for another, a county or province or watershed assembly for another, and so on. This will seem very odd to those who do not see that there is any problem to solve; but if mortal man can suggest any other alternative to a completely centralised bureaucracy, let him speak now or be for ever silent. The Webbs argue their case for these two main reforms with all their familiar intellectual command of the situation and knowledge of the facts and of human nature. Those who desire to know more about the book must read it.

Editor's Notes

- This review was published in the *Observer*, 8 August 1920, in "Books of the Day," 3: 3–4. In bold type after the headline and title of the book is printed: "By Bernard Shaw." There is no indication of when Shaw wrote it. However, in spite of successful revivals of *Arms and the Man* (11 December 1919), *Pygmalion* (10 February 1920) and *Candida* (1 March 1920), box-office receipts were not princely; and in January 1920 Shaw confesses he is relapsing into "ephemeral journalism" because it means "ready money from America." His decision to review the Webbs' book may simply have been because of his long-standing friendship with Sidney and Beatrice, and his desire to counterbalance the negative reviews that had already appeared; but a further stimulus may have been his dining with the Webbs at 41 Grosvenor Road, London, on 27 May 1920, where Beatrice had arranged for him to meet his secretary-to-be Blanche Patch.
- Sidney and Beatrice Webb (see above, 139, 199) did in fact celebrate a real "golden wedding" anniversary on 23 July 1942!
- The metaphor "spot-barred" is drawn from billiards, and refers to a game in which only one winning hazard is allowed to be made in the top pockets.
- "Skibbereen" is a town on the southern tip of Ireland, less than fifty miles from Parknasilla, where Shaw spent so many summers.

18 September 1920

A POLITICAL CONTRAST* [C2298]

THIS book is something more than the latest literary product of a well known author. It is a trophy of the war for England. It proves what

---

* "Satan the Waster: A Philosophic War Trilogy." With Notes and Introduction. By Vernon Lee. (Lane. 10s. 6d. net.)

everyone has lately been driven to doubt, that it is possible to be born in England and yet have intellect, to train English minds as well as English muscles, and to impart knowledge to Britons. The problem remains, how is it then possible for a nation to produce a woman like Vernon Lee, and at the same time choose Mr. Lloyd George and Sir Edward Carson as its dictators? The contrast is overwhelming. Put the Prime Minister's most important speech—say that on the Polish crisis the other day—beside the most trifling of Vernon Lee's notes to "Satan the Waster," and it immediately becomes apparent that Mr. Lloyd George leads the English people only as a nurserymaid leads her little convoy of children, by knowing her way about within a radius of half a mile or so, and being quick at guessing what promise or threat will fill them with childish hopes or terrors, as the case may be. As for Sir Edward, he becomes the policeman who misdirects the nurserymaid because he has rashly undertaken fixed point duty in a strange district much too big for his powers of comprehension. One sees the nurserymaid turn in her bewilderment from the policeman who does not know his job to the soldier who does, raising her little song of "Another little war, and another little war, and another little war won't do us any harm." "Certainly not," says the soldier: "it will do you a lot of good. Besides, it is absolutely necessary to prevent another big war." And the poor nurserymaid is not clever enough to ask why wars should be prevented if they are so wholesome. So she takes on the airs of a nursery-governess, and gives a history lesson, starting with the announcement that the independence of Poland is indispensable to the peace of Europe, the children being too young to know that Poland has been dependent and subjugate for a century and a half or so without protest from the nurserymaid, and with a most pacific effect on Central Europe, whatever the effect may have been on the Poles themselves. What the Foreign Office wanted her to say was that Polish independence may be worth a war from the point of view of Balance of Power diplomacy now that there is a possibility of Russia and Germany combining *contra mundum*, the officially correct remedy being the establishment and maintenance of a buffer State between them. What will happen when the buffer State sees the obvious advantage of making a Triplice (as Belgium had to) with the two adjacent bogeys is a speculation outside the nurserymaid's half-mile radius. After all, the European reactions of a war are uncertain and remote: the khaki votes and profits at home are certain. Norman Angell said that wars do not pay; but the nurserymaid has never had her mouth so full of chocolates in her life, and therefore thinks she knows better. If it were not for the sudden appearance of certain hooligans (for so the nurserymaid scornfully classes the working man in Council of Action) with bricks in their hands, and a very evident disposition to shy them, the unfortunate children would be up to their necks in blood literally before they knew where they were, as in 1914.

The nurserymaid has, as she thinks, some clever ideas about war. For instance, why declare war on Russia? Just send Poland arms and ammunition and food, and make our gallant fellows in Dantzig work for her behind the lines whilst our splendid navy blockades and if necessary bombards the Russians. The Russians will not be able to retaliate because we shall not be at war with them; so that we shall have all the fun of being at war without any of the unpleasantness of being torpedoed or bombed or reading casualty lists. Do not suppose that the nurserymaid is sagacious enough to be calculating on what would actually happen: namely, that Russia would be forced to declare war on us, and that the moment she killed a British soldier we should rush to arms and accept conscription again. If she were Machiavellian enough for that, she would also have gumption enough to know that a forced choice between conscription or revolution might make Lenin master of the situation The nurserymaid cannot understand Lenin—finds him "incoherent" when every intellectually competent person in Europe finds him only too terribly logical. Lenin keeps on saying to the British workman "Why don't you remove these aristocratic Curzons and Churchills and these *bourgeois* Carsons and Georges who are standing in our way and yours? You know you will have to do it some day: why not do it now?" He is too much the gentleman and diplomatist to use a shorter word than remove; but his meaning is clear; only the poor nurserymaid cannot grasp it, because she is not accustomed to be spoken to like that. She takes refuge with Mr. Balfour, crying "Speak to this sarcastic man for me, will you sir?" And he, having wasted the last thirty years of his life helping political nurserymaids over stiles and escorting them past strange cows, does his best for a hopeless client.

Now why do I push this similitude of the nurserymaid so far? Because I cannot get away from it whilst Vernon Lee is standing beside Mr. Lloyd George. You cannot read a page of "Satan the Waster" without feeling like that about the Prime Minister. Vernon Lee has the whole European situation in the hollow of her hand: Mr. Lloyd George cannot co-ordinate its most obviously related factors. Vernon Lee knows history philosophically: Mr. Lloyd George barely knows geography topographically. Vernon Lee is a political psychologist: Mr. Lloyd George is a claptrap expert. Vernon Lee, as her dated notes to this book prove, has never been wrong once since the war began: Mr. Lloyd George has never been right, as his speeches will prove if anyone will take the trouble to dig them up. Vernon Lee, by sheer intellectual force, training, knowledge, and character, kept her head when Europe was a mere lunatic asylum; Mr. Lloyd George hustled through only because, in matters of wide scope, he has no head to lose. And remember, Vernon Lee is an Englishwoman. Had she been Irish, like me, there would have been nothing in her dispassionateness: the three devastated streets of Louvain would have been balanced (not to say overbalanced) by the three hundred devastated acres of Dublin; and "the broken treaty" would have meant for her the treaty of Limerick. No wonder I had a comparatively mild attack of war fever. But Vernon Lee is English of the English, and yet held her intellectual own all through. I take off my hat to the old guard of Victorian cosmopolitan intellectualism, and salute her as the noblest Briton of them all.

I will now ask the reader to look back a few lines to the string of contrasts which I have drawn between Vernon Lee and Mr. Lloyd George, and ask him to read them again, substituting the name of Lenin for that of our Prime Minister. They immediately become ridiculous; and that is a very serious matter for us. Lenin can say to Vernon Lee, "Let the galled jade wince: *our* withers are unwrung." Lenin has made mistakes of practice, and admitted them. Lenin has made, or at least been forced to tolerate, mistakes in industrial organization which the Sidney Webbs would not have made, and has scrapped them frankly and effectively. Like all the other European statesmen, he has had to wade through atrocities; though he alone has neither denied them nor pretended that they were all inevitable. But Lenin has kept his head; has talked no manifest nonsense; has done nothing without knowing what he was doing; has taken the blether of his enemies as he has taken the bullets their assassins shot into him, without flinching intellectually. And he has surrounded himself, as far as the supply would permit, with men of his own calibre. Lord Curzon was able to hang up the Russian question in England for many months because he was too uppish to communicate with Mr. Litvinoff, just as Lord Randolph Churchill was too haughty to speak to Mrs. Asquith at dinner, when she was "only a Miss"; but Lenin and his extremely able envoy Krassin[sic] were not too uppish to communicate with Lord Curzon, even when he was so absurd as to offer his services with a magnanimous air to negotiate between Russia and General Wrangel, as between one European Power and another, on the question of which shall possess that well-known dependency of the British Empire called the Crimea.

What can we expect if we go on pitting British rabbits against Russian serpents, British boodle and bunkum against Russian fanaticism and realism: in short, sixth-rate political intellects against first-rate ones, and the education and outlook of Henry VII., piously preserved by taxidermist pedagogues in scholastic museums, against the ideas and outlook of Buckle, Marx, Nietzsche, Bergson, and the rest of the live wires of our supercharged time? The whole capitalized world is bursting with an impulse towards "the dictatorship of the proletariat," because the proletariat means simply the whole body of people who live by working, as against the handful who, as the Duke of Northumberland put it, live by owning, or, as Ruskin put it, by begging and stealing. Mr. Smillie can floor Mr. Lloyd George by challenging him to prevent the coal strike, or any strike, by simply making industrial and social service compulsory for all classes (and all incomes) as Lenin has done. Democracy and liberty have no meaning except as affirmations of the vital need for this supremacy of the proletariat; and yet our Prime Minister, ignorant of the meaning of the words, thinks he has only to hold up the phrase as a bogey to the children he is nursemaiding to defeat an antagonist of Lenin's quality. If he can do no better than that with Red Armies ready to spring into existence in every country in Europe and every State in America at a wave of Lenin's hand, the sooner we put Vernon Lee into the position occupied three hundred years ago by Queen Elizabeth the better.

But this is by way of being a review of Vernon Lee's book, and not a phrenologist's chart of Mr. George's bumps. The book, of first-rate workmanship from beginning to end, is far too thorough to leave the reviewer anything to say about it that is not better said in the book itself; but to aid the contrast I have suggested between Vernon Lee's braininess and Mr. George's bumptiousness, I append a few samples of the good things with which "Satan the Waster" is stuffed on every page, merely adding that the dramatic power and stage dexterity with which the work has been framed are quite adequate, and that there is no reason in the world why Vernon Lee should not have been a successful playwright except that her subject matter is above the heads of our theatrical caterers, and, doubtless, of the suburban playgoers whose taste in high politics is for hanging the Kaiser.

"The long duration of this war has resulted less from its hitherto undreamed of military machinery, less from the even more unprecedented wholesale fabrication of public opinion, than from the spiritual mechanism of errors and myths which the vastness, the identity of this war's dangers and sacrifices automatically set up in the minds of all the warring peoples." (The word long should now be omitted, as the war is now seen to have been, in fact, an amazingly short one.)—(Page 20.)

"When war suddenly bursts out among people who are thinking of other matters, the first thing they become aware of is that, in the Kaiser's symbolic words, *they did not want it*. And feeling certain that it was not of their willing, they inevitably lay hold of the belief that the other party must have wanted and willed it."—(Page 22.)

"To the modern conscience in time of peace, war is a monstrosity complicated by an absurdity; hence no one can believe himself to have had a hand in bringing it about."—(Page 23.)

"I need not introduce to you our old friend, Clio, Muse of History by profession, but, may I say it? by preference and true vocation, dramatic critic."—(Page 33.)

"Self Interest, a most industrious fellow. It is he who, on week days, plays unremittingly the ground bass of Life."—(Page 34.)

"Sin, whom the all-knowing Gods call *Disease*."—(Page 35.)

"Hatred, the stupidest of all Passions, yet the most cunning in deceit, brought with him a double-bass of many strings: shrill and plaintive gut, rasping steel, and growling bronze, and more besides; some strangely comforting in their tone like a rich cordial, although they heartened men to massacre each other."—(Page 36.)

"Ye are going forth, O Nations, to join Death's Dance even as candid high-hearted virgins who have been decoyed by fair show into the house of prostitution."—(Page 45.)

"Calamities of this kind do not spring from the small and negligible item which suffering and angry men call *guilt*."—(Page 94.)

"Not the air and the waters and the earth's upturned soil, nor the grass and the forests, nor the moon and the stars, are, as our ancestors thought, full of unseen and malevolent spiritual dwellers; but a place more mysterious and perilous, namely the spirit of man, where they lurk unsuspected, and issue forth working subtle or terrific havoc. The spells by which they are let loose are *words*. And the thoughtless magician's apprentice, the unhallowed hierophant, who plays with them, is the man or woman whom we pay to teach us, preach to us, and, above all, to write."—(Page 134.)

"Certain states of the nerves, nay of the muscles, are incompatible with certain thoughts: a clenched fist, for instance, with the notion that there is something to be said for the other side."—(Page 161.)

"The importance of the notion of evolution and all it has brought with it, lies largely in its teaching us to think genetically, which means thinking in terms not of stability, but of change. And this has led a small school of thinkers of to-day, whose thought will perhaps be dominant to-morrow, to the recognition that, in order *to understand what a thing is,* we must ask ourselves: What has it been, and what will it become?"—(Page 178.)

"What was the name of that retired Admiral who went about the country sowing acorns in order that England might never lack for oaken timbers, just at the very moment when the first iron ships were on the stocks? We are like that old gentleman; only, instead of acorns, we are sowing hatred, injustice, and folly." [Collingwood. But where is the first iron ship? Nothing of the kind is visible so far except a coffin ship with League of Nations painted on it, and a black flag in its locker. Perhaps something better may come out of the Russian dockyard.]—(Page 180.)

"Indeed, our optimistic talk about *extracting good out of evil* is, perhaps, one of Satan's little ironical tricks for, in his way, extracting evil out of good."—(Page 191.)

"Patriotism, as a collective though compound passion, requires for its existence segregation, opposition, antagonism, and I venture to add: hostility. . . . Patriotism can be considered virtuous or vicious only according to circumstances; and hence cannot be called virtuous or vicious taken in itself and, so to speak, in its own right."—(Page 234.)

"Statesmen prudently insisting on Preparedness, imprudently overlook that it calls forth Preparedness on the other side; and that the two Preparednesses collide, till both parties find themselves at war; and, in immeasurable, honest (or well-feigned) surprise, accuse the other party of breaking the peace, thus elaborately and expensively safeguarded."—(Page 245.)

"But what the poor world of reality really requires are heroes who can be heroic, and saints who can be saintly, on their own account, without a crowd to back them."—(Page 285.)

"Indignation (let us admit and try to remember this depressing truth!), Indignation is a passion which enjoys itself."—(Page 287.)

"Our guides and guardians, moralists, philosophers, priests, journalists, as much as persons in office, stand to cut a sorry figure before posterity, singling out, as they do, one of themselves, *e.g.*, the deposed and defeated Kaiser, as most convenient for hanging, but with no thought for some quiet Potter's Field suicide for themselves."—(Page 289.)

"The Nations were not aware of what war might do with their bodies and especially with their souls. But how about their guides and guardians?"—(Page 291.)

"Freedom of the Will, in the least metaphysical, the most empirical sense, is not, as theologians used to teach, a permanent possession of the soul. Its very essence is that it lapses by surrender; and that nine times out of ten, the freedom to do, or to refrain, is lost by the initial choice; and, as regards love or war, can be recovered only when the new circumstances which that decision has brought about, and that new self of yours, have run their course and been exhausted. You are a free agent so long as you have not set that stone, *yourself*, a-rolling. Once the push given, the brink left behind, the forces outside and inside yourself, the strange unsuspected attraction, weight and velocity, reduce you to helplessness."—(Page 295.)

G. B. S.

Editor's Notes

■ This review was first published in the *Nation* 27 (18 September 1920): 758, 760. It was reprinted in the *Bodleian* 12 (October 1920): 1894–97; also in Bernard Shaw, *Pen Portraits and Reviews* (1931). The alterations Shaw made at that time are slight: a hyphen is introduced in "well-known author;" "bogeys" is spelt "bogies (and "bogey" becomes "bogy"); and the quotations from Vernon Lee's trilogy are in the same size type as the rest of the article.

▪ There is no indication of when Shaw wrote the above review. He had been from 19 July 1920 at Parknasilla, on the Kerry coast, revising *Back to Methuselah* into "five plays and colossal preface," translating (and transforming) Siegfried Trebitsch's *Frau Gittas Sühne* into *Jitta's Atonement*, and, although he complained he had no time for it, catching up on correspondence.

▪ Vernon Lee [pseud. of Violet Paget] (1856–1935), English writer. Her first major work *Studies of the Eighteenth Century in Italy* (1880) was critically well received, but her first novel, a satirical picture of the aesthetes, *Miss Brown* (1884), was not so successful; thereafter she turned her attention to short stories and essays. Her attitude to the First World War was substantially the same as Shaw's; and, indeed, he was one of the few who spoke in favor of *Satan the Waster* in 1920. In later life Lee grew rather deaf and was obliged to resort to an ear-trumpet, which she also employed when talking to herself. She was famous also for appearing in the first line of a poem by Browning: "Who said 'Vernon Lee'?" She continued writing almost until her death.

▪ Lloyd George (see above, 317).

▪ Edward [Henry] Baron Carson (1854–1935), British politician and judge. Born in Dublin, he became Q.C. of the Irish Bar in 1880, and of the English Bar in 1894. He was Conservative M.P. for Dublin University from 1892 to 1918, during which time he was attorney-general (1915); first lord of the Admiralty (1917); and a member of the War Cabinet from 1917 to 1918. At the time of the above review he was M.P. for the Duncairn division of Belfast, which he remained until 1921.

▪ Poland had received substantial territory under the terms of the Treaty of Versailles (adopted on 28 June 1919), including the so-called Polish corridor extending along the River Vistula to the Baltic Sea, and large sections of Posen [later Poznan] and West Prussia. Responsibility for determining the eastern frontier of Poland was given to the League of Nations, whose proposal, announced on 8 December 1919, and popularly known as the Curzon Line (after George Nathaniel, Marquis Curzon of Kedleston, 1859–1925, the new British foreign secretary), failed to meet Polish demands, notably for Vilna in Lithuania, and the "old boundaries" of 1772. In March 1920 the Polish government forwarded a note to the Bolshevik government of the Soviet Union, requesting that the old boundaries be restored. The Polish demands were rejected, and on 25 April 1920, after several weeks of failed negotiations, Poland declared war on the U.S.S.R., being actively supported by France. The combined Franco-Polish armies inflicted a series of defeats on the Soviets, and the war ended on 12 October 1920, the Treaty of Riga (the following year) securing for Poland a major portion of its territorial claim. In fact, as Shaw mentions, the possibility of Russia and Germany combining *contra mundum* was a great fear in Europe; a fear falsely diminished when Poland signed its nonaggression pacts first with the U.S.S.R. (in July 1932) and Germany (in January 1934), and rekindled when World War II began, with German armies overrunning western and central Poland, while Soviet forces invaded the country from the east.

- Shaw "adapts" the chorus of Clifford Grey and Nat Ayer's song, "Another little *drink* wouldn't do us any harm" (see above, 366):

> Oh, there was a little hen, and she had a wooden leg,
> The best little hen that ever laid an egg.
> And she laid more eggs than any hen on the farm . . .
> *Chorus*
> And another little drink wouldn't do us any harm.

- [Sir] Norman, [Ralph Norman Angell Lane] Angell (1872–1967), English writer and pacifist, who wrote *The Great Illusion* (1910), to prove that wars are economically disastrous, even for the winners; and reiterated his beliefs in *The Great Illusion, 1933* (1933), in which year he won the Nobel Peace Prize.
- [Arthur James, first earl of] Balfour (1848–1930), Scottish statesman and philosopher. His distinguished parliamentary career saw him as secretary for Scotland (1886) chief secretary for Ireland (1887), first lord of the Treasury (1892–93), and prime minister (1902–6). He followed Churchill to the Admiralty in 1915 and under Lloyd George was foreign secretary from 1916 to 1919, at which point Lord Curzon became foreign secretary, Balfour remaining in cabinet as lord president of the Council. At the time of Shaw's article Balfour was representing Britain at the first assembly of the League of Nations.
- The Treaty of Limerick (see above, 381).
- [Vladimir Ilyich] Lenin [formerly Ulyanov] (1870–1924), Russian revolutionary leader. He developed an underground Social Democratic party with the intention of assuming leadership of the working classes against Tsarism. His idea of a professional core of activists leading the revolution, set out in *What Is To Be Done?* (1902), was adopted by the majority [Bolsheviks] arm of the party at the London congress in 1903; but was opposed by the minority [Mensheviks.] From 1907 to 1917 Lenin spent his time strengthening the Bolsheviks against the Mensheviks, interpreting the work of Marx and Engels, and organizing underground work in Russia. After the October Revolution, when the Bolsheviks took power, Lenin inaugurated the "dictatorship of the proletariat" with the formal dissolution of the Constituent Assembly. However, for three years he had to grapple with war from without (see above) and from within (between the "Whites" and the "Reds"). In 1919 Lenin initiated the formation of the Third International, with headquarters in Moscow; the Bolsheviks became the Communist Party; and Lenin, as virtual dictator, was able to put his policies into practice. He died after several strokes on 24 January 1924, his body was embalmed, and his tomb in Red Square, Moscow, became a Soviet shrine.
- Hamlet, watching "The Mousetrap," says to the guilty Claudius: "Your

Majesty, and we that have free souls, it touches us not. Let the galled jade wince, our withers are unwrung" (*Hamlet*, III. ii.).

▪ [Maxim Maksimovich] Litvinov (1876–1951) [real name Meyer Wallach], Soviet politician and diplomat. At the Revolution he was appointed Bolshevik ambassador to London (1917–18). In 1921 he became deputy people's commissar for foreign affairs, and commissar for foreign affairs (1930–39). In this capacity, he was instrumental in bringing about United States recognition of the Soviet Union in 1934, and, following the admission of the U.S.S.R. to the League of Nations, was a member of the Council of the League (1934–38). In May 1939, on the eve of the German-Soviet nonaggression pact he was dismissed from office (on a charge of neglect of duty); but reinstated following the German invasion of Russia. From 1941 to 1943 he was ambassador to the United States, and from 1943 to 1946 vice minister of foreign affairs.

▪ Lenin's "extremely able envoy" was [Leonid Borisovich] Krasin (1870–1926). An early revolutionary and a supporter of Lenin in the Bolshevik/Menshevik split (see above), he was at this time commissar for Foreign Trade and for Transport. His foreign trade duties took him to Sweden and Denmark early in 1920; and he entered Britain as head of the Soviet trade delegation—but subordinate to Foreign Affairs Commissar Chicherin (see below, 478). However, he was an important figure, possessing a conciliatory attitude and elegant manners, and managed to persuade Lloyd George that trade concessions would help moderate people (like himself)to improve their position in the Bolshevik leadership! The trade agreement was signed on 16 March 1920.

▪ [Baron Pëtr Nikolaevitch] Wrangel (1878–1928), Russian military leader. Late in 1917, after the Bolsheviks seized power, Wrangel joined the anti-Bolshevik forces (known as the White Army) in southern Russia, becoming their commander-in-chief in 1920. However, the Soviet-Polish armistice of 12 October 1920 (see above), enabled the Red Army to concentrate its power against Wrangel who, in November, fled to Constantinople [now Istanbul], Turkey, with 150,000 followers. In the last years of his life Wrangel returned to mining engineering in Brussels, Belgium.

▪ [Henry Thomas] Buckle's (see above, 151) unfinished *History of Civilization in England* (1857–61) was much admired by Shaw.

▪ Marx (see above, 21).

▪ Nietzsche (see above, 192).

▪ Bergson (see above, 336).

▪ [Robert] Smillie (1857–1940), Scottish politician. He was president of the Scottish Miners' Federation from 1894 to 1918, and again from 1921. From 1912 to 1921 he was president of the Miners' Federation of Great Britain, and from 1923 to 1929 Labour M.P. for Morpeth.

▪ Vernon Lee's call for "saints who can be saintly, on their own account, without a crowd to back them" may have set Shaw thinking about Joan of Arc, who was canonized in this very year (1920), and who had certainly become the subject of a Shavian play by autumn 1922.

19 February 1921

THE OLD REVOLUTIONIST AND THE NEW REVOLUTION* [C2318]

MR. H. G. WELLS shocked the Bolsheviks the other day by blaspheming against Marx's beard. That set us laughing; but, let us hope, it set them thinking. William Blake, following a tradition as old as the Olympian Jove, always represented God as a man with an impressive beard. Marx grew a beard so godlike that, as Mr. Wells maintains, it could not have been unintentional. But he did not look like God in Blake's Job. Bakunin, a rival revolutionist who loathed Marx, also cultivated a beard, but was still less like the God of Blake and Job. But Mr. Hyndman, who would as soon have thought of aiming at a resemblance to Samuel Smiles as to Jehovah, was born with exactly the right beard (at least, no living man has ever seen him without it), and has always resembled Blake's vision so imposingly that it is difficult to believe that he is not the original, and Blake's picture the copy. Nobody in the British Socialist movement has ever produced this effect or anything approaching it. Mr. Wells is so hopelessly dehirsute that his avowed longing to shave Marx may be the iconoclasm of envy. Mr. Sidney Webb's beard *à la Badinguet* is not in the running. My own beard is so like a tuft of blanched grass that pet animals have nibbled at it. William Morris's Olympian coronet of clustering hair, and his Dureresque beard, were such as no man less great could have carried without being denounced as an impostor; but he resembled the Jovian God in Raphael's Vision of Ezekiel, not the Jehovah of Blake. Mr. Hyndman alone, without effort, without affectation, without intention, turned his platform, which was often only a borrowed chair at the street corner, into a heavenly throne by sheer force of beard and feature. Even he himself could not ignore his beard, though he was the only man who could not see it. It compelled him to wear a frock coat when his natural and preferred vesture would have been a red shirt. He had to preach the class war in the insignia of the class he was fiercely denouncing. When in desperation he discarded his silk hat, the broad-brimmed soft hat that replaced it immediately became the hat of Wotan, and made him

* "The Evolution of Revolution." By H. M. Hyndman. (Grant Richards. 21s.)

more godlike than ever. Mr. Wells has succeeded in making Marx's beard as ridiculous as a nosebag. Let him try his hand, if he dares, on Mr. Hyndman's. He will try in vain. A glance at the excellent portrait which forms the fontispiece to Mr. Hyndman's latest book will carry conviction on this point.

I expatiate on this solitary majesty of Mr. Hyndman's because it is significant of his part in the Socialist movement. As a Socialist leader—and he was ever a leader—he was never any good for team work. It was not that he was quarrelsome (though on occasion he could be a veritable Tybalt); for there was not another leader in the movement who was not quite ready to meet him half-way at any moment in this respect. Nor can it have been that the beard carried with it the curse of the first commandment. It was that he had what is very rare among practical politicians in England, the cosmopolitan mind, the historical outlook, the European interest. For mere municipal Socialism, which he called Gas and Water Socialism, he had no use. Also, as a thorough revolutionary Socialist, he knew that Trade Unionism is a part of Capitalism, being merely the debit side of the capitalist account, and that Co-operative Societies within the capitalist system are no solution of the social question.

Now it happened that during the most active part of Mr. Hyndman's public life, the Co-operative Wholesale was developing prodigiously, and the huge new machinery of Local Government throughout this country made an unprecedented extension of Gas and Water Socialism possible for the first time. Mr. Sidney Webb saw the opening, and jumped at it with the Fabian Society behind him. Mr. Hyndman disdained it, and would not admit that the road to Socialism lay through the suburbs and along the tramlines. Morris, always fundamentally practical, was no fonder of the suburbs than Mr. Hyndman; but he saw that Webb's work had to be done, and gave it his blessing from a distance with the apology (for the distance) that it was not an artist's job. Sidney Webb saw, too, that the efforts made by Morris and Hyndman to organize the workers in new Socialist societies had failed as hopelessly as the earlier attempts of Owen and Marx, and that the Socialists must accept the forms of organization founded spontaneously by the workers themselves, and make them fully conscious of this achievement of theirs by making its history and scope known to them. Hence the famous Webb "History of Trade Unionism" and the treatise on "Industrial Democracy": a labor of Hercules which nobody but Webb and his extraordinary wife would face or could have accomplished. Mr. Hyndman, interested in the evolution of revolution, frankly scorned such spade work. He was eloquent about Chartism, Marxism, and the First International, but simply bored by the Amalgamated Society of Engineers and its past.

The result was that during the last ten years of the nineteenth and the first ten years of the twentieth century Mr. Hyndman was often sidetracked, whilst Municipal Trading and the organization of a Parliamentary Labor Party by the Trade Unions were being hurried up at a great rate. It was not a business that needed a striking figure-head; and Mr. Hyndman is nothing if not a striking figure-head. But it occupied all the capable Socialist subalterns and staff officers very fully; and thus it happened that Mr. Hyndman was left with a retinue devoted enough, but incapable and disastrously maladroit. Look at his portrait, and you can see in his face a sort of sarcastic despair left by his continually disappointed expectation of intellectual adequacy in his colleagues. But for them he would certainly have won the seat in Parliament which he very nearly did win in spite of them. But it is not clear that he could have done anything in that doomed assembly: he has never suffered pompous fools gladly; and the beard does not conceal his contempt for people who cannot think politically in terms of a very comprehensive historical generalization: that is, for ninety-nine hundredths of his fellow countrymen, and ninety-nine point nine per cent. of their chosen representatives. His real work, like that of Marx, was the pressing of that generalization, in season and out of season, on a civilization making straight for the next revolution without the least sense of its destination or its danger.

It is with this generalization that Mr. Hyndman challenges us in his latest book. It is a conspectus of history, and an important one, because it propounds a Sphinx riddle that cannot be answered by mere opportunists. Conspectuses of history are in the air just now. Mr. Wells has put his masterpiece into the form of an outline of the world's history. Mr. Chesterton, having taken the Cross and followed Godfrey of Bouillon to Jerusalem, has come home in a historic ecstasy. Mr. Belloc urges the view of history that the Vatican would urge if the Vatican were as enlightened and as free as Mr. Belloc. And all this at a moment when the threatened dissolution of European civilization is forcing us to turn in desperation to history and social theory for counsel and guidance.

I am not sure that Mr. Hyndman's book is not the most pressing of all these challenging essays. Mr. Wells, though ultra-revolutionary, has deliberately, and for his purpose necessarily, excluded theory from his *magnum opus,* simply preparing a colossal explosive shell crammed with all the relevant historical facts, and hurling it, with a magnificent gesture of intellectual power, at the incompetence, ignorance, obsolescence, and naïve brigandage of the State as we know it. Mr. Chesterton, though he never has a theory, has a cry and a theme; and his extemporizations and variations on them are imaginative, suggestive, inspiring, resounding to the last human limit of splendor in that sort of literary orchestration; but the cry is "Back to the Middle Ages," and the theme is "*Cherchez le Juif*": neither of them in the line of evolution or within the modern conception of the Fellowship of the Holy Ghost. Mr. Belloc is leading a forlorn hope; for Ibsen's Third Empire will not be the Holy Roman Empire. All three either ignore evolution or virtually deny it. Mr. Chesterton and Mr. Belloc even ridicule it, not without plenty of material, thanks to the antics of some of its professors. But Mr. Hyndman has a theory, and an evolutionary one. It is not complicated by Medievalism, official Catholicism, and Judophobia. It has proved itself capable of engaging the faith of small bodies of thoughtful Europeans, and the fanaticism of large bodies of thoughtless ones. The march of events has confirmed it, not only before its promulgation by Marx and Engels (all theories fit the past on the day of publication because they are made to fit it), but since. Mr. Hyndman's clear, close writing, always readable, always carrying you along, never confusing or seducing you by the extravagances, the audacities, the extemporary digressions of writers who, having no military objective, stop repeatedly to play with history, obliges us to entertain his book seriously, and either confute it or let his case win by default. It is quite competently put, with no nonsense about it. There is no attempt to conciliate the reader or propitiate public opinion. Mr. Hyndman does not believe, nor pretend to believe, that *tout comprendre, c'est tout pardonner*: on the whole, he rather concludes that the better you understand history the more you condemn its makers. He spares neither invective nor eulogy; and he words them without the smallest concession to any feeling but his own. He uses tact to make his presentation of his case effective, never to make himself agreeable. In the end you may dislike him, especially if he dislikes you; but his case is there to be answered, and is furthermore a case that must be answered. Mr. Wells's case is unanswerable; but its acceptance does not commit you to Marxist Communism. Mr. Belloc has a very strong case against Parliament, and would have us discard it and face a really responsible monarchical (not royal) Government by a President and Cabinet; but he associates this with a strenuous advocacy of private property on the ground that it will do us no harm if we have little enough of it and are as ignorant as Tennyson's Northern Farmer. It is

Mr. Hyndman who shows you that if there is anything in history, private property, in its modern reduction to absurdity as Capitalism, is tottering to its fall, and that we must make up our minds to be ready for the new Communist order or for a crash.

But Mr. Hyndman has yet another claim to urgent attention over his competitors in the survey of history. His book comes just when the hugest of the European Powers is putting its doctrine to an experimental test on an unprecedented scale. And this situation is made piquant by the unexpected fact that Mr. Hyndman repudiates Lenin as completely as he repudiates Cromwell or Robespierre. The English arch-Marxist has been confronted with the fulfilment of all the articles of his religion: the collapse of Capitalism, the expropriation of the expropriators, the accouchement of the old society pregnant with the new by *Sage Femme La Force,* the dictatorship of the proletariat, and the obliteration of the *bourgeoisie* as a social order. And instead of crying *Vive la Révolution!* and packing his traps for Moscow to inaugurate the latest statue of Marx, he out-Churchills Churchill in his denunciation of the Bolsheviks. This is interesting: we want to know how he justifies it. At first sight he seems to cover his position by setting up the mature Marx as a historic materialist against the immature Marx of the Communist Manifesto, apparently forgetting that in a previous chapter he has knocked historic materialism into a cocked hat. Bolshevist Marxism, I may explain, is the Marxism of the Manifesto, taking a hint from Rousseau by calling its administrators Commissars. Mr. Hyndman declares that to make Force the midwife of progress is to discard the full Marxist doctrine (insisted on at the end of every chapter in his book) that Force cannot anticipate the historic moment, and that premature revolutions are bound to fail, like the Peasants' War and the insurrection of Baboeuf.

But this, though true, does not prove Bolshevism premature. The undeniable fact that no midwife can deliver the child alive until its gestation is complete by no means shakes the historical likelihood that the birth will be a difficult one, needing a strong hand and a forceps, and possibly killing the mother. Who is to say that the historic moment has not come in Russia? Certainly not Mr. Hyndman, who has so convincingly proved from history that the historic moment is as often as not a psychological moment. All that the Marxian historic moment means when analyzed is the moment when the *bourgeoisie* loses its grip on industry and on the armed forces of the Government, and lets them slip into the hands of the leaders of the proletariat when these leaders are what Marx calls class-conscious: that is, fully aware of the relations, actual, historical, and evolutionary, between the *bourgeoisie* and the proletariat, and well instructed as to the need for and nature of the transition from Capitalism to Communism which they have to operate. Surely these conditions are realized in Russia at present as nearly as they are ever likely to be anywhere. Lenin is as doctrinaire as Marx himself; and the *bourgeoisie* is down and out without having struck a blow. The Soviet Government has made none of the mistakes for which Mr. Hyndman reproaches the Luddites and the Paris Commune of 1871. Far from destroying machinery, they are straining every nerve to develop production and open up foreign trade. Instead of superstitiously respecting the banks, and humbly borrowing a little money from the Rothschilds to go on, they have promptly seized all the specie, bullion, and jewellery they can lay their hands on and made any attempt to hold it back a capital offence, like the Apostles. They have, on the whole, pounced on the right things, and shot the right people (from the Marxian point of view). They are as ruthless in dealing with the counter-revolution, and with attempts to carry on habitual commercialism, as they are tolerant of mere sentimental regrets for the imaginary good old times of the Tsardom. They have shown themselves able to handle and dominate both the *bourgeoisie* and the Militarists. Koltchak [sic], Denikin, and Wrangel successively have tried to play the part of Gaston de Foix, only to be cracked like fusty nuts by Trotsky, in spite of the gold of Churchill (*ci-devant* Pitt) and the munitions of Foch. Is there any likelihood of the conditions under which Feudalism and Capitalism accomplished their transformation of society being reproduced more exactly for the transformation of Capitalism into Communism? If, as Mr. Hyndman contends, Bolshevism is not real Marxism, but a murderous imposture, what does he think the real thing will be like? He owes us an answer to this question.

If one may infer his answer from his indictment of Bolshevism, he relies on the fact that the colossal peasant proprietary which forms the bulk of the Russian nation is unconverted. This is true; but if Socialism is to wait until farmers become class-conscious Marxists, it will wait for ever. The *bourgeoisie* did not wait for the approval of the farmers before they consummated the Capitalist transformation by establishing Free Trade, which all but abolished British agriculture. We should still be in the Stone Age if Hodge had always had his way. I cannot suspect Mr. Hyndman of that romantic cockney idolatry of a politically stupid and barely half-civilized occupation which makes Mr. Chesterton and Mr. Belloc offer us mud pies as castles in Spain.

The antagonism between city civilization and rural primitiveness has underlain all the revolutions just as it underlies this one. Mr. Hyndman quotes with indignation a general order to the Red troops in the Don district to exterminate the Cossacks; but it needs only a little hypocrisy and the requisite alteration of names to be eligible for Sir Hamar Greenwood's "Weekly Summary." The French Revolution did not stop to convert the farmers of La Vendée: the two parties tried to exterminate one another until the peasants were crushed, as they always are by the city men, because if the peasants had their own way there would not be any towns at all; and the peasants, having by this time forgotten how to make their own clothes and ploughs, cannot do without towns. Mr. Hyndman does not deny that the Russian farmers are better off than they were before the revolution: what he insists on is that they refuse to feed the towns, and will produce no more than enough for their own consumption. Now it would perhaps be better, as far as we can judge at a distance, to tax the farmers frankly to their capacity and compel them to produce by compelling them to pay the tax, by distraint if necessary, than to pretend, as the Soviet does, to buy their surplus produce with worthless paper money. But the Soviet leaders disclaim reliance on this expedient: they declare that they are surrounding their factories with communal farms, and that they will extend this system until individual proprietary farming is crowded off the earth in Russia. It is absurd to contend that the historic moment for this has not arrived: far more plausibly might it be alleged that it is overdue. The historic moment is the first moment at which it can possibly be done.

Mr. Hyndman, steadily intellectual as a historian at long range, is (being human) prejudiced as a current politician. During the war he was what he still is, a vehemently patriotic "Majority Socialist." But he denounces the German Majority Socialists fiercely for voting the German war credits and not coming out as pro-Britons and Pacifists. Yet he has no words scathing enough for Lenin, because Lenin refused to vote the Russian war credits, and recognized the necessity for securing peace at any price that could be paid by a Micawber note of hand. He is equally intolerant of "the unfortunate Bolshevism and Pacifism of some of the French leaders." He can forgive neither the Germans for fighting us, nor the Bolshevists for surrendering at Brest-Litovsk when they were hopelessly beaten, instead of bleeding to death as England's auxiliaries. This is neither Socialism nor philosophy of history: it is naïve John Bullism. Why should John reproach Fritz because he, too, found in the hour of trial that blood is thicker than gas and water?

However, Mr. Hyndman's anti-Bolshevism is not always mere Jingo resentment of the Brest-Litovsk Treaty. There are moments when he seems to be revolted by the institution of compulsory labor by the Soviet Government, and by the imposition of the will of an energetic minority on the Russian people. But in his own vivid and very favorable sketch of Peruvian Communism under the Incas, he recognizes that suppression of idleness and ruthless punishment of sloth and ca' canny was the political secret of the prosperity and happiness of these people who always sang at their work and did not know what poverty was. For my part, I cannot understand how anyone who has the most elementary comprehension of Socialism can doubt that compulsory labor and the treatment of parasitic idleness as the sin against the Holy Ghost must be fundamental in Socialist law and religion. If Lenin has abolished idleness in Russia, whilst we, up to our eyes in debt, are not only tolerating it, but heaping luxury upon luxury upon it in the midst of starvation, then I am much more inclined to cry "Bravo, Lenin!" and "More fools we!" than to share Mr. Hyndman's apparent horror. As to the Bolshevists being in the minority, Mr. Hyndman cites with approval "the marvellous transition effected by Japan in forty years from Feudalism to Capitalism." Immediately before this he says that "permanent social revolution and Communist reconstruction can only be successfully achieved when the bulk of the population understands and is ready to accept the new forms which have, consciously or unconsciously, developed in the old society." But he cannot believe that the Japanese man-in-the-street understood what was happening when Capitalism was substituted for Feudalism, or accepted it in any other sense than letting it happen to him, just as the British laborer let the New Poor Law and the enfranchisement of the *bourgeoisie* happen to him. There never has been any such conversion of the majority of a people: all the changes have been imposed by energetic minorities. We should still be under the rule of the shepherd kings if Mr. Hyndman's Liberal generalization were true or even one-fifth true. What is true enough for practical purposes is that until the live wires of the community are charged with a new current, or with a higher potential of the old one, neither the majority nor the minority can change the system. Even Peter the Great, with all his gibbets and racks and knouts, could not have imposed his ideas on old Russia if his retinue of able blackguards had not been as tired of old Russia as he was. The old Russians were in a stupendous majority all through. What Mr. Hyndman stigmatizes as "the tyranny of the minority" is an indispensable condition not only for moving society forward (or backward, as at present), but for keeping it alive where it stands. In England the majority will never be converted to the need for government at all: nine-tenths of us are born anarchists.

Finally, Mr. Hyndman falls back once more on Historic Determinism, and declares that the Bolshevists must fail because the economic conditions are not ripe. This impales him on the point of his own spear, because one of the best chapters in his book, called "The Limits of Historic Determinism," contracts those limits to a tiny space in which there is room for a monument inscribed *Hic jacet* Carolus Marx, but not room for Russia. It is, he says (and proves it) "a demonstrable truth that similar forms of production sometimes have wholly dissimilar Governments imposed upon them." He shows that a single man with a conviction, like Mahomet, can start a movement which will conquer half the civilized world, whilst movements that have the sympathy of four out of every five men in the country wither and are stamped out by a few unpopular rascals. Does not Mr. Hyndman then, as a Socialist leader, take an unnecessarily heavy risk in denouncing as untimely an attempt to do for Communism what Mahomet did for Islam, when he himself has shown that none of the Determinist arguments against the possibility of its success will hold water? His real reason seems to be that he has set his heart on England being the Holy Land of the Communist faith: John Bull again! Also, curiously enough, on the transition being a peaceful parliamentary one. The old Internationalist is a patriot at heart, the old revolutionist a pacifist.

The petulance of the days when Mr. Hyndman was a spoilt child of Nature and Fortune still flashes out from time to time in this book. One can see that he can no more work in double harness to-day than he could when he and Morris kicked over the traces of the Democratic Federation nearly forty years ago; but the general effect is one of mellowness, which encourages us to believe that Mr. Hyndman's later years have not been the least happy of his tempestuous life. Certainly his beard never became him better than it does to-day.

G. B. S.

Editor's Notes

- The above review was first published in the *Nation*, now the *Nation and The Athenaeum* 28 (19 February 1921): 703–5. It was also published as

"Beards, Bolsheviks and Bourgeoisie," in *Hearst's Magazine* (New York) 40 (August 1921): 13, 73–74, and reprinted in Rosalind Travers Hyndman's *The Last Years of H. M. Hyndman* (London: Grant Richards; New York: Brentano's, 1924.) It was also reprinted by Shaw in *Pen Portraits and Reviews* (1931), the only alterations being the removal of inverted commas around titles, and the removal of periods in "Mr," and hyphens in "to-day."

- There is no indication of when Shaw wrote the review of Hyndman's book; but it was undoubtedly typed by his new secretary, Blanche Patch, at 10 Adelphi Terrace, and when finished simply sent downstairs to the *Nation*, whose staff occupied the ground and first floors of No. 10. A possible clue to its date of composition lies in a letter Shaw wrote to Boris Lebedeff on 22 November 1920, in which he uses the same form of words about Wells's book *Russia in the Shadows* (1920), that he uses in the opening two sentences of the article, saying: "Wells has given a human touch to his descriptions by his iconoclasm about Marx; but *by making us laugh at Marx's beard* and at the absurdly uncritical deification of him by the Bolshevists he has created a much more goodnatured atmosphere" (*Collected Letters 1911–1925*, 702; my italics).

- H. M. Hyndman (see above, 20).

- H. G. Wells (see above, 346–47).

- William Blake (1757–1827), English poet, painter, engraver, and mystic. His twenty-one *Illustrations to the Book of Job* (1826), completed when he was nearly seventy, are considered to be unequaled in modern religious art for sheer imaginative force and visionary power.

- Bakunin (see above, 21).

- Samuel Smiles (1812–1904), Scottish writer and social reformer, whose most celebrated book, *Self-Help* (1859), containing short "lives" of great men, and the admonition "Do thou likewise," became the archetypal Victorian school-prize. He wrote many other "improving" works, including *Character* (1871), *Thrift* (1875), and *Duty* (1880).

- "Badinguet" was a nickname of [Charles Louis] Napoléon [Bonaparte] III (1808–73); and "Dureresque" means presumably like the beard of Albrecht Dürer (1471–1528) as revealed not in the 1493 beardless painting, but in the 1498 self-portrait, where the painter's ringlets suggest the "Olympian coronet," though the beard is still not as full as that of William Morris.

- Raphael's "Vision of Ezekiel," currently in the Pitti Gallery, Florence, was probably painted in 1517, and depicts an amply bearded and moustached god, supported by cherubs, an eagle, a winged lion, and a winged bull.

- Wotan, otherwise known as Odin, Wuotan, or Woden, was the highest god of the Northern races. When seated on his throne he wore his eagle helmet. However, when he descended to earth (as he did frequently to see what men were doing), Wotan wore a broad-brimmed hat, drawn low over his forehead to conceal the fact that he had only one eye.

- Tybalt, Juliet's cousin in *Romeo and Juliet*, quarrels with and is killed by her husband, Romeo, which precipitates the latter's exile and is indirectly the cause of Juliet's death.

- The First Commandment is "Thou shalt have no other gods before me."
- Morris (see above, 165).
- Webb (see above, 139).
- Owen (see above, 20–21).
- Wells's book was *The Outline of History* (1920); Chesterton (see above, 331–32), who, like the French nobleman Godfrey of Bouillon, or Godefroy de Bouillon (1061?–1100), leader of the First Crusade, had made a pilgrimage to Jerusalem a year after the war ended, wrote *The New Jerusalem* (1920); Hilaire Belloc (see above, 379) had written *A History of England* (1915), and, went on to complete a four-volume reinterpretation of English history finishing in 1931, crossing swords with H. G. Wells over the latter's *Outline of History.*
- Engels (see above, 149).
- For Shaw's earlier invocation of Tennyson's Northern Farmer, see above, 402.
- Lenin (see above, 425).
- [Oliver] Cromwell (1599–1658), English revolutionary, who became the Lord Protector of England from 1653 to 1693.
- [Maximilien Marie Isidore de] Robespierre (1758–94), French revolutionary, who became supreme ruler of France in 1794.
- The bloody but unsuccessful Peasants' War took place in Germany from 1524 to 1526 between the working classes and the nobles and clergy. Both sides committed atrocities, and thousands were killed, but the peasants won no concessions by their revolt.
- The insurrection of [François Noël] Baboeuf [or Babeuf], whose pen name was Gracchus Babeuf (1760–97) was his attack upon the French Revolution (which he had originally enthusiastically supported) because it had not developed along the lines of his own socialist theories. He took part in a plot to overthrow the Directory in 1796, and was executed.
- The Luddites were English mechanics who, in violent reaction against the replacement of handicraft by machinery in the period 1811 to 1816, set about destroying machinery in the midlands and north of England. Their name is allegedly taken from from one Ned Ludd who lived in a Leicestershire village in 1779, and who, in a fit of fury, broke up two frames in a stockinger's house.
- After the surrender of Napoleon III [emperor of France] at the Battle of Sedan in September 1870, Paris capitulated to the Germans, and the National Assembly (the majority of whom were royalists) agreed to the peace terms dictated by the German statesman Otto von Bismarck. The socialists in Paris considered the terms of the peace humiliating, and led a successful uprising against the national government, setting up a proletarian dictatorship in its place in March 1871. A municipal council (the Paris Commune) was elected which proposed various measures for the benefit of the working man; but before they could take effect, the National Assembly sent troops into Paris, where bloody fighting led to the downfall of the Commune on 28 May, with the loss of 20,000 Communards.

- In the Acts of the Apostles (2:44 et seq.) we learn that the apostles had all things in common, selling their possessions and goods, and dividing the proceeds with all as every person had need. However, in chapter 5 we hear of Ananias and his wife who sold some land, and "kept back part of the price"; whereupon Peter said, "Ananias, why hath Satan filled thy heart to lie to the Holy Ghost, and to keep back part of the price of the land? why hast thou conceived this thing in thine heart? thou hast not lied unto men, but unto God." It is then reported that Ananias "hearing these words fell down, and gave up the ghost: and great fear came on all them that heard these things . . ."
- [Aleksandr Vasilievich] Kolchak (1874–1920) was a Russian naval commander in World War I, who went to Omsk after the 1917 Revolution as war minister in the anti-Bolshevik government. As leader of the White Russians, he cleared Siberia in conjunction with the Russian soldier [Anton Ivanovich] Denikin (1872–1947), who had been in the army man and boy and had risen to the rank of lieutenant-colonel in the First World War. When Omsk fell to the Bolsheviks, Kolchak was shot. Denikin went on to win the Ukraine, but was defeated by the Red Army at Orel in 1919, and the following year resigned his command and escaped to Constantinople. He lived in exile in France from 1926 to 1945, and thereafter in the United States.
- Wrangel (see above, 426).
- Gaston (de) Foix (1489–1512), French nobleman and soldier. This nephew of Louis XII of France, who became duke of Nemours in 1505, displayed such bravery and acumen in the Italian wars that he became known as the "Thunderbolt of Italy." Twice he defeated the Swiss, chased the pope's troops from Bologna, took Brescia from the Venetians, and defeated the Spanish forces at Ravenna, where he himself was killed.
- [Leon] Trotsky (see below, 447).
- [Sir Winston Leonard Spencer] Churchill (1874–1965), English statesman. Successively soldier, war correspondent, member of Parliament, cabinet minister, first lord of the Admiralty, secretary of state for war, and prime minister of Great Britain from 1940 to 1945, when he was an inspiring wartime leader. In the general election at the conclusion of the war, however, Churchill was defeated and became leader of the Opposition in Parliament. He became prime minister again in 1951. In 1953 he was knighted. Advancing age caused Churchill to resign as prime minister in 1955, but he continued to serve in the House of Commons until 1964. Noted as a painter, a wit, and a writer as well as a politician, in his book *Great Contemporaries* (1937), Churchill describes Shaw as "one of my earliest antipathies"; but after his mother (who was interested in literary celebrities) took Churchill to lunch with Shaw in the early years of this century, he confessed to being "instantly attracted by the sparkle and gaiety of his conversation." The polar opposite of Shaw in politics, Churchill, in his account of him, perhaps not surprisingly, dwells almost exclusively upon Shaw's charm and levity, likening him to a jester, thus reducing Shaw's serious thought to triviality. And yet in the same

chapter, he describes Shaw as "the greatest living master of letters in the English-speaking world."

- [Ferdinand] Foch (1851–1929), French soldier and marshal of France. Born in Tarbes, and educated at the Ecole Supérieure de la Guerre, he became professor of strategy there in 1894 and commandant in 1897. He was instrumental in winning World War I, first with his strategy at the Marne and at Ypres (September and November 1914), and at the Somme (1916); then as commander-in-chief of the Allied armies from March 1918 when he orchestrated the engagements that forced the German retreat and eventual surrender.
- Sir Hamar [formerly Thomas Hubbard] Greenwood (1870–1948), Canadian-born British politician. In 1895 he moved to England. He was called to the bar by Gray's Inn in 1906, in which year he became Liberal member for York and acted as Sir Winston Churchill's parliamentary private secretary for four years. When war broke out he himself raised the 10th Battalion, South Wales Borderers, and commanded it at the front in France. In February 1915 he was created a baronet. In August 1916 he returned to politics; three years later he became undersecretary for home affairs, and in April 1920 joined the Cabinet as the (last) chief secretary for Ireland. As such he was responsible for reinforcing the Royal Irish Constabulary with 5,800 recruits, chiefly soldiers who had been demobilized, who, because of their mixed uniforms, were known as "Black and Tans" (from a famous pack of Limerick hounds). These also included some fifteen hundred auxiliary police, some of them ex-convicts, all of them inappropriately trained, whose infamous and violent conduct against the civilian population of Ireland was defended by Greenwood in his "weekly summaries" of the conflict, in the House of Commons.
- La Vendée is a Department of France, whose capital, La Roche-sur-Yon is about two hundred miles SW of Paris. During the French Revolution much of this area was controlled by Royalist and Roman Catholic insurgents until June and July 1794 when harsh treatment was meted out. The Nantes Tribunal, headed by Jean Baptiste Carrier, dealt with those who aided the rebels in La Vendée and sent more than eight thousand people to the guillotine in three months.
- Shaw's view that it would be "better to tax the farmers frankly to their capacity and compel them to produce by compelling them to pay the tax, by distraint if necessary, than to pretend, as the Soviet does, to buy their surplus produce with worthless paper money" was adopted two months later by Lenin (see below, 444).
- Wilkins Micawber (see above, 338).
- Peter I [known as Peter the Great] (1672–1725), czar of Russia (1721–25) developed Russia into a great European power by introducing many Western European scientific, technological, cultural, and political concepts. However, he did this at a price. He regimented his subjects ruthlessly; and his reforms and swift, cruel reprisals for not honoring them, made a powerful impression upon the Russian people.

■   The belief that "nine-tenths of us are born anarchists," was repeated (and extended) in Shaw's Preface to the Webbs' *English Local Government* (written the following winter) in which he writes, "Both Americans and Englishmen are born Anarchists."

7 January 1922

TROTSKY, PRINCE OF PAMPHLETEERS*
[C2376]

WHATEVER his terrified bourgeois critics may think or say of Trotsky as Archcommunist-Terrorist, they must admit that when he takes his pen in his hand he is a Nailer. To say that he outshines Junius and Burke means nothing nowadays, not that the horses they flogged are dead or even moribund (they are all alive and kicking), but because we have now no more use for Junius and Burke than for George III. But this cannot be said of Karl Marx, a superb pamphleteer, Trotsky's old master in the art; yet in everything but length of wind the pupil surpasses the master. For one thing, Trotsky has a much better temper. Marx, in his hatred of the bourgeoisie and his jealousy of Proudhon and Bakunin, was implacable: there was no touch of gallantry in him. And his championship of the proletariat and criticism of its exploiters were so lacking in realism that one is repeatedly tempted to declare that he might as well have lived in Patmos as in Soho and on Haverstock Hill for all the evidence his works contain of his having ever seen a working man or talked to a financier or civil servant in his life. Trotsky is not like that. Making all allowances for the effervescence of his success—such a success as Marx never experienced—in cracking Koltchak [*sic*], Denikin, and Wrangel like three fusty nuts, and frightening Europe as nobody else since the Kaiser has frightened it, the gaiety of his controversial style must come from a genuine gaiety of heart. He is a ruthless and trenchant antagonist, but not a nasty one. Marx accused Bakunin of dishonesty, of treachery: he

* The Defence of Terrorism: A Reply to Karl Kautsky." By L. Trotsky. (Labor Publishing and Allen and Unwin.) 3s. 6d. net.

blackened his character more than he disparaged his brain. Trotsky is much kinder to Kautsky. When Kautsky makes a point, it catches Trotsky's intellectually honest eye at once; and he exclaims cheerfully, "Let us see whether we cannot find a grain of truth in this mass of drivel." Like Lessing, when he cuts off his opponent's head, he holds it up to shew that there are no brains in it; but he spares his victim's private character. Marx hit where he could, and often hit spitefully: Trotsky does not hit below the belt. He leaves Kautsky without a rag of political credit; but he leaves him with his honor intact.

There is another and a much more important difference. Mr. John Burns, early in his public life, said, "All the Anarchism I ever had in me was knocked out by the first ten minutes I spent on a County Council Committee." In saying so, he put his finger on a truth that needs to be remembered in these days when men of the non-governing classes may find themselves Cabinet Ministers and even Prime Ministers. Karl Marx never had to raise or spend a farthing of public revenue, nor to sign a death warrant. Trotsky and Lenin were in that position until 1917. They lived and let live like private men of moderate means until one day Lenin found himself full of bullets, some of which have not yet been extracted. The two realized then that Bolshevism was face to face with enemies who regarded a Bolshevist as a mad dog, and Communism as a heresy to be ruthlessly stamped out by the secular arm. They realized also that these enemies could not be converted and disarmed by kindly and cogent lectures on surplus value and economic evolution. Trotsky grasped the fact that Lenin had been shot because he had not shot the people who wanted to shoot him. Having the rare gift of profiting by experience, he rapidly organized his shooting resources, and soon laid out the whole reaction, domestic and foreign, Koltchak, Denikin, and Wrangel, capitalist, syndicalist, and anarchist, with such Napoleonic energy, that all Europe, though red with brothers' blood to its elbows, was horrified at his deplorable indifference to the precepts of the Sermon on the Mount. But order reigned in Moscow; Denikin found London a safer place; and Koltchak mouldered in the grave without his most devoted followers being able to pretend that his soul was marching on.

There is, however, one remarkable omission in Trotsky's defence of Proletarian terrorism. The romantic tradition in history demands that the sensation scene in a revolution must be a regicide. Why did the Soviet revive that tradition? It was found possible to get rid of Louis

Philippe without guillotining him. Napoleon the Third died in his bed. I have met many English Republicans and Communists; but not one of them regards a regicide as an inevitable incident of a change from Capitalism and monarchy to Communism and Republicanism. Even when regicide was still *de rigueur* we were content, after due trial, with The head of the Man of Blood: we did not lynch him, and his wife and children with him. The French executed both Louis and Louis' wife; but Marie Antoinette was formally and separately tried on a charge of unpardonable treason of which she was unquestionably guilty. Why did the Russian revolutionists not only go back to the obsolete tradition of regicide, but actually massacre the whole royal family without a trial, and in plain violation of the rights of its members as citizens of the republic?

Trotsky should have dealt with this if he meant his book to go to the whole European and American jury. The incident was an extraordinary one, because of its very curious combination of ruthless and lawless murderousness with a consideration for the feelings of the victims unprecedented in the records of regicide. Everything was done that could be done to make the event as little disagreeable to them as possible, except to spare their lives. Even their religious interests were carefully consulted by these slaughtermen who regarded such interests as imaginary and superstitious. It was contrived that a full choral service should be held, with singers imported for the occasion, in the royal household. The victims, thus unconsciously prepared for death, were allowed to go to bed in the usual domestic course. They were awakened and told that as there were some threatening disturbances in the neighborhood, it had been hastily decided to remove them by night to a place of safety. They rose, the women shewing the good faith in which they had received the news by carefully concealing their jewelry in their clothes. They assembled in an empty room to await their carriages. The Tsar asked for a chair, and was given one. Then a body of gunmen, having arranged exactly which person each should shoot, entered the room. The Tsar was dead within five seconds; and only the gunmen were alive within thirty.

If we compare this with the miseries and degradations of Marie Antoinette's imprisonment, and the suspense and public infamy of her ride in the tumbril to the guillotine, we have to admit that the Russian royal family was fortunate indeed in being so mercifully disposed of. What remains to be explained is why they were disposed of at all. What right had the Soviet Government to lay a finger on three obviously quite nice girls whom it had converted from grand duchesses into citizenesses? If the Tsar and Tsarina were as guilty of trying to overthrow the Government as Charles or Louis or Marie Antoinette, as of course they were, what emergency was there to justify lynching them instead of bringing them to trial?

Trotsky should answer that question. It is not enough to rely silently on the not very clear statements that have been made as to the innocence of the Soviet Government in the matter. It may be that this very methodical lynching was as unauthorized as the knocking out of Pussyfoot's eye in the streets of London by a mob of students. It may be that it was a pure revolutionary conventionality: an application of the rule "See what was done last time" by men whose knowledge of history was very superficial, and whose sense of constitutional procedure was nil. It may be that it was an excess of zeal in disregard of formal orders which the Soviet Government nevertheless meant to occur, like the excesses of the Black-and-tans in the reprisals campaign in Ireland. In any case Trotsky owes us a word about it. He would spare us any official humbug, we know; and even his personal view of the incident would be interesting. So far, it is indefensible from the bourgeois point of view. From the Communist point of view it is horrifying.

Howbeit, when the shooting was over, Trotsky found, as we did when our shooting was over, that his victory was only the beginning of his troubles. He might have shot the entire human race outside the Communist Party and those who accepted its government, without making it easier to keep Russia alive. Some of the laborers, no longer compelled by the Capitalist system to work for twenty-four shillings a month or starve, behaved like perfect capitalist gentlemen, and refused to work at all. Trotsky had to announce that the human animal is lazy, and that every advance in civilization is an expression of the desire to save labor. Thus is Trotsky also among the prophets of the Manchester School and its famous desideratum of a selfish Incentive to Labor. To supply that Incentive effectually, it was necessary to substitute for starvation the alternative of being shot; and quite a good many proletarians had to be shot before the others could be convinced that the Soviet was in earnest. The young heroines who had braved Siberia and the dungeons of Peter and Paul to teach the sacred duty of revolution against the tyranny of the Tsar were so scandalized by the shooting that they reverted to their old revolutionary habits; and Trotsky and Lenin, doubtless to their own astonishment, found themselves filling the fortress prison of Peter and Paul with precisely the same heroes and heroines that Stolypin had immured. Seditious newspapers, too, found themselves as ruthlessly suppressed as The Globe was by Mr. Lloyd George, or the Sinn Fein Press by Sir Hamar Greenwood.

Then there was the land question. The clever people who had helped themselves to unduly large estates in the *débâcle* had to be disposed of by allowing their less grasping neighbors to hang them and divide their acres more equitably. It was even necessary to send agitators to suggest the process when it did not occur spontaneously. But you cannot make a silk purse out of a sow's ear; and still less can you make a Communist out of a peasant proprietor, always an unbreakable vessel of the great original sin of property. In virtuous indignation at the Russian Hodge's want of respect for Karl Marx the Soviet seized his harvest and paid him in roubles, ten thousand roubles being equal to one cab fare. Hodge refused to produce harvests on such terms; and I suggested in these columns, in a review of a book by Mr. Hyndman, that the peasant should be taxed to a definite amount (as our landlords tax our Hodge's with a definite rent) and then let alone. Two months later Lenin announced that he had done this.

Then came the discovery that the organization of production and distribution was beyond the capacity of a new and undeveloped form of government; and it had to be sub-let to individual employers with permission to trade. This step was hugely chuckled over in the unregenerate west of Europe (mostly starving through the breakdown of Capitalism) as an ignominious return to Commercialism, as to which all that need be said is that if our Commercialists are satisfied they are welcome to their laugh as far as the Soviet is concerned.

Finally, it had all along been obvious to the few who really understood the economic revolution in Russia that though it was sound Marxism to expropriate the expropriators, it was one thing for a Russian Government to expropriate the Russian expropriators, and quite another to expropriate the French and English expropriators. The British Government, for example, expropriates its own millionaire subjects to the tune of eleven shillings in the pound annually, and, in addition, takes seven years income from them when they die; but if it were to inform the United States that its debt to them was subject to the same expropriative taxation, Admiral Lord Beatty would presently be plugging eight-inch shells into the people with whom he is now swearing Blutbruderschaft over the dinner table.

The recognition of this frontier limit to the power of a Communist Government is the latest step of the Soviet; and it has taken a famine to drive them to it, although it was the most obvious of all the first necessities of the situation. The Russian ex-capitalist will observe ruefully that his Government has been kinder to French and British investors than to him.

This concession to western Commercialism makes an end of the last excuse left to the Powers for refusing to recognize the Russian Government. It has been from the beginning the only Government in Europe that has earned the attention of thoughtful people. Our own Government has exhausted the possibilities of blundering without losing its ignorant complacency or prescribing any remedy for the monstrous mess it has got us into except a hair of the dog that bit us. During the war it was forced by the simple alternative of defeat and subjugation to organize national effort and set up a magnificent national plant, instead of depending on the profiteers who were supplying our batteries with one shell each a day at prices ranging from six to fifteen hundred pounds per shell. The success of this move was enormous; yet the moment the war was over, the Government set up a cry that national effort was corrupt and disastrous and its destruction economical. It deliberately disbanded the national workers; broke up the national plant; sold the national factories by the dozen for little more than it has since paid private contractors to set up single new ones; bribed the disbanded workers to idle about until the ruin was irrevocable; debased the currency; placed every possible obstacle in the way of the communications which are the very life circulation of industry by making travelling and postage dear under pretence of making them pay; plundered the vanquished of ships and coal, and met the obvious consequences to the workers of South Wales and the Tyneside by raising a new army to slaughter them if they did not consent to starve quietly; put taxes on German exporters which British importers had to pay: in short, did all the things for which Trotsky would have shot them.

Naturally the political authors of these exploits do not like Trotsky. Naturally, too, Trotsky has many admirers among the people who have been reduced to destitution by the Government policy. They perceive that as far as terrorism goes, all governments are alike: the policeman's truncheon and the rifles of the emergency force and the Black and Tans are the final arguments of the State, whether it be Communist or Capitalist. The difference lies in the use to which the force is put. Trotsky and Lenin use it, apparently, to abolish idleness and waste; to build up their nation by placing the welfare of its children first; to stop thieving and brigandage in high places; to destroy the tyranny of money and the superstitions of factitious nobility; to organize production and distribute income with the object of producing human welfare instead of perpetuating the squalid tragedy of Dives and Lazarus: in sum, to do what every famous teacher of mankind from Plato and Jesus to More and Ruskin have been preaching throughout the centuries. Because they have read the works of Marx and despise the works of the Fabian Society they have made some elementary blunders; but they have been the first to confess them (the Capitalist press owes its exultant knowledge of them, not to its own perspicacity, but to Lenin's speeches); and they have done their best to rectify their errors, instead of concealing them and persisting in them as we do. No wonder our politicians feel the earth shaking under them when such unheard-of innovations are perpetrated by men who are actually in power with Red armies at their command. What is more, the earth *is* shaking; and if we are not careful it will gape and swallow up our sham civilization.

This book of Trotsky's, not being a Fabian tract, does not throw much light on the technique and machinery of Communism. He will puzzle some readers at first because he begins with a military study of the Paris Commune of 1871 from the point of view of a Proletarian Minister of War who regards that episode, which to the British bourgeois is only a dimly remembered French riot, as the opening campaign of a war still in progress, the end of which will be the end of an epoch. He then makes hay of the pet democratic excuse of our *fainéants* that no political change should be made until a majority of the population understand, desire, and vote for it, which is as much as to say that no political change should ever be made at all. His demonstration of the necessity for abolishing the Constituent Assembly on the day of its birth is absolutely convincing: Mr. Balfour would have done the same. Trotsky declares, in effect, that Communists must do what their opponents have always done: that is, impose Communism on the people the moment they find themselves able to do so, knowing that the people will upset it in the long run if they find it intolerable to them, but having at least had the opportunity of sampling it and growing up under it instead of reading silly tirades against it in the papers when their drudgeries leave them any time for reading at all. Our own governing classes can say no less. Only, they could not say it so well. Trotsky has learnt his lesson from the realities and responsibilities of Government; and but for that prejudice of his against idleness (Cecil Rhodes expressed it in the one clause of his will which we never mention) he would be a man after Mr. Winston Churchill's own heart.

BERNARD SHAW

Editor's Notes

- This review was first published in the *Nation and The Athenaeum* 30 (7 January 1922): 560–61. It also appeared modified and shortened, as "Concessions to Commercialize End Powers' Excuses for Refusing to Recognize Russia," in the *New York American*, 5 February 1922, vol. 2, p. 2:1–8.
- There is no indication when Shaw wrote the above. In December 1921 and January 1922 he was revising his pamphlet, originally intended as a Preface to the Brockway-Hobhouse Report from the Committee (chaired by Lord Olivier, and on which Shaw served) on the conditions of English prisons, for inclusion as a Preface to Sidney and Beatrice Webb's *English Local Government*. It was withheld from the report because Shaw widened its scope beyond the limits imposed by Hobhouse, particularly in regard to "the sixth commandment." Shaw's cheerful acceptance—indeed promotion—of the death penalty for crimes other than murder in that Preface makes one better understand his review of Trotsky's pamphlet, as does his description of deterrence in the criminal justice system as a euphemism for terrorism.
- Leon Trotsky [otherwise Lev Davidovich Bronstein] (1879–1940), Russian revolutionary, who was arrested when only nineteen as a member of a Marxist group and sent to Siberia. In 1902 he escaped, joined Lenin in London, and took part in the abortive 1905 revolution, ending up in Siberia again. Escaping a second time, he became a journalist among Russian émigrés in the West, returning to Russia in 1917. He joined the Bolshevik party and, with Lenin, was mainly responsible for organizing the November Revolution. As commissar for foreign affairs he negotiated with the Germans the peace treaty of Brest-Litovsk, and in the civil war as commissar for war he expanded the Red Army from 7,000 to 5,000,000. His influence did not long survive Lenin's death, however; and Stalin finally exiled him to Central Asia in 1927. He continued to repeat Lenin's warnings against Stalin, with the result that he was expelled from Russia two years later; but his continuing intrigue and agitation in exile led to his being sentenced to death *in absentia*. In 1937 he found asylum in Mexico City, where three years later he was assassinated by Ramon del Rio with an ice-pick.
- Karl [Johann] Kautsky (1854–1938), German Socialist leader. Like Shaw he denounced World War I as an imperialist venture, but unlike Shaw he was a pacifist. He disagreed with the Russian Bolshevik revolution of November

1917, and refused to follow a large section of his party into the newly formed United German Communist Party, which supported the Soviet regime. He wrote a number of polemics against the Bolshevik leadership, including "Dictatorship of the Proletariat" (1918). After World War I he lived mainly in Vienna, directing the activities of the Austrian Socialists; but after Hitler's annexation of Austria in 1938, Kautsky went to Amsterdam, where he died. Among his numerous publications perhaps his most famous are his four-volume *Theories of Surplus Value* (1905–10) (based on manuscripts and notes of Marx, and intended as the basis for a fourth volume of Marx's *Das Kapital*), *Ethics and the Materialist Conception of History* (1907), and *Foundations of Christianity* (1908).

▪ A "Nailer" is slang (c.1818) for a marvelous specimen, or a very skillful hand at something (*OED*).

▪ "Junius" was the pseudonym of the author (whose true identity has never been discovered) of a series of shrewd and well-written letters that appeared in the *Public Advertiser* between 1769 and 1771, attacking public figures from a Whig standpoint; and [Edmund] Burke (1729–97), Junius's contemporary, was the Irish statesman and philosopher whose eloquence against the prevailing abuse and governmental mismanagement of his day is also preserved in his writings and speeches.

▪ George III (1760–1820), king of England, popularly supposed mad, is now thought not to have been, though his behavior was certainly strange.

▪ Proudhon (see above, 129–30).

▪ Bakunin (see above, 21).

▪ Koltchak, Denikin and Wrangel (see above, 432, for the identical simile of "nuts," and 426 and 438 for information about the three).

▪ Shaw adapted the witticism about Lessing—when he cuts off his opponent's head, he holds it up to shew that there are no brains in it—when he wrote *The Apple Cart* (1928), a play that deals with the attempted dissolution of a monarchy. King Magnus is speaking with Boanerges, the President of the Board of Trade:

MAGNUS. Not only have I to sign the death warrants of persons who, in my
    opinion ought not to be killed; but I may not even issue death warrants
    for a great many people who in my opinion ought to be killed.
BOANERGES [*sarcastic*] Youd like to be able to say "Off with his head!"
    wouldnt you?
MAGNUS. Many men would hardly miss their heads, there is so little in them.

He also repeated it in *Everybody's Political What's What* (1944).

▪ [Gotthold Ephraim] Lessing (1729–81), German dramatist and critic, one of the leaders of the Enlightenment. He founded, with the German philosopher Moses Mendelssohn (1729–86) and the German critic Christoph Friedrich Nicolai (1733–1811), a critical journal *Briefe, die Neueste Literatur Bettrefend* [*Letters on the latest in literature*] (1759–65) to which he contributed a remarkable series of essays that were instrumental in getting rid of French influence in German literature. He also wrote numerous highly successful (and seminal) plays that have become classics of the German stage.

- John Burns (see above, 270).
- Tsar Nicholas II [Nikolai Aleksandrovich] (1868–1918), the last emperor of Russia (1894–1917). After his forced abdication on 17 March 1917, he and his German-born wife Empress Alexandra Feodorovna (1872–1918) and their children were imprisoned in Siberia, where, at Ekaterinburg [now Sverdlovsk] on 17 July 1918, they were all shot to death.
- [William Eugene Johnson] (1862–1945), known as "Pussyfoot," American reformer and prohibition propagandist. His nickname came from his catlike policies in pursuing lawbreakers in the "Indian Territory." He was chief special officer in the U.S. Indian Service from 1908 to 1911, during which time he secured 4,400 convictions. He also became well known as a temperance organizer, and came to England in 1919 to drum up support for the cause. He lost an eye at a prohibition meeting at Essex Hall, London, when he was struck and dragged from the platform by medical students.
- Courcelles, in Shaw's play *Saint Joan*—which he was to begin writing in less than a year—was also a man with a superficial sense of history. His call for the torture of Joan is refused by the Inquisitor:

COURCELLES. Your lordship is merciful, of course. But it is a great responsibility to depart from the usual practice.

JOAN. Thou art a rare noodle, Master. Do what was done last time is thy rule, eh?

- Black-and-tans (see above, 439).
- The Manchester School (see above, 412).
- [Petr Arkadevich] Stolypin (1862–1911), Soviet chairman of the Council of Ministers. As a consequence of his perceived success as district marshal in Kovno Province [Russian Poland] (1889–1902), he was sent to provinces troubled by unrest—particularly Saratov—where he proved cruelly effective in bringing the peasantry under control. In 1906, while retaining his ministerial post, he was appointed minister of the interior. Stolypin was both monarchist and nationalist, and formulated repressive policies toward non-Russian minorities under Russian control (Finns and Poles), though he did, for pragmatic reasons, try to discourage the popular anti-Semitism of the time. He took a great deal upon himself, including sweeping agrarian reforms until his own popularity with the increasingly autocratic Nicholas became shaky, and he probably would have resigned or been dismissed had he not been shot at point-blank range (at the opera house in Kiev) by Dmitri Bogrov, for reasons that have never been made clear, though a political conspiracy is probable.
- [Sir Thomas] More (1478–1535), English statesman, whose lord chancellorship under Henry VIII was marked by simplicity and virtue.
- [David Beatty,] first Earl Beatty (1871–1936), English naval commander, had a distinguished war record (sinking three German cruisers in Heligoland Bight at the outbreak of the war, and another near the Dogger Bank in 1915,

and taking part heroically in the Battle of Jutland (31 May 1916). He was
made First Sea Lord in 1919.

- Cecil Rhodes's sixth (and last) will, dated 1 July 1899 (with codicils of
January and 11 October 1901, and 18 January and 12 March 1902) left his
beautiful house on the slopes of Table Mountain for the use of the premier of
a federated South Africa, and his Suffolk estate at Dalham to his own family,
with the clause that, according to Shaw, we "never mention": namely, that no
"loafers" should inherit it.
- Winston Churchill (see above, 438–39).

11 March 1922

CHESTERTON ON EUGENICS, AND SHAW ON CHESTERTON* [C2385]

A criticism of Mr. Chesterton is in the nature of a bulletin as to the
mental condition of a prophet. Mr. Chesterton has disciples. I do not
blame him: I have some myself. So has Mr. Wells. All sorts of people
have disciples, from osteopaths to tipsters. But most of them do not get
into our way politically. Mr. Chesterton's do. Therefore it is important
that his pulse should be felt, and his condition reported on; for if he
were to go—well, may I say, for the sake of alliteration, off his
chump?—the consequences might be serious. He has many magical
arts and gifts at his command. He can make anything that can be
made with a pen, from a conspectus of human history to a lethal jibe
at the Lord Chancellor; and to utilize this practically boundless technical equipment he has enormous humor, imagination, intellect, and
common sense.

Now in respect of the humor and imagination, his integrity can be
depended on; but when you come to the intellect and common sense,
you have to be careful, because his intellect is fantastic and his common sense impatient. That is because his humor and imagination will
creep in. It is such fun to take some impossibly obsolete person—say a
Crusader—and shew that he was right in his ideas, and that the
sooner we get back to them the better for us, that no humorist inge-

* Eugenics, and Other Evils. By G. K. Chesterton. (Cassell, 6s.)

nious enough to do it can resist it unless he has the dogged cerebral honesty of an Einstein. And here again it is so funny to *épater les savants* by arguing that Einstein, being a Jew, invented Relativity to popularize his longnosed relatives, and that Ptolemy, who thought the earth flat, was on solid ground, that the cumulative temptation sometimes strains even Chesterton's colossal shoulders. To give way is such an amiable weakness too! When he does it I am always amused; and I am never taken in: at least if I am I do not know it, otherwise, of course, I should not be taken in. But other people may be. Besides, Mr. Chesterton may take himself in. He may stray up an intellectual blind alley to amuse himself; for it is the greatest mistake to suppose that there is nothing interesting or useful to be picked up in blind alleys before you run your head into the *cul de sac*. A man like Mr. Chesterton finds more diamonds in such an alley than an ordinary man walks over pebbles in the clearest logical fairway. By stopping to pick the diamonds up, like Atalanta, he may not get far enough to discover that the alley is blind. Even if he does, he may find a way out by pretending that he has found one, as the mathematician overcomes an intellectually insuperable difficulty by pretending that there is such a quantity as minus x. Searchlights in blind alleys have illuminated the whole heavens at times; and men have found courage and insight within their limits after finding nothing but terror and bewilderment in the open desert.

Thus Mr. Chesterton, who once lived near the Home for Lost Dogs in Battersea, has a whimsical tendency to set up Homes For Lost Causes, in competition with Oxford University, in his half-explored blind alleys. Like the Home in Battersea, they are not popular with the lost ones; for the final hospitality offered is that of the lethal chamber. The Lost Causes like their last ditches well camouflaged. Mr. Chesterton scorns concealment: he stands on the parapet, effulgent by his own light, roaring defiance at a foe who would only too willingly look the other way and pretend not to notice. Even the Lost Causes which are still mighty prefer their own methods of fighting. The Vatican never seems so shaky as when G. K. C. hoists it on his shoulders like Atlas, and proceeds to play football with the skulls of the sceptics. Pussyfoot's chances of drying the British Isles seldom seem so rosy as they do the morning after Mr. Chesterton has cracked the brainpans of a thousand teetotallers with raps from Gargantuan flagons waved by him in an ecstasy in which he seems to have ten pairs of hands, like an Indian god.

Nature compensates the danger of his defence by the benefit of his assault. He went to Jerusalem to destroy Zionism; and immediately the spirit of Nehemiah entered into him, and there arose from his pages such a wonderful vision of Jerusalem that our hearts bled for the captivity, and all the rival claimants, past and present, silly Crusader and squalid Bedouin in one red burial blent, perished from our imaginations, and left the chosen people of God to inherit the holy city. He attacks divorce with an idealization of marriage so superhuman (without extraordinary luck) that all his readers who have not yet committed themselves swear that nothing will induce them to put their heads into the noose of that golden cord. He stated the case for giving votes to women so simply and splendidly that when he proceeded to give his verdict against the evidence it passed as a misprint. Really a wonderful man, this Chesterton; but with something of Balaam in him, and something of that other who went whither he would not.

His latest book is called "Eugenics, and Other Evils." It is a graver, harder book than its forerunners. Something—perhaps the youthful sense of immortality, commonly called exuberance—has lifted a little and left him scanning the grey horizon with more sense that the wind is biting and the event doubtful; but there is plenty of compensating gain; for this book is practically all to the good. The title suggests the old intellectual carelessness: it seems mere nonsense: he might as well write Obstetrics and Other Evils, or Dietetics or Esthetics or Peripatetics or Optics or Mathematics and Other Evils. But when you read you find that he knows what he is about. The use of the word Eugenics implies that the breeding of the human race is an art founded on an ascertained science. Now when men claim scientific authority for their ignorance, and police support for their aggressive presumption, it is time for Mr. Chesterton and all other men of sense to withstand them sturdily. Mr. Chesterton takes the word as a convenient symbol for current attempts at legislative bodysnatching—live-bodysnatching—to provide subjects for professors and faddists to experiment on when pursuing all sorts of questionable, ridiculous, and even vicious theories of how to produce perfect babies and rear them into perfect adults. At the very first blow he enlists me on his side by coming to my own position and reaffirming it trenchantly. "Sexual selection, or what Christians call falling in love," he says, "is a part of man which in the large and in the long run can be trusted." Why after reproducing my conclusion so exactly he should almost immediately allege that "Plato was only a Bernard Shaw who unfortunately made his jokes in Greek," I cannot guess; for it is impossible to understand what the word "only" means in this sentence. But the conclusion is none the less sound. He does not follow it up as I do by shewing that its political corollary is the ruthless equalization of all incomes in order that this supremely important part of man shall no longer be baffled by the pecuniary discrepancies which forbid the duchess to marry the coalheaver, and divorce King Cophetua from the beggar maid even before they are married. But that will come in a later book.

Mr. Chesterton is implacable in his hostility to the Act for dealing with the feeble-minded. How dangerous these loose makeshift categories are when they get into the statute book he brings out thus: "Even if I were an Eugenist, then I should not personally elect to waste my time locking up the feeble-minded. The people I should lock up would be the strong-minded. I have known hardly any cases of mere mental weakness making the family a failure: I have known eight or nine cases of violent and exaggerated force of character making the family a hell."

This is a capital example of Mr. Chesterton's knock-out punch, which is much more deadly than Carpentier's. It is so frightfully true, and illuminates so clearly the whole area of unbearable possibilities opened up by this type of legislation, that it makes the reader an Anarchist for the moment. But it does not dispose of the fact that the country has on its hands a large number of people, including most authors, who are incapable of fending for themselves in a competitive capitalistic world. Many of them do quite well in the army; but when they are demobilized they are in the dock in no time. As domestic servants they are often treasures to kindly employers. Provide for them; organize for them; tell them what they must do to pay their way, and they are useful citizens, and happy ones if the tutelage is nicely done, as between gentlemen. But freedom and responsibility mean misery and ruin for them. What is to be done with them? Mr. Chesterton says "Send them home." But that solution is already adopted in most of the cases in which it is possible. How about those who have no home? the old birds whose nest was scattered long ago? You cannot get rid of a difficulty by shewing that the accepted method of dealing with it is wrong. Mr. Chesterton's demonstration of its danger actually increases the difficulty; for it is quite true that many of the most hopeless cases are cases not of Defectives but of Excessives. If the Prime Minister were to say to Mr. Chesterton to-morrow, "You are quite right, God forgive us: the Act is a silly one: will you draft us another to deal with these people properly?" Mr. Chesterton could not fall back on the eighteenth century and cry *Laissez faire*. All the king's horses and all the king's men cannot set that lazy evasion up again. If Mr. Chesterton were not equal to the occasion, Mr. Sidney Webb and his wife would have to be called in; for the facts will not budge; and it is cruel to abandon the helpless to a mockery of freedom that will slay them.

Mr. Chesterton joins the campaign against the quackeries of preventive medicine with zest. "Prevention is not better than cure. Cutting off a man's head is not better than curing his headache: it is not even better than failing to cure it." He shews that the dread of religious superstition is itself a superstition, possible only to a Press that is a century out of date because its journalists are so hurried and huddled up in their stuffy offices that they have no time to observe or study anything, and can supply copy to the machines only by paying out any sort of old junk that has been current for a century past. He says with a sledge-hammer directness that reminds me of Handel: "The thing that is really trying to tyrannize through Government is Science. The thing that really does use the secular arm is Science. And the creed that really is levying tithes and capturing schools, the creed that really is enforced by fine and imprisonment, the creed that really is proclaimed not in sermons but in statutes, and spread not by pilgrims but by policemen—that creed is the great but disputed system of thought which began with Evolution and has ended in Eugenics. Materialism is really our established Church; for the Government will really help to persecute its heretics. Vaccination, in its hundred years of experiment, has been disputed almost as much as baptism in its approximate two thousand. But it seems quite natural to our politicians to enforce vaccination; and it would seem to them madness to enforce baptism."

This, except for the slip by which the essentially religious doctrine of Evolution is confused with the essentially devilish doctrine of Natural Selection, is undeniable, whether you believe in vaccination or not; and it is well that we should be made sharply aware of it, and also of the fact that as much hypocrisy, venality, cruelty, mendacity, bigotry and folly are using Science (a very sacred thing) as a cloak for their greed and ambition as ever made the same use of Religion. Indeed this is an understatement as far as the mendacity is concerned; for what priest ever lied about the efficacy of baptism as doctors have lied, and are still lying, about such shallow and disastrous blunders as Lister's antiseptic surgery, or have laid hands on children and gouged out the insides of their noses and throats in the spirit of the Spanish grandee who admired the works of God, but thought that if he had been consulted a considerable improvement might have been effected?

But we must not let our indignation run away with us. Let us contemplate a typical actual case. Scene: a school clinic. Present: a doctor, a snuffling child, and its mother. A dramatic situation has just been created by the verdict of the doctor: "This kid has adenoids." The mother is not in the least in a Chestertonian attitude. Far from objecting to State surgery, she holds that her child has a right to it in virtue of the doctor being paid to be there; and she is determined to insist on that right in spite of what she considers the natural disposition of all men, including doctors, to shirk their duties to the poor if they can. Far from crying, "Hands off my darling: who but his mother should succor him and know what is good for him?" she demands, "Ain't nothing to be done for him, poor child?" The doctor says, "Yes: the adenoids had better be cut out."

Now this may not be the proper remedy. It is on the face of it a violent, desperate, dangerous, and injurious remedy, characteristic of the African stage of civilization in which British surgery and therapy still languish. A better remedy may be one of the formulas of Christian Science, or the prayer and anointing of St. James and the Peculiar People, or that the child should say every morning between sleeping and waking, "My nose is getting clearer and clearer," twenty-five times over. A million to one the real remedy is half a dozen serviceable handkerchiefs, a little instruction in how to use the nose in speaking and singing, with, above all, better food, lodging, and clothing. The mother does not "hold with" the mystical remedies. Of the two which are not mystical, the last mentioned means spending more money on the child; and she has none to spend, as the doctor very well knows: else, perhaps, he would honestly press it on her. Thus there is nothing for it but the knife. The hospital will cost the mother nothing; and it will be rather a treat for the child. She does not consider the hospital a disgrace like the workhouse: on the contrary, all her human instincts and social traditions make her feel that she is entitled to help in case of sickness, for which her very scanty household money does not provide. Accordingly, the interior of the unfortunate infant's nose is gouged out; and possibly his tonsils are extirpated at the same time, lest he should be overburdened with tissues which surgeons consider superfluous because they have not yet discovered what they are there for.

Now observe that here the mother does not protest: she insists. The doctor operates because there is no money to pay for sane natural treatment. The alternatives are to do nothing, or to throw the mother back on some quack who would promise to cure the child for a few shillings. All the responsible parties, the mother, the doctor, the schoolmaster, and presumably Mr. Chesterton, are against doing nothing. What, then, is Mr. Chesterton protesting against? He is protesting against adapting the treatment of the child to the low wages of its parents instead of adapting the wages of the parents to the proper treatment for the child. And he is quite right. From the point of view of the welfare of the community the decision of the doctor can be compared only to that of Grock, the French clown, who, when he finds that the piano stool is not close enough to the piano, moves the piano to the stool instead of the stool to the piano. We have managed to bedevil our social arrangements so absurdly that it is actually easier for our Parliamentary Grocks to move the piano to the stool. But nobody laughs at them. Only exceptionally deep men like Mr. Chesterton even swear at them.

Mr. Chesterton is, however, too able a man to suppose that swearing at the Government is any use. All Governments are open to Shakespear's description of them as playing such fantastic tricks before high heaven as make the angels weep, just as all men who undertake the direction of other men are open to William Morris's objection that no man is good enough to be another man's master. But when a job has to be done, it is no use saying that no man is good enough to do it. Somebody must try, and do the best he can. If war were declared against us we could not surrender at discretion merely because the best general we could lay hands on might as likely as not be rather a doubtful bargain as a sergeant. Or let us take a problem which arises every day. We are confronted with the children of three mothers: the first a model of maternal wisdom and kindness, the second helpless by herself but quite effective if she is told what to do occasionally, and the third an impossible creature who will bring up her sons to be thieves and her daughters to be prostitutes. How are we to deal with them? It is no use to pretend that the first sort of mother is the only sort of mother, and abandon the children of the others to their fate: the only sane thing to do is to take the third woman's children from her and pay the other two to bring them up, giving the second one the counsel and direction she needs for the purpose. Of course you can put the children into an institution; only, if you do, you had better be aware that the most perfectly equipped institution of the kind in the world (it is in Berlin) acts as a lethal chamber, whilst in the mud-floored cabins of

Connaught bare-legged children with a single garment, and not too much of that, are immortal. You have to do something; and since the job is too big for private charity (which is abominable, tyrannical and humiliating: in fact everything that raises Mr. Chesterton's gorge in public maternity centres and school clinics and the like is a tradition from the evil days of private charity) it must be organized publicly; and its organizers must be taught manners by Mr. Chesterton and the few others who know that insolence to the poor, though compulsory in our public services, acts like sand in an engine bearing.

But it remains true that as most people do not become "problems" until they become either poor or rich, most of the bad mothers and fathers and sons and daughters could be made passably good by simply giving them as much money as their neighbors, and no more. I am not so much concerned about their freedom as Mr. Chesterton; for it is plain to me that our civilization is being destroyed by the monstrously excessive freedom we allow to individuals. They may idle; they may waste; when they have to work they may make fortunes as sweaters by the degradation, starvation, demoralization, criminalization, and tuberculization of their fellow citizens, or as financial rogues and vagabonds by swindling widows out of their portions, orphans out of their inheritances, and unsuspecting honest men out of their savings. They may play the silliest tricks with the community's wealth even after their deaths by ridiculous wills. They may contaminate one another with hideous diseases; they may kill us with poisons advertised as elixirs; they may corrupt children by teaching them bloodthirsty idolatries; they may goad nations to war by false witness; they may do a hundred things a thousand times worse than the prisoners in our gaols have done; and yet Mr. Chesterton blames me because I do not want more liberty for them. I am by nature as unruly a man as ever lived; but if Mr. Chesterton could guess only half the inhibitions I would add to the statute book, and enforce by ruthless extermination of all recalcitrants, he would plunge a carving knife into my ribs, and rush through the streets waving its dripping blade and shouting *Sic semper tyrannis*. I see in the papers that a lady in America has been told that if she does not stop smoking cigarettes her child will be taken from her. This must make Mr. Chesterton's blood boil; for he tells us with horror that when he was in America, people were admitting that tobacco needs defending. "In other words," he adds, "they were quietly going mad." But the truth, I rejoice to say, seems to be that they have given up the defence. What right has a woman to smoke when she is mothering? She would not be allowed to smoke if she were conducting a bus or selling apples or handkerchiefs. A man should be able to turn away in disgust from a railway smoking carriage without being reminded of his mother.

But unless I tear myself away from this book I shall never stop. If, as Mr. Chesterton seems to insist, I am to regard it as another round in the exhibition spar with Mr. Sidney Webb which he continues through all his books, I must give the verdict to Mr. Webb, because the positive man always beats the negative man when things will not stay put. As long as Mr. Webb produces solutions and Mr. Chesterton provides only criticisms of the solutions, Mr. Webb will win hands down, because Nature abhors a vacuum. Mr. Chesterton never seems to ask himself what are the alternatives of Mr. Webb's remedies. He is content with a declaration that the destruction of the poor is their poverty, and that if you would only give each of them the security and independence conferred by a small property on its owner (when he is capable of administering it) your problems would vanish or be privately settled. Nobody is likely to deny this: least of all Mr. Sidney Webb. But Mr. Chesterton's Distributive State, which is to bring about this result by simply making us all dukes on a small scale, would not produce that result even if its method were practicable. To many men—possibly to the majority of men, property is ruinous: what they need and desire is honorable service. They need also a homestead; and though for some of them the ideal homestead is a flat in Piccadilly, others want a house in the country, with a garden and a bit of pleasure ground. That is what Mr. Chesterton enjoys; but if you were to offer him these things as industrial property, and ask him to turn his garden into a dirty little allotment and make money out of it, he would promptly sell himself as a slave to anyone who would employ him honorably in writing. So would I: so would Mr. Belloc: so would Mr. Webb. In short, this distribution of property of which Mr. Chesterton tries to dream, but to which he has never been able to give his mind seriously for a moment, so loathsome is it, would be an abominable slavery for the flower of the human race. Every Man his Own Capitalist is the least inspiring political cry I know; and when Mr. Chesterton raises it my consolation is that it cannot be realized. I urge Mr. Chesterton to go on thundering against the tyranny of Socialistic regulation without Socialistic distribution (the Servile State) to his heart's content; but I warn him that if he persists in threatening us with the double curse of peasantry and property as an alternative, he will give the most fantastic extremes of doctrinaire Eugenics an air of millennial freedom and happiness by mere force of contrast.

G. B. S.

Editor's Notes

- There is no indication when Shaw wrote the above review, which was published in the *Nation and The Athenaeum* 30 (11 March 1922): 862–64, and reprinted in Bernard Shaw, *Pen Portraits and Reviews* (1931). In the reprint Shaw altered the clause "and that Ptolemy, who thought the earth flat," to "and that the saints who thought the earth flat"; removed the hyphen from "half-explored"; the inverted commas around titles; altered the colon after "Handel" to a comma; removed commas before opening inverted commas for speech (e.g., "Far from crying 'Hands off my darling' "); and removed the apostrophe in "Ain't," and the periods in "St." and "Mr."
- G. K. Chesterton (see above, 331–32).
- Albert Einstein (1879–1955), German-Swiss-American mathematical physicist, who published three papers in 1905 that revolutionized the human view of the physical universe, and helped lay the foundations for the nuclear age: one offered an explanation of the photoelectric effect that concerns the emission of electrons from metal surfaces exposed to light (a study that became a cornerstone of quantum theory, and in practical terms paved the way for television and automation systems); a second paper analyzed mathematically the theory of the Brownian movement—and provided a method for determining the dimensions of molecules; and the third was Einstein's initial presentation of the special theory of relativity, describing the relativistic nature of uniform motion and the interdependence of space and time, culminating in the famous equation postulating the equivalence of mass and energy [$E = mc^2$]. The paper entitled *General Theory of Relativity* was published in 1915, in which year Einstein was made a member of the Prussian Academy of Science, which provided him with a yearly stipend to allow him to devote himself exclusively to research. Shaw and Einstein first met at a dinner party in June 1921, nine months before the above review was published, when Einstein was visiting London. Afterward they kept in touch through the intermediary of Archibald Henderson, Shaw's biographer, who was also a scientist and who, in 1923, worked at the Kaiser Wilhelm Institute, where Einstein was the director. Einstein admired Shaw, congratulating him in 1926 on his seventieth birthday, and two years later praising and offering to promote his *Intelligent Woman's Guide to Socialism and Capitalism*. Shaw for his part had always been interested in science (he was a life member of the Royal Astronomical Society, and showed an interest in space travel when he was in his nineties), and was

delighted with the fact that Einstein considered himself an "artist-mathematician"; see Archibald Henderson *Table-Talk of G.B.S.* (London: Chapman and Hall, 1925), 139. When the German dictator Adolf Hitler came to power in 1933, Einstein, who had been a vocal opponent of National Socialism, was on a lecture tour in Belgium; and found that in his absence the German government had revoked his citizenship, confiscated his property, set a price on his head, and had him expelled from the Prussian Academy of Science. Many nations offered him refuge; but after spending a few months in seclusion in London, he went to the United States and became an American citizen in 1940, serving as professor of theoretical physics and head of the mathematics department at Princeton University until 1945, when he became professor emeritus.

▪ Atalanta's beauty gained her many admirers; but she was not to be won easily. She required her suitors to run a race with her. If any reached the goal before her he was to be her husband; but all whom she outdistanced were to be killed with her dart. As she was almost unbeatable in running, many suitors perished in the attempt, until Milanion (some say Hippomenes) appeared: Aphrodite had given him three golden apples from the garden of the Hesperides, and as soon as the race started he threw down the apples, and Atalanta, fascinated, stopped to pick them up, so that Milanion arrived first at the goal.

▪ The Home for Lost Dogs in Battersea was established in 1860, and moved to its present site (4 Battersea Park Road) in 1871. The number of dogs and cats brought in annually runs into thousands.

▪ It was Matthew Arnold (in the preface to the first series of *Essays in Criticism,* 1865) who described Oxford University as "Home of lost causes, and forsaken beliefs, and unpopular names, and impossible loyalties!"

▪ Pussyfoot (see above, 449).

▪ Balaam, requested by Balak, king of Moab to curse the invading Israelites, was warned by God not to do so. Yet he went on his donkey with the princes of Moab, and would have been killed by an angel standing in the way, if the donkey had not saved him: when he beat the donkey, the Lord opened her mouth and she reproved Balaam (Numbers 22–24). The "other who went whither he would not" was Saint Peter. In Saint John's Gospel, Jesus speaks to Peter: "Verily, verily, I say unto thee, When thou wast young, thou girdest thyself, and walkedst whither thou wouldest: but when thou shalt be old, thou shalt stretch forth thy hands, and another shall gird thee, and carry thee wither thou wouldest not" (John 21:18). In other words, there was something in Chesterton that refused to do the will of God, even when it was plain; just as there was something else in him that compelled him to carry out the will of God in spite of himself. (The image of Balaam is an appropriate one for Chesterton, who wrote a poem called "The Donkey" in the voice of the beast that carried Christ into Jerusalem.)

▪ King Cophetua, a legendary African king, cared not for women until he saw a beggarmaid "all in gray" with whom he fell in love. He married her, and together they lived "a quiet life during their princely reign." The tale is told in one of the ballads in Percy's *Reliques.*

- [Georges] Carpentier (1894–1975), French boxer. He won the French lightweight title at the age of fifteen, a European championship at seventeen, and was badly beaten at the hands of Americans Frank Klaus and Billy Papke. Shaw was always a keen follower of boxing; on 13 December 1919 he had reported in the *Nation* on the Carpentier–Joe Becket fight, which Carpentier won by a knockout. Carpentier won the world light-heavyweight title from "Battling" Levinsky in 1920, and subsequently defeated "Bombardier Billy" Wells and [Ted] "Kid" Lewis (though this victory was much disputed). However [William Harrison] "Jack" Dempsey, who had won the heavyweight title by defeating Jess Willard at Toledo, knocked out Carpentier in the fourth round of their fight in Jersey City, New Jersey, on 2 July 1921. Shaw had picked Carpentier to win (in an article in the *New York American* on 30 June 1921, with the headline "Bernard Shaw Says Georges Will Beat Dempsey Easily"). Shaw insisted in a letter to Lawrence Langner on 29 July 1921 that he had *not* picked Carpentier to win; but that he *had* said that the betting of 4 to 1 on Dempsey was absurd. He went on to claim that Dempsey had been lucky.
- The Webbs (see above, 139, 199).
- The Peculiar People were a Christian religious sect founded in England in 1838, taking their name from references in both Old and New Testaments, who rejected medical aid, trusting solely to prayer for the cure of disease.
- See the Epistle of James, chapter 5:

> 14. Is any sick among you? Let him call for the elders of the Church; and let them pray over him, anointing him with oil in the name of the Lord:
>
> 15. And the prayer of faith shall save the sick, and the Lord shall raise him up; and if he have committed sins, they shall be forgiven him.

- Shaw's ironic suggestion that a person's tonsils should be removed, "lest he should be overburdened with tissues which surgeons consider superfluous because they have not yet discovered what they are there for," is a reminiscence of Sir Patrick Cullen in *The Doctor's Dilemma* (1906), who says: "I know your Cutler Walpoles and their like. Theyve found out that a man's body's full of bits and scraps of old organs he has no mortal use for. Thanks to chloroform, you can cut half a dozen of them out without leaving him any the worse, except for the illness and the guineas it costs him."
- Grock was the stage name of Adrien Wettach (1880–1959), Swiss (not French) clown, whose first appearance in London was in 1911 under the aegis of C. B. Cochrane, the famous impresario. Thereafter he became world-famous in both circus and theater. The point of his act was a battle with a succession of musical instruments, none of which he succeeded in playing. In fact he was a good musician.
- The reference to government's "playing such fantastic tricks before high

heaven as make the angels weep," drawn from Shakespeare's *Measure for Measure,* was applied by Shaw to Sir Almroth Wright on 18 October 1913 (see above, 277).

- Morris (see above, 165).
- *Sic semper tyrannis.* "Thus shall tyranny always [perish]."

15 October 1926

SOCIALISM AND THE LIVING WAGE: LABOUR'S TWOFOLD TASK* [C2614]

ON the first page of this remarkable pamphlet, just issued by the Independent Labour Party, it is noted that "as if by tacit consent, the Labour Movement has hitherto avoided any precise statement of this far-reaching principle": that is, the principle of the Living Wage.

I venture to offer an explanation of this apparent omission. The Labour Party is partly a Trade Unionist Party and partly a Socialist Party. The Living Wage is a principle in Trade Unionism; but in Socialism it has no locus standi, because Socialism proposes that we shall live on our share of the national income and not by the sale of our labour as a commodity in the market for wages. Naturally, the Socialist leaders of the Party can hardly put forward as a principle something that they want to abolish on principle. Their business in the matter is to co-operate with their Trade Unionist colleagues in forcing on the Capitalist system, whilst it lasts, a minimum price for labour as a market commodity.

As a rule, the cheaper commodities are, the better. But there are exceptions. Cheap labour, cheap gin, and cheap cocaine snow are public calamities. It is desirable that they should be as costly and as difficult to buy as possible, pending the day when they shall not be purchasable at all.

What few of us seem to know is that the Living Wage is one of the principles of Capitalism. It is true that the Capitalist parties are as ignorant of this as an average forecastle hand is of astronomy and mathematics, without which his captain dare not lose sight of land. It

* *The Living Wage.* By H. N. Brailsford, John A. Hobson, A. Creech Jones, and E. F. Wise. (The I.L.P. Publications Department.) 6d.

is a fact, nevertheless, that Capitalism, which is a carefully-thought-out social and economic system, is based on a theorem that if private property and freedom of contract are secured by law, the first two needs of a progressive society will be provided for automatically. Number one: All proletarians will find employment at which they can earn sufficient to keep them alive, without ever earning enough to enable them to cease working. Number two: The proprietors will become so rich that even when they are gorged with luxuries they will still have so much more than they can spend that they must invest it as industrial capital to save it from rotting. That is, they must lend it to men of business who will feed troops of proletarians with it and set them to make railways and build factories and construct machines and so forth. When Turgot, Adam Smith, and their successors convinced William Pitt and Cobden and Peel and Company that Capitalism could and would carry out this tremendous undertaking, of which the older systems were becoming more and more incapable, Capitalism was established as a principle of government and given a free hand. It is precisely this free hand that the coal owners, led by a gentleman who seems to understand Capitalism, are now insisting on.

The general reply of the Labour Party, or rather the Labour Parties (for there are really two Labour Parties in coalition in Parliament to-day), is that Capitalism has failed to carry out its guarantee of a living wage. It has never provided the entire proletariat with that for a single day. It has had to confess that a reserve army of destitute unemployed is necessary to its operations. When it had a free hand it wiped out, as the saying was, nine generations of workers in one generation. It produced incredible death rates and horrible degradation among the survivors. Not until the free hand was tied by new laws which were all ruthless infractions of the Capitalist system were the worst of these horrors mitigated. The free hand for the owner and employer, called *laissez-faire* lest the proletariat should understand too much about it, is to-day hopelessly discredited.

All the same, we must make Capitalism work until we have replaced it by Socialism. Meanwhile the proletariat must live by the sale of its labour as a commodity in the market; and the political struggle on its domestic side must rage between the proprietors and their parasites who want labour to be as cheap as possible, and the proletarians who want it to be as dear as possible. If the price be left to the higgling of the market, it will fall far below subsistence point; therefore the proletarians, represented by the Labour Party, must insist on its regulation by law, directly and indirectly. If the price be left to the Trade Unions, it may rise beyond what the industry can bear, thus raising the question whether the industry, if socialised, could not bear a good deal more than it can as capitalised. And so the quarrels are endless; but the people must be fed somehow, quarrels or no quarrels, if the nation is not to perish.

We on the Labour side often fail to bring Capitalism to book effectively because we do not understand it sufficiently to know the obligations it undertook when it induced our ablest statesmen to adopt it. It was not established for the sake of its beautiful eyes: it was established because, at a time when the industrial revolution and a huge increase of population had dangerously outgrown the capacity of the old country gentleman and domestic handicraft system, it undertook to provide a living wage for the new millions of proletarians, and at the same time to guarantee a yearly saving of capital from every year's harvest, and its spontaneous application to the development of industry. As long as we continue to depend on Capitalism for the existence of the nation, it is the business of our statesmen and political parties to keep Capitalism to its word, and, when it fails, to step in with the strong arm of the State and do what it has left undone, just as a sanitary authority steps in and puts the drains right when the landlord has let them go wrong.

Thus we have two activities thrust on us: keeping Capitalism up to the mark by legislation, and getting rid of it altogether by constructive substitution of Socialism. Between the two we have our hands full; and we shall get muddled over the two jobs unless our minds are clear about them.

That is why the I.L.P. pamphlet on *The Living Wage* is necessarily much occupied with methods of compelling Capitalism to keep things going decently until we are ready to do without it. When this is clearly understood, our young innocents who imagine that social systems can be changed in a day by proclamation, will perhaps read it with the patience and attention it deserves.

It is impossible for me to deal here with the financial part of the pamphlet; but I will take the opportunity of saying that it is still far too true that, as Keir Hardie confessed, we know nothing about finance. I am horrified at the extent to which Labour papers are allowing themselves to be captured by the Inflation Swindle. Nobody who understands what we have seen since 1918 can believe that any government or any people, Capitalist or Socialist, can yet be trusted with an inconvertible paper currency. Unless we return to gold and stick to gold, rejecting all manipulated stabilisations, we shall be in the soup with France and the others.

And yet we find Labour papers publishing stuff about "the horrors of Deflation": that is, the horrors of elementary honesty! When the subject is currency or classical music, you can put anything across a British editor, especially a Labour editor.

Editor's Notes

- The above review, subscribed "by G. Bernard Shaw," was published in the *New Leader* 13 (15 October 1926): 4:4. The *New Leader* was the weekly organ of the Independent Labour Party.
- The pressure of work on the sixty-nine-year-old Shaw made him ill in the spring and early summer of 1925, and Charlotte Shaw arranged a tour of the Orkney and Shetland Islands from July to October. She believed that the principal culprit was his *Intelligent Woman's Guide to Socialism and Capitalism* on which he was working. A dispute in the coalfields turned into the General Strike of May 1926, which finally went against the strikers, as the British public rallied to the defense of the government. Shaw was not in favor of the strike, either: "It is as if the crew of a ship, oppressed by its officers, were advised by a silly-clever cabin boy to sink the ship until all the officers and their friends the passengers were drowned, and then take victorious command of it. The objection that the crew could not sail the ship without navigating officers is superfluous, because there is the conclusive preliminary objection that the crew would be drowned, cabin boy and all, as well as the officers"; see Bernard Shaw, *The Intelligent Woman's Guide to Socialism and Capitalism* (London: Constable, 1929 [first published 1928]), 448. By 1926 Shaw's reputation was global. Successful productions of his *Saint Joan* (1923) in New York, London, Paris, Berlin, Moscow, Rome, Madrid, Belgrade, and Tokyo, plus his award of the Nobel Prize for Literature in 1925, had made his name known to the uttermost parts of the civilized world. In the hot August of 1926 the Shaws were holidaying at the Regina Palace Hotel, Stresa, on the shores of Lake Maggiore. It was perhaps here that Shaw wrote the above article.
- H[enry] N[oel] Brailsford (1873–1958), English Socialist author and political journalist. In 1907 he joined the Independent Labour Party, and edited the *New Leader* from 1922 to 1926. He was an ardent supporter of women's suffrage, sympathetic to the plight of the Irish, a promoter of India's claim to independence, and a believer in the aims of Soviet Russia. He was not anti-British, but he was decidedly anti–imperialist. He was a leader writer to such newspapers as the *Manchester Guardian* and the *Daily Herald,* and wrote

several books, including *Shelley, Godwin and their Circle* (1913), *How the Soviets Work* (1927), *Voltaire* (1935), *Subject India* (1943), and *Our Settlement with Germany* (1944).

- Hobson (see above, 129).
- A[rthur] Creech Jones (1891–1964), English politician. He joined the Independent Labour Party and in 1913 became honorary secretary of the Camberwell Trades Council and Borough Labor Party, of which he was cofounder. During World War I, Creech Jones (like Fenner Brockway and others) served three years in prison for refusing to obey orders given to him after being drafted against his will. And—as in the case of Brockway—his prison experience interested him in penal reform. He later denounced capital punishment and sentences of flogging and hard labor still practiced occasionally in some parts of the Commonwealth. In 1922 he brought the nonmanual workers in ports, docks and harbors into the Transport and General Workers' Union. During the Second World War, Creech Jones became parliamentary private secretary to Ernest Bevin (1881–1951); he also visited West Africa to investigate native labor conditions, a prelude to his being made parliamentary undersecretary of state for the Colonies after the Labour victory in the 1945 election. His colonial successes included constitutional reform in Cyprus, and presiding over the granting of independence to Ceylon in 1948. This set the pattern for other ex-colonies to follow in the next fifteen years. In the general election of February 1950 Creech Jones lost his seat at Shipley, but in 1954 he was again returned to Parliament, representing Wakefield.
- E[dward] F[rank] Wise (1885–1933), English economist. Born in Bury St. Edmunds and educated at King Edward VI School in that city, and finally at Sidney Sussex College, Cambridge, he took a B.A. in 1906 (mathematics and natural science triposes), and was a junior clerk in the House of Commons in 1907, and a subwarden at Toynbee Hall (Whitechapel) in 1911, in which year he was also called to the Bar (at the Middle Temple). During the First World War he was secretary of the Anglo-Russian supplies committee (1914–15), assistant director of army contracts, in charge of clothing and raw materials (1916), and principal assistant secretary to the minister of food (1917). In 1929 he was returned as Labour M.P. for East Leicester, which he remained until 1931.
- Turgot (see above, 364–65).
- Adam Smith (see above, 199–200).
- Shaw refers either to William Pitt, first earl of Chatham (1708–78), known as Pitt the Elder, or to his second son William (1759–1806), both of whom were prime ministers of Britain.
- Cobden (see above, 337).
- Peel (see above, 77).
- [James] Keir Hardie (1856–1915), Scottish Labour leader. The first-ever Labour candidate, he represented West Ham (South) (1892–95), and Merthyr Tydfil from 1900 for fifteen years. In 1891 he had joined the Fabian Society; but two years later backed the new Independent Labour Party, of which he was

chairman till 1900 and again in 1913 and 1914. He began the newspaper the *Labour Leader,* and handed it over in 1903 to the I.L.P. Though Shaw and Hardie were not close—Shaw once described him to Webb as "a Scotchman with alternate intervals of second sight (during which he does not see anything, but is suffused with afflatus) and common incapacity"—nevertheless, Shaw had campaigned for Hardie in Merthyr in 1910 and, on Hardie's death, wrote a tribute published in the local newspaper at Merthyr Tydfil, and in the *Labour Leader,* 14 October 1915.

12 March 1927

THE LATEST FROM COLONEL LAWRENCE* [C2636]

THIS abridgment of the famous Seven Pillars (itself an abridgment) contains as much of the immense original as anyone but an Imam has time to read. It is very handsomely and readably printed, and has not a dull or empty sentence from end to end. It contains sixteen reproductions of the illustrations to the Seven Pillars, including a portrait of Feisal, the superb drawing of Mr. D. G. Hogarth, and a magical one of the author by Mr. Augustus John; a remarkable Chino-Johnian group by Mr. Cosmo Clark; three portraits by Mr. W. Roberts, which are triumphs of the draughtsmanship that sprang from Cubism; and seven of the portraits of Arab chiefs which Mr. Eric Kennington went into the desert to make so consummately and humorously skilful in their combination of the popular style of the pavement artist (to disarm the chiefs) with his own very original and independent modernity: the Perfect Futurist turned Perfect Screever. The book does not, like the original, leave you with a sense of having spent many toilsome and fateful years in the desert struggling with Nature in her most unearthly moods, tormented by insomnia of the conscience: indeed it is positively breezy; but that will not be a drawback to people who, having no turn for "salutary self-torture," prefer a book that can be read in a week to one that makes a considerable inroad on a lifetime.

* "Revolt in the Desert." By T. E. Lawrence. (Jonathan Cape.) 30s.

Among the uncommon objects of the worldside, the most uncommon include persons who have reached the human limit of literary genius, and young men who have packed into the forepart of their lives an adventure of epic bulk and intensity. The odds against the occurrence of either must be much more than a million to one. But what figure can estimate the rarity of the person who combines the two? Yet the combination occurs in this amazing age of ours in which we sit holding our breaths as we await wholesale destruction at one another's hands. In Mr. Apsley Cherry-Garrard's *Worst Journey in the World* we have a classic on Antarctic exploration written by a young man who endured it at its blackest. And within ten years of that we have "Colonel Lawrence" (the inverted commas are his own) appearing first in the war news from Arabia as a personage rather more incredible than Prester John, and presently emerging into clear definition as the author of one of the great histories of the world, recording his own conquests at an age at which young company officers are hardly allowed to speak at the mess table.

The fate of the man who has shot his bolt before he is thirty, and has no more worlds to conquer, may be compared curiously with that of the genius who dies unwept, unhonored, and unsung, and is dug up and immortalized a century later. Nobody will ever be able to decide which is the more enviable. But it is mitigated if the hero has literary faculty as a second string to his bow; and Colonel Lawrence has this with a vengeance. He can re-create any scene, any person, any action by simple description, with a vividness that leaves us in more complete possession of it than could "the sensible and true avouch of our own eyes." He packs his narrative with detail that would escape nine hundred and ninety-nine out of a thousand observers; so that when he has made you see the start of Feisal's motley legions as plainly as he saw it himself, he has also left you with an exact knowledge of how an Arab mounts a camel and arranges his outlandish clothes for riding, and how he manages to carry a slave with him (when he has one) as a western might carry a portmanteau. As to the landscape painting, no padding novelist gravelled for lack of matter ever approached Col. Lawrence's feats in this art. And the descriptions are not interpolated: they are so woven into the texture of the narrative, that the sense of the track underfoot, the mountains ahead and around, the vicissitudes of the weather, the night, the dawn, the sunset and the meridian, never leaves you for a moment.

You feel, too, the characters of the men about you: you hear the inflections of their voices, the changes in their expression, all without an instant of reader's drudgery. There is a magical brilliance about it; so that you see it at once with the conviction of reality and with the enchantment of an opera. Auda after his roaring camel charge, with his horse killed, his field glass shattered, and six bullet holes through his clothes, unhurt and ascribing his escape (under Allah) to an eighteen-penny Glasgow Koran which he had bought as a talisman for a hundred and twenty pounds, is at once a squalidly realistic Arab chieftain and a splendid leading baritone. The description has the quality of orchestration. Lawrence's own famous camel charge, which was checked by his having the camel shot under him, and ended, after a whole Arab tribe had thundered over him, in the irresistible anti-climax of the discovery that he had shot the camel himself, makes a page that reduces Tennyson's Charge of the Light Brigade to minor poetry.

These blazing climaxes of adventure stand out from an inferno of tormented bodies and uneasy souls in which one is glad to meet a rascal for the sake of laughing at him. The subjective side which gives Miltonic gloom and grandeur to certain chapters of The Seven Pillars, and of the seventy and seven pillars out of which they were hewn, plays no great part in this abridgment: Lawrence's troublesome conscience and agonizing soul give place here to his impish humor and his scandalous audacities; but it will interest the latest French school of drama to know that their effect remains, and imparts an otherwise unattainable quality to the work, even though they are not expressed.

The political side of the revolt, important and extraordinary as it is, need not be dwelt on here: it is now public property; and the value of the national service rendered by its author is patent to everybody, except, apparently, those whose function it is to give official recognition to such services. It is characteristic of the author and hero of this book that he has provided most effectively against the possibility of his ever making a farthing by it; and it is equally characteristic of the powers that be, to assume that he is amply provided for by it. He is left in his usual ultra-scrupulous attitude; but the nation can hardly claim to have left itself in a generous one. For it is England's way to learn young men not to know better than their elders. Nothing could have been more irregular than the methods by which Lawrence disabled Turkey in the Great War by hurling an Arab revolt on her rear; and to encourage and reward irregularity would be to set a bad example to the young.

G. BERNARD SHAW.

Editor's Notes

- The above review was first published in the *Spectator* 138 (12 March 1927): Literary Supplement, 429. Also published as "Shaw Calls Lawrence Hero, Genius," in the Literary Review of the *New York Post* 16 April 1927, 1 and 13. Reprinted in German translation as "Bernard Shaw urteilt über Lawrence," in Lawrence's *Aufstand in der Wüste* (Leipzig: Paul List, 1927), [6]– 8. Also reprinted in *Bernard Shaw's Nondramatic Criticism,* ed. Stanley Weintraub (1972).

- Though he exclaimed at the enormity of Lawrence's original manuscript of *The Seven Pillars of Wisdom,* Shaw wrote the above review while he himself was laboring toward the end of the 200,000-word *Intelligent Woman's Guide to Socialism and Capitalism,* which he had begun in 1924 at the request of his sister-in-law, Mary Cholmondeley. He finished the book four days after the above review was published. *The Seven Pillars* seems unconsciously to have influenced Shaw's own book, not only as to length but also in prompting him to produce two special copies of the *Guide* (one for Lawrence, and the other for his sister-in-law), to use the artist Eric Kennington (see below) to design its dust jacket, and to seek to make the printing and binding as aesthetically pleasing as possible.

- T[homas] E[dward] Lawrence (1888–1935) [known as "Luruns Bey" or "Lawrence of Arabia"], Anglo-Irish soldier and author. He was brought up in Oxford, where he attended Jesus College. He became a member of a British Museum archaeological expedition in 1910 to the ancient Hittite city of Carchemish (now Karkamis, Turkey). At the outbreak of the first World War he joined the British Military Intelligence service in Egypt. In 1916 he helped in the British relief of the Arab prince Feisal [later King Feisal I (1885–1933), king of the Hejaz] in Saudi Arabia. Lawrence was accepted by the Arabs as a military adviser, unified their armed forces, and led them against their Turkish rulers. In 1918 Lawrence and Feisal entered Damascus together in triumph before the arrival of the British army. Lawrence took part in the Paris Peace Conference in 1919, but was unsuccessful in his attempts to obtain Arab independence. He was attached to the Middle East division of the British Colonial Office from 1921 to 1922, in which year he resigned and enlisted in the Royal Air Force as an aircraftman under the assumed name of John Hume Ross, in an attempt to escape from the publicity his own name had given him; but his identity was discovered. Accordingly, in 1923 he adopted the name T. E. Shaw, and joined the Royal Tank Corps. In 1925 he rejoined the R.A.F. and served for ten years. Soon after his discharge in 1935 he was killed in a motorcycle accident. Lawrence was first brought to meet Shaw at Adelphi Terrace on 25 March 1922 by Sydney Cockerell. Lawrence had written *The Seven Pillars of Wisdom* (about 300,000 words) and on 17 August 1922 he asked Shaw for his opinion of this work. Shaw read it while he was writing *Saint Joan,* and Stanley Weintraub has suggested a most plausible connection between Shaw's Saint and the unworldly Lawrence, both charismatic military leaders who puzzled and infuriated politicians. Later, Shaw based his character of Private Meek in *Too True to be Good* (1931) squarely on Lawrence, who was delighted with the portrait. Shaw edited the MS of *Seven Pillars of Wisdom,* correcting and altering ambiguities, and Charlotte proofread it. Lawrence in fact developed a close friendship with Charlotte Shaw, whose sensitive and friendly eye saw into Lawrence's troubled soul. For practical help he turned more to G.B.S. Lawrence prepared a £30 each subscription *édition de luxe* of *The Seven Pillars of Wisdom,* which unfortunately cost him £90 each to produce, thus running himself into financial difficulties. To meet the costs he therefore agreed to the publisher Jonathan Cape bringing out a much-abridged version of the work entitled *Revolt in the Desert* in March 1927. This is the book reviewed above. Shaw had previously written to the prime minister, trying for a Civil List pension for Lawrence; and now wrote again, but to no avail. Later, Lawrence sent his literary view of the Royal Air Force (entitled *The Mint*) to Charlotte in installments, and again she proofread the work. This book, clandestinely printed and privately distributed, was not published until after Lawrence's death because of the objection of Sir Hugh Trenchard [marshall of the Royal Air Force], and because of its references to Lawrence's fellow airmen. He also translated *The Odyssey,* and wrote *Oriental Assembly* (1929), and *Crusader Castles* (1936). The Shaws were generous to Lawrence; indeed, the motorcycle on which he died in a Dorset lane was a present from them.

- D[avid] G[eorge] Hogarth (1862–1929), English archaeologist and keeper of the Ashmolean Museum, Oxford, from 1909 to 1927. He made "digs" in Asia Minor, Syria, and Egypt, and in the First World War was also involved in organizing the Arab revolt against the Turks.
- Augustus [Edwin] John (1878–1961), Welsh painter. He excelled in portraits, producing memorable studies of Shaw, (three of) T. E. Lawrence, Thomas Hardy, and Dylan Thomas. Indeed, it was his portrait of Shaw that precipitated the latter's meeting with Lawrence, since Sydney Cockerell had come to Adelphi Terrace to collect Shaw's portrait for the Fitzwilliam Museum, Cambridge, of which he was curator.
- [John] Cosmo Clark (1897–1967), English painter. He was an art student in London and Paris from 1912 to 1914, in which year he joined the London Regiment and served in France until the war's end, achieving the rank of captain and receiving the Military Cross. After the war, he resumed his studentship until 1921, in which year he was awarded the Royal Academy gold medal in painting and a travel scholarship. In 1938 he became head of the Hackney School of Art. When war broke out again in 1939, Clark became deputy chief camouflage officer with the ministry of home security until 1942. He continued painting after the war, was elected a member of the New English Art Club in 1946, and won the silver medal of the Royal Society of Arts in 1948. His paintings are to be found in many art galleries.

- W[illiam Patrick] Roberts (1895–1980), English artist. He was associated with Roger Fry, Wyndham Lewis (as a Vorticist) and represented at the "London Group" exhibition in 1915, and the New York exhibition of 1917, in which year he joined the Royal Field Artillery until 1919. In 1922 he provided illustrations for the full-length work of Lawrence's *Seven Pillars of Wisdom,* three of which were reproduced in this edition. During both world wars he was an official war artist, and used a "formal Cubist, or rather cylindrical style, with a certain satirical emphasis." He was given a retrospective exhibition at the Tate Gallery in 1965, and the following year was elected R.A.
- Eric [Henri] Kennington (1888–1960), English painter and sculptor. He was also an official war artist in both the world wars, and was primarily known for his studies of the daily life of ordinary soldiers, and the R.A.F. in the Second World War. Between the wars he mainly painted portraits, but also did book illustration (including the ones for Lawrence). He was elected R.A. in 1959.
- The word "screever" is London slang (c. 1851) meaning a pavement artist (from the Latin *scribere,* to draw or engrave).
- Apsley [George Benet] Cherry-Garrard (1886–1959), English polar explorer. One of the youngest of the civilian officers on the ill-fated expedition of Robert Scott to the South Pole in 1910, he nevertheless quickly gained Scott's confidence, and shared all the major journeys, including a desperate one with Wilson and Bowers to hunt for Emperor penguins' eggs in the freezing darkness of an Antarctic winter. He said goodbye at the Beardmore Glacier to the five who were to try to cross the last three hundred miles to the Pole; but back at base bad weather and sickness decreed that only Cherry-Garrard and a Russian boy dog-driver would set out to bring relief supplies to Scott and his companions on their homeward journey. Not a good navigator, and with the Russian boy in a state of collapse, Cherry-Garrard halted at One-Ton depot, though ever afterward he was haunted by the thought that he might have gone further south to meet his leader. He was one of the party who, the following spring, discovered the bodies of Scott and his friends buried in the snow. Invalided out of the service in World War I, he spent the remainder of the war under the care of his doctors at his ancestral home of Lamer Park, Wheathampstead. Thus he was a neighbor of the Shaws at Ayot St. Lawrence. *The Worst Journey in the World* (1922) was Cherry-Garrard's description of the ill-fated Scott expedition to the South Pole; and Shaw gave editorial advice and made alterations to the manuscript, just as he had with Lawrence's book.
- Prester John ["Priest John"], an alleged Christian priest and medieval king, originally supposed to reign in the Far East, beyond Persia and Armenia; but from the fifteenth century generally identified as a king of Ethiopia or Abyssinia. Marco Polo identified Prester John with a certain Un-Khan (a historical person who died c. 1230), who received tribute from the Tartars but was finally slain by Genghis Khan.
- Horatio reacts to the appearance of the Ghost in the first scene of Shakespeare's *Hamlet* by saying:

Before my God, I might not this believe
Without the sensible and true avouch
Of mine own eyes.

8 October 1934

H. G. WELLS AND THE DEAN* [C3068]

"*I cannot understand how anyone can wish to write an autobiography, unless, indeed, he wants to leave a flattering and by no means honest selfportrait.*"

Having thus pontificated, our quondam Dean and much loved Divine Doctor proceeds to write an autobiography which will stand with the Confessions of St. Augustine and Grace Abounding as a supreme justification of the practice he denounces. I swallowed it at a single gulp with great delight. It is called Vale, or Goodbye; but I hope and believe that the divine doctor will prove one of those visitors who say "Well, I must be going," and then talk for another hour on the doorstep. By the way, when you are asking for his book at the shop, do not make Vale rhyme to fail or sale. Try Vahlay.

*   *

*

Now Dr. Inge is quite right in his estimate of the autobiography which is a combination of *apologia pro vita mea* with a string of pointless reminiscences by an egotist who believes himself to be unique, not having enough interest in other people to have noticed that we are for all practical purposes 99.9 per cent. exactly alike, so that any palmist can astonish you by persuading you that he is telling you the intimate history of your life when he is actually only telling you the history of his own.

But Mr. Wells knows this as well as Dr. Inge. Why, then, does he write a very elaborate and intimate autobiography, not like Dr. Inge and the lady in Byron's poem who, "swearing she would ne'er consent,

* "Experiment in Biography." By H. G. Wells. Vol. 1. (Gollancz, Cresset Press.) 10s. 6d.
"Vale." By the Very Reverend William Ralph Inge, K.C.V.O., D.D. (Longmans Green.) 3s. 6d.

consented," but quite deliberately on the assumption that what has happened to him is of intense interest and importance to everybody?

The explanation is simple. Dr. Inge attaches little importance to external circumstances. That is not only because the .1 per cent. in which he differs from the rest of us is of so magnificently fine a quality that it almost removes him from the human species, but also because he has had no direct experience of the crushing weight with which external circumstances press on nine-tenths of the inhabitants of this unspeakably miserable island.

He is a modest man by nature, shrinking when the world touches its hat to him, as it always has, and having, as he confesses, all but run away from Asquith's inspired offer of the Deanery of St. Paul's because "nothing could make an ecclesiastic of me." But he does not know, as Wells knows, the part played by external circumstances in a capitalist world. His one brief experience as a parish priest was at All Sinners, Ennismore Gardens, which should really have been dedicated to Saint Dives, where he actually accumulated church funds for his successor.

*   *
*

He is impatient of the sort of clergyman who, as he puts it with characteristic frankness and amazing innocence, drags "the condition of the people" into the spiritual business of the Church. As a Socialist, I have conspired against capitalist society with some of these clergymen. They had mostly been curates in a slum parish, and had learnt by soul-desolating experience how hopeless it is to try to make a woman hunger and thirst after righteousness when her children are hungering and thirsting after more bread and milk.

I am not sorry that he missed that experience; for it is one that would not be possible in an honestly organized society, and that does no man any good, though it may make him useful in social emergencies as a revolutionist. If Dr. Inge had read Karl Marx when he was twenty-six as I did, and had lived ever since, as I have, with a sense of living on the thinning crust of a revolutionary volcano instead of under the comfortable illusions of Asquithian prosperity and security, he would understand me better, he would understand his own times much better, and he would not mistake his greatest political contemporaries, Lenin, Stalin, Trotsky, Chicherin, Litvinoff, Sokolnikoff, and Maisky for a rabble of bloodthirsty gangsters and guttersnipes.

But then he would have been dragged into the revolutionary arena and spoilt for more permanent things. But I wish he would let Russia alone. It is becoming more and more evident every day that in my own unvarying support of the Soviet Government since 1917, I have been backing the right horse, and our anti-Bolshevists backing the wrong one, even from the ultra-imperialist balance-of-power point of view in the east.

*   *
*

There is a fundamental absurdity in a man of Dr. Inge's quality taking part against the most intellectual aristocracy the world has yet known with the insolent snobbery of, say, the late Lord Curzon trying to snub Chicherin, and being at last snubbed as an upstart by that equally haughty scion of a long line of nobles.

Dr. Inge is as anti-plutocrat as Lenin and as anti-ecclesiolator as George Fox, and therefore as revolutionary a force as Ruskin or Wells or myself. That is why he is so affectionately admired by those he has done least to conciliate.

*   *
*

Wells's attitude is entirely different. He is a born sociologist. Concern for the condition of the people is not to him the stigma of a rather silly sort of clergyman but the whole business of his life. His autobiography is not an *apologia pro vita sua* (very much the reverse, in fact, in many of its pages) but a document recording facts of first rate importance to our present urgent problems in political, social, and religious life.

The jackals of posthumous calumny will never be able to debunk Wells in volumes entitled The Real Wells, The Truth About H. G. Wells, or the like: he has debunked himself as amusingly and unmercifully as he has debunked Mr. Polly or even Mr. Parham. The man who succeeds in getting an inch more fun out of Wells than Wells has got out of himself will be a greater genius than he. For Wells is not only a born sociologist and story teller, but a born comedian whose scope embraces both high and low comedy. His passion for sociological truth is reinforced by his passion for making people laugh; and he knows that the biggest laugh the comedian can draw is the laugh at himself. He explicitly says that enlightenment comes to him first as derision.

Dr. Inge, in spite of his discarded gaiters, is also tempted to wield the hot poker of Grimaldi occasionally. His definition of a great man as one with such a sense of his own dignity that he keeps on looking like a stuffed owl even in his bath is not only irresistibly funny but also a guarantee that here at least is an author who will play the game and not try to make his celebrity impose on you the purely romantic category of Great Man. I am a Great Man myself; and I know.

*   *

*

These two intensely interesting and eminently important men, Wells and Inge, are both Platonists in the origin of their several missions to our time, and both committed by their writings to "mysticism based on a foundation of reason," which is my own persuasion, though I think Dr. Inge really means mysticism strictly audited by facts; for reason is an extremely corrupt referee. Both of them are a little bothered by superstitions from the Victorian pseudo-science which was really a masked attack on that ancient deity whom William Blake called Old Nobodaddy. Wells's Huxleyan biology seems to me simply physiology with all the biology left out and all the facts that upset Paley's Evidences emphasized. The Dean, who does not care a damn (saving his reverence) for either Huxley or Paley, and says masterfully that "to ascribe infalliblilty to the pronouncements of the institutional Church seems almost monstrous," does not yet laugh heartily enough, to my taste, at bugaboo astronomy and physics.

*   *

*

But that does not greatly matter. The striking contrast is in the fact that these two contemporary Platonists, both of them gifted with every talent of expression and with daimonic mental honesty, are very unlike, neither of them mentioning nor counting the other (so far) in their pilgrimages, and both almost certain to quarrel violently if they should ever be elected a duumvirate to rescue us from our political confusion. Still, the coincidence of their two autobiographies is an unparalleled piece of luck for us; and I cannot imagine any intellectually alive and humanly curious person not making a rush to read both.

Editor's Notes

■ The above review, subscribed "by Bernard Shaw," was first published in the *Daily Herald,* 8 October 1934, 10:3–7.
■ In the intervening years since the previous article, Shaw's reputation had continued to grow around the world, and he had followed it. Charlotte was an inveterate traveler, always seeking to curtail the enormous demands of work Shaw made upon himself, and a large portion of each year was spent abroad: in Italy, the French Riviera, Yugoslavia, the Mediterranean, South Africa,

Greece, India, Hong Kong, Japan, and North America. Everywhere he landed, Shaw was mobbed by the press, and gave controversial speeches and interviews. These seven years also saw him sparring with the two people whose works he reviews above. However, although in January 1928 he had gone into print against Dean Inge in an article in the *Evening Standard* over "The Inquisition, the Star Chamber and the General Medical Council," his admiration and friendship persisted, and in 1931 he had read *Too True to be Good* to the dean (supposedly too deaf to hear it in the theater). With H. G. Wells, too, he had stirred old hostilities, attacking him on the vivisection issue in the summer of 1927, and receiving a blast from Wells in the *New York Times* later that year. Lawrence Langner, in a letter to Shaw, defended him against "the ridiculous attack" made by Wells, and concluded by hoping that Shaw would answer Wells's article very thoroughly. To this Shaw's secretary, Blanche Patch, replied on 30 December: "Mr. Shaw wishes me to let you know that he is not going to answer Wells's article. They are very good friends, and it is quite understood that Mr. Wells may blow off steam like that whenever he feels like bursting"; quoted in Lawrence Langner, *G.B.S. and the Lunatic* (London: Hutchinson, 1964), 114. Despite Shaw's inveterate good humor, he differed with Wells in print again over Radclyffe Hall's controversial *The Well of Loneliness*, the following October.

- H. G. Wells (see above, 346–47).
- W.R. Inge (see above, 411–12).
- [Aurelius Augustinus, also known as] Saint Augustine [of Hippo] (354–430), greatest of the Latin Church Fathers, and one of the most eminent doctors of the Western Church. He is the author of some of the most powerful Christian works, including his theological philosophy of history *The City of God* (413–426), but his best-known work is his *Confessions* (400) referred to by Shaw above, which is both a spiritual autobiography and an original work of philosophy, containing a famous discussion on the nature of time.
- The full title of John Bunyan's (1628–88) spiritual history is *Grace Abounding to the Chief of Sinners, or the brief Relation of the exceeding Mercy of God in Christ to his poor Servant John Bunyan* (1666).
- Shaw's skepticism over palmistry is not reflected in his first experience of it, as recorded in his *Diary* for 14 September 1886, when he "met about a dozen men at Molloy's, all strangers to me except Oscar Wilde and Dowling. Heron Allen, a chiromantist, told my character by my hand very successfully" (198). Though I have never seen it suggested before, Wilde's short story about Septimus Podgers, the chiromantist, entitled *Lord Arthur Savile's Crime* (1887) may well owe its origin to this occasion; in which case, we might detect Shaw as a bit-player in the opening scene, where "a celebrated political economist was solemnly explaining the scientific theory of music to an indignant virtuoso from Hungary."
- The lady in Byron's *Don Juan* (1819–24) did not swear; she whispered:

> A little still she strove, and much repented,
> And whispering "I will ne'er consent"—consented.

- Asquith (see above, 186–87).
- Dean Inge was for a time vicar of All Saints, Ennismore Gardens, Kensington, a rich parish (hence Saint Dives).
- Shaw had worked in the 1880s with Christian Socialists like the Rev. Stewart Headlam (1847–1924), upon whom Shaw partly based his character James Mavor Morell in *Candida* (1895), who had founded in 1877 the Guild of St. Matthew, a small Anglican society that addressed itself to social problems.
- Lenin (see above, 425).
- Stalin [real name Josif Vissarionovich Djugashvili (1879–1953), Soviet dictator, who ousted Trotsky (see above, 447).
- [Georgi Vasilevich] Chicherin (1872–1936), Russian revolutionary and diplomat. As Shaw hints, Chicherin was born into a distinguished family of gentry, tracing its nobility back five centuries to an Italian ancestor [Cicerini] who had come to Moscow in the suite of Princess Zoe Paleologue in 1472. It was in the capacity of Trotsky's deputy commissar of foreign affairs that the British knew him best, when the Bolsheviks had abandoned force in favor of peaceful coexistence with the Western Powers. Between 1921 and 1924 Chicherin and his colleagues obtained diplomatic recognition for the new Soviet regime from all of the great powers (except the United States), and from many smaller nations. The Genoa Conference in 1922 showed Chicherin at his diplomatic best, defending the Soviet position on every issue, and calling for sweeping disarmament. Thereafter, however, with the gradual withdrawal of Lenin from affairs of state, Chicherin lost his principal ally on the Politburo, and in 1927 tendered his resignation.
- Litvinoff (see above, 426).
- [Grigori Yakovlevich] Sokolnikoff (1888–1939), Russian revolutionary and diplomat. It was in the early 1920s Sokolnikoff reached the height of his prestige: he had been a successful people's commissar of finance (1922), bringing about much-needed currency reform, and he was elected a candidate member of the Politburo in 1924. Then he ran foul of Stalin, by espousing the "leftist" Zinoviev opposition and calling for freedom of discussion within the Party and economic reforms. He was immediately dropped from the Politburo, and in 1929 was sent as Soviet ambassador to the United Kingdom, where he remained until the year of the above book review. He was then recalled to Moscow and demoted again, before being tried in 1936, sentenced to ten years in prison where he either died or was shot in 1939.
- [Ivan Mikhailovich] Maisky (1884–1975), Russian diplomat and historian. From 1922 Maisky was a diplomat in the Commissariat of Foreign Affairs, assisting in forming and signing the Soviet-Finnish nonaggression pact of 1932 in which year he was named ambassador to Great Britain, taking over from Sokolnikoff. He remained in that post until 1943, a turbulent period of Anglo-Soviet relations since it included Stalin's great purges (which he was forced to defend), the Munich conference, the Nazi-Soviet pact (which the Soviet government neglected to inform him about), and the Russo-Finnish war. When Hitler invaded the U.S.S.R. and Churchill offered an alliance with Russia, Maisky again found himself at the center of difficult diplomatic negotia-

tions. In spite of the fact that he did very well (participating in the first important inter-Allied conference in 1941 and establishing diplomatic relations with Canada), he was replaced as ambassador in 1943 by an inexperienced diplomat, and was appointed a deputy foreign commissar in Moscow. Although Stalin could not do without Maisky at the Yalta and Potsdam conferences in 1945, he eased Maisky out of the Foreign Ministry in 1946 by having him elected to the prestigious Academy of Sciences, where he devoted his time to teaching and research. In February 1953 he was arrested, but was saved by the death of Stalin two weeks later; though he remained in custody and was in fact tried for treason and espionage in 1955, but found only guilty of certain "errors" in the performance of his diplomatic duties. He went on to receive many honors, and died in Moscow at the age of ninety-one.

- Lord Curzon (see above, 424).
- George Fox (1624–91), English religious leader and founder of the Society of Friends (or "Quakers"). He was a great egalitarian; in consequence his life was a succession of persecutions and imprisonments. He and his followers (for he had nearly a thousand) refused to take the oath of abjuration. He visited Wales and Scotland, America, Barbados, Jamaica, Holland, and Germany, eventually accompanied by William Penn and Robert Barclay.
- Ruskin (see above, 65).
- Wells's *The History of Mr. Polly* was published in 1910; his *The Autocracy of Mr. Parham* in 1930.
- [Joseph] Grimaldi (1778–1837), the most famous of all English clowns; he is said to have appeared on the stage first as a dancer at the age of two. His great success was at Covent Garden in 1806, and he reigned there as singer, dancer, actor, acrobat, and mime until his retirement in 1823. His memoirs were edited by Charles Dickens. Because of him, clowns were frequently called "Joey;" a name by which Shaw often referred to himself.
- Huxley (see above, 112).
- Paley (see above, 308).

1 August 1936

ACE MORALITY: A DOCUMENT* [C3157]

THIS is a book which everybody should read. It is the autobiography of an ace, and of no common ace, either. We are all much concerned just now with the danger of being bombed, gassed, and burnt alive,

---

* "Sagittarius Rising. By Cecil Lewis. (Peter Davies.) 8s. 6d.

women, children and all, with our water and electricity cut off when we have become helplessly dependent on them. Well, the hand that can release these judgments on us is the hand of the ace. And the ace may be a lad of 17. Indeed, it is not clear that such an age limit is necessary. The late Sir Horace Plunkett learnt to fly when he was over 80, having been recommended to take mountain air for sleeplessness. I believe I could have taken a plane into the air and released a bomb when I was 15.

Under such circumstances the moral training of our lads might be expected to rouse some concern or at least some curiosity. Apparently it is not even thought worth mentioning. When Prime Ministers and Secretaries of State for War in their great rearmament speeches proposed the enlistment and training of several thousand youths to rain destruction on the capital cities of the world, it never occurred to them to give any particulars as to the course of Diabolonian education which is to fit them for a delight and pride in this new and very startling department of human activity. How are we to test and select for the requisite high spirits, sense of mischievous humour, and moral irresponsibility which must go to make a boy ready to convert a city of God (more or less) into a City of Destruction?

Mr. Lewis solved that problem for himself without any misgivings. At the age of 16 he found himself so "air minded" that he transferred himself from his famous public school to the Flying Corps in the spring of 1915 without consulting anyone. Now, if the public school had been Eton, Harrow, Winchester, Rugby or the like, Mr. Lewis would have been a ready-made Diabolonian. But it was not: it was Oundle: Oundle under Sanderson the Great, who cordially agreed with me as he showed me round the scene of his triumphs that Eton and all the rest of them should be razed to the ground and their foundations sown with salt. Thus Mr. Lewis had a quite special Sandersonian-Wellsian pacifist schooling. His father was and is a distinguished sky pilot, not a bomber, but one who has never left the ground, nor rained anything but sermons on his fellow-creatures. The boy was not the usual young public-school Caliban whom nothing can tame or humanise: he had all the noble tastes and qualities, love of nature, love of beauty, love of poetry, soaring imagination, and physical gifts that eventually carried him to a height of six feet four inches, with a brilliant endowment of good looks. In short, one of the best, perhaps the very best, of all the recruits of 1915. He could have won his Military Cross and his promotions on his appearance alone.

As a matter of fact, he won them by committing all the atrocities of
air warfare with an enjoyment that lasted until his demobilisation
with unbroken nerve and unscathed limbs at the end of the war. He
had a charmed life in every sense of the word. And throughout it all
he never disliked a German except for twenty minutes on a black
night when the Gothas were bombarding London, and somebody he
loved was on the ground beneath. That brought on a fit of Berserker
fury in which he deserted his defensive post and plunged vengefully
into the thick of our own anti-aircraft barrage in search of a Gotha to
bring down. But the Gothas eluded him in the darkness; and the fit
passed very quickly.

And now comes the test question. How did the exceptional humanity of this prince of pilots react to the demand for atrocities made upon
him by his duties? As it happened he was never a bomber. He won his
cross on observation patrol, which needs daring, intelligence, reckless
exposure to Archies, but has not slaughter for its direct object. In the
second phase of his service, which was offensive patrol, he was a
duellist, guiltless of the blood of women, children, and civilians. It
was, as he puts it, Hector and Achilles, a battle of champions, fought
in flying chariots with machine guns instead of Homeric spears. So
far, nothing unpardonably Diabolonian.

Unfortunately, there was one incident which spoils the chivalrous
picture. It reminds me of something that happened to myself one
evening many years before the war. One cheerless evening, walking
through Battersea Park, I came upon a vast ruin that had old associations for me. It was one of those enormous glass structures that came
into vogue in the middle of last century with Paxton's Crystal Palace,
originally the Hyde Park Exhibition. These monsters were as movable
as bird cages. One of them appeared during my boyhood in Dublin as
an exhibition building on the site now occupied by the Catholic University. It was taken away to England, where it was re-named The
Albert Palace; and, after what wanderings I know not, got finally
stranded and abandoned in Battersea Park, where it confronted me in
the dusk like a ghost from my nonage. There was something spectral
and tragic about it; for all Battersea's boys had thrown all Battersea's
stones (there were stones in the streets in those macadamised days) at
its million panes, leaving nothing unshattered save its monstrous and
miserable skeleton. You can imagine with what bitter reflections on
the wanton destructiveness of my species I passed on.

Suddenly an unbroken pane of glass caught my eye. It was irresistible. I believe I should have been shying stones at that pane to this day

if the appearance of a park-keeper and the dignity of my professional position had not forced me to pass along harmlessly with every fibre of my being crying out against leaving that pane unshattered.

To return to Mr. Lewis. He was in the sky on a bloodless observation patrol contemplating a desolated terrain over which the tides of war had swept in and out. I had a glimpse of it myself in 1917, when, sightseeing round the Front, I found places where villages had been with nothing left of them but a prostrate signpost with a name on it, or a wheelwright's emplacement showing through the snow. Mr. Lewis's reflections were no less sombre, his generalisations no less tragic than mine in Battersea Park. The pilot in him sublimated into the poet and philosopher, as so often happened to him in the empyrean.

Suddenly he noticed a solitary house that had not been demolished. His observer saw it, too. And the same strange call of nature gripped them both. They had no bombs: bombing was not their business, nor was their machine equipped for carrying or launching any such projectile. No matter: they returned to their station, wangled a bomb, shipped it at great risk of being blown to pieces by it, and returned to hover over the dwelling that war at its worst had spared. Lewis brought all his mental powers into play to ensure a direct hit. He calculated his height, his distance, his speed and that of the wind with a conscientiousness which made success mathematically certain; and at his word the observer managed to heave the bomb overboard, again at considerable risk of its resenting such improper manhandling by a premature explosion.

The story lacks its tragic consummation. The house stands to this day presumably; and the pit dug in the earth by the bomb a mile or two away has long since been filled up. But the page from the real psychology of war remains. Mr. Lewis, like all sane men, loathes war. Nobody could sing more fervently than he: "How beautiful are the feet of them that bring the gospel of peace!" But he had a shot at that house all the same. Had the war lasted another month he would have bombed Berlin. So should I, I suppose, had I been in his place. Mr. Lewis has a good deal to say about it, and says it very well; for he is a thinker, a master of words, and a bit of a poet. But there are the facts at first hand. The funniest passage in the book deals with the disappearance from the dinner table of two of his messmates who were smashed by one of our own shells. The passage is: "The battery rang up to apologise." Why must we laugh? Because, I suppose, if we took war seriously we should all go mad.

Some people like war. There is to all of us a side that likes it. We should provide for the gratification of that liking as a sport, even if we have to suppress its political exploitation. It could be done every year on Salisbury Plain. And as there is no fun in poison gas, and mechanised warfare has reduced courage to absurdity, we might reconsider Fielding's remark that battles might be fought just as well with fists as with musketry.

Mr. Lewis was clearly not deficient in natural tenderness. He was apparently always in love with some lady; and it cannot be doubted that many ladies were always in love with him. Touching these matters with an admirable delicacy, he never tells us that it was not always the same lady; but as his heart was broken again and again by tragic partings seen dimly through his vein of poetry, one may suspect him of inconstancy, but not accuse him of indiscretion or insensibility.

BERNARD SHAW.

Editor's Notes

- The above review was first published in the *New Statesman and Nation,* n.s., 12 (1 August 1936): 162, and reprinted in *Living Age* (New York) 351 (October 1936): 165–67. It was also reprinted in *Bernard Shaw's Nondramatic Criticism,* ed. Stanley Weintraub (1972). The book reviewed has also been reprinted, both in 1966 and 1983.
- Cecil A[rthur] Lewis (b. 1898), English author. Lewis's life to the time of the above review is substantially the one narrated by Shaw. Like Cherry-Garrard and T. E. Lawrence, Lewis was another of the attractive young adventurers whom Shaw befriended in the years following World War I. After the war Lewis became manager of civil aviation for Vickers Ltd. (1919) and flying instructor to the Chinese government in Pekin in 1920 and 1921, in which year he also became a founding member of the British Broadcasting Corporation. Lewis aroused Shaw's interest in the new technology of radio; in return Shaw concerned himself with Lewis's budding career, introducing Lewis (by letter) to Lawrence Langner of the New York Theatre Guild in January 1930. Lewis spent time in New York, but went on to Hollywood to try and sell some of Shaw's picture rights, notably *Arms and the Man*. Twentieth Century–Fox, however, already had in mind the unauthorized musical version (*The Chocolate Soldier*); frustrated, Lewis returned to England. Later Shaw chose Lewis to direct a film of *How He Lied to Her Husband* (though Lewis knew nothing of filming); and the finished product was shown in London in January 1931. It was not particularly well-received. In April 1932 Shaw gave Lewis the go-ahead to film *Arms and the Man*, which was also not a success. Undaunted,

Shaw still allowed Lewis to be one of the script adaptors of the highly success-
ful film version of *Pygmalion*, begun in March 1938, produced by Gabriel
Pascal, directed by Anthony Asquith and Leslie Howard. In the Second World
War Lewis served in the R.A.F., and after the war went sheep-farming in South
Africa, served with the radio and television department of the United Nations
Secretariat in New York, worked in commercial television in London, and on
the *Daily Mail* from 1955 until his retirement in 1966. Among his many other
books are *Broadcasting from Within* (1924), *Pathfinders* (1943), *Yesterday's
Evening* (1946), *Farewell to Wings* (1964), *Turn Right for Corfu* (1972), *Never
Look Back* (his autobiography, 1974; filmed for TV, 1978), *Gemini to Joburg*
(1984), *The Gospel According to Judas* (1989), *The Dark Sands of Shambala*
(1990), and *Sagittarius Surviving* (1991).

- Sir Horace [Curzon] Plunkett (1854–1932), Irish agricultural reformer.
He founded the Irish Agricultural Organization Society, was M.P. for Dublin
Co. (S) from 1892 to 1900, and chairman of the Irish Convention (which
Shaw advised) in 1917 and 1918. He and the Shaws were friends.

- In Bunyan's *The Pilgrim's Progress,* Christian fled from the City of Destruction to the Celestial City.

- [Frederick William] Sanderson (1857–1922), English schoolmaster, whom
Shaw calls "Sanderson the Great," was elected headmaster of Oundle School (a
fifteenth-century foundation in Northamptonshire) in 1892. He revolutionized
the school, whose fortunes had declined disastrously, by reorganizing the
teaching, and particularly by introducing fresh subjects of study such as bio-
chemistry and agriculture; by building an observatory, a meteorological station, botanical gardens and an experimental farm, workshops, laboratories,
metal- and woodshops, a drawing office, a forge and a foundry: in short by
revitalizing the school until the number of boys attending rose from ninety-two
(in 1892) to five hundred (in 1920). By the time of Sanderson's death, the
reputation of Oundle was extremely high.

- "Sky pilot" (slang for a clergyman) refers to the pilot who directs the
course of a ship, and thus was originally applied to a seaman's missionary.

- Caliban, the half-human half-demon monster in Shakespeare's *Tempest,*
according to Coleridge, "is all earth, all condensed, and gross in feelings and
images; he has the dawnings of an understanding without reason or the
moral sense."

- The German Gotha G.V. was powered by two 260 hp Mercedes engines,
had a maximum speed of 87 mph, and could carry about a half ton of bombs
at fifteen thousand feet. Between 2 September 1917 and the end of the year,
Gothas from Bombengeschwader 3 mounted fifteen night raids, of which
nine penetrated to London.

- Berserker: "A wild Norse warrior, who fought on the battle-field with a
frenzied fury known as a 'berserker rage' " [*OED*].

- "Archies" were anti-aircraft guns, or occasionally gunners. The slang,
dating from 1915, probably derives from the music hall song having the
refrain "Archibald, certainly not!"

- [Sir Joseph] Paxton (1801–65), English architect, responsible for the glass and iron structure that covered twenty-one acres in Hyde Park, and was originally erected for the Great Exhibition of 1851. The Crystal Palace, as it came to be known, was re-erected in Sydenham, and became famous for its concerts, many of which Shaw attended and reported on. It was destroyed by fire in the year of this review.

• The actual words (adapted from Isaiah 52:7) of the soprano aria from Handel's *Messiah* are "How beautiful are the feet of them that *preach* the gospel of peace, and bring glad tidings of good things."

• Fielding's belief that "battles might be fought just as well with fists as with musketry" is found in *Tom Jones*, book 5, chapter 12, when Tom, interrupted in his love-making with Molly Seagrim by Thwackum and Blifil, fights with them both and leaves them bloody-nosed upon the ground: "Here we cannot suppress a pious wish, that all quarrels were to be decided by those weapons which Nature, knowing what is proper for us, hath supplied us; and that cold iron was to be used in digging no bowels but those of the earth."

1 August 1937

THE WEBBS' MASTERPIECE* [C3200]

Books about Russia have crowded the market for some years past. Interesting as they are—for it is hardly possible to be dull about Russia—they have been written at the disadvantage that the authors did not know what they were writing about. They were like men writing about the moon before astronomy became a science. This was not noticed here, because most books written about England, and all speeches by Cabinet ministers decorated with Old School Ties, have the same drawback. "What do they know of England that only England know?" was asked dithyrambically by an author who died without having discovered that an Englishman who knew England would be a phenomenon so extraordinary that pilgrims might well come from the ends of the earth to contemplate him.

That, I suppose, is why pilgrims actually do come from the ends of

---

* "Soviet Communism: a New Civilization?" By Sidney and Beatrice Webb. New and revised edition with up-to-date Postscript. Price of the Left Book Club edition, 5s.; price of the edition for the general public, £1 15s.

the earth to contemplate the Webbs, who really do know their England. The late Earl of Oxford has left on record his estimate of Sidney Webb as a saint who has written countless volumes which nobody could read. He had evidently never tried; for, granted the least interest in their subject and some capacity for it, the Webbs are never unreadable. But Asquith was a university man who believed, as such, that he knew everything and had no need for any further instruction. If he had read the works of the Webbs from beginning to end the history of England might have been different. At all events he would often have caught out Mr. Lloyd George instead of being bowled helplessly by him.

For just consider what knowing England means. What is the real working constitution of England as far as England is constituted at all? Not blatherskite about democracy and imperialism mouthed by orators who understand neither, but Consumers' Co-operation, Trade Unionism, industrial organisation, and Local Government. Which of us had any conception of co-operation as a working force in society until Beatrice Webb wrote its history and drew its moral? And when Beatrice and Sidney got together and wrote the history of Trade Unionism on such a basis of personal contacts and exhaustive investigation as Marx and Engels had never dreamt of, a most dangerous gulf in our social consciousness was filled up and built upon. The following volume on industrial democracy shewed the incidence of industrial facts and forms on our civilization—the substance of the Marxian thesis—with an actuality that brought down Marx's generalization to tin tacks and made it an effective force in modern thought. Then came the monumental history of local government, completing the great Webbian diagnosis of the English Constitution. It seemed the climax of their life and labours. The question became "What dont they know of England, these Webbs who all things know?"

Yet when the Russian revolution plunged a sixth of the globe with a crash into an epoch of professed Communism it presented the apparently superannuated couple with a job which they—and they alone on earth—had qualified themselves by a long and arduous apprenticeship to undertake. Instead of overwhelming them it rejuvenated them. They rushed to Russia and tackled it without a moment's hesitation. They knew where to go and what questions to ask and what to look at. No Russian had any such knowledge. They went and asked and looked. They discovered a new civilization where a British officer had immortalized himself by the concise report "Russia is a slum." To that officer a slum was only a place where you held your nose. The Webbs understood slums. They understood everything, and disentangled the amazing multiple social structure, quite new in the world, which has grown up almost spontaneously in a society relieved of the stranglehold of what we call property and are coming more and more to realize as simple robbery.

The result is set down in these two volumes entitled Soviet Communism by Sidney and Beatrice Webb. It is absolutely unique as a conspectus and interpretation of this New Russia that is so much more than Russia. Nobody who has not read it ought henceforth to be allowed to write about Russia; for without this groundwork nothing that is happening there is really intelligible.

It needs hardly any further recommendation to the members of the Left Book Club.

Editor's Notes

- The above review was first published in *Left News,* no. 16 (August 1937): 467, with the subscription "by Bernard Shaw." It was also published as "The Webbs on Russia," in *First and Last* 1 (8 November 1937): 24.
- According to Michael Holroyd, on his second voyage to South Africa (in April 1935) Shaw had taken with him the proofs of the first edition of Webb's *Soviet Communism: A New Civilization?* (see Michael Holroyd, *Bernard Shaw.* Vol. 3, *1918–1950. The Lure of Fantasy* [Chatto and Windus, London, 1991], 283). In the early summer of 1937, he paid his annual visit to the Webbs, and this time helped them with the revised edition of the book. Since the last two books reviewed coincide with their authors' need (Lewis's need for employment, and the Webbs' ill-health and straitened circumstances—to alleviate which Shaw had given them £1,000 in 1934), such enthusiastic endorsements of his friends' work seem as much motivated by Shaw's desire to help them as to inform the public.
- The Webbs (see above, 139, 199).
- Rudyard Kipling (see above, 207) had died on 17 January, the previous year. He wrote in "England's Answer to the Cities,"

Winds of the World, give answer! They are whimpering to and fro—
And what should they know of England who only England know?

- The "late Earl of Oxford" was, of course, Herbert Henry Asquith, first earl of Oxford, who had died in 1928 (see above, 186–87).

27 March 1942

THE TESTAMENT OF WELLS* [C3441]

HERE, under the title of *The Outlook for Homo Sapiens,* is the Testament which Herbert George Wells has bequeathed to the world in 287 pages (say 130,000 words) for eight and sixpence, or for the asking at the nearest public library. It is well worth the money if you have any; and if you are in the TRIBUNE reader class you must read it because it is indispensable political news. And when H. G. is the writer, reading is a treat and not a labor. Anyhow, you must read it.

The last sixty years have seen the rise of two new sects, the Wellsians and the Shavians, with a large overlap. The overlap may suggest that as our doctrine must be the same, our mental machinery must be the same also. But in fact no two machines for doing the same work could be more different than our respective brains. Ecologically (H.G's favourite word) and intellectually I am a seventeenth century Protestant Irishman using the mental processes and technical craft of Swift and Voltaire, whilst Wells is an intensely English nineteenth century suburban cockney, thinking anyhow, writing anyhow, and always doing both uncommonly well. The doctrine in my hands is a structure on a basis of dispassionate economic and biological theory: in his it is a furious revolt against unbearable facts and exasperating follies visible as such to his immense vision and intelligence where the ordinary Briton sees nothing wrong but a few cases that are dealt with by the police. He has neither time nor patience for theorizing, and probably agrees with that bishop whose diocese I forget, but who said very acutely that I would never reach the Celestial City because I would not venture beyond the limits of a logical map. These differences between us are very fortunate; for our sermons complement instead of repeating one another: you must read us both to become a complete Wellshavian.

When Wells burst on England there were no Wellshavians; but there were Webbshavians, *alias* Fabians, who had the start of him by ten years, and had the advantage of having been caught by the literature of Socialism when they were just the right age for it: that is to say

---

* "The Outlook for Homo Sapiens." By H. G. Wells. (Published by Secker & Warburg.)

in their mid-twenties, when he was in his teens, too young to take it in to its full depth.

At first the ten years were all to the bad. Wells, throwing himself into the Fabian movement to reform everything that was wrong in the world as well as the economic system, found himself confronted by a disillusioned Old Gang of wily committee men and practised speakers whose policy it was to keep the Fabian Society to the economic point and head off all excursions into religious controversy, party controversy, and sex controversy. Against this policy Wells hurled himself furiously, smashing down its compromises and platform tricks with a one-man artillery barrage of vituperation, reckless of whether he contradicted himself in every second sentence or even in the same sentence. He called for a society of millions of members and an expenditure of hundreds of thousands of pounds. It was a glorious episode in the history of the Society; but the Old Gang, with their ten years' experience and hard training, knew the possibilities only too well; and H.G. shook its dust off his feet after kicking up a prodigious cloud of it, leaving the Old Gang in possession.

He never thereafter worked with any existing Society of practising politicians or became a committee man with committee manners, broken-in to accept the greatest common measure of a council of colleagues as the limit to which things could for the moment be carried, and with an eye always on the jury. He would not fit himself into any movement or party, though he raged through them all, playing for his own hand and leaving his mark wherever there was stuff plastic enough to take an impression. Far from keeping an eye on the jury he no sooner took up a question than he forgot everything and everybody else and charged into it, kicking out of his way everyone, friend and foe, who obstructed him for a moment, and always being forgiven and getting away with it. He insulted all his friends and never lost them, and made no enemies except the simpletons whose enmity hallmarks its object as a friend of humanity. He obeyed no rules of conduct except his own, and scattered invective in all directions as an R.A.F. pilot scatters bombs; but nobody has ever accused him of doing a malicious injury or being capable of it. He is the most ungovernable man of his rank in ability in England; but his fundamentally noble and generous nature keeps his halo undimmed all the time. And he is the best of good company: one of the few writers of whom it can be said that if his conversation could have been reported and all his books destroyed, the gain to his reputation might have been greater than the loss.

*   *   *

Wells, as a very English Englishman, is subject to attacks of a sort of mental gout or Berserkeritis which the Elizabethans called the spleen, the symptoms of which are in war reckless violence and in peace wild vituperation. When he sickens in this way, woe to the individual whom he dislikes and selects as whipping boy for his educational campaigns. Now it happens most unfortunately and quite unaccountably that his pet aversion is Karl Marx. The story of that famous exile is so pitiable that it hardly bears thinking of by any humane person. Marx's first beloved children died of slow starvation, which wrecked his health and shortened his own life. His two youngest daughters committed suicide. His wife was driven almost crazy by domestic worry. And yet he managed to write a book which changed the mind of the world in favor of Wells and nerved Lenin and Stalin to establish a new civilisation, largely Wellsian, in Russia. Yet Wells, when the fit is on him, loses his head and pursues this unhappy great man with a hatred so foreign to his own nature that one has to laugh it off as brain fever. Mention Marx to him and with the ink still wet on his chapters on the Class War and the woes of "the unpropertied," he will deny that there is any class war or any such thing as a proletariat, both being Marxian lies. He will belittle the Russian revolution and declare that the vital issue between experimenting with Socialism in a single country and waiting for an impossible world revolution was only a wretched personal squabble between Stalin and Trotsky.

Happily, after raving like this for pages and pages, he comes out at last on the perfectly sound ground that it is England's business not only to make the same inevitable revolution in its own way in its own country (Stalinism) but to make an equally successful job of it without any of the mistakes and violences that would have wrecked Bolshevism had not we and the other western powers rallied all Russia to its side by senselessly attacking it and making its leaders national conquerors and saviours as well as international Communists. Which is excellent Fabianism.

If H. G. in the next edition of his Testament will stick to his conclusion and drop his vituperation of Marx with a handsome apology, asking himself what would have become of him and of me if we, luckier than Marx, had not chanced to possess a lucrative knack of writing novels and plays, he will, I think, gain in authority and consistency.

There are moments too when our Protestant anti-clerical habits get the better of Wells's Socialism. He is at the top of his form when he shews that the Reformation is still only half finished; but he is a bit hard on the Roman Catholic Church when he blames it alone for the poverty and ignorance that have made civilisation a disease and that none of the Churches have been able to cure. It is true that the Roman Catholic Church, in desperation, has made a merit of "holy poverty" and pleaded that without it we should be without the virtue of charity, whilst the Protestants have on the contrary made a supreme merit of prosperity ("holy riches"). But both persuasions are equally helpless against the economic consequences of private property. Without an economic Reformation none of the attempts to realise the ideal of a Catholic Church, which has never yet existed in Rome or Geneva or Moscow or anywhere else, will succeed. Meanwhile the Ulster slogan "To Hell with the Pope!" is only a red herring across the trail of Socialism.

I suppose I must honestly conclude by warning readers that my opinion of any work by Wells is so prejudiced in his favor by my personal liking for him that I do not myself know how much it is worth. Anyhow, his books have to be read, and not merely read about.

Editor's Notes

- The above review was first published in the *Tribune,* no. 274 (27 March 1942): 13–14, with the subscription "By Bernard Shaw." It was reprinted in *Tribune 21,* ed. Elizabeth Thomas (London: McGibbon and Kee, 1958).
- The Shaws were at Frinton-on-Sea, Essex, when the Second World War began on 3 September 1939. Revivals of his plays were very popular during the war, but Shaw did what he had done in the First World War; that is, revert to a flood of journalism about the conflict, much of which appeared in the Labour press. In 1941, in the mornings, Shaw began writing *Everybody's Political What's What* (1944), which he described as an elementary textbook on politics.
- H. G. Wells (see above, 346–47).
- Although Shaw's description of himself as a seventeenth-century Irish Protestant links him with Swift (see above, 119), who was gifted with a similar taste for irony, Shaw has nothing of the latter's bitterness and misanthropy.
- Voltaire (see above, 113).
- Berserkeritis (see above, 484).

10 March 1943

WHAT WOULD MARX SAY ABOUT BEVERIDGE?* [C3474]

MARX, buried in Highgate Cemetery, and certified by the doctors as having died on March 14, 1883, is in fact much more alive to-day than he ever was in the 65 years before that date. For me he began to live just then; for it was then that I read Das Kapital, and had to read it in Deville's French version because there was no translation in English and my scraps of German were not enough for tackling the original text. It made another man of me, as it did fourteen years later of Lenin.

*

By now it has changed the mind of the world, and produced a new civilisation in Russia known to Marx as the biggest and most backward State on earth. A hundred years ago North America was the land of the free and hope of the world. Russia was its despair. Twenty years ago Sasha Kropotkin said to me, "Russia will save the world's soul." And Russia is keeping her promise.

The nineteenth century began with such a high opinion of itself that Macaulay, its most brilliant historian and honest politician, thanked God he lived in its golden age of what Gladstone called prosperity increasing by leaps and bounds. Marx's torpedo hit it between wind and water in its middle, and blew the golden lid off hell. After that we found it hard enough to believe in the benevolence of God, much less thank Him. Compare Macaulay's pre-Marxian history of the 1688 revolution with the post-Marxian history of Spain by Madariaga! One is a trumpery budget of Reform Club gossip; the other is world history. The vainglorious nineteenth century died on the defensive, apologising for being the wickedest page of human history.

As far as any such change can be accredited to a single man, this was the work of Marx. He is still doing it in spite of the tombstone in Highgate Cemetery, which ought, by the way, to be replaced by a towering monument, and no doubt will be some day.

---

* "Karl Marx: Selected Works." Vols. 1 and 2, ed. V. Adoratsky. (Lawrence and Wishart.) 10s. 6d.

*

And yet, though all this and much more is true; though there are now only two orders of statesmen, the pre-Marx fossils and the post-Marx live wires; though Marxism is now a religion, with the first volume of Capital for its Bible, the Russian revolution has proved that militant Socialists whose tactics are exclusively Marxist have to be shot before his principles can be carried into practice. In Fabian Essays, which I edited nearly 60 years ago with the ablest team of young Socialists ever assembled in England, Marx's name is not mentioned, nor his peculiar economic theory and philosophic method even alluded to, much less made a basis of the Fabian case against Capitalism. This omission was spontaneous on the part of my colleagues. On my part it was intentional. I was determined to produce for England a book of English Socialism by English writers reasoning in the English way instead of trying to impose German Socialism on England in the repulsive jargon, half Germanised English and half Anglicised German, that did duty in those days for translations of Marx and Richard Wagner. The Marxian Dialectic, useful enough for German university students, nursed on the philosophy of Hegel, was mere botheration in England. It was pitiable to hear its exponents expatiating incomprehensibly on it when they should have been preaching British Socialism in its native language.

*

I shall at once be asked whether this policy of British Socialism for British Socialists has not been proved a blunder by the apparent fact that Marxian Internationalism has achieved an epoch-making success in Russia whilst Fabian Socialism has been an ignominious flop in England. My reply is that the apparent fact is a delusion. What has actually happened is that Marxian tactics broke down ruinously in Russia, and under sheer pressure of circumstances had to be replaced by Fabian tactics. The revolution in Russia was saved from utter wreck by Lenin's readiness to recognise and remedy his mistakes, and Stalin's sagacious realism and saving sense of humour. Lenin's New Economic Policy was Sidney Webb's Inevitability of Gradualness under a Russian name. Stalin made the supreme change when he declared for Socialism in a Single Country, and exiled Trotsky the Internationalist Marxian. Socialism in a Single Country is the Socialism of Fabian Essays. And Sidney Webb, the real inventor of Fabian Socialism (for I, had I been left to myself and Marx, might have made most

of the mistakes of Lenin) is to-day the leading English exponent of the
Russian system, and its most thoroughgoing champion. If ever one
man was entitled to say to two hundred millions "I told you so," Webb
is that man.

*

But what about the flop of Fabianism in England? Well, it was
meant for the workers and offered to the workers when the Fabians
planned the Labour Party in the tract, drafted by Webb and myself,
entitled A Plan of Campaign for Labour. But we could not publish it
for the workers without publishing it for the capitalists as well. And
the capitalists, cleverer than the workers, seized it and turned it to
their own account by combining the enormous productiveness,
power and scope of State financed enterprise with their private property on its sources, and thus producing the new form of Capitalism
called Fascism or Nationalism—Nazi for short in Germany. The
Labour Party, dominated by the power of the Trade Union purse,
simply missed the bus.

*

And now, what has all this to do with the two volumes of selections from
the essays and correspondence of Marx which have just been issued by
Messrs. Lawrence and Wishart, and which I am supposed to be reviewing? Well, they contain gems enough to be well worth their cost; but
they also contain some dead wood. Marx is greater than ever; but his
dialectic of historical materialism belongs to the days when Tyndall
startled the world by declaring that he saw in matter the promise and
potency of all forms of life. But what interest has this for us who have
learnt from the brothers De Broglie that what Tyndall and Marx called
matter is as much alive as we are, and always in furiously rapid motion?
And now that we know that Marx's attempt to measure value by abstract labour power when he should have measured it by abstract desirability, and his treatment of both as mathematical constants instead of
as variables, can lead only to nonsense and bankruptcy, is it not waste of
paper to reprint the old controversies on the subject? All that stuff
should be skipped by our readers; and Mr. Adoratsky, the editor of its
two handy volumes, whose many informative notes cannot be too
highly praised, should have cut it out ruthlessly, and concentrated on
essays like the famous Eighteenth Brumaire, which should be read
carefully with Sir Oswald Mosley substituted in our minds for Louis
Napoleon, bar the invectives which Marx hurled at all anti-Marxists.

For though Marx could analyse capitalist policy, bourgeois policy, and proletarian no-policy like a god, nobody could guess from his writing that he had ever in his life met or spoken to a real natural capitalist, bourgeois, proletarian or living human being of any description.

*

If he were alive now he would probably denounce Sir William Beveridge as a rascally Appeaser trying to ransom Capitalism for another spell by his Report. And though that is precisely what Sir William is doing, and what the Diehards are haggling over, Sir William is not a rascal, but a very capable friend of humanity who has worked out the best terms the proletariat can obtain for the moment from the Diehards backed by the intense proletarian Conservatism which has just in one of our leading cities returned Lady Apsley to Parliament and turned down Jennie Lee.

*

Marxian strategy is all right; but what Marxian idolatry and bigotry can do without Fabian tactics may be learnt from Fenner Brockway's history, entitled "Inside the Left," of his honest and devoted self and of the Independent Labour Party. It is a heartbreaking record.

The Fabian Society has wakened from its long cataleptic sleep and is up and active again, lacking nothing for a revival of its ancient vigour and astuteness except perhaps an Irishman to checkmate its British quarrelsomeness. And now it can claim that the ablest, most successful, powerful, and communistically souled ruler in Europe, Stalin (Uncle Joe, if you like), is also Europe's arch-Fabian.

And that, I think, is enough for the present.

Editor's Notes

- The above article was first published in the *Daily Herald* 10 March 1943, 2:4–7. Above the title is printed "KARL MARX died sixty years ago next Sunday;" and after the title is the subscription "by George Bernard Shaw, Who here reviews "Karl Marx: Selected Works," Vols. 1 and 2, edited by V. Adoratsky (Lawrence and Wishart, 10s. 6d.). When he sent us his manuscript Mr. Shaw wrote: 'Please follow copy and don't alter the paragraphing.' In deference to Mr. Shaw's wishes we therefore leave his article in a state of solidity. The reader should not let himself be discouraged by this." Shaw made more than fifty contributions to the *Daily Herald*, which, we are told by Blanche Patch, was the newspaper (formerly the *Daily News*) that Shaw habitually read over the breakfast table, while Charlotte read the *Times*. There is no indication of when Shaw wrote this review, but it was evidently between bouts of writing *Everybody's Political What's What*, which again Blanche Patch reports she and Shaw worked on "most of the war"; see Blanche Patch, *30 Years with G.B.S.* (London: Victor Gollancz, 1951), 170.

- V[ladimir Viktorovich] Adoratsky (1878–1945), Russian Marxist historian and editor. Involved in revolutionary activities since 1900, Adoratsky joined the Bolshevik Party in 1904. The following year he was arrested and exiled to the province of Astrakhan. In 1906 he left Russia and continued his studies of Marxism abroad; he was probably in touch with Lenin at this time. After the Revolution, Adoratsky worked from 1920 to 1929 in the administration of the Central Archives and was director of the Marx-Engels-Lenin Institute. He became a Stalinist, claiming that Stalin was "the most outstanding Leninist theoretician." He did not live to see the policy of de-Stalinization which began in Russia in the 1950s. In addition to the above work, he wrote *Dialectical Materialism: The Theoretical Foundation of Marxism-Leninism* (1934), *The History of the Communist Manifesto of Marx and Engels* (1938), and edited *Karl Marx and Frederick Engels: Selected Correspondence, 1846 to 1895* (1942).
- Sasha Kropotkin (n.d.), daughter of the Russian geographer, revolutionary, and nihilist Prince Peter Kropotkin (see above, 207), and Sofia Grigorevna Ananeva, whom he married in 1879. From 1886 to 1917 she lived in England, first in the London suburbs, and then at Brighton. Later she lived in the United States. Shaw had breakfasted with her on his first arrival in New York on 11 April 1933.
- Macaulay (see above, 119–20).
- Gladstone (see above, 87).
- Salvador de Madariaga (1886–1978), Spanish writer, scholar, and diplomat. In 1928 he became professor of Spanish studies at Oxford, until 1931, when he became Spanish ambassador to the United States; and the following year Spanish ambassador to France. As an internationalist, his publications at that time sought to interpret his land and people to outsiders. The best example (to which Shaw undoubtedly refers) is his historical essay *Spain* (1930). In opposition to the Franco regime, Madariaga was exiled from Spain until Franco's death.
- Wagner (see above, 113, 167 et seq.).
- Hegel (see above, 56–57).
- Lenin (see above, 425).
- Stalin (see above, 478).
- Tyndall (see above, 87).
- [Louis César Maurice Duc] de Broglie (1875–1960), French physicist who carried out important research in radioactivity, X-rays, and the ionization of gases. His more famous brother [Louis Victor Pierre Raymond Prince] de Broglie (1892–1987), was also a French physicist, who in 1923 made a major

contribution to the theory of quantum mechanics with his studies of electro-magnetic waves. For his discovery of the wave nature of electrons he was awarded the 1929 Nobel Prize in Physics.

- Sir Oswald [Ernald, sixth Baronet] Mosley (1896–1980), English politi-cian, successively Conservative, Independent, Labour, and finally leader of the British Union of Fascists, sometimes called the Blackshirts. He entered the House of Commons in 1918. His followers fomented discontent in the East End of London in the late 1930s and in 1940 he was taken into custody under the Defence Regulations and not released until 1943. Shaw's displea-sure at the detention of Mosley was expressed in a statement published in the *New York Sun* on 19 November that year.

- Sir William [Henry, first Baron] Beveridge [of Tuggal] (1879–1963), British economist. As a member of the food ministry in World War I, he instituted a plan for wartime rationing. He was director of the London School of Economics from 1919 to 1937 in which year he became master of University College, Oxford. However, he is particularly remembered for (and Shaw refers to the report that preceded) the Beveridge Plan, a blue-print for social security and the welfare state. Other proposals by Beveridge that were subsequently adopted included those for medical insurance.

- Lady [Violet Emily Mildred Bathurst] Apsley (1898–1966), English politi-cian. Born Violet Meeking, in 1923 she married Lord Apsley, who had been elected Conservative M.P. for Southampton the previous year. Lady Apsley became president of the Southampton Women's Conservative Association in 1924; and when her husband, as parliamentary private secretary to the secre-tary of the Overseas Department of the Board of Trade, was sent to Australia to investigate complaints about the treatment of "assisted" emigrants there, she joined him, and later coauthored the book *The Amateur Settlers* (1925), which chronicled their experiences. In 1930 Lady Apsley obtained her pilot's license (and was a director of Western Airways from 1936 to 1955). Her husband was killed in an aircraft accident in the Middle East in 1942, whereupon Lady Apsley stood as Conservative candidate for Bristol in the resulting by-election. Although there were four candidates, her principal opponent was Jennie Lee (see below). Lady Apsley was returned with a majority slightly larger than her husband's; but in the 1945 election she lost to her Labour opponent.

- Jennie [Baroness] Lee [of Ashridge] (1904–88), Scottish politician. Born a miner's daughter in Lochgelly, Fife, she graduated from the University of Edinburgh with degrees in education and law, and at twenty-four became the youngest member of the House of Commons as Labour M.P. for North Lanark. In 1934 she married Aneurin Bevan and, setting aside her feminist principles, quietly supported him as he rose within the Labour Party. Although, as Shaw recounts, she lost to Lady Apsley in that particular by-election, her own parlia-mentary career was distinguished: in 1964, as Britain's first minister for the arts, she doubled government funding for the arts, and was instrumental in beginning the Open University. She was the author of two autobiographies *Tomorrow is a New Day* (1939), and *My Life with Nye* (1980).

- Fenner Brockway (see above, 284).

28 May 1943

FABIAN SOCIALISM* [C3480]

SIXTY years ago the Fabian Society was created and christened by Hubert Bland, Edith Nesbitt (Mrs. Bland), Frank Podmore and Edward Pease.

Its first tract, *Why Are the Many Poor?* and its clever title, which proclaimed its education, attracted me when I was looking out for a Socialist group that could work on my level and in my ways. This Fabian Society seemed just what I wanted. I inspected it, joined it, and saw that what it needed, and what I myself needed, was the enlistment of a recent discovery of mine in the person of a young man named Sidney Webb, then resident clerk at the Colonial Office. I brought him along; and he brought with him the other resident clerk, Sydney Olivier, another young man of extraordinary character and exceptional capacity, quite unlike either of us. We easily collared the new and quite willing Society, and made it substantially what it is at present. We began by imposing on the Liberal Party at Newcastle a Socialist programme which it threw over when it won the next General Election, whereupon the Fabians, who had foreseen this betrayal, avenged it by driving the Liberals from power until, under Asquith, Grey and Haldane, they became imperialists, and were confronted at Westminster by a new proletarian party which became the official opposition. We started the new London County Council with a Progressive Party representing municipal socialism; abolished the old London School Board; founded the London School of Economics, which has produced Beveridge; added *The New Statesman* to the weekly press; established an Independent Labour Party in Parliament; and achieved or initiated more advances than had seemed possible in 1884, when the Liberal Party, supposed to be the progressive side in Parliament, was easily distanced when Lord Randolph Churchill, as a Tory Democrat, added free education to the Tory programme.

We made history in this fashion until, in the course of nature, we young upstarts became an Old Gang, and were assailed furiously as such by a very gifted recruit ten years younger, by name H. G. Wells. But the Society, though keenly interested in him, would not throw us over for him; and he shook our dust from his feet, and

* "Fabian Socialism." By G. D. H. Cole. Allen & Unwin. 7/6.

withdrew with all his guns in action and more popular in the Society than ever.

We, the Old Gang, held on for 27 years, and then voluntarily resigned to make room for young blood.

But the Society, by this time middle-aged, not to say elderly, did not want young blood. It settled down comfortably to mark time, and made so little mark for a considerable interval that its existence was pretty nearly forgotten; whilst its old leaders, like Wells, became famous so widely beyond the limits of the little Society, never then numbering more than 2,000, that they had ceased to be thought of as Fabians, and were individual celebrities with the general public.

But young blood will not be denied leadership for ever, though it may have to age a bit in gaining it. Wells was only ten years younger than the Old Gang when he attacked it. He was followed in due time by an insurgent who was thirty years younger, and who, like Webb, had a very able partner in his wife. He had a ready pen, and an imposing collection of initials. He was educated, cultivated, and, like Beatrice Webb, was a genuine self-made Socialist and not a convert made by reading the Socialist scriptures. He had simply looked at the capitalist world, and, hating it, devoted his life to establishing something better. He made his mark in the Society by describing the Old Gang and their following as fools, and, when called on to withdraw, explained that he wished to correct his statement, as he should have said bloody fools. He then stalked out of the meeting in a manner which made it clear that he thoroughly meant what he said. I was boundlessly delighted by this demonstration, and used all my arts to prevent his quarrel with us from pushing him out of the Society. I succeeded in convincing both sides that Guild Socialism, from which he was then suffering acutely, was not inconsistent with Fabianism.

His much-initialled name was G. D. H. Cole; and he is now chairman of the Society he has revived.

The wheel has come full circle: G. D. H. and Margaret Cole are now the Fabian Old Gang; and of the seven Fabian Essayists of the 'eighties the only survivors are Webb and myself, both octogenarians lagging superfluous, and very apologetic for that liberty. Be patient with us: we shall not be long now.

Cole's new book, which I am supposed to be reviewing, is Fabian Essays brought up to date. Like the Essays, it is addressed to the secondarily educated. The fundamental doctrine is the same, but the atmosphere is different; for the readers at which the book is aimed are much less behind the times than ours were. We had to discredit *Laissez-faire* and prophesy the decay of capitalism through its Manchester School bigotry. But it did not decay. Cole is confronted with a capitalism that has stolen our thunder and revived with tenfold power as an organisation of monster monopolies, deliberately restricting production, smothering invention, and muzzling science to keep up scarcity prices and millionaire profits. Organised Labour, from which we had hoped so much when we pushed it into Parliament and induced it to call itself Socialist, applied the same policy to its one commodity, labour. Cole, the up-to-date Fabian, hopes nothing from it. His appeal is to the proletarianised business and professional intelligentsia, of whom we must make Socialists if we are to hold our own against the Fascist financiers.

I have long since ceased to haunt the Fabian Society, which is no place for ghosts. Last year I had to emerge from my superannuation for a moment to take part in a conference at the London County Hall. Sir Harold Webbe, the leader of the Conservative Opposition on the County Council, was present in that capacity. When I had put my case he rose and said that his further attendance was unnecessary, as the opposition was quite safe in the hands of that fine old Tory Mr. Bernard Shaw. I did not take the laugh as being at all against me. Tory Democracy did not get Lord Randolph Churchill far. It has deferred Winston's premiership to his seventh decade, and would have put it off for ever had not his Party's fear of him been overcome by its greater fear of Hitler. But modern progressive Toryism, begun by Disraeli, is another matter. Gladstone would have classed Mr. Eden as a mad Bolshevik if that obsolete Grand Old Man had ever heard of Bolshevism. Had he lived to read the articles of Mr. Boothby and Mr. Nicholas Davenport in *The New Statesman* he would have thought that the whole world was going mad. Toryism is now a more likely soil for Fabian seed than Liberalism. Mr. Cole and I, as old gangsters, are the Tories of Socialism.

Yet Mr. Cole is not a fine old Tory: he still bears traces of the fine old Liberalism which, though really moribund, was the first faith of many of the original Fabians. There is a passage in his book which I venture to advise him to expunge from future editions. On page 113 he writes:

> "I am not a Communist but a Liberal Socialist, with a passionate belief in the value of certain rights and freedoms which do exist substantially in Great Britain, in Scandinavia, and in cer-

tain other West European countries, but do not exist at present in the Soviet Union."

Now if Mr. Cole is not a Communist he is not a Socialist. Socialism without Communism is Fascism, which is the enemy the Fabian Society has to overthrow now that its old adversary Cobdenism is prostrate. And it is precisely those freedoms which the Soviet Government has had to abolish that the Fabians must disclaim also, because they are the most potent weapons of Capitalism, being in fact the right to be idle and do what you like, which Mr. Winston Churchill has explicitly given up. The Russians are the freest civilised people in the world at present; and the English so busy bawling that they never, never, never will be slaves that they do not notice that they have never been anything else.

Another point that needs clearing up is the transfer of political power from the landlords and monopolist financiers to the proletariat. What does "power" mean? If it means that government, which is an art that has to be learnt, and is far too difficult and recondite to be mastered by more than five per cent. or so of the population who have the gift of it, then it means wreak and ruin, with Napoleon or Hitler to the rescue at best, and Titus Oates, Lord George Gordon, or Horatio Bottomley at worst. The ninety-five per cent. who cannot govern, to say nothing of those who could but won't, must have the power to choose from the five per cent. and to revoke their choice (not too suddenly) when they change their minds. They must have a parliament in which to criticise the Government, to ventilate their grievances, to move resolutions and votes of confidence or no confidence, so that the Government may have its ear to the ground and learn where the shoe pinches. They must have power not only to upset Parties and Cabinets in the lump, but to get rid of individual ministers regardless of party. They must have power to suggest remedies and draft bills for the consideration of the Government. Their powers of suggestion should be unlimited; but if they are given power to legislate and execute, then we shall get what we have got wherever government by anybody selected by everybody has been given its head. Mr. Cole insists that "the fundamental necessity is a wider diffusion among those who lead popular opinion of an understanding of the age's basic conditions and requirements." True, and such diffusion is still the mission of the Fabian Society. But what about those who are incapable of such understanding?

"A social structure which will call for the active participation of as many as possible of the citizens in the work of political and economic government and administration" is a fine phrase, like the phrases in the Atlantic Charter; but it suggests to most citizens a nation of bureaucrats, whereas they want to be a nation of prosperous workers and artists practising all their talents, enjoying their leisure, and being well governed without having to bother themselves about it. A taste for public affairs is peculiar to Fabians (a few thousand in thirty millions) and by no means always a happy one. I was a Fabian, and knew more about public affairs than most people; but I do not regret having preferred playwriting to a parliamentary career.

On this point I think G.D.H. might be a little more cheerful and realistic; but his book is good enough for the occasion and better; and nothing that I have said about it must be taken as a disparagement of it as a knowledgeable and important exposition of Fabianism up to date. He is, if anything, too modest; for the enormous success of Socialism in Russia has been a triumph of Fabian tactics over revolutionary catastrophism. When William Morris closed down his hopelessly incompetent Socialist League, he said: "I suppose it will come in Mr. Webb's way: let us leave politics and make Socialists." Mr. Webb's way is the way of Stalin, who saw the other ways tried; and the U.S.S.R can now be quite properly called in this country the U.S.F.S.R.

Editor's Notes

- The above review was published in the *Tribune,* no. 335 (28 May 1943): 11–12, and reprinted in *Tribune 21,* ed. Elizabeth Thomas (London: McGibbon and Kee, 1958).
- There is no precise indication of when Shaw wrote the above piece, but he was still working on *Everybody's Political What's What,* from which this is clearly a spin-off.
- G[eorge] D[ouglas] H[oward] Cole (1889–1958), English economist, historian, and detective-fiction writer. He was converted to Socialism by reading William Morris's *News from Nowhere,* and had joined the Independent Labour Party before he went up to Balliol College, Oxford. His university days were distinguished academically, but his main interests lay outside his studies, in the areas of politics and literature. When he joined the Fabian Society (under the auspices of the Webbs) Beatrice confided to her 1914 diary that he was the "ablest newcomer since H. G. Wells." However, Cole's energy almost destroyed the Fabian Society as it was in those days, since he became a leader in the Guild Socialist movement, seeking for something more imaginative than the Fabianism of that time. He often collaborated in

his writing with his wife Margaret Isobel Cole, whom he married in 1918 (see below, 518–19). In 1929 he became Labour candidate for the King's Norton division of Birmingham, but a breakdown in health was discovered to be the result of diabetes, and he gave up his candidature. Nevertheless, his political and literary life continued unabated. He was Chichele Professor of social and political theory in Balliol College, Oxford, in 1944, and became president of the Fabian Society in 1952. He also wrote many books on Socialism, including a history of the British working-class movements 1789–1947 (1948).

- Hubert Bland and Edith Nesbit (Mrs. Bland) (see above, 66–67).
- Frank Podmore (1855–1910), English writer. In his youth a Spiritualist, he joined the Society for Psychic Research in 1882. Two years later, he was a founding member of (and named) the Fabian Society, and his rooms (at 14 Dean's Yard, Westminster) were frequently its meeting place. He was also on its executive for some years, coauthoring with Webb the Fabian tract *Government Organisation of Unemployed Labour*. However, Podmore's interest seems to have become focused increasingly on the Society for Psychic Research, of which he served as honorary secretary from 1888 to 1896, and about which he wrote several books. Podmore's death in 1910 looked suspiciously like suicide.
- Edward [Reynolds] Pease (1857–1955), English social activist and founding member of the Fabian Society. It was Pease who invited fifteen people to his lodgings (17 Osnaburgh Street) on 24 October 1883 to discuss the formation of the new society that was to become the Fabians, though many of his guests were already members of Socialist or revolutionary organizations. Shaw knew Pease well throughout the mid-1880s, visiting him at 17 Osnaburgh Street, or talking with him in endless walks home from the Fabian executive meetings (which in those days were regularly held in Pease's office). Later, Pease was taken on by the Fabians as their first paid secretary, performing, as Wells said, "the work of cabinet minister for the salary of a clerk." He served the Society well through its most tumultuous years, writing several of its tracts, and when he finally relinquished his secretaryship in 1913, it was Shaw who presented him with a set of the *Encyclopaedia Britannica* as a retirement gift at a banquet the following year. Pease enjoyed a forty-year retirement, during which he followed keenly the fortunes of the Society he had helped found, and whose first history he wrote in 1916.
- Webb (see above, 139).
- Sydney Olivier (1859–1943), English civil servant and Socialist. Olivier, educated at Corpus Christi College, Oxford, joined the Fabian Society in 1885, at which time he and Shaw were close associates. Olivier was a regular lecturer for various groups, and Shaw frequently attended his lectures, dined with him, and visited his house. In 1888 Olivier was elected to the executive of the Society (with Shaw and Webb); and in 1889 he assisted Shaw in the production of *Fabian Essays* (contributing his own essay "The Moral Basis of Socialism"). Olivier was in the West Indian department of the

Colonial Office for some years, and in autumn 1899 was appointed colonial secretary to Jamaica. After the 1923 election, Olivier became secretary of state for India in the government of [James] Ramsay MacDonald (1866–1937), Scottish politician and first Labour prime minister. From 1929 to 1930 Olivier paid his last visit to Jamaica as chairman of the West Indian sugar commission. He eventually retired to the Cotswolds; moved to Sussex, and died three months before the above article was published. Among his publications are those that reveal his interest in racial problems, particularly *The Anatomy of African Misery* (1927), and *White Capital and Coloured Labour* (2d ed., 1929).

- Asquith (see above, 186–87).
- Grey (see above, 285).
- [Richard Burdon, first Viscount] Haldane (1856–1928), Scottish jurist, philosopher, and Liberal statesman. In 1879 he entered Parliament as a Liberal. He supported the Boer War, and as secretary of state for war (from 1905 to 1912) was responsible for remodeling the army, establishing a scientific research department, and founding the Territorials. After 1909 Haldane served in an advisory capacity on education (his recommendations resulting in the establishment of provincial universities and evening college courses). From 1912 to 1915 he was Lord Chancellor, as he was again in the Labour administration in 1924. He also enjoyed a great reputation as a judge.
- Beveridge (see above, 497).
- As Shaw indicates, Lord Randolph [Henry Spencer] Churchill (see above, 269–70) was a "Tory democrat." In 1880 the defeat of the Conservatives prompted Randolph Churchill to form a small band of independents of the Conservative and Tory Parties; he attacked the domestic and foreign polices of Gladstone, particularly over Ireland. In the ensuing general election, which defeated Gladstone and brought Salisbury back as prime minister, although re-elected, Randolph Churchill's views did not accord with Salisbury's traditional Conservatism and he resigned the chancellorship four months later.
- Wells (see above, 346–47).
- Sir Harold Webbe (1885–1965), a member of the London County Council Education Committee since 1925, and its chairman a year later, he became the leader of the Municipal Reform Party, L.C.C., from 1934 to 1945. He was also M.P. for the Cities of London and Westminster from 1950 to 1959.
- Disraeli (see above, 56).
- Gladstone (see above, 87).
- [Robert] Anthony Eden, first Earl of Avon (1897–1977) English politician. In 1923 he was elected to the House of Commons as Conservative candidate, where from 1926 to 1929 he was parliamentary secretary to Sir Joseph Austen Chamberlain, then secretary of state for foreign affairs. It was in the foreign office that Eden made his mark. Under Churchill, Eden was appointed secretary of state for war and minister of foreign affairs until the war's end. During this period he led the British delegation to the 1945 San Fran-

cisco Conference, which established the United Nations. Defeated by Attlee's Labour Party in 1945, Eden became a leading member of the opposition; again became foreign secretary in Churchill's last cabinet in 1951; was knighted in 1954; and, upon Churchill's retirement the following year, became briefly prime minister. However, when, in November 1956, he ordered British and French forces to occupy the Canal Zone ahead of the invading Israeli army, his action was condemned by the United Nations, and early the following year, in failing health, he resigned the premiership.

- [Sir Robert John Graham, first Baron] Boothby [of Buchan and Rattray Head] (1900–1986), Scottish politician. He was elected in 1924 as M.P. for East Aberdeenshire, a seat he held until 1958. From 1940 to 1941 he was parliamentary secretary to the Ministry of Food, and later served in the R.A.F. In 1948 he was one of the original members of the Council of United Europe. He was a powerful and refreshing speaker, frequently on T.V. in his later years, exposing with candor the follies and hypocrisies of public life. He published *The New Economy* in the same year as the above article appeared, *I Fight to Live* (1947), and *My Yesterday, Your Tomorrow* (1962).

- [Ernest Harold] "Nicholas" Davenport (1893–1979), English economist, businessman, and writer. After studying history, being called to the bar, and trying his hand at stockbroking, he found his true vocation in journalism. He worked as a regular correspondent with the *Guardian* and the *New Statesman*. Shaw's comments about him reveal his belief in a mixed economy: he was close to the Fabians and the Labour leadership in the 1920s and 1930s; but was also a friend of R. J. G. [later Lord] Boothby (see above), and also of [Sir] Winston Churchill. His economic ideas appear in two books, *Vested Interests or Common Pool?* (1942), and *The Split Society* (1964), in which he made the case for reconciling private with public enterprise. His interest in films resulted in his helping fund Gabriel Pascal's film version of Shaw's *Pygmalion* (1938). Davenport also wrote a play *And So to Wed: A Play and a Postscript on Marriage and Procreation*, published in 1946, which contains lines of dialogue written by Shaw. Moreover, Davenport states that Shaw had sent him "an encouraging criticism, giving me rare advice on technical points of construction, which of course I gladly followed" (cited in Dan H. Laurence, *Bernard Shaw: A Bibliography in Two Volumes* [Oxford: Clarendon Press, 1983], 1:457).

- Cobden (see above, 337).

- Shaw quotes the chorus of the patriotic song "Rule Britannia," written in 1740, probably by James Thomson:

> Rule Britannia! Britannia rules the waves!
> Britons never, never, never shall be slaves!

- Titus Oates (1649–1705), conspirator and perjurer, whose monstrous plot (which implicated the Catholics in the destruction of the monarchy) led indirectly or directly to more than thirty-five judicial murders, mob violence, and his own imprisonment.

- Lord George Gordon (1751–93), another anti-Catholic agitator, mob leader, trouble maker, and consumer of the public purse, who, after causing riots, carnage, and great destruction of property, was tried for high treason.
- Horatio Bottomley (see above, 348).
- Morris (see above, 165).

14 October 1945

HEARTBREAK HOSPITAL* [C3613]

UP to a point the history of medicine is a dictionary of medical biography. So far Dr. Guthrie's job of packing it into 400 pages is learnedly and readably done, amusingly and instructively illustrated, and beyond criticism in no better light than that of such scholarship and clinical experience as I possess. But when he reaches the span of my lifetime I am floored by the extraordinary discrepancy between his history and my knowledge and experience, which is common knowledge and experience, in no way peculiar or idiosyncratic to myself, and, as I am not a doctor, free from professional economic bias, my interest in the matter being that of a patient. How is this to be explained? I pause for a reply. I have been pausing for more than sixty years; and no reply has come. I am supposed to have "a down on doctors," like Molière and Napoleon, Florence Nightingale and Mrs. Eddy; but this will not wash: doctors have been among my best friends since I was a boy of fifteen. Most of what I know about medicine has been learnt from them. What professional etiquette and the tyranny of the General Medical Council (their trade union) forbids them to say I say for them. When I was invited to deliver the Abernethy lecture at St. Bartholomew's every medical school in London pressed me to repeat it. Its title was "The Disadvantage of Being Registered."

*

First, let me make it clear that I do not for a moment suggest or suspect that Dr. Guthrie has deliberately and corruptly suppressed or

* "A History of Medicine." By Douglas Guthrie, M.D., F.R.C.S.Ed., F.R.C.E. (Nelson.) 30s.

distorted facts or invented the fables which have imposed on him. He is obviously as honest as the daylight. Incredible as it may seem, he, a registered certified Doctor of Medicine, a Fellow of the Royal College of Surgeons, does not know what every man in the street who has paid any attention to it knows about medicine and surgery in the nineteenth and twentieth centuries, and is still in the stage of a chemist I knew when I was eight years old, who played the violoncello in an amateur orchestra and believed in phlogiston. Bleeding was still a medical panacea: when you were ill you sent to the apothecary for leeches as a matter of course; and children in the nursery were ruthlessly purged every month, or oftener, ill or well. Treatments changed just as the patients changed, because people got tired of them; and doctors, like milliners, had to be in the fashion. Syphilis was treated with mercury. It "drove in" the infection and suppressed its natural cure until, years later, it broke out in the horribly disfiguring and destructive form called tertiary syphilis, though it was really mercurial poisoning. Iodide of potassium, guaranteed infallible, replaced it for a while, but proved so immediately allergic in many cases that it gave way to arsenic in a formula numbered 606 and its later modifications. Yet doctors persisted in prescribing mercury as well, just to make sure.

A parallel case was that of the treatment of malaria by quinine, under which it was incurable and became a yearly visitation.

*

There were fashions in surgical operations also; and as they were exempt from coroner's inquest they were all passed as successful if the operator could get his patient off the table alive. Extirpation of the uvula had its vogue; ovariotomy was the rage for a long season; tonsil removals and wholesale teeth extractions struggled for supremacy with extinction of the appendix. At present the emphasis is on a prostate operation which sometimes goes to the limit of human endurance of pain. Dr. Guthrie's sole relevant remark on all this is that "surgery had been rendered painless by the introduction of anaesthesia," which shocks one as a thundering lie at its first impact, but of course means only that the patient does not feel the touch of the surgeon's knife or saw.

Anaesthesia was followed in fracture cases by immobilisation in plaster jackets, with all the mischief that might have been expected from treating a broken living human body as if it were a broken chair or a leaking cistern, and a surgeon only a specialised carpenter and plumber. Heart patients were, and still are, immobilised and stimulated with whiskey until they die of hypertrophied liver. Even midwifery is threatened by this mechanistic theory which makes no distinction between a live body and a dead one. We now have young practitioners assuring us that in the near future all child-births will be effected by the Cæsarian operation instead of by vulgar midwifery.

*

Dr. Guthrie mentions these fashions only as incidents in the lives of the practitioners who introduced them, and confesses himself puzzled by the fact that Spencer Wells, who made ovariotomy almost safe, was scrupulously clean in his habits before Lister blundered into antiseptic surgery. He attributes Spencer Wells's success to this cleanliness but that was not Wells's own account of the matter. I never met him; but I knew an intimate friend of his who talked a good deal about him. The secret was simply keeping the patient in an unvarying temperature. Cleanliness was nothing new; for another successful surgeon of that day was Lawson Tait. Both he and Wells drew the water for their operations from the common pipe, teeming with microbes. The microbes gave them no trouble. Dr. Guthrie knows this as well as I do. But here is what he says.

> Spencer Wells operated on a thousand cases of ovarian tumour with an astonishingly low mortality, and was in high repute as a "safe" surgeon. His success lay in his insistence upon the most scrupulous cleanliness. Yet he could not explain why cleanliness was so important; and he did not possess that genius for detached observation which led Lister to the summit of his success.
>
> Lawson Tait was strongly opposed to Lister's views, and he denied the bacterial nature of sepsis. Nevertheless he always insisted on absolute cleanliness, and this was no doubt the cause of the remarkable success of his operations.
>
> Many were the eulogies of Lister which appeared at the time of his death, but none more aptly worded than that which appeared in the Royal College of Surgeons' report: "His gentle nature, imperturbable temper, resolute will, indifference to ridicule, and tolerance of hostile criticism, combined to make him one of the noblest of men. His work will last for all time; humanity will bless him evermore and his fame will be immortal."

Who would gather from this that Lister, a shallow reasoner and according to his dressers a maladroit operator, bedevilled surgery for years by substituting carbolic acid for pipe water and carbolic spray for fresh air, with the result that his incisions would not heal, and his ridiculous "donkey engine" had to be utterly discarded. It was founded on the germ theory of disease which I, knowing something of the outbreaks of gangrene in the Dublin hospitals, had challenged for its failure to account for their mysterious cessations when according to the theory they should have spread and depopulated the earth.

Such success as Lister had as an operator was due to the aesthetic cleanliness already established by Tait and Wells. Sir Almroth Wright, our brainiest bacteriologist, gave Listerism the *coup de grâce* in his controversy with its last champion, and re-established pipe water, with ten per cent. of salt in it, as the best available wound dressing. Wright's is now the standard treatment in England; and he arrived at it, not as a bacteriologist, but by analysing the prescription of soap and sugar poultices for wounds by the peasant women of Ireland. He also—and this may prove his most pregnant achievement—put his finger on the cardinal point of the success of cleanliness by his dictum that the effect of sanitation is aesthetic.

Not a word of this from Dr. Guthrie. Any student equipped with nothing but his book would be left under the impression that the germ theory and antiseptic surgery are an unchallenged part of the most modern medical science and surgical art, and that Lister was an immortal genius.

*

Another impression left by his history is that smallpox was abolished by vaccination. As a matter of fact vaccination, founded a century and a half ago on amateur statistics put forth by doctors who had never heard of "controls," and described one out of two cases as 50 per cent., lived on the credit of sanitation, which meanwhile made an end of plague, cholera, and typhus epidemics and of endemic fever. Vaccination was made compulsory in 1853, and enforced by ruthless persecution. The sequel was that whilst the epidemics of cholera and typhus (the controls) ceased, smallpox persisted and culminated in two appalling epidemics in 1871 and 1881. It did not give way until 1885, when compulsory isolation stopped it. That was the end of vaccination for anyone who had given half an hour to the history of it. The fierce persecution by which it was enforced provoked an equally fierce revolt against it.

The Jennerians circulated photographs of babies disfigured by con-
fluent smallpox, and were countered by more horrible photographs of
babies dying of generalized vaccinia. Leicester and Gloucester discarded vaccination and were met by prophecies of their speedy depopu-
lation by smallpox. Nothing of the kind occurred; and compulsion was
finally swept away by popular fury in an astonished Parliament which
was still in the 1853 stage of infatuation and delusion on the subject.
But the fashion persists, and has brought into existence a flourishing
trade in vaccines guaranteed to protect the inoculees from every disease under the sun. Lawrence of Arabia told me that he had been
inoculated 40 times and thought nothing of it, as his healthy blood
made short work of every pathogenic germ that was injected into him.
At present vaccination is more fatal and revaccination more disabling
than smallpox, and is suspected of including in its sequels not only the
known horror of generalized vaccinia, medically certified as indistin-
guishable from hereditary syphilis at its worst, but also of producing
infantile paralysis and other troubles.

*

Not a word of all this from Dr. Guthrie. His date in 1945 on the
subject is 1853. Not a hint that it is now as plain as the sun in the
heavens that pathogenic microbes are products of the zymotic diseases; that these diseases are products of ugliness, dirt, and stink
offending every aesthetic instinct and thus depressing the *vis medica-
trix naturae* (the Life Force); that dirt and squalor and ugliness are
products of poverty; and that though the Life Force is still an ultimate mystery, zymotic diseases can be abolished by abolishing poverty, the practical problem being one of economic distribution. If Dr.
Guthrie knew this he could hardly have thought it not worth mentioning. Such omissions are not history.

Our State regulation of the medical profession has for its organ a
Committee of the Privy Council called the General Medical Council.
Its proper function is the protection of patients against abuse of the
extraordinary privileges, including practically impunity for homicide
and mayhem, which doctors enjoy. Yet it is insanely manned by registered doctors, as if the criminal law should be executed by judges and
juries of convicted criminals. It has inevitably become a trade union of
the very worst type as classified by the Webbs, unquestioned as the
leading authorities on that subject. I agitated for years to have laymen
appointed as representatives of the patients. I succeeded only in inflict-
ing on the Council a very distinguished layman who was at once given

another whole time job which made it impossible for him to take any part in the Council proceedings or to retain his seat on it.

It should consist of laymen exclusively, with doctors acting as experts and assessors only. Nothing can be plainer nor more pressing; yet in the recent discussion of a reformed public health service not a word has been said about it.

*

All the journalists and all the political agitators seem to agree that the medical profession must be regulated by practising doctors with an overpowering pecuniary interest in illness and operations. As against it we have the imposing array of Christian Science Churches and the warning of their prophet Eddy that some day there will be a massacre of doctors. We have seen the Council snubbed by the Crown twice; once when our most famous manipulating surgeon, Herbert Barker, denounced and persecuted by the Council as an ignorant and dangerous bone-setter, came into the honours list with a knighthood, and again when the physicians of George V. included an osteopath. Naturopaths, osteopaths, herbalists, homeopaths, Battle Creek clinics, and unregistered practitioners are at work everywhere, earning higher fees than the registered slaves of the Council. And Dr. Guthrie either does not know of them, or considers them beneath the dignity of a history of medicine. I can account for Dr. Guthrie's reticences on no other grounds.

But I know more of the matter than he because my medical education, such as it is, has been wholly controversial and up to date. Every doctor should be controversially educated; and the examination slate should be cleaned every five years instead of, as in Dr. Guthrie's case apparently, every 100 years if at all.

Do not forget, however, that as a most readable dictionary of modern medical biography his so-called history is unique and well worth its price.

Editor's Notes

- The above review, subscribed "by Bernard Shaw," was published in the *Observer,* 14 October 1945, 3:4–6. It was also serialized in four parts in the *New York Journal-American,* as "Shaw Assails Medical Men's Fabled 'Cures' " (30 October); "Shaw Bares Old Vogues in Surgery (31 October); "Shaw Explains Best Means to Treat Wounds" (1 November); and "Shaw Charges Health Service Snubs Laymen" (2 November).

▪ This, one of Shaw's last flings at the medical profession, is a reminder of his lifelong dialogue with doctors both on and off the stage. His first dramatic hero was a doctor; his unfinished novel (begun in 1887) was entirely about doctors; in *The Philanderer* (1893) he mounted an attack, further developed in *The Doctor's Dilemma* (1906); until, in *Too True to be Good*, written in his seventy-fifth year, his final dramatic attack replaces scientific discussion by the presence on stage of a huge microbe: a grotesque emblem of the excesses of the New Germ Theory of half a century before. Shaw had grown up in an age of great medical progress, with the pioneer work of Pasteur, Lister, and Koch in the closing decades of the nineteenth century. Yet from the beginning, Shaw, with his slowly developing notion of a "Life Force," opposed the scientific reduction of human beings to a collection of chemical reactions, just as his belief in the individual will caused him to reject Darwin and embrace Butler and Lamarck. Nevertheless, as Shaw himself says, doctors had always been among his best friends: his Uncle Walter was a doctor; and he was on excellent terms with several prominent medical men, including James Kingston Barton (whom he had known since the previous century) and Sir Almroth Wright (see above, 276–77), on whose deaths he was to write generous tributes in the last years of his life.

▪ Douglas Guthrie (1885–1975), Scottish physician, surgeon, and author. Educated in Edinburgh, Jena and Paris, he became MB.BCh. (1907), and did postgraduate study in Hamburg, Jena, Berlin, and Vienna. He became a Fellow of the Royal College of Surgeons in 1913. After the war he specialized in otology and laryngology. In 1919 he was ear and throat surgeon for the Royal Hospital for Sick Children, and surgeon to the Ear and Throat Infirmary in 1920, in which year he became F.R.S.M. From 1945 to 1956 he was Lecturer on the History of Medicine at Edinburgh University. Apart from the above book, he authored *Lord Lister, His Life and Doctrine* (1949), *From Witchcraft to Antisepsis* (Clendening Lecture, 1954), *Janus in the Doorway* (1963), and numerous papers on otolaryngology and the history of medicine.

▪ Molière [Jean-Baptiste Poquelin] (1622–73), French dramatist, whose irritation with the medical profession (possibly resulting from his mother's early death) is revealed in such satirical works as *Le Médecin Malgré Lui* (1666) and *Le Malade Imaginaire* (1673), during a performance of which he died himself.

▪ Napoleon (see above, 263) mistrusted doctors; Florence Nightingale (1820–1910), British nurse and hospital reformer, converted her anger at the primitive sanitation methods and inadequate nursing facilities at the large British barracks-hospital at Üsküdar (now part of Istanbul, Turkey) into active nursing in the Crimean War; and Mary Baker Eddy (1821–1910), American founder of the Church of Christ, Scientist, who was plagued by ill-health but unable to find relief from the medical profession, finally did so through a spiritual revelation.

▪ Phlogiston is a nonexistent chemical that, before the discovery of oxygen, was thought to be released during combustion.

▪ [Sir Thomas] Spencer Wells (1818–97), English surgeon. In 1863 he went to Trinity College, Dublin; and in 1839 he entered Saint Thomas's Hospital, London. Admitted to the Royal College of Surgeons in 1841, after six years in the navy, he set up practice in London (chiefly as an ophthalmic surgeon) in 1853. The following year he was elected surgeon to the Samaritan Free Hospital for Women; and it was here that he devoted himself to perfecting the technique of ovariotomy, completing his first successful one in 1858. The practice however, was not generally accepted until 1864. By 1880 he had performed one thousand of the operations successfully. He filled all the chief offices of the Royal College of Surgeons in England, was made an Honorary Fellow of the King's and Queen's Colleges of Ireland and became surgeon to the queen's household in 1863, a position he maintained until 1896. In 1883 Victoria conferred upon him a baronetcy. He published many works, perhaps his most famous being the seminal work *Diseases of the Ovaries: their Diagnosis and Treatment* in 1865.

- [Joseph, Lord] Lister (1827–1912), English surgeon, and "father of antiseptic surgery," who was by turns lecturer on surgery at Edinburgh, Regius Professor of Surgery at Glasgow (1859), and professor of clinical surgery at both Edinburgh (1869) and King's College Hospital, London (1877–93). He made many important discoveries relating to the coagulation of the blood, inflammation, and so forth, but he is most widely recognized for his introduction of the antiseptic system in 1867, which revolutionized modern surgery. Shaw's antipathy to Lister, according to Frank Harris, derived from his own abscess on the instep (in 1898) which led to necrosis of the bone: "Unfortunately for him, at that time the Listerian antiseptic treatment of wounds was still in vogue; and the sinus left by the operation was stuffed with iodoform gauze at every dressing, with the result, now well understood, that it would not heal; and Shaw was an invalid on crutches for eighteen months until the Listerian antiseptic was discarded for pipe water, when he immediately recovered, and became a furious anti-Listerian just as, after his smallpox, he had become a furious anti-Jennerian"; see Frank Harris, *Bernard Shaw. An Unauthorised Biography Based on Firsthand Information* (London: Victor Gollancz, 1931), 204.

- Lawson Tait (1845–99), Scottish surgeon, specializing in diseases of women. He became surgeon to the Birmingham Hospital for Women in 1871, residing in that city until he died. He specialized in abdominal surgery, and perfected numerous new surgical procedures, becoming widely known and respected. He was also interested in politics, and contested one of the divisions of Birmingham. He published many books and papers, including essays that won the Hastings Gold Medal of the British Medical Association in 1873.

- Shaw himself was a victim of the smallpox epidemic of 1881, and spent that June recuperating at the home of his Uncle Walter, a physician.

- [Edward] Jenner (1749–1823), English physician and discoverer of vaccination. In 1773 in his native village of Berkeley, Gloucestershire, he began investigating the truth of the traditional belief that having cowpox was a protection against smallpox. In 1796 he injected a young boy with cowpox; six weeks later attempts to produce smallpox in the boy were unsuccessful. Two years later Jenner published his discovery in *An Inquiry into the Cause and Effects of the Variolae Vaccinae*. There was, however, great disagreement among physicians about the efficacy of Jenner's treatment, until finally seventy London physicians and surgeons signed their name to an endorsement of the practice. Shaw was not "furiously anti-Jennerian," as Harris claims: he was furiously against the idolatry of Jenner, the worship of miracle cures, and the extremism of compulsion. He deals with vaccination in his Preface to *The Doctor's Dilemma* (1906), and again in the Preface to *Back to Methuselah* (1918–21).

▪ The "State regulation of the medical profession" referred to by Shaw in the above article is not the National Health Service, which, although envisaged in the Beveridge Plan, did not come into force until 5 July 1948 with the passage of the National Health Service Act.

▪ [Sir] Herbert Barker (1869–1950), English manipulative surgeon. He was apprenticed to John Atkinson, the bone-setter of Park Lane, and before he was twenty-one had set up in practice himself, and was successful in Manchester and Glasgow before he established himself in London. He was soon persecuted by the medical profession, since he had no traditional training, and the controversy was much discussed in the press, particularly when Dr. F. W. Axham was struck off the the medical register in 1911 for acting as Barker's anesthetist. Many medical men took up Barker's cause, but the General Medical Council still refused to recognize Barker, who, nevertheless, was knighted in 1922. Shortly afterward he retired from regular practice. The medical profession slowly ceased its persecution: in 1936 Barker demonstrated his skill before the British Orthopaedic Association at Saint Thomas's Hospital, and the *Lancet* reported the case histories in detail.

▪ In Calhoun County, Michigan, on the Kalamazoo River, about 120 miles west of Detroit, the Seventh-Day Adventists in the nineteenth century started a medical boardinghouse that grew into the famous Battle Creek Sanitarium, under the direction of Dr. John Harvey Kellogg. To vary the vegetarian diets of his patients, Dr. Kellogg invented about eighty grain and nut-food products, including peanut butter and flaked breakfast foods. It was his younger brother W. K. Kellogg (and C. W. Post) who developed these products for worldwide sale.

20 October 1945

THE HISTORY OF A HAPPY MARRIAGE*
[C3615]

MRS. COLE's biography of Beatrice Webb, very readably written and extraordinarily well informed and competent, is beyond criticism be-

---

* "Beatrice Webb." By Margaret Cole. (Longmans.) 10s. 6d.

cause no critic, with the possible exception of myself, knows half as much about the Webbs, or understands that knowledge, as Mrs. Cole. Nothing better can be done until the time comes when Beatrice Webb's diary, written up from day to day, emerges from its veil of privacy and of her desperately illegible handwriting, and takes its place among the notable diaries of the last five reigns. Meanwhile Mrs. Cole's final verdict, "one of the greatest women of our generation," stands established by her book, which does not contain a superfluous or thoughtless word.

I have, however, a word to say about it that has not yet been said. It gives us not only the public life of a great woman, but a very intimate and fascinating account of a happy marriage. If all marriages were as happy, England, and indeed the civilized world, would be a Fabian paradise. Unfortunately it was not only a childless and exceptional one, but from a very common point-of-view an ascetically joyless one. Our national sports and pleasures, well within their means, were simply distasteful to the Webbs. Beatrice betting in the ring at the Derby or Grand National, Sidney in at the death at a fox-hunt, were inconceivable. Exercise they took religiously; Beatrice could walk me off my legs; and bicycling was not only permitted but rigorously prescribed for many years until Sidney's odd habit of fainting occasionally without symptoms or sequels overtook him one day on his bicycle, and she, riding as usual ahead of him and missing him, rode back and found him comfortably unconscious in the ditch with nothing else the matter with him. After that he was not permitted to walk by machinery.

Their life, therefore, presents itself to most of us as one of almost Trappist asceticism, except that it was by no means silent; for neither of them ever stopped talking when they were not reading or writing. Yet they enjoyed it thoroughly. I lived with them a good deal before my own late marriage, and was quite accustomed to be with them at work, and to see Beatrice every now and then, when she felt she needed a refresher (Sidney was tireless), rise from her chair, throw away her pen and hurl herself on her husband in a shower of caresses which lasted until the passion for work resumed its sway and they wrote or read authorities for their footnotes until it was time for another refresher. Meanwhile I placidly wrote plays, but was confirmed in my peculiar doctrine that a point will be reached in human mental development when the pleasure taken in brain work by St. Thomas Aquinas and the Webbs, and by saints and philosophers generally, will intensify to a chronic ecstasy surpassing that now induced momentarily by the sexual orgasm, and produce a normal enjoyment of life such as I have only experienced a very few times in my long life in dreams. The census most needed at present is of the few people who would not prefer unlimited champagne and expensive cigars, ropes of pearls in a box at the opera on the grand tier, and a fleet of Rolls-Royces, to the Webb-Aquinas routine.

Looking through the index of Mrs. Cole's book for personal contacts made and cultivated by the Webbs, one is struck by the absence or scarcity of the references to the aesthetic and histrionic celebrities within their reach. William Morris, their greatest Communist contemporary, is not mentioned except once in a reference to his house but not to himself. Cunninghame Graham, most picturesque of all their Socialist contemporaries and a story writer of genius (he figures in my play *Arms and the Man* with Webb in strong contrast), is not mentioned at all. Among the Fabians nothing is made of the conspicuously able pro-consul Olivier, who went his own way so unscrupulously that if his impulses had not been those of a good man he would have been a first-rate scoundrel. Hubert Bland, with his phenomenal muscular strength and prowess as a pugilist, his ferocious monocled scrutiny (his eyesight was defective), was dismissed by Beatrice after a brief investigation as "a mask," though as a typical suburban Tory converted to Socialism by falling among the primitive Fabians his point of view counted for a good deal in the development of Fabian policy.

These and other instances provoke the notion that the Webbs were Philistines, insensible to literature and art. They were far too intelligent to be anything of the sort; but they were supreme social investigators, and had to deal with men in the mass as citizens and not as geniuses. Beatrice was puzzled and repelled by individuals whom she could not class: she was not at her ease with me until she had classified me as a sprite. She catalogued Ramsay MacDonald as "a façade" and A. J. Cook as "an inspired goose." As an investigator, she would not be bothered by unclassable and incalculable people; but she was by no means stupidly insensible to their talent. Her choice of Webb was a stroke of genius; for to her relatives and in her social set the general opinion was voiced by a graceless nephew who raised the alarm in the family by announcing that Aunt Bo was marrying a seditious cockney cad.

Never was there a man less of a cad than Sidney. Within my experience he was the only man who combined prodigious ability and encyclopaedic knowledge with entire simplicity and integrity. When as practitioners of the arts of public life we were all posing, acting, dramatizing ourselves as best we could, Webb never posed, never acted, never courted popular favour or any other favour, and

was never in danger of becoming a humbug and a living fiction, not
to say a living lie.

This rare virtue in him had its disadvantages. When he had made
his work intelligible and authentic he would not spend a moment in
making himself or his style fascinating: such tricks never entered his
head. In the House of Commons he would hardly make himself audi-
ble. He was sometimes impatient with people because he gave them
all credit for being as gifted as himself, and could not imagine that
what was obvious to him instantaneously was Greek to them. Lady
Astor said of him that she had no doubt that he knew everything, but
that he should remember occasionally that other people didn't. His
advice was not always as gracious as it was good.

As both he and Beatrice conscientiously refrained from forming their
conclusions until they had with inexhaustible industry investigated all
the available evidence, they had furious disputes with me at almost
every step. I am not a complete apriorist, because I always start from a
single fact or incident which strikes me as significant. But one is
enough. I never collect authorities nor investigate conditions, I just
deduce what happened and why it happened from my flair for human
nature, knowing that if necessary I can find plenty of documents and
witnesses to bear me out in any possible conclusion. This is a shorter
method than that of the Webbs; and by it I sometimes reached their
conclusions before they did, and had them fiercely contested accordingly. When we were living together on Milford Common, Mrs. Green,
widow of the historian, paid us a visit, and was so startled at our first
after-dinner discussion that she could not believe that we could remain
on speaking terms after it, and was relieved to find next morning that it
had made not the smallest change in our personal relations and was part
of our daily routine. Certainly our work never suffered from lack of home
criticism; and as Socialism begins at home, and yet is so international in
its practical problems that when they have been solved for the British
carpenter or chemist they have been solved for every carpenter or chemist in the civilized world, we did not concern ourselves with diplomacy.
That is why there was no Webb foreign policy, nor any Shavian one until
1913, when I woke up to the threatening danger of war, and urged the
declaration of the Pact made years afterwards at Locarno when it was too
late and no expert believed in it nor in the equally futile Kellogg Pact
which followed. I saw the situation too clearly, being in England that
most foreign of all foreigners an Irishman, completely objective in my
criticism of that curious freak called God's Englishman. This objectivity
was so unbearable in England that though I was pro-English when it

came to fighting Kruger, Kaiser, or Hitler when they went all out for race hegemony, I ran some risk of being lynched, and did not try to drag the Webbs with me in my incursion into foreign affairs.

Besides, having been converted to Socialism not by Marx's dialectics and his erroneous capitalist theory of value, but by the tremendous impact of his English industrial facts and figures, I knew that the Cease Fire that followed his death could be ended by Webb, who alone could out-Marx Marx in his command of that atomic sort of ammunition. Until the Russian Revolution turned their eyes abroad the Webbs ignored diplomacy because they had something better to do, not that they were less conscious of it than Lord Vansittart. This was proved when they made their last great study of the Soviet constitution, and went all out in its acceptance as a new and more hopeful civilization.

It is impossible within the limits of a review to fill in half the details of this extraordinary ménage. Mrs. Cole has said enough and said it very well. But the moral is that not until it ceases to be extraordinary and becomes typical in English political society will it be possible to Fabianize England any farther than the Soviet has been forced to Fabianize Russia by sheer drive of circumstances after its disastrous trial of catastrophic change in 1917–20. Webb's Inevitability of Gradualness remains inexorable as to economic change, though changes of paper constitutions or lists of Cabinet Ministers may be as easy and sudden as lynching.

Editor's Notes

- The above was published in the *Times Literary Supplement*, no. 2281 (20 October 1945): 493–94, subscribed "by Bernard Shaw." It was also published in the *New York Times*, 18 November 1945, and was published as a pamphlet in the same year. There is no indication as to when Shaw wrote it.
- [Dame] Margaret Isobel Cole (1893–1980), English Socialist and writer, educated at Roedean School and Girton College, Cambridge, where she read classics. In 1914 Margaret Cole took her first teaching job at Saint Paul's Girls' School. Here she met Mary Hankinson, the Fabian (who gave occasional games lessons); in a letter to the present editor, Dame Margaret Cole explained how, through her, she came to meet her husband: "[Mary Hankinson] shared a cottage in the Chilterns with a full-time mistress named Ethel Moor, who was a Fabian. I stayed with them once or twice and was told about a dangerously subversive young man who was trying to break up the Fabian Society: his name was G. D. H. Cole. I became a volunteer in the Fabian Research Department, which had been captured by the rebel Guild Socialists" (Dame Margaret

Cole, unpublished letter to Brian Tyson, 25 August 1977). It was in 1918 that she married G. D. H. Cole and began a most remarkable political partnership that ended only with his death in 1959. During the 1930s the Cole partnership established the Society for Socialist Inquiry and Propaganda and the New Research Bureau, and Margaret began publishing on a large scale, *The New Economic Revolution* (1937), and *Marriage Past and Present* (1938) being two of her significant works. She continued to publish after World War II: *Makers of the Labour Movement* (1948), her edition of Beatrice Webb's *Diaries* (1952–56); a history of the Fabian Society in 1961; and ten years later a biography of her husband. Her autobiography had been published in 1949.

- *The Diaries of Beatrice Webb* (edited by Norman and Jeanne MacKenzie) were published again in four volumes from 1982 to 1985.
- Sidney and Beatrice Webb (see above, 139, 199).
- Saint Thomas Aquinas (see above, 381).
- William Morris (see above, 165).
- [Robert Bontine] Cunninghame Graham (1852–1936), Scottish author and politician. Shaw met Cunninghame Graham for the first time on 25 February 1888, but was never a close friend, though they corresponded from time to time. Cunninghame Graham became the first president of the Scottish Labour Party in 1888. From 1893 to 1898 he traveled extensively in Spain and Morocco, where an incident described in his book *Mogreb-El-Acksa* inspired Shaw's play *Captain Brassbound's Conversion* (1899). According to the above article, he had already furnished the inspiration for Sergius Saranoff (in opposition to Webb's unlikely Bluntschli) in *Arms and the Man* (1894)! Cunninghame Graham himself wrote a great many books (mainly of travel), but is chiefly remembered for his flamboyant essays and short stories.
- Olivier (see above, 503–4).
- Hubert Bland (see above, 66).
- Ramsay MacDonald (see above, 504).
- A[rthur] J[ames] Cook (1883–1931), Welsh miners' leader. Born in Wookey, Somerset, he became a coal miner in the Rhondda, and a leader of the South Wales branch of the miners' union. He became general secretary of the national union in 1924, and was a leading figure in the General Strike of 1926.
- [Nancy Witcher Langhorne, Viscountess] Astor (1879–1964), American-born British politician. Born in Greenwood, Virginia, she married Viscount Astor (her second husband) in 1906. In 1919, when her husband was raised to the House of Lords, she succeeded him as Conservative M.P. for Plymouth and became the first woman to take a seat in the House of Commons. She remained an M.P. until her retirement in 1948, a notable champion of women's rights, temperance, and progressive education. Notwithstanding their political differences, Shaw maintained a friendship with Lady Astor from 1928 until his death. The Shaws often stayed with the Astors (Shaw finished writing *The Apple Cart* on 29 December 1928 while staying at her country home), and Lady Astor was a frequent visitor to Whitehall Court, where a terra-cotta bust of her by Strobl stood in the hall. She accompanied Shaw on his trip to Russia in 1931 (with Charlotte's blessing) and, during the

Second World War, she would often arrive "with two or three Americans in a large American car with a service driver"; see Blanche Patch, *30 Years with G.B.S.* (London: Victor Gollancz, 1951), 151.

▪ Mrs. Green was presumably the widow of John Richard Green (1837–83), the Oxford historian who contracted tuberculosis in 1869 and, since active work became impossible, set about writing the first complete social history of England, entitled *Short History of the English People* (1874). Its success encouraged a larger edition published from 1877 to 1880.

▪ Locarno, a vacation resort on the north shore of Lake Maggiore, Switzerland, was the site for the signing on 16 October 1925 of the Locarno Treaties—seven treaties for mutual security—whose signatories were Germany, Britain, France, Belgium, Italy, Poland, and Czechoslovakia. The treaties were ratified in London on 1 December 1925, and the so-called spirit of Locarno prevailed until the Germans peremptorily invaded Czechoslovakia in 1938.

▪ The Kellogg Pact, more properly the Kellogg-Briand Pact or Pact of Paris, was a multilateral treaty renouncing war as an instrument of national policy, signed by fifteen nations in Paris on 27 August 1928. It was named after Frank Billings Kellogg (1856–1937), U.S. secretary of state, who sponsored and drafted it, and Aristide Briand (1862–1932), then foreign minister of France. In fact for his part in sponsoring the treaty, Kellogg was awarded the 1929 Nobel Peace Prize. Ratified by the United States Senate on 15 January 1929, the Kellogg Pact was invoked by the League of Nations in a vain attempt to halt the Japanese invasion of China; and later, in a still more spectacularly futile gesture, by sixty nations to protest the Italian invasion of Ethiopia in 1936.

▪ [Robert Gilbert,] first Baron Vansittart [of Denham] (1881–1957), English diplomat. In 1930 he became permanent undersecretary for foreign affairs. A trip to Germany to meet Adolf Hitler in 1936 confirmed him in his uncompromising opposition to the Nazi dictator; and he constantly warned of the coming catastrophe unless Britain armed herself to meet the German threat. In 1937 his continued agitation brought him into conflict with Neville Chamberlain, and from 1938 he was pushed aside politically. In 1941 he retired and was raised to the peerage.

23 December 1945
PAINTER AND PARTNERS* [C3622]

WATTS was one of the rarest of painters and sculptors. He was born able to draw and paint anything he wanted to draw and paint, or to

---

* "The Laurel and the Thorn: A Study of G.F. Watts." By Ronald Chapman.

model it in any plastic material. The resulting picture or statue was not only recognisably like its original but a revelation of qualities and possibilities in it which were invisible to ordinary mortals. And it was always what he intended it to be.

This last gift, though we are apt to take it as a matter of course, is not at all common. Even so great an artist as Rodin once showed me a head he had modelled with fingers on its lips, and asked me whether it suggested anything to me, as he did not know what to call it. I told him that De Quincey had written of things that are beyond speech as "the burden of the incommunicable." He liked this, and evidently meant to use it, though whether he ever did I do not know. Our mediocre artists paint the best model they can find and afford, and label her Juliet or Francesca or Deirdre, unless they have a turn for nudes, in which case she is catalogued as Venus.

This purposelessness never occurs in Watts's work. His worst picture, called The Dead Knight, can hardly be called a picture at all: it is an ugly surface with his favourite quotation scrawled on it; but it says what he means and means what he says; and in this it is typical of all his works.

*

What more is there to be said of Michael Angelo and Leonardo? Really nothing but the size of their jobs. Nobody gave Watts a Sistine Chapel or a Medici mausoleum or a church to decorate. But as far as his canvases went he could fill them with pictures of men and women, not as they could be seen at any moment in the streets but in their highest and utmost which reveal them as prophets, sibyls, poets. His portraits are precious beyond pearls. His Tennyson I cannot answer for, as I never saw Tennyson; but in the portrait and the gigantic statue in Peterborough we have the poet even if the man never looked quite like that. I knew William Morris and Walter Crane well enough to be very familiar with their appearance; and I knew their minds as far as such knowledge is possible. Watts's portraits of them are great because, though they are not photographic, they are psychographic, and give you the true Morris and the true Crane in their full depth and grace. The only other painter known to me who could do this was John Butler Yeats, father of the poet, an Irishman who lived neglected in Bedford Park when all the celebrities were having themselves painted by Millais and Frank Holl.

In Watts's day the grand tradition of Raphael and Michael Angelo, with its cant of chiaroscuro, "marvellous foreshortenings," "morbidezza of Andrea del Sarto" (the first open-air painter), and all the other slogans of the academic exhortations to carry on the work and win the overwhelming prestige of Michael Angelo, had produced so many huge daubs, quite unsaleable, that there was nothing for it but an uncompromising return to pre-Raphaelite visible realism. Watts, instead of being swept away by this movement, took not the smallest notice of it, and made for the shining light along the straight and narrow path, as if it had never ended in another city of destruction. His only tragedy (it was Rodin's also) was that a commercialised Europe had no Sistine Chapels for him to paint.

Such work as his must be seen as a life's work, as it can be now at Compton. Single pictures of his at the Academy exhibitions were outglared by the blazing reds and yellows, reeking from varnishing day, when all the other exhibitors worked up their canvases competitively to concert pitch. Millais, for instance, was colour-drunk. Watts's Hope hung beside Millais's blazing Beefeater is murdered. Such crimes made Burlington House a Chamber of Horrors in those days. Only a pilgrimage to Compton (I spent a year within a mile of it) can add Watts to one's parish temples of the great god, Art.

*

Mr. Chapman tells the story of Watts's five spiritual wives and an absurd legal union with an incipient genius, the girl model Ellen Terry, when he was a middle-aged, lukewarm gentleman and she an actress with a vocation as irresistible as his own. On the only occasion on which Ellen mentioned it to me, she described how, when she was only Watts's model, she came home one day and informed her mother triumphantly that she was going to have a baby. Watts had kissed her; and she was young enough to believe that babies were the result of kisses. For both of them the marriage was an entirely negligible episode which left no ill feeling. Watts tried legalised union again, very successfully this time, if I may judge by my acquaintance with his widow. Ellen tried four other men, but died an independent single woman.

*

As a polygamist Ellen Terry and her discarded husbands was easily surpassed by Watts, though he went through the legal ceremony only twice, both times with women young enough to be his daughters. A man who makes the creation of works of the highest art his sole and supreme business in life needs before all things a woman to be his servant, his mother, his nurse, his devotee, his housekeeper, and not at all necessarily his bedfellow. Clearly Ellen Terry, herself a genius, could not spend her life in this fashion: what she needed was a husband who would do it all for her; and she was not lucky enough to find one. Watts was extraordinarily lucky. As a child he was not mothered; but he was fathered until he was taken on successively by Lady Holland, Lady Duff Gordon, Mrs. Prinsep, Mrs. Cameron, Mrs. Russell Barrington, and finally (at 74) by his second legal wife, an amiable, comely woman with whom anyone could be happy, and capable enough to create and run the Compton pottery, manage the Compton gallery, and take the care of Watts in her stride quite easily. Such polygamy leaves Casanova nowhere. As Watts could paint and sculpt in the grand manner as easily as other men can walk or talk, he must be ranked as one of the most fortunate of mortals and yet the most dependent on women.

*

There was nothing surprising to me in this. Although from fifteen to twenty I took over and did the responsible office work of a man of forty, and did it as well as it needed to be done by anyone who hated it as much as I did, I abandoned it at twenty and threw myself on my mother until after years of failure I began to earn a little money. My management of my income consisted wholly of handing it to her and asking her for a pound when my pockets were empty. At forty I could afford to marry, and had to open a bank account and manage my copyrights and invest my savings; but as to my daily life, it was the same story: everything else was done for me by my wife and her servants. Only, being a bit of an economist and biologist, I did not take my dependence as a matter of course, like most men; I knew it, and was led by it to my belief that Eve came before Adam, and created him as her hunter and warrior, and finally as the feeder of her imagination and of the aspiration towards godhead of the Life Force in her. Many of her creations are only drones; but the geniuses are fastened on by susceptible women and have everything done for them except their own highest work.

*

This book by Mr. Ronald Chapman, THE LAUREL AND THE THORN (Landor's description of his laurel), is almost too well and thoroughly done. His description of Little Holland House throws over completely its reputation as Macaulay's pulpit, and shows that it was Watts's temple. When it was demolished and replaced by the Melbury Road studios its glory departed; for Topsy Morris, the idle singer of an empty day, who would have none of the Watts's grand manner, nor Macaulay's

Whiggery, and was not only pre-Raphael, but pre-Shakespear and arch-Chaucerian, came along with young Burne-Jones and a retinue of craftsmen who despised academic painting at his back, and decided that the Little Holland House set were high art snobs, and drove Watts out of London to the Isle of Wight, and finally to his end in Limnerslease by the Hog's Back in Compton.

Editor's Notes

- The above review was first published in the *Observer*, 23 December 1945, 3:4–6 It was reprinted as "Ellen Terry as George Bernard Shaw Saw Her," in the *New York Journal-American*, 14 April 1946, *American Weekly* supplement, 6–7. There is no indication of when it was written.
- Ronald [George] Chapman (1917–?), English author and librarian. Born in Compton, Surrey, he grew up in the house of G. F. Watts, and was educated at Eton and New College, Oxford, where he took his B.A. in 1942. He became a library assistant at the Bodleian Library, Oxford (from 1942 to 1962)— taking his M.A.in 1943—and was from 1962 to 1964 assistant librarian and superintendent of Radcliffe Camera. From 1960 to 1962 he was editor of *Oxoniensa*. In 1963 he had to give up nearly all reading, since he suffered from a myopic degeneration of the retina. He and his wife continued to live on their small farm in Buckinghamshire, stocked mainly with poultry and sheep. In addition to the above book, Chapman also wrote a picture book, *Scenes from the Life of Christ* (1951), and *Father Faber* (1961).
- G[eorge] F[rederic] Watts (1817–1904), English painter and sculptor. His professed artistic purpose was to ennoble mankind by preaching in paint and stone on the problems of wealth, the power of love, and courage in the face of death. In 1864 he married Ellen Terry; but parted from her within a year of the marriage. In 1867 he was elected a member of the Royal Academy, and received numerous honors and prizes thereafter. Watts married for the second time in November 1886 (see below). It is estimated that Watts painted about three hundred of what Shaw called on one occasion "incomparable" portraits, including those of Giuseppe Garibaldi, and the poets Tennyson and Browning. He presented 150 of his portraits to the National Portrait Gallery in 1904; and these are today considered his best work. But in his lifetime his allegorical work enjoyed great popularity, among his better-known allegorical paintings being *Love and Death* (1877), *Watchman, What of the Night?* (1880), and *Hope,* (1886). Shaw, in Annie Besant's journal *Our Corner* in June 1885, described one of these allegories: "Life is represented by a narrow rocky path. A young girl is painfully traversing it, helped along by Love in the shape of an agreeable youth with wings and an encouraging smile. The absence of roundness in the outline of the girl's limbs produces a cadaverous appearance which sensibly diminishes her beauty, but intensifies the impres-

sion of sadness and weakness conveyed by the whole composition" (quoted in *Bernard Shaw on the London Art Scene*, 51). Watts's well-known sculptures include the memorial to Tennyson mentioned above by Shaw, and the big equestrian statue that features as part of a monument to the South African statesman Cecil Rhodes (in Kensington Gardens, London).

- [François Auguste René] Rodin (1840–1917), French sculptor. In 1880 he was commissioned by the French government to produce the *Porte de l'enfer* [The gate of hell], inspired by Dante's *Inferno*, for the Musée des Arts Décoratifs; during the next thirty years he was engaged in creating the 186 figures for these bronze doors. The work was never completed; but many of Rodin's best-known works were originally conceived as part of its design, among them *Le Baiser* (1894), and *Le Penseur* (1904). His statues include those of a nude Victor Hugo, and Honoré de Balzac in a dressing gown (which last was refused recognition by the Société des Gens de Lettres, which had commissioned it.) He made many famous portrait busts, including one of Bernard Shaw in 1906.

- The "head . . . with fingers on its lips" sounds exactly like Rodin's *L'Adieu* (1892), modeled from the head of Mademoiselle Claudel.

- De Quincey's (1785–1859) phrase "the burden of the incommunicable" is found in the preface to *Confessions of an English Opium Eater* (1856).

- Morris (see above, 165).

- Walter Crane (1845–1915), British painter and illustrator. With William Morris he is considered to be a leader in the Arts and Crafts movement, as well as the "Romantic movement" in decorative art. He illustrated numerous books, his most famous being Spenser's *Faerie Queene* between the years 1894 and 1896. He was also an author of books on aesthetics, an influential teacher of art (he was director of three schools, including the Royal College of Art in South Kensington), and an active Socialist, contributing political cartoons to socialist journals and founding the Art Workers' Guild.

- John Butler Yeats (1839–1922), Irish painter. Among his five children were the poet William Butler Yeats (1865–1939) and the painter Jack Butler Yeats (1871–1957). In 1867 John Butler Yeats went to London and studied at Heatherley's Art School. In the early 1880s he returned to Ireland, began to exhibit successfully, and was a fair portrait painter. Many of his portraits of leading figures in Irish literary and political life are now in the National Gallery of Ireland. In 1908 he went to the United States, intending to stay for only a short time, but spending the rest of his life there, acquiring a reputation as one of the best conversationalists in New York. He lectured and wrote essays for *Harpers Weekly*. *Early Memories, a Chapter of Autobiography* was published after his death.

- [Sir John Everett] Millais (1829–96), English painter. Although a founding member of the Pre-Raphaelite brotherhood in the late 1840s, from the 1870s onward, Millais became chiefly famous as a fashionable portrait painter noted for brilliant color, strict attention to detail, arrangement, and clarity. In 1856 he was elected an Associate of the Royal Academy; in 1885 he became a baronet. Shaw's art criticism reveals that he admired the early Millais, occasionally used him as a stick to beat younger landscape or portrait artists, and always praised him for his color. Stanley Weintraub even suggests that several of Millais's paintings may have influenced Shaw's own dramatic settings (see the introduction to *Bernard Shaw on the London Art Scene, 1885–1950*).

- [Francis Montague] "Frank" Holl (1845–88), English painter. Admitted as a student at the Royal Academy in 1861, he first exhibited there in 1864, and thereafter was a regular exhibitor until his death. In 1876 he began portrait painting, which he was to do almost exclusively thereafter. From 1879 to the time of his death Holl painted 198 portraits of almost all the celebrities of his day, including the Prince of Wales. In 1886, Shaw described a John Collier portrait as "one of those opaque clayey faces in a black quagmire which Mr. Holl has made fashionable."

- Burlington House, Piccadilly, named after its original owner in 1664, the first earl of Burlington, and extensively remodeled over the centuries, assumed its present neo-Italian Renaissance appearance in 1873. It was converted to the use of the Royal Academy about 1768, and has since housed, as well as a permanent display of art treasures, the Academy's annual summer exhibition of contemporary work.

- [Dame] Ellen [Alice] Terry (1848–1928), English actress. After her brief marriage to Watts at the age of sixteen she married two years later Edward William Goodwin, the architect, by whom she had two children, Edith and Edward Gordon Craig; when that marriage broke, in 1877 she married the actor Charles Wardell, from whom she separated in 1881. In 1878 she joined Henry Irving in a twenty-four-year acting partnership at the Lyceum, during which time she became the leading lady of the British stage, enjoying her greatest success in 1882 as Beatrice in *Much Ado About Nothing*. Shaw admired her and in 1895 his friendship deepened into a love affair of letters that he and Ellen Terry kept up for five years. He wrote *The Man of Destiny* (1896) for her; but the mutual jealousy and professional irritation existing between himself and Irving (whom he wished to play Napoleon) interfered with the possibility of its production. Later he tried (unsuccessfully) to persuade Ellen Terry to create the role of Lady Cicely Waynflete in *Captain Brassbound's Conversion* (1899). She did, however, go to see the play, and met Shaw for the first time, by chance, under the stage of the Strand Theatre. Later, after Irving's death, she did play the role of Lady Cicely, and other roles by Shaw. Indeed, she toured the United States with *Captain Brassbound,* and in 1907 married James Carew, the American actor who played Captain Kearney in the play. Her friendship with Shaw diminished to an acquaintanceship as the years went on. She lectured on Shakespeare in England, the United States, and Canada; in 1925 she was made a Dame of the British Empire; and her correspondence with Shaw was published after her death.

- Watts's second (legal) wife was Mary Fraser Tytler (1849–?] the daughter of a Scottish landowner, brought up in the Highlands, who wished to be a painter herself after visiting Watts's studio. In 1876 she sent him presents and an intimate friendship began, but when she became too adoring Watts rebuked her idealization of him, concluding by saying that he hoped one day she would come with the news that she was going to be married. However, when Mary Tytler had passed through the Slade and South Kensington Schools of Art and began to paint in a rented studio at Epsom, she became engaged to a man who modeled for her; and this upset Watts to the point where he persuaded her to break her engagement, and finally to marry him.

- The other women in Watts's life were Mary Augusta Vassall-Fox, wife of fourth Baron Holland, whom Watts met in Italy in 1843; she modeled for him and they became quite intimate. In 1845 the Hollands left Florence and Watts, handing over the villa at Careggi to Lady Caroline Duff Gordon, wife of Sir William Duff Gordon, second baronet and Watts gave her two daughters drawing lessons. With one of the daughters (Georgiana Duff Gordon), he enjoyed a close relationship for a time. Next he met Mrs. Thomas Prinsep, wife of a distinguished Indian civil servant, and she dominated Watts's life for twenty years. They lived in London, and he met her in 1849 after his affair with "Georgie" Duff Gordon. In 1850, thinking him a "starving artist," Mrs. Prinsep took him to live with her and her acquiescent husband Thoby (in consequence known as "dog Thoby"). It was while he lived with the Prinseps that Watts married the sixteen-year-old Ellen Terry in 1864 (see above). Julia Margaret Cameron was the sister of Mrs Prinsep: she had married an Indian jurist, and was a person of extraordinary energy. She was a photographer who delighted in photographing (among others) Ellen Terry, Watts's first legal wife. When Mrs. Cameron left with her invalid husband for Ceylon, her place was taken by the equally vigorous and managerial Mrs. Russell Barrington, who took the house next door to the Prinseps' London home at 6 Melbury Road. Watts's friendship with her was intimate: she was his confidante (she also wrote a book about him), and so resented his second marriage to Mary Fraser Tytler (see above) that she had to be discouraged from making visits.

- Walter Savage Landor's poem, from which the title of the book is taken, reads as follows:

> Lately our poets loiter'd in green lanes,
> Content to catch the ballads of the plains;
> I fancied I had strength enough to climb
> A loftier station at no distant time,
> And might securely from intrusion doze
> Upon the flowers thro' which Illissus flows.
> In those pale olive grounds all voices cease,
> And from afar dust fills the paths of Greece.
> My slumber broken and my doublet torn,
> I find the laurel also bears a thorn.

▪ [Sir Edward Coley] Burne-Jones (1833–98), English painter. In 1861 he became a founder member of Morris, Marshall, Faulkner and Co. (later Morris and Co.) for which he designed tapestries and stained glass.

19 May 1946

IDOLATRY OF THE GLORY MERCHANT IS SHEER ILLUSION* [C3646]

AT this moment, when human equality is so urgently at issue between Socialists and Reactionaries, both of them all at sixes and sevens about it, it is a pity that so few military geniuses are also literary geniuses.

Marlborough, pen in hand, was a booby. Exceptions are Cæsar, Napoleon, Wellington and Montgomery: two Irishmen, a Corsican and an ancient Roman. And of these only two, Napoleon and Montgomery, have written about the qualities which made them victorious generals instead of Blimps.

Napoleon was so excessively professionalised (he was sent to a military school at the age of 11) and so completely indoctrinated with the academic 18th century battle tactics, which he practised with such extraordinary ability and aptitude that he fought his last pitched battle exactly as he had fought his first.

To him Wellington was an amateur; for you cannot make a thorough soldier of an English or an Irish general: they are not caught and trained young enough, and are gentlemen first and soldiers after.

The greatest of them gave up their profession, like Marlborough and Wellington, in horror and disgust at its butcheries; it is only the failures, like the Kaiser and Hitler, who try to establish themselves as tyrants by pushing military terrorism to extremity. Montgomery would have stopped the war at any moment had that been possible.

Napoleon seems an exception, as he was certainly not a failure as a general; for he won battle after battle, and at Waterloo believed with good reason up to late in the afternoon that he had won. Wellington

---

* "Military Leadership." By Field-Marshal Viscount Montgomery of Alamein. (Geoffrey Cumberledge, Oxford University Press.) 2s. 6d.

admitted that it was a very near thing, and would not allow a history of it to be written because the British artillery ran away.

But Napoleon was driven to his fatal attack on Russia not so much by ambition to conquer the world as by the fact that it was only as a great glory merchant that he had been deified in France, and that only by continued French victories could he maintain that idolatry. Lord Montgomery, who omits this snag in the plans of all conquerors, goes so far as to declare that the idolatry of the glory merchant is mostly sheer illusion. As a matter of fact ambitious conquerors do not last as long as fundamentally pacifist ones, who with thrones within their reach, throw away the sword and end as political duffers and constitutional reactionaries.

The power of the military leader is a function of the helplessness of the led. We all know how to do something. But for comprehension of where to do it, when to do it, why to do it, where to buy the materials for it and to sell the product after we have done our bit, we are in the hands of the 5 per cent or so who can decide all these questions for us. Unless the 5 per cent are available and given effective authority, no economic or political system can work except to the extent of doing what was done last time on the authority of Diehards, Duffers and Stick-in-the-Muds.

Now nobody who has not first-hand administrative experience can imagine the effect of authority conferred on duffers. It goes to their heads at once. They parade their privileges pompously, giving orders, often very cruel and stupid orders, for the sake of showing off their greatness and power.

Field-Marshal Montgomery stresses a desire to dominate among the qualities that make a great military leader, and attributes it to Napoleon; but he forgets, I think, the frightful rabble of political wind-bag nincompoops who were in power in Napoleon's early days and whose massacres, wholesale drownings (*noyades*), and insane cruelties of every description made the French Revolution stink in the nostrils of history just as the corruption by power of the German Government under Hitler did in our nostrils after 1933.

Napoleon rose and superseded these gangs of blackguards not by lust for domination but by sheer gravitation. Command came to him because France had to be governed; and he was the only man capable of the job. To such men power is not a luxury, but a responsible and very hard-working duty.

Lord Montgomery rose to the top in a whirlpool of, at best, student soldiers who knew very thoroughly what was done last time and could be trusted to do it again every time, not in the least because he wanted to dominate, but because he knew what to do next time and how and when and where to do it when his Haig-ridden comrades did not.

In the face of the appalling mess and deadlock of our sham democracy, as Hitler truly called it, which enables any brainless filibuster to hold us up for months when Europe is starving, we are tempted, after reading Lord Montgomery's pamphlet, to make him absolute totalitarian Kaiser, Fuehrer, Emperor and Dictator of Europe for the next five years with plenty of plutonium at his disposal.

In that five years more would be done than our Conferences will do in fifty. And he would refuse to be worked to death for longer. Napoleon said that a general lasts six years.

Montgomery would certainly not pay anyone £2,000 a year to oppose him, worry him, discredit and delay him. He might possibly have to shoot postulants for this function if they become too troublesome. He would tolerate no opposition for the sake of opposition. He would perhaps establish concentration camps for popular orators and debaters. At all events he would find that he could not govern without authority and power; that his success must be judged by the results of five year plans carried out in the teeth of popular Anarchism disguised as Liberty; and that Democracy is practicable not as misrule or no rule by ignoramuses, but as a choice between qualified rulers after (say) five years' trial.

The Russian period is three years, the American four, the British five; but instead of democratic authority there are constitutional guarantees to the man in the street that he shall not be governed at all, which is just what the poor mug desires. And so Britons always will be slaves.

Editor's Notes

■ The above review was published in *Reynolds News*, 19 May 1946, 2:2–4, with Shaw's first sentence italicized, his article interrupted four times by small headline phrases (which I have thought fit to omit) taken from the body of the text, and the following caption: "A copy of Field-Marshal Viscount Montgomery's lecture on military leadership came into Reynolds News office last week. It contained Viscount Montgomery's assessment of the relations between political and military leadership, summed up in the sentence, 'The whole training and experience of the soldier makes him less rather than more fitted to be a politician.' We asked Bernard Shaw, the world's most biting commentator on soldiers and politicians, to write this review." The paragraphing seems un-Shavian; but I have left it as originally printed.

- Taking the above caption as true, since *Reynolds News* was published on a Sunday, and thus since Montgomery's lecture was presumably received by them between 13 and 17 May 1946, we must assume that their request was made and Shaw's review written in the same period.
- [Bernard Law, first] Viscount Montgomery of Alamein (1887–1976), Irish-born English soldier. In World War II he commanded the 3d Division, and shared in the retreat to Dunkirk in 1940. The following year in North Africa, the 8th Army had only recently recovered from its pummelling at the hands of Axis forces, when Montgomery was appointed to its command. He quickly restored morale and the will to win, and at El Alamein in 1942 he launched a successful battle against the German general Erwin Rommel, followed up by a series of engagements that drove the German-Italian forces back to Tunis. His subsequent achievements in Sicily and Italy, where he served under the American General Dwight Eisenhower, as commander-in-chief of the British armies on the Western Front, were characterized by caution, but also tenacity. It was Montgomery who accepted the German surrender on Lüneburg Heath in 1945, and who commanded the British Occupied Zone in Germany from 1945 to 1946, in which year he became chief of the general staff. He was chief of NATO forces from 1951 to 1958. Apart from the above lecture, his publications include *Normandy to the Baltic* (1947), and *Memoirs* (1958) in which Montgomery makes much of his meeting with Shaw on 26 February 1944, in the studio of Augustus John (see above, 471) who was painting "Monty's" portrait. However, his claim that "Bernard Shaw looked in at the studio for a chat with Augustus John and remained there during the remainder of the sitting," is false. The truth, according to both Blanche Patch and Augustus John, is that "Monty" said that he would like to meet Shaw, and this is confirmed by Shaw's note to Blanche Patch: "I come up on Saturday to meet Gen. Monty at Augustus John's. He is sending a car for me there and back"; see Blanche Patch, *30 Years with G.B.S.* (London: Victor Gollancz, 1951), 110. Montgomery liked Shaw, finding him "most amusing, and with a penetrating brain," and clearly agreed with his critique of the portrait (Shaw thought Augustus John "not interested in the man"); for Montgomery refused it when it was finished.
- [John Churchill, first duke of] Marlborough (1650–1722), English soldier, who by a combination of good fortune and military skill rose to become earl of Marlborough in 1689, under William III, and enjoyed high office in the reign of Queen Anne and George I. After Marlborough's death, his wife Sarah edited her husband's papers for publication. It is to these last that Shaw refers.
- Colonel Blimp is a cartoon character invented c. 1938 by the English political cartoonist David Low (1891–1963). Colonel Blimp is a fat, pompous old gentleman with a walrus moustache, who has a rooted antipathy to change, hates the working classes of all societies, detects "Red" influences in

everyone but himself, and "makes even Neville Chamberlain look like a tool of Moscow."

- Haig (see above, 356).

6 November 1949

MORE ABOUT MORRIS.* [C3881]

GREAT men are fabulous monsters, like unicorns, griffins, dragons, and heraldic lions. But "this side idolatry," as Jonson put it, William Morris was great not only among little men but among great ones. All who knew him declared that he was the greatest man they had ever known. Scores of books will be written about him; but whatever record leap to light he never shall be debunked.

So far the most authoritative biography of him is Mackail's. But Mackail regarded his Socialism as a deplorable aberration, and even in my presence was unable to quite conceal his opinion of me as Morris's most undesirable associate. From his point of view Morris took to Socialism as Poe took to drink.

The latest biographer, Mr. Lloyd Eric Grey, is free from this prejudice. He does his utmost to appreciate Morris's political acumen, prophetic farsight, and eminence not only as poet, artist, and craftsman, but as a philosopher. His book, illustrated by a superb portrait of Morris by Cosmo Rowe, and by Burne-Jones's funny drawings, has no taint of academic snobbery. His hero worship is pushed to the limit, as it should be. The more widely it is read, the better.

*

It has, of course, trifling faults as well as deep qualities. It labours overmuch to determine Morris's place in literature. This is waste of time: Morris was no schoolman. He read everything that did not bore him, and, like Molière, took his goods where he could find them. He knew about Poe and Browning and Tennyson and Swinburne as all literary people know about them; but the only poets who influenced

---

* "William Morris, Prophet of England's New Order. By Lloyd Eric Grey. (Cassells.) 15s.

his beginnings were Chaucer and Rossetti. Being a born storyteller his pet modern authors were Dickens and Dumas. One day, when he had been desperately uncomfortable at a police court, going bail for some of the comrades, I found him rubbing it all off by reading "The Three Musketeers" for the hundredth time or so. On one such occasion his co-bailsman was Bradlaugh, and he envied the assurance with which that platform athlete ordered everyone about and dominated the police staff as if he had been the Home Secretary. He was nothing of a bully in spite of his pathological temper, and when physical courage came under discussion said: "I am a funkster; but I have have one good blow in me."

Mr. Grey is wrong about the famous outbursts of temper: he thinks that Morris laughed at himself for them. They were eclampsias, and left him shaken as men are shaken after a fit. The worst sorrow of his life was when his daughter Jenny became a hopeless epileptic, and he knew that it was an inheritance from himself. Mr. Grey, in one passage, suggests that he was lonely and affection-starved at Lechlade because Mrs. Morris neglected him for Rossetti, who never tired of painting her. This is a mistake. Morris adored Jenny. He could not sit in the same room without his arm round her waist. His voice changed when he spoke to her as it changed to no one else. His wife was beautiful, and knew that to be so was part of her household business. His was to do all the talking. Their harmony seemed to me to be perfect. In his set, beauty in women was a cult: Morris had no more reason to be jealous of Rossetti than Mrs. Morris of the gloriously beautiful Mrs. Spartali, or of Lady Burne-Jones, whose memoir of her husband shows that Morris was her hero.

*

Like Hyndman, Morris had something of the petulance of the born rich, though he could not endure the society of average ladies and gentlemen. I have said from clinical observation that his rages were pathological. I go farther, and believe that his lack of physical control when he was crossed or annoyed was also congenital and not quite sane. No two human beings could be less like one another than he and H. G. Wells; yet neither of them could be depended on to behave always sensibly. Being a great man, Morris could face and bear great trials; but on some utterly negligible provocation anything might happen, from plucking hairs out of his moustache and growling "Damned fool, damned fool," to kicking a panel out of a door.

*

I ask Mr. Grey to reconsider his estimate of The House of the Wolfings as more advanced than News From Nowhere. The Wolfings is, like all Morris's tales, lovely as a tissue of musical prose; but it is only his first attempt to restore Don Quixote's destroyed library, full of impossible sword fights and Dulcinea, and a very biased contrast between Roman and "barbarian" society. News From Nowhere is a picture of a possible future, with no fights and forlorn maids rescued from enchanters. Mr. Grey writes that it is unreal because there are no crimes in it. He forgets: there is a murder in it. There are even motor-boats in it.

When I went through Morris's Merton factory with him, I dared to say, "You should get a machine to do that." He replied, "I've ordered one."

Editor's Notes

- The above review was published in the *Observer* 6 November 1949, 7:6–7. There is no indication of when it was written.
- Shaw was still energetic throughout 1949, his ninety-third year, correcting biographer's errors (see below), giving a speech at the presentation of a gate for Ayot St. Lawrence's demolished abbey, and adapting a ten-year-old collection of personal reminiscences into *Sixteen Self Sketches*. On 13 August *Buoyant Billions* (begun in 1936) received its British première at Malvern (it later failed in London); and in the autumn Shaw completed *Bernard Shaw's Rhyming Picture Guide to Ayot St. Lawrence*.
- Lloyd Eric Grey [Lloyd Wendell Eshleman] (b. 1902), American author, critic, and educator. Born in Lancaster, Pennsylvania, he was educated at Dickinson College, Yale and Princeton Universities, obtaining his Ph.D. from the latter in 1937. His dissertation topic was William Morris; and a slightly revised version of this, entitled *A Victorian Rebel: The Life of William Morris* was published in 1940. The book reviewed above is, in fact, another issue of the same book with a replacement title. Eshleman also wrote *Moulders of Destiny: Renaissance Lives and Times* (1938), and was a contributor to the *New York Times Book Review*, the *New York Sun*, the *Commonweal*, and the *Journal of Modern History*.
- Ben Jonson (1572–1637), Shakespeare's contemporary and friend, spoke about his fellow playwright after his death: "I remember, the players have often mentioned it as an honour to Shakespeare, that in his writing (whatsoever he penned) he never blotted out a line. My answer hath been, would he had blotted a thousand. Which they thought a malevolent speech. I had not told posterity this, but for their ignorance, who choose that circum-

stance to commend their friend by, wherein he most faulted, and to justify mine own candour, for I loved the man, and do honour his memory (on this side idolatry) as much as any"; see Ben Jonson, *Timber: or, Discoveries; Made upon Men and Matter* (1641), in Ben Jonson, *Workes* (1640 title-page), 97–98).

- [John William] Mackail (1859–1945), Scottish classical scholar. His two-volume *The Life of William Morris*, published in 1899, was reviewed by Shaw in the *Daily Chronicle* on 27 April that year, and reprinted in *Pen Portraits and Reviews* in 1931. In it Shaw describes "the real history of Morris's plunge into politics as distinguished from the account given by Mr. Mackail."

- Cosmo Rowe's drawing of William Morris is the frontispiece of the book.

- Burne-Jones (see above, 527–28).

- "Il m'est permis, disait Molière, de reprendre mon bien où je le trouve." [It is permitted to me, said Molière, to take my good [fortune] where I find it] (quoted in Grimarest, *Vie de Molière* [1704], 14).

- Edgar Allan Poe (1809–49), American poet and short story writer. His many stories—to the writing of which he resorted through economic necessity—are fascinating narratives, often distinguished by grotesque inventiveness. His poetry, thematically sad, has haunting meters and melodies.

- Geoffrey Chaucer (c.1343–1400), the father of English poetry, author of *The Canterbury Tales* and several other masterworks, was a seminal influence on most subsequent writers. His burial plot in Westminster Abbey caused the surrounding area to be known ever after as Poet's Corner. The great folio copy of Chaucer, with Morris borders and eighty-seven illustrations by Burne-Jones, was produced in 1896, and has been described as one of the finest books ever made.

- Browning (see above, 28–29).

- Tennyson (see above, 113).

- Swinburne (see above, 355).

- Rossetti (see above, 237).

- Dickens (see above, 113).

- [Alexandre] Dumas [Davy Pailleterie] (1802–70), French novelist and playwright. He was a prodigious worker, with about twelve hundred volumes being published under his name. Best known in France for his plays, he is better known outside France for his historical romances, of which he produced a great number from 1844 to 1854, including such novels as *Les Trois Mousquetaires* (1844; English translation *The Three Musketeers*, 1846), and *Le Comte de Monte Cristo* (1844; English translation *The Count of Monte Cristo*, 1846) together with volumes of history, journalism, *causerie*, and ten extraordinary volumes of *Mes Mémoires*.

- Bradlaugh (see above, 83).

- *Funkster* seems to be Morris's coinage: the word *funk* meaning "cowering fear," deriving (possibly) from the eighteenth-century Dutch or Flemish dialect word *fonck*, was also used as the noun meaning "coward;" though sometimes the word *funker* was used.

- "Mrs. Spartali" became "Mrs. Stillman." According to May Morris: "W. J. Stillman, an American journalist and man of letters, was another of the friends who gathered round Rossetti and Morris and the others. Mr. Stillman, for many years correspondent for *The Times* in Rome, was the more nearly drawn into the circle as the husband of Marie Spartali, my Mother's nearest friend, whose beauty and charm will always be part of the romance of those days"; see May Morris, *William Morris, Artist, Writer, Socialist*, 2 vols. (New York: Russell and Russell, 1966), 1:74.
- Hyndman (see above, 20).
- H. G. Wells (see above, 346–47).

13 January 1950
A TRIBUTE TO A GREAT CHURCHMAN*
[C3895]

IT is puzzling to be born a Quaker, bred a Churchman, and made a Prelate. Dean Inge must often have said to himself "For which among the rest was I ordained?" In his Diary he confesses to the Quaker; but I, now one of his few remaining contemporaries, being often challenged to denominate myself, and being much of the Dean's various opinions, have ceased to reply that my nearest to an established religion is the Society of Friends, and, while calling myself a Creative Evolutionist, might also call myself a Jainist Tirthankara as of 8,000 years ago.

When the Dean and I were young the religious world was a battlefield of controversy and persecution. Draper's Conflict between Religion and Science was a textbook. I preached Fabian Socialism in Victoria Park to my little crowd with a Christian Endeavour Apostle preaching on my right and an atheist doing the same on my left: the one vociferating that all atheists had been in the dock at the police court or divorced for adultery, and the other calling the inn at Nazareth the Pig and Whistle, both of them convinced that they were uttering the profoundest religious doctrine and the most unquestionable scientific truth respectively. All the controversies were in terms

---

* "Diary of a Dean." By Dr. W. R. Inge. (Hutchinson.) 21s.

of what old photographers called Soot and Whitewash, and Ibsen's Brand All or Nothing. If the Nazareth inn had the sign of the Pig and Whistle, God did not exist. If the translators of the Authorized Version changed a negative into a positive to save the doctrine of the resurrection of the body, if the Ark was too small to hold all the earth's fauna in couples, if Joshua could not have stopped the sun in the Valley of Ajalon without putting the whole universe out of action, if asses and serpents could not have conversed in human speech with Balaam and Eve, then the Bible was untrue in every word and sentence from beginning to end. If a Secularist lecturer had been convicted of having travelled by rail without a ticket or kept a mistress (or being kept by one), or advocated birth control, then all Secularists were thieves, fornicators, swindlers, rascals and prostitutes; and only the ruthless exercise of the Blasphemy Acts could save us from moral chaos and material ruin. Association of ideas passed for logic.

A Divided Church

Even within the Church of England itself there was controversy. There were muscular Christian rectors who, determined to show that they were no killjoy mealy mouthed parsons, wore nothing clerical except jampot collars buttoned at the back, and were as assiduous at sports as in services. There were Anglo-Catholics who wore birettas and cassocks, called themselves priests, held up two fingers in blessing, and advertised their services as Masses. There were artist parsons who hung pictures of nudes all round their rooms to show that they had no sympathy with the zealots who held that sex is original sin. There was the Reverend C. L. Marson, who maintained that the first Article of the Church of England is, from the point of view of Jehovah's Witnesses and the Plymouth Brethren, flat atheism. The vehicle in which he made his rounds was a donkey cart; and the donkey's name was Sarah Bernhardt. He collected Folk Songs, which his humbler parishioners classed as debauchery, as they did all fine art and merriment. There were the Christian Socialists organised in the Guild of St. Matthew: some of them in the Church and Stage Guild with ballet stars and Lion Comiques, notably Jolly John Nash, who made his living by singing the praises of champagne, and was sincerely pious in private. And there were those who followed Herbert Spencer in holding that God is unknowable and unfathomable: in short, Neo-Jainists.

"No" TO BISHOPRIC

Into this boiling cauldron of controversy Ralph Inge was born, foredoomed by heredity and environment to be a minister of the Church of England, and destined to be that unique phenomenon, a famous Dean who refused a bishopric and became a famous journalist. It is no part of my business to describe or explain the steps of this unusual development. I know only too well the annoyance and corruption of doctrine caused by people who write and read about noted authors instead of reading what the authors themselves have written, mostly much better. All a reviewer has any right to say of another man's book is "Read it" unless his verdict is "Dont read it," in which case he should give his reasons. But in the Dean's case, the word is so emphatically "You must read it" that I shall permit myself only a note or two.

LASTING FRIENDSHIP

Many years ago I received for review a book entitled *Outspoken Essays,* and had hardly read three sentences before I smelt that very precious rarity, an original mind and a first-rate literary craftsman. As I was a bit in this line myself I was intensely interested, and reviewed it to that effect. My estimate has never changed. It led to a friendship which has made the kindly references to me and my late wife in the *Diary* so dear to me that any pretence of impartiality on my part would be ridiculous. There was no difference between us that mattered. But there was a difference. He had met many people I had met, and read many books I had read. But I had read Ruskin, Ibsen and Marx; and my classics were Orlandus Lassus and Sweelinck, Palestrina and Monteverde, Bach and Handel, Haydn, Mozart and Beethoven, Rossini, Meyerbeer and Verdi, whereas in the index to the *Diary,* Ruskin, Ibsen and Marx are not mentioned; and the Dean, surfeited with the strains of Jackson, execrates music. I divide sages into pre-Marx and post-Marx. The pre-Marxists, brought up on Macaulay and Gladstone, regard and regret the nineteenth century as an age of prosperity increasing by leaps and bounds. To the post-Marxists it is a bottomless pit of hell from which Marx lifted the lid. In the *Diary* Sidney Webb is referred to only once, and then in a quotation from a noodle who described him as a negligible nobody. And the Diarist records how, when we met, he found himself in unexpected agreement with me, but could not understand my obsession about Russia. Had he read Marx and discovered the Fabian Society he would have understood. On this point he dates as does another famous friend of mine, Gilbert Murray. He withdraws his description of Gilbert Chesterton's scriptures as the "elephantine capers of an obese mountebank" but does not define him as what he was: an extraordinarily gifted Peter Pan who never grew up.

"Two Thundering Lies"

Curiously enough, though he never mentions Ibsen, he was bothered, as Ibsen was when he wrote *Ghosts*, by a Darwinian turnip ghost. For Ibsen, disease, especially syphilitic dementia, was inevitably inherited. For the Diarist it was the cooling of the sun, and the freezing to death of mankind on an ice-cap over the whole solar system. Science has since made hay of both these prospects; but they started the notion that Ibsen and Inge were pessimists.

Clerically, the Dean escaped the worst trial of a parson's intellectual conscience: that of having to countenance superstitions he does not share with his more primitive parishioners, yet finding it impossible to cure their souls on any other terms. Rousseau told the world two thundering lies, both of which the Churches swallowed with shut eyes and open mouth. Number one: men are born free. Number two: Get rid of your miracles and the whole world will fall at the feet of Jesus.

Had Rousseau been born an employer he would have known that we are all born slaves to our necessities: bread and water, clothes and shelter, sleep and play and sanitation. Until these are satisfied there can be no freedom. Had he been a priest in a slum parish he would soon have learnt that if he got rid of the miracles his flock would go straight to the devil. An Irish Catholic statesman of my acquaintance was advised by a clever political lady to adopt a certain not quite straightforward stroke of diplomacy. He refused. She asked why. He replied "Because I happen to believe that there is such a place as hell." Jesus had to warn his missionaries that if they tried to weed the superstitions out of an established religion they would pull out the wheat as well as the tares. Mahomet, who when the Arabs were worshippers of sticks and stones made Unitarians of them at the risk of his life, found that he could not govern them without promising them a paradise of houris, threatening them with a loathsome hell, and claiming divine revelation for his oracles.

Were I an Irish priest and all my parishioners peasants I should say nothing of my own creed of Creative Evolution, which they could neither believe nor understand. I should educate the women in the cult of the Blessed Immaculate Virgin. I should bind and loose in the confessional. I should redeem the dead from purgatory for a cash consideration. I should elevate the Host as the real presence. Only so could I give them a religion they could believe and a spiritual director they could revere.

All this would have been hard on Ralph Inge if his living had been in Hoxton or the Isle of Dogs. He would soon have been in trouble like Colenso or Bishop Barnes. Happily he graduated clerically in Ennismore Gardens, where his parishioners were—how shall I put it?—up to snuff. Thereafter as Dean of St. Paul's in London City he had no slums to visit, and could speak his mind, leaving unspoken the brimstone specialities of the Little Bethels. Even I was invited to preach in the City Temple, and did so with complete acceptance more than once.

THE MAHATMAS

In the *Diary* the reason given for our getting on so well together is that we both had "no faith in Democracy." This must be interpreted as no faith in government and administration by parliaments of any-bodies or nobodies elected by everybody. Administration is a highly skilled profession; and government is possible only for the five per cent. or so born with the extra mental range it requires. Call them Mahatmas. The diarist, having that extra range, knows that the re-maining ninety-five per cent. do not possess it, and are a continual obstruction and a tyranny to those who do. Young Mahatmas, uncon-scious of their scarcity, and supposing all their fellow-creatures to be as wise as themselves, are always puzzled at first by the stoppage of common minds at the point where the next step seems to the Ma-hatma to be glaringly obvious, and yet is inconceivable, invisible, and impossible to Monsieur Tout le Monde. History soon convinces him that at best Monsieur elects Second Bests doing only what was done last time, and at worst Titus Oates, Lord George Gordon, favourite actors and soldiers (Henry Irving and Lord Roberts, for instance), the backbone of law and order all the time being the Vicars of Bray who obey any government that happens to be in power, and mind their own business "whatsoever king shall reign." The real use of votes for everybody is to prevent us from being governed better than we can bear, as in the case of Prohibition of intoxicating drink in the U.S.A., which had to be repealed in spite of its proved betterment. The Welfare State is not possible with an Illfare constitution. Nobody knows this better than the exceptional thinkers, the geniuses, the authentic Peculiar People like Ruskin, William Morris, and Inge, to say nothing of myself. But we were none the less Democrats not Plutocrats. Government, we hold, should be for the benefit of all, not for the enrichment of a class. The people must choose their rulers, but not from the mob but nature's limited supply of born Mahatmas. Nature (*alias* Providence) always supplies not only enough of whatever and whoever is necessary but in sufficient excess to allow of a choice. What we need is a sound anthropometric test; and on this the diarist and I were democratically agreed, though we may also agree with Hitler that Western parliamentary democracy is a fraud. Both prosperity and adversity make strange bedfellows.

LOOKING AT FACES

We knew also that mental capacity cannot be measured by money, and that, as Mr. A. L. Rowse rightly contended in the correspondence columns of *The Times,* secondary education is wasted on primitive minds. I go further and insist that education beyond capacity is gravely injurious. When it was pushed ruthlessly to extremes in Hohenzollern Germany professional crammers testified that it destroyed the minds of two out of every three successful examinees. Belief in the equality of human faculty is the most undemocratic of ideological superstitions, and produces anticlerical Deans, mystic scientists, Communist Conservatives, pious Freethinkers, insular Liberals, anti-Communist Socialists, Jainist temples full of idols and miracles, Christian Churches worshipping barbarous tribal deities, and anomalies and contradictions of all sorts.

On the first page of the introduction to the *Diary* his friends will enjoy a laugh which the diarist did not intend. He describes himself as a "shy scholar handicapped by a ridiculous inability to remember faces." In fact, there was nothing wrong with his memory. He could not remember faces simply because he never looked at them. This habit may have begun when he was young and shy, as we all are if we are not congenitally impudent. But the Dean's hundreds of sermons must have cured him of that. When anyone looks at me candidly straight in the face when making an assertion, I know at once that he (or she) is lying. We are all taught that liars can never do so, though as a matter of fact they never do anything else. The Dean cannot do it. He never looks at you at all. I have known only one other man who had this trick. Sir Frederick Pollock, if he sat facing you, shifted round inch by inch, and left you addressing the nape of his neck. He was none the less a clever man and a wit.

The illustrations in the *Diary* really illustrate it, and are most interesting. The Dean, an extraordinarily handsome intellectual, with an enchanting smile, should have been depicted in his gaiters; for the full dress of a dean is more becoming than any other now in vogue, except its one rival, the evening dress of a Scottish chieftain.

Editor's Notes

- The above review was published in the *Church of England Newspaper* (*and the Record*), n.s., 69 (13 January 1950), 1:1–5, and 5:1–3. The caption was followed by the subtitle "Thoughts on the Diary of Dean Inge By Bernard Shaw," and illustrated by one of the photographs in the book, of Dean Inge and Bernard Shaw "taken when the two were together on a Hellenic cruise." The article was also published in the *Atlantic* (Boston) in May 1950, and as a pamphlet in the same year. There is no indication of when Shaw wrote it.
- Jainism, a religion of India, is similar to Buddhism (of which it was a rival in India) and was founded by a contemporary of Buddha, namely Vardhamana Jñatiputra (599–527B.C.), called "Jina" (spiritual conqueror). Jains, like Buddhists, deny the divine origin and authority of the Vedas (the ancient sacred books of Hinduism) and revere saints (preachers of Jainism from the distant past) whom they call "tirth ankaras" (prophets, or founders of the path). At the time of this article the Jains numbered only about 1,500,000; but their influence was disproportionate to their numbers.
- [John William] Draper (1811–82), American scientist and historian. Perhaps his most influential book was *History of the Conflict Between Religion and Science* (1872), which was reprinted several times.
- Christian Endeavour Societies began with the Young People's Society of Christian Endeavour founded in 1881 in Portland, Maine, by Dr. Francis Edward Clark (1851–1927), a Canadian-born, American Congregational clergyman. The movement swiftly spread to Europe, and by the time of Shaw's

review was to be found in seventy-five nations boasting members from eighty different denominations. The World's Christian Endeavour Union was established in 1895 and together with the International Society for Christian Endeavour holds conventions from time to time, both organizations being headquartered in Ohio.

- "Pig and Whistle" (see above, 377, 382).
- The eponymous hero of Henrik Ibsen's play *Brand* (1866) is a clergyman who is contemptuous of the fainthearted, compromising Christianity he sees around him, and who believes that "all or nothing" should be the principle of religious faith.
- Secularists were members of the National Secularist Society.
- Reverend C[harles] L[atimer] Marson (1858–1914), English clergyman and author. He wrote interpretations of the Psalms, translated Plato, helped Cecil J. Sharp collect Somerset folksongs, and directed pleas for religious education to all the archbishops and bishops of England. In 1884 he crossed swords with Edward Aveling over the latter's pamphlet *Christianity and Capitalism*.
- The first of the Thirty-Nine Articles, which form the doctrinal basis of the Church of England is "Of Faith in the Holy Trinity"; a notion not subscribed to by Jehovah's Witnesses (a Christian sect founded by the American Charles Taze Russell (1852–1916) in 1872); nor the Plymouth [or Exclusion] Brethren (a Christian sect established in Dublin in the 1820s, its first English church being in Plymouth in 1831).
- Christian Socialists (see above, 62. Also, for Shaw's contributions to their official journal, see 20, 32, and 39).
- "Jolly John Nash," real name James Taylor (n.d.), English entertainer who sang a number of laughing songs, including "I Couldn't Help Laughing, It Tickled Me So," and "The Little Fat Grey Man," and made a great hit with one called "Sister Mary Walks Like This," which was accompanied by a comical hobble. Shaw, however, might well be thinking of his song "Racketty Jack," which he made famous singing before the Prince of Wales (later King Edward VII). With Arthur Lloyd, Nash was the first music hall performer to play privately to royalty, and the prince (according legend) joined lustily in the nonsensical chorus:

> Hey, hi. Stop, waiter! Waiter! Fizz! Pop!
> I'm Racketty Jack, no money I lack,
> And I'm the boy for a spree!

- Herbert Spencer (see above, 112).
- Shaw's comment on the annoyance caused by people who write and read about noted authors instead of reading what the authors themselves have written was heartfelt. On 15 January 1949 Shaw had written "Conversation Pieces," a letter to the *Times Literary Supplement* questioning the truthfulness of Stephen Winsten's book *Days with Bernard Shaw* (1949); a letter that was reprinted as "G.B.S. Gives a Warning" in the *World Digest* in March.

In fact Shaw had for years remonstrated with biographers like Archibald Henderson and would-be biographers like Demetrius O'Bolger over their "interpretation" of his life and work.

- For Shaw's review of *Outspoken Essays,* see above, 406 et seq.
- Ruskin (see above, 65).
- Ibsen (see above, 103).
- The list of Shaw's musical composers appears to be largely chronological: the Franco-Flemish composer Orlandus Lassus (c.1532–92), the Dutch composer Pieter van Sweelinck (1562–1621), Italians Giovanni da Palestrina (c.1525–94) and Claudio Monteverdi (1568–1643), as well as J. S. Bach, Handel, Haydn, Mozart, Beethoven, Rossini, Meyerbeer, and Verdi. The striking omission is Richard Wagner (see above, 113, 166 et seq.). whom Shaw championed for years before he was musically accepted. Perhaps a reassessment of Nordic myth in the light of World War II had something to do with Wagner's absence from the list.
- Shaw refers either to William Jackson (1730–1803), English organist and composer from Exeter, or William Jackson (1815–66), English organist and composer from Masham. The former, in addition to numerous secular vocal and dramatic works, composed anthems, services, and hymns; and the later composer, although less prolific, did so too; and Jackson of Masham certainly composed a Full Service in G (1864) which would, of course, have included a Te Deum.
- Macaulay (see above, 119–20).
- Gladstone (see above, 87).
- Sidney Webb (see above, 139).
- Gilbert Murray (see above, 316).
- G. K. Chesterton (see above, 331–32).
- Rousseau (see above, 397).
- In calling the followers of Islam "Unitarians" Shaw uses the word in a special sense: Muhammad [or Mahomet] exhorted the Meccans to abandon polytheistic religious customs and worship the "one true God." The word "Unitarian" is more commonly used to refer to the non-Trinitarian Christian faiths, like the Congregationalists.
- "Houris" are beautiful virgins promised in paradise for all faithful Muslims.
- Hoxton is a poor part of north London, near Old Street; and the Isle of Dogs is the low-lying north bank peninsular created by the great bend in the River Thames opposite Greenwich.
- [John William] Colenso (1814–83), English prelate. In 1853 he was appointed bishop of Natal. He soon learned the Zulu language, compiled a grammar and a dictionary, and translated the prayer-book and part of the Bible. However, his *Pentateuch and the Book of Joshua Critically Examined* (1862–79), which cast doubts upon the accuracy of the Bible, was considered heretical. He also made enemies by championing dispossessed Negroes; and his metropolitan, Bishop Gray of Capetown, made great (and finally successful) efforts to have him deposed, even publicly excommunicating him.

Colenso was eventually deposed in 1869. Shaw comments on this in his Preface to *Androcles and the Lion* (1916).

▪ [Ernest William] Barnes (1874–1953), English prelate. He was ordained in 1908, became a Fellow of the Royal Society in 1909, and Master of the Temple in 1915. In 1924 he became bishop of Birmingham; but his modernist and pacifist views made him a constant bête noir within the Church of England. Shaw praised his intellectual honesty in an article in *Outline* on 12 May 1928, though five years later he was to cross swords with him in print on the subject of compulsory sterilization, which the bishop favored.

▪ Titus Oates and Lord George Gordon are the examples given above when Shaw is making a similar point (501).

▪ Henry Irving (see above, 113).

▪ Lord Roberts (see above, 284–85).

▪ Shaw quotes the chorus of the eighteenth-century political song "The Vicar of Bray" about the time-serving priest who changed his coat according to the political winds, which runs:

> And this is law I will maintain,
> Until my dying day, Sir,
> That whatsoever King shall reign,
> I'll still be the vicar of Bray, Sir.

Shaw had taken the opening line of this song for the title of one of his plays: *In Good King Charles's Golden Days* (1939).

▪ A[lfred] L[eslie] Rowse (b. 1903) English historian and author. Educated at Christ Church, Oxford, he became a Fellow of All Souls; from 1962 to 1969 he was senior research associate at the Huntington Library, California, and has lectured at Cambridge and McGill Universities, besides being a Fellow of the Royal Society of Literature, and president of the English Association. He has produced a prodigious number of books on English history and on literary history, including his (often controversial) views on Shakespeare. He has also written books of poetry, and books about his own county of Cornwall. His autobiography *A Cornishman at Oxford,* came out in 1965. In 1982 he was awarded the Benson Medal by the Royal Society of Literature. In the above review, Shaw refers to the series of letters by Rowse to the *Times* on educational expenditure, written in August and September 1949.

▪ Sir Frederick Pollock (1845–1937), English jurist. Called to the Bar in 1871 he became professor of jurisprudence at University College, London in 1882, Corpus Professor of Jurisprudence at Oxford the following year, and professor of common law in the Inns of Court from 1884 to 1890. He became judge of the Admiralty Court of Cinque Ports in 1914. His publications, which went through several editions, include *Principles of Contract* (1875), *Digest of the Law of Partnership* (1877), and *Law of Torts* (1887). His Oxford lectures were also published.

26 March 1950

OLD BACHELOR SAM BUTLER* [C3904]

AT the beginning of my career, when I was a nobody reviewing books for the old Pall Mall Gazette, now long extinct, I received a book entitled Luck or Cunning, and, on reviewing it at some length, was infuriated when some fool of a sub-editor treated the book and its author as of no importance, and cut a great chunk out of it. I learned later on that this truncated article of mine seemed almost epoch making to the author, an old bachelor named Butler living in Clifford's Inn, who, though having won a certain select celebrity by a queer Utopia entitled Erewhon (Nowhere backwards), was carrying on a metabiological crusade against Darwinism which was being ignored by the Press and the biologists of that day to such an extent that he had to publish his polemics at his own expense, always at a loss which made marriage an economic impossibility for him.

As I was then under the same disability myself (I was over forty before I could afford to marry) and completely boycotted as a playwright, I was myself a compulsory bachelor and controversialist *contra mundum*. Moreover, as I was one of the select few who had read Erewhon and swore by it, I was to that extent in Butler's camp.

Exactly when and how I made his acquaintance I do not remember. He was 21 years my senior; and I was married before we met. Among his many oddities, he was a strict monogamist yet by no means a celibate; for he remained faithful to the French lady whom he visited once a fortnight, and was wholly innocent of polygamy.

*   *   *

He had never had any literary ambition, though he was a born writer; and this was my own case; for in my boyhood I aspired to be, not a Shakespear, but successively a pirate, an operatic baritone, and above all a Michael Angelo. Butler, too, tried for years to be a painter, just as his fellow student in Heatherly's [*sic*] Art School, Forbes Robertson, aspired to be a Titian or a Velasquez, never to be an actor. To this day I have to impress on young would-be authors that the strongest taste for high art does not imply any talent for its

* "The Essential Sam Butler." Edited by G. D. H. Cole. (Jonathan Cape. 12s. 6d.)

practice, and that for a born genius it is as tasteless as water is because it is always in our mouths.

When Butler at last gave up the hope that he could ever be anything more in pictorial art than a mediocre painter aiming at correctness of representation instead of self-expression, he took to composing music in the style of Handel, collaborating with his friend and biographer Festing Jones, a musical barrister of genuine talent who told me that Butler never could manage any tempo more elaborate than two or three crotchets in a bar, and that Beethoven was quite beyond him. So this also was a failure; and Butler, though his simple imitations of Handel might almost pass as uninspired originals, had to become Festing's librettist and supply him with some screamingly funny oratorio texts. He hated his father, Canon Butler, who had "beaten Latin grammar into him line by line," but dared not quarrel with him lest he should be disinherited. He despised his mother because she wheedled confessions from him and then betrayed him to his father and got him another whipping. He set no store by his sisters because they stood by their father, and did not consider that Sam got more than he deserved. Canon Butler was a genial old gaffer out of doors, but at home was tyrant, judge, jury and executioner all in one. A hydrogen bomb could not have blasted his reputation more devastatingly after his death than his undutiful son did with his novel called The Way of All Flesh. Yet Sam was himself a chip of the old block in controversy. He probably never heard of the priceless precept of Robert Owen, "Never argue: repeat your assertion." Sam certainly repeated his assertions; but he argued endlessly, and always treated his opponents as moral delinquents as well as damned fools.

*   *   *

Now all these traits do not suggest a Great Man, nor even an agreeable one, much less the likeable and considerate friend my wife and I always found him. Yet Sam was a great man as great men go. Mr. Cole, editor of the book now under review, holds that as The Way of All Flesh is a great novel, its author must have been a great man. But some of its readers think it proves that he was a little man. He himself put the secret of his greatness into a single sentence of six words, which he addressed to me as we were crossing the courtyard of the British Museum together. He said, with the most intense emphasis, "Darwin banished mind from the universe." He added," My grandfather quarrelled with Darwin's grandfather; my father quarrelled with Darwin's father; I quarrelled with Darwin; and my regret for having no son is that he cannot quarrel with Darwin's son." As a matter of fact Darwin had converted Butler for six weeks, because in those days we clever people who called ourselves Secularists, Freethinkers, Agnostics, Atheists, Positivists, Rationalists, or what not, and were classed by the orthodox as Infidels doomed to eternal damnation, were Anti-Clericals snatching at any stick big enough to whack the parsons; and as the biggest stick then was the Natural Selection of Darwin and Wallace, carried to absurdity by Weismann, we all, Butler included, grabbed it and layed on joyously. Butler alone thought it out deeply and quickly enough to grasp the horror of its banishment of mind from the universe.

The ensuing controversies only obscured this fundamental issue. They did not affect me because I had read the Patmos Evangelist's "In the Beginning was the Thought" and come up against the neo-Darwinist shallowness as flatly as Mazzini of whom I had never read a word. In my preface to Back to Methuselah I dealt with it, and have neither space nor need to expatiate on it again here. (Darwin, by the way, was no more a Darwinist than I am a Shavian.)

* * *

I will not pretend to criticise Mr. Cole's editing of the selection from Butler's writings of which the book in question consists. To Mr. Cole the job is child's play calling for no recommendation from me. That is why I tell my own tale at first hand. However, may I suggest that Butler should be classed in the roll of fame neither as novelist nor biologist but as metabiologist, just as we class Hegel not as physician but as metaphysician. This perhaps is because I call myself a metabiologist, and was the first, as far as I know, to bring that necessary term into the vocabulary.

I must also warn readers that Butler's guess that the author of the Odyssey was a woman is not an Erewhonian joke, and that it is now impossible to read it again without being at least half convinced that he was as right as Dickens was about George Eliot.

Editor's Notes

• The above review was published in *The Observer*, 26 March 1950, 8:2–5, and illustrated by a reproduction of one of Butler's own paintings from the book "Family Prayers." Butler had written, "I did this in 1864, and if I had gone on doing things out of my own head instead of making studies, I should have been all right." The article was also published in the *Saturday Review of Literature* (New York) 33 (29 April 1950): 9–10.

- This was Shaw's last book review. He was still active, however, still quoted in the newspapers, and still widely interested in current affairs. In the month of his ninety-fourth birthday he was to write *Why She Would Not*, a comedy in five scenes, finishing it on 23 July. That summer he received his last visitors, including India's first prime minister Jawaharlal Nehru, and his old friends the Langners. On 10 September, Shaw fell while pruning a tree in his garden, was admitted to hospital, suffered two bouts of surgery, and returned to Ayot St. Lawrence on 5 October. A month later (on 1 November) he lapsed into a coma, and the following day he died.

- G. D. H. Cole (see above, 502–3).

- For a comment on Shaw's review of Butler's *Luck, or Cunning?* see above, page 270. In Shaw's clipping of his own article, pasted in a scrapbook, he indicated omissions in his text, and at the end, in shorthand, wrote, "This is most annoyingly mutilated."

- Butler (see above, 306–7).

- Shaw's autobiographical chronology is convenient rather than accurate here. By 1887 his dramatic work consisted of a never-to-be-finished "Passion Play," and two acts of another unfinished piece initially called "Rheingold," which he had begun in 1884 in collaboration with William Archer, and that would not be finished (as *Widowers' Houses*) until five years later, in 1892. Moreover, Shaw met Butler in 1888, ten years before he married Charlotte Payne-Townshend.

- Butler for a time attended Thomas Heatherley's School of Art in Newman Street.

- [Sir Johnston] Forbes-Robertson (1853–1937), English actor. It is generally held that he studied painting at the Royal Academy before going on the stage in 1874 and for forty years winning a great reputation for his Shakespearean and modern roles. Shaw knew Forbes-Robertson, had read *The Devil's Disciple* to him (and Mrs. Patrick Campbell) in February 1897 (Forbes-Roberton played the part of Dick Dudgeon in 1900, though Shaw never liked him in the role); wrote the part of Caesar in *Caesar and Cleopatra* expressly for him; and had briefly shared the stage with him on 18 March 1913, when they both addressed a suffragist demonstration in the Kingsway Hall against forcible feeding. Forbes-Robertson, for his part, admired Shaw, declaring that of all the many dramatists he had come across only A. W. Pinero and Shaw knew how to impart their views at rehearsal in a practical manner.

- Festing Jones (see above, 394).

- Darwin (see above, 36, 112).

- Wallace (see above, 36).

- Weismann (see above, 309).

- The Patmos Evangelist is Saint John, who, according to legend, on the island of Patmos in the Ægean Sea, saw the visions of the Apocalypse. His Gospel begins with the line usually translated "In the Beginning was the Word"; but Shaw's translation is a more accurate rendition of the Greek word Λογοσ, which means "reasoned thought."

- [Giuseppe] Mazzini was a passionate theist, desiring to rescue democracy from materialism and secularism. Mazzini Dunn, a character in *Heartbreak House* (1916–17), is named for the Italian revolutionary.
- Hegel (see above, 56–57).
- Dickens received and read a copy of George Eliot's *Scenes of Clerical Life* in 1858, and although he had no idea who the author was he guessed her gender. He wrote to her on 18 January 1858: "I have observed what seem to me to be such womanly touches, in those moving fictions that the assurance on the title-page is insufficient to satisfy me, even now. If they originated with no woman, I believe no man ever before had the art of making himself, mentally, so like a woman, since the world began."

INDEX

All entries that have been uppercased are articles or authors reviewed by Shaw.